Social
Work

Dedicated to Judy, Andrew and Paul

THE BLACKWELL ENCYCLOPAEDIA OF

Social Work

Edited by
MARTIN DAVIES

Assistant editor
ROSE BARTON

BLACKWELL
Publishers

Copyright © Blackwell Publishers Ltd 2000
Editorial matter and organization copyright © Martin Davies 2000

First published 2000

2 4 6 8 10 9 7 5 3 1

Blackwell Publishers Ltd
108 Cowley Road
Oxford OX4 1JF
UK

Blackwell Publishers Inc.
350 Main Street
Malden, Massachusetts 02148
USA

British Library Cataloguing in Publication Data
A CIP catalogue record for this book is available from the British Library.

Library of Congress Cataloging-in-Publication Data

The Blackwell encyclopaedia of social work / edited by Martin Davies.
      p. cm.
   Includes bibliographical references and index.
   ISBN 0-631-21450-X (hb : alk. paper)—ISBN 0-631-21451-8 (pb : alk. paper)
     1. Social service—Encyclopedias. I. Davies, Martin.

  HV12 .B53 2000
  361.3′2′03—dc21

00-037953

Typeset in 9 on 10½ pt Sabon
by Best-set Typesetter Ltd., Hong Kong
Printed in Great Britain by TJ International, Padstow, Cornwall

This book is printed on acid-free paper.

Contents

Editorial Advisers

Professor Norma Baldwin, *Dundee University*
Dr Carol Dawson, *Independent trainer and consultant, Norwich*
Margaret Flynn, *National Development Team for People with Learning Disabilities, Manchester*
Professor Adrian L. James, *Bradford University*
Professor Joyce Lishman, *The Robert Gordon University, Aberdeen*
Professor Audrey Mullender, *Warwick University*
Dr Judith Phillips, *Keele University*
Professor Colin Pritchard, *Southampton University*
Dr Ian Shaw, *University of Wales, Cardiff*

Preface

How to use the Encyclopaedia

It is tempting for an editor, having devoted two years of his life to the task of creating a new Encyclopaedia, to share with his readers some of the thoughts that have passed through his mind as he has undertaken the work – to reflect upon, for example, the significance of the use of language in practice, or to point to the parallel existence of two strands in much of what is here presented: the ideological or value-based element, and the empirical or evidence-based element. But it is a temptation I shall resist.

The Encyclopaedia, with its 412 entries, written by 250 authors, must stand and will be judged in terms of its own inherent value. Read as a whole (as I have read it), it provides a fascinatingly reflective profile of social work today; but readers generally will use the Encyclopaedia more selectively.

The aim of the book is to provide accurate, up-to-date and lively explications of key topics in social work and in fields that are closely related to social work theory or practice. There is a particular emphasis on the research framework relevant to the development of social work knowledge.

Objectives vary for different categories of reader:

- Teachers may wish to make available to students some of the longer entries so as to stimulate seminar discussion; they may use the book to update their own lecture material, to react quickly to questions raised by students which fall outside their own area of expertise, or to keep themselves abreast of current debates or developments in the field.
- Students may use the Encyclopaedia to obtain a quick and efficient sense of social work as a broad-based discipline, to identify definitions of key terms and concepts, and to help in the production of written assignments.
- Practitioners may find in it the most conveniently accessible route to up-dates on their subject, or to explore related topics relevant to post-qualifying study.
- Readers outside the field of social work will have access in the Encyclopaedia to a broad perspective on this often controversial sphere of professional activity and its knowledge base.

There are three levels of entry:

(a) 1,000-word major items, usually with three suggestions for further reading;
(b) 200-word glossary items giving a brief explanation and suggesting further reading;
(c) 100-word short items, providing a definition.

Immediately following this Preface, there is a detailed LEXICON. The lexicon facilitates speedy access to those topics which relate most closely to the reader's own particular sphere of interest; it gives instant access, in alphabetical order, to all those entries, for example, which cover *child care and child protection*, or *learning disabilities*, or *social policy*. The longest listing in the lexicon identifies those entries which lead the reader to a comprehensive but concise coverage of *social work methods*.

Used proactively, the lexicon offers a kind of mini-textbook on key social work fields of practice or related policy disciplines, providing *passim*, an up-to-date list of recommended references which, together, enable the reader to pursue his or her interest to an advanced level of scholarship.

The reader will find only a limited amount of cross-referencing in the body of the text, but, where it occurs, I have used the standard convention of noting associated topics in small capitals.

At the end of the Encyclopaedia, there is a list of contributors; and subject and author indices. The subject index, in particular, will lead the reader to mentions of topics (for example, *Down's Syndrome* or *total institutions*) that might otherwise have been expected to appear in the main listing.

It is anticipated that *The Blackwell Encyclopaedia of Social Work* will go into new editions, and the editor will welcome, not just comments and criticisms, but suggestions for future entries. A policy decision was taken to omit from the listing all named organisations or individuals; and to avoid undue emphasis on the legislative context of social work in the United Kingdom.

Acknowledgements

The Editor is pleased to acknowledge the advice given by many friends and colleagues: Caroline Ball, Neil Bateman, Isabel Clare, Chris Clark, Annette Gurney, David Howe, Barbara Hudson, Sonia Jackson, Elizabeth Lancaster, Jill Manthorpe, Teresa Munby, Joan Orme, Andy Pithouse, Katie Prince, Jackie Rafferty, Harry Shapiro, Steven Shardlow, Brian Sheldon, David Smith, Nigel South, Nigel Stone, Neil Thompson, Anthea Tinker, Tony Vass, Dave Ward, Chris Warren and Brian Williams.

He is especially grateful to members of the Mental Health Group in the University of Southampton for their erudite contributions on aspects of psychiatry.

He also would wish to express his gratitude to Ann Steed for her secretarial help at a critical time in the final stages of manuscript preparation, and to Keith Porter for his provision of help, advice, support and magical solutions whenever the IT failed to work as it should.

Grateful acknowledgement is made to all the contributors who gave generously and enthusiastically of their time, expertise and academic commitment in their willingness to play an active part in the launch of this publishing venture.

Martin Davies
Hethersett, Norwich
April 2000

Lexicon

Child development

Community care

Development disorder

Disability

Domestic violence

Elder care

Theories for social work practice

Training for social work

Transnational issues

User perspectives

Tables

Figures

A

Abuse in Residential Care

Abuse in residential care refers to the physical, sexual, emotional or psychological abuse or neglect of children and young people living in residential care settings. It may be classified as individual abuse, organized abuse, programme or sanctioned abuse, or systems outcome abuse.

In the past, the main cause of abuse has been seen as the 'bad' individual adult care worker. However, major inquiries have highlighted the extent of programme or sanctioned abuse including the use of regression therapy in some Leicestershire children's homes, the Pin Down system of control in Staffordshire and the use of confrontational physical restraint methods at Aycliffe School. There is also evidence of organized paedophile activity in children's homes.

Systems outcome abuses can be described as the failure of law, policies, practices and procedures to protect, compensate and promote the optimum outcomes for 'looked-after' children and young people. This includes poor management which may lead to abusive cultures where bullying is rife, unsatisfactory placement policies, inadequate recruitment and staffing policies, and the general failure of care to compensate children and young people developmentally, emotionally and educationally, resulting in unacceptably poor outcomes.

Safeguarding children and young people from abuse will require major improvements:

- in staffing, management, selection, recruitment, training and inspection;
- in developing a comprehensive national strategy for residential child care;
- in involving young people and their families far more in decision-making processes.

For Further Reading
Utting, W. 1997: *People Like Us*. London: The Stationery Office.

MIKE STEIN

Abuse of Women

See DOMESTIC VIOLENCE.

Acceptance

Acceptance in counselling and therapy means prizing people as they really are, including the 'best and the worst' in them, without censure. Conveying acceptance involves making a distinction between the client's self – where there is a need to respect the client's worth and dignity – and his or her behaviour. The counsellor and therapist, appropriately, may convey disapproval of the behaviour. Acceptance is not all or nothing: there are degrees of acceptance. Thus negotiating and demonstrating acceptance becomes an important part of the counselling and therapeutic relationship. Self-acceptance – a key person-centred goal – means prizing yourself in the same way.

CHRIS WARREN-ADAMSON

Accountability

Accountability, though at first sight a simple concept, is in reality complex when applied to the practice of social work. There are at least four answers to the question: 'To whom is the social worker accountable for her or his actions?'

There is the traditional professional idea that the practitioner is accountable, first and foremost, to the client; but, although many social workers cling to the principle, the reality in public sector practice – when compared, for example, with private-sector counselling – often makes such an ideal impractical – hence the tendency to refer to social work as a 'semi-profession'.

Much social work practice is influenced by, constrained by or prescribed by statute, and to that extent, the social worker is wholly accountable to legal mandate. The duties of the approved social worker, the child protection worker or the probation officer are clear examples of this.

Many entrants to social work have strong personal, religious or political motivations, and the notions of 'helping people', 'doing good', 'serving society' or 'righting political or economic wrongs' remain powerful factors in their lives – hence they view themselves as being accountable to their own ideals or to a sense of personal duty.

Finally, most social workers operate within hierarchical systems, and they are, as in any bureaucracy, directly accountable through line management structures to their immediate superiors, thence to chief officers and, ultimately, to employing committees or councils. Complaints panels, disciplinary procedures, referral to the Ombudsman and, on rare occasions, the use of dismissal make such accountability explicit.

For Further Reading
Davies, M. (ed.) 1997: *The Blackwell Companion to Social Work*. Oxford: Blackwell.
MARTIN DAVIES

Action Research

Action research is a type of research which aims to develop a greater understanding and improvement of practice in the context where the research takes place. Action research engages the participants and researchers in active collaboration and collective self-reflection at all stages of the research process. Collaboration between these two groups enables practitioners to define the practice to be changed and to produce and act upon solutions for that practice. Researchers are able to gain a wider access to their field of study. Action research is a cyclical, dynamic process that bridges the gap between theory and practice.
ANITA GIBBS

Activities of Daily Living

Activities of daily living (ADL) is a global term used to indicate the range of occupational tasks required for:

- basic survival (for example, eating and drinking)
- self-care (for example, dressing and grooming)
- hygiene (for example, bathing/showering and hair washing)
- communication (for example, verbal and non-verbal expression)
- social relations (for example, initiation and maintenance of social and sexual relationships).

Competence in these tasks follows a developmental sequence. For example, the very young child normally progresses from gross motor to later fine motor skills required for independent feeding. In later childhood and adolescence, independence in ADL is achieved, and is potentially maintained throughout life.

Competent performance of ADL is required for individuals to assert their individuality, and to conform to overt personal and societal norms. Disease or disability can lead to an adverse impact (transient or permanent) on individuals' capacity to perform these tasks to their premorbid level. Maintenance, or improvement, of ADL at the highest possible level is vital for individuals to retain dignity, self-respect and sense of self within their immediate society.

For Further Reading
Hagedorn, R. 1997: *Foundations for Practice in Occupational Therapy* (2nd edn). London: Churchill Livingstone.
CHIA SWEE HONG AND ROD LAMBERT

Adolescence

Adolescence refers to the social and personal maturation process commencing with puberty, and leading to social acceptance as an adult in society. Though pubertal maturation leads to maturity during adolescence, it is not recognized as equivalent to the socio-cultural status of adulthood. Research into adolescence has come from history, philosophy, anthropology, sociology, psychology, clinical psychology/psychiatry, and related disciplines. The focus of research has varied among these disciplines, in that they have emphasized areas of interest particularly relevant to their perspectives.

History

From the historical perspective, Plato (427–347 BC) believed that rational and critical thought developed in adolescence, and that these should be fostered through mathematic and scientific training. Aristotle (384–322 BC) divided the developmental stages into infancy, boyhood, and young manhood, and this view was generally accepted during the Middle Ages. Rousseau (1712–1778) identified four stages of development and believed that teaching should correspond to these developmental stages of infancy, savagery, youth, and adolescence. In general, however, the concept of adolescence is believed to have been little recognized before modern times.

The modern age began with Darwin (1809–1882), whose theory of evolution by natural selection (1859) was applied by Freud and especially by G. Stanley Hall (1844–1924) who is recognized as the founder of the scientific study of adolescence. Stanley Hall also divided child development into four stages of infancy, childhood, youth, and adolescence, with the latter stage characterized by adolescent *storm and stress*. In 1923, Margaret Mead's findings with adolescent girls in Samoa challenged this *storm and stress* view. However, the 'roaring 1920s' were a time of rapid economic and social change, characterized by new-found social and sexual freedom in young people, and fashionable trends developed among youth in clothes, music and film which were emulated by adults. At this time, and despite Prohibition on alcohol in America, adolescents frequently drank illegally. However, these freedoms were halted with the onset of the Great Depression and, subsequently, World War II.

By 1950, the contemporary period of adolescence arrived with the economy fully recovered from the war. There were expanding opportunities in higher education, the development of television, advertising, and the drive to establish careers in a booming Western economy. In the 1960s, increased public attention came from protests against inequality for African–Americans in education, housing and employment. Public discontent peaked between the late 1960s to early 1970s when America entered the Vietnam War, with youth leading the most violent protests. In the 1970s, women's rights movements also culminated in public protest. At the same time, teenage sex and pregnancy increased, as did cohabitation before marriage. However, by the mid-1970s, much of the revolutionary fervour declined among adolescents and in society as a whole. In place, there was a return to achievement-oriented educational aspirations, with a desire for material consumption and wealth.

Psychology

An early theoretical perspective into adolescence came from Freud's psychodynamic theory of the psychosexual stages, with the overcoming of the Oedipal complex and attainment of the *genital* stage of mature sexuality at puberty and adolescence. With this influence, Harry Stack Sullivan's social psychiatric perspective considered the early and late adolescent crises of development in terms of escape from the frustrations of lust and anxiety towards comfort in security and intimacy. Subsequently, Erikson's adolescent crisis stage of 'identity versus identity confusion' was reworked by J. Marcia into four identity types of crisis/exploration within a developmental trend from *identity-diffused/confused, foreclosed, moratorium to identity-achieved* subjects.

The cognitive-developmental perspective has been represented by Lewin's theory of adolescent 'life-space' which encapsulates the adolescent experience as a field-and-time perspective expansion beyond the child-field, but not yet to the adult-field; Piaget's adolescent 'formal operations' stage of mental reasoning; Kohlberg's perspective on the development of adolescent morality and Gilligan's feminine critique of it; Selman's social cognition and interpersonal understanding, characterized by the in-depth and societal perspective-taking stage in adolescence; and Loevinger's ego-stage development in adolescence in the domains of impulse control and character development, interpersonal style, conscious preoccupations, and cognitive style. In contrast, a non-stage-based cognitive approach came from Bandura's social learning/social cognitive theory of adolescence, with an emphasis on vicarious reinforcement and modelling, imitation, and identification involved in adolescent aggression and the effects of television violence.

continued

More broad developmental approaches have included the developmental contextualist perspective of Lerner, which situates adolescent development within the various factors of the socio-environmental context; and the ecological model of Bronfenbrenner, which illustrated the concentric spheres of interrelationship within the microsystems (for example, family, friends, church), mesosystem (interaction of the microsystems), exosystem (for example, parents' employer, local education authority, local government), and macrosystem (for example, national government, state religion, mass media) domains in the social ecology. Finally, the evolutionary, particularly the ethological, approach considers parent–offspring relations, puberty, reproduction, and developmental life-history across species with implications for parent–adolescent conflict, aggressive or antisocial behaviour, psychopathology, and clinical psychology/psychiatry.

With some exceptions, most theories of adolescence involve a stage-like progression from infantile, childhood, and adolescent development towards adulthood. This approach involves both developmental and clinical aspects, as appropriate attainment of each successive stage at the relevant age reflects adequate psychosocial development throughout the life-span. Characteristics of the theory also influence the research area; for example, the more psychodynamic theories (for example, those of Freud or Stack Sullivan) tend to have particular clinical and psychiatric dimensions, with an emphasis on psychosexual development. By contrast, the less psychoanalytically influenced developmental/cognitive and ecological theories tend to have more directly relevant educational and social work dimensions and applications, which include implications for parental socialization of adolescents, the role of education, identity development, puberty and sexuality, friendship and peer influence, the effects of mass media, deviance, psychopathology, class, gender and ethnicity, and work experience and career.

For Further Reading
Adams, G. R., Montemayor, R. and Gullotta, T. P. (eds) 1996: *Psychosocial Development During Adolescence*. London: Sage.
Coleman, J. 1999: *Key Data on Adolescence – 1999*. Brighton: TSA.
Muuss, R. E. 1996: *Theories of Adolescence* (6th edn). London: McGraw-Hill.

KENNETH KIM

Adoption

Adoption involves the permanent transfer of all legal rights and responsibilities from birth parents to a new family. Once the adoption order is made legal, parentage is completely and irrevocably transferred to the adoptive family. An adoption order cannot be set aside except in the most unusual situation. Legal security is one of the cornerstones of adoption.

Modern adoption in the Western world dates back to the middle of the nineteenth century when the first adoption law was enacted in the State of Massachusetts. England introduced its first Adoption Act in 1926, and Scotland in 1930. Since then, adoption legislation has often been amended to reflect social changes and new knowledge, mainly of what is seen to be best for children.

As a basic human experience, adoption transcends most cultures. It usually adapts to reflect social changes in such matters as attitudes to non-marital births, sexual relationships, marriage, infertility, child bearing and inheritance. Motives for adopting have changed too, with adoption having become much more about relationships, intimacy, love and loss, commitment and challenge, than to further religious beliefs, political ambitions or financial gain. The onset of globalization has itself introduced a new dimension: that of intercountry adoption. However, this, along with transracial adoption, has been surrounded by controversy.

Around two-thirds of the 7,000 or so children adopted annually in the UK are adopted by relatives, mainly step-parents. The children adopted by non-kin are mostly those of parents who are unable, unwilling or legally prohibited from caring for a child. Who can adopt, who can be adopted and who can arrange adoptions differs across countries. In the UK, unlike most other countries, it is illegal for parents to arrange the adoption of their child by a non-kin, either directly or indirectly through an intermediary such as a doctor, lawyer or priest. Only approved agencies can do this.

Adoption is open to both couples and single people. Barring certain conditions, such as a lower age limit, almost anyone can adopt. In practice, it is more complex. Adoption agencies have a responsibility, when placing children, to safeguard and promote their long-term interests and welfare. As a result they are obliged to undertake a series of background investigations about the applicant(s), including their health and other social and personal circumstances relevant to the rearing of a child not born to them.

The evolution of adoption

For about twenty years after the end of World War II, adoption came to be viewed mainly as a solution to the separate 'problems' of infertility and non-marital births. With few exceptions, only infants and healthy babies were then seen as adoptable. This form of adoption became very popular among the middle classes, and it reached its peak in the late 1960s. Since then, adoption has become far more diverse involving, not only a much wider range of children, but also adopters from varied social backgrounds. In fact, because of severe shortages, only an insignificant number of in-country babies and infants are now adopted. The shortages came about mainly because of changes in attitudes towards having a non-marital child, the extensive use of contraception, the legal availability of abortion facilities and improved social conditions.

The scarcity of babies for adoption led agencies to turn their attention to children who did not fit with the traditional image of adoption. These were older children within the public care system, with some having a learning, physical or other disability and/or displaying emotional or behavioural difficulties. They came to be known as 'hard to place' children, or children with 'special needs'. Encouragement for this new type of adoption came from research which suggested that, given a new nurturing environment, children who had previously experienced the trauma of neglect, separations and other adversities could recover within certain limits. The decades that followed saw a concentration, mainly in Britain and partly in North America, on this type of adoption. Most other Western countries went for intercountry adoption. Because of this new type of adoption, agencies now undertake extensive preparatory and introductory work with both adopters and children to prepare them for what is to come, and offer extensive post-placement support where needed.

Adoption outcomes

Studies suggest that, on the whole, the adoption of infants and of very young children works as well as natural parenting and that psychosocial parenting is a reality. Furthermore, adopted people have been found to function not differently from others in the community. The studies have also been recording high levels of satisfaction with the adoption experience by both adoptive parents and adopted people.

Turning to the adoption of older, 'special needs' children, an overall breakdown rate of around 20 per cent can be expected. The older the child, the higher the level of difficult and disruptive behaviour; and the more depriving and rejecting the child's earlier experiences, the more likely it is that the arrangement will break down. Most breakdowns occur during the early placement stage and before the adoption order is granted.

continued

The quality of re-attachments and new relationships, the way the child is integrated into the new family and the quality of the child's previous experiences all have a bearing on the outcome and quality of the adoption experience. For some children, recovery from earlier traumatic experiences can be limited, and expectations have to be tempered.

Other recent research findings detailing the important contribution of genealogical and other background information to the identity and self-concept of the adopted person have helped to open up adoption records which were previously held in secret. These and other studies also give cautious support to the idea of more open forms of adoption and to adoption with contact, especially in the case of older children, some of whom may have had important emotional and physical links with members of their birth families. Siblings are more likely to be placed together now than be separated.

For Further Reading
Brodzinsky, D. and Schechter, M. (eds) 1990: *The Psychology of Adoption.* New York: Oxford University Press.
Howe, D. 1998: *Patterns of Adoption.* Oxford: Blackwell.
Triseliotis, J., Shireman, J. and Hundleby, M. 1997: *Adoption: Theory, Policy and Practice.* London: Cassell.

JOHN TRISELIOTIS

Adult Protection

Adult protection describes policies designed to co-ordinate decision making on behalf of vulnerable adults who are, or are at risk of, being abused. Abuse is defined within these policies as any acts or mistreatment that violate human or civil rights. A consensus has emerged to include physical, sexual, psychological and financial abuse and neglect within this overarching definition.

New government guidance mandates local agencies to work together and share information in the interests of vulnerable adults. It sets out channels for reporting abuse and a framework for assessment and decision making in a case conference or similar forum.

Inevitably, there are ethical and practice dilemmas in this area of work, especially when working with adults who lack capacity, or with those who have been intimidated or exploited within a family or professional relationship. Procedures address separately the agendas to be followed on behalf of the victim of abuse, the perpetrator(s) and those managers or agencies who have a responsibility for the overall context in which abuse has occurred.

For Further Reading
Department of Health 2000: *No Secrets: Guidance on Developing and Implementing Multi-agency Policies and Procedures to Protect Vulnerable Adults from Abuse.* London: The Stationary Office.

HILARY BROWN

Adults as Service Users in Community Care

Community care services are generally provided to adults. A distinction between adults and children is made in the White Paper, *Caring for People* (Department of Health, 1990): although the legal onset of adulthood varies depending on circumstances, the White Paper makes it clear that 'community care means providing the services and support which people who are affected by problems of ageing, mental illness, mental handicap or physical or sensory disability need' (p. 3). This provision is separated from that which the 'Government is pursuing separately in the Children Bill' (p. 3). The White Paper adds 'people with drug or alcohol related disorders, people with multiple handicaps and people with progressive illnesses such as AIDS' as potential recipients of community care services. Although some of the language has changed since 1990, these remain the broad categories for potential service users. Who then receives community care services is determined by organizational processes such as the eligibility criteria published annually by each local authority in community care plans and by the assessment of need usually carried out by a care manager.

For Further Reading
Department of Health 1990: *Caring for People: Community Care in the Next Decade and Beyond.* London: HMSO.

MARK BALDWIN

Advocacy

Advocacy involves either a group or an individual and/or their representative pressing their case with influential others to gain access to, or improve, supporting services, or, more usually in social work, trying to prevent proposals seen as negative. Both process intent and outcome should increase the individual's or group's sense of power, help to increase confidence, enable them to become more assertive and increase choices. Advocates try to change structures – in contrast to counsellors.

Types of advocacy include: self, family, peer, citizen, collective, professional and service professional. The term *whistle-blowing* is commonly used to describe the last type where social workers complain about their employing service, often at considerable personal and professional cost.

Social work advocates are often torn between their responsibility to agency and to service users.

Advocacy skills involve:

• careful listening
• accurate note taking
• explaining the process
• taking instructions from clients
• gathering relevant information
• feeding back lucidly
• negotiating for improvements.

Evaluation is both *expressive* and *instrumental*. Clients should have confidence and trust in the advocate (expressive), but instrumental elements are crucial: does advocacy improve their practical situation?

For Further Reading
Brandon, D. 1995: *Advocacy – Power to People with Disabilities*. Birmingham: Venture Press.

DAVID BRANDON

Affective Disorders

See BIPOLAR AFFECTIVE DISORDER and DEPRESSION.

Ageism

The term *ageism* was first coined by Robert Butler in the 1960s. He defined it as a process of stereotyping and discrimination against people because they are old, just as racism and sexism accomplish this for skin colour and gender.

Ageism has a number of dimensions: job discrimination, loss of status, stereotyping and dehumanization. Ageism is about assuming all older people are the same, despite their different life histories, needs and expectations. Ageism not only affects the lives of older people, but, like ageing itself, it affects every individual from birth onwards, putting limits and constraints on experiences, expectations, relationships and opportunities.

Ageism is important because it affects workers and carers at a personal level. Contact with older people may be avoided because it is viewed as unrewarding or it reminds younger people of their own ageing. This is partly because young people have no direct experience of old age and therefore have to rely on social stereotypes; as these may be quite negative, they create perceptions of a future old age as a time of dependency, poor health, poverty and vulnerability, even though this may bear little relationship to the lived experience of many older people.

Ageism affects men and women alike but may be especially detrimental to older women since it adds to their already disadvantaged position in society. Women may experience a loss of identity and status in later life. Two-thirds of older people are women; they are much more likely than men to experience a range of chronic illnesses that go untreated, and to end their days in a residential institution of some kind.

So far as black people are concerned, ageism compounds the problems of racist discrimination and stereotyping that they experience throughout their lives, with the result that there will be aggravated problems of poverty, low self-esteem and vulnerability to abuse.

For Further Reading
Butler, R. 1980: Ageism: a foreword. *Journal of Social Issues*, 36 (2), 8–11.
Bytheway, B. 1995: *Ageism*. Buckingham: Open University Press.

CHRIS PHILLIPSON

AIDS

See HIV AND AIDS.

Alcohol and Alcohol Problems

Alcohol is a drug, a legal drug, which is relatively cheap and easily available. It makes a swift impact on the drinker; in Western culture, it is often associated with pleasurable consequences. It has a depressant effect upon the central nervous system which can lead to disinhibition, lack of control and impaired judgement.

Alcohol problems

Alcohol problems involve difficulties that can occur following excessive consumption of alcohol. Alcohol problems are associated with accidents, relationship difficulties, problems at work, physical and mental ill health and crime. Alcohol-related harm may be associated with 62 per cent of serious head injuries in males, one in seven of all fatal road traffic accidents and 30 per cent of drownings. In Great Britain, 8–14 million working days are lost each year on account of alcohol misuse. The financial cost of such absences has been estimated at close to £2 million per year. It has been estimated that people with alcohol problems are 40–50 times more likely to commit suicide, while 66 per cent of parasuicides are likely to have experienced alcohol problems. Alcohol problems are involved in 40 per cent of incidents of domestic violence, and one in four male hospital admissions. NHS responses to alcohol problems cost an estimated £150 million per year and 28,000 deaths each year are drink-related. In England and Wales, 8.5 million people (6 million men and 2.5 million women) drink above the medically recommended levels (21 units per week for men and 14 units for women) and nearly 3 million people are alcohol dependent.

Explanatory models

Different models are used to explain alcohol problems – the disease model, which is dominant in the USA and the social learning model, dominant in the UK. The disease model tends to concentrate on dependent drinkers who have been labelled 'alcoholic' and often require residential treatment and detoxification. Traditional disease models have emphasized the biological, biochemical or physiological consequences of alcohol misuse and suggest that people who have drink problems are 'ill', not responsible for the consequences of drinking, cannot control their drinking and should abstain completely.

Social learning models involve seeing drinking behaviours as overlearned habits for which the drinker has responsibility, and it is argued that they should be set in environmental and situational contexts. These habits can be unlearned or modified, often without the need for complete abstinence. Cognitive-behavioural interventions and skills acquisition are important aspects of this approach. The social learning model tends to be linked with a continuum of problem drinking which does not make rigid distinctions between *normal* drinking and *problem* drinking or *alcoholism*. Instead, a continuum ranging from intoxication, to regular heavy drinking and dependency is preferred, with individuals moving along this continuum.

Intoxication is occasionally experienced by most people who enjoy social drinking. Intoxication at the wrong time and in the wrong place can have serious implications such as becoming drunk before driving a car or being in a pub at closing time with a reputation for 'trouble'. Regular heavy drinking, often on a daily basis over a prolonged period of time, can be associated with legal and social difficulties; it has a cumulative effect and is associated with physical illness. Dependent drinking, involving physical and psychological dependence, (traditionally labelled *alcoholism*) can cause very serious health problems. Those who are physically dependent when ceasing to use alcohol, can experience withdrawal symptoms. Dependence has a relapsing, often repetitive nature, despite the risk, or actual experience, of harm.

Indicators of dependence

Key indicators of dependence over a period of one to twelve months have been outlined in Edwards and Grant (1977):

- Narrowing of the drinking repertoire; difficulty in controlling the amount drunk; difficulty in stopping drinking in order to achieve the required blood alcohol level
- Preoccupation with drinking and its effects, so that other activities and relationships are given lower priority than drinking
- Increased tolerance to alcohol which requires higher intakes of alcohol to achieve the same effects
- Repeatedly experiencing physical and psychological withdrawal symptoms such as tremor, nausea, sweating and mood change
- Drinking regularly to relieve or avoid experiencing withdrawal symptoms
- Relapse after abstinence to previous patterns and levels of drinking, and continuing use despite knowledge of problems and harmful consequences
- Subjective awareness of a sense of compulsion to drink

The response to alcohol problems

Alcoholics Anonymous (AA) is the most widely known source of help for problem drinkers and is grounded in the disease model of *alcoholism*, focusing on the drinker's weakness *vis-à-vis* alcohol rather than on the wider environment. There are approximately 1,500 AA groups in England and Wales. There are also Councils on Alcohol or Alcohol Advisory Services which, next to AA, constitute the largest network of services for those experiencing alcohol problems within the voluntary independent sector. There are over 90 Councils in England, Scotland and Wales varying greatly in size and approach, but most of them tend not to regard the disease model as a basis for the alcohol problem; they rely heavily on trained voluntary counsellors.

Estimates of the prevalence of alcohol problems in social workers' family caseloads vary from 20 to 40 per cent. A survey of 3,000 probation officers revealed that 30 per cent of their caseloads had 'severe' problems with alcohol.

Many social workers have tended to stereotype negatively people with alcohol problems, to question their own right to intervene in such situations, to lack knowledge and skills in recognizing and assessing drink problems, to lack confidence in their interventions and to lack support from their managers, with deficiencies being noted in qualifying education and training courses. Social workers need to develop confidence, therapeutic optimism and commitment in working with alcohol problems – to develop role legitimacy, role adequacy and role support.

Social workers have a range of transferable skills that are valuable in work with those experiencing alcohol problems. These include generic assessment, interviewing and counselling skills based around, for example, systems approaches, cognitive behavioural, crisis intervention and task-centred work. Some additional more specialized knowledge and skills in working with alcohol problems can be bolted on to these generic skills: for instance, an understanding of the willingness and readiness of a person with alcohol problems to change behaviour – the importance of the precontemplation, action, maintenance and relapse stages which have significant implications for the types of intervention to be offered by social workers. Social workers need knowledge of the effects of alcohol, drinking units that are used in the assessment of amounts consumed when drinking, motivational interviewing skills and relapse prevention skills which are particularly significant in the earlier and later stages of intervention respectively.

continued

For Further Reading
Collins, S. 1990: *Alcohol, Social Work and Helping*. London: Routledge.
Collins, S. and Keene, J. 2000: *Alcohol, Social Work and Community Care*. Birmingham: Venture Press.
Edwards, G. and Grant, M. (eds) 1977: *Alcoholism*. Oxford: Oxford University Press.
Harrison, L. 1996: *Alcohol Problems in the Community*. London: Routledge.

STEWART COLLINS

Alternatives to Custody

Alternatives to custody are community-based court disposals which are imposed instead of a sentence of detention or imprisonment. Varying in form across jurisdictions, they can include community service orders and probation orders with or without a range of additional requirements. Critics have argued that they are often imposed instead of other non-custodial sentences, such as fines, and that the net of formal social control can be widened as a result. The 1991 Criminal Justice Act in England and Wales resulted in existing alternatives to custody being re-conceptualized as community sentences which are imposed as sentences in their own right.

GILL McIVOR

Alzheimer's Disease

Alzheimer's disease is one of a number of dementing illnesses, which is characterized pathologically by the presence of senile plaques and tangles in brain tissue.

There are approximately one-third of a million people suffering from Alzheimer's disease in the UK. Increasing age is the most robust risk factor for this disease and the number of new cases seen per year, per 2,500 individuals, is approximately four between the ages of 65 and 69 years, rising to approximately 150 between the ages of 90 and 94 years.

Apart from increasing age, the clearest associated risk factor for Alzheimer's disease is that of a positive family history, amounting to an approximately three-fold higher risk in first degree relatives of patients with Alzheimer's disease. Alzheimer's disease is multifactorial, but studies looking for environmental risk factors have been largely disappointing, and it is clear that a large proportion (60–70 per cent) of Alzheimer's disease is due to genetic factors.

Symptoms and management of the disease

A wide variety of symptoms occur in Alzheimer's disease, but memory loss is the most common. Memory loss is usually the presenting complaint, with patients having difficulty in learning new information such as the names of visitors. Later on in the disease, more distant memories are also affected. Other cognitive deficits include difficulties with speech, difficulties in motor activities, difficulties in recognizing objects and difficulties executing complex tasks. These cognitive changes relate more clearly to the disease progression than any other symptoms and have led to the widespread use of cognitive scales such as the Mini Mental State Examination. Other symptoms, however, are also very common. These include changes in behaviour, mood, thought, and auditory and visual hallucinations.

Historically, the management of patients with Alzheimer's disease has been largely influenced by the lack of specific treatments that can affect the course of the disease. Although this is changing, the management of Alzheimer's disease patients is still largely focused on helping carers to cope with the increased physical dependence of patients as the disease progresses, or with the treatment of troublesome behavioural disturbances. Commonly employed approaches include the use of community psychiatric nurses, domiciliary support, day care and respite care. Institutional care is usually reserved for patients with more physical or persistent non-cognitive symptoms.

In the early stages of the disease, a person with Alzheimer's disease may still have the capacity to consent to treatment. Clearly, as the dementing process progresses, the ability of the patient to perform the components of capacity will become diminished. However, there are no clear guidelines to state at what point that occurs during the dementing process, and each patient's capacity has to be assessed in its own right. When patients with Alzheimer's disease no longer have capacity and are refusing the treatment deemed necessary, then the only course of action is the implementation of the Mental Health Act. Patients with advanced Alzheimer's disease, while not having the capacity to consent to treatment, are often given treatment because of their lack of dissent. In this situation, the Mental Health Act Code of Practice Guidelines states that patients should be treated in accordance with the common law doctrine of necessity as long as it is in the patient's best interests.

The patient's financial affairs

With the diagnosis of Alzheimer's disease come a number of questions regarding a subject's ability to manage his or her own financial affairs. The four major processes of law implemented in these situations are power of attorney, enduring power of attorney, court of protection and appointeeship.

Power of attorney is a legal document whereby one person (the grantor) enables another person of his/her choice (the attorney) to act on his/her behalf with respect to financial matters. The attorney can then act as though he/she were the grantor. In English law, ordinary power of attorney becomes invalid if the patient becomes demented to such a degree that he/she can no longer manage his/her own affairs. Because of this, patients who are at the early stages of Alzheimer's disease should be encouraged to take out an enduring power of attorney.

With an *enduring power of attorney*, the grantor can require the enduring power of attorney to take effect at once and can continue despite subsequent incapacity, or to take effect only if the grantor should become incompetent. An enduring power of attorney can be made without the help of a solicitor; however, in practice, it is wise to ask a solicitor to ensure that the form has been correctly completed and questions of competence have been addressed. If the attorney believes that the grantor has become mentally incapable, the enduring power of attorney must then be registered with the court of protection.

The *court of protection* exists to supervise the management of the financial affairs of those who are mentally incapable of doing so themselves. The applications to the court of protection should occur when a patient who has taken out an enduring power of attorney is no longer mentally capable, when it is believed by the social worker that the patient is incapable of managing his/her own affairs because of mental capacity, when there is a dispute among the family about who should handle the patient's financial affairs or when there are no relatives.

Appointeeship may be appropriate if a patient has few or no assets and if his/her main sources of assets have been in the form of benefits from the Department of Social Security. The appointee is usually the local benefits supervisor who can claim social security benefits and allowances on behalf of a patient unable to do so because of a dementing illness.

For Further Reading

Arie, T. 1996: Some legal aspects of mental capacity. *British Medical Journal*, 313, 156–8.
Burns, A., Howard, R. and Petit, W. 1997: *Alzheimer's Disease: A Medical Companion.* Oxford: Blackwell Science.
Department of Health and the Welsh Office 1999: *Code of Practice, Mental Health Act 1983.* London: The Stationery Office.

CLIVE HOLMES

Anger Management

Anger management is a cognitive and behaviourally based intervention programme designed for corrective work with offenders. On the basis that individuals behave in accordance with learned responses, anti-social behaviour can therefore be unlearnt and pro-social modifications to maladaptive behaviour be learnt.

Anger management is often undertaken in group settings as a compulsory component of statutory community sentences. It focuses on an offender's responses to individual anger-stimulant situations such as frustration. It encourages a subjective recognition in offenders of potential loss of control and teaches avoidance strategies and control techniques such as constructive self-talk, negotiation and 'time-outs'.

HAZEL KEMSHALL AND PAUL HOLT

Animation

Animation entered social work language late and derives from European, particularly French social action. A Children's Society family centre employed an animateur as early as 1980. The animateur/animatrice develops community groups, runs play schemes, engages in community arts, and runs adult education programmes. Cultural animation is informed by community development and radical educational ideas – for example, those of Paulo Freire. His theory of conscientization enables the poor to embark on journeys of adult learning as well as an understanding of oppression. Outcomes are personal development and collective initiatives against poverty.

For Further Reading

Reisch, M., Wenocur, S. and Sherman, W. 1981: Empowerment, conscientization and animation as core social work skills. *Social Development Issues*, 5 (2–3), Summer/Fall, 109–20.

CHRIS WARREN-ADAMSON

Anorexia Nervosa

Anorexia nervosa is characterized by the core symptoms and behaviours of eating disorder, coupled with low body weight with a body mass index of less than 17.5 (weight in kilograms divided by the square of the height in metres, range 20–25). Initial treatment is often as an inpatient; it includes the correction of physical complications and nutritional rehabilitation as a starvation state maintains symptoms. Management often includes the individual and the family, in addition to the provision of support and monitoring. The disorder is often relapsing and remitting, though 44 per cent have a good outcome; there is 20 per cent mortality at twenty years.

CLAIRE KENWOOD AND RAY VIEWEG

Anti-discriminatory Practice

Anti-discriminatory practice is an approach to social work which emphasizes the various ways in which particular individuals and groups tend to be discriminated against and the need for professional practice to counter such discrimination.

Discrimination can occur on the basis of differences arising from ethnicity (racism), gender (sexism), class (classism), age (ageism), disability (disablism), sexual identity (heterosexism), mental health (mentalism), language (linguistic oppression) and various other less formally codified or documented forms of unfair or oppressive differentiation.

All such forms of discrimination can be seen to occur:

- at a personal level, in terms of individual attitudes and actions;
- at a cultural level, in terms of shared meanings, assumptions, values and stereotypes;
- at a structural level, in relation to the way society is organized *vis-à-vis* the distribution of power and life-chances (Thompson, 1997).

The background to anti-discriminatory practice

The radical social work movement of the 1960s and 1970s raised awareness of the significance of poverty and deprivation, and drew attention to the ways in which class-based inequalities underpinned the life context of so many recipients of social work services and interventions. The 1980s saw a greater awareness of, and emphasis upon, inequalities based on gender and race or ethnicity. This further fed into a greater sensitivity to various forms of discrimination (for example, in relation to age, disability or sexual identity). In turn, this led to a recognition that social work theory, policy and practice needed to take account of the full range of discriminatory factors that can reinforce patterns of inequality and can thus intensify or add to existing levels of oppression.

Anti-discriminatory practice can therefore be seen as an attempt to move away from traditional approaches to practice that concentrate primarily on the individual and/or the family context, with a view to promoting more emancipatory forms of practice which take greater account of the social context and the various ways in which the cultural assumptions and structural patterns of society stack the odds against certain disadvantaged or disenfranchized groups and individuals.

Power is an important underlying theme of anti-discriminatory practice insofar as discrimination arises from an imbalance of power. Indeed, the oppression associated with discrimination can be seen to arise from either the unintentional *mis*use of power (as a result of ignorance or misunderstanding, for example) or the deliberate *ab*use of power – with a clear intention to act against the interests of the group concerned. Power is also very relevant because the power that accompanies the social work role can play a crucial part in either challenging discrimination and oppression or adding significantly to them.

One problem standing in the way of developing anti-discriminatory practice is that of reductionism. This refers to the tendency to reduce a complex multilevel phenomenon such as discrimination to a simple matter of personal prejudice (*psychological reductionism*) or structural disadvantage (*sociological reductionism*). By failing to appreciate the subtleties and complexities of discrimination and the related concepts of inequality and oppression, we can encounter a number of significant problems, some of which may actually increase discrimination and/or its effects (Thompson, 1998).

The importance of language
A key feature of this approach which is often misunderstood is that of language. The importance of language stems from the fact that discrimination is often reflected in, and perpetuated by, forms of language. Language can be exclusive, in the sense that certain people are excluded by such usage – for example, using masculine forms of language to refer to people in general has the effect of excluding and devaluing women and the part they play.

Language is just one example of the range of subtle social processes that maintain patterns of inequality. Developing anti-discriminatory practice involves recognizing these processes and thus avoiding, challenging or undermining them.

Indeed, 'challenge' is an important word in the anti-discriminatory vocabulary. This is because patterns and processes of discrimination operate all around us – in attitudes and values, in many of the assumptions we take for granted, in organizational structures and patterns and in the way society is organized in terms of 'social divisions' such as class, race, gender, age, disability, sexual identity, linguistic group and so on. The task, then, is not simply to avoid forms of discrimination in our own actions and attitudes (*non-discriminatory practice*), but also to challenge them in other aspects of the situations we encounter in our work roles (*anti-discriminatory practice*).

The nature of anti-discriminatory practice
The primary goal of anti-discriminatory practice is the promotion of equality and social justice. This reflects both the value base of social work (with an emphasis on humanitarian goals and practices) and the very nature of the social work enterprise (tackling social problems at the level of personal social services).

Anti-discriminatory practice is not a separate or discrete social work theory or method, but rather a value stance to underpin practice in general – an approach premised on a commitment to countering unfair discrimination, inequality and oppression.

continued

Basic principles of the approach include working in partnership, empowerment, a focus on rights, and affirming diversity.

- *Working in partnership* involves moving beyond traditional medicalized views of the social worker as an expert who 'diagnoses' the problem and 'prescribes' a remedial course of action towards one based on open consultation and shared responsibility.
- *Empowerment* relates to the process of helping people to gain greater control over their lives by seeking to remove, alleviate or navigate around personal, cultural or structural obstacles to progress.
- *A focus on rights*: while providing caring interventions can be seen as a legitimate humanitarian activity, such caring also has to be seen in the context of rights. That is, respecting, safeguarding and promoting rights (for example, the right to be treated with dignity) is an essential complement to care.
- *Affirming diversity*: recognizing and valuing social differences is an important foundation on which to build emancipatory forms of practice. Such differences should be seen as social assets, rather than as problems.

For Further Reading
Lesnik, B. (ed.) 1998: *Countering Discrimination in Social Work*. Aldershot: Arena.
Thompson, N. 1997: *Anti-Discriminatory Practice* (2nd edn). London: Macmillan.
Thompson, N. 1998: *Promoting Equality: Challenging Discrimination and Oppression in the Human Services*. London: Macmillan.

NEIL THOMPSON

Anti-oppressive Practice

Anti-oppressive practice is a radical social work approach which is informed by humanistic and social justice values and takes account of the experiences and views of oppressed people. It is based on an understanding of how the concepts of power, oppression and inequality determine personal and structural relations.

Practitioners are required to analyse how the socially constructed divisions of race, age, gender, class, sexuality and disability, and the impact of differential access to resources, interconnect and interact to define the life experiences of individuals and communities. From this position, practitioners are provided with the means to recognize and challenge situations of oppression within their work.

Anti-oppressive practice is based on a belief that social work should make a difference, so that those who have been oppressed may regain control of their lives and re-establish their right to be full and active members of society. To achieve this aim, practitioners have to be political, reflective, reflexive and committed to promoting change.

For Further Reading
Dalrymple, J. and Burke, B. 1995: *Anti-oppressive Practice: Social Care and the Law*. Buckingham: Open University Press.

JANE DALRYMPLE AND BEVERLEY BURKE

Anxiety Disorders

The term *anxiety disorders* encompasses the large group within the old rubric of *neurotic disorders*. Historically, psychiatric symptoms and disorders have been separated into *neuroses* and *psychoses*. Neurotic symptoms are experiences that are normal in form but abnormal in their setting, severity or duration; low mood, fearfulness, anxiety, lack of motivation and lack of energy are common examples. Psychotic symptoms are abnormal in form: for example, delusions and hallucinations. Psychiatric disorders and syndromes have, in the past, been divided in this way depending on the group in which the symptoms predominantly lay. However, research into the epidemiology, prognosis and treatment of psychiatric conditions has demonstrated this classification to be flawed, and, as a result, there has been a move away from the term *neurotic disorders*.

Symptoms

Many of the specific disorders are discussed under their own headings; this section concentrates on common themes relating to the anxiety disorders as a whole. The symptoms of anxiety are common to all these diagnoses and fall into two groups – psychological and physical. The psychological experience of anxiety is a combination of several related feelings such as fear, thoughts of dread or impending doom, worry, restlessness and tension. The physical, or somatic symptoms include dry mouth, palpitations, hand tremor, sweaty palms, 'butterflies and knots in the stomach'. These physical symptoms are due to arousal of the sympathetic nervous system.

Non-psychiatric medical conditions such as overactive thyroid glands, cardiac chest pain and asthma can also present with anxiety symptoms and such conditions should be excluded in the assessment of the person.

Anxiety symptoms also occur in other psychiatric conditions such as schizophrenia and depression, and these illnesses can co-exist with anxiety disorders. If either of these two conditions is treated in their own right, the anxiety symptoms often improve considerably. Consequently, there is a need to determine whether the presenting problem is primarily an anxiety disorder or is secondary to another condition.

Substance abuse (particularly the abuse of alcohol and benzodiazepines) is associated with anxiety symptoms and disorders. The relationship is complex. Individuals may abuse substances in an attempt to self-medicate against the symptoms. Substance misuse also paradoxically produces anxiety symptoms, while drug withdrawal states may precipitate severe anxiety symptoms.

Causation and prevalence

The theories surrounding the cause of anxiety disorders are not mutually exclusive. The biological theory states that patients with anxiety disorders have different brain function with abnormal function of the serotonin and noradrenaline neurotransmitter system. Genetic, brain imaging and drug therapy studies support this, seen in the greater concordance rates in monozygotic (identical) twins, compared to dizygotic twins. Functional brain scans have shown differences in the brain activity (oxygen metabolism) in the basal ganglia of patients with anxiety disorders. Antidepressant drugs that have direct pharmacological effects on the serotonin and noradrenaline neurotransmitter systems have been shown to produce clinical improvements. The psychodynamic theory argues that anxiety symptoms are a psychological defence against more painful (unconscious) psychological conflicts. Behavioural theory sees anxiety as a learned fear response that has been generalized.

The prevalence of formal anxiety disorders in the general population is approximately 10 per cent. Up to 25 per cent of patients seen by general practitioners have significant anxiety symptoms, as do up to 40 per cent of young adult (18–35) probation and social services clients. Anxiety disorders are more common in women, and tend to present in early adult life, but can present at any age.

A trigger or 'stressor' precipitates anxiety symptoms, though specific stressors are discussed under subsequent headings (for example, in relation to *post-traumatic stress disorders*). The stressor may be closely related in time to a recent event or to one of many years ago, which often occurs in the development of phobias; for example, a child frightened by a dog can develop a dog phobia in later years.

The management of anxiety disorders

The management of anxiety disorders begins with a clear formulation of the patient's condition and understanding the factors that have contributed in that particular

continued

case. A combination of psychological, social and pharmacological treatments can be used.

Psychological interventions are the mainstay treatments in mild to moderate anxiety disorders, and are generally cognitive and behavioural in nature, consisting of education, relaxation and *in vivo* desensitization when appropriate. A range of professionals are active in such approaches, including community psychiatric nurses, psychologists and social workers, and most patients are treated wholly in primary care.

Social interventions should identify the factors which precipitate and maintain the condition, and attempts be made to alleviate them. This is an important area for social work expertise.

The two main classes of drug used are the anxiolytics (anti-anxiety) and the antidepressants. The anxiolytics, usually benzodiazepines such as diazepam and lorazepam, are very effective symptomatic treatments. They reduce the psychological and physical symptoms considerably, but there is a risk of tolerance and dependence occurring, especially after a month of regular use. They are best used in anxiety states which are precipitated by a clear trigger and are likely to be short lived. They can be used, however, for longer periods in cases where clinical benefits outweigh the risks. They are best avoided in less severe cases and non-drug approaches should be used first.

Treatment should be tailored to the individual, and may range from simple interventions to an intensive treatment package involving a combination of the above treatments, utilizing a range of professional inputs.

The prognosis of anxiety disorders is variable and depends on many factors. The majority of anxiety disorders are short lived and settle within six months. However, 80 per cent of disorders that persist for more than six months are still present after three years. Generally speaking, the more severe the symptoms, the poorer the prognosis.

For Further Reading

Buckley, P., Bird, J. and Harrison, G. 1995: *Examination Notes in Psychiatry: A Postgraduate Text*. Oxford: Butterworth Heinemann.
Gelder, M., Gath, D., Mayou, R. and Cowen, P. 1996: *Oxford Textbook of Psychiatry*. Oxford: Oxford University Press.
Wilkinson, G. 1992: *Anxiety: Recognition and Treatment in General Practice*. Oxford: Radcliffe Medical Press.

CLAIRE KENWOOD AND RAY VIEWEG

Appropriate Adult

In England and Wales, the Police and Criminal Evidence Act 1984 recognizes the special vulnerability of suspects detained for questioning at a police station who are aged under 17 or are mentally disordered or 'handicapped'. In such instances, the police must arrange for an *appropriate adult* to attend to assist the suspect. Though this task is commonly undertaken by a parent or relative, an informed social worker is more likely to take an active, assertive role in the interests of justice.

An appropriate adult's tasks should not be confused with legal representation, but include:

• aiding the suspect's understanding of the process

• facilitating communication with the suspect
• ensuring that interviews are conducted properly and fairly
• safeguarding the suspect's rights and welfare.

The appropriate adult has the right to inspect the custody record, to interview the suspect in private, to obtain legal advice for the suspect and to intervene if unfair interview tactics are used. Vulnerable suspects are more likely to be more suggestible when questioned, to give incriminating accounts that are inflated or invented, or to be more readily manipulated into confessing crimes when ill-informed of the basis for their detention or without understanding the legal implications of their admissions. Intervention at this early stage can help to gain rapport and build a supportive relationship that may enhance future work.

For Further Reading
Littlechild B. 1996: *The Police and Criminal Evidence Act 1984: The Role of the Appropriate Adult*. Birmingham: BASW.

NIGEL STONE

The Approved Social Worker

Approved social work in England and Wales originated in the Mental Health Act 1983. An approved social worker (ASW) is a professionally qualified social worker who has completed a nationally approved, assessed course in mental health law, policy and practice.

ASWs hold statutory rights and duties. Primarily, in respect of a person believed to be suffering from a serious mental illness, they have a duty to make an application for admission to hospital or guardianship where necessary, having regard to the least restrictive alternative to compulsory admission. ASWs have a right to enter premises where a mentally ill person may be living. This is not a power to force entry; if access is denied, ASWs may apply to a magistrate's court for a warrant to enable forced access. ASWs are required to assess people whom the police have detained in the belief that they are suffering from a serious mental illness.

An ASW may only be appointed by a social services department. Authorities recommend that the role of the ASW should be wider than solely considering the matter of compulsory admission to hospital. This might include the prevention of admission, the provision of advice, counselling, continuity of care and family work.

ASWs are accorded by statute independence of judgement. Yet they are also required to work in collaboration with other professionals and service users; and they are unable to perform their duties satisfactorily unless they do so.

For Further Reading
Pringle, N. N. and Thompson, P. J. 1999: *Social Work, Psychiatry and the Law*. Aldershot: Arena.

PAUL THOMPSON

Art Therapy

Art therapy refers to the process of making visual images within the context of a psychotherapeutic relationship. Theoretical underpinnings are based on the disciplines of the visual arts, psychotherapy and psychology. The emphasis is on the creative process of image making through engagement with art materials and the therapeutic dialogue between client, image and therapist.

Art therapy is primarily a non-verbal process which aids communication and the expression of feeling. It facilitates the exploration of areas of interpersonal difficulty appropriate to the client, and brings unconscious concerns to consciousness at a symbolic and concrete level, enabling verbal understanding and insight.

Art therapy is widely used in groups and individually with adults, adolescents and children with mental health difficulties, as well as for those not usually offered the benefits of psychotherapeutic help such as older people, those who are terminally ill, and people with learning disabilities.

Art therapy is a state-registered profession involving two years of full-time postgraduate training; its practitioners are increasingly found working in services offering psychological and emotional support to clients in social services settings, special education and the penal system.

For Further Reading
Case, C. and Dalley, T. 1992: *The Handbook of Art Therapy*. London: Tavistock/Routledge.

PHILIPPA BROWN

Asperger Syndrome

Asperger syndrome affects ways of communicating. Hans Asperger identified the syndrome in 1944; his work was translated in the 1980s. There is continuing debate about whether Asperger syndrome is part of the autistic spectrum or whether it constitutes a separate diagnostic category.

In Asperger syndrome, behaviour is characterized by difficulty in understanding and performing communication tasks in three areas: the literal interpretation of language, leading to distress, for example, if 'the cat's got your tongue'; a failure to understand non-verbal communication, for example, eye contact, turning away; and difficulty with social cues, for example, 'I'm tired' is not heard as a message asking you to leave.

For Further Reading
Cumine, V., Leach, J. and Stevenson, G. 1998: *Asperger Syndrome: A Practical Guide for Teachers*. London: David Fulton.

CLARE BECKETT

Assertive Outreach

Assertive outreach is a system of intensive client-centred community support, including health care and social support, for people with severe mental illness who have difficulty in engaging with services. It is characterized by low caseloads and a high level of regular and persistent contact with clients.

The assertive outreach model was developed in the USA and Australia, but has now spread to a number of developed countries. Some other terms have been used to describe intensive community care of this kind including 'Programme of Assertive Community Treatment' (PACT), 'Intensive Case Management' (ICM) and 'Mobile Community/ Intensive Treatment Teams' (MCTT/MITT).

Assertive outreach teams

There is good evidence that this system of care can engage and maintain contact with even the most difficult of clients. How the assertive outreach function is delivered can vary from area to area. Generally speaking, in areas with high psychiatric morbidity, an assertive outreach team will be required. This will consist of a suitable skill-mix of the relevant professionals, primarily mental health nurses, psychiatrists, occupational therapists and social workers, and may often include unqualified support workers. Where morbidity is low, the assertive outreach function can be provided from a generic Community Mental Health Team. The team or function can be located in a variety of statutory or non-statutory agencies.

Assertive outreach teams deliberately select people with the most severe and complex problems. The typical user of such services is a younger adult male who has suffered from a schizophrenic illness for a long period of time. He may experience one or more of the following factors:

- History of self-harm
- History of violence
- Non-compliance with medication
- Recent hospital admission(s)

Typically, clients of assertive outreach will require help with a range of issues extending well beyond physical and mental health care to support with benefits, housing, and the skills of daily living.

Achieving effectiveness

Assertive outreach requires a high level of commitment from staff. Typically, a team member might work with around ten clients, spending considerable time in face-to-face contact, and in the co-ordination of care. There is evidence and argument that deviation from the core principles of assertive outreach prevents achievement of good outcomes. Where assertive outreach is effective most of the following factors are usually present:

- The team delivers a good proportion of the required services, including clinical services, from within the team.
- Teams are multi-disciplinary and trained to deliver the outreach function.
- The team has control over hospital admissions.
- A range of relapse prevention techniques are deployed.
- There is a range of support services available locally for assertive outreach workers to connect with.
- There is a single point of access for the client.
- Each service user should have an identified key worker who co-ordinates a team-based approach to care.

- Clients are not discharged from the care of the team (unless their needs significantly decline).
- Team workers go out and meet clients in their usual community settings.

In addition, experience of setting up and managing assertive outreach demonstrates the importance of:

- establishing clear referral criteria in the context of a multi-agency agreement about the role of the team;
- choosing the right staff to work with clients;
- providing adequate clinical and managerial supervision of staff.

Outcome evidence from the USA, Australia and the UK shows that teams can maintain contact with up to 95 per cent of clients over time, and that there are improvements in symptomatology and social functioning. Clients of assertive outreach report high satisfaction with services and improved quality of life. Carers also report satisfaction with this care model.

Young people with higher levels of symptoms showed the greatest improvement in some services. There is evidence of greater stability of clients' housing placements when receiving assertive outreach. There is strong evidence that assertive outreach can reduce bed utilization (both the number and duration of admissions), and that it is a more efficient and lower cost form of care than hospital-based care.

Continuity of care is a vital component of assertive outreach – this is one reason why a multi-disciplinary approach, including psychiatry, is important. The team needs to maintain continuity of responsibility during any hospital admissions, otherwise stays remain long and the integration of care is lost. The effects of assertive outreach tend to diminish rapidly once it is withdrawn.

Given the current levels of interest in assertive outreach among governments and senior managers in public agencies in the UK and elsewhere, we can expect to see a significant growth in this function. Attention will therefore have to be paid to the organization and resourcing of such services, and particularly to the recruitment, development and retention of suitable staff.

For Further Reading
Marshall, M., Lockwood, A., Green, R. and Gray, A. 1998: Case management for people with severe mental disorders. In C. Adams, J. Anderson and J. De Jesus Mari (eds), *The Cochrane Database of Systematic Reviews (The Schizophrenia Module)*, Oxford: Software Update.
Stein, L. I. and Test, M. A. 1980: Alternatives to mental hospital treatment: 1. A conceptual model, treatment programme and clinical evaluation. *Archives of General Psychiatry*, 37, 392–7.
The Sainsbury Centre for Mental Health 1998: *Keys to Engagement*. London: The Sainsbury Centre for Mental Health.

ANDREW McCULLOCH

Assessing Motivation

The direct *assessment of motivation* is an additional measure when determining the nature of a person's difficulties and deciding upon the most appropriate treatment or intervention. Two approaches have been developed so far; the *decisional balance* and *readiness to change*. The *decisional balance* considers the extent to which the costs of a particular behaviour begin to be outweighed by the benefits to be obtained by amending it. *Readiness to change* is judged by asking the client directly about their willingness to change. Assessing motivation assists in determining whether to intervene and what type of intervention would be most beneficial.

ELIZABETH LANCASTER

Assessment in Child Care

Assessment is the process that controls the nature, direction and scope of social work interventions. It is particularly important in work with children because of its potential to initiate or influence life-changing decisions in relation to vulnerable individuals. *Child care* is used here to refer to the service provided to children and families where the child is looked after by a local authority or is at risk of being removed from home because of the inability of parents to provide care of an acceptable standard.

There are two main aspects of assessment in child care: the first is concerned with decision making, the second with outcomes.

Assessment related to decision making

A principal aim of British child care practice since the end of World War II has been to enable children to grow up within their own families and to end unavoidable separations at the earliest opportunity. The comprehensive Children Act 1989 laid great emphasis on continued parental responsibility and involvement, even when placement away from home was unavoidable. It also underlined the importance of cultural, ethnic and racial diversity. As a result, assessment has to encompass a wide range of factors which may impinge on a family's present and future ability to care for its children. The social worker must select the most relevant information to formulate an assessment which both describes the current position and attempts some prediction of the likely consequences of different placement decisions.

To assist in carrying out this task, social workers need to view assessment within an ecological framework, taking into account the children's cultural, socioeconomic, and ethnic characteristics, the parent–child relationship, the composition of the extended family, the degree of neighbourhood and community support available to the parent or principal caregiver, and the child's own age, development, functioning and behaviour, in addition to the interaction between all these factors. It is a legal requirement in Britain, as well as good practice, that children should be encouraged and enabled to express their ideas about their own situation and where they should live, an aspect of child care that was seriously neglected in the past and is still absent from discussion in much of the US literature.

The assessment should provide the basis for a plan for the child which offers the best prospect of promoting satisfactory development and future well-being and a stable living situation. In order of desirability the plan might be as follows:

1 *Family preservation*: the child to remain at home with social work support and monitoring
2 *Respite or shared care*, with parents looking after the child for part of the time
3 *Foster care* with relatives
4 *Short-term foster care* with a view to early return
5 Placement for *adoption*, with or without contact (if there appears to be no prospect of reunification)
6 *Long-term foster or residential care* with direct or indirect contact with parents/family members

If the decision is that remaining at home would cause harm to the child, the social worker then has to assess the suitability of possible alternative homes to meet that particular child's needs. Research on placement stability or breakdown has underlined the importance of carefully matching the child and prospective carers to ensure clear expectations. Problems arise when there is a limited choice and placements are made on the basis of expediency rather than skilled assessment of child, family and carers.

Assessment is not a one-off activity, but a continuous process which needs to take account of changing family circumstances and the child's growing capacity to take an active part in decision making. Time is needed for the social worker to assess the potential strengths of the family and its ability to change. On the other hand, there are strong arguments for setting firm boundaries to avoid the phenomenon of drift in care. Based on the evaluation of an intensive family reunification project, Fein and Staff (1993) recommend a time limit of six months for assessment before an alternative plan is initiated.

Assessment of child care outcomes

In the late 1980s, the drive for efficiency and effectiveness in public services led to increased interest in the outcomes of child care and welfare interventions. Reinforced by studies of young people leaving care showing them to be severely disadvantaged by comparison with their peers, this resulted in a Department of Health working party which developed instruments for assessing outcomes, the *Looking After Children* materials. The core of the system is a set of age-related *Assessment and Action Records* providing evidence of children's progress in a number of different developmental domains: health, education, identity, family and social relationships, emotional and behavioural development, social presentation and self-care skills. The *Records* specify desirable outcomes in all domains for each age group and ask questions about whether the 'parental' actions likely to lead to their achievements have been carried out. The assessment thus leads directly to an action plan to be co-ordinated by social workers in association with carers and other professionals. Aggregating the data from *Records* also offers an opportunity to build a bridge between assessment of individual and organizational outcomes.

The theoretical basis for this model of outcome assessment is described by Parker et al. (1991). It has been adopted by over 90 per cent of local authorities in Britain, translated into seven languages, and adapted for use in numerous other countries. The *Looking After Children* system can be seen as part of a general trend to standardize assessment procedures by the use of scales and instruments. However, such standardized instruments can only be a guide, in no way replacing the need for the social worker's skilled professional judgement of individual children's characteristics, needs and circumstances.

For Further Reading

Fein, E. and Staff, I. 1993: Last best chance: findings from a reunification services program. *Child Welfare*, 62 (1), 25–40.
Milner, J. and O'Byrne, P. 1998: *Assessment in Social Work Practice*. London: Macmillan.
Parker, R., Ward, H., Jackson, S., Aldgate, J. and Wedge, P. 1991: *Looking After Children: Assessing Outcomes in Child Care*. London: HMSO.

SONIA JACKSON

Assessment in Community Care

Assessment in community care involves the formation of a judgement concerning the needs of an adult which may result in their requirements being met by social care provision.

The nature of assessment

The aim of community care assessment is for a client's needs to be ascertained so that an individualized package of care can be provided. The assessment process occurs at the point when agencies engage with individual clients, make decisions about specific services and commit resources. An imaginative assessment of needs can result in creative service provision that allows people to live as independently as possible in the community, rather than in residential or nursing home care, with a better quality of life for themselves and their carers. There is an underlying assumption that there will be equal access to social care provision of an appropriate quality. However, this is difficult to manage as clients' needs are diverse and are sometimes difficult to distinguish from 'wants'; resources are scarce and there may be different funding levels available depending on the client group or geographical area.

Community care assessment is an information gathering exercise carried out with the participation of client and carer to obtain a holistic picture of their needs; this then forms the basis for decision making. There is an initial screening that determines the level of assessment, whether the presenting problem is appropriate to the agency, and whether eligibility criteria are applicable. The community care assessment combines agency policy, professional appraisal and client viewpoint. It shows the client's position at a certain point in time and results in the formulation of a care plan that is implemented and regularly monitored to ensure that changing needs continue to be met appropriately.

Assessing officers will try to establish trusting relationships with the client, within which sensitive information can be shared. The process can be complex and will involve input from other professional workers and agencies with specialized knowledge. There is a balance to be achieved between obtaining sufficient information for the worker and client to make informed decisions and the risk of intrusion which may leave the client feeling oppressed rather than enabled. It is important that this process be carefully managed, as the client's future quality of life may be dependent on the resulting resources provided.

Assessment will cover the clients' health needs, physical and mental capacity, emotional needs, financial support, addictions, suitability of living environment, occupational requirements and carer support. This will be in the context of the client's present situation, including stress and risk factors to themselves and others. The purpose is to construct a comprehensive picture of the clients's needs, strengths, limitations and existing support structures.

The provision of resources

National legislation requires agencies to make service provision available for people with social care needs, but there are limited resources and it is professional workers who usually gatekeep access to them, using assessment as a rationing tool. The demand for resources is increasing for many reasons, including the growing number of people aged over 80 and the movement of people from institutions into community care. There is a political restriction on the funding available for social care provision, as governments make choices about how to spend taxpayers' money; this creates problems for those who make decisions about meeting assessed needs: agencies use *eligibility criteria* to target those most in need without exceeding their budgets.

Eligibility criteria are systems of bandings which assign people to particular categories depending on their level of capability. They are used as a tool by agencies to decide whether someone is in sufficient need to qualify for services. They consist of a series of questions that help the worker to make a judgement about the level and type of provision that may be applicable and to assist in prioritizing client need: clients who are banded in a high-risk category will be eligible for more resources. Assessment may not result in services being allocated in the way that clients want, and agencies have complaints systems in place to give clients redress. The judicial system can also be used to challenge agency decisions.

Client involvement is central to the concept of community care assessment, and professional workers strive to empower clients to participate fully. This may sometimes be difficult as ways have to be found to explain the complex processes of assessment, taking into account any impairments that may affect communication or the client's ability to understand. Two other factors may inhibit client empowerment: first, the agency retains power over the allocation of resources; and, second, the client may be overwhelmed by the involvement of a number of professional workers.

Ideally, clients would be in a position to self-assess their own needs; but, sometimes, they may be reluctant to take part in the assessment process, seeing it as yet another source of stress at a time when they may be at a life crisis point. Sometimes, professional workers find that they are only able to involve the client to the extent of giving information about the process of assessment and telling them how to complain if they wish to.

Assessment is crucial to social care delivery, and is used as a tool by agencies to provide fair access to resources according to need. Professional workers want to work in partnership with clients to ensure that their needs are being individually met, though the concept of people having *needs* rather than *rights* may itself be disabling.

From the client's viewpoint, assessment may give access to increased independence and improved quality of life through sensitive service provision. It may also seem to be an intrusive process and raise expectations of choice that agencies are unable to deliver.

For Further Reading
Bounds, J. and Hepburn, H. 1996: *Empowerment and Older People – A Practical Approach*. Birmingham: Pepar.
Coulshed, V. and Orme, J. 1998: *Social Work Practice – An Introduction (3rd edn)*. London: Macmillan.
Mandelstom, M. 1999: *Community Care Practice and the Law*. London: Jessica Kingsley.
LEONNE GRIGGS

Assessment in Work with Offenders

Assessment can be described as a process of professional judgement or appraisal of the situation, circumstances and behaviour of the offender. It is one of the central tasks of the probation service at point of sentence, during community supervision, and for early release from custody.

The nature of assessment
The aims of assessment have changed as the roles and tasks of the service have been changed by legislation and penal policy. The traditional psychoanalytic and diagnostic approach has been superseded by attention to those criminogenic factors which research has indicated are associated with reoffending. These factors can either be dynamic and linked to environmental and situational factors such as accommodation, unemployment or anti-social attitudes and peer group networks, or they can be static, such as age,
continued

gender and previous convictions (Andrews, 1995). Assessments which combine both sets of factors are seen as the most useful. The purpose of assessment is the accurate identification of those factors associated with the individual offender's likelihood to reoffend. This been defined by Andrews as the *risk/needs principle*.

Assessments of risk of harm or dangerousness are also carried out by probation staff. These require the identification of those offenders who have the potential to carry out offences which present a risk of physical harm or psychological trauma to others. Assessments which combine attention to antecedents, behaviours and circumstances have the most efficacy (Kemshall, 1996). Research has established the factors most often associated with violent behaviour as age (17–25); gender (male); past behaviour and motivations (for example, aggressive behaviours and anti-social attitudes); the presence or absence of internal inhibitors (the absence of brakes on aggressive predispositions); availability of weapons and preparedness to use them; and access to victims.

The main format for carrying out assessment has remained the one-to-one interview, supported by information collection from other sources and reference to previous records where available. Interviewing can be supported by formalized assessment methods which can structure professional judgement, supplement it, or replace it.

Checklists of relevant risk factors assist interviewing by directing practitioner attention to the most pertinent areas. Formalized assessment methods which provide a probabilistic calculation of risk can be used to supplement clinical judgement. All methods are designed to improve the reliability and consistency of assessment, although the total eradication of professional judgement has been questioned. Personal and contextual knowledge pertinent to the likelihood of reoffending cannot be supplied by the actuarial method alone.

Assessments should promote equality, diversity and anti-discriminatory practice, and be verifiable through the cross-referencing of information. Consultation with other agencies is an important feature of offender risk assessment.

The preparation of reports

Assessments are most often presented in reports to sentencers and parole boards, or are contained in community supervision plans. Assessments in court reports are required to provide an analysis of the offence, relevant information about the offender and an assessment of the 'risk to the public of reoffending' (Home Office, 1995). Probation officers have a statutory duty to provide such assessments and can propose sentencing options to courts aimed at the reduction of risk, although sentencers are not obliged to sentence accordingly. Such assessment are informed by professional judgement, and, in some probation areas, by the use of formalized assessment tools for the prediction of reoffending. They are unlikely to take the form of statistical predictions of reoffending.

Pre-release reports are also required to provide a risk assessment in addition to an assessment of home circumstances and likely response to supervision. Assessment for community supervision should identify the criminogenic factors associated with reoffending, the possibility of risk to the public, and any factors such as alcohol or drug dependency requiring specialist provision. In addition, all assessments should establish the offender's motivation to change together with the level of responsiveness or the type of programme delivery most suited to the learning style of the offender.

The appropriate identification of risk level, criminogenic factors, motivation to change and responsiveness are the key features of offender assessment.

Assessment is central to the appropriate matching of offenders to interventions and to rationalizing the allocation of resources. This has resulted in a reduction of individual probation officer discretion and a managed approach to assessment, programme intervention and evaluation. Assessment has become one component of case management with an emphasis upon managed and evaluated practice, evidence-led assessment and intervention, and rational and objective systems for the allocation of resources.

For Further Reading
Andrews, D. A. 1995: The psychology of criminal conduct and effective treatment. In J. McGuire (ed.), *What Works: Reducing Reoffending. Guidelines from Research and Practice.* Chichester: John Wiley.
Home Office 1995: *National Standards for the Supervision of Offenders in the Community.* London: Home Office.
Kemshall, H. 1996: *Reviewing Risk: A Review of Research on the Assessment and Management of Risk and Dangerousness – Implications for Policy and Practice in the Probation Service.* London: Home Office Research and Statistics Directorate.

HAZEL KEMSHALL AND CHARLOTTE KNIGHT

Assisted Conception

Assisted conception refers to a range of techniques that enable involuntarily childless adults to achieve parenthood. These include interventions of varying technical complexity and may utilize embryos, eggs or sperm provided by the recipient individual or couple, or embryos, eggs or sperm provided by a third party whose identity may or may not be known to the recipient(s). While the medical profession has assumed the dominant role in the provision of assisted conception services, social workers – especially in the UK, the USA, Australia and New Zealand – have increasingly sought to influence service development and to ensure that the human and social implications of forming families in this way are not subordinated to the pursuit of technical efficacy.

Social work interest has focused on two broad areas: encouraging the provision of high quality counselling for those seeking treatment and for donors; and consideration of the implications for people born as a result of assisted conception services both as children and as adults, especially issues relating to the provision of access to information about genetic origins where donated embryos or gametes have been used.

For Further Reading
Blyth, E. 1999: The social work role in assisted conception. *British Journal of Social Work,* 29 (5), 727–40.

ERIC BLYTH

Attachment Theory

Attachment theory is a theory of behaviour and personality development in close relationships. It offers an explanation of the origin of people's emotional and relationship styles. The theory considers why certain patterns of attachment behaviour either persist or change, over time and across relationships. In its applications, attachment theory is used whenever social workers seek to change people's internal experience, interpersonal relationships or external social behaviour. In its earliest formulations, the theory and its applications concentrated on the quality of parent–child relationships, but it has now been developed and expanded to consider relationships and emotional behaviour across the lifespan. It is therefore relevant to work with all client groups.

The origins of attachment theory
The main features of attachment theory were developed and presented over several decades, beginning in the 1950s, by the British child psychiatrist, John Bowlby. Early clinical and research observations by Bowlby noted that many young children who had

continued

suffered either long periods of separation from their parents or severe emotional adversity went on to develop a range of behavioural and mental health problems. With his colleague, James Robertson, Bowlby also recognized that young children separated from their parents displayed a highly typical sequence of distressed behaviours. An initial phase of protest and crying was followed by a second one of despair, apathy and listlessness. If the loss and separation continued for some weeks, the young child would then enter a third, defensive phase of quiet detachment and withdrawal. It therefore appeared to Bowlby that young children form strong bonds, or attachments, with their main caregivers, which, if broken, cause great anxiety and distress. Out of his attempts to see links between these two observations – early adversity leading to later emotional and behavioural problems, and young children's attempts to cope psychologically with the loss of a parent – emerged the first formulations of what was later to become known as attachment theory.

The second main figure to appear in the history of attachment theory was Mary Ainsworth, an American-born psychologist. Originally a research student with Bowlby, Ainsworth later carried out a number of ethological studies in Uganda where she observed mother–baby interactions in the natural setting of the home. Recognizing that the quality and character of caregiving provided by mothers varied, Ainsworth, on taking up a post in the USA, developed a laboratory test (the 'strange situation' procedure), supported by further home observations, that was able to describe and classify different types of infant attachment behaviour within a variety of distinct caregiving environments. It was the combination of Ainsworth's rigorous research observations and Bowlby's groundbreaking theoretical formulations that showed the links between children's experience in close relationships and the character of their subsequent psychosocial development.

The nature of attachment

Attachment behaviour is an instinctive biological drive that propels infants into close, protective proximity with their main carers whenever they experience anxiety, fear, or distress. As well as distressors such as illness, hunger, fatigue and danger, the physical or psychological loss or unavailability of the child's main carer is a major trigger of attachment behaviour. The loss of the carer poses particular emotional difficulties for the infant. Loss of the attachment figure not only causes anxiety, it also entails the absence of the very person who is able to help soothe the child and return them to a more relaxed psychological condition. Prolonged or repeated psychological 'losses' of the attachment figure, whether physical or emotional, might therefore subject children to sustained periods of unresolved distress. Attachment figures who are emotionally unavailable and unresponsive are just as likely to cause anxiety and distress as those who are physically absent or dangerous. Attachment theory is therefore a theory that demands great interest be taken in the interaction between individuals and their social environment. The character of these interactions is believed to have a profound bearing on children's long-term social and emotional competence, well-being and psychopathology.

The connection between the quality of the child's external social world and their emerging internal psychological make-up is made via the *internal working model*. This cognitive model is an attempt by the child to represent mentally the self, other people, and the relationship between them. Depending on the quality of the child's close caregiving experiences, the self and other people can be represented as either positive (loved, valued, effective, etc.) or negative (rejected, ineffective, unworthy, etc.). As attachment relationships become psychologically internalized, the quality of a child's external social experiences becomes an internal mental property of that child. The mental inside is then able to influence the child's view of the self and others as well as social behaviour.

Attachment styles

In their efforts to defensively adapt to their caregiving relationship, children develop one of four basic internal working models which give rise to distinct attachment styles:

1 *Secure* attachment patterns: children experience their caregiver as available and themselves positively.
2 *Ambivalent* patterns: children experience their caregiver as inconsistently responsive and themselves as dependent and poorly valued.
3 *Avoidant* patterns: children experience their caregivers as consistently rejecting and themselves as insecure but compulsively self-reliant.
4 *Disorganized* patterns (often associated with children who have suffered severe mal-treatment): children experience their caregivers as either frightening or frightened and themselves as either helpless or angry and controlling.

Each pattern is associated with a characteristic set of emotional and relationship behaviours.

Attachment behaviour is now recognized as occurring across the lifespan. It is particularly pronounced in emotional and behavioural terms in childhood, adult sexual relationships, and in adults in their role as parents. Attachment theory is used to make assessments, particularly in child care and family work (including adoption), work with offenders, and psychiatric social work. It guides and informs a wide range of interventions, many of which recognize the therapeutic and developmental importance of consistent, supportive, reflective, attuned relationships between partners, parents and children, and social workers and service users.

For Further Reading
Bowlby, J. 1973–1980: *Attachment Trilogy: Volumes I–III*. London: Hogarth Press.
Howe, D. 1995: *Attachment Theory for Social Work Practice*. Basingstoke: Macmillan.
Howe, D., Brandon M., Hinings D. and Schofield, G. 1999: *Attachment Theory, Child Maltreatment and Family Support*. Basingstoke: Macmillan.

DAVID HOWE

Attempted Suicide

See SUICIDE and SELF-HARM.

Audit in the Public Sector

Auditors were first appointed in the 1840s to inspect the accounts of authorities administering the Poor Law. Audits ensured that safeguards were in place against fraud and corruption, and that local rates were being used for the purposes intended. These founding principles remain as relevant today as they were 150 years ago.

In 1982, the government brought local authority auditing in England and Wales under the control of a single, independent body, the Audit Commission, which began work in 1983. In 1990, the Commission's role was extended to include NHS authorities, trusts and other bodies. Under the Local Government Act 1992, the Commission was given additional responsibilities relating to the production of annual comparative indicators of local authority performance. The Audit Commission Act 1998 consolidates almost all legislation relating to the Audit Commission.

The Commission operates independently and derives most of its income from the fees charged to audited bodies. The Commission's main functions are as follows:

• To appoint auditors, from District Audit and private accountancy firms, to all local government and NHS bodies in England and Wales
• To set standards for those auditors through the *Code of Audit Practice*
• To carry out national studies designed to promote economy, efficiency and effectiveness in the provision of local authority and NHS services

27

- To define the comparative indicators of local authority performance that are published annually

Public funds need to be used wisely, as well as in accordance with the law, so today's auditors have to assess expenditure not just for probity and regularity, but also for *value for money*. The Commission's value for money studies examine public services objectively, often from the user's perspective. Findings and recommendations are communicated through a wide range of publications and events.

Today, the Commission's remit covers more than 13,000 bodies, which between them spend nearly £100 billion of public money annually. The Commission aims to be a driving force in the improvement of public services by promoting proper stewardship of public finances, and by helping local authorities and the NHS to deliver economic, efficient and effective public services.

For Further Reading
Audit Commission 1997: *The Coming of Age: Improving Care Services for Elderly People.* Abingdon: Audit Commission Publications.
GENA KENNEDY

Autism

Autism describes a range of developmental disorders recognized by observation of clusters of related behaviour, communication and interaction characteristics. Individuals have a *triad of disorder*, creating impairment of social interaction, impairment of communication and impairment of imagination (flexible thinking, play).

Leo Kanner, in 1943, identified children who never participated in the social world and were characterized by extreme isolation and insistence on sameness and routine. The diagnosis of autism shows different characteristics between children, and in different children at different stages. Reactions can range from rage to passivity either between individuals or at different developmental stages in the same individual. Autism can be diagnosed in conjunction with other disabilities and can also be experienced with high ability and performance in specific areas.

While autism is recognized through observation of behavioural characteristics, and behavioural therapies are often successful in managing its manifestation, diagnosis indicates cognitive and developmental disorder.

Frith (1991) identifies specific difficulty in recognizing 'other' people and models of thinking. However, no causal theory has been shown to be valid for all people tested who show the *triad of impairment*, and research is highly active.

For Further Reading
Frith, U. 1991: *Autism and Asperger Syndrome.* Cambridge: Cambridge University Press.
CLARE BECKETT

Autistic Spectrum Disorder

Autistic spectrum (or *autistic continuum*) was a term introduced by Lorna Wing in 1992 to differentiate between degrees of impairment within the specific syndrome of autism.

Autistic impairment can be a seamless continuum, with grey areas where individual ability and impairment severity interact to create different behaviour. Diagnosis can be made in conjunction with other impairments. Autistic spectrum or continuum disorders are different from each other in degree, but not in nature of impairment. All diagnosed autistic people will experience the *triad of impairment* (see *AUTISM*), but will display different behavioural and communication skills.

CLARE BECKETT

B

Bail

Though probation officers and social workers continue to concentrate effort post-conviction, earlier intervention during the *bail* period can have substantial merit, particularly with young or mentally disordered defendants.

Custodial remands constitute a quarter of the prison population and, while sometimes offering a period of respite and reflection, can erode accused persons' stake in society. Only 34 per cent of those imprisoned before trial are subsequently sentenced to custody.

This opportunity zone can be summarized as follows:

- Assisting courts to make greater use of bail by inquiries regarding defendants most likely to be remanded in custody, for example, establishing their home circumstances, community ties and sources of support, or negotiating with their families/community agencies to offer accommodation or help, thus affording a more realistic assessment of their chances of absconding or reoffending; better informed prosecutors can be more selective in deciding when to oppose bail.
- 'Containing' accused persons at a time when they may be feeling fatalistic about their prospects and are thus at risk of further offending, either by referral to bail hostels or by offering community 'bail support' – packages of oversight, activities, reconciliation initiatives within families and referrals to other agencies.
- Protecting vulnerable defendants from the negative consequences of custody, including risks of bullying, drug misuse and self-harm.
- Gaining a better understanding of defendants and their motivation which can enhance pre-sentence assessments and increase the uptake of proposed community-based disposals.

NIGEL STONE

Behavioural Social Work

See THE COGNITIVE-BEHAVIOURAL APPROACH.

Bereavement

See DEATH, DYING AND BEREAVEMENT.

Best Value

The term *best value* encompasses economy, efficiency, effectiveness and quality in service delivery. In 1998, the government White Paper, *Modernising Local Government*, made it clear that the concept would be tested against public and consumer opinion.

The philosophy of best value is not dissonant with the delivery of social services nor with social work values, but some characteristics of social services present a particular challenge, and the four parameters by which best value is defined are difficult to assess. Among the most problematic characteristics are the following:

- Social services are poorly understood, have a poor public image and a hostile press.
- The users are among the most vulnerable and the least politically organized.
- The services themselves are complex and have multiple objectives.
- They are difficult to evaluate, especially in terms of public and consumer satisfaction.

Practical delivery of best value requires redefinition into components which can be assessed, such as quality, scale and cost. The three are interdependent but have distinct criteria which do not overlap. Their impact on each other and on clients, carers, staff and the public can be evaluated.

For Further Reading
Fletcher, K. 1998: *Best Value Social Services*. Caerphilly: SSSP Publications.

KEITH FLETCHER

Bipolar Affective Disorder

While lifting of mood is part of the usual response to good fortune, elation can occur without an obvious cause; alternatively, it may seem excessive or rather too prolonged. Elation may be a symptom or sign of several psychiatric syndromes, including manic episodes, acute schizophrenic episodes and certain drug-induced states. The abundant energy and increased activity of people experiencing manic episodes is usually accompanied by an exaggerated sense of subjective well-being, although many feel irritable and exasperated and the euphoric mood is sometimes tinged with sadness. Typically, elation is reflected in excessive talkativeness and the quick succession of grandiose ideas and unrealistic plans: this impairment of judgement can lead to financial or sexual indiscretions that may ruin personal and family life. Insight into the changes in mood, activity and interpersonal relationships is usually impaired, contributing to the high rates of compulsory admission to hospital.

Manic episodes rarely occur in isolation: more characteristically, episodes recur irregularly, becoming interspersed with depressive episodes, which may become relatively more frequent with time. The cyclical pattern of mania and depression has been called *manic-depressive psychosis*: the current terms of *bipolar affective disorder* or *bipolar illness* are preferable, as many patients with the marked disturbance of affect do not experience psychotic phenomena, such as delusions or hallucinations. By convention, someone experiencing a first manic episode still receives the diagnosis of bipolar disorder, as depressive episodes invariably develop over the ensuing years.

Epidemiology and aetiology

Bipolar affective disorder is not a rare condition. Community surveys in industrialized countries indicate that the lifetime risk for bipolar disorder is around 1 per cent. Similar rates are seen in other cultures, although, as with depression, rates of bipolar disorder are higher in urban areas. Women and men are affected as frequently; the mean age of onset is 21 years; and there is no convincing association with particular social class.

There is no single cause for bipolar affective disorder: like depression, individual episodes usually result from the combination of familial, biological, psychological and social factors. The genetic 'loading' for bipolar illness seems greater than that for unipolar depression: for example, the concordance rate for bipolar disorder among identical twins is approximately 70 per cent. However, attempts to identify possible genetic markers for the condition have not been successful. As is the case for unipolar depression, abnormalities in the level of function of the neurotransmitters serotonin and noradrenaline may be important in bipolar illness. Manic episodes may be associated with over-activity in dopamine pathways within the brain, as mania can be provoked by dopamine-releasing psycho-stimulants, such as cocaine and amphetamine. Manic episodes occurring after childbirth have been linked to abnormalities in the pituitary release of growth hormone which follows experimental challenge with investigational compounds that act on dopamine receptors.

Psychosocial factors, particularly family dynamics, are undoubtedly important in influencing the course of bipolar illness once established; however, their role in causing the condition to appear is unclear. Studies of the impact of adverse life events have produced contradictory findings, although bereavement can be a common precipitant for a manic relapse.

Treatment

It is usually advisable to admit patients with manic episodes to hospital; even the less severe (hypomanic) episodes are disruptive and can lead to reckless behaviour or financial destitution. Considerable nursing skill is required to settle the euphoric, often overactive and insightless manic patient. The acute treatment of mania usually involves anti-psychotic drugs or lithium, sometimes in combination: anti-psychotic drugs are more quickly effective, but less well tolerated.

Lithium is more frequently used as a prophylactic treatment, designed to reduce the risk of future manic or depressive episodes. When prescribed rationally and when taken regularly, lithium can have startling effects, altering the course of illness dramatically; many patients will derive benefit and experience only side-effects such as thirst, tremor and weight gain. Anticonvulsant drugs, more frequently used in the treatment of epilepsy, can be effective in patients who respond only partially to treatment with lithium, or in those with particularly 'rapid-cycling' affective disorder. Psychological approaches to the long-term management of bipolar illness have not been studied extensively; however, 'self-management', including heightened mood awareness, the acquisition of appropriate assertiveness, and the spacing apart of activities and life events, has been advocated enthusiastically.

For Further Reading
Jamison, K. R. 1993: *Touched with Fire. Manic-Depressive Illness and The Artistic Temperament*. New York: Free Press Paperbacks.
Mulligan, S. and Clare, A. 1993: *Depression and How to Survive it*. London: Ebury Press.
DAVID S. BALDWIN

Birth Families
The term *birth family* refers to the family from which a child has originated biologically. The term has replaced the term 'natural' parents (which carried the implication that other forms of parenting are other than natural) in the world of child welfare, and is frequently used in contrast to adoptive, foster or other substitute parents. Most birth parents raise their children well, whereas, when birth parents live under stress, in poverty or have learning difficulties, physical handicaps, or psychological and personality problems, it is possible that parenting is compromised for some and they can be vulnerable to the scrutiny of the state and possible removal of their children.

The development of an alliance between parents and the state, giving birth parents greater participation in, rather than exclusion from, the investigative process, is seen as the key to helping families to remain intact and to bring up their children satisfactorily. An increase in intensive home care services is then needed to prevent family break up.

Birth parents who may wish to contest local authority plans often face great challenges, and sources of independent advocacy and support are frequently lacking. It is a difficult area of practice for social workers who are required to operate in partnership with parents although they may find themselves in adversarial relationships with them.

For Further Reading
Grotevant, H., McRoy, R., Christian, C. and Bryant, C. 1998: Birth mothers – adjustment and resolution of grief. In H. Grotevant and R. McRoy (eds), *Openness in Adoption*, London: Sage.
ALAN RUSHTON

Black Offenders, Working with
Effective work with *black offenders* will be based on the following principles:

- Black people are not a homogeneous group.
- All black people are likely to have experienced racism.
- It is necessary to promote equality by means of anti-racist, anti-discriminatory and ethnically sensitive practice.
- It is necessary to incorporate black perspectives.
- The worker must be aware of the likely impact of internalized racism and oppression on black offenders.

continued

- There must be shared responsibility for effective work with black offenders by black and white practitioners and managers.

There are differences *between* black communities based on cultural, social, religious, political, linguistic, generational, economic, geographical and historical factors; and any lack of understanding of these (as well as of the fundamental differences between black communities and the majority white communities) can lead to assessments and interventions which will perpetuate racist practice, encourage stereotypes and the pathologization of black offenders, and lead to a denial of access to ethnically sensitive service delivery.

The reality of racism

A common thread among black people is their daily experience of racism – personal, cultural and institutional – which overtly or covertly affects every aspect of their lives; it has an impact on their feeling of security, their livelihood, their general well-being and the access they have to public and private sector services. (This is reflected in the criminal justice system, where black people are over-represented as clients and under-represented as staff.) An understanding of the racist oppression of black people – past and present – is therefore a prerequisite for effective practice with black offenders.

Assessments and interventions with black offenders must use *proactive* anti-racist and anti-oppressive forms of practice; workers will engage in affirmative action by challenging racism and other oppressions at personal, cultural/societal and institutional/structural levels through an emphasis on equity in service planning and delivery. Recognition of the importance of black perspectives must not pathologize the black offender as 'problematic' because of skin colour, but should acknowledge that the experience of racism will lead to differences in the black offender's perception of the criminal justice system and in his/her attitudes towards the need to address offending behaviour.

The use of anti-racist and anti-discriminatory practice and the active acknowledgement of black perspectives will ensure that black offenders' needs are met through ethnically sensitive service delivery, allowing appropriate access to black resources within criminal justice and community organizations. To facilitate this, criminal justice agencies must set about rectifying the under-representation of black staff, particularly at management and decision-making levels.

Recognition of the impact of internalized racism, which can manifest itself in the form of anger, low self-esteem or psychological withdrawal, is imperative for effective practice with black offenders so as to avoid them being labelled as uncooperative or unmotivated. The effective practitioner needs to be aware of the multi-dimensional nature of racism or oppression and of internalized racism or oppression which will vary for each black offender. Assessments and interventions must be tailored to meet each individual's unique needs and their cycle of offending.

Achieving effectiveness

Evidence of effective work with black offenders can include the following:

- An offending behaviour groupwork model serving the needs of an all-black group led by black practitioners, promoting black perspectives and incorporating affirmation and positive identity work with a focus on black community cultures
- Assessment and intervention plans that articulate the impact of racism and other oppressions on the individual black offender
- The design of realistic and achievable strategies that enable the black offender to challenge and eradicate racist or oppressive barriers within his/her life and to address factors which appear to be contributing to offending behaviour
- The provision of access to equitable service resources

- The provision of access to specialist black resources, where these are requested by the black offender

Black offender surveys on their experience of the criminal justice system have indicated that:

- they value honesty;
- they appreciate being accorded respect as human beings and not just labelled as criminals;
- they want practitioners to understand their experience of being black and they want to be respected for it;
- they want to be given the choice of having a black worker or of joining an all-black offence-focused group;
- they want assessments and interventions to maintain a balance between their offending behaviour and their individual needs – with particular reference to employment, education and training, housing, and other public sector services – all of which are likely to incorporate elements of institutional racism;
- they want practitioners to involve them in reviews of their progress and to share in discussions about the worker's plan of intervention.

Effective work with black offenders can be achieved if all practitioners – black and white – adhere to the key principles of practice, and if white practitioners acknowledge their own internalized racism and demonstrate a willingness to address it. Much can be gained from recognition of the fact that none are true experts on this issue, that all have much to learn, and that all should feel able to articulate their fears and anxieties and acknowledge their ignorance and mistakes.

Practitioners have immense power at their disposal as agents of social change, and this needs to be harnessed individually and collectively so as to counteract the oppressions that are faced daily by black and white offenders. This can only be achieved through a shared ethos of promoting anti-oppressive practices as black and white workers, and through articulating this ethos to black and white offenders alike.

For Further Reading
Dominelli, L. (ed.) 1995: *Anti-Racist Probation Practice*. Aldershot: Arena.
Kay, J. and Gast, L. (eds) 1998: *From Murmur to Murder: Working with Racially Motivated and Racist Offenders*. Birmingham: Midlands Probation Training Consortium.
Tucklo Orenda Associates 1999: *Making a Difference: A Positive and Practical Guide to Working with Black Offenders*. London: Tucklo Orenda Associates.

BIJAL SISODIA

Black Perspectives on Social Work

Historically, the term *black* has carried emotive and negative meanings, relating particularly to skin colour. This and other essentialist ideas about racial difference, drawn from the natural and social sciences, were used to construct a notion of 'other' which resulted in individuals, groups and communities labelled as 'black' suffering discrimination and inequality.

The politicization of 'black' communities and the growth of black consciousness led to the positive reclamation of the term *black* and a change in its usage. The term started to be used to describe people mainly of South Asian, African, Caribbean or Chinese origin. However, individuals and communities continued to contest their inclusion and exclusion under such a term, which they argued could result in the loss of individual

continued

histories and identities. For example, this has been articulated by people who are of Asian and Chinese origin and people who describe themselves as being of 'mixed race' or 'mixed parentage'. The changing boundaries of who is included within the term *black* and its definition, need to be taken into account in any discussion of *black perspectives on social work*.

We see the term *black* as a unifying political force which has provided a forum where different minority ethnic groups have been able to challenge existing discrimination and inequalities. The expression of these experiences and ideas is found in what may be referred to as *black perspectives*.

The development of black perspectives

The main thrust in the development of black perspectives on social work arose out of the need to respond to racist practices based on assumptions about black people, their culture, ethnicity, identity and needs. These practices were supported by racist ideologies within social science and legislative frameworks. It was a political movement which gave opportunity to minority ethnic groups not only to empower themselves but to redefine their own needs. It highlighted the impact of structural racism on the planning and delivery of services.

Black perspectives had its roots in the civil rights and black liberation movements of the 1960s and 1970s, gathering strength in the 1980s with the growing radicalization of black communities, professionals and academics in the UK. This, alongside changes in anti-discriminatory legislation, brought challenges to institutional racism at all levels in society. In welfare organizations such as social work, the anti-racist movement became the drive to change the pervading Eurocentric ideologies which had historically influenced the relationship between social work and the black communities.

In 1983, the establishment of the Association of Black Social Workers and Allied Professions (ABSWAP) was one response to the failure of the state to provide equitable and appropriate services to meet the needs of members of the black community. Bodies involved in the training of social workers, such as the National Institute for Social Work's Race Equality Unit and CCETSW's Black Perspectives Committee, produced materials which were highly critical of contemporary social work practice. These developments during the 1980s and early 1990s provided opportunities for black social workers to discuss issues around race and racism, and to develop different ways of working with the black community. Established black organizations and community groups also mobilized and made demands for the provision of relevant welfare services.

The nature of black perspectives

A black perspective is more than merely a response to race and racism. It provides a framework for developing an alternative to practice that is based on taken-for-granted assumptions about black people, their culture, needs, and identities. This framework is underpinned by a critical understanding of the varying nature of power and powerlessness, and therefore has the potential to analyse the complexities of the experience of oppression. The experience of racism is mediated by class position, gender, sexuality, disability, age and health status; any black perspective must therefore include the total experience of marginalized groups.

A black perspective in social work has these fundamental elements:

- It is a political philosophy, motivated by principles of equality, rights and justice – where the personal is political.
- It is informed by black people's diverse and changing experiences of race and racism, both past and present, national and international.
- It challenges existing beliefs, ideologies, practices and procedures of individuals and systems, and is transformative at these levels.

- It informs anti-racist and anti-oppressive practice, providing a means through which black and white workers can work together to combat racism and other oppressions.
- It provides black workers with the intellectual and political space to develop and consolidate ideas and practice.
- It demands collective action and networking.
- It has a user focus and is driven by community activism.
- It values and works with the differences and strengths of individuals and communities so that practice is both applicable and accessible; it thus develops a professional response sensitive to, and takes account of, the diverse family patterns, cultural traditions and values of black communities.
- It reclaims and recognizes the history, cultures, language, religions, traditions and spirituality of black people, allowing black people to reassert their black identities.
- It incorporates an understanding of the range of human need, requiring assessments of need and risk to be holistic in their approach.
- It provides social work practitioners with the basis from which to challenge Eurocentric interpretations of human experiences.

Providing one definition of *black perspectives on social work* is problematic. Black communities in the UK are not a static entity: they consist of different and sometimes competing minority ethnic groups who are constantly in a process of change as they respond to local, national and international events. A black perspective must be able to take into account, incorporate and respond to, those dynamic changes. It has the potential to provide an intellectual and practical tool for social workers to work with black individuals, communities and colleagues which is challenging and effective.

For Further Reading
Ahmad, B. 1990: *Black Perspectives in Social Work*. Birmingham: Venture Press.
Modood, T. and Berthoud, R. 1997: *Ethnic Minorities in Britain*. London: Policy Studies Institute.
Shukra, K. 1995: From black power to black perspectives: the reconstruction of a black political identity. *Youth and Policy*, 49, 5–19.

BEVERLEY BURKE AND PHILOMENA HARRISON

Bonding

Bonding is a term used to summarize specific patterns of social interaction, usually between parent and child, that function to establish or maintain proximity.

The term *bonding* stems from ethology where it is used to describe a special relationship between individuals: for example, 'pair bonding' in birds. In social work, the term describes human interactions that include both publicly observable behaviours (for example, lifting up a crying baby, reaching out, protecting and taking care of a child) and private behaviours (for example, feelings of love, fond thoughts and protective emotions).

Originally, bonding was thought of as a process that, to build a life-sustaining relationship between mother and child, had to happen more or less immediately after birth. Poor bonding was thought to lead to untold difficulties in the child's later life. Today, the term is understood as a summary label for a behavioural pattern that develops over time, and can be established at different times and between different people. It is now understood that delays in the establishment of this interaction pattern do not necessarily have detrimental side-effects.

For Further Reading
Gewirtz, J. L. and Kurtines, W. M. 1991: *Intersections with Attachment*. Hove: Lawrence Erlbaum.

KAROLA DILLENBURGER

Bulimia

Bulimia is an eating disorder characterized by binge-eating and purging in the context of normal bodyweight. Treatment can usually be in the community, unless complicated by additional physical or psychiatric factors. Treatment is focused on the resumption of a normal eating pattern with the aid of cognitive-behavioural techniques. Anti-depressant medication has been shown to be useful in reducing the binge–purge cycle associated with low mood. Little concrete is known of long-term prognosis, but medical complications can be life threatening. Up to 70 per cent report reduction in symptoms at six years after active treatment.

CLAIRE KENWOOD AND RAY VIEWEG

Bullying

Bullying is the aggressive behaviour arising from the deliberate intent to cause physical or psychological distress to others. It can be both physical and psychological, short-term or long-term, but always the bully intends to inflict pain.

Bullying among adults is sometimes referred to as harassment, mental cruelty, assault or extortion. Bullying covers a wide range of aggressive activities; included are physical attacks, name calling, malicious gossip, spreading sexual slurs, damaging or stealing the property of victims, or coercing them into acts which they do not want to do.

Up to 25 per cent of school-age pupils will experience bullying and, for 4 per cent, the consequences are severe. Post-traumatic stress disorder is not uncommon among both child and adult victims. Child and adolescent victims with unresolved post-traumatic symptoms may develop 'victim' characteristics which predispose them to become victims of harassment as adults. This includes domestic violence as well as workplace harassment.

Child and adolescent victims need adult intervention to stop the bullying. In the UK, teachers and governors of schools have a duty of care to children defined by the Department for Education and Employment Circular 8/94, *Pupil Behaviour and Discipline*.

For Further Reading
Randall, P. E. 1997: *Adult Bullying*. London: Routledge.

PETER RANDALL AND JONATHAN PARKER

C

Capacity/Incapacity

Capacity is a legal term to describe the ability of a person to make, take and act on decisions which will be treated, in law, as being valid. The ultimate decision as to whether a person has capacity rests with a court.

A person may be said to lack capacity if they are unable to make a valid decision (as opposed to a correct or right decision) or unable to give or withhold valid consent to medical or other treatment.

Capacity can be affected by virtue of age, mental disorder or mental impairment.

- *Age* A child reaches the age of legal capacity at 18 years. However, this may be at a younger age and will be determined by 'when the child achieves a sufficient under-standing and intelligence to enable him or her to understand fully what is proposed. It will be a question of fact whether a child seeking advice has sufficient under-standing of what is involved to give a consent valid in law' (*Per Lord Scarman in Gillick v West Norfolk and Wisbech AHA* [1986] AC 112).
- *Mental disorder* An application for compulsory detention under the Mental Health Act 1983 to carry out an assessment or treat a mental disorder will, *de facto*, be made without consent. Legal safeguards exist to protect patients so detained con-cerning types and length of treatment and discharge.
- *Mental impairment* The position is the same as that which applies in cases of mental disorder. In addition, case law has determined that a person may be 'informally' admitted and detained under s.131 of the Mental Health Act 1983 which 'permits the admission of compliant incapacitated patients where the requirements of the prin-ciple of necessity are satisfied' (*Per Lord Steyn R v Bournewood Community and Mental Health Trust ex p L* 1998, *Times*, 30 June HL).

Necessity is a common law principle which requires that there must be a necessity to act when it is not practicable to communicate with the patient, and that the proposed action must be that which a reasonable person would take acting in the best interests of the patient. This could therefore encompass both those with a learning disability and those who are elderly mentally impaired.

Social workers and issues of capacity

Decisions and actions about which a person may be considered to lack capacity can include financial and legal decisions, consent to medical treatment, day-to-day living, and civil and criminal liability for actions. A person who is considered to lack capacity may be made subject to one of a variety of different legal provisions and court orders depending on their circumstances:

- The administration of elderly incapable or mentally disordered persons' affairs may become subject to enduring powers of attorney or (upon application) the Court of Protection or an appointee under Social Security Regulations.

continued

- Someone with severe mental impairment, that is, associated with abnormally aggressive or seriously irresponsible conduct, may be received into guardianship under s.7 of the Mental Health Act 1983.
- Where a (usually elderly) person is unable to care for him/herself adequately, an application to forcibly remove them from their home under s.47 National Assistance Act 1948 may be made to a magistrates' court on the recommendation of a community physician.

Legal safeguards exist to protect those who lack capacity and to ensure that the treatment given, necessarily without consent, is appropriate.

Social workers working with young people, older people and those with disabilities or mental disorders may, it is clear, encounter the issue of capacity in different areas when working with clients.

For Further Reading
Kennedy, I. and Grubb, A. (eds) 1998: *Principles of Medical Law*. Oxford: Oxford University Press.

TERESA MUNBY

Care Management and Planning

Care management refers to the processes of identifying and organizing more individualized and appropriate packages of care to vulnerable individuals requiring long-term care, usually in their own homes. Such a definition is insufficient however, and six elements considered together enable a more precise definition to be formulated (Challis et al., 1995):

1　The performance of a set of core tasks, from assessment to review
2　The function of co-ordination of care
3　Explicit goals for care management, such as extending community tenure
4　A focus upon people with long-term care needs, and hence targeting care management
5　An emphasis upon particular features which differentiate care management from the activities of other community-based professionals, such as length and intensity of involvement with the client and the breadth of services spanned
6　The dual functions of care management, influencing services at client level and at a more aggregated level, influencing the pattern of services overall

There are broad similarities in the changing pattern of services for older people in different countries. These involve shifting or maintaining the balance of care in the face of rising demand. These changes may be characterized in simple form as:

- a move away from institution-based provision of care;
- the extension of home-based care;
- for individuals with more intense needs, the development of mechanisms of care co-ordination, usually through the medium of case or care management.

Care management can thus be seen as being at a pivotal position in long-term care, balancing individual needs with equity in the allocation of care.

The background to care management
Care management was introduced into UK government policy in the late 1980s, when the White Paper *Caring for People* identified assessment and care management as the cornerstones of high-quality care. At the practice level, this required ensuring that placement decisions of vulnerable people in residential and nursing homes were appropriate,

and that, for some people, the opportunity of more intensive, co-ordinated home support would be available. This followed a government review of arrangements for the community care of older people after a substantial increase in public expenditure for long-stay residential and nursing home care during the 1980s. The main research available focused on very targeted forms of care management concerned with high-risk groups such as those likely to require hospital or nursing home care. Demonstration studies ranged from the original Kent Community Care Project (Challis and Davies, 1986) to the more integrated health and social care initiatives linked with services such as geriatric medicine (Challis et al., 1995). These were of an intensive care management approach targeted on very vulnerable individuals, giving care managers much greater freedom to spend resources and create solutions for home through devolved budgets.

The nature of care management

The implementation of care management in the UK raised issues common to other countries. Definition was provided in detailed guidance (Social Services Inspectorate, 1991), but this left much room for local interpretation regarding the form, content and extensiveness of care management. In particular, care management came to refer to most of the assessment, service allocation and review processes of care for *all* users of services, regardless of their level of need. It has often not been targeted or focused on the very vulnerable.

Research evidence regarding assessment has indicated a great deal of variation in the content and quality of the documentation examined. Needs and problems appear to be poorly categorized and needs are described rather than analysed; information is collected and recorded in ways which lack reliability and validity. Care management appears to lack clarity about overall objectives, and its definition tends to be broad and focused on organizational process. Lack of budget devolution limits freedom of manoeuvre for individual care managers; there are difficulties arising from a rigid definition of purchaser and provider roles and, within agencies, there is a concern at the emergence of an administrative rather than a social work definition of care management. Care management is often seen as an assessment-oriented activity and, consequently, the review process is one characterized by neglect.

Lacking evidence of a shared and agreed definition used by agencies, care management risks having no more meaning than *the process by which people are processed through a major care agency*. Government and others have suggested the need for more differentiated forms of care management, so that the intensity of intervention is more commensurate with the level of need and required response by making a distinction between *co-ordinative care management* and *intensive care management*.

The need for targeting

Specific types of care management need to be related to specific types of need groups. For much long-term care provision, it is care management of the intensive kind which is likely to be required, characterized by a more professional orientation among staff, smaller caseloads and intensive responses to need. Interestingly, in social care terms, intensive care management may be more helpfully seen as a form of secondary care, and this provides an analogy for where the most valuable health care linkages may be made with care management. In the care of older people, services such as geriatric medicine and old-age psychiatry offer access to appropriate expertise for assessment for individuals with complex problems. Vertical integration of systems of health and social care focused upon particular need groups, such as dementia sufferers, may make feasible links between care management and rehabilitation, secondary health care and social care. It may also permit effective pooling of care budgets permitting a wider range of resources to become more flexibly distributed.

continued

Care management and social work

The relationship between care management and social work appears insufficiently well resolved and some clearer specification of the link between staff mix and model of care management might be beneficial in improving the efficiency of workforce utilization. Unresolved questions remain about the training content most appropriate for care management, and about which occupational groups possess the relevant attributes. In some countries, the turf of care management has been claimed by social work and, in others, this has not occurred. As health and social care become more closely integrated, the nature of the contribution of social work will need to be more clearly articulated. In the absence of clarity about the definition of care management itself, this is likely to prove difficult.

Care management has taken the responsibility for co-ordination and integration of fragmented systems of care at the micro-level. There is also a service development role for care management which may be *direct* through care management team activity or *indirect* through feedback of requirements to contracting. Service development through care management may well be neglected by agencies relative to the function of care co-ordination.

Overall, there is a need for further work in the areas of assessment, definition and differentiation of care management, and appropriate integration with health care. One positive development would be to see care management as providing a definition of social work in long-term care.

For Further Reading

Challis, D. and Davies, B. 1986: *Case Management in Community Care*. Aldershot: Gower.
Challis, D., Darton, R., Johnson, L., Stone, M. and Traske, K. 1995: *Care Management and Health Care of Older People*. Aldershot: Ashgate.
Social Services Inspectorate/Social Work Services Group (SSI/SWSG) 1991: *Care Management and Assessment: Managers Guide*. HMSO: London.

DAVID CHALLIS

Care Programme Approach

The *care programme approach* (CPA) was introduced in England in 1991 by the Department of Health to provide a 'safety-net' of care for people with severe mental illness in the community. It was, first, designed to minimize the risk of these users of services being discharged from hospital before there was a package of care in place to provide for their treatment and support in the community, whether this was in their homes or in residential accommodation. Second, it was to ensure identification of those currently in the community and to see that their needs were assessed and met.

The background to the CPA

Deinstitutionalization has been a major force in shaping services internationally. The USA and the UK have been at the forefront of this process. In both, there have been serious concerns expressed by statutory and non-statutory bodies about the care and aftercare of those who might previously have been admitted to institutions, and about the drift of mental health teams away from caring for the most severely mentally ill. Research that demonstrated relatively high levels of severe mental illness among the homeless and in the criminal justice system, also reinforced the need for improvement in the organization and delivery of services. The care programme approach is a policy response to these concerns. Its origins can be traced back to the Spokes Inquiry into the Care and After-care of Sharon Campbell. This concluded that there had been a breakdown in the delivery of services, effectively resulting in the death of Sharon Campbell's social worker, and the Inquiry Report recommended that the government provide a written summary clarifying local and health authorities' statutory duties to provide after-care for users with mental illness.

The care programme approach involves assessment of health and social care needs, nomination of a key worker to co-ordinate care, a written care plan, regular review of these needs and implementation of the plan, inter-professional collaboration and consultation with users and carers. It applies to all users accepted by mental health services, but multidisciplinary assessment and review is only required for those who are severely mentally ill. The key worker, who can be any mental health worker, should be the focal point of contact for the user, the carer and other professionals, especially the general practitioner, and is responsible for keeping in touch with the user and seeing that the agreed programme of care is delivered.

Team working and the multidisciplinary context

Team working is a fundamental principle of psychiatric practice as demonstrated by a range of research. However, networks with others, for example, housing officers, police and duty solicitors, who may have roles that are more generic, are also of importance. The CPA was developed as case (in the UK, named *care*) management was being introduced for all clients served by social services departments. This also involves assessment by a care manager who co-ordinates delivery of care and ensures review and monitoring of it. The care manager, unlike the CPA keyworker, usually has budgetary responsibility for purchasing care, and, particularly with those with severe mental illness, they may also provide care. Systems integrating CPA and care management for this group have been developed in most areas.

Individual assessment of health and social need and the development of mental health services to respond to these needs represent good professional practice, and the CPA reinforces this. It also places responsibility for the co-ordination of care on a keyworker whom users and carers, including GPs, can contact and who is responsible for seeing that care is delivered. Care plans are negotiated with users. The nature of severe mental illness is such that the user may not agree to part of a plan that seems essential to the team providing care. If a user refuses contact, a multidisciplinary discussion (although not necessarily a meeting) is often used to establish alternative ways of presenting a care plan which is acceptable to the user. The user may opt only to accept a part of the programme offered and, as far as possible, the programme will be sufficiently flexible to accommodate this. However, even if the programme is wholly rejected, the offering of contact on a regular basis in consultation with the user's GP continues. The carer is also offered assistance on a regular basis and provided with a reliable point of contact.

Maintaining contact with the person, and any carer involved, is a continuing responsibility for the keyworker. At a later stage, the user may have a change of mind or, in some instances, need care under the Mental Health Act. Intervention needs to be prompt to limit deterioration and risks to self or others. Targeting of resources on severely mentally ill people is necessary as community mental health teams have been prone to move away from care of the severely mentally ill. Similar guidance has been issued to GPs. Adequate mental health information systems have been developed to ensure that information is readily available when required, for example, about risk status, name of key worker or timing of reviews.

The provision of appropriate care for people with severe mental illness in consultation with them, and their informal and formal carers, is a most complex activity. Research into the implementation of the CPA is showing that it is progressively focusing the limited resources available on those who need them most and maintaining them in contact with services.

continued

For Further Reading
Conway, A., Melzer, D. and Hale, A. S. 1994: The outcome of targeting community mental health services. *British Medical Journal*, 308, 627–30.
Kingdon, D. G. 1994: The care programme approach. *Psychiatric Bulletin*, 18 (2), 68–70.
Tyrer, P., Morgan, J., Van Horn, E., Jayakody, M., Evans, K., Brummeu, R., White, T., Baldwin, D., Harrison-Read, P. and Johnson, T. 1995: A randomised control study of close monitoring of vulnerable psychiatric patients. *Lancet*, 345, 756–9.

DAVID KINGDON

Carers

A *carer* is someone who looks after, or helps to look after, a relative, neighbour or friend who has additional needs as a result of disability, illness or ageing. The care given is informal in that it does not form part of a paid contract; instead, it relies on a sense of responsibility for and commitment to the other, driven by feelings of love, duty or concern.

The background to caring

The concept of 'being a carer' is a relatively recent phenomenon; the emergence of carers as an identifiable group and their increasing importance in social policy terms was marked by the Carers (Recognition and Services) Act 1995. Although people provided assistance to neighbours, relatives and friends long before they were recognized as carers, they would not have used this term, or identified themselves as belonging to a special category. Two main forces drove this 'social construction' (Bytheway and Johnson, 1998, p. 241): as deinstitutionalization shifted provision from institutions into the community, informal carers moved higher up the agenda as essential providers; at the same time, carers' interests were advanced by pressure groups campaigning from within their ranks.

The General Household Survey suggests that one adult in eight is providing informal care and that 5.7 million adults could be termed 'carers' (Rowlands, 1998, p. vi). Although these statistics indicate the vast scale of informal care-giving, their accuracy is compromised by the lack of any fixed point at which 'everyday helping' becomes caring. Illness, physical or learning disability, sensory impairment, mental disorder and incapacity occur throughout the life course, presenting different challenges at different stages, and informal care may be complex or low-key, transient or enduring. Individual interpretations of what it means to be a carer are necessarily subjective, but the care provided by informal carers is characterized by responsibilities that extend beyond those expected in relationships unaffected by disability, illness or ageing. Informal caring is sometimes seen as a series of one-way transactions in an asymmetric relationship between *carer* and *dependant*. A systems approach to the understanding of caring relationships is a more useful model as it has the capacity to represent the complexity, multiplicity and reciprocity of real-life care arrangements.

The identity of the carers

Carers, and those they provide care for, vary in terms of culture, race, class, age and sexual orientation, and their values and perspectives shape the caring relationships that are formed between them. Women in their middle years without paid work are disproportionately likely to assume the primary caring role, whereas men, children and women in employment usually take on supplementary support responsibilities. Some informal carers remain 'invisible': they may not be identified by statutory agencies, they may not recognize that they fall within the definition, or they may see their caring tasks as an integral part of being a partner or parent. Formalizing the role by labelling individuals as 'informal carers' is not universally welcomed and may be perceived as intrusive, culturally insensitive or as an inappropriate delegation of professional responsibility.

Unlike assistance provided on a contractual basis, where detached servicing of needs is sometimes possible, informal caring is often bound up with being in relationship. Caring is emotionally and physically demanding work, heavily influenced by interpersonal dynamics, individual and joint histories, and cultural norms. Roles and relationships do not always adjust to accommodate the changing circumstances of people's lives, and individuals who are closely related are not necessarily comfortable caring for one another. Provision of intimate care without the protection afforded by professional distance may breach established boundaries and taboos, and provoke distress.

The apparent ordinariness of caring is deceptive, and the role played by informal carers is often undervalued by health and social care workers. The shifting boundary between lay and professional care has resulted in the performance of increasingly complex tasks by carers, who often have difficulty accessing adequate information and resources. Many carers derive satisfaction from their role, but the rewards of caring can be outweighed by the burdens of financial disadvantage, social isolation and restricted employment opportunities. When they are left to cope unsupported, the quality of care may be compromised, placing carers, and those they care for, at risk.

Not everyone who needs care as a result of illness, disability or ageing wishes to be 'cared for'. Some feminists have suggested that informal care is intrinsically exploitative and propose a return to collective, group-living care arrangements that lift the burden from individual carers. On the other hand, some disabled people have insisted on their right to care for, and be cared for, by the people they are in relationship with, and have asserted their right to a life style of independent or interdependent living, supported by direct payments.

Health and social care professionals often fail to recognize the legitimacy of the carer's perspective; it is, after all, the carers who have day-to-day involvement with service users. Although the needs of users and carers may sometimes seem to be irreconcilable, both may be equally in need of service, and both can equally contribute to an understanding of the situation that they share.

The absence of the carer's voice in user-centred research is striking and, although the recognition and support of informal carers is now firmly enshrined in policy, in practice, they remain isolated, disadvantaged and marginal to the decision-making process, with little sense of working in partnership with professionals.

For Further Reading

Bytheway, B. and Johnson, J. 1998: The social construction of informal carers. In A. Symonds and A. Kelly (eds), *The Social Construction of Community Care*, Basingstoke: Macmillan.
Morris, J. 1998: Creating a space for absent voices: disabled women's experience of receiving assistance with daily living activities. In M. Allott and M. Robb (eds), *Understanding Health and Social Care. An Introductory Reader*, London: Sage.
Rowlands, O. 1998: *Informal Carers*. London: The Stationery Office.

ROSE BARTON

Case Conferences

A *case conference* is a meeting of family and professionals concerned with a vulnerable person so as to exchange information and plan together. The case conference is central to child protection procedures and is referred to as the *child protection conference*. It symbolizes the inter-agency nature of assessment, treatment and the management of child protection.

There are two kinds of child protection conferences: the *initial* and the *review* conference. An *initial conference* is normally convened by social services after a child protection investigation. At an initial conference, a decision is made whether to register a child; if a child is registered, a multi-agency plan is formulated. Before a child is registered, the conference must decide that there is already, or is a likelihood of, significant harm leading to the need for a child protection plan.

The purpose of the *review conference* is to review the arrangements for the protection of the child and to consider whether registration should be continued or ended. The participation of parents, carers and children, if age-appropriate, is positively encouraged, unless it would be prejudicial to the child's interests.

For Further Reading
Department of Health 1991: *Working Together: Under the Children Act 1989*. London: HMSO.

ANNA GUPTA

Case Management

Case management is a client-centred approach to the co-ordination of services to meet the needs of vulnerable individuals. It targets elderly, mentally ill or disabled people, enabling them to live in the community by accessing appropriate help. Its goals are continuity of care and individualized support through assessment, care planning, intervention, monitoring and review.

There are many models of case management. That implemented across the UK since 1990 and termed *care management* involves assessment of need and the purchase and co-ordination of services, with emphasis on cost-effective allocation of resources. Intensive case management models emphasize provision of practical and therapeutic support by social workers or others. Case management may promote consumer choice and advocacy, but assertive community treatment with mentally ill people may also involve compulsory supervision requirements with reluctant clients.

Standards vary widely, and research highlights the importance of local variables and the difficulty of making comparisons between systems. Administrative models enable the equitable rationing of resources. Intensive case management is more expensive, but has shown significant positive outcomes for clients.

For Further Reading
Huxley, P. 1993: Case management and care management in community care. *British Journal of Social Work*, 23 (4), 365–81.

WILLIAM HORDER

Case Recording

Case recording is the process of writing accounts of events and social workers' actions in a case for agencies to retain. Case records are part of case files containing information about clients and their circumstances, family members, other workers involved and copies of documents, letters and reports about the case.

Case records have many, sometimes conflicting, uses:

- Maintaining continuity of practice over time and between workers
- Acting as evidence in professional supervision
- Securing accountability for the worker's practice

Writing records may help workers to order their thoughts and assessments about the case. Clients sometimes share in recording, and often have rights of access.

Records usually comprise brief narrative accounts of contacts with and about clients, summaries and plans of work covering a period of time and visual records, such as family trees. Longer accounts may be made of important, difficult or potentially controversial contacts. Case records may be poor, distorted by only containing workers' perspectives, by workers' self-justification of their actions and by restrictive or inadequate agency forms and systems. Many records are incomplete because workers give greater priority to contact with clients.

For Further Reading
Prince, K. 1996: *Boring Records? Communication, Speech and Writing in Social Work*. London: Jessica Kingsley.

MALCOLM PAYNE

Casework

Casework involves focusing on identified problems and those experiencing them, and trying to understand the relationship between them. Hence, it is often described as a psychosocial approach. Casework is sometimes referred to as one-to-one work, but a case can involve an individual, a couple or a family; the emphasis is on each person as an individual. All people are seen as a product of their unique circumstances. Casework provides a sustaining and nurturing relationship over time, and works with the individual to try to answer the question: 'Why?'

Social workers might use a number of therapeutic interventions (for example, counselling or crisis work) when analysing a particular situation or problem, but the focus is always on the person or people involved in the situation and their perceptions of it. Although casework is sometimes criticized for holding people responsible for their problems, more accurately, it sees people as having the capacity to resolve them. This is achieved by the worker actively listening, showing empathy, trying to give insight but recognizing that those involved are self-determining and ultimately responsible for their own decisions.

For Further Reading
Coulshed, V. and Orme, J. 1998: *Social Work Practice*. Basingstoke: Macmillan, ch. 7.

JOAN ORME

Challenging Behaviour and its Management

Challenging behaviour is a term which is widely used within services for people with learning disabilities (and less widely in services for other client groups) to refer to 'culturally abnormal behaviour(s) of such an intensity, frequency, or duration that the physical safety of the person or others is likely to be placed in serious jeopardy, or behaviour which is likely to seriously limit use of, or result in the person being denied access to, ordinary community facilities' (Emerson, 1995). Such behaviours include self-injury, potential criminal offences such as physical aggression, destruction of the environment, sexually unacceptable acts and fire-setting, and a range of rarer and more idiosyncratic activities, such as faecal smearing or stereotyped behaviour.

The term 'challenging behaviour' is a label applied by those wanting to share information and obtain specialist support and treatment from educational, health, and social care services. The label may be misused, however, to support policies of inappropriate discrimination or exclusion. Properly used, its main advantages over earlier terms (for example, 'problem behaviour') are in drawing attention to the impact that an individual's behaviour has on his or her life, and in defining the 'problem' as, in part, that of those around the person. 'Problem behaviour', managed successfully, no longer presents a 'challenge'.

Prevalence and risk factors
Challenging behaviour is common among people with learning disabilities. Studies in the UK suggest a rate of 10–15 per cent among children and adults known to specialist learning disabilities services. Since most people with mild learning disabilities have no contact with specialist services after leaving school, there is also a group of adults identified as having learning disabilities only when their behaviour brings them into contact with mental health services or the criminal justice system.

Though of variable relevance for different individuals and across different forms of behaviour, a number of factors appear to be associated with challenging behaviour among people with learning disabilities:

- Gender: boys and men more than girls and women
- Age: a particular risk occurring during adolescence and early adulthood
- Severity of the disability: those with more severe impairments being more vulnerable

continued

- Impairments of vision or hearing
- Impairments of expressive and receptive language
- Epilepsy
- Specific biologically based syndromes, such as Fragile-X, associated with hyperkinesis and attentional problems, or Prader-Willi Syndrome, associated with over-eating
- Autistic spectrum disorders, characterized primarily by impairments of social interaction, imagination, and communication
- Mental health difficulties, including psychiatric disorders
- Histories offering limited opportunities to experience secure attachments
- Victimization through emotional, physical or sexual abuse
- Living in institutional, particularly hospital, settings – the relationship is complex, but it appears that institutionalization is usually now a consequence, rather than a cause, of challenging behaviour

Understanding challenging behaviour

In recent years, some integration between different frameworks for understanding challenging behaviour has been achieved by the acknowledgement that, rather than being arbitrary, the behaviour has *meaning* (or 'function') for that particular individual in the context of his or her history and current experiences. Attempts to manage challenging behaviour in the absence of an understanding of its possible meaning are likely to be unsuccessful and will often be unethical.

Generally, challenging behaviour helps the person to gain some control over his or her feelings or thoughts, or aspects of his or her physical or social environment, but its precise meaning is likely to be different for different individuals, even for behaviour which has a similar form (for example, self-injury by head-hitting). Within the same person, the meaning may also vary across time and settings, or across different forms of behaviour (for example, physical aggression and fire-setting).

The purpose of assessment is to develop an account of the likely meaning(s) of the person's behaviour. Assessment may be complex and time-consuming and may involve a variety of methods including:

- archive material
- self-report measures, such as interviews and questionnaires
- reports from other people, such as carers
- assessment of the individual's skills and abilities
- direct observations in different settings.

Increasingly, attention has been given to assisting people with learning disabilities to express their thoughts and feelings for themselves, even if they have limited or no expressive verbal language.

A comprehensive assessment will also include an understanding of the social context in which the person's behaviour developed and now takes place. The majority of people with learning disabilities have lives characterized by limited opportunities for social and intimate relationships, long periods of inactivity, and the disadvantages associated with poverty. These are all factors likely to lead to more challenging behaviour. Though individuals in social care provision are more likely to have support, this is often provided by frequently changing and inexperienced carers. Too often, the impact of carers on the person's challenging behaviour has been neglected.

All the information needs to be integrated in a summary which provides:

- an understanding of the way in which the person's challenging behaviour has developed and been maintained; and
- a rationale for the different interventions which will be used to manage the person's behaviour and improve his or her quality of life.

Increasingly, such summaries are presented in visual form because this increases their accessibility to people with learning disabilities and their carers.

Management

Successful management of a person's challenging behaviour increases access to, and benefits from, experiences and opportunities which are typical for his or her peers. Achieving this usually requires an approach which is multidisciplinary and, particularly when the person's needs are complex (for example, if he or she has additional substance misuse problems, or is at risk of contact with the criminal justice system), also multiagency. The framework devised by LaVigna et al. (1989) is often used for co-ordinating the different aspects of management. It comprises both proactive and reactive strategies.

Proactive strategies are designed to decrease behaviour over time and consist of ecological manipulations, positive programming and direct treatment.

- *Ecological manipulations* produce changes in behaviour by amending the person's physical and social environment, for example, by participating in the recruitment of staff in a staffed housing project, or arranging greater access to enjoyable activities. Social workers are particularly likely to be involved in these interventions.
- *Positive programming* is used to develop competencies which will enable more effective coping, for example, improving communication skills, providing psychotherapy, and/or training in relaxation techniques.
- *Direct treatment* is used to achieve rapid change, for example, medication for a diagnosed psychiatric disorder, or providing clearer expectations and feedback around the individual's behaviour.

Reactive strategies are designed to contain incidents of challenging behaviour. Such strategies may have, at times, to incorporate physical interventions that are individualized, carefully monitored and implemented by staff with the requisite training.

The development and implementation of both reactive and proactive strategies requires careful consideration of issues relating to consent.

While the approach described here may often be successful in a person's existing environment, it requires careful monitoring and may, at times, also need to be supplemented by designing life arrangements which are highly specific to a particular individual's needs. Such solutions, although expensive in the short term, may, in the long term, be both more effective and more efficient.

For Further Reading

Department of Health 1993: *Services for People with Learning Disabilities and Challenging Behaviour or Mental Health Needs* (The report of a project group chaired by Professor J. L. Mansell). London: HMSO.

Emerson, E. 1995: *Challenging Behaviour: Analysis and Intervention in People with Learning Disabilities*. Cambridge: Cambridge University Press.

Emerson, E., Hatton, C., Bromley, J. and Caine, A. 1998: *Clinical Psychology and People with Intellectual Disabilities*. Chichester: John Wiley.

Koegel, L. K., Koegel, R. L. and Dunlap, G. 1996: *Positive Behavioural Support – Including People with Difficult Behaviour in the Community*. Baltimore: Paul H. Brookes.

ISABEL CLARE AND PETER MCGILL

Changing Behaviour

See THERAPEUTIC INTERVENTION.

Character Disorders

See PERSONALITY DISORDERS.

Child Abuse

Child abuse is a process whereby, either through inaction or actions that are injurious, a child's safety, health or development is compromised to a degree that substantially offends against prevailing standards of childcare.

The nature of child abuse

Any concept of child abuse implies an identified standard of physical, emotional and psychological well-being and a general understanding of the value and meaning of childhood against which the lived experience of children can be set. As the scientific and popular idea of childhood changes, so too do different forms of behaviour become identified as abusive. Accordingly, child abuse is to be understood as an historically and culturally specific phenomenon that is not susceptible to a fixed or universal definition. In this way, abuse is to be distinguished from any literal injury or other harm inflicted upon a child, which may or may not be regarded as abusive; for example, legally sanctioned corporal punishment is routinely excluded from accounts of child abuse.

As well as being contingent upon cultural norms, what constitutes child abuse is also determined by public policy and the relationship that this describes between the individual, the family and the state. Moreover, that which is legislatively or executively defined as 'abuse' is substantially influenced by the professional aspirations and discourses of those whose job it is to work with abused children. Most Western democracies can trace broadly similar histories in this regard from mid-nineteenth century private and philanthropic concerns with poverty and public health to twenty-first century state welfarism and concerns with a child's inner world.

Contemporary accounts of child abuse are commonly classified under three broad headings:

- Events or processes which fall under the heading of *physical abuse* conventionally include non-accidental injury to a child, or denying a child adequate means of subsistence, protection or care through their physical neglect.
- *Sexual abuse* usually refers to the involvement of minors in sexual activities that they do not fully comprehend, and to which they have not given their informed consent. Such activities may include the commercial exploitation of children for the purposes of prostitution or pornography, as well as engaging the child in developmentally or age inappropriate sexual acts.
- *Emotional abuse* describes the active or passive disregard of a child's maturational, emotional and psychological needs through, for example, persistent and excessive criticism, shaming, threatening or anxiety-inducing behaviour on the part of carers.

One further broad classification might be termed *ecological abuse*, whereby a particular group or class of children is subject to abuse by virtue of their group or class membership. Examples might include exploitative child labour or those who are victims of natural disasters or war.

None of these categories are mutually exclusive or independent: for example, physical abuse may imply emotional abuse, and sexual abuse may involve physical harm. Nor do any of the categorizations predict either the site of the abuse or the nature of the formal relationship between the abuser and the child. Abuse occurs in family homes, within privately run or state institutions, and between children and their parents, peers or strangers.

The causes of child abuse

The definitional imprecision of child abuse has fostered a variety of causal accounts. Some explanatory theories emphasize social and environmental factors such as poverty of means or expectation which produce stresses on and within families. Similarly, at the macro-political level, the relative powerlessness of children in economic and political terms has been said to make them inherently vulnerable to exploitation and victimization. Other theories focus more on the individual as the proximate cause of child abuse. Such theories tend to focus on the nature of the relationship between carers and children, as well as on the personal characteristics of those involved in the process of abuse. For example, failures in attachment between the child and its primary carer, as well as psychiatric or other pathological conditions in the adult, have been cited as predictive or aggravating factors in the aetiology of abuse. Particular characteristics of the child, such as illness or congenital abnormality, may also increase a child's vulnerability to abuse, particularly where this leads to the frustration of parental expectation.

Mono-causal accounts and those which seek to integrate different perspectives offer different levels of explanation of the phenomenon of abuse and have originated widely divergent strategies for detecting, preventing and responding to its occurrence. Consequently, calculation of the prevalence, incidence and consequences of abuse is problematic.

The prevalence and consequences of child abuse

Most formal or administrative measures of child abuse record either notifications of reports of abuse or adjudicated cases requiring further professional involvement. Data extrapolated from surveys of clinical populations or studies of victimization throughout the general population, invariably report the prevalence of abuse to be higher than those estimates deriving from administrative data, although the relationship between the level of identified abuse and that which goes unobserved or undetected is not clear.

Depending on the nature of the abuse, victimization data do indicate age and gender effects. Boys are more likely to be physically abused than girls, and girls are more likely to be sexually abused than boys. The age of those who are sexually abused is likely to be higher than that of those subject to physical abuse, although abuse remains essentially a hazard of infancy and early childhood.

The consequences of abuse for a child are a function, not only of the nature and severity of the abuse, but also of the personal resources of the child and what help, support and protection they receive. Constellations of symptoms consequent on abuse may include immediate and persistent physiological and psychological responses to trauma or neglect, more or less functional adaptations to stress, damage to a child's self-esteem, self-destructive or socially unacceptable behaviour, or psychiatric illness. It is increasingly recognized that survivors' own accounts are critical in understanding the experience, meaning and the consequences of abuse.

For Further Reading

Butler, I. and Williamson, H. 1994: *Children Speak: Children, Trauma and Social Work.* Harlow: Longman/NSPCC.

Corby, B. 1993: *Child Abuse – Towards a Knowledge Base.* Buckingham: Open University Press.

Wilson, K. and James, A. (eds) 1995: *The Child Protection Handbook.* London: Baillière Tindall.

IAN BUTLER

Child Abuse Inquiries

Child abuse inquiries are mechanisms for examining the circumstances in which children known to (or in the care of) state agencies are subjected to serious and fatal abuse. They usually arise from considerable public concern about the handling of such cases. In Britain, the publication of the Maria Colwell report in 1974 laid the foundation of the country's child protection system. Between then and 1997, there were 65 further inquiries resulting in publicly available reports; see Table 1. Inquiries are most

Table 1 Child abuse: Key inquiries in the UK 1974–92

Year	Title	Type of abuse	Area	Key findings	Impact
1974	Maria Colwell	Physical	East Sussex	Lack of interprofessional co-operation	Interprofessional system for responding to child abuse first developed
1985	Jasmine Beckford	Physical	London Borough of Brent	Insufficient focus on protection needs of children	Child protection to be given primacy in work with families. 1988 Working Together guidelines[a]
1987	Cleveland	Sexual (121 cases)	Cleveland	Insensitive and intrusive intervention into families	Greater emphasis on the wishes of children and rights of parents in child abuse investigations Children Act 1989
1991	Pindown	Physical abuse in residential care (132 cases)	Staffordshire	Abusive regimes to control children with challenging behaviours not detected by management	Guidelines for better recruiting, training, management and monitoring of residential social workers. Utting Report 1991[b]
1992	Orkneys	Ritual abuse (9 cases)	Orkneys	Poorly conducted investigations and insensitive interviewing techniques	Guidelines for joint police and social work interviews in cases of child abuse. 1992 Memorandum of Good Practice[c]

[a] Department of Health and Social Security 1988: *Working Together: A Guide to Interagency Cooperation for the Protection of Children from Abuse.* London, HMSO.

[b] Utting, Sir William 1991: *Children in the Public Care: A Review of Residential Care.* London, HMSO.

[c] Home Office (in conjunction with the Department of Health) 1992: *Memorandum of Good Practice on Video Recorded Interviews with Child Witnesses for Criminal Proceedings.* London, HMSO.

50

commonly used to examine the deaths by physical abuse and neglect of individual children living in their own families but supervised by state agencies. They are also used to examine child sexual abuse, ritual, organized and institutional abuse of children in residential and day care settings. Inquiries vary in type and process. Those ordered by central government have wide-ranging powers and are conducted in the manner of court hearings; those established by

local authorities have limited powers and operate more informally. The findings of child abuse inquiries continue to exert considerable influence on the development of child protection policy in the UK.

For Further Reading
Corby, B., Doig, R. and Roberts, V. 1998: Inquiries into child abuse. *The Journal of Social Welfare and Family Law*, 20, 377–95.

BRIAN CORBY

Child Care Policy and Practice

Child care (or child welfare) policy and practice covers a range of services provided to assist children and families who have encountered a major difficulty affecting the well-being, care or control of the child. Parents and other family members may be unable to provide adequate physical and emotional care of the child, perhaps on account of death, abandonment, health problems or multiple life stresses. In some cases, an adult in the family has seriously or repeatedly ill-treated the child. Outside intervention may also be invoked by family conflicts or the behaviour of the child, including law-breaking, aggression or school-related difficulties. Many child care problems derive from family disruption, poverty or social upheaval.

In such circumstances, formal agencies intervene with the aim of caring for or protecting the child, or in order to influence the behaviour of the child or family. Usually, central and local government have the main responsibility for the welfare of child citizens, but direct services or legal powers and duties may be assumed by non-government organizations too. In many parts of the world, international agencies such as Unicef, Caritas and Save the Children play an important role.

National and local differences in geography, wealth, political system, cultural values and history all affect the ways in which child care problems are created, defined and responded to. Each country has its own social policies and specific legislation affecting children. However the principles of the UN Convention on the Rights of the Child of 1989 are widely influential. Article 3 of the Convention asserts that, in all actions concerning children, 'the best interests of the child shall be the primary consideration'. Other rights impose duties on governments and others to promote children's survival, health and development, identity and family belonging, all on a non-discriminatory basis. The Convention also stresses the importance of taking account of children's views. Countries differ in the extent to which these principles apply equally to children who are judged to 'do wrong' and who have been 'wronged' by the absence or poor quality of family care. Hence, youth justice systems are to varying degrees integrated with, or separated from, child welfare systems.

Varieties of child welfare provision
Services may be provided to support children within their family home or a child may be placed away from home on account of the severity of the problems or the paucity of facilities. Depending on a country's socio-economic position and policy stance, an array of family support or preventative services can help families to alleviate or resolve their difficulties. The availability of universal provision like social security, education and housing is a crucial foundation affecting the likelihood that families may run into difficulties or can cope with them. Specialist services are also required to help individuals, nuclear families or extended kin networks to apply or improve their caring and

continued

coping strengths. Other measures can promote the capacities of groups or communities of parents, children and others to provide mutual support or engage in social action directed at ameliorating their environment, or making agencies and professionals more responsive.

The salience and roles of social workers vary greatly within and between countries. Commonly, field social workers assess, plan and review family circumstances. They can provide direct help (for example, by counselling, therapy or life-story work) and/or organize access to services. These include financial and housing assistance, day support, educational provision, specialist guidance, mediation or treatment, and out-of-home care. In certain circumstances, such as responding to allegations of abuse or arranging adoptions, preparation of reports and court appearances are essential tasks. Social workers can also be employed in residential establishments, either providing daily care or assuming a more specialist role, usually to work with residents' families.

Both research evidence and principles based on partnership ideals suggest that successful child care social work entails open negotiation with family members to define problems and agree aims and responsibilities, recognizing that the wishes and interests of different family members may conflict. Awareness of cultural considerations and close attention to practical needs is required. In certain circumstances, notably child abuse or youth offending, legal powers from a court or its equivalent are used to give official agencies authority to impose on children or parents compulsory monitoring, guidance or attendance at specified provision.

Out-of-home care

The three main forms of service away from home are foster families, residential homes and schools, and adoption. Out-of-home care is provided for children whose families are unable to care for them or do not want to, as well as for some placed under a legal order. Children may be away for any period, from a day or two up to their whole childhood. Some have repeated episodes away from home. The impact of separation, discontinuity and disrupted relationships and schooling can be very negative unless the transitions are well handled and the alternative care arrangements are of high quality. Consequently, experts agree that placement away from home should only occur after serious consideration and when it is clearly in the child's interests. Nevertheless, some children have been shown to want and benefit from alternative care.

The role of the state in family life

Both the general role and the specific decisions and actions of social workers reflect everchanging ideas embodied in policy and practice. Particularly important are perceptions of the role of the state in family life:

- The sometimes competing rights and needs of children and parents
- Risks posed to children by other family members or the wider environment
- Children's vulnerability, attachments, identities and competencies

At different times, in different places and depending on the particular family circumstances, the balance varies between a 'child rescue' approach with ready use of legal powers or removal of children from home to 'better' alternatives, and voluntary assistance aimed at helping families to stay together or be re-united.

For Further Reading
Downs, S. W., Costin, L. B. and McFadden, E. J. 1996: *Child Welfare and Family Services*. White Plains: Longman.
Hill, M. and Aldgate, J. 1996: *Child Welfare Services*. London: Jessica Kingsley.
Pringle, K. 1998: *Children and Social Welfare in Europe*. Buckingham: Open University Press.
MALCOLM HILL

Child Development

Child development refers to the process by which dependent infants grow through child-hood and adolescence into autonomous adulthood. The changes cover a number of areas of growth: physical, behavioural, cognitive, emotional, social and educational. Each area has its own body of research-based knowledge, but it is the pattern of progress across different areas which will explain the individual child's functioning, whether it be the development of language in a two-year-old or the achievement of educational success in a ten-year-old.

The child in the environment

The process of change over time involves an interaction between the child and the environment – for example, an interaction between what the infant brings physically, intellectually and temperamentally and what the environment provides in terms of care, protection and stimulation. The final outcome in terms of the quality of adult functioning will therefore depend on the characteristics of the child, the environment and the interaction between them. Although we are most familiar with the idea that the environment shapes the child, for better or worse, it is now accepted that the child also shapes the environment. The temperamentally easy child will bring out the best in the anxious parent. The child with a severe physical disability or with autistic tendencies will challenge even the best efforts of the committed and competent parent. The quality of such interactions will affect the way in which children master their maturational tasks. Therefore, although it is possible to identify some broadly similar stages of development, there will be individual differences, mostly within what we could call the normal range but, in some cases, jeopardizing the progress towards healthy adult functioning.

Social work and child development

For social workers, applying knowledge of both normal and problematic developmental processes in childhood has always been an important part of fulfilling the role required of them by society. The need to understand the development of children and to place it in a theoretical context is an essential part of the social work task, primarily because it under-pins the work of assessment and intervention in cases where there are concerns about children's welfare. Social workers are required to be alert to individual children who are in need of help or protection; their needs can only be properly determined if social workers employ a framework for measuring the development of those children against what is known to be within the normal and acceptable range. What is more, in a working environment where resources are limited, knowledge of where a child fits in the developmental framework facilitates the targeting of effort and services to those children and families who are most in need of help and protection. Certain key questions have to be addressed. Is this child's development within the normal range? Is the parenting in this family environment good enough to ensure that developmental tasks are successfully undertaken and age-appropriate goals achieved? If not, what can social work agencies, normally in collaboration with health, education and other agencies, do to make a difference? Social workers are particularly well-placed to address these questions because they are trained to take into account both the inner and outer worlds, the psychosocial development of the self in the context of the physical and relationship environment.

It is important to consider the role of knowledge of child development in different areas of social work practice. In the area of family support or preventative work, social workers become involved in providing an assessment of children's developmental needs and whether they are being met. To identify need and provide effective help, social workers use a theoretically based knowledge of the range of normal development and the kinds of parenting which promote it. Accurate assessments of a four-year-old child,

continued

for example, should mean that the parents receive the right kind of help and advice and that the child receives the appropriate kind of pre-school provision. This increases the likelihood that the child will make a smooth transition, intellectually and socially, into school, a particularly important watershed developmentally for most children.

In the field of child maltreatment, the protective function of social workers hinges on their capacity not only to define and identify abusive or neglectful parental behaviours, but on their ability to document and evaluate the impact of certain parenting behaviours, acts of omission and commission, on the child. Knowledge of child development is supplemented here by familiarity with the research on the impact of maltreatment on development. Research can provide evidence which aids assessment and planning, such as the long-term consequences of particular kinds of maltreatment. It is often in the area of child protection that social workers are most likely to be called upon by inter-agency conferences and courts to provide reports and recommendations, which will have far-reaching consequences for the child. Social work assessments which place the individual child's current and likely future development in a theoretical framework provide the most persuasive arguments for their professional recommendations.

Finally, where children are separated from their families and brought up in foster care or adoption, understanding of child development, both in adequate family environments and in the context of maltreatment, is supplemented by awareness of the impact of separation and loss on development. Without such explanations, carers will be at a loss as to how best to promote healthy growth and placements are put at risk.

Social work decision making and intervention with children, the identification of risks and protective factors, relies on knowledge of child development. In this area of practice, social workers draw on other disciplines, particularly psychology, to ensure that they make the most effective use of the responsible role that they have been given to promote the care and safety of children.

For Further Reading
Bee, H. 1997: *The Developing Child*. New York:Addison-Wesley Educational Publishers.
Howe, D., Brandon, M., Hinings, D. and Schofield, G. 1999: *Attachment Theory, Child Maltreatment and Family Support*. Basingstoke: Macmillan.
Schaffer, H. R. 1998: *Making Decisions about Children* (2nd edn). Oxford: Blackwell Publishers.

GILLIAN SCHOFIELD

Child Neglect

Neglect can be defined as a condition that occurs when children's basic needs for adequate shelter, nutrition, clothing, education, stimulation, nurturance, encouragement, supervision and medical care remain un-met. Though neglectful conditions can exist on a continuum ranging from optimal to extremely harmful, in social work terms, neglect is generally understood to mean those situations which prevail to the extent that they cause significant risk to the physical and emotional health, development and safety of children. *Neglect* is essentially defined by its cumulative, severe and persistent nature, which differentiates it from intermittent episodes of inadequate caring. While perpetrators of neglect are generally perceived to be a child's caretakers, it can also be seen as the responsibility of communities and society at large.

The causes of child neglect
Neglect is the most widely reported form of child maltreatment, though its prevalence is difficult to calculate, both because of definitional difficulties and a tendency among

practitioners to regard children subject to neglect as 'in need' of support rather than 'at risk' of abuse, thus omitting them from official child abuse statistics. The former categorization evolved mainly from a reluctance to stigmatize and label families where the boundaries between inadequate parenting and general deprivation seemed unclear. Cultural differences are often cited as impediments to the recognition of child neglect, though it has been well established that serious deficits in child safety and welfare transcend cultural and ethnic norms. Equally, it is possible that concerns about child neglect are masked by the presence of the more prominently profiled categories of physical or sexual abuse in the same cases.

The knowledge base on neglect is limited by a dearth of methodologically sound research in the area. Study populations are often predetermined by the nature of their contact with welfare or clinical services, and researchers sometimes fail to differentiate between neglect and other forms of abuse. Equally, research has tended to be very gendered, concentrating principally on mothers and underrating both the negative and positive effects of men's involvement in child care.

While child neglect is by no means the inevitable consequence of adversity, it is frequently associated with parental factors such as low self-esteem, poor educational attainment, health problems, substance abuse, depression, learning disability, lone parenthood, experience of neglect as a child, prolonged contact with social services and poor management skills. Environmental factors often linked with neglect include sub-standard housing, social exclusion, social isolation and poverty.

Attachment and cognitive theories are often used to explain the aetiology and process of neglect, in terms of deficits in the carers' own developmental experience which can affect their adult behaviour, impeding their ability to appropriately perceive, interpret and respond to the needs of their children. Hopelessness and powerlessness are frequently manifested by neglectful carers.

Although neglect is often regarded as the least dangerous form of child maltreatment, its impact has been shown to be long-lasting and often more damaging than that of physical or sexual abuse. Physical effects of neglect include chronic health problems, malnutrition, enuresis, stunted growth, and serious injury or death either through preventable accident or disease. Psychological effects include delayed language and cognitive development, impaired concentration, attachment disorders, passivity, disruptive behaviour, poor coping and problem solving abilities, low self-esteem, inability to make or sustain relationships, and educational underachievement.

The social work response to child neglect

Neglect cases are more likely than any other category to be filtered out of the child protection system early, often without any offer of service. Criticisms of the way in which neglect cases have been handled by professionals include failure to understand the seriousness of its effects on children, lack of child centredness, under-use of developmental models, unwarranted optimism about carers' ability to change, and an overconcentration on parental compliance and recent individual events. Factors to be taken into consideration when assessing neglect should include the child's physical health, emotional state and developmental progress, his or her relationship with carers and experience of separations or losses. Carers should be assessed in respect of their relationships and any present or pre-existing issues which may impact on their current functioning, including physical and mental health, disabilities, addictions and recent adverse life events. The child and family's external environment should also be considered, including formal and informal supports and relationships with professionals, including school. Assessment should strive to highlight positive factors in relation to the children themselves, such as intelligence and resilience, as well as positive aspects of their familial and social networks which may be reinforced and developed.

continued

Given the persistent and cumulative nature of neglect, interventions should aim to enhance the overall quality of care that the child is exposed to over a period of time, rather than a concentration on individual acts of commission or omission. The actual interventions should be determined by the different stages of a child's development and targeted in a holistic fashion at the factors highlighted in the assessment. Work with neglectful carers is rarely achievable on a short-term basis, and commitment to longer-term engagement is usually necessary. Interventions need to be made at a co-ordinated multi-service level, involving welfare, housing, health and education services as necessary. Therapeutic work aimed at increasing parental competency and building on existing strengths has been found to be most successful when conducted in a group context which incorporates individual tuition and counselling. Effective models of intervention include family therapy and task-centred work. Direct services for neglected children which are likely to be beneficial include home, school and community-based play and tuition, therapy, and day or short-term respite care. Efforts should also be made to strengthen informal support networks. While the aim should be to work in partnership with parents as much as possible, there may be instances in which it is necessary to use legal sanctions to ensure a child's safety and welfare.

For Further Reading
Crittenden, P. 1993: 'An information-processing perspective on the behaviour of neglectful parents. *Criminal Justice and Behaviour*, 20 (1), 27–48.
Iwaniec, D. 1995: *The Emotionally Abused and Neglected Child: Identification, Assessment and Intervention*. Chichester: Wiley.
Stevenson, O. 1998: *Neglected Children: Issues and Dilemmas*. Oxford: Blackwell.

HELEN BUCKLEY

Child Protection

Child protection is a term which has both general and specific meanings in social work. The UN Convention on the Rights of the Child takes a broad approach to the protection needs of children. It refers to the protection of children from abuse (Article 19), from the illicit use of drugs (Article 33), and from economic, sexual and all other forms of exploitation (Articles 32, 34 and 36). This general view sees children as vulnerable to a wide range of abuses and mistreatment from both within and outside the family as a result of the relatively powerless state of childhood. The Convention seeks to address this vulnerability by requiring member states to assert the rights of children in their national policies for child protection.

Britain is a signatory to the UN Convention, but does not have its own children's bill of rights in this broad sense. Rather, it has developed a legal framework for the protection of children from abuse by their parents and immediate carers. For England and Wales, this framework is currently set out in the Children Act 1989. It is supported by criminal legislation such as the Children and Young Persons Act 1933 and the Sexual Offences Act 1956 which define a range of offences against children, and by guidelines for the practice of those agencies with child protection responsibilities. Scotland and Northern Ireland have separate, but similar legislative frameworks for ensuring child protection: The Children (Scotland) Act 1995 and the Children (Northern Ireland) Order 1995.

The need for the state to actively intervene in families to protect children was developed in late Victorian times with the formation of the National Society for the Prevention of Cruelty to Children (NSPCC). In more recent times, the child protection role in

England and Wales has fallen to local authority social services departments. Concerns about child mistreatment have, therefore, persisted for over 100 years, but with varying degrees of emphasis and different focuses.

Child protection in the late twentieth century

The late 1960s and early 1970s saw an upsurge of interest in physical child abuse and neglect. From the mid-1980s, there was an ever-increasing concern about sexual (and, to a lesser extent, emotional) abuse of children. The 1990s saw the emergence of new forms of physical and sexual abuse:

- Organized abuse, or the abuse of one or more children by two or more linked abusers
- Ritual abuse, or organized abuse carried out with ritualistic (usually Satanic) accompaniments
- Institutional abuse, or the physical and sexual mistreatment of children in day centres and residential homes by staff of these establishments.

In response to these concerns, and particularly as a result of the large number of public inquiries that reported after 1974, a system for responding to child abuse referrals and allegations developed. This system was originally established following the report of the Maria Colwell inquiry. In 1986, it was termed the child protection system following the inquiry into the death of Jasmine Beckford. It has three key features:

1 The establishment of area child protection committees (ACPCs), consisting of managers from all agencies with responsibilities in the child protection field – social services and probation departments, health agencies, the police and education authorities – and responsible for developing child protection policies at a local level, and for overseeing and monitoring their implementation
2 Arrangements for calling inter-agency child protection conferences in specific cases where children are considered to be at risk of significant harm
3 The creation of child protection registers identifying children considered to be significantly at risk

National guidelines provide a blueprint for these local arrangements. The key message of the guidelines is the need for a co-ordinated inter-agency response. They delineate the roles of the different agencies, and identify key issues relating to the timing and conduct of interdisciplinary child protection conferences. Finally, they outline the procedures for investigating cases where children are killed or seriously injured as a result of abuse (known as Part 8 reviews).

Child protection work grew considerably during the last two decades of the twentieth century, and, in the UK, became the dominant form of state child welfare intervention. In England, in 1996, there were 35,000 children (3 per 1,000 under 18) on child protection registers (including 10,400 for physical abuse, 8,900 for physical neglect, 7,500 for sexual abuse and 4,700 for emotional abuse). There were 30,000 registrations and 30,000 deregistrations in the year up to the end of March 1996.

The need for a tighter focus

In the mid-1990s, there was a shift in thinking about child protection in Britain. Major inquiries into sexual and ritual abuse of children in Cleveland and the Orkneys seemed to confirm a public view that social workers and other professionals were becoming obsessed with child protection concerns and overzealous in their interventions into family life. Research sponsored by the Department of Health supported this view. The main findings of the research were that the child protection system was acting like a giant filter, drawing into its net large numbers of deprived families, and focusing resources on those identified as the most serious cases of abuse. However, in this process,

continued

many of the sifted-out families felt insensitively dealt with and the researchers found that, often, their need for support was disregarded despite evidence of considerable deprivation, social problems and health deficiencies.

The Department of Health, in response, encouraged child protection professionals to be more discriminating in their assessments of families referred for child protection concerns, and to tackle their needs in more supportive and participative ways. In particular, it stressed the need for greater focus on the issues of persistent neglect and inadequate parenting.

The likelihood is that, in the twenty-first century, child protection services will be more integrated into broader child welfare systems. The challenge will be to establish a balance that ensures that families can be helped in a way that also ensures the protection of children within them.

For Further Reading
Department of Health 1995: *Child Protection: Messages from Research*. London: HMSO.
Parton, N. (ed.) 1997: *Child Protection and Family Support: Tensions, Contradictions and Possibilities*. London: Routledge.
Wilson, K. and James, A. (eds) 1995: *The Child Protection Handbook*. London: Baillière-Tindall.

BRIAN CORBY

Child Sexual Abuse

Although *child sexual abuse* (CSA) was rarely addressed as a social work problem before 1980, it is now clear from retrospective accounts of adults that CSA does frequently occur and often has negative consequences for child and adult mental health. Surveys of randomly selected adults in community mental health surveys indicate consistent findings: some 30 per cent of girls (up to age 16) have experienced at least one episode of unwanted, physical sexual contact. Prolonged CSA occurs in about 10 per cent of females and 5 per cent of males. About 1 per cent of biological fathers incestuously abuse their daughters. The rate for stepfathers and mother's cohabitee is much higher, up to 1 in 10 of these unrelated men in the girl's household imposing a long-term sexual relationship on the child. About 60 per cent of those who sexually abuse a female child are related to her (including stepfathers). Stranger assault is quite rare: about 5 per cent of all cases.

About half of victims will have some mental health problems, with about 20 per cent of these having prolonged and severe mental health problems, including depression, anxiety, suicidality, body image and eating disorders, sexual problems and various physical symptoms including pelvic pain. Sexual abuse by females is rare (less that 5 per cent of assailants); abusers of boys are overwhelmingly male. Male victims seem to be more severely affected by CSA than females, with higher rates of suicidal behaviour. The reason for this is not clear. The adult recall surveys indicate that the victim never told anyone about CSA in 80 per cent of cases; only for 5 per cent did authorities intervene, and then often ineffectively.

The prevalence figures for child sexual abuse estimated from adult recall studies are almost certainly underestimates, since only those with stable lifestyles are located in these surveys. Those living on the street or with high residential mobility will be missed. It is now established that young teen runaways, street kids and adolescent sex trade workers have rates of prior, prolonged and intrusive CSA of at least 50 per cent. There is a danger of blaming victims of CSA for their aggressive, suicidal and acting-out behaviour, punishing them without addressing the real causes of disturbed behaviour.

Social work approaches

CSA presents child protection workers with challenges of the utmost difficulty. While the primary aim of intervention is to ensure the child's safety, this is often achieved by removing the child from home, leaving the alleged offender in place. Children may experience guilt at throwing their family life into chaos, and face pressures to retract. If the offence is denied and prosecution is pursued, therapy for the child (which would be seen as interfering with the evidence he or she might give) must be postponed until after completion of the criminal trial. These trials, despite special measures (for example, screening the child from the accused), are known to be traumatic for many children, and trauma following revelation may be worse than trauma imposed by the abuse itself. Many cases, for this reason, never come to trial: but there is also evidence that some children feel cheated when the offender goes scot free. A complex array of professionals may be involved, and case conferencing is often necessary to ensure smooth transition of the child through an often adversarial system.

A complicating factor is that CSA only atypically occurs independently of other family problems, including disordered family relationships, emotional and/or physical abuse of children, and introduction of different father figures. While CSA can occur in any kind of family, it is clear that prevalence rates are much higher in disorganized blue-collar families. These families are more likely to contain children with low self-esteem reflecting prior emotional and/or physical abuse. These children are less likely to resist sexual advances by a family member or someone outside the family who offers the young person sex in exchange for emotional attachment. Comparison of children who have suffered sexual abuse without any other types of abuse with those suffering emotional abuse alone indicates that CSA has less negative impact than emotional abuse *per se*.

The mothers of victims

Mothers have a key role in supporting their child through the traumatic factors surrounding revelation of CSA. Social work interventions should seek to support the mother as well as her child. Mothers may often have unresolved trauma issues from their own abusive childhoods, even though they were rarely aware that their own child was being abused. Sometimes, mothers disbelieve their child's accusation against a family member, or, if believed, blame the child for the abuse. This means that the young person has a double burden of guilt to bear, and mental health outcomes for such stigmatized children are often poor.

Special problems

Some children cope with CSA by dissociating from it. These self-induced hypnotic states can lead to actual forgetting of the abusive events, but with an underlying pattern of traumatic reactions evidenced by post-traumatic stress disorder, dissociative personality disorder, and in extreme cases, multiple personality. Memories of CSA can be repressed, but can also suddenly reappear in consciousness, typically when the abuser dies. Nevertheless, expert consensus now seems to be that memories of CSA recovered in therapy should be treated with caution, and do not constitute *prima facie* evidence for legal or other accusations to be made.

Resilient children who survive CSA without apparent ill-effects are likely to have had close emotional support with someone during the abuse; to have had relatively good self-esteem prior to the onset of abuse; and to have been able to use conscious distancing strategies, belittling the abuse and the abuser without actual dissociation.

Physical examinations of children who are alleged victims of CSA have proved generally unhelpful, since most types of CSA leave few discernible physical signs after 72 hours. Over-reliance on such physical examination (which is itself often humiliating and traumatic) has led to débâcles such as the large-scale removal of children into care in Cleveland, which provoked a backlash against social work interventions, to the extent

continued

that social work in the late 1990s in both Britain and North America now treats CSA investigations with undue caution.

Children from emotionally barren and physically abusive homes may be drawn into sex rings, run by paedophiles living on or close to run-down areas of public housing. Paradoxically, many children stay in these sex rings because they offer companionship and reward which they did not receive at home. Children in care are also easily recruited into such rings, especially those who have experienced prior CSA. In some cases, these sex rings are staging posts for juvenile prostitution. These sex rings are also a source of child pornography, which may have a clandestine but widespread clientele. The showing of such pornography to children is one method by which paedophiles encourage potential victims to engage in sexuality with adults.

Adult survivors

Given the known prevalence of child sexual abuse, the number of adult survivors who might benefit from therapies designed to address problems stemming from sexual and other abuse in childhood is potentially very large. A common factor in the lives of survivors of CSA and other abuse is that of attachment problems arising from chaotic socialization. This has formed the basis of one school of group therapy (Alexander), but several different and competing models exist for treating adult survivors. Any group treatment which can reduce feelings of guilt, enhance self-esteem and increase social support appears to be successful, regardless of the theoretical rationale underlying the therapy. Individual counselling with adults using cognitive restructuring of irrational beliefs stemming from the CSA appears to be particularly successful.

The abusers

Adult recall surveys of males indicate that up to 10 per cent have at least a passing sexual interest in minors, while the number of men with a strong sexual attachment to prepubescent children is about 3 per cent of the total population. Finkelhor's 4-factor model, for CSA to occur, identifies four situations:

1   An underlying sexual attachment to children
2   Internal justification that such behaviour is, in some way, right
3   Relative absence of external controls about sexuality involving children
4   Actual access to children

Fixated paedophiles may enter professional or voluntary roles which give such access, and then abuse literally hundreds of children during their lifetime. At the opposite end of this continuum are regressed offenders, weak men who regress within their families to a sexual relationship with a daughter. These men seem to carry on their abuse within an aura of personal shame which is communicated to the victim. On revelation, there is a danger that they may commit suicide, leaving an additional burden of guilt for the victim and her family.

The largest number of abusers are men who often have other criminal records, and who casually abuse their own and others' children. While the majority of fixated offenders were themselves CSA victims, only about 30 per cent of abused males will acquire a tendency to prefer boys as sexual targets.

For Further Reading
Bagley, C. 1997: *Children, Sex and Social Policy: Humanistic Solutions for Problems of Child Sexual Abuse*. Aldershot: Ashgate.
Bagley, C. and King, K. 1990: *Child Sexual Abuse: The Search for Healing*. London: Tavistock/Routledge.
Bagley, C. and Thurston, W. 1996: *Understanding and Preventing Child Sexual Abuse: Critical Research Summaries, Vols. I and II*. Aldershot: Arena.

CHRIS BAGLEY

Childhood Temperament

The idea that children have basic *temperamental styles*, observable at birth, emerged from the New York longitudinal studies of Chess and Thomas. They identified three types:

1 *Easy*, describing an infant who is tractable, smiling and adapts well to new routines (about 70 per cent of all children)
2 *Slow-to-warm-up*, describing an infant who is rather fearful and clinging, and adapts poorly to novel experiences (15 per cent)
3 *Difficult*, describing an infant who tends to be fretful and aggressive, to cry without being comforted, and to react with rage to frustrations (15 per cent)

For the stressed parent, the *difficult* child is one who may be excessively punished, rejected or abused. Chess and Thomas show that goodness-of-fit between parental care and a child's temperament means that a difficult temperament by no means predicts the development of later conduct disorders. However, when a difficult child is punished excessively, abused and rejected, the likelihood of deviant outcomes is high. The models of child temperament have been successfully applied in work with adoptive and foster children, and in general parenting courses. Studies of delinquent youth show that early difficult temperament is strongly predictive of later aggressive behaviour, indicating that more focused intervention in the early years of disadvantaged children might divert children from delinquency by improving the match between child temperament and parenting style.

For Further Reading
Carey, W. and McDevitt, S. 1995: *Coping with Children's Temperament: A Guide for Professionals*. New York: Basic Books.
Chess, S. and Thomas, A. 1986: *Temperament in Clinical Practice*. London: Guildford Press.

CHRIS BAGLEY

Children in Care

Children in care is a term that was used prior to the passing of the Children Act 1989 to describe all children 'in the care of local authorities', whether as a result of voluntary admissions to care or as a result of statutory interventions. It has since been replaced by the term *looked-after children*. The term *children in care* is, however, still in use and denotes those 'looked-after children' who are placed with local authorities as a result of care proceedings, emergency protection orders and remands pending further court hearings.

BRIAN CORBY

Children's Experience of Domestic Violence

Children who live with *domestic violence* face both direct and indirect risks of harm.

Many men who abuse women also abuse children; the overlap on the child protection register may reach two-thirds. Children risk injury by intervening. Most know that their mother is being abused and are present or nearby during attacks; some see their mother killed. Fleeing home, sometimes repeatedly, disrupts lives, but the high risk of behavioural and psychological problems can recede once children feel safe.

Statutory intervention is problematic. Unfocused thinking – employing phraseology like 'dangerous families', 'marital conflict' – fails to name the dangers that the male perpetrators present. Female victims are blamed for 'failure to protect'. Contact orders permit continued abuse. Exclusion orders in child care proceedings are under-used. Confidentiality about whereabouts is too often breached. Expecting women to separate can escalate the dangers.

Ensuring the safety of abused mothers would constitute effective child protection. Recognition as 'children in need', family support services, groups and counselling would all help children directly. Meanwhile, refuge childwork, responses of the child care charities, work in schools and inter-agency co-operation are already developing apace.

For Further Reading
Mullender, A. and Morley, R. (eds) 1994: *Children Living with Domestic Violence*. London: Whiting and Birch.

AUDREY MULLENDER

The Children's Hearings System

The Children's Hearings system in Scotland was established under the Social Work (Scotland) Act 1968. The system has a welfare orientation, integrating decision making for children who offend and for those lacking care or protection. An official, *the Reporter* (usually qualified in law or social work), receives all referrals and must decide if there is sufficient *prima facie* evidence to establish a condition of referral, and, if so, whether a child is in need of compulsory measures of supervision. The courts are involved only where the facts of a case are disputed, or for appeals, or for dealing with more serious offences.

The hearing is a tribunal of lay volunteers, intended to provide a community view of a child's best interests. It involves three lay members, a parent(s) or guardian, the child in the majority of cases, a social worker and the Reporter who provides legal advice. Parent(s) and/or the child may bring a representative, who may be a friend or a legal adviser. Where a supervision requirement is made, there is provision for an annual review.

For Further Reading
Lockyer, A. and Stone, F. 1998: *Juvenile Justice in Scotland: 25 Years of the Welfare Approach*. Edinburgh: P. and P. Clark.

LORRAINE WATERHOUSE

Children's Rights

Children's rights fall into three broad groups: the right to resources, the right to protection, and the right to be heard. Internationally, children's rights are defined by the UN Convention on the Rights of the Child (1989). Although most countries, including the UK, fall considerably short of the standard set by the Convention, it provides a benchmark against which to assess government policies and a focus for organizations campaigning on behalf of children. Under the terms of the Convention, countries are required to report progress on implementation and to respond in each subsequent report to the comments and suggestions made in relation to the previous one.

Almost every part of the UN Convention has relevance for social work, but the main principles are crucial: that rights apply to all children without discrimination (Article 2); that the best interests of the child must be a primary consideration (Article 3); and that children have the right to express their views on all matters affecting them and to have those views taken seriously (Article 12).

For Further Reading
Hodgkin, R. and Newell, P. 1998: *Implementation Handbook for the Convention on the Rights of the Child*. New York: Unicef.

SONIA JACKSON

Class
See SOCIAL CLASS.

Client
See USER.

Clinical Psychology
Clinical psychology is the application of psychology to problems in health and community care. These problems may be emotional, behavioural or physical, and may present as acute, treatable conditions or in the context of long-term disabilities. The focus of work may be on the individual, the family or other social group or at the organizational level, and will always take account of the lifespan developmental context. Clinical psychologists are concerned with clients across a wide range of service settings for vulnerable children and adults.

The clinical psychologist draws on psychological theories, findings and methods to assess the problems presented and to develop a clinical formulation. This aims to provide an explanation by clarifying the problems experienced and providing a theory of how and why they developed and are maintained. It will give an account of the factors which will facilitate or constrain progress and thus identify realistic goals for intervention. The formulation should thus help to inform an appropriate intervention which will be chosen and implemented on the basis of empirical evidence of what is effective.

For Further Reading
Marzillier, J. and Hall, J. 1992: *What is Clinical Psychology?* (2nd edn). Oxford: Oxford Medical Publications.

MALCOLM ADAMS

The Cognitive-behavioural Approach

Cognitive-behavioural social work means the use within social work of procedures derived from cognitive and learning theories. These procedures are used to analyse or to change behaviour – both *covert* behaviour (feelings and thoughts) and *overt* behaviour (behaviour that can be directly observed). The subjects of the social worker's study or intervention may be clients or others in the clients' environment, or, indeed, social workers themselves or their colleagues. (The term *cognitive-behaviour therapy* often refers more specifically to work with people suffering from a mental illness or emotional distress.) As the hyphen in the term implies, the approach is made up of two overlapping sets of techniques, their attendant psychological theories and bodies of empirical research.

Behavioural social work

The behavioural tradition, built on the work of Thorndike, Pavlov, Watson, Skinner and Bandura, focuses on how behaviour changes as a result of experience. Our behavioural repertoire is largely the product of learning. This vast range of possible responses is acquired through lengthy interaction with the physical and social environment. (Clearly, genetic and other biological factors also influence behaviour in a more general sense, and there is an interaction between these and environment.)

Three broad processes of associative learning account for the acquisition and maintenance of motor, verbal, cognitive and emotional responses:

1 *Classical* or *respondent* conditioning/learning, identified and mapped in the work of the physiologist Pavlov
2 *Operant* or *instrumental* conditioning/learning, detailed in the work of the psychologists Thorndike and Skinner
3 Bandura's idea of *vicarious* learning, or *modelling* – second-hand learning – which contains elements of both respondent and operant associations as well as a major cognitive component

These bodies of theory underpin behavioural intervention.

Respondent learning theory

Respondent learning theory proposes that responses – particularly emotional responses such as fear, anger or sexual arousal – which are triggered by 'unconditioned' stimuli, become associated with other, previously neutral, stimuli either through dramatic single 'pairings' (anxiety about strangers after an attack, for example) or through repeated associations (a build-up of bad experiences in a day-centre group producing more and more avoidant reactions). Thus it may be possible to *unlearn* conditioned anxiety reactions by *controlled exposure* to threatening circumstances or by more gradual *systematic desensitization* methods based on hierarchies of threat.

Operant theory

Operant theory proposes that behaviour is a function of its consequences. The interventions derived from it focus on arranging changes to rewarding, punishing or relief-giving consequences; for example, by ignoring attention-seeking behaviour in a child; by rewarding attempts at negotiation rather than aggression; or by using more elaborate sets of procedures such as points systems or family contracts. These and other procedures are used to teach, increase or decrease behaviours.

continued

Modelling theory

Modelling theory suggests that we learn much through imitation. Thus the techniques in that field are built upon providing more suitable examples so as to remedy learning deficits (for example, in parent training, by demonstrating how to divert a child before they become over-emotional; or, in assertion training, by showing how to remain calmly persistent when being put upon).

Usually, behavioural procedures are not used singly, but are combined in 'packages' or 'programmes'. Examples where this happens include social skills training, parent training, communication and problem-solving training.

Cognitive-behavioural social work

In the last quarter of the twentieth century, there was growing interest among adherents of both behavioural and cognitive psychology in the idea that the increasingly well-founded propositions of the other might be incorporated in their practice. To an extent, this was a recognition of the practical realities of work with clients, in that no sensible behaviourist could afford to neglect how a person in difficulty *construes* the nature and origins of that difficulty. Similarly, no sensible cognitivist could afford to neglect practising new patterns of behaviour to collect evidence or to ensure that new cognitions translate into new patterns of behaviour.

The cognitive tradition is built on three propositions:

1   Above the level of basic physical reflexes and associations, human beings do not simply respond to stimuli, they *interpret* them.
2   Thought patterns can cue and maintain patterns of unwanted behaviours and mood states.
3   Unreasonable, illogical, self-defeating patterns of thought are a major and hitherto neglected component of the triad of closely linked aspects of behaviour: emotion, overt behaviour and cognition. Particular distortions of cognition occur which are associated with personal and socio-psychological problems. These include: *selective perception*, for example, focusing on failures and ignoring successes; *misattribution*, explaining one's own behaviour or current state by inappropriately assigning triggers and causes externally or internally (for example, youth offenders bemoaning the provocation they suffer through poor vehicle security; or depressed people blaming themselves for everything).

Most erstwhile 'behavioural social workers' have become 'cognitive-behavioural social workers'. Their work has been enriched by the theoretical and practice innovations which focus on intentions, self-control mechanisms, attitudes to self, situation and the future, and cognitions and their emotional and behavioural sequelae. Where irrational, counterproductive beliefs and 'automatic thoughts' are implicated in the client's difficulties, client and worker in partnership define, identify, track and then challenge these, using both verbal and behavioural strategies.

Cognitive procedures are particularly relevant in work with depression and anxiety, and form a major part of programmes for anger control, offending behaviour and drug and alcohol problems. It is now common within the cognitive-behavioural approach for, say, the design of an effective parenting group to begin with desensitization procedures – gently bringing parents to break down problems they may have been avoiding into a hierarchy of least-to-most-threatening items; then reviewing the thought patterns parents bring with them ('he is a monster, no one can control him', or 'I am just a hopeless mother'); then modelling problem-solving and positive reinforcement techniques.

Such amalgams show up increasingly well in outcome research and have found effective application in fields such as child-behaviour problems, offending, depression, relapse-prevention in drug and alcohol problems, and skills acquisition in learning disability. In social work, such approaches have been a major factor affecting the upturn in our fortunes in the effectiveness literature. The problem of access to training for sufficiently large numbers of staff remains. Nevertheless, a disciplinary merger has been effected with surprisingly little pain and steadily growing promise.

In conclusion

Cognitive-behavioural social work is characterized by certain key principles. The work is based on scientific theories, and is evidence-based: 'what works' evidence is sought out and acted upon, while, in addition, each intervention is assessed in terms of its effectiveness by the individual worker, wherever possible by means of a baseline followed by repeated measurements of progress. The main focus is on contemporary causes of behaviour (overt and covert antecedents and consequences). Explanations and intervention plans are shared with the client, and, drawing on research from other fields, working relationships are founded on empathy, warmth and genuineness on the part of the worker. In addition, practitioners use their interpersonal skills to give positive reinforcement for problem-solving, task-oriented behaviour. Drawing on research on effective modelling, workers highlight similarities with their clients and try to provide an example of 'coping' successfully. A good working relationship is a necessary but not sufficient condition for being an effective helper in this field.

Being psychology-based, the cognitive-behavioural approach is, of course, limited in what it can achieve in face of the life difficulties that confront so many social work clients. Consequently, the cognitive-behavioural social worker needs many other kinds of skills and knowledge: law, welfare rights, understanding of physical and mental health issues, and much more. It is this mix of skills and knowledge that distinguishes the cognitive-behavioural social worker from similarly oriented colleagues in other helping professions.

The cognitive-behavioural approach has been developed through a process of research and evaluation and, because it is so based, it is subject to modification and addition as new findings emerge.

For Further Reading

Cigno, K. and Bourn, D. (eds) 1998: *Cognitive-behavioural Social Work in Practice*. Aldershot: Ashgate.

Sheldon, B. 1995: *Cognitive-behavioural Therapy: Research, Practice and Philosophy*. London and New York: Routledge.

Sundel, M. and Sundel, S. S. 1999: *Behavior Change in the Human Services: An Introduction to Principles and Applications* (4th edn). Thousand Oaks: Sage.

BARBARA L. HUDSON AND BRIAN SHELDON

Cognitive Development

Cognitive development is the maturation of thinking capacity. Cognitions are a person's knowledge, thoughts and reasoning about the world. Cognitive development is the process by which the capacity to reason and create internal mental representations of the world develops. As children physically mature, their intellectual processes also become increasingly sophis-ticated and more able to cope with abstract concepts. Piaget, whose theory of cognitive development has been highly influential, proposed that cognition develops through assimilation, whereby a new idea is fitted into existing ways of thinking and accommodation, and existing thought processes are adjusted to fit new information.

BRIGID DANIEL

Cognitive Psychology

Cognitive psychology is the study of the psychological processes involved in perceiving, interpreting and interacting with the environment.

A major impetus for the development of cognitive psychology came from dissatisfaction with the attempts of early learning theorists to make sense of human life purely in terms of directly observable stimuli and behavioural responses. The rationale for concentrating upon what could be observed had been based on the desire to establish psychology as a scientific discipline. However, the strict behaviourist perspective was gradually modified when a reappraisal of what could count as scientific inquiry was combined with the increasing plausibility of the claim that mental phenomena must have a substantive role in any adequate account of human functioning.

The cognitive approach in psychology

The central thesis of cognitive psychology is that human beings process and act upon information in ways that depend upon beliefs, concepts and habits of interpretation. Each person adds something 'cognitive' to the raw data of their experience, and what they add is crucial to their subsequent behaviour. This can be illustrated in terms of the therapeutic practice which has developed from the theory base of cognitive psychology. Cognitive interventions normally aim to review and modify ingrained responses to life situations, thus bringing about both cognitive and behavioural change. The basic assumptions are that there are significant variations in the ways in which people view themselves and their circumstances, and that this variation includes potentially dysfunctional psychological constructs which might be the subject of effective therapy.

Work with drug abuse provides a specific example of this, the cognitive approach being used to understand and, where appropriate, to challenge individual beliefs and attitudes to drug taking. Various techniques may be adopted, including work aimed at reappraisal of the difficulties in a drug user's life. These difficulties may, for example, include financial and relationship worries, which might seem so intractable that they prompt the use of drugs. Therapy would look at the extent to which drug abuse contributed to the personal problems, even though, in the short term, drugs may be experienced as an essential part of life. In addition, negative self-images may be discussed and challenged, particularly if they undermine the idea that coping without drugs may be a practical possibility. Using strategies of this kind, the key objective is to encourage within drug abusers the habit of questioning taken-for-granted ways of framing and responding to problems.

Social work in the criminal justice system has also been influenced by cognitive methodology. Programmes focused on offending behaviour are designed to make offenders reflect on the consequences of their actions, both for themselves and others. In work of this type, alternatives to crime are examined, the idea being that it is possible to become more skilful in pursuing different and legal ways of acting in those situations that have previously led to offending. As in the case of work with drug abusers, interventions would address the personal problems in an offender's life, examining ways of thinking and behaving which often contribute to a destructive cycle whereby the stress induced by personal problems is followed by ill-considered behaviour which then leads to more stress.

The social context

The application of cognitive psychology in social work is sometimes criticized on the grounds that it may reduce major social concerns such as crime and drug misuse to matters of personal psychology, as though the key to tackling these social problems lay merely in working with certain groups of people to change their attitudes and beliefs. For this reason, in noting the potential value of cognitive approaches in social work, it is important to recognize that there are socio-economic factors such as poverty and unemployment which often dominate the lives of clients. Cognitive psychology provides a theory-base which can be useful in scrutinizing and possibly improving personal responses to stressful life circumstances, but it is not a substitute for a broader political strategy which would tackle inequalities in social and economic conditions.

It should also be said, with regard to the social work relevance of cognitive theory, that although its use directs attention to psychological analysis, it does so in a way which builds on the environmental perspective which was so crucial to the formulation of learning theory; and this highlighting of the human impact of environmental influence matches social work's view of the significant extent to which people are shaped by their backgrounds. Indeed, cognitive theory offers ways of understanding, in detail, how social context can influence behaviour. For instance, if someone is faced with extreme financial hardship, criminal activity can appear essential to survival. There is a role for social work here, both in attempting to contextualize individual responses to such adversity, and in working with these responses to examine alternative courses of action. A background of long-term unemployment might have contributed largely to financial problems, but the difficulties may be worsened by behaviour which repeatedly results in arrest, imprisonment and social dislocation.

In conclusion
Generally speaking, the usefulness of cognitive theory depends on its effectiveness in bringing about cognitive and behavioural change. Cognitive approaches are, in fact, comparatively effective in these terms. The most successful interventions are those which provide the basis for enhanced control, so that people feel less driven by events and are more able to direct the course of their lives. It needs to be said, however, that the application of cognitive theory, although potentially valuable, is not a cure-all. In particular, for many social work clients, gaining a sense of 'enhanced control' will depend on the satisfaction of fundamental material requirements, such as securing a house and an adequate income. Social work that is influenced by cognitive psychology needs to be flexible and sensitive enough to take into account basic concerns such as these.

For Further Reading
Beck, A. T., Wright, F. D., Newman, F. C. and Liese, B. S. 1993: *Cognitive Therapy of Substance Abuse*. New York: The Guildford Press.
Eysenck, M. W. 1993: *Principles of Cognitive Psychology*. Hove: Erlbaum.
Sheldon, B. 1995: *Cognitive-behavioural Therapy*. London: Routledge.

MALCOLM MILLAR

Collaboration in Community Care and Primary Care

Collaboration refers to working together to achieve common goals. The term *collaboration* has both positive and negative connotations for it also implies sharing information and strategies with 'an enemy'. Both the positive and the negative interpretations of the term can be applied to the context of agencies and individuals working together to provide health and social welfare services in the community. Collaboration and conflict are 'both sides of the same coin' in that conflict may be part of the process of achieving collaboration; the process of working together may lead ultimately to a relationship that ends in either conflict or collaboration. Successful collaborative effort is often overlooked when the situation is unproblematic, but is quickly noticed when difficulties arise. The organization of welfare and the division of agencies' responsibilities will vary according

continued

to the context: countries or localities may have different ways of managing their health and social services. Crucial to successful collaboration, or the acknowledgement of those conflicts that need to be addressed, is the extent to which policies or legislation provide positive structures for working together.

Community care is a concept with a variety of meanings. One interpretation is for social services and health agencies to work in collaboration to deliver better services to users in their own homes. The intention of the policy makers in the UK set out in government policy documents and in legislation is that agencies should work together to achieve better community care: by entering into collaborative arrangements, and thereby pooling resources, skills and ideas, agencies have the potential to create new and better services. By working together, agencies have the opportunity to clarify their responsibilities to deliver 'seamless services'.

Primary care groups are responsible for determining the health and care needs of their localities. The major focus is on the health care of populations in localities and the use of resources to meet local needs. There is representation from medicine, nursing, social services and other local organizations in the primary care groups. In essence, the overall policy focus is on agencies working together across the health and social services divide to provide seamless services for users in their localities. In England and Wales, although the word collaboration appears in policy documents, it is not a word that is used in the legislation; and, in practice, a variety of other terms have been used to mean working together including co-operation, co-ordination, consultation and partnership.

Co-ordination, consultation, collaboration and partnership

However, *collaboration* can be differentiated from other words such as *co-ordination*, *consultation* and *partnership*. These terms can be conceptualized as a continuum, indicating a process through various states from isolation to full collaboration, or as a ladder of participation that implies a potential development from non-participation to citizen power. Co-ordination and consultation would appear as precursors to collaboration, with partnership being a further and possibly ultimate goal. A distinction can be made between co-ordination (which means the bringing together of various ideas or activities), consultation (which may mean listening to other people's views) and collaboration (which incorporates a notion of working towards shared goals or beliefs). Collaboration may be interpreted as a stage that leads to partnership, a term that implies a fuller commitment; indeed partnership has been the preferred term of the government in relation to primary care.

Collaboration can operate at three levels:

1 Individuals in everyday practice working together
2 Agencies working together at local level
3 Broader interpretations of working together by local agencies in order to influence government policy

To work collaboratively with others requires an understanding of one's own values, knowledge and skills, as well as of those of others (Hornby, 1993). To work both across agencies and between agencies requires an understanding of differing organizational perspectives (Øvretveit, 1993). To work in collaboration with service users means being aware of the values, knowledge and skills that people possess by enabling them to achieve their own goals (Trevillion, 1993). Both the personal and the organizational dynamics of working together reflect the power dimensions that are part of the process of collaboration.

Barriers to collaboration

There are a number of barriers to collaboration in community care and primary care. In some instances, economic factors have been translated into competition between agencies through internal markets which have provided a perverse disincentive to collaborate. Even in societies without internal markets, competition about professional status and power to allocate resources can act as a hindrance. Professional tribalism and differences in the priorities of individuals from different disciplines can militate against successful working together to achieve common goals. Differences in administrative and managerial systems can cause communication problems and delays. Both organizational and personal strengths and weaknesses play a part in the success or failure of collaborative work. Self-interest and threats to autonomy and domain are powerful negative influences; there will always be contextual disincentives to collaborate.

Collaboration and conflict often exist side by side – they are part of a process. Collaboration is a realistic term to apply to the changing context of health and social care when it is conceived as a term that denotes the process of working towards achieving shared goals rather than being seen solely as a functional outcome. Collaboration is an emergent process: it relates to a multi-dimensional, cyclical and iterative development that forms part of the contemporary reality of practice in community care and primary care.

For Further Reading
Hornby, S. 1993: *Collaborative Care: Interprofessional, Interagency and Interpersonal.* Oxford: Blackwell Science.
Øvretveit, J. 1993: *Coordinating Community Care: Multidisciplinary Teams and Care Management in Health and Social Services.* Buckingham: Open University Press.
Trevillion, S. 1993: *Caring in the Community: A Networking Approach to Community Partnership.* London: Longman.

HELEN GORMAN

Communication Theory

Communication theory developed from cybernetics (the study of control systems) and family process theory. Communication theory is most commonly associated with systems thinking. *Communication* relates to the sharing of meaningful interactions with other people in the world. It concerns the passing of, receiving and acting on information.

The theory examines the processes that communication involves: the selection of a means of conveying a message (language, gesture, writing), the decoding of the message by the recipient (hearing, seeing, reading), and making a response on the basis of the interpretation (reply). Understanding the rules and structures of communication can help to formulate sensitive and appropriate professional interactions with the service user.

PETER RANDALL AND JONATHAN PARKER

Community Care

Community care may be defined as the provision of long-term care in less restrictive settings than has traditionally been the case.

The emergence of community care
The definition of the term *community care* in the UK has tended to lack clarity, sometimes including all non-hospital environments as the community, at other times referring to home-based care. This is because the definition initially reflected the concern of government with the closure of psychiatric hospitals, and more recently with the uncontrolled growth of residential and nursing homes (Challis, 1993). For a comparison of developments in the UK with other countries, the terms *care at home* or *home care* are likely to be the most appropriate.

continued

From the 1960s onwards, UK government policy was supportive of community care, although issues of funding and organizational arrangements were not addressed. However, the 1980s can be seen as the period when financial constraint finally provoked a review of community care policies. Efforts were made to improve co-ordination of care in the community and to transfer finance from health to social care.

Nonetheless, despite the commitment to community care, co-ordination was seen as essentially a top-down activity pursued by service planners rather than field-level practitioners. Only the effects of financial restraint led to more profound structural change. In the face of increasing needs arising from an ageing population, the only substantial source of funds available for care was from the social security system, which enabled older people to receive their care in private and voluntary residential and nursing homes, whereas the funding for community health and social services was restrained under a policy to reduce overall public spending. Consequently, a serious policy distortion emerged, whereby the number of beds in homes increased very substantially, with the cost of this increasing from £10 million in 1980 to £1,000 million in 1989. Entry to homes was, at the time, determined not by assessment of need but by financial eligibility.

Analysis of the implications of these developments by efficiency audit, carried out by the Audit Commission, criticized:

- the perverse incentives arising from the funding
- the problems of organizational fragmentation
- the failure to match resources to needs in community care.

In 1988, a government sponsored review of community care arrangements (The Griffiths Report, *Community Care: Agenda for Action*), recommended a more co-ordinated approach to the funding and management of care. It proposed placing the responsibility for the allocation of public funds, assessment of need and co-ordination of care with social services departments, with care management seen as contributing to the more efficient use of resources. In general, these recommendations formed the content of the 1989 White Paper, *Caring for People*, and were implemented through the NHS and Community Care Act 1990.

These were radical changes, establishing social services departments as the lead agency, being the source of most public funding for the long-term care of vulnerable people, with the incentive to consider developing alternative and, where possible, less costly community-based care. Care managers were to identify, on the basis of assessment, the combination of services best suited to the needs and circumstances of an individual service user. Hence, community care reform was designed, at least at the margin, to produce a degree of downward substitution in the provision of care, moving away from institutional to enhanced home care and developing improved co-ordination at the client level through care management. The pursuit of similar changes in other countries makes the genesis of the UK reforms of interest.

Care management and the social work role

The development of a coherently articulated framework for community care through public policy intervention, rather than the process of exhortation which constituted earlier policies, provides real opportunities for social work. Given that the bulk of the work in community-based care is with older people, the community care policies for care management offer a clearer role for social work in long-term care that was previously absent. Indeed, traditionally UK social work has been less clear about its contribution to meeting the needs of those requiring long-term support such as older people. It remains to be seen to what extent social work can identify a more explicit definition of its functions through the community care changes, with care management perhaps being seen as social work in long-term care situations, and other roles such as short-term interventions being appropriate for less chronically impaired individuals. The clarification of the role of social work in community-based care as a consequence of more explicit government policies with clear field-level implications is a welcome development.

Another UK White Paper in 1998, *Modernising Social Services*, together with other policy documents in the 1990s, reaffirmed key features of the previous policy and stressed the objectives of rehabilitation and prevention, and the maintenance of independence. These provide ways in which health and social care will need to come closer together at the service level.

Other exciting areas conspicuously underdeveloped in the community care changes have been ways of linking the activities of secondary health care with community care. This is evident in old-age services more so than in mental health. Both the Australian Aged Care Reforms and demonstration studies in the UK suggest that there are real opportunities for social work and care management to link more closely with specialist geriatric medicine and old-age psychiatry. This could contribute to improved assessment prior to placement in residential and nursing homes and provide expertise to the more effective home care of very vulnerable older people (Challis et al., 1995, 1998). The prevention and rehabilitation initiatives from government only serve to stress this point.

The need for housing

It must be remembered that effective community care is not dependent upon the efforts of health and social care alone, important though these are, but also on the provision of adequate and suitable housing. There are examples of care management schemes that have failed precisely because of this lack. It is probable that our conception of community care is likely to become more subtle over time, as the development of more finely differentiated forms of supported housing breaks down the current binary distinction between home care and 'non-home care'.

For Further Reading

Challis, D. 1993: The effectiveness of community care. *Clinical Gerontology*, 3, 97–104.

Challis, D., Darton, R., Johnson, L., Stone, M. and Traske, K. 1995: *Care Management and Health Care of Older People*. Aldershot: Ashgate.

Challis, D., Darton, R. and Stewart, K. (eds) 1998: *Community Care, Secondary Health Care and Care Management*. Aldershot: Ashgate.

DAVID CHALLIS

Community Care Rights

Community care rights entitle frail, ill, vulnerable and disabled people of all ages and their carers to receive the information, advice and social services they need to enable them to live independently in the community or in a range of supported residential or nursing home accommodation, and to exercise control over the planning and organization of their services. These individual rights to community care services are underpinned by a complex maze of post-war legislation, case law, government directions, regulations and guidance, charter rights and local authority policies, liable to varying interpretations and influenced by the availability of resources.

The growing need for expert guidance through the community care maze inspired a consortium of local agencies, the Oxfordshire Community Care Advice and Action Group, acting collectively as an informal watchdog, to set up in 1995 the first independent, specialist community care rights advice service in the UK, providing comprehensive information and legal expertise to enable people and their carers to gain access to assessments and services and/or support with negotiations, challenges and complaints.

For Further Reading

Coombs, M. A., with Sedgwick, A. 1998: *Right to Challenge: the Oxfordshire Community Care Rights Project*. Bristol: Policy Press and the Joseph Rowntree Foundation.

MARGARET COOMBS

Community Mental Health

See THE CARE PROGRAMME APPROACH.

Community Mental Health Nursing

Mental health care, particularly within community settings, lies in a notch between social and health care systems. In theory, *mental health nurses* provide long-term clinical intervention, social support and accommodation.

The reality is that, in the UK's mixed economy of care, both nursing and social work professions may assume key worker roles – the nurse within the care programme approach, the social worker within care management. As assertive outreach services develop, so the working relationship between nursing and social work becomes more entwined, especially as both may act as case managers within case (as opposed to care) management.

Increasingly, community mental health teams are becoming jointly funded and managed by both health and social services. This means that people with serious or enduring mental illnesses receive some generic care equally from both professions and some which is specific to their professional background and training. However, the intended outcome of this collaborative and integrative form of working is to provide a more seamless response to patient or client needs, to meet their individual requirements and promote their social role valorization, or normalization.

For Further Reading

Leff, J. (ed.) 1997: *Care in the Community – Illusion or Reality?* Chichester: John Wiley.

MARTIN F. WARD

Community Service Orders

Community service orders are a sentence of criminal courts under which an offender aged 16 or over is required to undertake between 40 and 240 hours of unpaid work, intended to be of benefit to the community. The orders are organized and supervised by the probation service (in Scotland, by social work departments). Introduced in 1973, they quickly proved popular with courts, probably because they contain elements of punishment, reparation and rehabilitation. Similar measures have been adopted in other countries. In 1991, the 'combination order' was introduced, bringing together the requirements of community service and probation orders.

DAVID SMITH

Community Social Work

Community social work aims to establish and provide support to local groups and help to develop and sustain social support networks within communities. It contrasts with more individualized approaches to social work, and is usually practised within patch-based or neighbourhood-based teams. Starting from the position that most personal care is provided by relatives, friends and neighbours rather than professionals, community social work encourages mutual forms of help and attempts to harness the community's own resources to identify and provide for their own needs, if they are given appropriate support.

GORDON JACK

Community Supervision in Mental Health

See the CARE PROGRAMME APPROACH (CPA) and REGISTERS.

Community Work

Community work refers to the methods and skills used to work with groups of people around a shared interest or concern. At the core of the methods and skills is the idea of organizing: helping people to come together to form an autonomous group.

The nature of community work

Most community work takes place on a neighbourhood basis around issues which are important for people living in the same locality. Community work is also undertaken on the basis of common interest – a faith community or a women's network, for example. Similar kinds of local organizations also form themselves into federations. Community work practised in a neighbourhood provides opportunities for regular face-to-face contact between workers and residents and, equally important, it makes more feasible the testing job of organizing people around a common issue.

Running strongly through community work is a creative tension between the object-ive of helping a group achieve a particular outcome, such as arranging a safe play area for children, and the intention of encouraging a group – and individual members of it – to develop and change. Community workers and their employing organizations place different emphases on this balance between *task* and *process*. For those favouring the latter emphasis, the connections with community-based adult education become very important.

Values are of paramount importance in community work. They inform and permeate the methods and skills, and are concentrated on the idea of achieving greater equality and social justice through the redistribution of power and resources. Different ideolo-gies inform practice – conservative, liberal, radical and Marxist. Furthermore, commu-nity work has been championed for a variety of political purposes: individualistic forms of self-help alongside community empowerment programmes for the most excluded groups of people in society.

Community work can be thought of as a combination of vision, energy and a set of tools which drive forward community action, community development, social planning, community organization and service extension.

Community work in the twentieth century

Community work has been pushed and pulled between different social movements and professions. It began at the beginning of the twentieth century in the work of bodies such as the Charity Organisation Society and some of the university settlements. Between World War I and World War II, it was associated with the formation of community asso-ciations on council estates and, from the late 1940s, the creation of new towns. In the 1960s and early 1970s, it was linked with the Home Office Community Development Projects and with radical campaigning groups active at that time, notably the Campaign for Nuclear Disarmament (CND) and the squatters movement. At the same time, it was taken up by both the education and social work professions. The Seebohm Report in 1968 gave clear recognition to community work and it was this, along with the announcement of the urban programme in the same year, that gave it a definite identity. A similar, albeit more muted recognition of community work within social work came with the growth of community social work in the late 1970s and early 1980s.

The idea that community work is the third method of social work, complementing individual and group work, provided a theoretical basis for community work during the 1970s. The theory came from the USA and was influential world-wide. This way of understanding community work can still be found in a number of countries.

In the UK, the ties between community work and social work weakened from the mid-1980s. The possible exception was Scotland where, because of Scottish legislation and the strong political commitment of some of the local authorities, community work remained a more visible part of social work. In general, however, community work in the 1990s related much more to economic regeneration, planning, housing, recre-ation, health and social inclusion than to social work. The Labour Government elected in 1997 introduced policies and programmes for regeneration, social inclusion and health which emphasized the importance of community involvement. The NHS and Community Care Act 1990 and the Children Act 1989 both provide for the re-introduction of community work into a social work context, but the opportunity was not immediately taken up.

Community work in the developed world has had an overwhelmingly urban focus. In areas of multiple deprivation, it has been seen as a very relevant way both of engaging with local residents and of working with service providers. Work in rural communities has developed more slowly, and community work's approach and methods have been adjusted to this different context.

continued

In the early 1980s, there were just over 5,000 paid community workers in the UK. Studies carried out subsequently suggest that the total number of community workers has increased to approximately 7,000. As part of the strengthening of community work, training opportunities for unqualified workers and community leaders have been made available: short courses, accreditation of prior learning and mentoring. These opportunities provide stepping stones to longer training courses which offer a qualification – either a vocational qualification, a diploma in youth and community work, or a degree. Local authorities and regeneration agencies have increasingly sought to employ staff who have community work knowledge and skills.

There is a national organization for community work training (the Federation of Community Work Training Groups), a membership organization (the Association of Community Workers), an umbrella organization for community development (the Standing Conference for Community Development) and a non-departmental public body (the Community Development Foundation). There are networks which bring together community workers and other practitioners on a regional basis and in each of the four nations – Scotland, Northern Ireland, Wales and England.

For Further Reading
Francis, D. and Henderson, P. 1992: *Working with Rural Communities*. Basingstoke: Macmillan.
Harris, V. 1994: *Community Work Skills Manual*. Newcastle: Association of Community Workers.
Twelvetrees, A. 1991: *Community Work*. Basingstoke: Macmillan.

PAUL HENDERSON

Competence
See ACTIVITIES OF DAILY LIVING.

Complaints Procedures
Complaints procedures provide a statutory mechanism which allows clients of social services departments to complain about services and seek redress. The Children Act 1989 and the National Health Service and Community Care Act 1990 introduced a three-stage procedure. When a complaint is made, an informal investigation followed by remedy or apology generally satisfies the complainant. If there is no resolution, formal investigation of the complaint is undertaken by a senior manager. Clients who are still not satisfied may proceed to an independently chaired panel which reviews the complaint and reports, with recommendations, to the Director. Dissatisfied clients are required to use the complaints procedure before resorting to the Ombudsman, or seeking judicial review in the High Court.

Despite statutory regulation, complaints procedures vary immensely. The key issues include accessibility, support for vulnerable complainants, the composition of the independent panel, financial compensation, and the use made of clients' complaints to review and improve services. There is a general recognition that the procedures may work for very angry, very articulate – or well-supported – clients, but that the most vulnerable rarely pursue complaints.

For Further Reading
Lowe, N. and Douglas, G. 1998: *Bromley's Family Law* (9th edn). London: Butterworths, 596–610.

CAROLINE BALL

Compulsory Admission to Hospital
See SECTIONING.

Conciliation
See MEDIATION.

Conditioning
See LEARNING THEORY.

Confidentiality
Confidentiality is an ethical principle requiring workers and agencies to respect the privacy of service users by taking responsible care of infor-

mation gained during professional activity, and, in the absence of special circumstances, divulging it only with permission from subjects or informants. Evidence of danger to vulnerable people and matters of public interest exemplify such exceptional circumstances. Preventing 'careless talk', ensuring secure storage and disposal of paper or computerized records, and sharing material only on a 'need to know' basis respects the value of personal information given by service users.

Issues of confidentiality merge with the idea of *freedom of information*. The civil liberties movement of the 1970s emphasized clients' moral right of access to records about themselves; the Data Protection Acts 1984 and 1998 and the Access to Personal Files Act 1987 provide legal frameworks for record-keeping practice in social work. Subjects can read and copy material not judged harmful to themselves or others.

Particular problems of confidentiality arise where records relate to more than one person (in family and groupwork, for example) or are compiled by co-workers in multi-agency teams: the right of access by one person may breach the confidentiality of another.

For Further Reading
Prince, K. 1996: *Boring Records?* London: Jessica Kingsley.

KATIE PRINCE

Contact (between Birth Family and Child)
See PARENTAL CONTACT.

Contracts between Social Workers and Service Users
Contracts involve the drawing up of verbal or written agreements between social worker and user which bind both participants, are the outcome of discussion and negotiation, and provide a framework for practice which structures worker/user interaction.

Contracts can be used in work with individuals, couples, families or groups. They cut down misunderstanding and the avoidance of issues in worker/user interaction, provide greater scope for openness and honesty, and recognize the user as an active empowered partner. They involve explicitness, a drawing together, reciprocal obligations, mutual accountability and responsibility.

Contract content includes identification of the realistic, positive aims of both parties, user rights, tasks that will be performed, the means to achieve these tasks, time and place for meetings, and frequency and length of sessions. The contract also may involve clarification of those who will be present at meetings, ground rules for behaviour, limits on confidentiality, record keeping and access, procedures for reviewing and ending the contract, and action to be taken if those involved do not keep the agreed conditions.

For Further Reading
Collins, S. and Rojek, C. 1992: Should social workers use written contracts? In E. Gambrill and R. Pruger (eds), *Controversial Issues in Social Work*, Needham Heights, MA: Alleyn and Bacon.

STEWART COLLINS

Counselling

Counselling involves a paid or voluntary worker offering explicitly to give time, space, care and attention which focuses upon the concerns of another – the client. Clients have the opportunity to explore and clarify their strengths and weaknesses, to improve the quality of their life and to move towards greater well-being. Counselling involves the worker observing, listening, understanding, responding, evaluating and acting in partnership with the client. It can involve short-term or long-term work. The counsellor uses psychological theories and communication skills, values, experience and personality characteristics to help the client work on personal concerns and problems. There is an emphasis on planned facilitation rather than advice giving. Counselling takes place within social, economic, political and organizational contexts. The interaction between worker and client will be influenced by social divisions such as class, gender, race, age, sexual orientation, language, religion and disability. Counselling has largely developed within Western cultural values.

continued

Counselling usually places considerable emphasis on the helping relationship between worker and client. Trust, respect and confidentiality are seen as important so that clients can feel safe to disclose and explore the emotional and practical realities of their lives. If counsellors are experienced by their clients as genuinely concerned and understanding, then it is more likely that clients will benefit. If counsellors are experienced as over-involved or intrusive or under-involved, cold and detached, then these factors can be associated with client harm and, therefore, counselling can be harmful as well as beneficial. Empathic understanding, genuine concern and respect are important to facilitate emotional release by clients, to enable them to explore themselves and their life situations. It is intended that clients begin to see themselves, other people and the world more positively, becoming more accepting of themselves and their strengths and weaknesses. Some clients may require more than this – they may need to develop a different perspective and new skills in their day-to-day lives.

Approaches to counselling

There are a wide range of approaches to counselling based on different theoretical perspectives. There can be overlap and disagreement both within and between these approaches. Each approach has an explanatory framework, a conceptual scheme that provides an explanation for the client's concerns, a therapeutic perspective and a set of tasks in which, to meet the client's goals, worker and client engage. There are four main approaches to counselling – psychodynamic, humanistic, cognitive-behavioural and eclectic.

The *psychodynamic approach* is based upon the work of Freud, Jung, Klein and others. Emphasis is placed on the interaction of the *id* – the basic instinctual drives – the *super ego* – the moral conscience and voice of restraint – and the *ego* which mediates between the two and deals with the demands of the outer environment. Attention is given also to the psychosexual stages of development – the oral, anal, oedipal and latency stages. Some emphasis is placed on the impact of the past upon the present. Defence mechanisms such as projection, denial and rationalization are seen as important, while transference and counter transference are acknowledged – i.e. the impact of past relationships with parental figures or parental substitutes upon the present relationship between worker and client. Attachment, loss and separation may also receive attention. This approach has been, traditionally, a long-term one.

The *humanistic approach* reflects the influence of existential and phenomenological perspectives after World War II. It includes rational emotive, reality therapy and transactional analysis, but a major figure here is Carl Rogers and client-centred/non-directive therapy. Rogers placed emphasis on three core conditions seen to be 'necessary and sufficient' for effective helping – empathy, congruence and unconditional positive regard. The humanistic tradition emphasizes subjectivity, meaning, freedom, choice and potential for growth.

Cognitive-behavioural approaches have been influenced by the thinking of early behaviourists such as Pavlov, Watson and Skinner. Eysenck, Bandura and Wolpe have also been significant. There are various types of behavioural approaches based on classical or respondent and operant conditioning. Learning through experience, rehearsal and modelling of behaviour is seen as important. The focus is on learned behaviour, unlearning and changing specific behaviours. Behaviour is shaped and reinforced by its consequences. There is an emphasis on observation, measurement and change. Cognitive aspects focus on thoughts and feelings and how these affect behaviour. There is a tendency towards short-term helping, and the approach can be useful, for example, in working with behavioural problems in children, 'neurotic' conditions such as anxiety states, offending, drinking and drug problems.

Eclectic approaches are linked more closely to meeting particular user needs and circumstances. The worker uses a combination of psychodynamic, humanistic and cognitive-behavioural approaches to understand, develop and focus relationships. Hence, the counsellor chooses the best or most suitable ideas from a range of theories.

Social work's use of counselling skills

Counselling is often used by social workers in an eclectic form. Humanistic, client-centred and cognitive-behavioural approaches are particularly influential in social work. The attractions include the sound empirical base, and the emphasis on a positive forward-looking growth-based approach. Counselling skills may not be practised by social workers in a 'pure' form; they are more likely to be used alongside other skills and knowledge within the organizational context of voluntary, independent or statutory agencies, may be linked to the needs of particular client or user groups, and will be limited by worker accountability to statutory and legal requirements. Counselling skills underpin or link with social work theories, such as, for example, systems approaches, task-centred and crisis work. They are also relevant in the social work process, in initial interviews, assessment, ongoing intervention and termination, and always need to be integrated with anti-oppressive perspectives. Egan's (1998) model, which combines client-centred and behavioural ideas, is useful for social workers to help them to explore, understand, act and evaluate their interventions with users of social work. It is both responsive and systematic – a key requirement for effective counselling in social work.

For Further Reading

Atkinson, D. R. and Hackett, E. 1995: *Counselling Diverse Populations*. Madison: Brown and Benchmark.
Brearley, J. 1995: *Counselling and Social Work*. Buckingham: Open University Press.
Egan, G. 1998: *The Skilled Helper: A Systematic Approach to Effective Helping* (6th edn). Pacific Grove, California: Brooks Cole.

STEWART COLLINS

Co-working in Practice

Co-working in practice is a form of organizing work whereby two or more workers jointly facilitate sessions with a group or with a family. During the sessions, the co-workers may vary the organization: sometimes adopting different roles and sometimes amplifying each other's interventions. Clients may benefit from co-working when they see how each of the co-workers reacts to various issues. Co-workers can be aided, too, as one gathers observations, while the other is more actively involved. Because of the complexity of co-working, an honest and strong working alliance has to be carefully developed between the co-workers themselves.

ODED MANOR

Crime and Delinquency

Crime and delinquency have been a major focus for social work intervention for as long as social work has existed: involvement with young offenders goes back to the reformatory school movement of the mid-nineteenth century, and work with adult offenders was incorporated into the criminal law in 1907, with the Probation of Offenders Act. However, despite this long history, the role of social work in criminal justice has remained contested, and its place in the system has never been wholly secure. This is because work in this field raises sharp questions about the balance between care and control, and because crime has a much higher political salience than most of the problems with which social workers are concerned. This inherent uncertainty about

continued

the purposes of social work in criminal justice was heightened in the UK from the 1980s by the rapid pace of legislative change, as governments sought sometimes to reduce the prison population by encouraging the use of community-based measures, and sometimes to demonstrate the toughness of their law and order policies by encouraging an increased use of imprisonment.

The welfare approach

In the immediate post-war period, policy on juvenile offenders stressed concern with their welfare: they were to be helped or treated as children in trouble, not punished as criminals. The emphasis changed in the mid-1970s, however, under the influence of the 'back to justice' movement originating in the USA, and of research evidence, also mainly American, which, it was claimed, demonstrated that 'nothing worked' in the sense of being effective in reducing reoffending. As a result, and with the further support of the labelling perspective in sociology, social workers in juvenile justice re-interpreted their role as essentially one of damage limitation – diverting young people from the criminal justice system, or minimizing their involvement with it. Although originating in pessimism about the extent to which social work could help young people change in positive ways, this stance achieved considerable success in contributing to a reduction in the number of juvenile offenders sent to custody in England and Wales. From the 1990s, however, legislation increased the severity of the available penalties for young offenders, allowing custodial sentences for children as young as ten years old. At the same time, the range of community-based sentences was widened, and social workers were encouraged to work with other agencies in developing local strategies to reduce youth crime.

In Scotland, a welfare orientation to young offenders persisted, incarnated in the Children's Hearing system, in which (up to the age of 16) an offence is regarded as only one of several 'grounds for referral': the system prioritizes the welfare of the young person over all other considerations, social workers are central to the operation of the system, and – except in very serious cases – punishment is regarded as irrelevant.

Tough programmes of supervision

In Scotland, a separate probation service ceased to exist in 1968, and work with adult offenders was incorporated into unified social work departments. In England, Wales and Northern Ireland, the probation service retained a distinct identity. Probation officers were influenced, like workers with young offenders, by the 'nothing works' message of the 1970s, and their task was increasingly defined in terms of providing supervision in the community as an alternative to custody, rather than (as in the original legal definition) as a duty to 'advise, assist and befriend' people on probation. To dispel the supposed public perception of probation as a soft option, probation services were instructed to develop programmes of supervision that were tough and demanding, and could be presented as 'punishment in the community'.

Legislation in 1991 sought to ensure that probation officers worked exclusively with relatively serious offenders, and conceived probation and other forms of community sentence primarily as a punitive restriction of liberty, the degree of restrictiveness being determined by the gravity of the offence. Probation orders, which had historically been made *instead of* a sentence, became sentences in their own right. In the late 1990s, the requirement that offenders should consent to the making of a probation or community service order was abolished, and the training of probation officers was formally separated from that of social workers.

Paradoxically, probation officers at the same time began to recover some faith in the potential effectiveness of social work with offenders, in the light of new research evidence. This suggested that programmes that employed a cognitive-behavioural approach, concentrated on offending and related problems, were well structured and explicit in their aims, and offered a range of learning methods, were likely to produce good results in terms of known reoffending.

The interests of victims

Although the extent and gravity of crime and delinquency are often exaggerated by the media or for political purposes, all the most reliable evidence suggests that the volume of crime, and especially of violent crime, has increased dramatically in all developed countries (except Japan) since World War II. Crime is a major source of fear and distress, particularly in the areas of social and economic deprivation where the risk of victimization is highest. Social workers in criminal justice have traditionally thought of the offender as their 'client', setting to one side the question of what their responsibilities might be to victims or to the community at large. The policy emphasis on public protection and the needs of victims which developed from the late 1990s meant that social workers had to acquire a different sense of purpose, one that explicitly included the assessment of the risk to others posed by offenders, attention to victims' views and interests, and a commitment to 'effectiveness-based' forms of practice.

The offender can no longer be the sole beneficiary of the values of respect, care and humanity which social work has historically brought to the criminal justice process.

For Further Reading

Brownlee, I. 1998: *Community Punishment: A Critical Introduction*. Harlow: Longman.
Cavadino, M. and Dignan, J. 1997: *The Penal System: An Introduction*. London: Sage.
Mair, G. 1997: Probation and community penalties. In M. Maguire, R. Morgan and R. Reiner (eds), *The Oxford Handbook of Criminology* (2nd edn), Oxford. Clarendon Press.

DAVID SMITH

Crisis Intervention

Crisis intervention is a theoretical method which focuses on the opportunities for growth and positive change arising from the emotional energy generated by the experience of crisis. A crisis is defined as a turning point, the result of the breakdown of *homeostasis* or psychological equilibrium when the individual's coping resources have been surpassed and a new approach has to be developed.

Often misunderstood as referring to an emergency, a crisis does not need to be an urgent situation. For example, admission to residential care for an older person may constitute a crisis, even where such an admission has been carefully planned and prepared-for well in advance. Conversely, many urgent situations are dealt with effectively by the person concerned without evoking a crisis of any kind. It is therefore important not to confuse crisis intervention with emergency response work (which may be employed, for example, in the wake of a local disaster).

The aim of crisis intervention is to capitalize on the energy generated by the crisis and hence to promote growth, learning and enhanced coping resources. In this respect, it can be seen as a form of empowerment, supporting people in drawing out the positives from the changes they are experiencing.

For Further Reading

Thompson, N. 1991: *Crisis Intervention Revisited*. Birmingham: Pepar.

NEIL THOMPSON

Crisis Management

Crisis management is the means by which people in a state of acute psychological disequilibrium are enabled to regain and strengthen their capacity to cope through a staged process of intervention. Such intervention combines immediate emotional and practical support at onset with therapy which is time-limited to coincide with the restoration of equilibrium and the establishment of new coping skills. While a crisis can be precipitated by stressful events, it is the emotional reaction that constitutes the crisis, not the situation itself. The severe psychological discomfort experienced in the crisis state propels the person into a search for new coping strategies. In this way, a crisis is a turning point. The enhanced state of readiness to change of a person in crisis demands dynamic intervention as disequilibrium is temporary – typically four to six weeks.

A number of crisis management models have been developed following foundational work in the 1950s in the USA. All have in common a set of procedural steps for helping a person work through the crisis by exploring and then changing affective, cognitive and behavioural patterns. Earlier ego psychological orientations have been giving way to cognitive approaches.

For Further Reading
Roberts, A. R. 1996: *Crisis Management and Brief Treatment: Theory, Techniques and Applications*. Chicago: Nelson Hall.

BARRY LUCKOCK

Critical Thinking

Critical thinking denotes an approach to evidence, argument and decision making which is closely related to scientific reasoning. It draws attention to sources of error, bias and distortion in both the process and content of intellectual activity, and shows how these can undermine the quality of decision making within the helping professions with serious consequences for the welfare of service users.

Critical thinking advocates the teaching of particular skills to practitioners to enable them:

- to assess accurately the quality of evidence, whether from research or from practice experience;
- to recognize common fallacies and errors in reasoning and counter them in a professional context;
- to recognize how affective biases (for example, a desire to please, a concern not to be ostracized) and cognitive biases (for example, memories of a vivid case, a tendency selectively to perceive evidence for a preferred position) can adversely influence the quality of our own judgements, and see how they can be used by other people to promote a particular point of view or strategy not consistent with good quality decision making or problem solving (cf. advertising or propaganda); and

- to establish a *modus operandi* which promotes accuracy or truth over winning the argument.

For Further Reading
Gambrill, E. 1997: *Social Work Practice: A Critical Thinker's Guide*. New York: Oxford University Press.
Gibbs, L. 1991: *Scientific Reasoning for Social Workers: Bridging the Gap between Research and Practice*. New York: Macmillan.

GERALDINE MACDONALD

Curfew

Curfew generally means a restriction on movement in a specified area for some part of the day. In criminal justice, it often refers to a restriction on an individual's movements as a condition of bail. Courts have the power (rarely used) to include similar conditions in supervision and probation orders, and, since 1994, to make curfew orders, alone, or with a probation order, monitored by electronic tagging. In Scotland, a 'child safety initiative', involving police intervention with young children out on the streets after dark, foreshadowed legislation in England and Wales (1998) providing for local child curfew schemes.

DAVID SMITH

Cycle of Change

Cycle of change is a theoretical framework describing the process an individual goes through in attempting to change any problematic behaviour; the phrases *wheel of change* or *stages of change* are also used.

The model is used to frame interventions in respect of various compulsive/addictive behaviours (for example, alcohol and drug abuse) and with the perpetrators of sexual crime. It was developed following observation of the behaviour of cigarette smokers. Its principal characteristics are the idea of:

- a cyclical rather than a linear process of change;
- clearly identifiable stages through which people pass; and
- the likelihood of relapse into the problematic behaviour.

The change cycle is divided into stages: contemplation, determination, action, maintenance and relapse. An additional stage, precontemplation, lies outside the cycle. These stages describe different states of readiness for change on the part of the client, suggesting that social workers need to vary their intervention accordingly. Thus task-centred work is appropriate to the action phase, and motivational interviewing is particularly helpful in the contemplation phase.

For Further Reading

Prochaska, J. O., DiClemente, C. C. and Norcross, J. C. 1992: In search of how people change. *American Psychologist*, 47 (9), 1102–14.

ELIZABETH LANCASTER

D

Dangerousness

Dangerousness is most often defined as an individual's potential or capacity to cause serious physical harm or psychological trauma to others. The key components of an assessment of dangerousness are:

- the identification of the behaviour of concern;
- the potential damage or harm likely from that behaviour; and
- the probability that it will occur and under what circumstances.

Frequency and imminence have also been considered as important features. While violent and sexual offending are most easily encompassed by the term dangerousness, the likely extent and nature of potential harm has become the key principle of definitions of dangerousness.

Two approaches to assessment can be discerned:

1. The *clinical method* is derived from the medical and the mental health fields: it is an individualistic diagnostic assessment of the personality and situational factors deemed to be relevant to dangerous behaviour; it has low predictive accuracy due to error and bias.
2. *Actuarial assessment* has its roots in the insurance industry and is based upon statistical calculations of probability; it has greater accuracy, but only in general terms about groups of people or types of actions.

Combined approaches using actuarial base rates and structured interviewing techniques are advocated.

For Further Reading
Walker, N. (ed.) 1996: *Dangerous People*. London: Blackstone Press.

HAZEL KEMSHALL

Day Care for Children

Day care for children is care provided by someone other than the child's parents, excluding residential and foster care. Day care is usually used by parents while they are working or studying. However, social workers also use day care: they purchase places for children in need, and this practice is known as sponsored day care.

Day care can be full-time or sessional, group- or family-based and provided by the private, public or voluntary sector. Forms of day care include day nurseries, pre-school playgroups, childminders, nannies and relatives. Day care for more than two hours a day, other than relative care, must be registered and inspected under the Children Act 1989.

Concern has been raised about the harmful effects of day care on young children's development, particularly mother–infant attachment. Research does not substantiate the view that children will be harmed by daily separation from their mother. Good quality day care does not put children's development at risk. Neither does it prevent children developing attachments to their mother or other adults caring for them.

For Further Reading
Mooney, A. and Munton, A. G. 1997: *Research and Policy in Early Childhood Services: Time for a New Agenda*. London: Institute of Education.

ANN MOONEY

Day Care in Adult Services

Day care is the provision of community care resources to adults needing care outside their home but not requiring residential care. The term includes resources traditionally provided in segregated buildings. Day care can be split into two types:

1. Specialist day care services, providing both relief to carers, and assessment, rehabilitation and monitoring for adults who might lose their independence
2. Day facilities, providing informal care focused on entertainment and social relationships

Day care is provided in the statutory, voluntary and private sectors. In times of resource constraint, services focus on people with higher support needs, reducing the element of recreation and companionship. Community care, emphasizing user choice, has led to the development of day resources outside of identified buildings, and within the broader community. This avoids users being grouped together and offered standard services, and seeks to fulfil the diversity of their individual needs through employment and education in ordinary settings.

Collaborative decisions on day care provision are made, based on service users' expressed needs.

For Further Reading
McIntosh, B. and Whittaker, A. 1998: *Days of Change: A Practical Guide to Developing Better Day Opportunities with People with Learning Difficulties.* London: King's Fund.

MARK BALDWIN

Deaf People, Social Work with

Social work with Deaf/deaf people involves individuals, groups or communities with experience of deafness, or their carers, or advocates.

Work includes involvement with the *Deaf community* who share language, culture, history and experience of oppression; this group use the term with a capital 'D' to denote a pride in their situation. It includes involvement with deaf children and their families, including child protection work, with deafened adults and Deaf/deaf people who have additional impairments, and with hard-of-hearing people.

Social workers use advocacy, counselling, the promotion of self-advocacy and community care liaison. There is a recognition of the interweaving nature of socio-political discrimination and oppression. Deaf/deaf people have normal needs for social work, but additional needs may exist because of rejection by 'hearing people', due to discrimination in access to services, or because of negative historical perceptions of Deaf/deaf people.

Social workers with Deaf/deaf people require skills in sign language and other systems of communication.

For Further Reading
Jones, S. 1997: *Sensory Impairment, Pathways 3, 4 and 5.* London: Central Council for Education and Training in Social Work, 67–117.

SUE JONES

Death, Dying and Bereavement

Death, dying and *bereavement* are fundamental aspects of human experience, and are therefore relevant to many areas of professional social work practice. While there are clearly some social work posts which specifically address these issues (hospice social workers, for example), all social workers are likely to encounter the challenges of responding to death, dying and bereavement at certain points in their work. This applies across the life course, from social work interventions in relation to miscarriages, deaths in childbirth or soon after, through to natural deaths in old age, as well as deaths due to illness, accidents, suicide or homicide.

To understand death, dying and bereavement as important factors in social work, it is important to be clear about the meaning of key concepts. *Bereavement* literally means 'robbed' or 'deprived' (consider the related term of 'bereft') and therefore refers to the actual loss experienced. *Grief* is the term used to describe a person's psychological response to the loss. It is commonly thought of in terms of the emotional response, but cognitive and behavioural aspects of grief also have an important part to play: grief is not restricted to emotion. *Mourning* refers to broader patterns of response to the loss and includes social factors such as the use of rituals, religious or otherwise.

The theoretical and research-based literature on bereavement overlaps to a certain extent with the literature relating to crisis theory. Traditional approaches to loss theory draw on the notion of a set of stages or phases, or a set of tasks parallel with the idea of developmental tasks used in life-course psychology. However, more recent developments in the theory base have tended to criticize such approaches, and have sought to develop more sophisticated explanations; for example, see Corr et al. (1996) in relation to dual process theory.

continued

There are a number of myths or common-sense assumptions that much of the theory-based literature challenges: for example, the notion that young children do not grieve, or that older people are immune to grief because they become accustomed to it. Such assumptions can be not only inaccurate, but profoundly discriminatory and oppressive.

Hospice

The social work task in relation to death, dying and bereavement has a number of aspects, not least those of hospice work and bereavement interventions. The hospice movement was founded by Dame Cicely Saunders and began in the UK in 1967. Hospice care refers to a philosophy of care, rather than to a specific building or service, and can be delivered in a wide range of settings to people who have a life-threatening and terminal illness. Central to this philosophy is the emphasis on quality of life. The philosophy of hospice is based on the premise that dying is a normal part of living: it *affirms* life, neither hastening death nor postponing it. Both the physical and psychosocial well-being of people who are dying are promoted by means of a palliative care approach. Key principles underpinning this approach are outlined by the National Council for Hospice and Specialist Palliative Care Services:

- An emphasis on the whole person
- The provision of care which encompasses both patients and those who are significant in their lives
- An emphasis on open and sensitive communication, including the provision of sufficient and appropriate information about diagnosis and treatment options
- Upholding the value of respect for patient autonomy and choice
- A focus on quality of life, including good symptom control

Interdisciplinary teams of professionals and volunteers collaborate to work within a shared and explicit philosophy to address the physical, psychological, emotional and spiritual needs of the person who is dying and those who are close to him or her. Psychosocial support involves assessing the impact of the illness and the need for ongoing support; the provision of support for the bereaved usually continues after the death. This assessment should be sensitive to the social, cultural and linguistic context of the situation, and should take account of the changing and variable needs of those living with life-threatening illnesses. Social workers with an understanding of, and skills in, dealing with loss and change, together with knowledge of statutory and voluntary resources, are well placed to provide psychosocial assessment and intervention before and after death.

A feature of hospice is the provision of ongoing bereavement care, offering social, psychological, emotional, practical and spiritual support to those in need of help to cope with their loss and the new challenges they face. Social workers and other key personnel can be involved in identifying those people who might be at special risk in bereavement and then in providing appropriate forms of support.

Conclusion

While bereavement counselling can be an appropriate and effective intervention in certain circumstances, there is a need to avoid equating the social work role with that of counselling. Bereavement interventions are likely to be on a much wider scale, incorporating financial, housing and other practical matters; child care concerns; care planning and co-ordination; and possibly statutory interventions. Care should be taken to avoid the common mistake of assuming that any person who has experienced a bereavement is therefore in need of counselling – the need for any bereavement intervention has to be carefully assessed.

Questions relating to death, dying and bereavement may be significant even at times when no one has recently died or is dying. Social work assessments may be made or interventions performed where the memory or fear of a bereavement has significance in the situation, or is affecting the way in which one or more individuals are responding to it.

For Further Reading
Corr, C. A., McNabe, C. M. and Corr, D. M. 1996: *Death and Dying, Life and Living*. Pacific Grove: Brooks/Cole.
Dickenson, D. and Johnson, M. (eds) 1993: *Death, Dying and Bereavement*. London: Sage.
Stroebe, W., Stroebe, M. and Hansson, B. (eds) 1993: *A Handbook of Bereavement: Theory, Practice and Research*. Cambridge: Cambridge University Press.

DENISE BEVAN AND NEIL THOMPSON

Debt Counselling
see MONEY ADVICE.

Decentralization
Decentralization is a process in which decision making and control over the delivery of services is transferred from a central location to a number of more local settings, closer to the populations being served. It often involves the establishment of neighbourhood committees which include representatives of local residents, and the creation of neighbourhood offices delivering a range of services. Decentralization aims to make services more accessible, accountable and responsive to locally defined needs and priorities. Within neighbourhood (or patch) offices more generic forms of practice are often developed, with different professional groups working collaboratively to provide fully integrated services.

GORDON JACK

Decision Making in Social Work

Decision making is a process of making a choice between two or more options. The ability to make decisions is a core professional competence in social work, but there are differing perspectives as to its principle components. There is a difference between descriptive theories of what social workers do in practice and prescriptive theories of what they could or should do. Social workers potentially have a number of decision-making roles, including facilitating clients to make informed life decisions, making professional judgements, participating in processes of partnership decision making with clients and other stakeholders, or making recommendations to courts, panels and other decision-making bodies.

Sound decisions and effective decisions
Social situations are complex and uncertain, requiring a distinction between *sound decisions* and *effective decisions*. Decisions are *sound* when appropriately made according to established criteria, while *effective* decisions achieve the decision makers' goals. Sound decision making includes involving the client to the highest feasible level, consultation between the stakeholders, careful framing of the decision situation and making a systematic choice between options. Well-made decisions increase the chances of beneficial outcomes, but, in conditions of uncertainty and complexity, they may not always be effective. The relative lack of influence social workers have over wider social factors, such as poverty and the level of resources, can limit what sound decision making alone can achieve.

There are different *levels of client involvement*:

- Being informed of a decision that has already been made
- Being consulted about a decision yet to be made

continued

- Jointly making decisions in partnership
- Clients making decisions for themselves

A principle of sound decision-making practice is for clients to have the highest feasible level of involvement, but they may not always feel sufficiently empowered to make decisions, and social workers may be too ready to take over. If clients are to have an effective say, energy needs to be directed towards client empowerment and anti-oppressive practice. Client autonomy may not always be feasible – for example, when clients have a mental impairment that affects their decision-making capacities, or if children are considered not to have sufficient understanding, or when there are issues of unacceptable risk, or when resources need rationing.

When involvement needs to be limited to consultation, there is the accompanying danger of unjustified paternalism. In such circumstances, practitioners need to take care that they do not go against the client's wishes unless there are both ethical and legal justifications. There are potentially a large number of *stakeholders*, in addition to the client, that may need to be involved and many decisions in social work are made at reviews, conferences, panels and meetings of various other kinds. Stakeholders need to consult with each other to share information but the presence of clients at these meetings is not sufficient in itself to ensure their involvement. Active steps may be required to prevent them being excluded from meaningful participation.

Decision framing is a process of constructing a mental image that structures the decision situation and can include the identification of key factors, decision goals and a set of options. A sound decision frame is based on careful assessment using the most up-to-date information available to paint a valid picture of the situation. Social workers require sufficient discretion to be able to respond to the unique features of decision situations, but can be constrained by agency procedures and regulations. Decision frames need to be sensitive to a wide range of factors but agency attempts to standardize practice can conflict with professional endeavours to construct holistic assessments. Effective intervention requires that longer-term goals be kept firmly within the decision frame, alongside feasible and creative options. Critical reflective practice is necessary to ensure that decision frames do not contain distortions, based on stereotypes, that lead to unsound and discriminatory decisions.

Social workers are subjected to contradictory demands and intense emotions, and can face difficult choices when all options are likely to have undesirable consequences. The *choice between options* can be made in a number of ways, including the decision makers believing that they have an obligation to take a particular course of action or need to choose the option most likely to bring about a beneficial outcome or the least detrimental outcome. The former approach relates to deontological ethics, being concerned with what is the inherently good or right action, irrespective of outcome. The latter pertains to utilitarian ethics and focuses on deciding which option promotes good consequences for the client. Clear and systematic thinking is required, but paralysis would occur if every decision was subjected to detailed analysis.

Intuitive decisions are made without deliberation, while *analysis* breaks down the decision, and subjects the parts to explicit examination. Inexperienced workers may lack the necessary expertise to make intuitive decisions, while experienced practitioners still need to use analysis when faced with particularly difficult decisions. There are a number of ways options can be analysed, including balancing positive and negative consequences of implementing courses of action or assessing the degree of risk that an undesirable outcome will occur. There is a danger that such aids to decision making are used in a mechanistic way, rather than as guides in the formation of professional judgements.

The tracing and evaluation of *decision outcomes* provides feedback to decision makers that can be used to improve decision-making practices and focuses on whether the decision makers' goals have been achieved. When to evaluate the outcome, what method to use and from whose point of view, are problematic issues that require resolution before a judgement can be made as to whether the decision is effective. This needs to be distinguished from the evaluation of decision making that focuses on whether the processes involved in making the decision were sound. When harmful outcomes occur, it is relatively easy to look back and conclude that obvious errors were made. However, at the time the decision was taken, the situation may have been far from straightforward.

For Further Reading
O'Sullivan, T. 1999: *Decision Making in Social Work*. Basingstoke: Macmillan.

TERENCE O'SULLIVAN

Deinstitutionalization

Deinstitutionalization is both a *policy* – of hospital closure – and a *process* – of relocating people into the community. The policy of hospital closure gained ground for a variety of interrelated reasons. Institutions came to be seen as totally unsuitable places for people to live in: not only were they routinized, regimented and dehumanizing places from within, but they were remote from the rest of the everyday world; they were also expensive to run.

At the same time as institutions came into question, so the ideas of normalization and ordinary living came into vogue, especially for people with learning difficulties. Clearly, people could not lead 'ordinary lives' in institutions. The institutions had to go. Deinstitutionalization, in this sense, is the closure of the long-stay hospitals.

It is also a process of resettling people from hospital into the community. To work well, deinstitutionalization goes beyond relocating people to a new address. It means supporting them in making choices about their own lives, and enabling them to take their place in society as ordinary citizens.

For Further Reading
Mansell, J. L. and Ericsson, K. 1996: *Deinstitutionalisation and Community Living: Intellectual Disability Services in Britain, Scandinavia and the USA*. London: Chapman and Hall.

DOROTHY ATKINSON

Deliberate Self-harm

See SELF-HARM and SUICIDE.

Dementia

See ALZHEIMER'S DISEASE.

Demography

Demography is the scientific study of the size and structure of human populations, and how these change over time. At its core is the quantitative description of population change. It is also usually considered to include the scientific study of how social, economic and cultural factors influence population change, and the social and economic impact of changes in the size and structure of populations (Daugherty and Kammeyer, 1995). Demography also encompasses population projection (the forecasting of population size and structure), and the study of population policies.

What demographers study

The size of a population changes for three reasons: birth, death and migration. Thus, the three key processes which demographers study are fertility, mortality and migration. In addition, all human populations have 'structure' in that their members can be classified according to their sex, age, marital status, ethnic origin, educational attainment, occupation and other factors. For the demographer, sex, age and marital status are the most important of these characteristics. The study of changes in a population's structure therefore involves the analysis of other processes, for example, marriage and divorce.

continued

Demographic data come from three types of sources. First, population censuses are taken every ten years in many countries; these collect information about each person's name, sex, date and country of birth, marital status, relationship to the head of the household in which they live, usual address, usual address one year ago, ethnic origin, occupation and educational qualifications. Second, vital registration of births, marriages and deaths provides data on the number of these events, and on the characteristics of parents and those who marry and die. Third, surveys are used to furnish more detailed information about specific topics. Examples include the British National Child Development Study, which is a longitudinal study of a cohort of children born in 1958; and the British annual General Household Survey.

Births, marriages and deaths

Demographers use data from these sources to chart trends in the important demographic processes (Coleman and Salt, 1992). Between 1970 and 2000, mortality in the UK fell by around 50 per cent for children and by between 20 and 25 per cent at ages over 70 years. Fertility fell during the late 1960s and early 1970s. At the rates prevailing since around 1980, the average woman can expect to have fewer than two children in her life. The greatest fall in fertility has been among women in their twenties; there has actually been an increase in fertility among older women, associated with an increasing participation in the work-force.

The last three decades of the twentieth century saw a large rise in the proportion of men and women 'cohabiting' (living together in informal unions). Both legal marriages and informal unions have become more unstable. One result of this has been that the proportion of children born outside legal marriages increased very greatly during this period, such that by the mid-1990s more than one in three children were born to parents who were not legally married. A large proportion of these parents were living together.

Because of these changes, demography has developed a particular focus on marriage and family life, which includes the study of the transitions into cohabitation and married life; childbearing; separation, divorce and widowhood; and remarriage. It analyses the forces which promote and retard these processes, and examines the impact of these processes (and the changes in population structure which they produce) on social and economic life. For example, increased rates of divorce and remarriage lead to increases in the proportion of children living with a single parent, a tendency for households to be smaller and for family and kinship ties to be more numerous but looser. Reduced mortality, combined with increased divorce rates, has resulted in a rise in the proportion of households which contain only one person.

Age structure

A population's fertility and mortality largely determine its age structure. A key aspect of the age structure is the dependency ratio, or the ratio between the number of people below school leaving age and above the statutory retirement age, and the number of people of working age (see table 2). As people live longer and have fewer children the proportion of the elderly rises and the proportion of children and of people of working age falls, a phenomenon known as *population ageing*.

Changes in the age structure are associated with changes in the proportion of the population suffering from various types of ill health and disability. For example, in England and Wales in 1988, about a quarter of those aged 45–64, two out of every five persons aged 65–74, and half of those aged 75 and over were suffering from a long-standing illness which limited their activities. The demand for health care increases as the proportion of the population in these age groups rises.

The Office for National Statistics is responsible for collecting and processing the majority of demographic data in the UK. Its quarterly journal, *Population Trends*, contains up-to-date information on the country's population structure, and on trends in fertility, mortality, marriage and migration. A wide variety of statistics is also available on-line at http://www.statistics.gov.uk.

Table 2 Age structure of the UK population, 1971–91 and projected age structure, 2001–21

	1971	1981	1991	2001	2011	2021
Total population (thousands)	55,928	56,352	57,808	59,618	60,929	62,244
Percentage at ages						
0–14	24	21	19	19	17	17
15–29	21	23	23	19	19	18
30–44	18	19	21	23	20	19
45–59	18	17	16	19	21	21
60–74	14	14	14	13	15	17
75 and over	5	6	7	7	8	9
Dependants per 1,000 persons of working age						
Under 16	438	371	331	327	296	282
Pensionable age	280	297	299	292	310	305
Total dependants	718	668	630	619	606	587

Sources: Estimated from Office for National Statistics (1998, p. 57) and Shaw (1998, p. 43).

For Further Reading
Coleman, D. and Salt, J. 1992: *The British Population: Patterns, Trends and Processes.* Oxford: Oxford University Press.
Daugherty, H. G. and Kammeyer, K. C. W. 1995: *An Introduction to Population.* New York: The Guilford Press.
Shaw, C. 1998: 1996-based national population projections for the United Kingdom and constituent countries. *Population Trends 91*, 43–49.

ANDREW HINDE

Depression

Unhappiness is part of the usual reaction to adversity, but can also occur without an obvious cause: the symptom of *depressed mood* is present when unhappiness lasts longer than expected, appears out of proportion to circumstances, or seems out of control. Depressed mood occurs in certain physical illnesses (such as hepatitis or glandular fever) and in many psychiatric syndromes: the characteristic features of the depressive disorders include low mood, reduced energy and loss of interest or enjoyment. Other common symptoms in depressive episodes include poor concentration, reduced self-confidence, guilty thoughts, pessimism, ideas of self-harm or suicide, disturbed sleep and altered appetite. The designated severity of episodes varies, dependent upon the number and intensity of symptoms, and the associated impairment at work and in personal or family life.

Variations in the clinical picture
Many depressed patients also describe anxiety symptoms: in some, these may be more prominent, the underlying depressive symptoms being found only after direct questioning. Certain so-called 'biological' depressive symptoms (including weight loss, feeling worst earliest in the day, and early morning wakening) tend to predict a better response to antidepressant drugs. Some severely ill patients hold delusional beliefs or experience distressing hallucinations, these reflecting the low mood – believing oneself to have irre-

continued

deemably sinned, or hearing derogatory voices, for example. This state is usually called 'psychotic depression', and can respond well to electro-convulsive therapy (ECT). Depression is usually an intermittent condition, most patients experiencing multiple episodes over their lifetime; individual episodes varying in length, severity and impairment, and in the response to treatment.

Consequences of depression

Depression causes much personal suffering, and imposes a significant burden on society: the under-recognition and generally poor treatment of depression together constitute a major public health issue. For the individual, depression causes psychological distress, reduces quality of life and increases the mortality from suicide, accidents and cardio-vascular disease: it can contribute to marital and family breakdown, and, in depressed mothers, can delay the development of their children. The economic burden on society arises not from health and social care costs, but rather from the costs of reduced work productivity in patient and carers, and from the costs of premature mortality, due to suicide, which is the cause of death in approximately 10 per cent of patients with a severe recurrent depressive disorder.

Epidemiology and aetiology

In western societies, community surveys indicate that significant depressive symptoms are reported by approximately 15 per cent of the population: some 10 per cent of consultations in primary care settings are probably due to depressive disorders. Women are twice as often affected as men, the lifetime expectancy being around 20 per cent and 10 per cent, respectively. Although the prevalence of depressive symptoms increases with age, major depressive illness may be no more common in the elderly. Recent studies reveal a rising incidence of depression in younger age groups: in young men, this may be linked to the rise in suicide rates. While depressive symptoms are more frequent in the socially excluded and economically disadvantaged, depressive illness affects people from all sections of society. Depression in childhood or adolescence is no longer regarded as a rare condition.

Depression has many causes: in most patients, depressive episodes arise from the combination of familial, biological, psychological and social factors. Genetic influences are most marked in patients with more severe depressive disorders and 'biological' symptoms: the morbid risk in first-degree relatives is increased in all studies, this elevation being independent of environment or upbringing. The response of depressed patients to antidepressant drugs, and the results of certain investigations suggest that abnormalities in the level or function of the neurotransmitters serotonin, noradrenaline and dopamine may be important, although this evidence is not conclusive. Low self-esteem, an obsessional personality, the experience of adversity in childhood and maladaptive negative patterns of thinking about oneself and others, are all psychological risk factors for depression. Social factors include excessive undesirable life events, usually involving loss (such as bereavement, divorce and redundancy), and persisting major difficulties including being a lone parent, prolonged unemployment, poverty, and lack of social support or intimacy.

Treatment

Because most depressive episodes result from the combination of biological and psychosocial factors, the optimal treatment of depressed patients usually involves integrating psychological and physical treatment approaches with practical social support. Physical methods of treatment include the judicious use of antidepressant drugs and, occasionally, ECT; light therapy may be helpful for some patients with seasonal affective disorder (SAD or 'winter depression'). Neuro-surgery is used exceedingly rarely, being restricted for severely and chronically ill patients who derived no benefit from multiple, combined, specialist treatment approaches. Antidepressant drugs include the tricyclic antidepressants (TCAs), mono-amine oxidase inhibitors (MAOIs), selective sero-tonin re-uptake inhibitors (SSRIs) and a disparate group of other compounds. In stan-dard practice, some 70 per cent of patients with moderate or severe episodes will be substantially improved within three months of starting treatment: by continuing with antidepressants, the risk of relapse can be halved, and longer-term treatment can prevent the emergence of new depressive episodes. However, the antidepressant drugs are not ideal, side-effects limiting their use in some patients. The older drugs (for example, the TCAs) can cause drowsiness and interfere with work, and are dangerous when taken in overdose: newer drugs (for example, SSRIs) are somewhat better tolerated, and relatively safer, but treatment-emergent sexual dysfunction is common.

Many of the mildly depressed patients seen in primary care settings can be helped by simple counselling and instruction in problem-solving techniques. However, moderately or severely ill patients generally require more intensive psychological approaches, such as cognitive therapy or interpersonal therapy. These directive, problem-focused, time-limited treatments are effective in the short term, and possibly have some value in delaying the onset of new depressive episodes. Unfortunately, access to specialized psychological treatments is variable and, often, limited. Marital or couple therapy can be a useful accompaniment to other treatment methods; and many patients describe some benefit from complementary approaches such as the Alexander technique or meditation, although scientific evidence for this efficacy is lacking.

For Further Reading
Healy, D. 1997: *The Antidepressant Era*. Cambridge, Mass, USA: Harvard University Press.
Milligan, S. and Clare, A. 1993: *Depression and How to Survive It*. London: Ebury Press.
Thompson, C. 1996: Mood disorders. *MEDICINE, Psychiatry*, 24 (2), 1–5.

DAVID S. BALDWIN

Developmental Psychology

Developmental psychology is the study of social, cognitive, affective and behavioural changes that occur over time through maturation and learning.

Social developmental psychology is concerned with understanding and explaining the changes that occur through the lifespan in our ability to interact with, form and main-tain relationships with other people. Social development also includes the development of gender roles and social identity. Developmental psychologists may also be interested in *affective* or *emotional* changes that occur through maturation and learning; for example, the development of humour, empathy and love.

Cognitive developmental psychology is concerned with the changes that occur in our thought processes and abilities from birth to old age. The study of developing language, intelligence, perception and attention are within this category.

Clinical developmental psychology is the study of the idiopathic development of children and adolescents who exhibit problem behaviour. Attempting to under-stand and explain behaviour problems – such as conduct disorder, depression and anxiety disorders – is crucial in determining the best interventions for the children concerned.

The nature / nurture debate

Many changes in social, affective or cognitive processes occur through the gradual maturation of both physical and psychological processes. In addition, changes occur

continued

as a result of learning. Much of our behaviour is a result of an interaction between the things we experience and the genes we are born with. There are few aspects of development that can be considered entirely a result of either *nature* or *nurture*: the complexity of human development is a result of the interaction between nature *and* nurture.

Important theories of child development

Jean Piaget's (1950) work on the cognitive development of children suggested that children progress through the same set of stages, at approximately the same ages, during their intellectual development. The first of these is the *sensori-motor stage*, which begins at birth and focuses on the development of motor and sensory abilities. The final stage is that of *formal operational intelligence* which begins during early adolescence, where logical, abstract and scientific thinking develops. The stage of cognitive development influences the child's ability to understand certain types of questions and affects the types of answers given by the child. There has been much development of Piaget's work in this area which has suggested that Piaget underestimated the age at which children achieve cognitive developmental milestones such as *object permanence*: the knowledge that an object exists when it is out of sight.

Later research in children's cognitive development has focused on *theory of mind*. By the age of four years old, children are aware that other people may have beliefs that are different to their own, or beliefs that are inaccurate. Prior to this stage, children behave as if their own beliefs are a reflection of reality, and that everyone shares these beliefs. Theory of mind is important in terms of both cognitive and social development; having a theory of mind allows us to predict what other people's behaviour or intentions might be and to understand other people's feelings.

The moral development of children is an important area to consider: whether a child of a certain age can judge right from wrong has profound implications for issues such as determining criminal responsibility. Lawrence Kohlberg (1963) suggested a *stage theory* for moral development, which implied that many children and adolescents do not have fully developed moral understanding. Stages of moral reasoning, from pre-conventional, through conventional to post-conventional reasoning, see the motivation for moral behaviour ranging from a wish to avoid punishment from authority (stage 1) to following universal, ethical principles that are beyond rules (stage 6). Age ranges are rarely given for the stages of Kohlberg's model because people progress through these stages at widely varying rates. Critics have pointed out that both Kohlberg's and Piaget's theories are specific to western culture. Kohlberg's theory has also been criticized as being biased against women. Differences in parenting style have a significant effect on the moral reasoning of the child. Culture and education are also considered to be critical factors.

Social learning theorists suggest that children learn behaviour not only as a result of being rewarded and punished for their actions, but as a result of observing other people's behaviours and the consequences of those behaviours. For example, children who observe that aggressive behaviour achieves a reward or pay-off are more likely to use aggressive behaviour themselves.

Attachment theory

Social and emotional development in children is widely researched, particularly the development of attachment to caregivers. Infants develop an attachment to their caregiver during their first year of life, and the quality of this attachment depends on the responsiveness and availability of the caregiver. This caregiver need not be the mother, and an infant can have multiple attachment figures without adverse effects. Many studies have suggested that an insecurely attached child might have more problems later in life than a securely attached child is likely to have. However, children's *internal working models* of attachment can alter; attachment classification at one year does not necessarily predict outcome in later life.

An understanding of developmental psychology is invaluable to practitioners in determining age-appropriate behaviours and abilities, and assessing the many factors that affect a child's development.

For Further Reading
Herbert, M. 1998: *Clinical Child Psychology: Social Learning, Development and Behaviour.* Chichester: Wiley.
Schaffer, H. R. 1996: *Social Development.* Oxford: Blackwell.
Shaffer, D. T. 1996: *Developmental Psychology.* California: Brooks/Cole.

JACKIE BLISSETT

Direct Care Payments
Direct care payments are monies paid to an individual by an agency which has a duty to provide services to that person, in lieu of those services. The individual then assumes the responsibility of purchasing their own services to meet the assessed need. In England and Wales, the Community Care (Direct Payments) Act 1996 enabled local authorities, for the first time, to make cash payments to certain classes of individual who require support. The Act defines a direct payment as 'a payment made by a local authority to an individual whom it has assessed as needing community care services'.

CAROL DAWSON

Direct Work with Children
Direct work with children encompasses a range of activities involving communication with children, usually on a one-to-one basis. Direct work may be undertaken for purposes of assessment or care planning and is often used in placement preparation work. It also covers treatment or therapy for children who have experienced loss, are suffering from the effects of abuse, or have behavioural difficulties. Social workers in child care settings undertake such work, but, increasingly, contract direct work out to other organizations and professionals.

It is worth distinguishing between activities designed to promote playful but purposive dialogue with children, and sustained therapeutic interventions. Many of the techniques in the former group, such as the use of dolls or puppets and life story work are derived from the practice of play therapists and, as with play therapy, their validity rests on the belief that play is a natural medium for communicating with children. Therapeutic interventions include different forms of play therapy as well as behavioural and cognitive therapies, all of which aim to achieve change.

For Further Reading
Wilson, K., Kendrick, P. and Ryan, V. 1992: *Play Therapy: A Non-directive Approach for Children and Adolescents.* London: Baillière Tindall.

NICKY STANLEY

Disability
Disability is a highly contested term. Medicine and its allied professions conceptualize disability as damage to a person's body or mental functioning requiring diagnosis, care or professional treatment. By contrast, the *social model* of disability argues that 'the problem' should not be located within an individual person, but rather in a 'disabling environment' which excludes and denigrates disabled people. A third approach is psychological, addressing both conscious and unconscious experiences, such as disabled people's experiences of loss, trauma and stigma, and non-disabled people's fears, fantasies and emotional investments (for example, as carers) in disability.

In practice, medical, social and psychological thinking is rarely as clear-cut as the models of disability suggest. For example, much neuroscience acknowledges the importance of emotional experience in shaping brain physiology. Social constructionism increasingly recognizes that bodies cannot be ignored in discussions of disability. Finally, many psychological approaches examine ways disabled people internalize social and cultural oppression, and non-disabled people exercise power. Thus, there is growing concern to recognize the complex relationship between physiological, social and psychological dimensions and bridge different

93

models and to examine disability as an *embodied* and *relational* experience.

For Further Reading
Marks, D. 1999: *Disability: Controversial Debates and Psychosocial Perspectives*. London: Routledge.

Deborah Marks

Disability in Children

Disability in children is a disadvantage which may be created by physical or intellectual impairment, or by ill health. The disabling condition can result from a wide range of causes, including accidental and non-accidental injury before or after birth, disease which may be hereditary, or neglect. Disability can be progressive or life threatening.

The *social model* is an influential school of thought which holds that disablement is created as much by societal attitudes and responses to children who have impairments as it is by any limitations imposed by the condition itself. For example, a child who cannot walk is further disadvantaged if they are denied access to the same quality of education as a non-disabled child from the same community.

This discriminatory tendency can apply to social services if disabled children receive a different quality of response that would be considered inappropriate for non-disabled children of the same age and background. Mainstream child protection services have been criticized for excluding disabled children. An emphasis on professionals extending their existing knowledge and skills, and, thereby, applying the same childcare principles to all children leads to services being offered on a more inclusive basis.

For Further Reading
Middleton, L. 1999: *Disabled Children*. Oxford: Blackwell Science.

Laura Middleton

Discharge Planning

Discharge from hospital is the process by which people leave hospital after a period of in-patient care and return to life in the community. This may be to the person's own home, to hostel provision, or to residential or nursing home care. The need to plan for discharge and a successful transition for the individual back into the community concerns a range of service users, including older people, adults with learning disabilities, and those with mental health problems. The plan should be based on an individual's needs, and, in particular, the need for services, assistance or equipment once discharged from hospital; these should be provided as the individual leaves hospital or very shortly after.

The context for discharge planning

Discharge planning takes place in different hospital settings: acute and community hospital trusts; psychiatric hospitals and those providing for people with learning disabilities. Within acute hospital provision, there are differences in discharge arrangements and differences in the extent to which planning takes place on different wards: the emphasis will vary, for example, between specialist wards for older people or for people with terminal illnesses or progressive neurological conditions and general medical and surgical wards.

Discharge arrangements are based on legislation and policy guidance. This places responsibilities on local authorities (social services and other departments) and health authorities and providers (healthcare trusts and primary care providers) to work together to assess, plan and meet the needs of people leaving hospital.

Discharge planning is complicated when considering patients who are vulnerable and who have complex needs to enable them to return to the community. Even when the situation seems relatively straightforward, complications can arise. Much has been written concerning problems surrounding discharge from hospital and the transfer of care across the health and social care divide, between hospital and community.

It is apparent that changes in in-patient care, especially in acute care settings, and the resulting reductions in length of hospital stay mean that people are discharged 'quicker and sicker' with higher levels of dependency and disability than previously. Several difficulties surrounding the arrangements for discharge can be identified:

- Poor communication and information flow between community and hospital teams, before, during and after discharge from hospital
- Lack of adequate assessment and planning for discharge while in hospital
- Failure to identify individuals/carers who have special needs or who are vulnerable
- An apparent over-emphasis on the needs of the institution for early discharge, rather than a focus on individuals' needs
- Lack of service provision for individuals and subsequent reliance on informal support systems on discharge
- Inadequate involvement of individuals and carers in the planning process, including insufficient notice of discharge

The importance of discharge planning

In 1988, the British Geriatrics Society and the Association of Directors of Social Services issued a statement discussing the need for discharge plans to be made for patients leaving hospital. In 1989, the Department of Health published a circular concerned with the discharge of patients from acute hospitals. Health authorities were instructed to establish discharge policies for all client groups and to monitor the effectiveness of these arrangements. Particular emphasis was given to three key areas:

1 The importance of starting planning for discharge as soon as possible after admission
2 The importance of a multidisciplinary approach to planning
3 The importance of actively involving patients and their carers in discharge planning

Ways of implementing the guidelines were outlined in a booklet that accompanied the circular. Additionally, a further circular was distributed to local authorities to reinforce the original health guidance (Department of Health, 1989). Changes in NHS provision occurred following the implementation of the NHS & Community Care Act 1990 and the introduction of internal markets and the purchaser/provider split. Within this, acute hospitals have to contain costs and operate more efficiently. They have to maximize bed occupancy rates and usage. The need to ensure that beds are available for new admissions means that hospitals cannot afford to have beds 'blocked' by people who need resources to be provided for them in the community so that they can leave hospital but who do not need to remain in (expensive) hospital care.

The changes due to the NHS & Community Care Act 1990 meant that social services departments became responsible for public funding to finance community care, and the introduction of assessment and care management for adults in need of social care. These changes were initially focused on administrative and financial responsibilities as far as discharge from hospital was concerned. The changes were intended to reinforce arrangements for good practice already advocated.

However, the circulars were not adhered to locally, and were not monitored as to the effectiveness of their implementation at a local or national level. Discharge arrangements were thus included as one of the eight key tasks of implementation of community care reforms. Specific agreements between health and local authorities on nursing home placements and also discharge were required for local authorities to obtain community care monies from government. Similar requirements for funding followed in subsequent years. Further attempts were made to tackle some of the problems with discharge, for example by the Department of Health (1995b).

Hospital discharge arrangements are seen as a key issue of the post-1990 reforms, particularly for those individuals, most of them elderly people, who enter some form of

continued

care on leaving hospital. Hospital social workers are more involved in discharge planning activities than previously, and work with health care professionals, often in multi-disciplinary teams, to arrange and implement safe discharge from hospital. Systems of care management/discharge planning have developed and changed the traditional role of the hospital social worker. Studies, including Social Services Inspectorate inspections, have confirmed the need for social workers to be fully involved in discharge planning and implementation (Davies and Connolly, 1995).

For Further Reading
Davies, M. and Connolly, J. 1995: The social worker's role in the hospital. *Health and Social Care in the Community*, 3 (5), 301–9.
Department of Health 1989: *Discharge of Patients from Hospital*, HC (89) 5 and LAC (89) 7, London: HMSO.
Department of Health 1995b: *Hospital Discharge Workbook*. London: HMSO.

BRIDGET PENHALE

Discourse Analysis

The unitary term *discourse analysis* refers to a collection of research methods and analytical tools from diverse theoretical and disciplinary traditions. These methods are increasingly being used in social work research.

In this context, the term *discourse* can mean a number of things. It may refer to language used within organizations or in encounters with service users, as this is displayed in talk or in written texts such as case notes. It may also refer to ways of thinking, or 'knowledges' or 'discourses' about particular phenomena, such as gender, race, the family or mental health, and how these reflect particular political or moral positions.

Within discourse analysis, there is a preference for data which have 'naturally occurred' in the cut and thrust of everyday life. These are usually preserved on audiotape and transcribed using coding devices which attempt to represent as much of the detail of the interaction as possible. The context in which the talk takes place, or the audience for whom the accounts were written, is also of central importance in the analysis. Analysts would be interested in the ways in which social workers categorize and order their cases and their world, and how they use language strategically. However, the methods can also be used by practitioners themselves to help them reflect on their practice.

For Further Reading
Van Dijk, T. A. (ed.) 1997: *Discourse as Structure and Process*. London: Sage.

SUE WHITE

Discrimination

To experience *discrimination* usually implies that an individual or group is being excluded from opportunities to participate in some desirable aspect of social life, or is being excluded from access to equal opportunities or the enjoyment of scarce resources. There is a general sense of the person or group not being treated fairly.

Individuals may act purposively to discriminate against others, or social systems and structures may have unwanted or unexpected discriminatory consequences. Common grounds on which individuals experience discrimination include age, disability, ethnicity, gender, race, sexual orientation, religious affiliation and nationality.

Sometimes, discrimination is divided into *negative* and *positive* forms:

- *Negative discrimination* is the unwanted exclusion of one or more groups from desired objectives.
- *Positive discrimination* applies where a discriminatory act is intended to have desirable consequences – for example, where a member of a group that often experiences discrimination is protected from that form of discrimination by the exclusion of others.

All acts of discrimination have both positive and negative outcomes: some individuals are favoured and others are excluded.

Legislation has been introduced in the UK to afford *some* level of protection to *some* groups that experience discrimination in certain circumstances.

For Further Reading
Sayce, L. 1998: Stigma, discrimination and social exclusion: What's in a word? *Journal of Mental Health*, 7 (4), 331–43.

STEVEN SHARDLOW

Dissocial Personality Disorder
See PSYCHOPATHIC PERSONALITY DISORDER.

Diversion
Diversion refers to the process by which offenders are dealt with, using a variety of informal measures, as an alternative to formal processing in the criminal justice system. The concept of diversion has its roots in labelling theory, which emphasizes the potential for formal criminal justice processing to increase the risk of future delinquency and which advocates less intrusive responses to minor offending, especially among young people. It was central to the 'new orthodoxy' of juvenile justice in England and Wales in the 1980s, and was advocated as a key focus for the work of the probation service in the context of the *non-treatment paradigm* for probation practice.

Although offenders may be diverted at different points in the criminal justice process, the term is most commonly associated with diversion from prosecution. The form that it takes varies across jurisdictions and includes systems of police cautioning, mediation and reparation, family group conferencing and the provision of social work and other services to individuals whose offending is considered to reflect underlying personal problems. Diversion programmes have, however, been criticized for 'net-widening' by bringing more people under the control of non-justice agencies.

For Further Reading
Muncie, J. 1998: *Youth and Crime: A Critical Introduction*. London: Sage, ch. 6.

GILL McIVOR

Divorce and Family Court Welfare

When couples separate or *divorce* in England and Wales, a court may request a report concerning *the welfare of any children* involved if there are issues about which the parents disagree concerning the arrangements for their children's future, or where the court has any child welfare concerns. Under s.7 of the Children Act 1989, reports may be prepared by either the family court welfare service, staffed by probation officers specializing in such work, or by a local authority social worker. In practice, almost all such reports are prepared by the family court welfare service (but see final section below).

The developments of family court welfare
Following the Divorce Reform Act 1969, the number of divorces in England and Wales increased from 58,000 in 1970, reaching 158,000 in 1994 before falling to 148,310 in 1997. This takes no account of the increase in the breakdown of relationships between unmarried couples. Consequently, the number of requests from courts for welfare reports increased from under 4,000 in the early 1960s to 36,073 in 1997.

Such work was originally based on the investigation and reporting of the family's circumstances and any factors relating to children's welfare which the welfare officer deemed relevant. However, because of the adversarial legal process in England and Wales and the nature of the law on divorce, the system came under attack for exacerbating the conflict between couples, thus inflicting greater damage on the children. This, together with the increasing incidence of family breakdown and the demand for welfare reports, led to a growing interest in conciliation (first mooted in the Report of the Finer Committee on One-Parent Families in 1974) among family court welfare officers who, from the early 1980s, increasingly began to experiment with new approaches developed by conciliators and family therapists working with divorcing families.

This led to a reconceptualization of court welfare work as practice developed from simply investigating and reporting to include approaches which sought to address issues

continued

of family breakdown by using methods designed to reduce parental conflict, help them to settle their disputes and to agree arrangements for their children, thereby enhancing children's welfare and assisting with family reorganization post-separation/divorce. Such developments were not universal in England and Wales, however, and wide variations in practice emerged, leading occasionally to trenchant judicial criticism because of perceived failures to investigate adequately and to provide courts with the information they required.

The Children Act 1989 led to major changes. It was based on certain clearly articulated principles, all of which endorsed in various ways the further development of practices which would maximize family autonomy and parental responsibility, involvement and agreement, so as to minimize harm to children. In addition, changes to the Probation Rules in 1992 and the introduction of National Standards for Family Court Welfare Work in 1994 both endorsed the use of mediation (which had by then become the preferred term because of confusion surrounding the meaning of the term *conciliation*). Increasingly, therefore, the social work contribution to the judicial task of ensuring the paramountcy of the welfare of children in divorce came to be redefined in terms of reducing conflict and encouraging parents to agree about future arrangements for their children.

Although the Children Act encouraged minimal intervention by the courts, s.16 gave them the power to make a family assistance order in exceptional circumstances to assist families with any continuing problems post-divorce. There was no clear definition of the nature and purpose of such orders, however, and many more such orders have been made than was originally anticipated. In addition, in spite of the existence of National Standards, considerable variations in practice have continued.

The pattern is still evolving

In 1996, following a heated debate about the reform of the law relating to divorce, the Family Law Act was passed, introducing 'no fault' divorce, with irretrievable breakdown as the sole ground. The Act requires all those seeking divorce to first attend an Information Meeting intended to apprise them of the consequences of divorce, including its impact upon children, the likely costs, and the legal and welfare services (including mediation) available during the period of reflection and consideration that must elapse to demonstrate that a marriage has irretrievably broken down. During this period, the parties will be expected to agree about issues relating to children, finances and property. It also introduced publicly funded mediation and improved provisions for dealing with domestic violence. The Act's provisions relating to mediation and to domestic violence have been implemented. The debate about the main reforms has been extensive, however, although their eventual implementation remains a possibility.

In 1999, following a review of the work of family court welfare officers, Guardians *ad litem* and the Official Solicitor, the Government announced the formation of a new Children and Family Court Advisory and Support Service, combining these services into a single organization under the oversight of the Lord Chancellor's Department, thereby severing the link between family court welfare and the probation service.

Although there is some evidence of increasing convergence in the legal frameworks for divorce and in associated approaches to child welfare in many industrialized countries, the arrangements for the provision of family court welfare services in England and Wales are probably unique. In Northern Ireland, welfare reports are provided by social services departments (usually by Family and Child Care Teams), and, in Scotland, lawyers are also often instructed by courts to report on the views and interests of the child. In Australia, reports are prepared by counsellors employed by a specialist welfare service attached to the family courts. In many other jurisdictions, however, both elsewhere in Europe and in the USA, child welfare reports in divorce proceedings are frequently prepared by experts (often psychologists) who are appointed directly by the courts on a case-by-case basis.

For Further Reading
James, A. 1995: Social work in divorce: welfare, mediation and justice. *International Journal of Law and the Family*, 9, 256–74.
James, A. and Hay, W. 1993: *Court Welfare in Action: Practice and Theory*. London: Harvester Wheatsheaf.
James, A. and Sturgeon-Adams, L. 1999: *Helping Families after Divorce: Assistance by Order?* Bristol: Policy Press/Joseph Rowntree Foundation.

ADRIAN L. JAMES

Domestic Violence

Domestic violence is the term commonly used to refer to violence against women by a partner (husband or cohabitant, ex-husband or ex-partner) in the context of intimate relationships within the family. The terms *violence against women* and *woman abuse* as well as the older term *wifebeating* are also used. All of the terms generally refer to the physical and/or sexual abuse of a woman by her male partner/husband and may extend to include psychological abuse and other forms of controlling, aggressive and intimidating behaviours.

The common pattern in domestic violence

There have been three historical periods when violence against 'wives' became a public issue and was responded to by reformers and agencies of the state – the 1870s, the 1910s and from the 1970s to the present. At each time, the issue was publicly recognized, statistics were gathered, explanations were offered and new laws and policies were introduced. For each period, the move to public recognition and reform was lead by a vigorous women's movement. Increasing progress has been made away from the traditional acceptance of this form of violence in public opinion, professional practice and official legislation and policy to increasing intolerance of the violence, accompanied by diverse efforts meant to provide support for abused women and to eliminate men's violence.

Research findings show that, across time and across cultures, violence in marital and marital-like relationships is overwhelmingly asymmetrical, with men as the usual perpetrators and women the usual victims. While much of this violence remains unreported, findings from depth-interviews, crime statistics and victim surveys reveal that between 10 and 25 per cent of all 'married' women have experienced violence from their male partner at some time during their life. The nature of the violence ranges from slapping and shoving to domestic homicide. The most common form of physical attack is punching and kicking usually resulting in injuries such as bruising and cuts and, sometimes, broken bones and teeth. Evidence suggests that acts of physical violence are usually accompanied by threats as well as other acts of aggression, coercion and intimidation, and violent events may also include acts of sexual violence.

Across societies, homicides in domestic settings are, for the most part, the killing of wives – *uxoricide* – which usually occurs in the context of a history of sustained violence by the man against his woman partner. Abused women sometimes kill their husband or male partner, and this is commonly in the context of a history of his violence toward her. The rate of domestic or spousal homicides varies across countries, but it usually includes a history of male violence directed at the woman that is known to the police as well as to health care providers and the social services. While homicide is an unusual outcome of domestic assaults, it nonetheless represents a significant proportion of all the homicides of women and, in some countries, accounts for a considerable proportion of all homicides.

continued

Explaining and responding to domestic violence

Various explanations have been proposed including social and individual pathologies; interactional, situational and family dynamics; and institutional, cultural and ideological forces. Male domination, power and control are important elements in many of the theoretical perspectives. Historical, anthropological and contemporary research persistently reveals that conflicts associated with male sexual possessiveness of women and women's domestic labour (for example, food preparation, house cleaning and childcare) are frequently associated with men's violent responses. Individual backgrounds linked to the learning of male domination and violent behaviour are also important.

This problem simultaneously involves researchers, social activists and policy makers. Activists have been central in placing the issue on the public agenda, defining it as a problem of social importance and engaging the state and voluntary and statutory agencies in the process of changing policies and practices. Researchers have added systematic knowledge about the nature and extent of the violence itself, and undertaken evaluations of the effectiveness of various interventions. Policy makers have supported policies and programmes intended to reduce or eliminate the problem, and to provide support for abused women and their children. Particular attention has focused on providing housing and refuge for abused women, and on criminal justice responses. The evidence shows that housing and shelter provide important sanctuaries for women and children, and that criminal justice based cognitive-behavioural programmes for abusers are more effective in eliminating subsequent violence than other responses from the justice system.

Overall, the evidence about domestic violence tells a common story, of a problem that is fairly widespread in most societies, of violence perpetrated by men against women partners, of increasing public awareness, and of developments in legislation and interventions focused on different responses to abused women, to the men who abuse and to the children who witness and/or live in the atmosphere of such events. During the last quarter of the twentieth century, there were numerous changes in law and law enforcement, and in the social and health care services of many nations throughout the world. For the most part, these developments have followed a pattern of responses that reflect a growing awareness of the issue and innovations in responses to the women who are abused, the men who perpetrate the abuse, and the children who reside in such households and, thus, witness such violence and live with its consequences.

For Further Reading

Dobash, R. E. and Dobash, R. P. 1992: *Women, Violence and Social Change*. London: Routledge.
Dobash, R. E. and Dobash, R. P. 1998: *Rethinking Violence Against Women*. London and Thousand Oaks, California: Sage.
Mullender, A. 1996: *Rethinking Domestic Violence: The Social Work and Probation Response*. London: Routledge.

REBECCA EMERSON DOBASH AND RUSSELL P. DOBASH

Drop-in Centres

Drop-in centres provide day care for vulnerable people using a more informal approach than other services such as day centres. The nature and aims of each drop-in centre will largely depend on who runs the service. Most centres are run by voluntary organizations and staffed by professionals, although many encourage user involvement, and a few centres are run entirely by users.

The aim of drop-in centres is usually to provide advice, support and social contact for a specific group of service users. For example, drop-in centres run by local MIND groups generally aim to provide a safe space for people with mental health problems to talk with staff or other users. Informal social contact is the key element to many drop-ins, although some centres hold structured sessions, such as specialist advice or self-help groups. The informality of drop-in services is often beneficial to people with chaotic lifestyles who have difficulty keeping appointments, such as homeless people or substance misusers. Drop-in centres may therefore be seen as complementing other more formal services or as an alternative to them.

For Further Reading
Morgan, S. 1993: *Community Mental Health*. London: Chapman and Hall.

MARK DRINKWATER

Drug Misuse

Drug misuse may be defined as the socially disapproved and inappropriate consumption of illegal substances, possibly with undesirable consequences regarding physical and/or psychological health, social relationships, education and/or employment, and involvement with the criminal justice system.

A continuum of use can be described: from experimentation, through recreational use, to problematic misuse and increasing tolerance, to more chronic 'abuse' and a state of physical and/or psychological dependence or 'addiction'. However, the terms *abuse* and *addiction* are often seen as value-loaded. *Misuse* or *problem drug use* are usually preferred in care practice, although some clinicians may still adopt *addiction*, especially in the USA.

Different substances, different factors
Different substances, illegal or legal, have different effects: barbiturates, tranquillizers, heroin, alcohol are depressants; amphetamines, cocaine, caffeine, tobacco are stimulants; cannabis relaxes; LSD is hallucinogenic; Ecstasy (MDMA) produces mild visual distortion. Actual behaviour, patterns of use, physical responses and subjective experience will all be strongly shaped by other influences: personal characteristics (for example, the individual's physiology or mental health), expectations, specific context of use, culture and sub-culture, strength and purity versus adulteration of drugs. Internationally, the most commonly used illegal drug is cannabis, but heroin and cocaine arouse greatest social concern. In the UK, deaths caused by illicit drugs amount to a few hundreds per year, by no means approaching mortality figures related to alcohol- and tobacco-related disease. Media coverage tends to sensationalize messages about illegal drugs.

Certain drugs are designated as prohibited according to various domestic laws and international Conventions. In the UK, it is not drug use *per se* that is illegal but possession and/or trade (dealing/trafficking). The classification of illegal drugs is a tiered system reflecting official perceptions of their relative harmfulness: Class A drugs include strong opiates (for example, heroin), cocaine, LSD and Ecstasy; Class B include cannabis, amphetamines and barbiturates; Class C, tranquillizers and some mild stimulants. Maximum penalties are highest regarding Class A, lowest regarding Class C; they may take the form of custodial sentences, financial orders (confiscation of assets or fines) or diversionary sentences (referral to treatment and counselling, and/or community service). The links between drug misuse and crime are debated. Some argue the illegality of drugs makes them expensive and, hence, users must turn to crime (for example, burglary or shoplifting) to afford them. Others argue that it is participation within a delinquent/criminal milieu that will introduce an individual to subsequent drug misuse.

History, policy and practice in the UK
Use of heroin spread dramatically during the 1980s, then declined, but returned from the mid-1990s. The late-1980s saw considerable alarm about crack-cocaine: serious

continued

misuse in certain urban areas became evident but prevalence has not approached the levels once sensationally predicted or experienced in the USA. Through the 1990s, Ecstasy, amphetamine and LSD caused official concern.

Prohibition of drugs is relatively recent. The use of opiates was common in the nineteenth century. The early twentieth century saw emergence of a medical view of drug misuse as addictive or as a disease requiring treatment, and a moral/legal view of it as a vice requiring control (Berridge, 1998). By the 1970s, policy and legislation accepted a distinction between *soft* and *hard* drugs, and between *users* and *dealers*. In the UK, the Misuse of Drugs Act 1971 drew an enduring distinction between offences of *possession* and of *supply*. In the 1980s, the coincidence of the rise in heroin consumption (now by smoking the drug – 'chasing the dragon', as well as by intravenous injection) alongside fears about AIDS/HIV transmission by the shared use of syringes, encouraged the development of harm-reduction approaches to drug misuse. This new agenda challenged the clinical goal of 'withdrawal leading to abstinence', and opened up new directions in treatment, education, counselling, prevention and outreach work. Funding was provided to establish numerous new drugs agencies. In the 1990s, Drug Action Teams and Drug Reference Groups were new local fora for specialist and generic services with social care, prevention, health and enforcement remits.

Debates concerning *decriminalization* or *legalization* (not the same thing) of drugs are recurrent. One supporting argument is that, at present, illegal drugs cause less harm than legal drugs: it is their illegality that is responsible for related harm (for example, adulteration, crime). A counter-argument is that legal drugs are widely available, illegal drugs are not: the health, social and crime-related consequences of widespread legal availability of prohibited substances are unknown. The decriminalization/legalization arguments are unlikely to gain government support in the foreseeable future. In particular, the international prohibitionist agreements would be a source of powerful opposition. However, as a positive alternative, harm-reduction, recognition of drug misuse as related to social and environmental problems, and the need for integrated community responses, are all now accepted in the UK as central to policy and practice programmes.

One argument is that it is now non-acquaintance with drugs or drug-users that has become the 'deviation from the norm'. Others argue that drug use has not become 'normal': acceptance of prohibitions, peer-group resistance, parental attachment and preference for alternative activities remain central to the lives of most young people. Both arguments (South, 1999) have some validity across late-modern societies and their implications are profound for professionals in social care, probation, policing and drugs prevention.

For Further Reading
Berridge, V. 1998: *Opium and the People*. London: Free Association Books.
South, N. (ed.) 1995: *Drugs, Crime and Criminal Justice (Vols 1 and 2)*. Aldershot: Dartmouth.
South, N. (ed.) 1999: *Drugs: Cultures, Controls and Everyday Life*. London: Sage.
NIGEL SOUTH

Table 3 The principal drugs in use in the UK

I *Drugs that depress the nervous system*	
Alcoholic beverages	Available in the UK through 170,000 licensed premises; over 90 per cent of adults drink to some extent
Benzodiazepines – minor tranquillizers (e.g. valium, mogadon)	The most commonly prescribed drugs in Britain; also available on the illicit market
Barbiturates	Once common; particularly dangerous drugs; now rarely seen on the streets
Solvents and gases (e.g. glue, lighter fuel, cleaning fluids or aerosols)	Recent British studies have found that between 7–10 per cent of secondary school pupils have tried solvents, and that sniffing peaks around the third and fourth years of secondary school.
GHB (liquid ecstasy)	Available in sex shops, sometimes at clubs
II *Drugs that reduce pain*	
Opiates, opioids, narcotic analgesics	Illicitly produced and imported, heroin (which can be smoked, swallowed, sniffed or injected) is the most widely misused of this class of drugs. There are perhaps 100,000–150,000 regular users in the UK.
III *Drugs that stimulate the nervous system*	
Amphetamines (e.g. speed)	After cannabis, probably the most widely misused controlled drug
Cocaine (e.g. coke or crack)	Coke is sniffed or injected; crack is smoked; widely available on the illicit market, but more expensive than other stimulants
Caffeine	Taken regularly by the great majority of the British people in tea, coffee or cocoa
Tobacco	Although smoking is increasingly discouraged in public or work places, tobacco is widely available in shops; 38 per cent of UK adults smoke it.
Anabolic steroids	Available in some health clubs, its use is quite widespread and is increasing. In some needle exchanges, 50 per cent of the clients are steroid users.
Alkyl nitrates	Sometimes called *poppers*; the vapours are inhaled.
Hallucinogenic amphetamines (ecstasy or E)	Ecstasy use peaked in the early to mid-1990s. In 1996, it was estimated that 5 per cent of the UK adult population and one in eight of young people between ages of 20–24 had used the drug.
Khat	Used mainly by refugees from Africa
Legal highs (e.g. ephedrine)	Not widely available, but can be bought in some herbalists and at festivals
IV *Drugs that alter perceptual function*	
LSD (also called *acid*)	Commonly available on the illicit market, surveys show that up to 10 per cent of those aged 16–24 might have tried the drug.
Hallucinogenic (or magic) mushrooms	Surveys suggest that for the UK as a whole, one in ten school-leavers might have tried mushrooms, while one in five will have done so in some parts of Scotland and Wales. The mushrooms grow wild.
Cannabis	Smoked by itself or with tobacco, cannabis has the greatest non-medical usage of all drugs controlled in the UK under the Misuse of Drugs Act 1971: The British Crime Survey showed that a third of those surveyed in the 16–29 age range had tried cannabis, with a half of this group using it regularly.
DMT	Snorted or swallowed, but usually smoked; limited availability
Ketamine (or Special K)	Normally used for medical or veterinary purposes; sometimes diverted and sold on the illicit market

Extracted with permission and in an abbreviated form from *Drug Abuse Briefing (Seventh Edition)*, (1999), written and published by the Institute for the Study of Drug Dependence. Grateful acknowledgement is made to the ISDD for permission to reproduce this material; readers are referred to the Institute's *Briefing* for more detailed information about the effects of drug usage.

Drugs Principally Used in the UK

The drugs principally used in the UK are listed in Table 3.

For Further Reading
Coomber, R. (ed.) 1994: *Drugs and Drug Use in Society: A Critical Reader*. Greenwich: Greenwich University Press.
Gossop, M. 1996: *Living with Drugs* (4th edn). Aldershot: Arena.
Robson, P. 1994: *Forbidden Drugs: Understanding Drugs and Why People take Them*. Oxford: Oxford University Press.

DRUGSCOPE

Dual Diagnosis

The description of *dual diagnosis* is vague, subjective and confusing. Most frequently, it is used to describe co-existing problems: most commonly a person with mental health and addiction problems (either alcohol, illicit drugs or both). However, it can also be found as a label for people with learning disabilities and mental health needs, or substance-related problems, or eating disorders. Essentially, it refers to concurrent problems or needs – not always resulting from a medical diagnosis; these needs are frequently addressed by separate organizational or professional services. As with many terms, work in the USA has been influential; in the UK, the term *comorbidity* is often encountered across medical/psychiatric interfaces.

The challenges arising from dual diagnosis stem from efforts to distinguish between primary and secondary diagnosis, and the possible complex interactions between problems. A label of dual diagnosis may be associated with higher levels of unpredictable response to treatment and the service environment. Its use evokes possibilities of increased levels of violence, suicide and therapeutic pessimism.

The dual diagnosis label may also challenge services which lack experience and resources to cross traditional boundaries. Gaps in services have been identified and a variety of possible developments have been proposed – such as out-reach teams, intensive care management, co-ordinated services, joint training and collaborative working at professional and agency levels. Research points to a need for caution in applying the term but the high proportion of service users within social services, health and the criminal justice systems who have complex needs spanning services may explain the popularity of the term. The phrase *double jeopardy* may also be found, indicating the risk of co-existing problems.

For Further Reading
Rorstad, P., Cheinski, K., McGeachy, O. and Ward, M. (eds) 1996: *Dual Diagnosis: Facing the Challenge*. Kenley: Wynne Howard Publishing.

JILL MANTHORPE

E

Eating Disorders

Eating disorders are primary disorders of weight control by manipulation of eating behaviours. Overeating, associated with psychological problems, is classified as an eating disorder, but the central conditions are *anorexia* and *bulimia nervosa*. These are considered as separate entities, but share characteristic symptoms: morbid fear of fatness, (body image disturbance and linkage of self-worth) and behaviours (calorie restriction, purging possibly by vomiting, laxative or diuretic ingestion, and excessive exercise). Both disorders can lead to serious (sometimes fatal) physical complications but also need to be distinguished from physical conditions causing weight loss. They are often associated with other psychiatric conditions including depression, anxiety and personality disorders.

Although commoner in western adolescent women, they are increasingly reported outside this group. There are many theories of aetiology; one popular idea is that weight is one area of control in a life where much feels beyond control. There is likely to be a complex interplay between socio-cultural, biological and psychological factors, and these must all be given consideration in the process of management.

For Further Reading

American Psychiatric Association 1993: Practice guidelines for eating disorders. *American Journal of Psychiatry*, 150 (2), 208–28.

CLAIRE KENWOOD AND
RAY VIEWEG

Ecological Approach to Social Work

The *ecological approach to social work* adopts a systems framework and, to understand the ways in which personal functioning is affected, focuses on the mutual interactions between individuals, their families, communities and the wider society. Social work assessments within this approach consider the balance between stressors and supports, or risks and protective factors. There is an emphasis on people's subjective experience of their lives because many health and welfare outcomes have been found to depend upon an individual's interpretation of their circumstances relative to other members of their society.

An example of the application of this approach is provided by the work of Garbarino and his colleagues in the USA. They have revealed the way in which differences in the social support networks that exist in otherwise similar neighbourhoods affect rates of officially notified child maltreatment. The importance of the ecological perspective for social work lies in its ability to reveal the complex web of social interactions which help to shape personal behaviour and which need to be considered in the construction of preventative and therapeutic interventions.

For Further Reading

Jack, G. 1997: An ecological approach to social work with children and families. *Child and Family Social Work*, 2, 109–20.

GORDON JACK

Education and Training for Social Work

Social work education and training comprises the structures and processes of learning towards assessment for a professional qualification in social work which is recognized, where applicable, for registration, licence to practise, entry into jobs with protected title or activities, and membership of a professional association. This is known as the *professional* or *qualifying level*. It embodies definitions of purpose, learning models and participation by students in constructing their professional identities. The term also refers to learning for further and advanced qualifications in social work.

continued

Social work education and training at the tertiary educational level is found world-wide, but there is no single universal model. Its patterns and levels of growth are rooted in national histories which shape and mediate the forms of social work through the effects of economic policy, political agenda, legal frameworks and dominant ideologies, religions and cultures. Cross-national generalizations and statistics must be treated with caution.

The background to social work training

The precursors of modern schools of social work appeared in the UK, mainland Europe and the USA in the 1890s and early 1900s, initiated by charitable movements, labour groups, movements of women and the churches. Growth of new schools took place world-wide and, in 1928, the International Association of Schools of Social Work was founded in Paris. By 1937, there were 179 schools of social work in 32 countries, but international co-operation was disrupted by World War II and the long-term division of Europe. Social work practice and training grew and professionalized with post-war reconstruction, economic expansion and the demands of widening state services, although these trends were dislocated and reshaped by responses to the Western economic crisis of the 1970s and subsequent marketization, managerialism and long-term restructuring.

By the mid-1990s, there were approximately 1,700 schools of social work in 100 countries and annual intakes across 19 European countries were estimated at around 29,000. Social work education had re-emerged in China, in post-communist Central and Eastern Europe, and in Russia and the Republics. A century from their early origins, schools in the USA had close to 580 accredited programmes producing 28,000 qualified social workers (1997), while the UK's 96 programmes were producing around 4,500 social workers a year in 1998. Women, the main participants in the early programmes, still comprised 75 per cent or more of those qualifying in the UK and USA, and were in a majority in numerous other countries.

Structural questions

In UK and similar Western-based models, formal provision of social work education at the professional level typically confronts a number of structural questions. These include determining:

- the parts to be played in planning and delivering the programmes by educational institutions, service agencies, service users and students, and the sources of funding;
- the level of academic award, entry requirements, credit arrangements and equal opportunities policies;
- curriculum and assessment content, their generic and specialist components and their relationship to defined standards and future employment roles;
- minimum periods of study and structures for full-time, part-time or distance learning;
- requirements for practice learning and the qualifications of practice teachers;
- any pre-registration practice requirements and arrangements for progression to advanced learning;
- boundaries and overlap with adjacent professions and arrangements for interdisciplinary learning;
- measures for accrediting programmes, evaluating their outcomes and supporting development.

These are not neutral administrative questions, but areas of contest between key interests in social work education, the outcomes of which shape its nature and variations. Countries differ in how they are determined, arguing the respective merits of centralization and autonomy, but where there exists a national or state department, council or association with designated authority, responsibility for making or delegating the decisions commonly rests with such a body.

Models of learning

Social work education and training is also shaped by models of learning:

- A *technical* model is based on the acquisition of pre-defined knowledge and skills and their application.
- *Critical pedagogy* is concerned with understanding social position in power hierarchies constructed through class, gender, race and other dimensions of oppression and aimed at empowerment and social change.
- *Andragogy* utilizes the adult student's experience and motivation and fosters self-directed learning.

Andragogy articulates with *learner-centred* approaches and with the non-positivistic *reflective learning* school. Models may co-exist in programmes or one may predominate.

Purpose and priorities

Education and training is shaped further by ascendant definitions of purpose and priorities. Definitions may be professionally led by its teachers and practitioners, consumer-led by students or service users, or managerially led by employers or government. Managerially led, and some consumer-led definitions are associated with the pursuit of work-force competence through vocationalism which is favoured for its attention to outcomes and the sharpened objectives this can bring, but attacked for technical reductionism and de-professionalizing social work. Some professionally led definitions set aside the synonymous use here of *education* and *training*, and invoke *education* to signify the academic knowledge and development of critical skills necessary to effective professional practice and enhanced status of the qualification. The development of holistic models of competence encompassing higher-order abilities of cognition and reflection offers some reconciliation of the positions, although underlying disputes remain about curriculum priorities, for example, as between critical theoretical content and learning for efficient service delivery.

Despite national differences in social work education, cross-national commonalities are evident – for example, in the post-war influence of American practice methodologies and in the subsequent exploration of radical and postmodern alternatives. They are apparent in the recurrence, in academic and practice curricula, of human science derived paradigms, social services knowledge, law, social work methods and values. They appear also in the determination of African, Asian and Pacific, Central and South American and East European schools of social work in the post-colonial and post-communist periods to develop authentic, locally relevant curricula and pedagogies to augment or replace Western models. The globalization thesis predicts that both international influences and local nationalisms will increasingly affect the patterns and concepts of social work education and training, as the hold of older nation-states weakens.

For Further Reading

Gould, N. and Taylor, I. (eds) 1996: *Reflective Learning for Social Work*. Aldershot: Ashgate.

Usher, R., Bryant, I. and Johnston, R. 1997: *Adult Education and the Postmodern Challenge*. London: Routledge.

Watts, T. D. Elliot, D. and Myadas, N. (eds) 1996: *International Handbook on Social Work Education*. London: Greenwood Press.

COLIN WHITTINGTON

Education Social Work

Education social work refers to social work practice conducted within the education sector and directed towards children of school age – generally those aged between 5 and 16 years, although education social workers may also be working with both younger children and older young people – and their families. The aim of education social work is to ensure that children obtain optimum benefit from a meaningful educational experience.

Education social work in the UK has its origins in the school attendance enforcement service established in the late nineteenth century accompanying the introduction of universal compulsory education. The designation *education welfare*, rather than education social work, is employed in many parts of the country, while in a number of English-speaking countries world-wide, the term *school social work* is more likely to be utilized. Education social workers are employed by public education authorities throughout the UK, which also administer most schools within the public education system. Since there are no national standards or requirements concerning education social work practice or qualification, major variations between employing agencies exist concerning the deployment of staff, their training and their workload although, given their origins, the enforcement of school attendance remains a central brief.

Resourcing and deployment

Although reliable statistics are difficult to acquire, there is evidence of education social worker : student ratios ranging from 1 : 719 to 1 : 10,035, with a national average ratio of 1 : 2,443. This itself is considerably less advantageous than the ratio of 1 : 2,000 considered by the professional association, the National Association of Social Workers in Education, to be necessary to provide 'an effective professional service to ensure that children's interests are adequately safeguarded and effective preventative work carried out' (Blyth and Milner, 1997). It is estimated that approximately one-fifth of education social work staff throughout the country hold a recognized social work qualification, although some education social workers possess youth work or teaching qualifications. The general lack of qualifications is recognized as posing problems for the professional standing and credibility of education social workers in relation to other groups in both education and social work.

Resourcing pressures have been maintained as a consequence of the process initiated by the Conservative government in the 1980s to 'roll back the frontiers of the state' and reduce expenditure on publicly funded services. Within education, this resulted in disproportionate reductions for support services, such as education social work, as education authorities sought to maintain the value of resources directed towards schools.

The tasks of education social work

In addition to attendance work, education social workers may find themselves involved in a range of welfare activities concerned with school-age children, few of which would be unfamiliar to social workers employed in other settings:

- Working with disabled children and children with formal statements of *special educational need* in accordance with statutory provision
- Child protection
- Monitoring and regulation of the employment of school children
- Working with pre-school age children – for example, assisting parents/carers to obtain nursery placements

- Home–school liaison
- Interagency liaison
- Preventative programmes on misuse of alcohol, drugs and other substances
- Working with children exhibiting disruptive behaviour and/or at risk of exclusion from school
- Securing alternative education provision for persistent non-attenders and children excluded from school
- Providing individual and/or group work for children with particular difficulties (for example, regarding attendance, behaviour or relationship difficulties) and/or their parents/carers
- Providing information/advocacy/mediation for children excluded from school and their parents/carers
- Providing in-service training for other education staff
- Participating in the juvenile justice system
- Preparing reports for courts
- Providing advice/administration concerning welfare benefits
- Working with pregnant girls and school-age mothers
- Working with young people who provide care for sick or disabled family members
- Working with children from traveller families

The context of education social work practice

Contemporary education social work practice is influenced by increasing awareness of the value of education, as illustrated by the leader of the Labour party – and subsequently Prime Minister – during the 1997 UK general election campaign and the early establishment by the Labour government of a Social Exclusion Unit, whose first report, published in the summer of 1998, focused on truancy and exclusion from school. At the same time, the idea that schools have a valuable welfare role, in addition to their purely educational functions, gained increasing support (Gilligan, 1998). Examination of how schools impact on the behaviour and life experiences of their pupils has promoted development of the *whole school* concept – which ensures that responsibility for problem solving is shared among all members of the school community, and not simply regarded as the exclusive responsibility of specialist pastoral and welfare staff.

Finally, given the centrality of attendance-related work to education social work, dominant assumptions about non-attendance pose significant challenges for education social work. Government (both Conservative and Labour) belief in a causal relationship between non-attendance and involvement in juvenile delinquency has promoted a punitive, legalistic approach to the management of non-attendance, thus demonstrating the need for the continual assertion of social work values, especially given the failure of UK education legislation and practice to endorse the spirit of the UN Convention on the Rights of the Child.

Conclusion

Working practices in education social work, its role and relationships within both schools and the wider welfare network, need to respond to these pressures to ensure that children maximize their educational opportunities. While lack of professional qualifications, associated marginalized status and lack of clear national expectations pose obvious difficulties, the latter in particular and the freedom from the restrictions of the school timetable and statutory child protection responsibilities experienced by teachers and child-care social workers respectively, nevertheless provide opportunities for creative and innovative endeavour.

continued

For Further Reading

Blyth, E. and Milner, J. 1997: *Social Work with Children: The Educational Perspective.* Harlow: Longman.

Central Council for Education and Training in Social Work 1992: *Preparing for Work in the Education Welfare Service: Improving Social Work Education and Training, 13.* London: CCETSW.

Gilligan, R. 1998: The importance of schools and teachers in child welfare. *Child and Family Social Work,* 3, 13–26.

ERIC BLYTH

Efficiency, Economy and Effectiveness

See AUDIT IN THE PUBLIC SECTOR.

Elder Abuse

Elder abuse has been defined by Action on Elder Abuse as a 'single or repeated act, or lack of appropriate action occurring within any relationship where there is an expectation of trust, which causes harm or distress to an older person'. It owes its origins as a social problem to the identification of *granny bashing* or *battering* in the 1970s, when it evolved as part of a wider feminized consciousness concerning domestic and inter-personal violence. Its emergence can also be traced to a growing preoccupation with the poor quality of life among older people living in institutions.

The nature of elder abuse

The term incorporates mistreatment and neglect of older people, and has been categorized as taking the following forms: physical, emotional (or psychological), financial, sexual and neglect. There are clear parallels with the abuse of people with learning disabilities, and many statutory bodies have responded by creating multi-agency policies with procedures/guidelines to assist practitioners, some drawn up in relation to older people, others more broadly in respect of (vulnerable) adults.

Risk factors for elder abuse have moved from explanatory models of carer stress to an emphasis on dependency and, latterly, pathology within dysfunctional families and relationships. In institutions, the role of power and organizational cultures has been highlighted, while a feminist approach to abusive family dynamics has been developed.

Within the UK, the potential for current law to provide a framework for intervention has been questioned. There is no framework comparable to that for children. The Law Commission's reports in the 1990s sought to develop a system balancing imperatives for self-determination and protection, particularly relating to those lacking mental capacity.

Developments in the USA have been influential world-wide. US researchers have produced findings relating to prevalence and incidence. US models of intervention have been researched: the findings are presented through its National Committee for the Prevention of Elder Abuse (Baumhover and Beall, 1997).

The experiences and views of survivors of elder abuse have begun to inform research and practice. It is clear that while many older people who are abused may be very frail or have dementia, their status as adults requires them to be empowered to make choices, including the refusal of help and the rejection of simplistic labels of *victim* or *survivor*.

Counteracting elder abuse

Much writing on the subject reflects two contrasting discourses: the theoretical or conceptual, and the pragmatic or service-driven approach.

- *Theoretical explanations* draw attention to interpersonal issues and the characteristics of victims/survivors and abusers/perpetrators. Other theoretical analyses focus on the importance of ageism and the devaluing of care within social exchanges.
- *Pragmatic responses* require services and professionals to address 'new' problems and to reassure policy makers, the public and interest groups representing older people, that abuse will not be tolerated. Difficulties remain, however, in imparting assurance as 'abuse' remains definitionally unclear and policy initiatives subject to other priorities.

Campaigns on elder abuse have succeeded in attracting support from a wide range of professionals. Training and research has been devised for multi-professional audiences with areas of expertise developed by certain key professional writers (Bennett et al., 1997). Social models of elder abuse appear to be widely accepted and these have promoted inter-agency collaboration.

The development of practice responses and models to deal with elder abuse are at early stages. Parallel debates exist within family or domestic settings and the institutional arenas. Developments in inspection and regulation of institutions reflect long-standing concerns about quality rather than abuse, though the growing use of the label of abuse may be prompting more of a 'policing' culture. Wider public and political debate about whistle blowing has identified the need for institutions to be more open and accountable. New checks on staff and agencies in all sectors may be ascribed to a climate of concern about the possibility of abuse and career abusers.

Within the domestic arena, the possibility of abuse, or being at risk of harm or neglect, has entered the language of assessment. Uncertainties remain, however, about compulsory (mandatory) reporting, the ethics of intervention and the ability of practitioners to respond without possibly causing further harm or distress (for example, by removal of an older person from home). A value base encompassing anti-ageist practice, citizenship and empowerment has been promoted as relevant to all practitioners: much of this is derived from social work values.

Continuing debates

Critics of the elder abuse enterprise raise the possibility of its infringing individual rights through increased observations of older people and alienating those who provide care in difficult circumstances. They also point to the danger of sensationalizing abuse and portraying older people as victims. The individualization of abuse as interpersonal may also serve to disguise some older people's views that an ageist society is abusive. Links between older people and those involved in elder abuse debates are undeveloped. Other criticisms relate to issues of language with *abuse*, *victim* and *perpetrator* seen as rigid and offensive terms in what may be mistreatment or inadequate care.

Elder abuse has entered professional vocabularies and service statements. However, care staff in particular have debated whether abusive behaviour among residents or between an older person and his/her carer should be labelled as abuse. A similar debate exists in relation to people with learning disabilities, where the emphasis has been on sexually abusive men. Elder abuse literature explores such issues, but some definitions restrict it to abuse directed to older people.

The UK government has responded to the emergence of elder abuse as a social problem through development of policies, education and training initiatives. The policy agenda addresses the problem piecemeal, with early attention to the protection of those lacking

continued

mental capacity and the revision of the inspection and regulatory framework for services.

For Further Reading
Baumhover, L. A. and Beall, S. C. (eds) 1997: *Abuse, Neglect and Exploitation of Older Persons: Strategies for Assessment and Intervention*. London: Jessica Kingsley.
Bennett, G., Kingston, P. and Penhale, B. 1997: *The Dimensions of Elder Abuse: Perspectives for Practitioners*. Basingstoke: Macmillan.
Decalmer, P. and Glendenning, F. (eds) 1997: *The Mistreatment of Elderly People*. London: Sage.

JILL MANTHORPE

Eldercare

The term *eldercare* can be used as a convenient shorthand for the care of older people. Although *older people* is the more acceptable terminology (and certainly never *the elderly*), eldercare has the advantage of brevity.

Care can be interpreted in a number of different ways including wider issues about the concern that a community may express. In the context of care for older people, however, it may include physical (for example, feeding and washing), financial (for example, help with money) and emotional (for example, counselling) support.

Care may be a two-way process with older people both giving and receiving care. The image of older people being a burden often fails to recognize the important unpaid work, such as grandparenting, which they do.

Who needs care?

There is clear evidence of a greater incidence of both acute and chronic illness among older people compared with other age groups. Some diseases, such as coronary heart disease and cancer, are strongly age-related but also have important environmental causes. Numbers of older people with depression are thought to be greatly underestimated. The prevalence of dementia increases with age with about one in five over the age of 85 suffering from this condition. For most problems, there is an increase with age: for example, difficulties with locomotion (such as going up and down stairs), with self-care (such as washing and feeding), and with domestic tasks (such as shopping) tend to increase considerably after the age of 85.

However, generalizations about the need for care are dangerous. For example, there are gender differences with older women being more prone to problems of impairment and disability in later life. There are some differences for older people from black and ethnic minorities (although not a homogeneous group) and, for this group, there is evidence of under-use of some services such as health. There are also some myths, such as that they all live in self-supporting families with no need for other forms of care.

There are also wide variations in the health and ability to cope among older people, with some very old people remaining very fit. Professionals can be particularly prone to view ageing as a time of automatic physical and mental decline because those whom they meet tend to be ill or frail. Nearly half of people aged 65 and over have no long standing chronic illness. The emphasis on a healthy lifestyle for younger people and on active ageing may lessen the need for care in later life.

Who gives care?

In most Western societies, most eldercare is mainly given by families. The role of the state across the world varies between a minimum of intervention to a highly sophisticated welfare system. In Western Europe, some degree of financial support is given by the state to almost all older people as is health care. While there is great variation in the extent of state help (usually at a local level), with domestic, personal care and mobility tasks, the role of informal help, mainly from families, is far greater. The only exception is over specialized tasks such as nursing and cutting toenails. The ability to give care often depends on proximity and so co-resident care is where the greatest intensity of care usually takes place. This is most likely to mean care by a spouse, who is usually also older, or a daughter. For the latter, this may affect their employment and entitlement to a pension.

It is likely that future generations of older people will be less willing to accept care in any form without questioning either the source or the standard. The movement towards advocacy and empowerment is leading to a new generation of older people who may demand certain forms of care and refuse others. For example, there is already some indication from Scandinavia that some older people would prefer care to come from professionals rather than from families.

It is possible that technology such as the development of active and passive alarms, may enhance the independence of many older people, and thus reduce the need for care. However, for those most in need, including those with dementia and with severe physical disabilities, it is likely that hands-on care from a person is what is wanted.

Where does care take place?

Most older people live in homes of their own. In the UK, only 5 per cent live in some kind of institution. Of the remainder, 90 per cent live in non-specialized housing and a further 5 per cent in sheltered housing. For these two groups, most care is given by family and friends. Of greatest concern, in most countries, because of the ageing of the population, is long-term or continuing care for those older people who need a great deal of care. Institutional care is expensive and disliked by most older people. The challenge for research and service providers is to find ways that older people can be kept in a home of their own. Offering very sheltered housing with enhanced facilities, including 24-hour care available on site and the provision of some meals, is one option. Other rapidly developing forms of care include intensive home care schemes.

Conclusion

The problem and challenge of eldercare concerns those who are at the edge of institutional care, but it must not be forgotten that they are likely to be the minority, that most care will continue to be provided informally and that older people are often the providers of care for their own age group and for younger people. Nor must the value of simple basic services (such as help with the cleaning), especially those aimed at prevention, be ignored.

For Further Reading

Allen, I. and Perkins, E. 1995: *The Future of Family Care for Older People*. London: HMSO.

Bernard, M. and Phillips, J. 1998: *The Social Policy of Old Age*. London: Centre for Policy on Ageing.

Tinker, A. 1997: *Older People in Modern Society*. London: Longman.

ANTHEA TINKER

Elderly Mentally Infirm (EMI)

The term *elderly mentally infirm (EMI)* usually refers to the spectrum of mental health conditions in old age often described as the dementias – i.e. not the affective (depressive) disorders, nor the psychotic ones. The term can be used generically to encompass all elderly mentally frail people regardless of the aetiology of that mental frailty. Dementias are being given increasingly complicated classifications: Alzheimer's disease, multi-infarct dementia, and the dementias associated with alcohol or brain damage. The latter, for example, may occur as a result of boxing, when it is known as *dementia pugilistica*.

EMI as a concept also serves as a means of indicating the level of care that will be needed to provide quality services for this group; EMI units should have higher staff ratios, should concentrate on retaining function – for example, by the use of reminiscence therapy and regimens designed to retain continence and enhance the quality of care.

PAUL KINGSTON

Elderly Persons Homes

See RESIDENTIAL AND INSTITUTIONAL PROVISION FOR OLDER PEOPLE.

Electronic Monitoring

See TAGGING.

Emotional Abuse and Neglect

Emotional abuse and neglect are here considered in the wider context of child abuse generally. The terms are used to describe behaviour by parents or caretakers towards children which is damaging to their well-being and/or development in particular ways.

Since the late 1960s, there has been increasing awareness in Britain of the damage done to children and young people by different forms of abuse within their families and in institutions. As the years have gone by, however, we have come to understand that the concept of abuse is both complex and contentious. At first, physical injury dominated the discussion; then, in the 1980s, attention focused on sexual abuse, including, increasingly, the activity of paedophile rings. During the 1990s, there emerged widespread professional anxiety about the effects of emotional abuse and neglect on children. This is reflected in the numbers of children in the child protection register categorized under the headings of emotional abuse and/or neglect. These numbers, especially in regard to neglect, have been rising steeply, to the point when, in a majority of local authorities, they are higher than in the categories of physical or sexual abuse.

But what do these words mean? What is 'emotional abuse'? What is 'neglect'? Are they the same?

Neglect

To develop normally, all children from infancy require systematic attention by adults to a range of needs, physical, emotional, intellectual and social. In the early years, particularly, those needs are intertwined and are usually met in close relationships with parents or carers. Thus, *neglect* can, and often does, embrace all four dimensions. However, whether neglect is considered to be abuse is essentially about its extent and persistence. We may use the word neglect in its day-to-day sense ('omission of care') without implying that the child in question falls within the group which need protection from abuse.

The dilemma for all concerned professionals is to decide if the threshold has been reached when the formal designation of neglect is required.

The various dimensions of neglect should be taken into account in making such a decision. In the past, there has been a concentration on the obvious physical aspects of the problem – poor hygiene or diet, and dirty home conditions, for example. In seriously neglectful families, though, there are often other associated problems: for instance, a lack of attention to health problems, and difficulty in providing consistent warmth and attention. Just as worrying is neglect of young childrens' needs for intellectual stimulation: this has been least well understood by social workers.

There is ample research from many different fields to prove that such deprivation of care has adverse and sometimes irreparable effects on development; this evidence has been summarized by Stevenson (1998). However, there are many difficulties still within the judicial process in proving that a particular case of neglect is attributable to the omission of care by the adults (and, in criminal cases, that it is deliberate), and that it has caused or is likely to cause 'significant harm' – the legal test in the Children Act 1989. Obviously, it requires more detailed and holistic assessment than, for instance, abuse resulting in a fractured skull or abuse in the form of rape. However, it is increasingly accepted that persistent and pervasive neglect must be regarded as abusive and, hence, falls into the formal categories of abuse used within the British child welfare services. There is also much psychiatric, psychological and clinical evidence of the long-standing adverse effects of emotional abuse. (Iwaniec, 1995).

Emotional abuse

What of emotional abuse? Even if all serious neglect is emotionally abusive, the converse is not necessarily the case. Adults can be emotionally abusive to children in diverse ways: through sadistic threatening verbal behaviour or gross over-protection, for example. Such cases are much less common than those of neglect but they may give rise to much anxious concern in those who seek to help the children and see the pain which the children have to endure.

In both neglect and emotional abuse, questions are often raised about the relevance of different cultures to the application of the concepts. To what extent do we see these problems through the lens of our own particular society, class, ethnic or religious group? Would some adult behaviours be considered quite acceptable to some and unacceptable to others? Do social workers have a particular 'angle' on such matters? These are complicated matters. It is obviously true that there are many variations on child-rearing practices and the values (such as obedience) that underpin them. All social workers should be aware of the effects on their practice of their own cultural and familial experiences, and will need to distinguish between peripheral concerns (such as table manners) and basic tenets of 'good enough' child care. However, it is possible to become too 'hung up' about these matters, especially when one is, rightly, anxious to avoid accusations of ethnic or class bias. Especially in neglect, there is much common ground between cultures as to what constitutes necessary care, and, even in emotional abuse, the behaviour and reactions of the child can give a good picture of whether adult attitudes are damaging. Indeed, it is sometimes suggested that social workers accept lower parental standards than the neighbourhood community. Such discussion, however, needs to take into account that child abuse in general is a socially constructed concept – there is no absolute definition.

This discussion shows how difficult is the task of assessing neglect and emotional abuse within the formal parameters of child abuse and the systems in place to protect children. Social workers find it hard to separate the damage or potential damage to children from the issue of parental blame. If the parents are poor, themselves deprived or damaged, or of limited ability, for example, it is easy for sympathy for them to deflect attention from the primary goal of safeguarding children. It may be that more emphasis on early prevention and more family support will lessen this tension. However, there is research evidence (Gaudin, 1993) that changing the behaviour of neglectful parents within a time-scale that meets the children's needs is very difficult. It may be that greater emphasis on supplementary care for the children as well as helping the parents would pay dividends.

continued

For Further Reading
Gaudin, J. 1993: *Child Neglect: a Guide for Intervention*. Washington: National Center on Child Abuse and Neglect, US Department of Health and Human Services.
Iwaniec, D. 1995: *The Emotionally Abused and Neglected Child: Identification, Assessment and Intervention*. Chichester: John Wiley.
Stevenson, O. 1998: *Neglected Children: Issues and Dilemmas*. Oxford: Blackwell Science.
OLIVE STEVENSON

Emotional Development

Emotional development is the maturation of the expression of personal emotions and recognition of the emotions of others. Infants express only contentment or distress, but by a few weeks show basic emotions and, by eight months, display a wide range. During the first year, infants can distinguish and react to the emotional states of others. In some circumstances, they may check the emotion of the primary caretaker before responding (social referencing). From about eighteen months, they begin to talk about emotions, first their own and then those of others. From this age, they can also demonstrate active empathy towards others, although it is based on what they themselves would find comforting. In the third year, they develop an awareness that another person's feelings may be different from their own and can comment on the cause of emotional states. From the fourth year, the 'theory of mind' develops, whereby children infer mental states of others and recognize that their perspective can be different. At around six or seven, children understand more complex emotions that depend on the reactions of others, such as guilt, pride and shame.

For Further Reading
Smith, P. K. and Cowie, H. 1991: *Understanding Children's Development*. Oxford: Blackwell Publishers.
BRIGID DANIEL

Emotional Disorders

Emotional disorders have been used to denote a wide variety of clinical disorders including anxiety, depression, 'neurotic' disorder; the term is non-specific in application. The International Classification of Diagnoses [ICD-10] retains this as a group category in childhood disorders as the equivalent to adult neurotic disorders.

For Further Reading
World Health Organization 1992: *The ICD-10 Classification of Mental and Behavioral Disorders: Clinical descriptions and diagnostic guidelines*. Geneva: World Health Organization.
CLAIRE KENWOOD AND RAY VIEWEG

Empathy

Empathy is one of the three core conditions for the practice of successful therapy, together with genuineness and warmth, according to Carl Rogers's client-centred model. It requires the worker to listen and attend respectfully to the client in such a way as to form as full an understanding as possible of the client's situation in all its aspects, and to communicate that understanding to the client. This deeply interpersonal interaction resembles the 'encounter' that Rogers speaks of in relation to group experience. If the client feels empathized with, the safe framework thus established will facilitate the further exploration of problematic material.
CAROL KEDWARD

Empowerment

For service users, *empowerment* means challenging their disempowerment, having more control over their lives, being able to influence others and bring about change. There has been an explosion of interest in the idea of empowerment in social care. This reflects broader interest in a concept which transcends conventional politics and ideology, addresses both the *personal* and *political*, and seeks to unite the two. Empowerment has become a key concept in social work and social care. It is now central in political, social policy, educational, cultural, sexual, personal and managerial discourses, as well as entering popular usage. At the same time, there are concerns among social care service users and professionals that the term has been reduced to jargon through over-use and lack of clarity.

There is little agreement about the definition of empowerment. The political right, for example, based its use of the term on its view of the state's capacity to meet individual needs as problematic, defining empowerment as increasing people's control over public services through citizen's charters, chartermarks and government hotlines. Empowerment's dominant popular meaning is also individualistic, but generally signifies little more than *feeling* good or powerful.

Models of empowerment

Many different strands can be identified in the development of the idea and usage of empowerment. There are self-help, liberational, professional, managerialist and market models of empowerment. They are in complex relationship with each other. While there are overlaps between them, there are also important differences. Empowerment has become the site of key struggles over the nature and purpose of politics, policy, services and professional intervention. That is why its meanings are heavily contested and it is important to recognize its *regulatory* as well as its *liberatory* potential.

The two approaches to empowerment most in evidence in social work and social policy are the *professional* and *liberational* ones. Professional interest in empowerment developed in response to the new demands of the consumerist care market. The idea offers human service professions like social work, facing uncertainty and insecurity, new arguments for their own autonomy and consolidation by emphasizing the prior need for *their* empowerment if they are to empower service users. The concept has been embraced enthusiastically as providing a new paradigm for practice, giving it vitality, legitimacy and credibility. Empowerment is offered as both an aim for welfare staff and a means for them to achieve it.

The professional definition of empowerment sees professional intervention as the route to service users' empowerment. Disabled people's and social care service users' organizations are suspicious of these claims and aspirations. They have not only learned to be wary of the ambiguities of professional practice (its concern to regulate as well as to support), but they do not necessarily see it as having any role to play in their empowerment at all. Others see a role for professional workers and allies in *supporting* them to empower *themselves*, for example, by providing information and support, and increasing people's expectations and by valuing, supporting and involving service user's organizations.

Empowerment is an inherently political idea in which issues of power, the ownership of power, inequalities of power and the acquisition and redistribution of power are central. While professional approaches have focused on *personal* empowerment (bringing about change in the individual), the liberational approaches adopted by the disabled people's and service users' movements place equal emphasis on personal and *political* empowerment – bringing about broader change.

Some commentators in the disabled people's movement emphasize empowerment as an expression of their own *self-organization* and collective action, seeing the route to both personal and political empowerment as a collective process based on working and struggling together. Others, for example in the psychiatric survivors' movement, place more emphasis on the role of self-help, mutual aid and support in enabling their empowerment. There are both objective and subjective components to empowerment. It is concerned with increasing the actual power people have, and their personal capacity to use it.

The social worker's role in empowerment

While empowerment in social care goes far beyond professional practice, professional practice is still likely to have a role to play in service users' empowerment – for better

continued

or worse. Committing social work and social care practice to empowerment requires fundamental changes in its governance, form, process and objectives.

The direct payments schemes pioneered by disabled people's organizations, and adopted by government, offer important insights here, prefiguring change in the role, relations and purpose of professional practice. They have redefined the meaning of 'skills', created new occupational roles and, most important, have transcended traditional power relations in social work and social services by enabling the service user to become the employer rather than the 'client' of the worker.

Service users and their organizations challenge professional assumptions, still embodied in much professional training, that practitioners are equipped and competent to 'care' for others who are 'vulnerable', 'inadequate' and 'need' their 'help', assumptions which encourage unequal and unhelpful relationships between the two.

They highlight instead the importance of practitioners being open to learn and gain skills and understanding from the experience, knowledge, views and ideas of service users. This takes place at individual, collective and structural levels: in individual practice, through the involvement of service users and their organizations in the broader construction of practice and policy, and through equal opportunities training and employment policies in social care.

Practice is based on two-way traffic between service providers and users. It is about the growth and development of practitioners, as well as service users, each learning from the other. Such an approach to practice also gives a new meaning to the empowerment of practitioners. Instead of being based on workers having more status, power and resources, as some conventional commentators have suggested, their empowerment, like that of service users, is based on more equal relations rooted in trust, honesty, respect, reliability and openness – qualities which service users prioritize in professional practice and highlight as empowering.

For Further Reading
Jack, R. (ed.) 1995: *Empowerment In Community Care*. London: Chapman and Hall.
Oliver, M. and Barnes, C. 1998: *Disabled People and Social Policy: From Exclusion to Inclusion*. London: Longman.
Shera, W. and Wells, L. M. (eds) 1999: *Empowerment Practice in Social Work*. Toronto: Canadian Scholars Press.

SUZY CROFT AND PETER BERESFORD

Equal Opportunities

Equal opportunities is a set of principles, procedures, and practices to ensure that there is no unfair discrimination in either employment practices or service delivery. The minimum requirement is that organizations adhere to equal opportunities legislation which outlaws unfair discrimination on the basis of race, sex, and disability.

Social work and social care agencies in both the statutory and voluntary sector subscribe to a set of values which ensure that their practice often goes beyond the minimum legislative requirement by recognizing other oppressed groups (for example, gay men and lesbians, older people and those with mental health problems)

and by being attentive to the potential for unfair discrimination and oppression in all their activities. This involves identifying ways in which practices may directly or indirectly discriminate against minority and other groups who are oppressed or disadvantaged by assumptions, beliefs and organizational structures which privilege a dominant culture, and using positive action to ensure appropriate representation in both the work-force and among service users.

To achieve this, organizations develop policies which require the monitoring of outcomes of services and interventions, the publication of codes of practice to give guidance on procedures, and training to ensure that all workers follow them.

For Further Reading
Ahmad, B. 1991: *Equal Opportunity Training: A Guide for Practice*. London: National Institute for Social Work.

JOAN ORME

Ethics
See PROFESSIONAL ETHICS and VALUES IN SOCIAL WORK.

Ethnic Minorities
See RACE AND RACISM IN SOCIAL WORK.

Ethnography
The term *ethnography* encompasses a range of research methods originating in social anthropology and sociology which are used to understand people's daily lives and how these are shaped by interactions of various kinds.

Ethnographers often study organizations such as social services departments, generally spending large amounts of time as a participant or non-participant observer of events and conversations. There are a number of different types of ethnography, for example, analytic ethnography, critical ethnography and practitioner ethnography. However, these approaches all emphasize the ethnographer's *deep familiarity* with the subjects studied. Analysis is built upon detailed descriptions of persons and events. At the same time, it is often argued that, for them to be able to perceive aspects of an organization or culture which are normally taken-for-granted by the *members*, the researchers need to maintain some distance or strangeness within the setting.

There is some debate, therefore, about the integrity of ethnographic research conducted by practitioners, particularly where this is aimed at exposing, or providing a remedy for, 'poor practice'. However, ethnographic research can expose aspects of professional practice which have become routine and unquestioned. This can facilitate dialogue within social services departments, and between academics and practitioners. This dialogue has potential as a tool for the facilitation of disciplined and reflective social work practice.

For Further Reading
Hammersley, M. and Atkinson, P. 1995: *Ethnography: Principles and Practice*. London: Routledge.

SUE WHITE

European Perspectives on Social Work

The diversity of conceptual frameworks and practice traditions in social work in Europe seem to make it impossible to subsume them under the term *European social work* in more than a purely descriptive way. Indeed, any attempt at even finding a common title across the different European languages appears futile, while the diversity of professional identities at national level still strongly resists any merging of boundaries. A different mix of traditions prevails in each country. At the start of the twenty-first century, the term *social professions* appears to be gaining acceptance as the generic title; this facilitated the formation of a Thematic Network under the European Union SOCRATES Programme in higher education, bringing together at least social work and social pedagogy.

The historical background
The field is divided by the historically contingent manner in which each nation state recruited agencies and volunteers from its civil society to assist in the social integration of a residuum of disaffected victims of industrialization and modernization. In some contexts, the prudent administration of material welfare benefits came to characterize the profession's scope; in others, the teaching of socially acceptable habits; and, in others again, the provision of assistance with psychological coping mechanisms and emotional readjustment.

Accordingly, these fields adopted different academic disciplines as the core of their professional development and as a means of gaining a degree of autonomy and critical distance from the immediacy of the state mandate. Prevalent were the paradigms of applied social science, of psychology (particularly of the analytic kind) and of pedagogy

continued

in the sense of the life-long learning to realize one's full and active membership of a society. These academic contours gave rise to greater consistency in the emerging professional boundaries between different forms of the *social professions* such as social assistance, social counselling and social pedagogy/education. At this conceptual level, the emergence of a distinctly European exchange of discourses took shape at the beginning of the twentieth century, building on the humanistic and religious exchanges which had already been a feature of European charity organizations and their pioneers.

While the social work paradigm specifically received a strong impulse from across the Atlantic, symbolized by Mary Richmond's (1917) classical text *Social Diagnosis*, the vibrant internationalism of the 1920s was infused with European ideas, particularly those of social pedagogy and of psychoanalysis. The nature and extent of this formative period of European social work in the inter-war years has yet to be researched systematically. It is clear that this internationalism, inspired by the internationalism of the peace movement and of first wave feminism (and much less by that of socialism), activated political conflicts quite inevitably when national governments sought to commit social work more directly to a national agenda. This was the case most blatantly in Nazi Germany, which persecuted, exiled and killed countless social workers.

Social pedagogy and social work

The impression that social work proper commenced in most continental European countries only after World War II and with the aid of US- and UN-led training programmes, and that it imported US methods is misleading. Many of the protagonists of those programmes were, in fact, exiles from Europe (for example, Walter Friedlander, Gisela Konopka, Hertha Kraus) who had incorporated their formative learning and practice experiences into the emerging US discourse on social service delivery, social group work and casework respectively. However, these models now assumed the quality of universality and the attention to local, national, and European contexts was suspended, as was indeed the attention to cultural specificity. In most European countries, with the exception of the university sectors in Germany, Poland and latterly also in Italy, the social pedagogy discourse was, until recently, relegated to an academically inferior level. Immediacy to practice weighed more heavily on courses in the residential care and youth work fields, although Ireland and Sweden have recently commenced university courses in these fields.

The critique of the repressive potential of prevalent forms of casework and pedagogy gave community work a new impetus in the late 1960s, all over Western Europe. Ideas and strategies were gleaned in part from Paulo Freire's (1972) 'The Pedagogy of the Oppressed' but with little reference to the European origins of those concepts. A derivative in the form of *animation*, the mobilization of service users' own resources, established itself mainly in the French speaking parts of Europe and had also limited impact in Italy and Austria. However, the call for grounding social work generally in an expressly political analysis of its mandate failed to rally this rapidly differentiating professional field in Europe around a central concept.

Nevertheless, European exchange programmes have given the social professions a better understanding of their historic differences, and hence have increased the potential for closer co-operation. Contacts over the re-commencement of professional social work training in post-communist parts of Europe were largely conducted in the spirit of a growing awareness of the importance to social work of the concepts of culture, identity and 'difference'. Potentially universal components are reflected in a commitment to anti-discriminatory, anti-racist and citizenship-based methods. This may prevent social workers contributing to a *fortress Europe* approach by means of social policies and their discriminatory application in the way that their role in the past sometimes furthered exclusionary policies – as, for example, in their acquiescence in classification tasks under Nazism.

The major European organizations representing social pedagogy and social work (the European Association of Schools of Social Work, Formation d'Educateurs Sociaux Européens, and the European branch of the International Federation of Social Workers) collaborate closely in the Thematic Network for the Social Professions and are committed to an approach that addresses diversity and discrimination simultaneously. The journals *Social Work in Europe* and the *European Journal of Social Work* represent the first academic fora for the development of a distinct European discourse in the social professions.

For Further Reading
Cannan, C., Berry, L. and Lyons, K. 1992: *Social Work and Europe*. Basingstoke: Macmillan.
Lorenz, W. 1994: *Social Work in a Changing Europe*. London: Routledge.
Shardlow, S. and Payne, M. (eds) 1998: *Contemporary Issues in Social Work: Western Europe*. Aldershot: Arena.

WALTER LORENZ

The Evaluation of Effectiveness

The *evaluation of effectiveness* involves measuring the outcomes of social work intervention against its objectives. Such an endeavour is critical to the development of evidence-based social work policy and practice.

Experimental and other designs
However, this seemingly straightforward definition belies both conceptual and methodological complexities which relate to the contested nature of social work and the most appropriate mechanisms by which its effectiveness might be assessed. The *experimental design* – in which subjects are randomly allocated to either an experimental treatment group or to a non-treatment control – is said to offer the most rigorous test of the effectiveness of a service or model of intervention.

In social work, where for practical and ethical reasons random allocation is rarely achievable, *quasi-experimental designs* are more usual. Here, advantage is taken of naturally occurring 'experiments' in which different types of services or interventions whose intended effects are similar are provided to similar groups of service users. If differences in outcomes are observed, it is assumed that this must be attributable to the differential effectiveness of the services received.

In the *single case design*, a similar rationale is applied with respect to effects observed following the successive provision and withdrawal of intervention with individual cases.

Critics of the experimental design have pointed to its limited ability to elucidate the processes by which particular outcomes have been achieved. More generally, less attention is paid in evaluative research designs to the process of intervention than to the identification and measurement of outcomes. This limits the ability of the researcher to be specific about what precisely has brought about the desired results, and, hence, places limitations upon the ability of research to provide clear pointers for policy and practice.

Identifying objectives
It is, furthermore, rarely the case that there exists, among the various stakeholders, agreement as to what the objectives of intervention are and how their achievement might therefore be assessed. *Pluralistic evaluation* is an approach to the evaluation of

continued

effectiveness which recognizes the existence of multiple perspectives on effectiveness by inviting the various stakeholders to identify what they consider to be the key objectives of a social work service, and measuring the extent to which each has been achieved.

Although researchers may be able to identify a set of outcomes which can be measured relatively easily, others are less tangible. A distinction is often drawn between *service-based outcomes* and *outcomes for service users*. The former relate to the content and manner of service provision and the fit between what is intended and what is actually delivered. The latter are concerned with the effects of a service, for good or ill, on the different parties involved who may include direct service users, their families or carers, or the personnel of other services the effectiveness of whose own practice is dependent upon co-operation and collaboration with social work. In this context, effectiveness may be assessed in relation to measures of 'client state', judgements of the quality of life and indicators derived from user response.

Research models

The nature of knowledge and evidence in social work has been fiercely debated. This has implications with respect to the choice of yardsticks against which effectiveness might most appropriately be assessed and the choice of methods for doing so. Some advocate the incorporation of models derived from health research; for them, scientific knowledge is essentially positivistic and associated with quantitative measures derived from the use of experimental and quasi-experimental designs.

Others have questioned whether such an approach gives sufficient recognition to the differences between the health and social work sectors, to the wider methodological repertoire employed in the social sciences or to the increasing involvement of service users in the commissioning, design, implementation, interpretation and utilization of research. Instead of endorsing the traditional research values of neutrality and objectivity, proponents of user-led or user-controlled research question the relevance of these values and advocate, instead, the adoption of people's direct experiences as a basis for knowledge.

In a context of fiscal restraints on welfare expenditure, the effectiveness of social work intervention cannot be considered in isolation from the costs of alternative courses of action. The analysis of cost effectiveness, therefore, involves a comparison of the outcomes of different interventions with the costs associated with each. Especially where choices need to be made between a range of service options, the juxtaposition of cost and outcome data can facilitate informed policy making and resource management. However, economic data tends to be scarce, inconsistent in availability and quality, and rarely used coherently in decision making.

Evaluation, as the term implies, often requires judgements to be made about the relative value to be ascribed to particular combinations of outcomes and costs, or to the various objectives which are subscribed to by the different stakeholders in a social work service. It also differs from monitoring, even though the two terms are often used synonymously.

Monitoring involves the collection of information about what happens on a day-to-day basis in an agency. As such, the data obtained are essentially descriptive, though they may contribute to the evaluation of effectiveness, especially if the information collected sheds light on the extent to which service objectives are being met.

Ultimately the diversity of problems confronting social work, the methods by which they are tackled and the settings in which they are addressed encourage a pragmatic approach to the evaluation of effectiveness, in which no one approach is to be preferred for its potential to illuminate the impact of social work services and the fit between what is intended and what is, in practice, achieved.

The choice of evaluative methods will, additionally, be influenced by professional and epistemological perspectives on the relevance of different kinds of research, knowledge and evidence to social work policy and practice.

For Further Reading
Cheetham, J., Fuller, R., McIvor, G. and Petch, A. 1992: *Evaluating Social Work Effectiveness*. Milton Keynes: Open University Press.
Shaw, I. 1999: *Qualitative Evaluation*. London: Sage.
Shaw, I. and Lishman, J. (eds) 1999: *Evaluation and Social Work Practice*. London: Sage.

GILL McIVOR

Evidence-based Practice

Evidence-based practice denotes an approach to decision making which is transparent, accountable, and based on a consideration of current best evidence about the effects of particular interventions on the welfare of individuals, groups and communities. It relates to the decisions of both individual practitioners and policy makers.

The phrase *evidence-based practice* in respect of social interventions was adopted from developments within health, and acquired currency in the late 1990s.

Those who espouse an evidence-based approach to policy and practice recognize the importance of a range of factors in decision making, including societal and individual values, practice wisdom and resources. However, they argue that the influence of these factors should be informed by a rigorous consideration of current best evidence available of the *effects* of particular interventions.

Research design and methodological rigour
Social interventions are typically designed to bring about a number of outcomes, often for a range of stakeholders – the individual client, the community, the policy maker. Optimal decisions require as secure a knowledge base as possible, not only of what interventions best secure particular outcomes and at what cost, but also what adverse effects – unintended, unforeseen or simply undesired – are possible, and at what level of risk. Determining what shall count as 'a secure knowledge base' is pivotal to an evidence-based approach, and, therefore, a central feature of evidence-based practice is its attention to issues of research design and the methodological rigour of available sources of evidence.

Evidence-based practice does *not* argue that only experimental research methods such as randomized controlled trials are valid sources of evidence about the effects of interventions. It does, however, maintain that – all other methodological considerations being equal – the results of experimental studies are more secure than others with regard to their *internal validity*. That is to say, if presented with a variety of studies using different designs (for example, randomized controlled trial, matched group comparison, pre-post test, etc.) all of which were optimally designed and conducted, then those using experimental methodology afford us less reason to be concerned that their results might be attributable to other, confounding factors – such as the passage of time or unknown differences between a group of people who have received the intervention and another which has not.

Advocates of evidence-based social work argue that, both on ethical and technical grounds, our choices should reflect the degree of internal validity afforded by studies and that this is a function first of their design and, thereafter, of the methodological adequacy of the conducted study. The history of evaluation in social work and other areas
continued

of social welfare demonstrates clearly that we frequently overestimate social work's beneficial effects and underestimate social work's capacity for adverse effects. In general, the more rigorous the research design, the less dramatic the former and the more transparent the latter (Oakley, 2000).

Randomized controlled trials have come to be referred to by some as the 'gold standard'. However, despite their superiority in terms of internal validity, they are not always technically possible or ethically feasible within social work. For example, social workers often operate within nationally determined policies which allow limited or no scope for experimentation; it is rarely possible to 'blind' participants, workers or, indeed, data gatherers to which intervention participants are associated with; and it is often not ethically acceptable to withhold assistance of some kind to vulnerable people in need of services.

Literature reviews

In general, the examination of the effects of social work interventions remains a relatively under-researched area (Macdonald, 1998). Nevertheless, as a discipline which draws upon the work of other professionals, one of the challenges inherent in an evidence-based approach to decision making is the synthesis of available information, the gathering together and analysis of available evidence. Typically, literature reviews in social work journals are narrative in nature, do not make explicit the basis for the selection and evaluation of studies and afford the same weight to studies of varying design and methodology. These and other factors result, at best, in biased summaries of the available evidence. In paper form, they are also likely to be out-of-date by the time of publication, and are rarely updated in the light of new evidence. Evidence-based practice requires that decision makers have access to rigorously and transparently prepared, up-to-date syntheses of current best evidence. A scientific approach to research synthesis has been developed within health, and this model, appropriately adjusted to take into consideration the methodological challenges inherent in social welfare, is proposed as the basis of evidence-based social work. The approach is that of the 'systematic review'.

The Cochrane Collaboration is an international organization which prepares, maintains and makes accessible systematic reviews of health interventions. Its electronic journal, the *Cochrane Library*, is published four times a year. Though health dominated, the *Cochrane Library* contains systematic reviews of relevance to social work, particularly in the areas of health, disability, mental illness and community care. It also includes reviews relevant to those working in the fields of child care, criminal justice, and older people. In 1999, a parallel collaboration, the Campbell Collaboration, was launched. This organization prepares, maintains and makes accessible systematic reviews of social, educational, and criminal justice interventions. Its focus is not restricted to social problems but to social interventions more generally, and it works in close collaboration with the Cochrane Collaboration to avoid duplication of effort.

For Further Reading
Macdonald, G. M. 1998: Promoting evidence-based practice in child protection, *Clinical Child Psychology and Psychiatry*, 3 (1), 71–85.
Oakley, A. 2000: *Experiments in Knowing: Gender and Method in the Social Sciences.* Cambridge: Polity Press.
The Cochrane Library, Oxford: Update Software, updated quarterly.

GERALDINE MACDONALD

Evolutionary Psychology

Evolutionary psychology (or *sociobiology*) refers to the biological origins of social behaviour. With E. O. Wilson's (1975) textbook *Sociobiology*, the field became established, with comparative studies ranging from insects, mammals, primates and humans revealing the underlying evolutionary logic of social organization, interpersonal behaviour and conflict, and individual reproductive (genetic) success into subsequent generations.

From the late 1980s, the sociobiological emphasis on observable behaviour shifted towards 'psychological mechanisms' or ancestral evolutionary 'adaptations', which came to be recognized as often being maladaptive in modern society (hence, the shift away from analysis of behaviour). Further theoretical work continued with gene-culture co-evolutionary theory of language and culture, together with the evolutionary basis of ethnocentrism/prejudice/xenophobia, inter-group conflict and warfare.

Increasing acceptance of evolutionary thinking was found in psychology with applications to other areas, such as epistemology, religion, political science, economics, and ethological-based psychiatry. There are implications for sociology and social work, particularly concerning the genetic relationships involved in paternity uncertainty and domestic violence, step-parent–child conflict and abuse, and aggressive, antisocial, or maladaptive behaviour in adolescents which could persist through generations in resource-deprived, unstable familial and socio-environmental contexts.

For Further Reading

Buss, D. M. 1999: *Evolutionary Psychology*. London: Allyn and Bacon.

KENNETH KIM

Existential Social Work

Existential social work draws upon the work of existential philosophers, psychotherapists and novelists. It offers a framework for social workers and users to understand the fundamental questions of existence and to develop ways of coping with them. Emphasis is placed on the significance of subjective experiences, the uniqueness of each individual's perceptions of the world – a phenomenological approach – with an emphasis on partnership in helping.

Key concepts include the inevitable presence in existence of loneliness, suffering, despair, absurdity and death in a contingent, ever-changing world, while emphasizing that people always have freedom to choose, to rebel, to search for meaning, to engage and change their circumstances, however unpromising these may be. It is 'bad faith' to deny such opportunities. Authenticity is important. This involves responsibility and concern for others, as well as for oneself: a commitment to fellow human beings and the difficulties and suffering they face. The existential social worker helps users to face the doubts and uncertainties of existence, and helps them come to terms with anxieties and vulnerabilities by acknowledging and empathizing with problems while seeing positive, future movement as being an ever-present possibility.

For Further Reading

Thompson, N. 1992: *Existentialism and Social Work*. Aldershot: Avebury.

STEWART COLLINS

Extrinsic Ageing

Extrinsic ageing is caused entirely or partly by factors outside the body. In animal experiments, restricting calorie intake prolongs lifespan, while restricting exercise reduces it. In humans, tobacco smoking, a poor diet (low in fruit and vegetables, high in animal fat), a sedentary lifestyle and excess alcohol are all associated with a reduction in life expectancy and an increase in many of the common diseases of later life. Sunlight, chemicals, radiation, infections and other toxins can also damage parts of the body and speed up normal ageing processes.

PETER CROME

F

Factitious Disorder by Proxy

See MUNCHAUSEN SYNDROME BY PROXY.

Failure-to-thrive

Failure-to-thrive is a syndrome that describes infants and young children whose weights, heights (when older), head-circumferences and psychological developments (when measured over a period) are significantly below expected norms for their chronological ages, and whose well-being may give cause for concern. It can arise from physical illness (termed *organic failure-to-thrive*), from psychosocial reasons (*non-organic failure-to-thrive*), or from a combination of these and other factors.

Problematic mother–child interaction, especially during feeding, and poor nurturance are the commonest aetiological factors contributing to a condition associated with acute feeding difficulties, inadequate nutrition to promote normal growth, aversive temperamental attributes, disturbed mother–child relationships, insecure attachments, family dysfunction, poverty, neglect and emotional abuse.

DOROTA IWANIEC

Family-based Respite Services

Family-based respite services offer carers short breaks by linking their child or adult relative to another local family – or individual – on a one-to-one basis, care generally being offered in the latter's home. Respite carers receive training, support and remuneration from local schemes, usually run by statutory or voluntary agencies. Research has repeatedly shown a high rate of satisfaction among carers using these services. However, widespread homesickness among children has also been recorded.

The first family-based services in the UK were set up in 1976, and it is estimated that there are now 470 such schemes in the UK. These cater principally for disabled children, older people (including those with dementia) and adults with learning disabilities.

There has been much debate about the term *respite* because of the negative connotations of this word, implying that the disabled person is a 'burden' from whom relatives need frequent breaks. For this reason, many schemes use terms such as 'shared care' or 'short breaks'.

In addition, most services emphasize the importance of providing a positive experience for the individual directly receiving care.

For Further Reading
Stalker, K. 1996: *Developments in Short-term Care: Breaks and Opportunities.* London: Jessica Kingsley.

KIRSTEN STALKER

Family Centres

The term *family centre* is often assumed to refer to a neighbourhood setting where parents and children voluntarily take part in activities which seek to enhance child, family and community life. Such activities are usually organized by paid staff and/or volunteers and can also take place beyond the centre and in the homes of local people as well. Services are often aimed at younger families and might include positive play experience, pre-school day care, parenting skills, child development, groupwork, counselling, family welfare, adult education and community development.

Family centres emerged most prominently in the 1980s, and were hailed in Britain as an exciting development offering a new paradigm for integrated community-based family support. A defining aspect is their preventative orientation and the use of a physical location in which multiple functions are thought to provide a synergy beyond their separate parts, capable of developing family and community strengths in areas of social need often associated with children entering the care system.

Types of family centre

In the mid-1990s, there were estimated to be some 750 UK family centres run by local authority and/or voluntary agency providers. Approximately 450 were thought to be local authority funded but many of these were in partnership with voluntary agencies. Authoritative sources in respect of relevant law, policy, practice and theory can be found in Holman (1992) and Cannan and Warren (1997). From their work, we can identify four general types of centre.

1 A local *neighbourhood model* that offers open access services to parents and children and, by this and other means, seeks to invigorate family and community solidarities
2 A *community development model* that encourages families to initiate and run their own services in the belief that collective action will lead to improvements in social and environmental factors influencing family life
3 A *client orientated model* offering assessment and therapeutic services, and sometimes described as a specialist referred family centre, restricted mainly to families referred by welfare professionals, often where aspects of child protection or welfare are paramount
4 What might be described as a *bureau family centre* is usually local authority run, combines open access as well as more therapeutic/assessment facilities and also houses statutory social work staff who operate in the community. The centre may also provide a venue for other welfare and health professionals whom families may wish to visit. Such centres are likely to contain administrative staff and facilities required to progress statutory child care practice.

Some problems in running family centres

While centres sometimes combine elements of the above, they also share to some extent in a number of practical and philosophical problems in relation to *function*, *capacity* and *ownership*.

An example of a problem in relation to *function* can arise with the more informal open access model which often claims an holistic approach to families. Users are likely to be women with younger children, and it is not evident that others in a family (adolescents, adult males, or older people) are easily attracted or that centres can flexibly and swiftly reconfigure their operations to cater for such a range of potential users and welfare needs.

An example of a *capacity* problem might be found in those centres that offer a community development approach to tackle severe inequalities. Such projects face difficulties if they rely solely on the energies of local people and local professionals to regenerate communities without the aid of significant resources, a multi-agency strategy and also the commitment of business.

An example of an *ownership* problem can exist in relation to the thorny issue of who controls the policy and practice of family centres. Here, the involvement and influence of users will depend very much upon the type of centre and its purpose. There is a small but growing number of examples where voluntary organizations have set up centres and have gradually handed these over to be directly managed by local people. This would not easily be achieved for example at an open access centre run by a voluntary organization but funded by a local authority keen to reduce child care admissions in an area. Funders would likely want certain kinds of services in return for their investment and may not be sanguine if these were, in some way, impeded by local users keen to create a different project for the centre. Likewise, those specialist centres which take referrals where child protection issues abound are not usually open to negotiation with users over the business at hand. Similarly, a local authority run centre that offers a range of open

continued

127

access, client referred and professional welfare services cannot realistically divest itself of ownership or operational control to local families. In short, there can be tensions over user participation and control within family centres.

In conclusion

None of the above detracts from the innovative and progressive nature of much family centre practice. The history of family centres is one of adaptation and growth, stemming in significant part from convincing evidence that users rate highly their experience of open access and community-oriented types of service. While there are increasing examples of centres becoming managed by local people, there are also instances of centres helping communities to become directly engaged in ambitious regeneration schemes. Research also suggests positive outcomes for families referred to the specialist referred model. Family centres are generally thought of as an effective means of family and community preservation. There remains, however, a need for more longitudinal and comparative research. This is noted by Pithouse et al. (1998) who provide case studies of family centres together with examples of similar services in the USA and Hong Kong.

For Further Reading

Cannan, C. and Warren, C. (eds) 1997: *Social Action with Children and Families: A Community Development Approach to Child and Family Welfare*. London: Routledge.
Holman, R. 1992: Family centres. *Highlight*, 111. London: National Children's Bureau.
Pithouse, A., Lindsell, S. and Cheung, M. 1998: *Family Support and Family Centre Services: Issues, Research and Evaluation in the UK, USA and Hong Kong*. Aldershot: Ashgate.

ANDREW PITHOUSE

Family, The Changing Shape of the

The term *family* is used widely in everyday speech, almost invariably unquestioningly, as though an unambiguous, unique definition is self-evident. Most people would understand a family to include members who are related by blood or marriage, and most would probably add those connected through cohabitation. Yet this definition, based as it is on biological parenthood, kinship and sexual relationship, is not completely clear-cut; for example, should adoptive children and non-resident stepchildren or students be included, and where does one draw the line with distant relatives?

The issue is partly solved by contemplating a variety of alternative definitions ranging from the *nuclear* family to the *extended* family. Two additional criteria can usefully be considered: sharing a common residence (even if on an occasional or part-time basis); and emotional ties of affection, care or support. Of course, these two factors may or may not coincide; for example, an elderly relative living nearby may receive help and support, while a member of the extended family may live in the same household, but yet lead an entirely separate and independent existence from those of the nuclear family.

Theoretical concepts

Sociologists and social theorists have devoted considerable energy to identifying the different types of families and postulating how their evolution is related to developments in society and individuals' changing needs and roles. They have approached it from a number of different perspectives: biological, functional, social, psychological and political/ideological, as well as from an anti-family stance. In the course of these analyses, different terms have been used: conjugal families, extra-nuclear kin-bonds, classical extended family, modified extended family, reconstituted family, and the modern family.

As an example, the term the *modern family* signifies a structurally isolated nuclear unit which cherishes both husband–wife and parent–child bonds.

Understandably, most of the available statistical information on families refers to co-residential members – primarily because censuses and surveys are addressed to those resident in particular households, which in turn are easy to locate because each occupies a fixed physical space. Indeed, the concepts of *family* and *household* were scarcely distinguishable in official statistics until 1961, when a definitive typology was introduced into the census and became the basis for subsequent classifications.

Historical trends

About a century ago, most couples were married, with relatively large numbers of children by present-day standards, and usually living in larger, rented housing. Often, other relatives – elderly parents, aunts, uncles, cousins – lived with them, forming extended families. Many households contained domestic servants, who, although not members of either the nuclear or extended family, were nevertheless regarded as part of the family.

Since then, many factors have influenced the changing size and characteristics of the family, and, indeed, the symbiosis between the family and society in general. Women have had fewer children, and have lost fewer through infant mortality. (Adult mortality, too, was high at the start of the twentieth century compared with now, and widowed lone parenthood was much more common.) Extended families have declined in relative numbers, while the single (nuclear) family household has steadily gained ground to become the dominant type.

Divorce was comparatively rare before 1939 – apart from a peak just after World War I – but grew, particularly during the 1960s. As a result, divorced lone parenthood increased, as did remarriage after divorce (which, just after World War II, eclipsed the former importance of remarriage after being widowed). Remarriage after divorce in which one or both partners bring children from previous marriages into the new marriage leads to 'reconstituted' families involving stepchildren. Concurrent with the rise in divorce was that of cohabitation, both as pre-marital cohabitation – living together with one's future spouse – and in the form of informal unions, in place of marriage.

In the first part of the twentieth century, apart from temporary increases immediately after the two World Wars, the proportion of all births which took place outside marriage was relatively level at around 1 in 20, but, during the 1960s, it rose steadily, and after the mid-1970s increased at a very fast rate, resulting in the further growth of single (never-married) lone motherhood. A related trend occurred in the annual numbers of children adopted. The numbers peaked in the late 1960s and then fell continuously, so that the number of new families formed by the adoption of children is now negligible compared with the formation of new families by births or by the process of stepfamilyhood.

These historical trends may be summarized and put into a broader context, since other demographic and social changes occurred during the twentieth century which had an impact on families and households:

- Women having fewer children; childbearing at older ages; increasing childlessness
- The advent of modern contraception and the increased use of abortion
- Smaller household and family sizes
- A decline in extended families and multi-family households; overall fewer kin
- A growth in the numbers living alone
- A fall in infant mortality resulting in virtually all children surviving to adulthood

continued

- A decline in adult mortality; lower prevalence of widowed lone parenthood; and increased proportions of families spanning two, three or more generations
- More elderly people, either living alone, in institutions, or with their children or other relatives
- A decline in adoption; a growth in lone motherhood among never-married women
- An increase in births outside marriage, and consequent growth in cohabiting couple families and lone parenthood
- A rise in the prevalence of cohabitation; decline in first marriage; growth in divorce
- An increase in the proportion of remarriages among all marriages; and a consequent growth in married couple stepfamilies
- A growth in cohabitation of lone parents with new partners; and the creation of cohabiting couple stepfamilies

Of course, all these trends – some of which have been rapid and significant, others comparatively slow and of lesser importance – have a collective and cumulative effect, and as such are inter-related.

Families and households in recent decades

Fortunately, statistical data sources allow a greater insight into the changing profiles of families and households in recent years. Table 4 shows the trends in household composition since 1961. The proportion of all households which have consisted of a couple family with their dependent children has been falling since the early 1960s, both for couples with one or two dependent children, and for those with three or more. In fact, the latter kind of household has halved in relative numbers, as larger families have become less common. Multi-family households have declined too, from 3 per cent of all households in 1961 to just 1 per cent in 1998. However, there has been a substantial growth in one-parent households: one-family households consisting of a lone

Table 4   Households: by type of household and family in Great Britain, 1961–98

	1961 (%)	1971 (%)	1981 (%)	1991 (%)	1998[a] (%)
One person					
Under pensionable age	4	6	8	11	14
Pensionable age	7	12	14	16	14
Two or more unrelated adults	5	4	5	3	3
Single family households					
Couple[b]					
No children	26	27	26	28	28
1–2 dependent children[c]	30	26	25	20	19
3 or more dependent children[c]	8	9	6	5	4
Non-dependent children only	10	8	8	8	7
Lone parent[b]					
Dependent children[c]	2	3	5	6	7
Non-dependent children only	4	4	4	4	3
Multi-family households	3	1	1	1	1
All households (= 100%) (millions)	16.3	18.6	20.2	22.4	23.6

Dependent children are defined as those aged under 16 or from 16 to 18 (inclusive), and in full-time education.
[a] At Spring 1998.
[b] Other individuals who were not family members may also be included.
[c] May also include non-dependent children.
Source: Censuses and Labour Force Survey.

parent with dependent children formed 2 per cent of all households in 1961, but 7 per cent in 1998.

Another notable change has been the trend towards people living alone: since 1961, in relative numbers, one-person households have more than trebled for those under pensionable age, and doubled for those of pensionable age. In fact, the growth in living alone has been most marked among the most elderly – those aged 75 and over. It is notable that over 1 in 10 men aged under 45 was living alone in the mid-1990s – three times the proportion two decades earlier – reflecting the decline in marriage and the rise in separation and divorce.

During the 1990s, among men and women aged under 50, the proportions who were married fell somewhat, while the proportions cohabiting slowly but consistently increased. By the same token, the proportion of all families with dependent children which were married couple families declined slightly, while those which were cohabiting couple families steadily grew.

Turning to the profile of the different kinds of family with dependent children, the fullest available picture is shown in table 5. Just under 7 per cent – 1 in 15 – of all

Table 5   Stepfamilies, and other families with dependent children[a], and dependent children living in them, 1990–92, Great Britain

Type of family with dependent children[a]	Families with dependent children (%)	Dependent children within given family type		
		Type of child	Percentage	Mean number per family
Married couple stepfamilies				
Stepfather/natural mother	3.4	all	3.9	2.1
Stepmother/natural father	0.9	all	1.1	2.4
Stepfather/stepmother	0.3	all	0.6	3.5
All married couple stepfamilies	4.6	all	5.7	2.3
Cohabiting couple stepfamilies				
Stepfather/natural mother	1.6	all	1.6	1.9
Stepmother/natural father	0.3	all	0.3	1.8
Stepfather/stepmother	0.1	all	0.3	3.2
All cohabiting couple stepfamilies	2.1	all	2.2	2.0
One-parent families[b]				
Lone father families	2.0	own	1.8	1.6
Lone mother families	16.6	own	14.8	1.7
All one-parent families[b]	18.6	own	16.6	1.7
Couple families with natural children only				
Married couple families	71.2	own	72.8	1.9
Cohabiting couple families	3.5	own	2.7	1.5
All couple families with natural children only	75.6	own	75.5	1.9
All families with dependent children[a]/ all dependent children in all families	100.0%		100.0%	1.9
Sample size	6,882		12,764	

Components may not sum precisely to totals because of rounding.
[a] Dependent children are aged under 16, or from 16 to 18 and in full-time education.
[b] Where lone parent is not cohabiting.
Source: OPCS Omnibus Survey.

continued

families with dependent children were stepfamilies: almost 5 per cent were married couple stepfamilies and a further 2 per cent were cohabiting couple stepfamilies.

Among all couple families with dependent children – that is, excluding one-parent families – 8 per cent were stepfamilies. Among married couple families with dependent children, 6 per cent were stepfamilies, while about 20 per cent of all cohabiting couple families with dependent children were stepfamilies. That is, among cohabiting couple families with dependent children, families with only natural children were relatively less common.

In addition, couple families were four times as numerous as one-parent families, which, in turn, were almost three times as numerous as stepfamilies. Lone mothers out-number stepmothers by 10 to 1, but stepfathers outnumber lone fathers: there are over 2.5 times as many stepfathers as lone fathers.

Table 5 also shows that about 8 per cent of all dependent children in 1991 were living in stepfamilies; of these, 2 per cent were 'own' children, and the remainder, 6 per cent, were themselves dependent stepchildren. Of these, 4 per cent were in married couple stepfamilies, and 2 per cent in cohabiting couple stepfamilies.

Conclusions

The changing patterns of fertility, marriage, divorce, cohabitation and living alone have meant that family and household structures have become more diverse, and that individuals are more likely to experience living in a greater variety of types of family and household during their lifetime. This tendency has been reinforced by the increase in longevity and in re-partnering after the breakdown of marriage and informal unions. The pattern of parenthood has also changed: in general, women are having fewer children and at older ages – and an increasing proportion are choosing not to have any children at all.

In many respects, similar trends have been observed in most European countries.

For Further Reading
Elliot, F. R. 1986: *The Family: Change or Continuity?* London: Macmillan Education.
Ferri, E. and Smith, K. 1998: *Step-parenting in the 1990s.* London: Family Policy Studies Centre.
Haskey, J. C. 1998: *The Fragmenting Family: Does it Matter?* London: Institute of Economic Affairs.
Office for National Statistics 1997: *Social Focus on Families.* London: The Stationery Office.
© Crown Copyright   JOHN HASKEY

Family Court Welfare
See DIVORCE AND FAMILY COURT WELFARE.

Family Group Conferences

Family group conferences are child welfare and youth justice decision-making meetings involving young people and extended family as key decision makers. They are used in situations of high risk for children and young people, including child protection and when a young person offends. The youth justice conferences are based on restorative justice, and include the victim.

The conferences' family-oriented format, culturally respectful process and high level of service user control make them radically different from other apparently similar decision-making meetings (for example, case conferences with parents present). They were initially developed in New Zealand, and are now taking place in many other countries, sometimes with a legal basis and sometimes as a practice initiative.

The conferences have an independent co-ordinator, and provide a period of private family time. Around seven family members and two professionals attend 'average' conferences, which last for two hours or more.

The conferences have proved successful in involving extended family, and the outcomes are generally as good as or better than other approaches, but their radical nature has made their implementation a complex and challenging process.

For Further Reading

Marsh, P. and Crow, G. 1998: *Family Group Conferences in Child Welfare*. Oxford: Blackwell Science.

PETER MARSH

Family Support

Family support involves the provision of services for children living at home, and is often seen as an alternative to services for children living away from home in residential or foster care. In this context, family support policies are often described as 'preventative'. This definition has been used in the UK in respect of the Children Act 1989 and the provisions available under Section 17: for example, social workers are empowered to work with children in need living at home with their families; the Act allows for a broad definition of the term 'in need'.

The idea of *family support* has also been viewed as being in opposition to, or as an alternative to, child protection policies; but a Department of Health research overview (1995a) has demonstrated this to be a false theoretical proposition, and empirical evidence has shown that family support is the principal mechanism by which health and social services systems can seek to protect children from maltreatment.

The term *family support* is also employed as a general description for services aiming to relieve stress and to promote the welfare of children. Even when they are specified clearly, the aims of family support tend to be wide-ranging: the services designed to achieve these aims may include:

- universal pre-school day care;
- specialist projects for targeted populations – for example, *HomeStart* operating in many English local authorities and *NewPin*, still largely based in London, both of which seek to use parents who have overcome family problems to help those who are currently in difficulty; and
- family centres.

Family support is best defined in terms of tightly organized and evaluated programmes to deal with specified family problems, using skills drawn, as appropriate, from health, education or social services. Very few successful programmes exist in the UK, although Gibbons' (1990) evaluation of an intervention in Newpath gave room for encouragement; to date, it is the only robust UK study of family support and should act as a model.

A review of the literature (Little and Mount, 1999) suggests that the following would be worth further scrutiny:

- The aforementioned *Homestart* and *NewPin* programmes
- Health care and education for vulnerable mothers in the first months of a child's life – for example, the Elmira programme in New York State
- Help with parent–child interactions – for instance, the Instapje and Opstapje projects in the Netherlands
- Community-based education for vulnerable mothers, such as the Child Development programme in the UK, Ireland and South Africa

continued

The term *family support* has a particularly British flavour. It is akin to *family preservation* in the USA which offers intensive support to families comprising children on the threshold of separation to state care; in Northern Europe, the term is more closely associated with family therapy and is not normally linked to the idea of providing support for the child at home.

For Further Reading

Department of Health 1995a: *Child Protection: Messages from Research*. London: HMSO.

Gibbons, J. with Thorpe, S. and Wilkinson, P. 1990: *Family Support and Prevention: Studies in Local Areas*. London: HMSO.

Little, M. and Mount, K. 1999: *Prevention and Early Intervention for Children in Need*. Aldershot: Ashgate.

MICHAEL LITTLE

Family Therapy

Family therapy is a theoretical framework for understanding interactions between individuals in families, and between them and the economic, social, cultural and political systems of which they are a part. Family therapy is also a method of working. It aims to help individuals to understand and negotiate their relationships within the family. It focuses on the impact of influence and feedback between individuals and between family members and other, wider systems. It provides an opportunity for family members to look into their family from 'outside', while also exploring what may be happening 'inside'. The theoretical framework and methodological approach aim to offer family members a different way of perceiving the world, which may enable them to appreciate the intrapersonal, interpersonal, and structural constraints that have contributed to problem repetition. This may enable them to find different solutions to the problems that they experience.

Social work and family therapy

Social workers may doubt the relevance of family therapy for their practice, couched as it sometimes appears in jargon and technology. Indeed, they may criticize family therapy's apparent reliance on therapist expertise and techniques rather than on a partnership approach, and its slowness to engage with issues of power and anti-oppressive practice. Moreover, the field of family therapy is confusing. Different approaches or models exist, making it more accurate to refer to family therapies. However, even if social workers do not see themselves as family therapists, the theoretical perspectives and tools for understanding and intervention are useful in practice with individuals, families, groups and teams.

The focus is on the family and the interactions between its members, and between it and other systems with which the family connects. This provides an opportunity to explore internal dynamics and external difficulties, and any relationship between the two. It connects the personal with the social. Efforts for change may need to be directed at both. An underpinning principle, therefore, is the notion of circular causality. This hypothesises that, in any focus on 'causes', a search for a beginning is illusory. Any linear cause–effect sequence is an oversimplification. More useful is connecting people's transactions or patterns, to understand how their perspective and behaviours fit together, often in a manner that is preventing change.

Models of family therapy

Different models vary in the degree to which they focus on present concerns or past events. *Psychodynamic family therapy* emphasizes historical factors which continue to influence family members in their interactions. It employs tools such as geneograms to map historical information and its development. *Structural family therapy* focuses on the present and on how structures such as boundaries within a family may be dysfunctional. It uses tools such as enactment to clarify talked-about behaviour and to change how people interact. Other therapists may be more concerned with the meanings and beliefs that underpin complained-about behaviour, or with how the conversation unfolds between them and the family. Indeed, with any one family, a variety of approaches, or informed eclecticism, may be required to understand and then to change its tendency to return to a problematic steady state.

Nonetheless, despite these different theoretical frameworks, a systems perspective informs much family therapy. A distinction may be made between open systems (which maintain a capacity to evolve) and closed systems (that are characterized by resistance to change). Whether the focus is on rules, scripts, boundaries or the nature of communication, on myths, imbalances of power and repeated solutions, the task is to understand the meaning and force behind patterns and symptoms. The task is to explore differences and to examine alternatives, while making sense of what has prevented family members from redefining their relationships.

It follows that how the therapists engage with the family will vary. They may interact directly with the family or, rather, offer observations and comments. They may actively form relationships or alliances, generally or with different family members at particular times. Alternatively, they may maintain a position of neutrality; this involves challenging everything while eschewing judgements and taking sides. Similarly, their goals and interventions may vary: from aiming to promote insight or to resolve problems, to seeking more fundamental relationship change; from the suggestion of tasks, to paradoxical messages.

Family therapy has engaged with the principle of partnership. For example, family therapists will provide information about their approach to the work. Similarly, the technology that is used, such as one-way screens and teams, can be 'reversed', so that family members can observe and comment upon family therapists 'enacting' relationships or difficulties within the family, or discussing the family's problems and how best to intervene. These developments reflect a greater openness or transparency.

Questions of gender, ethnicity, sexuality, power and social context are on the agenda as significant influences on people's experiences and choices. Beliefs and assumptions held by family members and by therapists must be explored since they influence expectations about roles and behaviour, and the meaning that is derived from what others say and do. Key relationships, life-cycle phases and authority structures will vary between families and, for example, should influence who is included in meetings. Because of the gendered nature of families, the emphasis should not be just on problem solving but also on relationship building and understanding experience. It should include a focus on power – how it is used, in what context, with what effect.

Enabling people to stand back and view their experiences from a different perspective promotes curiosity and interest in understanding what is happening. Questioning assumptions and common responses promotes recognition that people may be part of the problem as much as the solution. Family therapy as a theoretical framework and method of intervention has a broader applicability therefore, not just with individuals and families, but also with groups, teams and organizations that may need to understand their experience and change their patterns of behaviour.

continued

For Further Reading

Jones, E. 1993: *Family Systems Therapy: Developments in Milan-Systemic Therapies.* Chichester: Wiley.

Reimers, S. and Treacher, A. 1995: *Introducing User Friendly Family Therapy.* London: Routledge.

Stratton, P., Preston-Shoot, M. and Hanks, H. 1990: *Family Therapy: Training and Practice.* Birmingham: Venture Press.

MICHAEL PRESTON-SHOOT

Family Violence
See DOMESTIC VIOLENCE.

Fatherhood
See PARENTING.

Feminist Theory and Practice

Feminist theory and practice is concerned with understanding and transforming the subordinate position of women in society. It dates back to the nineteenth century when feminists were involved in campaigns for the vote and the welfare of women and children.

The background to feminist theory

There have been different and competing feminist theories which have had implications for the practices engaged in. Divisions were particularly pronounced in the second wave of feminist activity which emerged in a number of Western countries in the 1960s. This generation of feminists tended to be more wide-ranging in their critique of society than their predecessors. For example, although liberal feminism with its emphasis on the inclusion of women in the existing social order was an important strand, the dominant strands were revolutionary/radical feminism and Marxist/socialist feminism. Both sought the transformation of existing society but differed in their analysis of the causes of women's oppression. For revolutionary feminists, the roots of women's oppression lay in the power men as a group wielded over women as a group, whereas Marxist/ socialist feminists saw capitalism also playing a central role.

A range of feminisms emerged subsequently. These included analyses which sought to integrate the experiences and understandings of black women. An example was the insistence by black feminists that their particular social location meant that the 'family' often did not carry the same oppressive set of meanings that it appeared to do for white middle-class women and that it acted as a bulwark against the racism they encountered in wider societal arenas, including those which encompassed white women. Psychoanalytic feminism became influential as many women discovered how difficult it was to change entrenched patterns of behaviour and desires. Postmodernism has become popular with some feminists, and has led to critiques of the attempts such as that of the revolutionary/radical feminists or Marxist/socialist feminists to develop *the* analysis which explained the position of women world-wide. Postmodern feminists also emphasized the importance of the differences within the category 'woman', building upon critiques which pointed to the importance of class, sexuality, 'race', age and disability in women's lives.

In terms of issues tackled, men's violence and abuse have been of key importance. A range of service organizations such as Women's Aid and Rape Crisis were developed and have survived, although often in precarious financial circumstances. Feminists have also been involved in developing organizations which address the needs of the survivors of child sexual abuse. The theories and practice developed in relation to child sexual abuse and, to a lesser extent, domestic violence have been feminism's most significant contribution to social work theory and practice.

Feminist theory and practice in social work

Early writings emphasized themes which have been subject to subsequent critique. Feminist social work was essentially about women workers working with women service users, and the commonalities in their experiences provided the basis for empowering practice. Women's well-being was prioritized. Organizations such as Women's Aid and Rape Crisis, which rejected bureaucratic forms of organizing, were promoted as providing progressive organizational models for social services departments. Men, either in the roles as workers or service users, were viewed with suspicion or pessimism in terms of their interest in changing or their ability to do so. The needs of children were, in the main, identified as synonymous with those of their mothers. In the 1990s, convergence with anti-oppressive and anti-discriminatory perspectives facilitated the development of analyses which incorporated 'race', disability and age, but this was confined to analyses of women and the differences between men were not explored (Langan and Day, 1992).

In terms of specific issues, the increased visibility of child sexual abuse is largely due to the work of feminists from within and outside social work. They have been concerned to demonstrate its prevalence and to contest understandings which locate such abuse as a function of personal pathology or family dysfunction. They have drawn attention to the preponderance of men as perpetrators of such abuse, and see it as related to wider power relations which legitimize men's sexual exploitation of women and children. Feminists have attempted to influence policy and service provision in this area, and there is evidence of some success. They have been less successful in placing domestic violence on the social work agenda when their main focus was the damage it did to women. However, the development of analyses which have established the links between such violence and increased risks to children have proved influential.

Many of these developments have been subjected to feminist criticism. Wise (1995) has cast doubt on the feasibility of feminist social work as it has been developed. She argues that non-statutory agencies are not appropriate models for statutory social work, and she offers a critique on the abstract universalism of approaches which prioritize women's well-being, advocating instead contextual approaches which work for the best interests of the most vulnerable in any given situation.

There are also differences between feminists in terms of understanding violence and abuse; Featherstone and Trinder (1997) argue that there has been a failure to acknowledge differences between men, and that accounts of why abusive men behave as they do have been overly reductive and rational.

It is probable that a feminist project, which concerns itself with the needs and welfare of women, inadequately addresses the complexity of men's lives and locates children's welfare as coterminous with their mother's will not be perceived as relevant to practitioners in the future. What is more likely to be required are approaches which recognize the importance of the massive social changes which are occurring (such as the increase in divorce) and address the implications for all concerned – women, men and children.

For Further Reading

Featherstone, B. and Trinder, L. 1997: Familiar subjects? Domestic violence and child welfare. *Child and Family Social Work*, 2 (3), 147–59.

Langan, M. and Day, L. (eds), 1992: *Women, Oppression and Social Work*. London: Routledge.

Wise, S. 1995: Feminist ethics. In R. Hugman and D. Smith (eds), *Ethical Issues in Social Work*, London: Routledge.

BRID FEATHERSTONE

Financial Advice

Financial advice aims to solve financial problems faced by people who use social work services. It involves providing information and other practical help. The close relationship between poverty and social care services means that service users will often experience financial problems. These may be related to difficulties in trying to live on social security benefits, problems caused by administrative failure in delivery of social security or personal debt.

Financial advice may involve welfare rights advice or money advice (sometimes called debt counselling). It can also involve practical advice on life skills concerned with living on a low income, obtaining funds from charities (to fill gaps in social security provision) and also using the legal powers of social care agencies to make discretionary financial payments. Financial advice may also occur in task-centred approaches or crisis intervention.

For Further Reading
Wolfe, M. 2000: *Debt Advice Handbook* (2nd edn). London: Child Poverty Action Group.

NEIL BATEMAN

Focus Groups

Focus groups are targeted group sessions which can be used for a variety of purposes and which follow a particular format.

In social work, focus groups can be used for qualitatively orientated, formative, process and outcome evaluations, quality assurance initiatives and community needs assessments. The advantages are that participants are actively involved in information generation, material can be gathered quickly, and accessible and applicable results can be produced. Disadvantages are that too much credibility can be attached to the views of focus group members and that it can be difficult to form a group which interacts productively.

One format, much utilized, comprises: a brief *introduction*; an opening *factual question* to generate interaction; *transition questions* which operate as a link between the introductory question and the key questions; the *key questions* which form the substance of the session and which clearly emphasize the topic of interest to the focus group facilitators; and *ending questions* which close the discussion and enable participants to reflect on what has been said. The optimum number of participants is eight and there are two group facilitators.

For Further Reading
Morgan, D. L. and Krueger, R. A. 1998: *The Focus Group Kit*. London: Sage.

BARBARA FAWCETT

Foetal Alcohol Syndrome

Foetal alcohol syndrome is a term devised by US researchers in the 1970s to describe the effects on the foetus of alcohol consumption by women in pregnancy. Research in the USA has pointed to short- and long-term effects: for example, low birth weight, attention deficit disorders, and brain damage. These findings are tentative, however, and there is ongoing debate about whether such effects are due solely to alcohol misuse. Most known cases of foetal alcohol syndrome are from very deprived backgrounds, and other forms of substance misuse (smoking and drug-taking) are frequently implicated. Foetal alcohol syndrome raises issues for preventive health and child protection work.

BRIAN CORBY

Foster Care

Foster care is an arrangement for the temporary care of a child separated from his or her family of origin whereby he or she is looked after in the home of another family, usually in return for some form of allowance or payment. It is to be distinguished from adoption, which implies the permanent transfer to substitute carers of all of the rights as well as the duties of birth parents.

The background to foster care
Historically, most societies have made informal, usually kinship-based, arrangements to assume responsibility for the care of children who could not be looked after by their

own parents. Such arrangements continue to be made, although the term 'foster care' is increasingly reserved for the more formal processes involving those agencies that have a statutory duty towards children. Foster homes comprise a variety of family forms and household structures, including lone carers and those without children of their own.

Contemporary forms of foster care can trace their more immediate origins to the nineteenth-century practice of 'boarding out' children who might otherwise have been looked after in institutional forms of care such as the workhouse, district school or penitentiary. Although slow to develop at first, the provision of family style care was given impetus by a more general failure of faith in institutional provision that emerged on both sides of the Atlantic after World War II. To this point, foster care was generally regarded as a long-term alternative to other forms of substitute care. It drew on the philanthropic or charitable instincts of host families and on immersion in the host family for its intended beneficial effects, generally to the exclusion of the child's birth parents.

The post-war preventative and rehabilitative ideal produced a more inclusive, short-term and task-focused form of foster care, and encouraged the use of foster homes as the placement of first resort for children in the public care. The pre-eminence of family forms of care was secured by several studies published in the 1970s which identified high failure rates for residential provision and rediscovered large numbers of children who had become 'lost in care'. Subsequently, a preference re-emerged among childcare professionals for earlier decision making and the securing of more 'permanent' foster-ing (or adoptive) arrangements for children. Such arrangements, it was argued, would enable children to receive adequate 'psychological' parenting, through continuity of reliable relationships and consistent nurturing care.

As well as changes in the means, this period also saw developments in the mode of foster care and the advent of the professional or treatment foster home. Such pro-grammes are defined by their more therapeutic, task-specific and contractual orienta-tion. Treatment foster carers are usually paid a salary, rather than an allowance, for the maintenance of the child.

The nature of foster care today

The movement towards consumerism in welfare services has seen the re-emergence of a model of foster care which once more aims to support rather than replace the family of origin as the primary locus of child-rearing, and which uses both traditional and treat-ment models of foster care.

Many of the tensions that have characterized the development of foster care remain unresolved and find echo in contemporary practice. Placements continue to be defined along such dimensions as intended duration and particular function. Both the relative status of foster carers and the place of the child's birth family in the fostering arrange-ment continue to be points of contention.

Accordingly, foster care practice is enormously varied. Short-term foster care might range from day-placements to a continuous period of several years. Placements may be voluntary or court mandated. Arrangements might be intended to accommodate the tem-porary absence of a child's carer, to offer relief or respite care to a child or their usual carers, as a remedial, restorative or therapeutic experience for a child who has suffered abuse or neglect or where family problems preclude the child's parents from looking after their child adequately, for the purposes of assessment, as preparation for adoption, or as a remand condition. In almost all cases, foster carers need to be able to respond to receiving children at short notice, often at a time of crisis, to be able to meet the psychological and emotional needs of children separated from their usual carers, to

continued

provide high standards of physical care, and to work as part of a multidisciplinary team, as well as with the child's birth parents, on resolving whatever difficulties are associated with the child.

Measuring the effectiveness of foster care

The effectiveness of short-term fostering can be measured against several outcomes, and in relation to each party to the process, depending on the purpose of the placement. Factors associated with success, broadly defined but especially where this implies the child returning to the care of his or her parents, include well-planned recruitment, selection and training of carers, careful preparation of the child for the placement, a structured process of matching and introductions, regular contact with the child's family of origin, close liaison among all those working with the child, and beneficial changes brought about through direct work with the child's family. In the UK, success rates of over 80 per cent have been claimed for placements providing temporary care in this way.

In practical terms, the distinction between long-term foster care and adoption may be difficult to sustain, in that the former can be a prelude to the latter and may not have family reunification (also sometimes termed *rehabilitation home*) as an objective. Long-term placement with relatives or friends is generally more successful than other forms of long-term placement. Across the full range of long-term placements, approximately 20 per cent will break down within five years. Decisive factors in success include age at placement, the degree of emotional and behavioural difficulty associated with the child, and the degree to which the child's pre-placement history and culture and their sense of their own origins is preserved and integrated with their later sense of personal identity. This has been shown to be particularly important in the case of cross-cultural placements.

For Further Reading

Berridge, D. 1996: *Foster Care: A Research Review*. London: HMSO.

Sellick, C. and Thoburn, J. 1996: *What Works in Family Placement?* Barkingside: Barnardos.

Triseliotis, J., Sellick, C. and Short, R. 1995: *Foster Care: Theory and Practice*. London: Batsford/BAAF.

IAN BUTLER

Freedom of Information

See CONFIDENTIALITY.

Functional Assessment and Analysis

Functional assessment and *functional analysis* are used for the identification of environmental contingencies of which the behaviour under investigation is a function. Functional assessment and functional analysis can be used with any client group: they are concerned with the function rather than the structure of behaviour; they are applied to clinically relevant and/or everyday behaviours; they lay the foundations for individually tailored treatment plans, and

they can be employed as treatment or a part of treatment.

Functional assessment and analysis are based on the knowledge that:

- functionally equivalent behaviour can be topographically different; for example, self-injurious behaviour or temper tantrums can both serve to avoid a task;
- topographically similar behaviour can serve different functions; for example, school refusal can serve to gain social attention or to avoid bullying.

Functional assessment is both a method for aiding hypotheses or clinical formulations about

FUNCTIONAL ASSESSMENT AND ANALYSIS

the function of variables causing behaviour (without explicit testing), and is descriptive of contingencies of which behaviour is a function (without experimental verification). Functional analysis is experimental: relevant antecedents or consequences are systematically altered in a range of test settings leading to the identification of exact circumstances that control the behaviour.

For Further Reading
Sturmey, P. 1996: *Functional Analysis in Clinical Psychology*. Chichester: John Wiley.

KAROLA DILLENBURGER

G

Gambling Addiction

Gambling addiction is a state of psychological dependence on the activity characterized by a felt need to take part in various types of gambling. It is associated with intermittent or continuous preoccupation with gambling, and the development of craving and tolerance for it. There is impaired control over gambling and 'chasing of losses', in spite of the realization that this leads to increasing problems. The resulting financial, social and psychological disorder is known as *pathological gambling*.

While it is an heterogeneous condition, personal aspects within the make-up, such as risk-taking characteristics as well as depression, play a part in causation. Interpersonal difficulties, especially within the family, may initiate the condition and maintain it. Public policy on gambling is also important, especially in relation to the availability of facilities and the encouragement of excess.

There should be a detailed assessment of the personal and social aspects of the situation and help provided for problems in these areas. Access to readily available money should be restricted, and repayments by the individual to creditors arranged. Initially, there must be total abstinence from gambling and this may need to be lifelong. Gamblers Anonymous, a self-help group, can offer valuable support and, in certain cases, is able to provide all the help necessary.

For Further Reading

Moran, E. 1995: Gambling. In M. Jacobs (ed.), *The Care Guide*, London: Cassell.

EMANUEL MORAN

Gatekeeping

Gatekeeping is a term, coined in the 1970s, intended to refer to actions designed to prevent individuals from entering social welfare systems, or to limit access to scarce resources. In juvenile justice, the concept was originally associated with resistance to a tendency (especially in the more preventative approaches such as intermediate treatment) for individuals to become subjected to increasing measures of formal control, out of proportion to the scale of their delinquent actions ('*net widening*'). Heavily rooted in social systems thinking, gatekeeping was viewed as a necessary precaution to prevent '*tariff escalation*' – i.e. the imposition of rapidly escalating sanctions following a further offence or other deviant behaviour.

Within contemporary social work practice, community care and criminal justice services, gatekeeping is more closely associated with the *rationing* of scarce resources. In the field of intensive probation for offenders at high risk of custody, this is carried out routinely as part of the pre-court assessment process, frequently utilizing *risk assessment* scales and measures. A similar approach is inherent in many community care assessment procedures.

In the wider fields of welfare and benefits, tightly prescribed criteria may exist which determine those particular groups to be *targeted* for greater levels of control or resources, according to political objectives.

BRYAN WILLIAMS AND NORMA BALDWIN

Gay Men

See LESBIAN AND GAY ISSUES IN SOCIAL WORK.

Gender

Gender refers to the set of characteristics, behaviours and practices associated with the sexual categories of male and female. Within social science, however, the definition of gender is dependent upon the theoretical framework which is used to explain it. The definition here is based on the principle that culture (for example, in terms of socially ascribed role taking), rather than biology, is responsible for shaping conduct; hence, the relationship between sexual category and gender is that of association. By way of contrast, biologically based explanations of gender would assume that behaviour is a direct result of the same internal phenomena (such as genes, hormones and chromosomes) which determine sex category. These two general ways of describing gender can be understood as essentialist: that is, gender is the inevitable product of either biology or culture. Alternatively, constructionist theorists might focus upon the way in which gender is created through language. Strong constructionists would argue that even sex cannot be understood only as a biological given: scientists undertaking their investigations do so by way of socially available concepts or linguistic systems. Given the influence of sociology and feminism, those researching and writing in the field of social work usually understand gender either as a product of culture or as a construction.

The importance of gender in social work

Feminists and anti-sexist writers, in their attempt to draw attention to the power relations and inequalities between men and women, have largely been responsible for making gender an important theme in social work research and literature. All aspects of social work – its knowledge base, education, organization and practice – have been scrutinized through the gendered lens. For example, it has been argued that most of the social science knowledge which informs social work is androcentric, with the result that women are either ignored or treated as the inferior Other. Feminists have responded by carrying out research from new perspectives and developing their own theoretical frameworks. Taking knowledge and curricula into account, strategies for ensuring anti-sexist social work education have been suggested. In terms of the organization of social work, attention has been drawn to the horizontal and vertical segregation of labour. With regard to practice, attention has been given to ways of working that are sensitive to the difficulties that women face, particularly in the context of a sexist society.

Variations in the feminist perspective

Feminists, however, are not a homogeneous group and different feminist perspectives employ different explanations of gender, gendered inequality and the means of achieving change. Liberal feminists take an individualist approach and see prejudice as the culprit in an otherwise satisfactory social system. In contrast, Marxist and radical feminists propound a structural analysis: Marxist feminists emphasize the fundamental injustice of a class-based society, and radical feminists draw attention to the ways in which men, by means of the patriarchal system, collude to maintain power and control over women. Radical feminists encourage women's alliance as a means of creating change. Post-structural feminists, as the name suggests, reject the idea that one single structure can account for gendered inequality. Instead, attention is given to the multiple, often contradictory, processes of gendered power relations.

Although this is not an exhaustive list of the different feminist perspectives, the description gives some indication of the theoretical frameworks most frequently used when feminists write about social work. The topic of gender and social work organizations serves to illustrate this point: liberals would suggest organizational equal opportunities measures as a means of achieving a more efficient meritocracy and an improved chance of promotion for women. Marxist feminists might advocate the elimination of pay differentials between managers and social workers, while radical feminists advocate the increased appreciation of feminine qualities. This would lead to more women managers, a different style of leadership, and, in turn, more caring organizations. Post-structuralist feminists might examine respondents' accounts of social work careers and the complex interplay of power which is inevitably involved when gender is linguistically constructed.

Men's role

Given that the oppression of women automatically implicates men, they too have been subjected to the academic gaze. Attention to men's role as oppressor has been one factor

continued

in the development of critical studies on men. Relevant for social work, for example, has been the critical reflection on men's violence in families. Partly in response to the focus on men as oppressors, there has grown concern with the more varied ways in which men can behave – as carers for dependent relatives, for instance. This may be motivated by a rejection of the feminist's arguments in total, or more particularly, a rejection of the one-dimensional hierarchy of power, and the essentialist notions of gender that are associated with some feminist analyses.

Sexuality is an integral part of gender and this, too, has been an important topic for social work research, theory, organization and practice. Sexuality and masculinity have been under particular scrutiny as men are, in the main, the perpetrators of child sexual abuse. Concern with sexuality has been broader than this, however, and attention has focused, not only on exploitation and the need to control sexuality, but also with facilitating sexual relationships, as in the arrangement of residential care for elderly or disabled adults. While heterosexuality has dominated the agenda, there is increasing recognition of the multiplicity of sexualities and the need for social work to take this into account.

For Further Reading
Hearn, J. and Maynard, M. (eds) (forthcoming): *Women, Men and Gender Relations.* Cambridge: Polity Press.
Langan, M. and Day, L. (eds) 1992: *Women, Oppression and Social Work: Issues in Anti-discriminatory Practice.* London: Routledge.
Pringle, K. 1995: *Men, Masculinities and Social Welfare.* London: UCL Press.

ELIZABETH HARLOW

General Anxiety Disorder

General anxiety disorder is a condition in which the patient experiences abnormal levels of anxiety without any precipitants. It usually presents in early adult life but can occur in later middle age. One-year prevalence rates are 2.4 per cent for men and 5.0 per cent for women. It is important to exclude a diagnosis of depression as patients often present with prominent anxiety symptoms. Psychological treatments, including relaxation techniques and education about anxiety, are beneficial. Medication is also helpful. Symptomatic relief can be gained by the use of beta-blockers and benzodiazepines such as diazepam. The latter are highly effective but have problems with the risk of dependence. Tricyclic and SSRI (selective serotin re-uptake inhibitors) antidepressants are also of benefit.

For Further Reading
Nutt, D. and Bell, C. 1997: Practical pharmacotherapy for anxiety. *Advances in Psychiatric Treatment,* 3, 79–85.

CLAIRE KENWOOD AND RAY VIEWEG

General Practice, Social Work in

Social work in general practice refers to the location of social workers in doctors' surgeries. It originates from the fact that people's health and social care needs overlap, and is based on the idea that they can best be met by co-ordinated interprofessional work. It is most often seen in services to older people.

The benefits are that it enhances preventative work, that access to services is less stigmatizing for service users, that services respond more holistically to need and that service quality is improved. The weaknesses – which help to explain why its development has been patchy – are that the social worker will have to manage conflicting priorities, while being professionally isolated and relatively unsupported. This isolation may also create managerial problems.

In practice, social work in general practice blurs the boundaries between health and social care. It is important to ensure that a social work identity is retained in a medically dominated environment. If this is managed, the strengths of the model outweigh the weaknesses, and it can prove a stimulating environment for experienced social workers.

For Further Reading
Lymbery, M. 1998: Social work in general practice: dilemmas and solutions. *Journal of Interprofessional Care,* 12 (2), 199–208.

MARK LYMBERY

Generic and Specialist Practice

Generic practice means individuals and teams working with all client groups, from the cradle to the grave, addressing a range of problems; using all or some social work methods; covering intake and long-term work. Occasionally, it means working across domiciliary, day and residential settings; and it can also mean working with one client group using various methods and/or settings.

Specialist practice means the opposite. It can mean either a division of labour or superior knowledge and skill about a client group, problem area, methods or settings. The specialist practitioner can be at the front line or specialism can extend up the organization.

Generic social work assumes a common core of knowledge, values and skills underpinning all practice. In the 1970s, this belief was, mistakenly, taken by social services departments to require teams and their members to work generically. This was never the case with non-governmental organizations. Now social services and social work departments in the UK have specialist posts, teams and sections, a change reinforced by legislation. There has been little research into whether the different practices have different outcomes. A question, of particular relevance for social work education, concerns the stage at which social workers should specialize.

For Further Reading
Fuller, R. and Tulle-Winton, E. 1996: Specialism, genericism and others: does it make a difference? *British Journal of Social Work*, 26, 679–98.

PHYLLIDA PARSLOE

Genetic Factors

Genetic factors refer to aspects of behaviour which are of inherited origin. Research in behavioural genetics has grown rapidly since the 1980s with twin study-based mathematical/statistical models which analyse the multivaried influences of nature, nurture, and their complex interactions.

Much evidence from the behavioural sciences has come to support the idea of genetic influences for domains including parent–child conflict; life events from childhood to adolescence; age at puberty and first sexual intercourse; divorce, linked to personality traits; behavioural and psychiatric disorders; and in most other investigated domains. Though the role of genetic influences is neglected outside psychology, psychiatry and medicine, the rapidly burgeoning findings have much relevance for social work, particularly in the genetic links involved in domestic violence, step-parent–child conflict and abuse, and IQ-linked childhood aggressive, antisocial, or maladaptive behaviour persisting through adolescence and adulthood. Recognition of the interaction of genetic and socio-environmental influences could minimize expression of these latent genetic risks.

For Further Reading
Marteau, T. and Richards, M. (eds) 1999: *The Troubled Helix: Social and Psychological Implications of the New Human Genetics*. Cambridge: Cambridge University Press.

KENNETH KIM

Geriatric Medicine

Geriatric medicine (also known as *medicine for the elderly*, *clinical gerontology* or *clinical geratology*) relates to the prevention, diagnosis, alleviation or cure of disease in older persons. Like all branches of clinical medicine, geriatric medicine is both a science based on evidence, and an art requiring skills and attitudes derived from experience. Geriatric medicine is particularly concerned with the promotion and maintenance of health, as well as remedial and social aspects of illness.

The specialty of geriatric medicine has become established in many developed countries over the last few decades, in response to ageing of the population. Developing countries are now facing similar demographic change as survival improves and birth rates decline. By the year 2025, it is predicted that there will be more than 100 million people aged above 80 years, over half of them in the developing world. There is no entirely satisfactory definition of *elderly*: using a particular age is administratively convenient and

continued

may relate to aspects of social provision (such as retirement pensions), but has little biological relevance. However, there are some illnesses (such as Alzheimer's disease or hip fracture) which become very much more common in later life, and, as a general rule, advanced age is associated with decreased physiological performance of most bodily functions. Although many people remain fit and healthy until very late in their lives, the last few years before death often comprise a period of increasing dependence and disability due to chronic disease. It is towards the healthcare needs of people during this period that geriatric medicine is primarily directed.

The medical needs of older people

Physiological decline with ageing varies from person to person, but may alter the presentation of disease in older people and complicate their treatment. In younger people, information gained from what the patient says, what the physical examination shows, and the results of investigations (such as blood tests or X-rays) is integrated to reach a single diagnosis. A different approach is often needed with older patients, many of whom suffer from several disorders at the same time. The major causes of disability are heart disease and stroke; loss of vision and hearing; arthritis and osteoporosis (thinning of bones); incontinence of urine; depression and dementia. Older people with any acute illness (such as pneumonia) may develop non-specific symptoms such as confusion, falls or immobility.

Older patients often take longer to recover from an acute illness than those who are younger, and they are more likely to have chronic disease which limits their functional ability. Rehabilitation is therefore a crucial component of geriatric medicine. The aim is to restore the person to the optimal level of ability within the needs and desires of that individual and his or her family. The patient (or client) is thus at the centre of the rehabilitation process: the therapeutic team must assess the degree of functional impairment and disability, make an informed estimate of the potential for recovery, and then negotiate goals which are relevant to that individual patient. Clearly such goals have to take into account the psychological and social frameworks within which the patient functions.

The context of geriatric medicine

In Britain, Australia and New Zealand geriatric medical services are led by specialists working predominantly from hospital bases, linking to the community through outpatient clinics, day hospitals and domiciliary outreach teams. Older patients with acute illness are either managed as part of the general medical services for all ages, or in separate facilities according to a given age. The choice of age cut-off is usually driven as much by resource considerations as clinical need.

In the USA, geriatric medicine has evolved mainly from nursing homes, with more emphasis on primary care (as opposed to secondary care in hospitals) and general (family) practice. To some extent, the pattern of health services for older people in a particular country reflects the funding arrangements and the degree of choice which patients (and doctors) are free to exercise within that system. In several countries, for example, patients may choose to refer themselves to a specialist. Whatever the system, the interfaces between primary and secondary care, and between health and social services, need careful planning and management.

Apart from the care of acutely ill older people and rehabilitation, geriatric medicine is involved in the provision of long-term care to a greater or lesser extent in different countries. In the community, various systems have been tried to identify unreported illness or unmet health needs in older people through screening or case-finding. Such schemes may best be targeted at those who are more obviously at risk (such as the very elderly, those with functional impairment, living alone, recently bereaved or discharged from hospital). However, these initiatives are not of proven benefit and require further research. For older people with overt complex health needs, comprehensive multidisciplinary geriatric assessment is of established value.

Reducing disability in old age

Perhaps the most important question facing geriatric medicine is how much we can reduce or postpone the period of disability at the end of life. Many of the relatively limited number of chronic disabling conditions in old age have their antecedents in middle age or even earlier. Modifiable influences such as smoking, diet and exercise have a substantial impact on outcomes. People with better health habits not only survive longer, but, in such persons, disability is postponed and compressed into fewer years at the end of life. Health policy will place increasing reliance on health promotion and prevention of disease through environmental and lifestyle patterns.

For Further Reading
Briggs, R. 1998: An historical overview of geriatric medicine: definition and aims. In M. S. J. Pathy (ed.), *Principles and Practice of Geriatric Medicine* (3rd edn), Chichester: John Wiley: 1–6.
Khaw, K.-T. 1997: Healthy ageing. *British Medical Journal*, 315, 1090–6.
Vita, A. J., Terry, R. B., Hubert, H. B. and Fries, J. F. 1998: Ageing, health risks and cumulative disability. *New England Journal of Medicine*, 338, 1035–41.

ROGER BRIGGS

Globalization and Social Work

Globalization is the idea that the world has become more integrated, economically, politically and culturally. In *economic* terms, it refers to the internationalization of production and trade and the increased mobility of capital. *Politically*, this is seen to have placed constraints on national policy making, although it may also lead to new supra-national forms of governance. *Culturally*, it is conceived of in terms of the compression of time and space, and the increased mobility of ideas facilitated by information technologies.

Globalization may affect social work in a number of ways. The purchaser/provider split has allowed multinational firms to become providers of care. Shifts towards more flexible patterns of work may affect both the organization of social work and the nature of its client base. Social policies premised on low tax levels and budget restraint reduce the resources available for social services. Funds may also be diverted away from highly dependent groups towards education and training to attract higher-wage investment. Finally, an intensified exchange of theories, practices and research findings between social work communities has become possible.

For Further Reading
Trevillion, S. 1997: The globalisation of European social work. *Social Work in Europe*, 4 (1), 1–9.

CHRISTOPHER HOLDEN

Good-enough Parenting

Good-enough parenting is a term introduced to child care social work by the British child psychiatrist, Donald Winnicott, who emphasized that there is no 'right' way to bring up children. Whether a parent is 'good enough' can only be assessed in the light of the needs of an individual child. Parenting which is good enough for an emotionally resilient child may fail to meet the needs of a child who is learning disabled or temperamentally vulnerable. The support available from a partner, relative or welfare agency can tip the balance between good-enough parenting and the necessity for out-of-home placement.

For Further Reading
Winnicott, D. W. 1965: *The Maturational Process and the Facilitative Environment*. New York: International Universities Press.

JUNE THOBURN

Group Homes/Groupcare

Group care takes place within both residential and day care services, and is a discrete area of practice which focuses on the differing formal and informal groups which occur when people, both users and staff, share the same life-space. *Group homes* provide a base for a range of people in need of care, and differ in their organizational aims. For some, the main aim is to provide residence to promote choice and independence, while others are primarily therapeutic communities. Many, while not

147

explicitly therapeutic, will seek to exploit the therapeutic potential of opportunity-led work derived from both formal and naturally occurring encounters.

Although the primary task and working methods will vary, in all homes there will be an emphasis on the "coordinated use of time through rotas, routine, etc." (Ward, 1993). The planned use of physical space and the interface between the staff and user-group will be more significant than in other practice settings. The complex patterns of interaction which occur within and between the differing groupings necessitate team interdependence, clear leadership, consistent ways of working informed by groupwork theory, and clarity of purpose.

For Further Reading
Ward, A. 1993: *Working in Group Care: Social Work in Residential and Day Care Settings.* Birmingham: Venture Press.

HILARY LAWSON

Groupwork

Groupwork refers to a method of social work practice which is concerned with the recognition and use of processes which occur when three or more people work together towards a common purpose. The term groupwork is also used to describe a context for practice, where social work practice is conducted in groups.

The use of the group in social work has a distinguished history. Indeed, groupwork occupied one of the four pillars of the classical edifice of social work practice, the other three being casework, family work and community work. Groupwork practice is well-researched and has proved effective with many different people in a variety of difficult circumstances; it has an international pedigree and supports two journals, *Groupwork* and *Social Work with Groups*. The power of groups and groupwork has entered the popular consciousness, especially through well-known experiments in social psychology which have demonstrated the potential of groups to achieve changes in the beliefs and behaviours of individual members.

The nature of groupwork
The archetypal social work group is led by two co-workers and consists of 6–12 participants, selected because of their common needs and problems, meeting once a week for 6–12 sessions. However, there is an extraordinary diversity of groups and groupwork, and this image of a stereotypical group is no more common than that of the 'typical' nuclear family.

It is not easy to pin groupwork down to a succinct definition. A gathering of people is not sufficient; 'groupings' frequently arise in residential and day care settings without necessarily giving rise to groupwork. Moreover, individual social work can be conducted in groups without the practice of groupwork; this has been described as 'work in groups' rather than groupwork. A further complexity arises from the fact that the orientation of groupworkers varies immensely, from behavioural to psychodynamic, and from a highly structured format to very loose, non-directive approaches; all can be described as groupwork.

Since there seem to be as many kinds of groupwork as there are social work practices, what are the distinguishing features? Groupwork involves the explicit use of group processes, where the group is an instrument for change or stability. The focus of the outcome of groupwork practice can be at the individual or the group level or both, but it amounts to more than 'work in groups'. Role theory has been influential in the development of a theory of groupwork, especially in terms of explaining individual behaviours in groups. Systems theory, too, has been significant in helping to consider the interaction between individuals, the group leadership, subgroups, the whole group itself and larger systems beyond the group. Empowerment models of groupwork practice have developed in response to broader concerns about power, oppression and anti-discriminatory practice in social work; groups are seen as microcosms of the wider society, with the potential to oppress.

The strength of groupwork lies in its ability to bring together people who face similar difficulties and to provide opportunities for people to experience companionship and to give as well as to receive. Gathering people together is, in itself, potentially empowering; paradoxically, the group also provides a powerful medium in which professionals can exert their authority, should they choose to do so. This is demonstrated especially in groups in probation settings, where offence-related groups are commonly used to change and control unacceptable behaviours.

Key issues in groupwork

Whatever the particular approach, there are several issues of universal significance to groupwork:

- The purposes of the group and how these are agreed
- The way individual members find out about the group and whether they are chosen, self-selected or 'involuntary'
- The optimum size and composition of a group (especially in terms of difference or sameness in the characteristics of group members)
- The boundaries of the group; whether group members have contact with each other outside the group
- The respective advantages and disadvantages of a time-limited or an open-ended group, and open or closed membership
- Styles of leadership and arrangements for co-leading or co-facilitating
- The leadership's ability to balance process skills and task skills
- The kinds of activity to be used in the group
- The methods used to record and evaluate the group, along with issues of confidentiality and disclosure
- The ways in which group processes are used
- The organizational context of the group and the 'fit' between groupwork and other aspects of the social work service
- The practical arrangements and organizational skills which groupwork entails should never be underestimated

The response to all of these central concerns depends very much on the orientation of the groupworker, but the issues themselves are generic.

The future of groupwork

There is some concern that groupwork, as opposed to work in groups, is in decline. Certainly, it is difficult to assess the extent to which groupwork is used as a practice method, but it is likely that the prevalence of groupwork is heavily influenced by agency policies. In common with many forms of social work practice, it is important to consider how dependent both the quantity and the quality of groupwork is on agency patronage. Groupworkers must, therefore, consider what agency supports there are for their practice: is it integral or an optional extra? A core activity of the agency or icing on the cake? A significant part of the agency's skill base or a perk for some of the staff? Even in those cases where there is evident commitment to groupwork, such as those probation services in the UK which rely heavily on groupwork provision, there is no guarantee that different kinds of groupwork will be allowed to flourish.

Groupwork has played a significant part in the history and development of social work practice. It is possible that the active use of group processes is becoming less common than 'work in groups', but an ability to recognize group processes, and to work with them, remains an essential social work skill.

continued

For Further Reading
Brown, A. 1992: *Groupwork* (3rd edn). Aldershot: Ashgate.
Doel, M. and Sawdon, C. 1999: *The Essential Groupworker*. London: Jessica Kingsley.
Mullender, A. and Ward, D. 1991: *Self-directed Groupwork: Users Take Action for Empowerment*. London: Whiting and Birch.

MARK DOEL

Groupwork – Some Practice Perspectives

Each *groupwork* initiative is unique, and any typification risks violating the reality of individual experience. We can, however, detect some core themes and patterns which will have meaning wherever groupwork takes place.

Context, planning and negotiation

Consideration of *context* is the key to groupwork practice. Most initiatives will aim to examine a number of levels:

- The different needs, interests and potential contributions of the various stakeholders involved: each bringing their own experience, expectations, beliefs, hopes and fears to the enterprise, all of which interacts to produce a synergy greater than the sum of the parts
- The values and assumptions which will inform decisions to be made about needs, assessment and the proposed methods of intervention
- Practical resourcing and support for the group and the availability of social work provision

The *planning* phase will involve:

- the formulation of clear aims and purposes
- naming the type of group and the criteria for membership
- the selection process, and the offer of service to individuals
- the identification of resources and organizational arrangements
- clarifying the nature of leadership styles
- the exploration of power differentials and potential for oppression within the group.

The establishment of the group requires *negotiation* and *agreement* about whether it will be:

- open or closed
- established or created
- heterogeneous or homogeneous
- long-lived or short-lived
- open-ended or time-limited
- large or small
- outward looking or inward looking
- voluntary or compulsory.

Different types of group

It is possible to identify four broad categories of group in terms of leadership, facilitation, and self-direction:

- *Problem-solving/task-centred groups* tend to follow a structured approach with specific aims and outcomes; they may use behavioural, cognitive and/or learning theories; they are functional. Examples of such groups might include social skills training groups, parents coping with child behaviour difficulties, offenders, or treatment groups.

- Some *psychotherapeutic/counselling groups* use psychodynamic theories (for example, drawing on Freudian or Kleinian ideas); other approaches may be humanistic and/or person-centred (for example, using transactional analysis or Rogerian ideas); yet others may have a cognitive emphasis (for example, cognitive, neurolinguistic programming, drama, art or music groups). The focus is on relationships, feelings, the achievement of personal change and increased self-awareness through group interaction. Examples might include debriefing from trauma, working with the survivors of abuse or domestic violence, or a disability forum.

- *Mutual support groups* are made up of participants who share common personal concerns, needs or interests; they might include groups catering for the carers of older people with Alzheimer's disease, those aiming to derive support at a time of loss or bereavement, or those aiming at self-help – for example, a black workers' group.

- In *action-oriented groups* participants collaborate around common social concerns to empower themselves and to campaign towards neighbourhood, political or social change (for example, black womanist groups or groups of tenants).

Group processes

Common practice supports the early negotiation of a group *contract* or working agreement. This incorporates aims and purposes with individual expectations and concerns, and establishes ground rules or a code of conduct. A critical element is the extent to which individual members feel engaged through this process, above and beyond their own personal needs.

Good practice suggests that issues of *power* and *authority* can then be explored as differences and similarities appear, and a partnership of co-equals is established. The sources of power which may be assumed, ascribed, or aspired to include:

- a dominant ideology (for example, race, gender, ability, age, class)
- position/status
- knowledge and skills
- control over resources
- personal attributes.

The impact of different or conforming styles of behaviour and leadership may then become evident, and the groupworkers may perceive different roles and relationships, emerging (for example, 'gatekeeping', 'scapegoating', alliances or subgroups).

The *group identity* grows and *norms* are agreed or tussled over as individuals seek to find common ground. Stages of development have been characterized as forming, storming, norming, performing and adjourning. The groupworkers usually take responsibility for the process *on behalf of the whole group*. Critical incidents may be explored while the negotiated content of the group programme continues. Key skills will include the balancing of task and process, and balancing individual and group needs.

Themes to the fore are likely to include co-operation and mutual compliance, conflict, dependency, exclusion and intimacy – a microcosm of society. Most groupworkers strive to understand the interactions and inhibitions present, and the interplay of different kinds of power and challenge – particularly their own potential to oppress because of their power as leaders or facilitators.

Even where communication is experienced as open and clear, the group may still value useful triggers, and could use *action techniques*:

- Hardware – for example, video, audio, pre-recorded tapes
- Written/printed material – for example, questionnaires, reports

continued

- Experiential programming – for example, exercises, games, simulation, role play
- Graphic material – for example, diagrams, photographs, use of flipchart
- Changing the shape – for example, using pairs, trios, small groups

Such techniques ultimately provide further opportunities for interaction between members and not simply between leaders and members. Shared activity helps to enhance the group's sense of identity through the promotion of interdependence, the facilitation of new relationships, and the opportunity for personal reflection. Communication leads to disclosure and the discovery of the beliefs, information and capabilities held by others; this, in turn, may make a difference to their lives.

Another significant consequence of these individual transactions is that some may choose to moderate their own more extreme positions to promote *group cohesion*. This process of negotiation and integration requires the groupworkers to be flexible in responding to unpredictable situations.

A group at the *performing stage* fully acknowledges member values, skills and resources. A climate of respect, trust and acceptance facilitates the achievement and evaluation of group tasks; individuals may ultimately lose self-limiting beliefs and develop more self-confidence as a direct result of this process of integration; and they may learn new skills transferable to other social situations.

Ending and evaluation
Before *adjourning* (or *ending*), to evaluate outcomes against its original aims, the group revisits its contract, thus enabling all members, including the leaders/facilitators, to express their appreciations before moving on.

The groupworkers may wish to *reflect* on their own practice and, finally, be required to evaluate professional outcomes in terms of the wider stakeholder interests.

For Further Reading
Brown, A. 1992: *Groupwork* (3rd edn). Aldershot: Ashgate.
Doel, M. and Sawdon, C. 1999: *The Essential Groupworker*. London: Jessica Kingsley.
Mullender, A. and Ward, D. 1991: *Self-directed Groupwork: Users Take Action for Empowerment*. London: Whiting and Birch.

CATHERINE SAWDON

Guardians *ad Litem*

A *guardian ad litem* is an independent social worker who is appointed by the court to represent and safeguard the interests of children in public law proceedings in England, Wales and Northern Ireland. In Scotland, the role of the *safeguarder* has some similarities to that of the guardian *ad litem*.

The court will normally appoint a guardian *ad litem* in all public law cases affecting a child, including applications for contact and secure accommodation orders. The guardian *ad litem* is represented by the child's solicitor, unless the child is believed competent to give instructions to a solicitor, and the instructions differ. The guardian *ad litem's* overriding duty is to provide an independent view to the court as to the best interests of the child and ensure his or her wishes and feelings are known. In addition, guardians *ad litem* are required to advise the courts on allocation and timetabling, and on how to keep delays to a minimum in the interests of the child's welfare.

A guardian *ad litem* may also be appointed in adoption proceedings where consent is refused or an independent view of the child's welfare is required.

For Further Reading
Department of Health 1992: *Manual of Practice Guidance for Guardians ad litem and Reporting Officers*. London: HMSO.

ANNA GUPTA

H

Health-related Social Work

Health-related social work is designed to provide a service to users who are in contact with health-care agencies – whether in the state or independent sectors. It can include work in primary health care settings (usually doctors' surgeries), psychiatric clinics or hospitals, general hospitals, hospices and nursing homes. Health-related social work has a strong interprofessional and interdisciplinary dimension, and it has been suggested that a major task for the social worker is to interpret bureaucratic medical systems to service users and, in turn, to represent the user's interests to other professionals.

GRETA BRADLEY

Health/Social Services Interface

The *health/social services interface* refers to the boundary between the responsibilities of the two services. Such boundaries are not necessarily coterminous; nor are health and social services single entities. A social services department may relate to a number of health authorities, trusts and primary care groups with differing and changing priorities, structures and legislative bases.

There can be difficulties for service users in obtaining appropriate help, most graphically illustrated by arguments about the *social bath*: the so-called Radox/Dettol divide. The management of the interface affects crucial areas such as hospital discharge and community care. Central government has made repeated calls for more effective working together as a seamless service. This can be facilitated through joint commissioning, multi-agency children's plans and the inclusion of social services personnel on health care management boards.

Those most likely to benefit from well planned interagency working are individuals who can least easily be fitted into the core business of either agency and whose needs are for both health and social care: for example, young homeless, people exhibiting challenging behaviour, people with learning disabilities, those with chronic illnesses, children leaving care and people with mental disorders.

For Further Reading
The Journal of Interprofessional Care. Basingstoke: CARFAX, quarterly.

LAURA MIDDLETON

Health Visitors

Health visitors are qualified nurses working in primary health care teams, having regular contact with and direct access to vulnerable families. They share active involvement with social workers in child protection work, and research has shown that many doctors delegate clinical responsibility in child abuse cases to health visitors; increasingly, health visitors represent GPs at case conferences, presenting the doctor's report or case notes as required.

Health visitors see their role as being one of prevention by the provision of support to families and the early identification of those in need of additional help.

MARTIN DAVIES

Helping

Helping is the process by which individuals are assisted in managing problem situations in their lives. It is the desired outcome of all social work interventions, in that they should improve the situation, alleviate suffering and leave people with a more positive sense of self.

One model of helping (Egan, 1998) involves four stages: exploring, understanding, action and evaluation. These stages depend on accurate communication which, by actively listening to, respecting and accepting people's construction of their world, can of itself be helpful; but accurate communication will also clarify understandings of the problem(s) to be managed and the changes that are needed, including changes expected by others in the case of involuntary referrals (for example, offenders).

Helping can involve practical support such as providing resources (including money or accommodation), undertaking tasks on behalf of an individual or ensuring that they acquire the necessary skills (for example, literacy skills and social skills). Other forms of helping can support changes in behaviour (for example, drug rehabilitation programmes).

Helping does not necessarily eradicate problems; the ultimate aim is to bring about positive change in the way that people manage their problems and, thereby, to empower them.

For Further Reading
Egan, G. 1998: *The Skilled Helper: A Systematic Approach to Effective Helping* (6th edn). California: Brooks/Cole.

JOAN ORME

Heredity
See GENETIC FACTORS.

Heterosexism
Heterosexism reflects the dominance of a worldview in which heterosexuality is used as the standard against which all people are measured; everyone is assumed to be *naturally* heterosexual unless proven otherwise, and anyone not fitting into this pattern is considered to be abnormal, sick, morally corrupt and inferior. The assumption of heterosexuality and its superiority is perpetuated through its institutionalization within laws, media, religions and language, which either actively discriminate against non-heterosexuals or else render them invisible through silence. Just as the concepts of racism and sexism have helped us to understand the oppression of black people and women, so the concept of heterosexism has assisted us in theorizing lesbian and gay oppression.

SUE WISE

HIV and AIDS

HIV (human immunodeficiency virus) is the retrovirus which may lead to the development of AIDS. *AIDS (acquired immune deficiency syndrome)* is a disease which causes a progressive weakening of the immune system. HIV is the primary cause of AIDS (Gant, 1998).

HIV attacks CD4 cells (also known as T4 cells and CD-4 lymphocytes and T-helper cells). CD4 cells are a type of blood cell important to the immune system. By reducing CD4 cells, HIV reduces the body's ability to fight infection. Healthy blood contains an average of 1,200 CD4 cells per cubic millimetre. HIV infection can cause this to drop into single figures. The body recognizes HIV as an agent which causes disease, and manufactures antibodies which fight against the virus. It is a test for these antibodies which reveals the presence of HIV (Gant, 1998; Milner, 1998).

The average time from HIV infection to the development of AIDS is twelve years. The 1987 CDC HIV Classification System, updated in 1993, views AIDS as a progression of HIV infections and identifies a number of disease stages:

- *Acute HIV infection* Following infection with HIV, antibodies are produced. The production of antibodies is known as seroconversion. Antibodies are not detectable with current tests for up to six months after infection. There may be some symptoms similar to flu, but people will not necessarily feel ill during this period.
- *Asymptomatic infection* There are no symptoms during this period and the majority of people will be unaware they have the virus.
- *Persistent generalized lymphadenopathy (PGL)* Symptoms such as glandular swelling, chronic diarrhoea and skin conditions may appear. They must be present for three months or more to constitute a progression of the illness.
- *AIDS-related complex (ARC) or active HIV infection* As the name suggests, illnesses resulting from the presence of HIV will develop. These may include neurological disease, secondary cancers and secondary infectious diseases. The immune system is greatly weakened, but not as severely as in AIDS.

- *AIDS* A person with AIDS will have a CD4 count of fewer than 200 cells per cubic millimetre of blood and will be HIV antibody positive (Milner, 1998).

Transmission

HIV is present in body fluids, including blood and blood products, semen, vaginal secretions, breast milk, urine, saliva and tears. HIV cannot survive outside the body. HIV is contagious, not infectious and it is very unlikely that the virus could be caught through casual contact such as coughing or sneezing. There are three routes of transmission.

1 *Sexual* The earliest reports of HIV were linked to gay men and, therefore, to the sexual behaviours of gay men. It is now known that the transmission of HIV is not linked to any particular sexual orientation, but to sexual activity.
2 *Blood* The main routes of transmission of HIV through blood are by transfusion of blood or blood products contaminated with the virus. In the UK, the Blood Transfusion Service now takes great care to ensure that all blood, and blood products, will be safe to use. The use of contaminated equipment, such as needles or syringes used for injection, carries a high risk of infection.
3 *Mother to child* It is possible that mothers who are infected with HIV can pass the virus on to their children during pregnancy, at the time of birth and through breast feeding. Approximately 25 per cent of children born to women who have HIV will be infected. If anti-HIV drugs are used during pregnancy, the risk of infection will be measurably reduced (Gant, 1998).

These methods of transmission enable the identification of high risk activities.

- *Sex-related activities* High-risk sexual practices include vaginal or anal intercourse without using a condom, and unprotected oral sex with mouth sores. Both these practices give a risk of the transfer of body fluids.
- *Blood-related activities* The sharing of needles and syringes may result in the transfer of blood left in the needle or syringe from one person to another. Needle exchange programmes have been found to reduce the incidence of HIV among injecting drug users, and education programmes are also important (Gant, 1998; Milner, 1998).

Epidemiology

The first cases of AIDS were identified in California in the early 1980s. Because the first people to be identified with AIDS were gay men, the disease was called gay-related immune disease (GRID). Early identification of the disease with gay men led to an hysterical reaction, talk of a 'gay plague' and persecution of the gay community. It is now well established that HIV, and its spread, is not confined to people of a particular sexual orientation. Rather, the disease will infect all persons who put themselves at risk by activities which expose them to contaminated body fluids by any one of a number of well-identified behaviours. AIDS is now a global disease. The World Health Organization estimates that there are 18.5 million adults and 1.5 million children infected with HIV. In the UK, at the end of 1997, 25,000 adults and children were infected with HIV (World Health Organization, 1999).

Service provision

In the UK, voluntary organizations were active from the early 1980s in the provision of support for people with HIV and AIDS. The best known of these organizations is the Terrance Higgins Trust, which led the way in developing services, and which still plays

continued

a major role. From the mid-1980s, the Government provided funds for health-related organizations, and for a public education campaign.

Treatment

There is no cure for AIDS, but drugs which slow down the disease process have been developed. The most recent development is a triple-combination antiretroviral therapy, which has been shown to be effective in controlling infections and symptomatic problems. However, it has adverse side-effects which make it a difficult regime to follow, and it is very costly, which limits its availability.

For Further Reading

Gant, L. M. 1998: Essential facts every social worker needs to know. In D. M. Aronstein and B. J. Thomson (eds), *HIV and Social Work: A Practitioners Guide*, Birmingham, New York: The Harrington Park Press.

Milner, K. 1998: The etiology and epidemiology of HIV disease. In M. D. Knox and C. H. Sparks (eds), *HIV and Community Mental Health Care*, London: John Hopkins University Press.

World Health Organization, http://www.who.ch/emc/diseases/hiv Accessed 8/9/99

JOANNA HESLOP WITH ADRIAN CROOK

Homelessness and Housing

To enjoy a minimum standard of living, a dwelling that is warm and damp-free, with bedrooms for all the occupants, is considered essential by a majority of people. However, nearly one million citizens in the UK lack these basics, and some are literally without homes. Homes are also 'properties' to be traded and rented. Residential dwellings in the UK are conventionally categorized by *tenure* – the manner in which they are owned. First, there is *personal ownership*, usually achieved by means of a mortgage, and most householders are owner–occupiers (67 per cent). Next, there are two forms of *renting*: the *social rented sector* provided by publicly funded bodies such as local authorities (20 per cent) and housing associations (4 per cent); then *private renting* from landlords who let commercially (10 per cent).

Housing

Housing can also be understood in terms of quantity, quality and access to the available dwellings. A surplus of dwellings above the number of households in society is necessary to provide flexibility in size, location and cost, which will allow for the residential mobility needed to accommodate demographic and economic changes and people's preferences. The surplus of available dwellings over demand narrowed from one million to 822,000 between 1979 and 1998. The Conservative governments between 1979 and 1997 decreased housing expenditure by 60 per cent, in an ideologically driven belief that the free market alone can satisfy housing need. However, a million of the UK's 23.6 million dwellings are unfit or unavailable, and half a million households are concealed within other households. If house building remains at the turn of the century figure of less than 200,000 per annum, as the social and economic changes work through, housing shortage is likely – leading to an increase in homelessness. Since 1986, the government has relegated the role of local housing authorities to that of 'enablers', and now housing associations lead building and letting in the social rented sector.

From 1945, local housing authorities were set to house the growing population and eradicate unfit dwellings. Circumstances, and their own ineptitude, prevailed against them managing to achieve those objectives. People lost confidence in local authorities as they fractured old communities only to 'replace' them with modernist housing estates constructed to low building standards in the 1960s and 1970s. People with sufficient income avoided living in them; others left when they could. Gradually the poorest, least socially powerful tenants came to dominate such estates. As the mass re-housing programme faltered, the neo-classical liberal economic project of the Thatcher administrations withdrew funding from public housing and gave tenants the *Right to Buy*. In 1980, local authorities rented 6.4 million dwellings most of which were traditional two-storey houses with gardens. Massive discounts made the *Right to Buy* a sensational success, so that, by 1995, 1.5 million dwellings had been sold. Local authorities had also lost stock to housing associations, trusts and private companies for renting, rehabilitation and resale. With just 4.5 million houses left by 1995, council estates had a different character because the dwellings which the sitting tenants preferred to buy were, in the vast majority of cases, houses with gardens, rather than flats or maisonettes. Hence, the social rented council estates remaining are now more distinctly separate in geographical location and architectural design, as well as in the social and financial circumstances of the tenants. Local authorities are left managing, with fewer resources, estates most of which are despised for their brutal modernist design, their isolation, crime, absence of amenities, and filthy environmental conditions. The tenures have been polarized and the public housing service residualized.

In 1998, a New Deal for Communities began, including 1,370 such estates, led by the Social Exclusion Unit which claimed to be developing an integrated and sustainable approach to the problem. Initially, 17 areas were chosen to become models of what could be achieved, on which is to be lavished £800 million.

Homelessness

Homelessness is the most extreme form of housing need in that it is a failure of access to a secure home. Social workers were happy to shed their former responsibilities for homeless families, but, although it is essentially a housing problem, homelessness is also about the breakdown of personal relationships. UK policy and law has always effectively made a *deserving–undeserving* distinction between homeless adults with dependent children and those without. Since 1977, there has been a statutory requirement on local housing authorities to house homeless people temporarily, pending investigation of their circumstances into eligibility for permanent, suitable re-housing. However, the only applicants who are likely to be helped are those with children, pregnant women, or who are otherwise deemed to be 'vulnerable' – because of old age, disability, chronic sickness, vulnerability to domestic violence, racial abuse, or because they are seen as young people 'at risk' of exploitation. That list is roughly in descending order of priority. Homeless persons officers may reject applicants because they are judged to have made themselves homeless intentionally and, if it can be shown, they have a 'better connection' with another local authority.

If an applicant passes these tests, they are deemed to be 'statutorily homeless'. In 1996, more restricted procedures were enacted. Now, the local housing authorities have the lesser duty to accommodate statutorily homeless households for up to two years, during which time they are put on the normal waiting list for social rented housing. Additionally, otherwise eligible applicants may be directed to 'other suitable accommodation' in the district and, if they do not take it, can be judged intentionally homeless. Homelessness grew during the 1980s to peak at 144,780 statutorily homeless households accepted in 1991, and fell to 120,810 in 1995 – the year before the changes.

continued

It is not known how many 'single homeless' people there are: perhaps around 100,000, of which a quarter may be in London alone. Many live in hostels and shelters provided by voluntary organizations, but more are 'dossing with friends', living in squats and sleeping out. Now, as in the nineteenth century, there is no other area of social services within which charitable organizations make the major provision of practical help and support – outside a statutory framework.

For Further Reading

Balchin, P. and Rhoden, M. (eds) 1998: *Housing: the Essential Foundations.* London: Routledge.

Burrows, R., Pleace, N. and Quilgars, D. (eds) 1997: *Homelessness and Social Policy.* London: Routledge.

Hutson, S. and Liddiard, M. 1994: *Youth Homelessness: the Construction of a Social Issue.* Basingstoke: Macmillan.

JOHN STEWART

Homophobia

Homophobia is a term coined in the early 1970s to describe the fear and loathing that many non-homosexuals feel about homosexuality (both male and female). It was conjectured that such feelings revealed deep psychological conflicts for individuals who were repressing their potential for homosexuality, which exists in all human beings. The term has now generally lost its pathological overtones and is used more generally to denote an individual's negative attitudes and responses towards lesbians and gay men. Although still used to describe a personality trait, it is now also used to describe forms of social organization and institutions: for example, to say that the legal system is homophobic is to comment on its oppressive nature for lesbians and gay men, in the same way that describing the legal system as racist or sexist is a short-hand way of referring to institutionalized oppression.

SUE WISE

Homosexuality

See LESBIAN AND GAY ISSUES IN SOCIAL WORK.

Hospital Admission

Admission to hospital refers to those situations in which an individual enters hospital to receive treatment as an in-patient; it may be either physical or psychiatric in nature, depending on the patient's health condition. Admission may be on an elective basis (planned in advance) or as an emergency following a traumatic accident or because of a developing health condition. The majority of admissions are to acute hospitals for intensive but time-limited interventions. There are a smaller but important number of admissions for progressive conditions in which the patient and/or the caregivers may require respite services, or in which medication regimes may need review and alteration.

Hospital social workers are ideally placed to assist individuals who are admitted to hospital with some of their concerns regarding practical support, welfare benefits or the longer-term implications of illness. Unfortunately, volume of work may mean that this is not possible in all cases, but, to achieve continuity and consistency of assessment and care planning, the role of the social worker in discharge planning should commence as close to admission as possible.

For Further Reading

Merry, P. 1998: *The NHS Confederation 1998/99 NHS Handbook* (13th edn). Tunbridge Wells: JMH Publishing.

BRIDGET PENHALE

Hospital Discharge

See DISCHARGE PLANNING.

Hospital Social Work

Hospital social work in the UK relates to the work carried out by professional practitioners in a range of hospital clinics, wards and out-patient departments in the state, private and voluntary sectors, including work done by social workers attached to hospices. Hospital-based social work practice has a long history, and remains crucial in health care.

The background to hospital social work

A recommendation from the House of Lords Select Committee on the abuse of hospitals in the metropolis (1892) led to the first almoner appointment in 1895. This post, occupied by Mary Stewart, on secondment from the Charity Organization Society (now the Family Welfare Association) was set up at the Royal Free Hospital, London. Other hospitals followed this approach: employing almoners to assist with high demands and to check that patients were not receiving free treatment if they could afford to pay. Their other functions were to promote access, treatment and public health among those in need. Early work centred on maternal and child services. The work quickly became professionalized with the introduction of the Hospital Almoners Council to oversee training and recruitment in 1907, and the London School of Economics awarding certificates for training in 1912.

During World War I, the role of almoners was encouraged in relation to the casualties of war. The 1920s focused again on means testing, but almoners also identified themselves with the emerging social work profession, particularly its work with children. The Hospital Almoners Association was formed in 1922 with 51 members, including those from outside London. The Royal Commission on Lunacy and Mental Disorder (1926) advocated a similar system to that of almoners for mental health – the genesis of psychiatric social work.

The almoner, a 'reserved occupation' during World War II, was freed by the creation of the NHS from financial assessment. The Institute of Almoners (a registration body formed in 1945) urged the employment of only qualified almoners. The Younghusband working party (1959) on training recommended a two-year training programme, followed by the 1962 Act to oversee training. In this post-war period, almoners developed psychodynamic casework approaches to social problems as well as relating to medical and social circumstances of patients in general or specialist health care settings. Baraclough (1995) describes their roles as brokerage, medication, reconciliation and service.

The Institute of Almoners changed its name to the Institute of Medical Social Workers in 1964. Medical or hospital social workers were traditionally attached to wards and outpatient departments in general/psychiatric hospitals. Their focus was on the impact of illness or disability on the personal and social situation of the patient/service user; to help them to adjust and come to terms with their changing health (physical) situation, and also to act on their behalf and liaise appropriately with other members of the multi-disciplinary team. The emphasis on the social aspects reflects a growing commitment to the social construction model. This work could be focused within the institution, involving attending ward rounds and meetings. For many, liaising with outside bodies was at a stage removed. Some hospital social workers continued to wear white coats within the hospital which was interpreted as their wish to identify with the medical profession. Other dynamics included the largely female composition of hospital social workers.

continued

Hospital social work today

The Seebohm Report (1968) and the ensuing changes meant that NHS social workers were transferred to local authority employment and the two-year medical social work training was subsumed into the general social work qualification. While, today, the title *hospital or medical social worker* may indicate the location or focus of the social worker's work, in many ways, the role of an almoner has been revalidated following the NHS and Community Care Act 1990. Depending on the circumstances, many will be involved in financial enquiries as part of holistic assessment and care management; others will be engaged in outreach or service development, particularly for patients with chronic conditions (including addictions). Some will be involved in social support for those with life-threatening conditions (for example, HIV/AIDS), and will see their remit as encompassing families and other care providers.

A tension clearly exists between the professional desire to offer a counselling or casework service and the prescribed role of care management. Equally, while the hospital or medical social worker continues to operate within health care settings, there may be strains in relationships at professional and agency levels. Pressure, for example, to increase in-patient turnover by movement to social care may be interpreted as detrimental to social well-being. A Social Services Inspectorate report (1993) classified hospital social work as being located at the interface; this can be interpreted at a variety of levels – interpersonally, interprofessionally and interagency. The role of the hospital social worker requires continual attention to these wider changes in welfare, to health provision in hospital and community settings in particular, and to interprofessional boundaries.

The role of hospital social work appears to be mirrored in other countries and Berkowitz's edited volume (1996) provides a series of examples of the potential for social workers to interpret bureaucratic medical systems to individuals and to represent individual interests. These examples suggest that *health-related social work* may be a term that more accurately describes practice than *hospital social work*, since hospitals are less commonly now the site of care and treatment. Nonetheless, the continuing importance and legitimacy of hospital-based social work, particularly in the area of discharge planning, remains in its own right.

For Further Reading

Baraclough, I. 1995: A cause for celebration. In *A Hundred Years of Health Related Social Work, Professional Social Work (Special Supplement)*, January, 9–12.

Berkowitz, N. (ed.) 1996: *Humanistic Approaches to Health Care: Focus on Social Work*. Birmingham: Venture Press.

Department of Health, Social Services Inspectorate 1993: *Social Services for Hospital Patients*. London: Department of Health.

GRETA BRADLEY

Housing

See HOMELESSNESS AND HOUSING.

The Human Life-cycle

The *human life-cycle* approach to developmental psychology is concerned with: the attitudes, feelings, thinking and behaviour of individuals in a social context throughout their lives; the changes that occur; and the factors that bring about those changes. The life-cycle approach is based on four premises:

1   Development is continuous, not just for children but for adults.
2   Maturity is relative.
3   Development occurs in a social context.
4   Developmental influences involve biological, cognitive and emotional factors, the social context, and their interaction.

Any consideration of a life-cycle approach must address the relative contribution of heredity and the environment to individual development. Learning theory contributes to our understanding of human development by postulating mechanisms throughout life by which we learn and adapt our behaviour. The life-cycle approach assumes that there are common developmental and emotional tasks which we all undergo at each stage of development. Piaget, Freud and Erikson postulate universal cognitive and/or psychosocial stages and tasks.

Piaget and cognitive theory

Piaget's stages of cognitive development are shown in table 6.

Table 6   Piaget's stages of cognitive development

Approximate age	Stage	Major characteristics
0–2 years	Sensorimotor	No/little language No sense of objective reality Reality is based on sensing and feeling.
2–7 years	Pre-operational	Egocentric thinking Reliance on perception rather than logic Development of language
7–12 years	Concrete operations	Concrete thinking Understanding of number, classes and relations, but tied to real events rather than abstract concepts
12–15 years	Formal operations	Ability to deal with hypothetical abstract thinking

There are weaknesses in Piaget's theory:

- It overestimates the importance of motor activity.
- It underestimates perception and the capacity of young children to process information.
- It lacks analysis of cognitive development in adult years.
- Piaget used a very small sample on which to base a general theory.
- It conceives the developmental stages as rigid, invariant structures.

Freud and psychoanalytic theory

Freud addressed early childhood emotional development and, like Piaget, ignored subsequent change. He postulated a three-part personality structure on which future development is built.

1   The *id* or the infantile personality is urge-led, based on a need to survive and procreate; it is instinctual with no sense of reality or conscience, but is based on a need for immediate satisfaction.
2   The *ego* reflects the impact and requirements of reality, and represents the rational, cognitive aspects of personality; it mediates between our infantile impulses demanding immediate gratification, the requirements of reality and the demands of our conscience.

continued

3 The *superego* addresses morals, values and beliefs and the behaviour which is required as a result of them; it deals with 'what we ought to do' in contrast to 'what is' (the *ego*) or 'what we want' (the *id*).

Freud's model (see table 7) is based on the idea that human mental life consists of *consciousness* (everything we are aware of), *pre-consciousness* (everything we can remember), and *the unconscious* where primitive and repressed impulses and emotions remain active but unavailable to consciousness, while nonetheless influencing behaviour.

Table 7   Freud's proposed model of development

Age	Stage	Characteristics
0–18 months	Oral	Predominance of the *id* Gratification of impulses by sucking
18 months–3 years	Anal	Development of the *ego* Gratification through the development and control of urination and defecation
3–6 years	Phallic	Development of the *superego* Concern with infantile sensual/sexual pleasure
6–11 years	Latency	Loss of concern with sexual pleasure Identification with parent of same sex and peers
11 years plus	Genital	Towards adult mature sexuality

Critiques of Freud focus on five points:

1 The lack of scientific evidence underpinning a theory based on selected observations
2 The ambiguity and lack of predictive ability of the theory
3 The overemphasis on sexuality and aggression
4 The unsatisfactory nature of the analysis of female development
5 The limitations of a theory based on a white male middle class European population

Erikson's eight stages and life-cycle theory

Unlike the work of Piaget or Freud, Erikson's life-cycle theory (table 8) spans childhood, adulthood and old age. He proposed that individuals encounter predictable life crises, creating conflicts with significant others and the environment. How these are addressed contributes to individual development.

Each life crisis involves a potential tension, and psychological health depends on the achievement of a balance between the extremes of these tensions or *pulls*. The opposing pulls at each stage constitute developmental crises which arise at different biologically or age-determined stages; they are denoted by the use of *versus*. The pulls influence how we behave, how we experience life, and our inner state, whether conscious or unconscious.

Erikson postulates these pulls and crises as universal. In some senses, they may be – facing death is an inevitable outcome of growing old. However, the model assumes a universality across culture, ethnicity and gender, which is difficult to sustain. As with Freud, there are criticisms:

Table 8 The eight stages of Erikson's life-cycle theory

Approximate age	Stage	Major characteristics
0–18 months	Trust v. mistrust	Need for regular, predictable, reliable and loving care-giving and feeding so that the baby develops an inner sense of goodness and trust in the outer world Failure to provide such care may result in a prevailing sense of mistrust.
18 months–2/3 years	Autonomy v. shame and doubt	Children develop mobility, language and sphincter control and a sense of separate identity. Potential for independence also leads to anxieties about separation. Successful development of mobility, language and sphincter control generates confidence and a sense of autonomy, but all children will experience some degree of inadequacy, leading to feelings of shame and doubt.
2/3–6 years	Initiative v. guilt	Children develop multiple relationships and a capacity to reason, deduce and plan and act independently. Children also engage in 'magical thinking' where to wish is to cause and to implement. Such assumptions of 'infantile omnipotence' or unconscious causation can lead to intense guilt, about the 'magical power' of wishes, which feature clearly in children's and adults' concerns about death.
6–11 years	Industry v. inferiority	Interaction with peers Measuring of competence and ability Importance of response of schools, teachers and peers in giving recognition and praise which develops a child's self-esteem
11–18 years	Identity v. role diffusion (adolescence)	Physically puberty occurs. Psychologically involves establishment of separate identity through work, peer relationships, sexual relationships and separation from parents. Structural influences (for example, unemployment) render separate work identity problematic. Peer influence and lack of societally valued roles may lead to exclusion identity based on an alcohol-, drug- or crime-related lifestyle.
Adulthood	Intimacy v. isolation	The emphasis is on achieving a balance of work, leisure, friendship and sexuality (albeit linked by Erikson to heterosexuality and procreation). The alternative, isolation, implies difficulty in engaging in relationships, whether at work, in friendship, or in personal intimate relationships.
	Generativity v. stagnation	Involves a commitment to help and provide for the next generation. This stage may involve children but is also about employment, productivity, useful learning and handing it on.
	Integrity v. despair	Integrity involves a realistic acceptance of one's life as it actually was, one's strengths and weaknesses, and the painful and pleasurable events in one's life. In contrast, despair implies bitter regret and lack of acceptance of what has happened, a sense of 'if only things had been better', and a consequent difficulty in facing death.

continued

- The lack of a research base to underpin such a general theory
- A lack of attention to specific cultural and gender issues which may diverge from such a broad, generic theory
- Overgeneralization, particularly in the adult stages, where diverse experience makes generalization problematic
- The assumption that earlier stages influence further adult development, whereas current research indicates how adult experience – for example, in positive attachments and role models – may compensate for early deficiencies

Conclusion

All life-cycle models have weaknesses – they overgeneralize for each stage about common experiences at the expense of individual differences, biological or environmental – and this weakness becomes greater in considering the range of adult experience, motivation and behaviour. The models are not, because of the multicausal nature of development, predictive; they do not adequately address class, society, gender and ethnicity and their contribution to difference.

Nevertheless, a life-cycle approach has merits in considering the main tasks for any individual at each developmental stage, and, given their culture, class, ethnicity and gender, how and why they are meeting them, or not.

For Further Reading
Lefrançois, G. 1990: *The Lifespan*. Belmont, CA: Wadsworth.
Lishman, J. (ed.) 1991: *Handbook of Theory for Practice Teachers in Social Work*. London: Jessica Kingsley.
Robinson, L. 1995: *Psychology for Social Workers*. London: Routledge.

JOYCE LISHMAN

Hypothesis Testing

Hypothesis testing is a statistical process that allows inferences to be drawn from sample data. Suppose we predict a relationship between two variables such as bereavement and suicide. We find in a sample of 75 cases of suicide coming before a coroner that 36 per cent were recently bereaved of a close relative, compared to 13 per cent of matched, living controls. Can we conclude that people in the population who commit suicide have more often experienced bereavement, or is this a chance finding due to sampling?

The researcher sets up two contradictory hypotheses, the working assumption that there is a relationship between independent and dependent variables (for example, in this case, between bereavement and suicide), and second, that there is no such relationship. The second is the *null hypothesis*, which will be statistically tested. Logically, we cannot prove the working assumption, but we may *reject the null hypothesis* if the sample data are distributed in a way which is unlikely to be consistent with it. The level of probability below which the null hypothesis is rejected is called the *level of*

significance of a statistical test, which by convention is often set at less than 1 in 20 ($p < 0.05$).

For Further Reading
Black, T. R. 1993: *Evaluating Social Science Research*. London: Sage.

JANE GIBBONS

Hysteria

Hysteria is a term with a chequered history which has been replaced because of confusions in meaning. The central characteristic is the physical expression of psychological pain. Associated care-seeking behaviour can be misdirected because of this linkage. There is a need to identify the psychological explanation. Physical explanations for the symptoms should be ruled out.

The symptoms occur in vulnerable personalities at times of stress, and are often short lived. However, they can become chronic and self-reinforcing. At this stage, they become difficult to manage effectively. All carry risk from multiple physical investigations.

The International Classification of Diagnoses [ICD-10] includes disassociative (conversion) disorder and somatoform disorder (somatization, somatoform disorder and hypochondriacal disorder) to cover these disorders. Disassociative disorder includes disturbance of higher mental function (for example, amnesia) and disturbance of movement and sensation (for example, convulsions, paralysis and mutism). Somatoform disorder is the repeated presentation of multiple and often changing physical symptoms despite medical investigation and reassurance. Two main distinctions are seen: somatization and somatoform problems where the focus is on the symptoms and symptom relief; and hypochondriasis where the emphasis is on the catastrophic meaning of the symptoms and their likely 'sinister' progression.

For Further Reading
Snaith, P. 1991: *Clinical Neurosis* (2nd edn). Oxford: Oxford Medical Publications.

CLAIRE KENWOOD AND RAY VIEWEG

I

Impairment
See PHYSICAL DISABILITY.

Incapacity
See CAPACITY/INCAPACITY.

Income Maintenance
Income maintenance is an umbrella term used to describe the different ways in which cash is transferred to and from the state and individual citizens. The term is usually associated with social security systems, concentrating upon the provision of subsistence-level incomes to poor people through contributory, categorical or means-tested benefits. More accurately, income maintenance refers to the wider patterns through which individual incomes are derived, such as taxation, fringe benefits in work and the cash-equivalences of education, health and other services. The incomes of the rich, as well as the poor, are thus influenced by income maintenance policies. Different elements overlap, so that it is possible to be both sufficiently well-off to pay tax and yet poor enough to claim social security benefits. As a result, the subject is ideologically contested, covering questions of citizenship rights, gender and the alternative approaches of poverty relief or poverty prevention.

In social work circles, income maintenance concentrates upon poverty, often aiming for *income maximization*, assisting service users to obtain the best outcome from a combination of the complex systems used to administer income maintenance.

For Further Reading
Hills, J. 1997: *The Future of Welfare: A Guide to the Debate*. York: Joseph Rowntree Foundation.

MARK DRAKEFORD

Incontinence
Incontinence is described as an 'involuntary loss of urine or faeces in an inappropriate place' (Bennett and Ebrahim, 1995). This suggests that the individual was not restricted by geographi-cal impairment from access to an appropriate place to pass urine or faeces. However, because of other factors, the person excreted inappropriately.

There are two forms of incontinence, urinary and faecal. The causes are described as stress, detrusor and overflow:

- *Stress* incontinence is caused by intra-abdominal pressure, for example, when a person laughs.
- *Detrusor* is caused by failure of the bladder neck.
- *Overflow* is usually noted by a constant dribble of urine.

For Further Reading
Bennett, G. and Ebrahim, S. 1995: *Health Care in Old Age*. London: Edward Arnold.

PAUL KINGSTON

Independent Living
Independent living, in its broadest usage, refers to living outside of residential care and institutions. It often implies an ability to do things for oneself, to be self-supporting and self-reliant. This usage has been challenged by the disability movement which adopts a wider definition set within the framework of human and civil rights. Independence is seen as the right to make choices, to assert control over one's own life, and the right to participate in society. Independent living, in this context, involves people living outside of institutions in homes of their own, having access to opportunities available to other citizens, and being in control of their lives. The latter includes being able to determine the nature and source of the support they require. The *independent living movement* became a campaigning force concerning the rights of disabled people internationally during the 1980s and, as a part of this, Centres for Independent Living (sometimes referred to as Centres for Integrated Living) were established.

For Further Reading
Swain, J., Finkelstein, V., French, S. and Oliver, M. (eds) 1993: *Disabling Barriers – Enabling*

Environments. Buckingham: Open University Press, and London: Sage.

CAROL DAWSON

Independent Sector
See PRIVATE RESIDENTIAL AND DAY CARE and VOLUNTARY ORGANIZATIONS AND SOCIETIES.

Inequalities in Physical Health
Social work, in its own right, can contribute to more equal chances of physical well-being and to greater equity when ill, through redressing social disadvantage.

Epidemiological and sociological research has established the powerful association between unequal social conditions and differentials in life expectancy, the onset of ill health and access to health care. Social work policy and practice may compound such inequalities through, for example, their involvement in rationing under-resourced services.

Nevertheless, social work, not confined to health care settings, characterized by lay/professional alliances and rooted in a commitment to tackle social inequalities, can contribute to greater equality across key dimensions to physical health: health maintenance, living with illness and facing terminal illness. This is exemplified respectively in work to reveal and counter domestic violence – a major health hazard for women; in measures to ensure equal access to home care for members of minority ethnic groups experiencing profound ill health: and in the development of gay men's AIDS care initiatives.

For Further Reading
McLeod, E. and Bywaters, P. 1999: *Social Work, Health and Equality.* London: Routledge.

EILEEN MCLEOD

Infancy

Infancy is the period of human development that extends from birth to around 18–24 months. However, the extent of the period of infancy is rather loosely defined and depends on social convention. Human infants are characterized by their initial total dependence upon more mature caretakers to meet all their needs. Such caretaking supports development in a number of domains.

Physical development
Physical development follows the cephalocaudal and proximodistal sequences, by which growth and control progresses from the head down to the feet, and from the centre of the body towards the extremities. In normal development, the sequence of development in different domains is the same for all children, but the rate varies.

During the first month, when prone, infants can lift the head. By the third month, they can hold the chest up and use the arms for support, and between three and four months can roll over. By about six months, they can sit without support, and from seven months many will crawl or shuffle. At about eight months, they can pull to a standing position, by ten or eleven months walk using support, and, at a year, walk independently. During the next few months, they improve walking skills, although they may still bump into obstacles. Locomotor skills are used to actively explore the environment.

In the first month, infants hold objects placed in the hand, and begin to make arm movements towards objects during the second and third months. Between four and six months, they develop reaching and grasping skills and take objects to their mouths. Between seven and nine months, objects can be transferred between hands. By nine months, finger and thumb grasp is present. Fine finger control develops over the next months and, by eighteen months, they can hold a pencil, draw simple shapes and pick up small objects. Fine motor skills are used to manipulate and explore objects.

continued

Perceptual development

Newborn babies can distinguish and prefer the sound of their mother's voice. At a week old, they can recognize their mother's smell. Babies appear to have an innate preference for looking at edges and lines. From two months, they begin to scan objects for internal features. The most powerful stimulus for infant looking behaviour is a human face. By two to three months, they can distinguish between the primary caretaker and other faces by sight. By five or six months, they can distinguish some emotional expressions.

Cognitive development

Understanding of cognition is influenced by Piaget's structural theory which distinguished infant cognition as 'sensorimotor'. Initially infants repeat reflex actions such as looking and sucking, then co-ordinate information from different modalities. At four to eight months, awareness of events outside the body develops, and actions aimed at achieving an end occur. There is increased awareness that objects persist even when out of sight (object concept). More purposeful trial and error behaviour develops, and, finally, representational thought emerges between eighteen and twenty-four months. Some studies suggest that object concept may develop earlier than Piaget suggested; however, the lack of symbolic thought is generally agreed to characterize infant cognition.

Infants make a variety of sounds and respond to the human voice. By six months, vowel and consonant sounds are used and babbling with a whole range of speech sounds begins. From nine months, understanding of words burgeons (receptive language). From twelve to thirteen months, the first words are used (expressive language), are added to slowly over the next few months before a spurt towards two-word sentences at around eighteen months. Initially, primary caretakers tend to fit their responses around the infant's sounds, but, increasingly, the child becomes involved in turn-taking of utterances as a foundation for later conversations.

Emotional development

Theories of socio-emotional development have been influenced by the work of John Bowlby and, despite some criticisms, there is general agreement that the primary emotional task of infancy is the development of secure attachment to at least one key person. Humans appear to have a basic biological need to seek and maintain contact with others, and to have the need for a particular person if distressed. In the majority of cases, attachment is formed towards the primary caretaker as it is promoted by the interactional process of expression of and meeting of needs. The attachment relationship is demonstrated from about six months when a fear of strangers may emerge. When separated from the primary caregiver infants manifest proximity seeking and separation protest which involves the expression of distress and efforts to be reunited with the attachment figure.

On the basis of early attachment experiences, an internal working model develops, which acts as a template for other relationships. Permanent separation from the primary attachment figure can impair a child's security and the associated exploratory behaviour. Infants demonstrate attachments to other key adults and siblings.

Mary Ainsworth demonstrated that it was possible to characterize different qualities of attachment by the age of one year: 60–65 per cent of infants demonstrate *secure* attachment which is characterized by a clear preference for the primary caregiver rather than a stranger and protest at separation. *Insecure* attachment can be of different types: *avoidant*, in which the child avoids contact with the primary caregiver; *ambivalent*, where the child protests at separation but is not easily comforted by the caregiver; and *disoriented*, where the child shows conflicting behaviour patterns. A secure attachment relationship creates a secure base from which a child feels safe to explore the world, and has been associated with high esteem and other positive characteristics in later child-hood. Insecure attachment has been associated with difficulties in making relationships in childhood.

It should not be assumed that trauma in infancy has a lesser impact than trauma at other stages of development. Severe malnutrition and physical neglect can have a drastic effect, especially upon brain development. Loss of the primary caretaker or experiences of abuse have the potential to affect emotional and cognitive development.

For Further Reading
Bee, H. 1994: *Lifespan Development*. New York: Harper Collins.
Fahlberg, V. 1994: *A Child's Journey Through Placement*. London: BAAF.
Santrok, J. W. 1994: *Child Development*. Iowa: Brown and Benchmark.

BRIGID DANIEL

Informal Care
See CARERS and YOUNG CARERS.

Information and Communication Technologies (ICT)
Information and communication technologies (ICT) support the social work processes of communication, information sharing, recording, retrieval, processing and exchange through computers. Single computers linked to local area networks (LANs) allow the sharing of data, printers, and electronic mail within offices. Wide area networks (WANs), such as the Internet, connect hundreds of thousands of computers across the globe.

Social work practice and management is increasingly reliant on ICT systems that can handle social welfare information. The focus is on client information systems, care management systems, and, increasingly, sharing information between health, social services and other agencies, as well as handling management processes and finance. In 1996, Barnes noted that '95 per cent of United Kingdom local authority agencies already register referrals on a computer record'.

Increasingly, ICT provides opportunities for social work:

- The potential for more effective support to be given to service users through the provision of better information
- The monitoring of needs and services on both an individual (service user and practitioner) and aggregate (reporting and policy) basis

There are also challenges:

- The need for sufficient resources
- The effective integration of different systems
- The preservation of privacy and confidentiality
- Ensuring access for all

In addition, there is unlimited potential for increased use of ICT for communicating, including video-conferencing facilities, computer mediated communication, research dissemination and the provision of improved access to information for socially excluded service users.

For Further Reading
Barnes, C. 1996: Where is 'IT' at in UK social services and social work departments? *New Technology in the Human Services*, 9 (4), Southampton: Centre for Human Service Technology, University of Southampton: http://www.chst.soton.ac.uk

JACKIE RAFFERTY

Institutional Abuse
Institutional abuse refers to forms of abuse that occur within institutional settings for vulnerable adults. The abuse may be physical, including sexual abuse and harassment, or psychological and emotional in nature. Situations of racial abuse are also included. Neglect, either active or passive, is usually included within definitions, as is material abuse or exploitation such as the misappropriation of money, property or possessions.

169

Institutional settings in which abuse or neglect may occur include those run by public, private and voluntary, or not-for-profit organizations: hospitals, residential and nursing homes, day care settings and occupational training centres. All vulnerable adults who use such institutions could be at risk of experiencing abuse or an abusive regime.

The abuse may be indicative of the type of institutional regime that exists, whereby individual residents or patients are mistreated and various rights (for example, the right to dignity and respect) denied. Abuse may be committed by relatives, care staff, other residents, or visitors to the home. It may be a continuation of a pre-existing abusive situation, or occur anew in this type of setting.

For Further Reading
Stanley, N., Manthorpe, J. and Penhale, B. (eds) 1999: *Institutional Abuse: Perspectives across the Lifecourse*. London: Routledge.

BRIDGET PENHALE

Institutionalization

Institutionalization refers to the generally negative aspects of institutional life which some individuals experience. In the late 1950s, Russell Barton, a psychiatrist, developed his work on *institutional neurosis* in an attempt to understand the way in which the residents of psychiatric institutions became apathetic and dependent. Later, it was observed that older people, and people with physical disabilities in care settings, also manifested the same behaviours.

In 1961, Erving Goffman published his seminal work on *Asylums*, in which he explored the processes of institutionalization as experienced by 'inmates'; he focused on the routines and structures of institutions, arguing that the removal of normal patterns of activity and identities provided a cultural and social context within which individuals became depersonalized. He developed a model of the *total institution* with four key features:

1 All aspects of life occur in the same place, controlled by one authority.
2 Each aspect of daily activity is carried out with others who are all treated the same.
3 All aspects are rigidly programmed.
4 The separation of staff and inmates is maintained.

Few institutions now fit Goffman's original definition, but the concept of institutionalization remains relevant.

For Further Reading
Jack, R. (ed.) 1998: *Residential versus Community Care*. Basingstoke: Macmillan.

BRIDGET PENHALE AND GRETA BRADLEY

Institutional Provision for Older People

See RESIDENTIAL AND INSTITUTIONAL PROVISION FOR OLDER PEOPLE.

Intensive Probation

Intensive probation is a term used to describe methods of supervising offenders on probation which involve more contact or supervision time than is usual for the average probationer. Intensive approaches to probation were developed particularly in the 1980s and 1990s in the USA (as *intensive supervision*) and in Britain (for example, as day centres requiring daily attendance, and later as programmes to develop social or cognitive skills and strategies to avoid offending).

Intensive forms of probation often fail to reduce either custodial sentencing or offending, with the exception of a small number of programmes which have been found to be effective.

PETER RAYNOR

Interagency Work

Interagency work describes collaborative arrangements and/or working relationships between agencies that enable members of the agencies to work together to meet the needs of identified groups of service users.

Interagency work can have a strategic focus such as *joint service planning*. In addition, or alternatively, the focus may be operational: for example, agreements may be reached between agencies for the provision of co-ordinated services.

Interagency work can be based on national guidance. For example, *Working Together to Safeguard Children* (Department of Health, 1999) outlines ways in which joint working arrangements to safeguard and promote children's welfare should be agreed, implemented and reviewed through an interagency forum, the Area Child Protection Committee.

Effective interagency work draws upon the different organizational and professional roles, resources and skills to meet the needs of service users. This is achieved when there are shared values and goals, together with a framework of identified standards of practice supported by policies, procedures and practice guidance. Interagency work is most effective when there is commitment from senior managers, and when formal systems are embedded in positive informal networks.

For Further Reading
Leathard, A. 1994: *Going Interprofessional – Working Together for Health and Welfare.* London: Routledge.

JAN HORWATH

Intercountry Adoption

Intercountry adoption involves the transfer of children from one country to be adopted in another. Depending on governmental arrangements, the adoption may be completed in the sending or receiving country.

The background
Large-scale intercountry adoption is a modern phenomenon. Leaving aside the thousands of British children who were sent to countries of the New Commonwealth from the end of the nineteenth century up to the 1960s to stay with foster carers or live in orphanages, intercountry adoption as such took off mainly after the end of World War II. In its initial stages, it was a mainly humanitarian response to the devastation caused by wars, such as those in Korea and Vietnam. However, by the 1980s, it had become a large-scale enterprise involving the transfer of thousands of children each year from poor Third World countries to more affluent ones in the West.

The dramatic decline in the number of children available for adoption in the West, which started in the 1970s, was the main reason for the large increase in intercountry adoptions. It is estimated that around 10,000 intercountry children are adopted annually in this way in the USA and nearly 20,000 in Western Europe. Until the Romanian revolution in 1989, only an insignificant number of children were adopted intercountry in Britain. This was mainly because of the strict immigration controls operating and the prohibition of third-party or independent adoptions. Attention, instead, was focused on older children, and those with special needs. Even now, the number of intercountry adoptions in the UK is estimated to number only a few hundred each year.

Policy and practice issues
Intercountry adoption poses many moral and theoretical issues which challenge its legitimacy and practice. Besides the absence of choice for most birth parents, caused mainly by the extremes of poverty, there have also been many well-documented cases of large-scale organized kidnapping, stealing, trafficking and trading in children. The failure of most governments in both sending and receiving countries to regulate the practice of intercountry adoption has helped to fan this market.

The Hague Convention for the Protection of Children has taken the initiative to regulate the practice by bringing together 65 countries to consider the legal and policy issues involved. The published Convention consists of a number of parts, each one dealing with an aspect of intercountry adoption. While progress has been made, members of the Convention failed to agree on the most fundamental clause providing for the prohibition of arrangements by non-accredited agencies, which could have helped to bring some order into the practice. Participating countries have been slow to sign the Convention.

continued

171

The outcome of intercountry adoption

Much of the evidence on the outcome of intercountry adoption comes from North America, Scandinavia and Holland. Research has mainly focused on two themes:

1 How the children are functioning on a range of developmental dimensions
2 The children's racial, ethnic and cultural identity

The children's functioning

Taking medical and health issues first, the main studies are agreed that, within a reasonable period of time, the children overcome the many physical and nutritional deficits displayed on their arrival. With regard to schooling and linguistic development, the findings are similarly encouraging, though older children on arrival face greater linguistic challenges. Turning to emotional and behavioural adjustment, the studies are again agreed that, on the whole, intercountry adopted children do well, and some do very well. Their overall development matches, or is just below, that of incountry adoptees. As with incountry adoption, the adjustment of intercountry adopted children is mediated by the quality of previous parenting experiences, their age on arrival and the quality of their new experiences.

Most of the studies confirm other research in child development, showing that adoption can assist the great majority of children to overcome past physical and psychological developmental deficits. Parental satisfaction with the adoption experience has been found to be high. Studies eliciting the views of the children or of adult adoptees also suggest that a significant majority express contentment with their adoption. However, where there are children of the family, integration is perceived to be somewhat less satisfactory.

Racial, ethnic and cultural identification

Besides the extra adjustment hurdles faced by all adopted children compared to non-adopted ones, there are additional tasks for those adopted intercountry. These mainly include an awareness and acknowledgement of the duality of their heritage, an acknowledgement of their difference in terms of appearance, and learning to cope with racism and negative discrimination, where prevalent.

The available studies convey a generally positive picture on this subject, but with also a number of concerns. For example, some children were found to be pre-occupied with their appearance, to display a rather poor sense of racial and ethnic identification, and, in certain areas, to be at the receiving end of negative racial discrimination. The experience of racism and discrimination appears to be relative to the part of the country where adoptees happen to live, such as the population mix of the area. Though accurate statistics are lacking, it is reported that a significant number of adoptees are now visiting their countries of origin to find out more about their roots and/or to establish contact with members of their birth families.

Overall, the achievement of a child-centred approach in intercountry adoption relies on several things:

- Close collaboration between the sending and receiving countries
- Strict adherence to the laws of the respective countries
- Following standards of good practice set by accredited agencies, such as in the preparation of adopters and birth parents
- Being freely entered upon
- No profit being involved
- Being covered by a comprehensive range of post-placement services

For Further Reading
Alstein, H. and Simon, R. (eds) 1991: *Intercountry Adoption*. New York: Praeger.
Bagley, C. 1993: *International and Transracial Adoptions*. Aldershot: Avebury.
Triseliotis, J., Shireman, J. and Hundleby, M. 1997: *Adoption, Theory, Policy and Practice*. Ch. 9, London: Cassell.

JOHN TRISELIOTIS

Interdisciplinary Practice

Interdisciplinary practice involves the integrated application of insights drawn from different branches of learning or science to the organization, discovery and/or transformation of specific aspects of the natural or social world.

Disciplines are reflected in, and largely determined by, the categorizations of intellectual areas within academic institutions and are defined by that aspect of the world that they seek to know: philosophy (the moral order); sociology (society), political science (the polity), anatomy (the body), psychology (the mind) and so on. As social constructions, the nature of disciplinary boundaries and the relations between them are subject to the interplay of social, political and ideological forces. Disciplinary areas are thus not fixed, but rather characterized by a continuous process of formation and re-formation in which sub-disciplines may emerge and consolidate over time into new disciplinary areas.

The nature of interdisciplinary practice

The term *interdisciplinary practice* is often used interchangeably with that of *interprofessional practice* but differs insofar as a discipline is both broader and more fundamental in scope than any branch of professional practice based upon it. The relationship between the intellectual disciplines and professional practice is one of symbiosis; professional practice is both the application of disciplinary theory and knowledge as well as one of the means by which the content and parameters of an intellectual discipline are reconstituted. In this way, the professional practice of nursing, for example, has developed out of the broad (and itself comparatively recent) discipline of medical science to lay claim to its own distinctive disciplinary focus.

A particular disciplinary area may inform the knowledge and practice of a number of related professional groups. Thus have the insights of sociology, or social science more generally, informed the professional practice of lawyers, psychologists, educationalists and many of the professions allied to medicine. In turn, the theoretical foundations of a particular profession may be underpinned by the insights of more than one discipline. The body of knowledge underpinning contemporary social work, for example, has been constructed (some would say less than coherently) from a range of different disciplines including psychology, sociology, public health, jurisprudence and education.

The term *interdisciplinary practice* is also often used interchangeably with that of *multi-disciplinary* practice, but can be differentiated in terms of the level of integration involved. Whereas multi-disciplinary practice involves the combination of disciplinary approaches, typically via the operational co-ordination of different professional groups, these approaches remain located within parallel, and distinctive, intellectual boundaries. Interdisciplinarity, in contrast, requires that the different

continued

insights are intellectually combined, or merged, in the identification and resolution of the problem at hand.

An illustrative example: child protection

The UK child protection process provides a good example of the distinction between interdisciplinary practice and other forms of professional collaboration. This process is both *multi-agency*, insofar as it combines the operation of a range of organizations delivering health, welfare, education and criminal justice services, and *multi-professional*, insofar as those agencies comprise the activities of a number of different professional groups. Thus, for example, the role played by the health service in the child protection process can involve the participation of, variously, paediatricians, GPs, health visitors and police surgeons. The child protection process however is less fully *interagency* or *interprofessional*, insofar as the involvement of other agencies/professionals typically characterizes only the initial stages of enquiries, with social services departments and social work professionals largely being left to see the process through. Similarly, while the process can be seen to be *multi-disciplinary*, in terms of the different bodies of theory and knowledge that underpin the work of the various professionals involved, it is rarely *interdisciplinary* in that those different theoretical positions are not typically merged into a single coherent and co-ordinated professional approach. Indeed, it is arguable that the child protection process is characterized by considerable tension between the different disciplinary approaches represented, and by the political and ideological privileging of some (namely the medico-legal) disciplinary standpoints over others.

Disciplinary domains

Tensions within *interdisciplinary practice* may derive from the different aspects or 'domains' of the natural/social world on which they focus. Some disciplinary domains may be closely related, such as those which comprise the biophysical disciplines (anatomy, biology, biochemistry, medicine, etc.) and some may be obviously complementary, such as those which focus on different aspects of the social world (sociology, law, political science). The relationship between others, however, such as those concerned with the domain of ideas (philosophy, ethics, literary and cultural studies) and those whose primary focus is on the material world (engineers, technologists, architects) may be less obvious and the achievement of interdisciplinary practice correspondingly more difficult. Even between those who share cognate or complementary intellectual domains, however, difficulties within interdisciplinary practice may arise from the different views of the nature of the world (ontology) and the way in which it is known (epistemology). Professional practice in many areas of health and social care is characterized by considerable tension between the broadly (and loosely) termed 'medical' and 'social' models of theory, enquiry and practice.

The value of interdisciplinary practice

A final comment must be made about the implicit assumption underpinning much of the literature on interdisciplinary practice that it is necessarily a desirable objective. As with *interagency* and *interprofessional* practice, it may be important in certain cases, both for the professionals themselves and for the client groups they serve, to maintain a degree of professional distinctiveness. The value for professionals of having their assumptions and practices challenged by those working within very different intellectual paradigms may be lost through an interdisciplinary collaboration which seeks to minimize or ignore those differences. More importantly, perhaps, the over-identification or collusion between different professional groups may diminish the opportunity for those who use their services to access alternative assessments of, or responses to, their situation. Assessment of the relative strengths and weaknesses of interdisciplinary and *uni-disciplinary* ways of working, and of the conditions under which the former may be provided is bedevilled by the lack of good quality research-based evidence.

For Further Reading

Berg-Weger, M. and Schneider, F. D. 1998: Interdisciplinary collaboration in social work education. *Journal of Social Work Education*, 34 (1), Winter, 97–107.
Monit Cheung, K. 1990: Interdisciplinary relationships between social work and other disciplines: a citation study. *Social Work Research and Abstracts*, 26, September 23–9.
Soothill, K., Mackay, L. and Webb, C. (eds) 1995: *Interprofessional Relations in Health Care*. London: Edward Arnold.

CAROL LUPTON

Intermediate Treatment

Intermediate treatment was introduced as a statutory facility in the UK in 1969 – at the height of the fashion for therapeutic welfare provision for youth offenders and those 'thought to be at risk of offending'. Legislation enabled local authorities to provide capital funding and staff resources to involve vulnerable or 'deviant' teenagers in group work, community projects or residential adventure programmes, designed to strengthen their characters and reduce the risk of criminality.

Unfortunately, research demonstrated that some of those subjected to intermediate treatment programmes tended – if they misbehaved or failed to conform – to be 'sucked into' the institutional or penal system more quickly than would have happened if they had never participated in the first place. Intermediate treatment, though still operating in some areas, came to be recognized as an example of the way in which well-intentioned welfarist innovations can have damaging and life-affecting consequences for vulnerable people.

MARTIN DAVIES

Interprofessional Education

Interprofessional education enables members of two or more professions to learn to work more effectively together by modifying reciprocal attitudes and perceptions, establishing common knowledge and value bases, reinforcing collaborative competence and/or heightening motivation. It reframes curricula into common and comparative studies, and employs interactive methods to enable the participating professions to learn from, and about, one another. It may be brief or extended, at college or work, and call upon one or more academic disciplines. Where cultivating collaboration is only one of several reasons for shared learning, interprofessional education can be seen to comprise a dimension or emphasis within a wider definition of multiprofessional education.

HUGH BARR

Interprofessional Practice

Interprofessional practice involves members of two or more professions working together to respond more adequately to the needs of individuals, families and communities, and to improve the quality of service provided. It also optimizes use of resources by avoiding duplication. It may be brief or extended in relation to one case or many, effected through teams, case conferences, networks and one-to-one working within, and across, agencies. It calls upon professions to exchange knowledge, and to combine their expertise to plan and provide co-ordinated services. Its success depends upon cultivating trust and mutual respect in a shared learning environment and is made easier where policies are coherent and management is supportive.

Social workers collaborate with doctors (for example, GPs and psychiatrists), housing officers, lawyers, nurses (for example, health visitors), occupational therapists, police officers, probation officers, psychologists, school teachers and others, the mix depending upon the field of practice. Particular emphasis is put on inter-professional practice in child protection, in community care (including work with people with learning disabilities and mental illnesses), in primary care and in hospitals.

For Further Reading
The Journal of Interprofessional Care. Basingstoke: Carfax, published quarterly.

HUGH BARR

Interviewing

Interviewing refers to the skilled direction of a purposeful encounter between two or more people conducted principally through the medium of language, including sign language, storyboarding, and fingerspelling. Tasks such as the completion of forms may be undertaken during the course of an interview, but most social work interviews are not activity-based. Exceptions include: interviews with children; when specific therapeutic techniques are employed, such as those derived from Gestalt or art therapy; and where assessment involves observing how a person accomplishes tasks or the obstacles they face. Interviews are usually face-to-face, but can be conducted over the telephone, by means of a video link, or through other communication technology.

The importance of language
Because the medium for interviewing is language, special problems arise when the people involved have no common language, whether that is sign language or a language associated with another country or region. In these situations, an interpreter will be needed – ideally, someone who is neutral, acceptable to both parties, capable of offering confidentiality and who understands the requirements of the interview. It is important to remember that people's ability to convey emotion is usually best done through the language they first learnt, unless they have long since abandoned that language as their main means of communication. Having to speak about their feelings in the language of the interviewer can create a false impression of a restricted range of emotion. Even when both people speak English, but have learnt it in different countries or regions, misunderstandings and unwitting discrimination can occur.

The purpose of the interview
The purpose of an interview determines its nature, making clarity of purpose indispensable. For example, is the interview intended to explore feelings, to assess parenting abilities, or to provide a social history for a report? It is the social worker's responsibility to explain how they understand the purpose, and to elicit the person's views. Wherever possible, the interview's purpose, nature, location, and likely duration should be shared and negotiated. A collaborative approach reduces some of the inevitable power imbalance between social worker and client, enabling the person to participate in a fuller and more equal way. Even when someone can hardly be expected to 'like' the social worker's agenda, as in some cases of child protection investigation or mental health assessment, they have a right to know what it is. Gender, ethnic or cultural background, class, sexual orientation, age and previous experience are some of the factors which influence people's expectations of a social work interview. Social workers who familiarize themselves with the particular concerns of the different kinds of people they encounter, and who approach them with openness about what might arise will make more effective interviewers.

First-order and second-order skills
Interviewing skills go beyond the everyday skills of conversation and discussion, although they have features in common. There are two distinct kinds of skill to be considered.

- *First-order skills* are those employed in communicating with the interviewee.
- *Second-order skills* entail thinking about and managing the process of the interview.

It is essential to pay close attention to what the person is saying, at both verbal and non-verbal levels, through *careful listening* and *observation*. Observation is more than seeing, and people with little or no sight can be accurate observers of, say, agitation expressed by pacing around, or hesitancy about answering a question.

Empathy involves understanding the experience of another person, particularly their emotional experience, and communicating that understanding in words. It is based on listening and observation and promotes the development of trust and rapport. Empathic responses, usually in the form of a statement, are useful whatever the nature or stage of the work. They are rarely a mistake, though empathy is not enough on its own to enable people to solve their problems. It is easier to empathize with the similar and the familiar than with the different. Developing interviewing skills entails extending the range of experience with which the social worker can empathize.

The *use of questions* is almost an art form, as there are a number of different types of question. Closed questions produce 'Yes/No' replies: for example, 'Do you get on well with your father?' Open questions such as 'How do you and your father get on?' or 'What's it like living with your Dad?' stimulate the person's reflective processes and elicit a wider range of material. Narrow questions – 'What job do you do?' or 'How long were you in hospital?' – are useful in obtaining factual information. A barrage of narrow questions is felt as an assault, and can easily be avoided, as only rarely is the sole purpose of a social work interview to obtain information. Questions can be used to clear up confusion, to help the person think more deeply about their circumstances, to challenge their perceptions, and to generate ideas about how to solve problems or what direction to take. Questions give rise to thinking, just as empathic responses catch emotion. Good interviewing creates a rhythm between the two.

The social worker also needs to *summarize* key points, to *clarify next steps* and to *bring the interview to a close*.

Second-order skills come into play when social workers use their reflective abilities to act as an internal supervisor. Choices about what to say or do next continually present themselves, requiring *judgements* to be made. The social worker has to *keep the purpose of the interview in mind*, and *direct* the interview accordingly. *Responding flexibly* to any unanticipated issues which arise is equally important. Interviewing is interactive in nature; the social worker is responsible for *monitoring* and *reflecting on* the impact of their own interventions, and for *retrieving errors* where necessary.

Conclusion
Interviewing is central to social work practice. The effective interviewer has sensitivity, imagination, a clear sense of role and purpose, and the ability to work collaboratively with a range of people.

For Further Reading
Egan, G. 1998: *The Skilled Helper: A Systematic Approach to Effective Helping* (6th edn). Pacific Grove, California: Brooks/Cole.
Kadushin, A. and Kadushin, G. 1999: *The Social Work Interview* (4th edn). New York: Columbia University Press.
Sue, D. W. and Sue, D. 1999: *Counselling the Culturally Different* (3rd edn). New York: John Wiley.

JULIET KOPROWSKA

Intrinsic Ageing

Intrinsic ageing results from the inborn or genetic factors that contribute to changes in body systems and appearance. Muscle and brain cells are not capable of division and, therefore, if they die, they are not replaced. Other cells are capable of dividing but experiments have shown that this process stops after a pre-determined number of divisions. Older cells are also less likely to repair any damage that they sustain. These intrinsic factors are complicated and are not fully understood. Their impact on the overall ageing process in any one person will also be modified by external environmental factors such as diet, chemicals and radiation as well as by disease.

PETER CROME

Involvement by Service Users

See USER PARTICIPATION and THE WORKING ALLIANCE.

J

Judicial Decision Making

See PROFESSIONAL DISCRETION AND JUDICIAL DECISION MAKING.

Just Deserts

Just deserts is a principle adopted by penal systems, according to which punishment should be proportionate to the seriousness of crime. Derived from Cesare Beccaria, this principle was originally intended to rectify the unfairness and arbitrariness of penal institutions in the treatment of offenders. While in the formulation proposed by the reformers of the Enlightenment, just deserts also included a notion of rehabilitation, in successive uses, the term became mainly associated with the notion of retribution. Supporters of just deserts are found among criminologists and penal policy makers who oppose judicial discretion and indeterminate or open sentences.

VINCENZO RUGGIERO

Juvenile Justice

See YOUTH JUSTICE.

K

Key Worker

The *key worker* is the designated practitioner offering a 'special relationship', and named to ensure that responsibilities are carried out and that users are not lost in complex systems. Case conferences name a key worker to implement plans, and the role has a particular status in child protection. Key workers are also identified in residential and day care group settings.

A balance is struck between the responsibility of the whole staff group for the user, and the need for a user to have contact with a practitioner seen to have specific responsibilities including an openness to a closer relationship.

CHRIS WARREN-ADAMSON

L

Labelling Theory

*Label*s are useful generalizations that help us make sense of, order and predict social life. Labels assign a quality or value which influences the way people respond to that which is labelled. *Labelling theory* describes the response and expectations of others to an act labelled deviant. This may create a situation in which the labelled person can do no other than respond in the ways expected. The processes by which this takes place are not fully understood but concern moral outrage and stigmatization which engender a sense of injustice leading to further 'deviance' and the perceived necessity of control and punishment.

PETER RANDALL AND JONATHAN PARKER

Language, The Use of

Language is the essential medium of all social influence and intervention. Social workers should use language that is clear, accessible and informative. Clients are not best helped by workers who use obscure, inaccurate, deceptive or demeaning language. Professionals are less effective on their clients' behalf if they cannot communicate precisely and persuasively.

There is no simple relationship between language and the external world. The choice of language, as well as its content, carries significance. Language thereby creates and sustains the relations of power. Social workers often aspire to empower the subjects of their work; but since they are themselves empowered by state authority and professional expertise, their professional language is also the medium of control.

Language not only represents and transmits our understanding of the world, but also supplies the very concepts that furnish and limit our understanding. This is conveyed by the idea of a *discourse*. There are competing discourses in subject areas. For example, the discourse on disability that represented it as the special problems unfortunately experienced by impaired individuals is being displaced by a discourse that represents disability as the wider failure of society to provide equitably for the full spectrum of human capacities.

Modes of reference and personal address

Custom and usage about ways of referring to people are currently changing rapidly. Preferences differ between social groups, classes and generations. Professionals must be especially sensitive to the connotations of different forms.

In referring to categories of people, English usage now generally prefers the form 'people with disabilities' to the forms 'the disabled' or 'disabled people'*. For some categories, the older form 'the unemployed' is still current. This is mostly a matter of fashion.

Social work has no universally applicable general term for its users. 'Client' is probably most widely used but has the disadvantage of tending to focus social work

continued

---

* The transient nature of 'appropriate' terminology is illustrated by the fact that the disabled peoples' movement has recently argued for the retention of the form 'disabled people', on the grounds that this form of words accurately reflects the view that people are rendered *disabled* by the attitudes of society and the restricted nature of environmental provision. See the entry on PHYSICAL DISABILITY [Editor].

concerns too narrowly. Terms such as 'service users' and 'customers' are sometimes advocated, but are apt to be disliked by those to whom they refer. 'Residents' is useful in appropriate contexts. A 'case' is properly an item of professional activity, not a person or a family.

In first contact with service users, it is better not to address an adult stranger by his or her forename unless the context clearly supports it: it may be perceived as an impertinence. The use of title and surname is respectful until mutual consent for more familiar address is established. The same applies to letters. As regards women, the addressee's preference for Mrs, Miss or Ms should be respected. Letter-writers can help their correspondents by showing their own preferences in their printed signature lines.

Agency staff should supply their surname as well as their forename. For the agency to know a service user's full name while the user knows only the staff member's forename places the user at a disadvantage. The appropriate use of business cards and name badges helps in establishing identities.

Plain direct language

Social work often deals with sensitive and complicated personal issues; raising them can be painful, embarrassing or threatening. Because strong emotional reactions tend to interfere with understanding, it is especially important to communicate clearly. Language conveys tone, attitude and intention; these should be consciously fashioned and accurately monitored.

A number of recommendations can be made:

* Use ordinary, age- and culture-appropriate terms for the matters of everyday life. Avoid quasi-psychiatric terminology (for example, 'attachment behaviour') and sociological technical terms (for example, 'informal carer').
* Use simple, direct forms of speech and writing. Avoid convoluted syntax, complicated constructions, and double negatives. Avoid exceeding the vocabulary of your listeners.
* Speak clearly using an easily understood diction, especially with people who may have sensory or cognitive impairments. Be ready, if necessary, to learn alternatives to ordinary speech, such as sign language.
* Formal written communications such as letters and reports should maintain high standards of grammar, literacy and presentation, because badly presented work discredits the content and the author. Case notes and other informal documents will use modified language conventions, but must always aim for accuracy and clarity in the context.
* Be thoughtful in the use of language forms that require much hidden contextual knowledge to be fully understood, such as slang, ellipsis, metaphor, allusion, irony, in-jokes, and usages peculiar to restricted groups and subcultures.
* Dialect and accent signify community membership, affiliation and allegiance; remember they can bring about solidarity or alienation.
* Do not dissimulate. If something is tentative, do not imply it is definite, and vice versa. Avoid over- and understatement. If making a request, do so directly.
* When working with people whose first language is different from yours, redouble all the preceding injunctions. Develop your understanding of their linguistic culture.

Technicalities and jargon

Every occupation develops its own esoteric vocabulary. Social workers work largely with disadvantaged individuals and groups, and must be especially careful that their occupational jargon does not further disempower clients. For normal conversational purposes, plain language should always be used in preference to arcane abbreviations. The use of jargon loosely derived from statute should be avoided unless essential. Thus for example: 'residential care' is more intelligible than 'Part III accommodation'; 'compulsory admission' (under the mental health legislation) is better than 'sectioning'; 'report for the court' is more accessible than 'PSR'. Do not expect the wider world to be conversant with modish terms such as 'needs-led assessment' or 'spot purchasing'.

Technical terms for types of service user or conditions they may suffer from are useful for clear diagnosis and specification of needs, but must be employed with care and caution. They are frequently perceived as derogatory and, for that reason, they obsolesce rapidly. 'Mentally handicapped', 'spastic', 'problem family' and 'coloured' are examples of fairly recently discarded labels. Their contemporary equivalents will probably soon look just as outdated.

For Further Reading
Pugh, R. 1996: *Effective Language in Health and Social Work*. London: Chapman and Hall.
Rees, S. 1991: *Achieving Power: Practice and Policy in Social Welfare*. North Sydney: Allen and Unwin.
Rojek, C., Peacock, G. and Collins, S. 1988: *Social Work and Received Ideas*. London: Routledge.

CHRIS CLARK

Law and Social Work

Social work is empowered, guided and controlled by its *legal mandate*. This mandate consists of three elements. The first is organizational, in that most social work in the UK is practised from within the structures of the statutory social services. The second is functional, in that the law determines the powers and duties with which social work is endowed. The third is procedural, in that the law largely determines the nature and extent of social work accountability, both to service users and to the community generally.

The statutory context of social work
One of the hallmarks of social work in the UK is that, in general, it is located within public, corporate bodies, such as local authorities. The powers and responsibilities assigned to such bodies in relation to social work practice are set out in a series of statutes, such as the Children Act 1989, the Mental Health Act 1983 and the NHS and Community Care Act 1990. They must also adhere to secondary legislation, such as Directions and policy guidance issued under s.7 of the Local Authority Social Services Act 1970, as well as taking account of general advice, as set out in practice guidance. This framework represents the statutory context of social work.

Since these legal powers and duties are placed upon the authority itself, they need to be translated into actual services for delivery to individual service users. The powers and duties may be delegated to voluntary organizations and independent sector providers. Examples here include the provision of residential care to vulnerable adults under the National Assistance Act 1948, and local authorities contracting with other agencies to provide family support services. Otherwise, the translation of the legal mandate into service provision is achieved by assigning legal functions to individual local authority employees. One means of achieving this is designation. For example, only approved social workers (ASWs), that is, social workers 'approved' in accordance with s.145, are designated with the necessary powers and duties to carry out certain functions under the Mental Health Act 1983. More usually, the means employed is delegation. The local authority delegates authority to its employees who, in turn, must adhere to the
continued

statute and the local authority's guidance on its implementation. Social work practice is thus shaped by its organizational context and the statutory powers and duties with which it is endowed.

It is these statutory powers and duties, outlined in statute and amplified through policy and practice guidance, which define, for example, the individuals towards whom social workers have responsibilities, such as children in need and their families, and vulnerable adults and their carers. They determine, in broad terms, the nature and extent of social work intervention, such as prevention, protection and rehabilitation. They also set out the conditions under which compulsory intervention is permissible, as well as the safeguards which ensure that intervention takes place in accordance with due process of law and adherence to the principles of natural justice. In this way, the law not only defines social work functions, but also encompasses certain basic social work values, such as the concept of partnership in relation to children in need and their families, and the rights of individuals to receive care, treatment and control in the context of the least restrictive alternative.

However, the legal mandate may, in certain circumstances, be more restrictive than social work's professional values. For instance, social workers do not have a legal mandate to intervene to protect vulnerable adults from financial, physical or other forms of abuse, which corresponds to the child protection mandate that they are given. Some service users are automatically excluded from provision that would enable them to purchase their own care directly, which corresponds to the value position of self-determination and promoting autonomy (Community Care (Direct Payments) Act 1996. Similarly, the recognition in the Children Act 1989 of the importance of race, culture, religion and language when planning and delivering services for children in need and for looked-after children is not mirrored so centrally in the legal and policy mandate for community care services.

Finally, certain procedural aspects of the law determine the processes by which social work practice can be made accountable, either through the courts or through non-judicial processes, such as judicial review, the Commission for Local Administration, and complaints procedures. Case law has identified principles by which local authorities should consult with 'clients' when assessing and making decisions on individual service provision, and with voluntary organizations and community groups when engaged in service planning and development. Service users have a right of access to information held about them, under the Access to Files Act 1987, and to information about services, for example under the Disabled Persons (Services, Consultation and Representation) Act 1986. Local authorities have responsibilities for the registration and inspection of such services as child-minders, residential homes and nursing homes.

It is these three elements – organizational, functional, and procedural – which constitute social work law. These elements enable the relationship between the law and social work practice to be described, analysed and defined.

Social welfare law

However, the law comes into the relationships between social workers and their clients not just as a result of this legal mandate. Social workers are also in a key position to perceive how the law may have a profound effect upon the lives of their clients, in relation to such issues as family breakdown, housing and income support. Social workers therefore need to know about other aspects of the law if they are to respond appropriately and adequately to the wider needs of service users. These aspects of the law may be termed social welfare law. As with social work law, included in social welfare law are statutes and case law, and, on occasion, secondary legislation and policy and practice guidance. It may also contain mechanisms through which organizational practice can be made accountable. Social welfare law may also encompass certain social work values, either endorsing or constraining them. The difference, for social workers is that social welfare law does not provide them with powers and duties that offer a specific mandate for practice. Rather, it provides the framework within which they might work with 'clients' through advocacy and offer them guidance.

Law and practice

The importance of law to competent social work practice has been officially recognized. It is found in a requirement set down by the Central Council for Education and Training in Social Work. To qualify for a Diploma in Social Work, students must demonstrate, through formal assessment, their ability to understand and apply the legislation relevant to the country in which they intend to practise. Law is the only subject in either the practice or the academic curriculum for which such specific requirements are delineated.

Nevertheless, the law may not, of itself, be sufficient to reflect all the complexity of practice and of service users' lives. The legal rules may be seen as the essential bone structure for social work practice. However, the flesh and blood of practice also comprises other elements: policy decisions; professional, administrative and social work skills and values; the availability of physical and material resources, as well as local variation in needs, funding and traditions. It is the totality of these elements which finally determines the nature and character of social work as a professional enterprise.

It is also this very totality that highlights the challenges for practitioners and managers when working at the interface between law and social work. First, the law may identify what action can be taken, but not necessarily when or how. For example, it may not define what is meant, in terms of process or outcomes, by choice, empowerment and partnership, themes that figure prominently in social policy and yet may be interpreted by different stakeholders in social work and social care. Moreover, the interpretation and funding of the legal mandate may be left to individual local authorities, generating concern about geographic variability in services and the absence of rights to a standard and quality of provision that can be enforced.

Second, different areas of the law may reflect different concerns and priorities, indicating that the law itself is neither uniform, consistent nor conflict free, but rather a social creation and not uncommonly a compromise between different discourses. The dilemmas that social workers encounter – for example care versus control, rights versus risks, needs versus resources, and individual versus group – have their roots here. The final challenge is the degree to which social work is just the creation and expression of a legal mandate – national standards, judicial involvement in decisions that once were the province of professionals alone, and a burgeoning amount of guidance and regulations. When working together with legal practitioners, 'clients' and other professionals, social workers must be clear when interactions are dominated by the language, methodology and values of the law or of social work or some combination of each. Making the elements of practice accessible to oneself and to others is the beginning of defining the principles, processes and goals of an effective service.

For Further Reading

Braye, S. and Preston-Shoot, M. 1997: *Practising Social Work Law* (2nd edn). London: Macmillan.
Preston-Shoot, M., Roberts, G. and Vernon, S. 1998: Social work law: from interaction to integration. *Journal of Social Welfare and Family Law*, 20 (1), 65–80.
Vernon, S. 1998: *Social Work and the Law* (3rd edn). London: Butterworths.

GWYNETH ROBERTS AND MICHAEL PRESTON-SHOOT

Learned Helplessness

Generally, individuals have a need to be in control of their lives and not at the whim of external influences. This need constitutes one of the major competence motives and is a crucial life-task for the developing child, one of great significance to his or her self-concept and notably to self-esteem. When people initially expect to exert control over the outcomes of their actions, their first experiences of not being in control are likely to produce *psychological reactance* – a reasserting of their freedom. However, repetitions of failure are likely to result in what Martin Seligman has described as *learned helplessness*.

When humans and animals discover that their behaviour and significant life events are independent (i.e. that nothing the individual does will make any difference), this learned helplessness tends to generalize. Depression may result as the individual comes to realize that trauma cannot be controlled and coped with. Learned helplessness is thought to be involved in drug abuse. There are important individual differences in disposition to learned helplessness, with some people more likely to see themselves as having little or no control over external forces – a theoretical concept known as *the locus of control*.

For Further Reading
Seligman, M. E. P. 1975: *Helplessness: On Depression, Development and Death*. San Francisco: W. H. Freeman.

MARTIN HERBERT

Learning Disabilities – The Social Work Role

The *social work role with people with learning disabilities* (see LEARNING DISABILITY) and their families is to facilitate access to services and opportunities, and to offer emotional support. In addition, social workers have a duty to protect children and some vulnerable adults with learning disabilities, and to make application to admit and detain in hospital for assessment and treatment certain groups of people with a learning disability.

The provision of support

Parents and families may require support and services which differ from those offered to the person with a disability, and the social worker must take into account the needs and perspectives of all parties involved. Any assessment and subsequent intervention should involve the person with a learning disability (and/or their advocate), and should not be based entirely upon the views of the parents or carers.

The level and nature of support offered to the person with a learning disability and to their families will vary according to the severity of the disability and any associated physical or sensory loss, the nature of their social networks, and the ages of the person and their family members. Some may require little support throughout their lives, whereas others may need almost constant social work intervention.

No one professional group has sole responsibility for the needs of people with learning disabilities and their families. The more complex a person's needs, the more support may be required from a range of professionals and organizations. Social workers specializing in work with people with learning disabilities may be found:

- within social services teams, in care management roles;
- in community-based multidisciplinary teams, often consisting of a consultant psychiatrist (specializing in learning disabilities or developmental psychiatry), nurses, occupational therapists, physiotherapists, language and speech therapists, psychologists and therapists in art, drama, music or horticulture; or
- in learning disability hospitals and the resettlement teams which seek to relocate patients within the community as part of the deinstitutionalization programme.

The provision of services

Services for people with learning disabilities are provided by local authority departments or other statutory agencies. Some, like housing, will be generally available to all members of the community, while others will be designed specifically to meet needs relating to the learning disability. Terminology and structures vary from place to place, but facilities can include *adult training centres* which tend to be work-based, *social education centres* which additionally focus on leisure and lifelong learning, and *community resource centres* designed to facilitate community integration (for example, by teaching people how to go shopping). Voluntary, private and charitable organizations offer a full range of services from residential care to information giving, and the provision of emotional support.

Advocacy and self-advocacy groups are increasing in number; in the UK, the major national group of self-advocates with learning disabilities is *People First* which has affiliated regional groups. Social workers may involve independent advocates in both the assessment of needs and in the planning process. *Circles of Friends* are groups of people who undertake to consider the welfare of one disabled person throughout their life. Parents and carers can find support and obtain information from national and local support groups established to meet their needs. Some groups are based upon specific clinical diagnoses; others have a concern with all forms of learning disability.

Sometimes, people with learning disabilities and their families can find it difficult to access ordinary community facilities. This may be due to the nature of the disability or because of attitudes expressed by others in the community to the presence of the disability. The social work role in facilitating access to opportunities includes the provision of resources, aids, information, education, training and emotional support to a disabled person and their family, but it also requires the social worker to provide support, resources, education and training to effect changed attitudes within the wider community.

Service accomplishments

The American policy maker, John O'Brien (1986), laid down five *service accomplishments* which have proved influential in the development of good social work practice. He argued that the services provided should be judged by the extent to which they improve the quality of life experience:

1 *Community presence* – the experience of sharing the ordinary places that define community life
2 *Choice* – the experience of growing autonomy in both small, everyday matters and large, life-defining matters
3 *Competence* – the experience of growing ability to skilfully perform functional and meaningful activities with whatever assistance is required
4 *Respect* – the experience of having a valued place among a network of people and valued roles in community life
5 *Community participation* – the experience of being part of a growing network of personal relationships which includes close friends

In 1993, the Social Services Inspectorate in the Department of Health reaffirmed its acknowledgement of the appropriateness of these five accomplishments and added a sixth:

6 *Partnership* – the experience of being involved in the planning process

Change and transition in the life cycle

The time of diagnosis is often a very traumatic time for the parents, siblings and extended family. Diagnosis may be prenatal, perinatal or post natal. The social worker can offer

continued

emotional support, provide information and practical assistance, and liaise with other relevant professionals and support groups.

During early childhood, there may be a need to liaise with a wide range of service providers: home support packages may be introduced; social workers and health visitors may combine to help parents develop the special skills needed to further their child's development; there may be involvement concerning access to playgroups; or education may need support.

Major life transitions, such as the move to senior school or school-leaving, present particular challenges. Life plans should be drawn up with the individual as part of the social work task. Individual Programme Planning was one of the earliest systems of planning with individuals devised in the early 1980s. This was followed by Personal Goal Planning, Shared Action Planning, Personal Futures Planning and Person Centred Planning. These methods of working place the individual at the heart of any assessment and planning, and have increasingly stressed the need for the social worker to work in partnership with the person in maximizing the opportunities to meet their personal aspirations.

A person with learning disabilities, and their parents, may need support during the complex process of adopting traditional adult roles and in securing resources. For example, gaining access to appropriate accommodation away from the parental home and in finding employment or day-time occupation. Some will need constant care because of the level of their disability, while others may need support around particular adult roles such as being a tenant, an employee, a sexual partner or a parent.

Changes brought about by ageing parents or the loss of parents through death can be especially traumatic emotionally and in practical terms. Older people with disabilities may need support in retirement. For some, the deterioration of the ageing process is accelerated, and this may necessitate intervention.

For Further Reading

Department of Health 1992: *Local Authority Circular (92)15: Social Care for Adults with Learning Disabilities (Mental Handicap)*. London: Department of Health.
Manchester Joint Project 1998: *People, Plans and Possibilities*. Brighton: Rowntree Trust/Pavilion Publishing.
O'Brien, J. 1986: A guide to personal futures planning. In G. T. Bellamy and B. Wilcox (eds), *A Comprehensive Guide to the Activities Catalog: An Alternative Curriculum for Youth and Adults with Severe Learning Disabilities*, Baltimore, Maryland: Paul J. H. Brooks.
Social Services Inspectorate 1993: *Whose Life is it Anyway?* London: HMSO.

CAROL DAWSON

Learning Disability

Learning disability is the term currently used in the UK to describe a group of people who have in common various patterns of disordered or delayed development. Normal human development progresses through a series of stages, from total dependency in infancy to increasing independence in childhood and adolescence, through to the achievement of competencies in the physical, psychological, social and intellectual domains in adulthood. People with learning disability have in common a *significant intellectual deficit*, defined as an IQ two standard deviations below the mean IQ, which is 100 for the general population, and a delay in the acquirement of, or a failure to acquire *basic learning and social skills* during the developmental period – considered to be up to the age of 18.

People with learning disability are a very heterogeneous group who differ:

- in the extent of their disability
- in the presence or not of other impairments and disabilities
- in the aetiology of the learning disability
- in the presence of behavioural or psychiatric disorder
- in the presence of medical disorders such as epilepsy
- in individual personality characteristics, and
- in social and family circumstances.

Terminology

People with learning disability were separated as a group from people with mental illness in the nineteenth century. Terms such as *idiocy*, *imbecility* and *moron* were historically used to describe levels of impairment. *Mental deficiency*, *mental subnormality* and *mental handicap* were terms adopted at different times during the twentieth century. *Learning disability* was officially adopted as the term by the Department of Health in the UK in the 1980s. *Mental retardation* is the officially used term in the medical DSM IV and ICD-10 Classification of Mental Disorders. Other terms used include *developmental disability*, *learning difficulty* and *intellectual disability*. *Mental impairment* is the legal term used in UK mental health legislation. In any society where intelligence and competency are highly valued, labels assigned to people with learning disability eventually acquire a pejorative meaning, and this accounts for the constantly changing terminology.

A very useful concept is that offered by the World Health Organization in its definition of impairments, disabilities and handicaps: *impairment* refers to the brain disorder (with many different causes) which gives rises to the *disability* – with respect to the process of learning and acquiring the skills necessary for independent living. The *handicap* is a reflection of the extent to which the person is disadvantaged from the impairment and the resulting disabilities.

Aetiology

The population of people with learning disability can be divided into two broad groups:

- those with *organic* causes, (for example, chromosomal, genetic, pre-, peri- or post-natal trauma);
- those where *subcultural* factors (such as a poor home environment, poor diet, poor education, general social disadvantage and polygenic effects) summate. The majority in this group have mild learning disabilities.

Epidemiology

Between 2.0 per cent and 2.5 per cent of the population fall more than two standard deviations below the mean IQ of 100 (IQ < 70). Of these, 80 per cent are said to have a mild learning disability (IQ = 50–69), 12 per cent have a moderate learning disability (IQ = 34–49), 7 per cent have a severe learning disability (IQ = 20–34), and 1 per cent have a profound learning disability (IQ < 20).

Changing attitudes

Societal attitudes to people with learning disability underwent a major shift during the twentieth century, moving from the notion that they should be segregated and institutionalized to a more humane attitude recognizing that they have the same legal and human rights as others.

The philosophy of normalization and its evolution, development and elaboration best exemplifies this shift. The earliest meaning of the principle was grounded in the human and civil rights movement, and, in 1971, was reflected in the UN Declaration of the

continued

Rights of the Mentally Retarded. It was later elaborated to emphasize the importance of the way disadvantaged people are perceived or portrayed by the public, and was reformulated with an emphasis on socially valued roles rather than culturally normative practices.

Inherent in normalization ideas are the beliefs that all individuals with learning disabilities are capable of growth and development regardless of their degree of disability, and that they have the same basic human and civil rights as others.

Considerable changes have taken place in the way services for people with learning disabilities are now provided, with a move away from institutional to community care. People with learning disabilities need support which will vary considerably depending on their needs, and, for some, these can be quite complex from both a social and health needs perspective.

In the UK, social services departments are the lead agency in the provision of social and residential care for people with learning disabilities. The role of the social worker is crucial, and there is a statutory requirement for the social worker to undertake a needs-led assessment for people with disabilities.

Health issues

There are much higher rates of physical and sensory impairments, medical problems, and psychiatric and behavioural disorders in people with learning disabilities. The increased rates of psychiatric/behavioural disorders are a result of the dynamic interaction between biomedical and psychosocial processes. Biomedical factors (such as genetic and chromosomal disorders, epilepsy, sensory impairments) and social factors (for example, impaired skills and language development, poor communication skills, a limited range of coping skills, low self-esteem, dependence on others, having little control over one's life and being negatively valued and labelled) all contribute to the high risk.

The well-delineated psychiatric disorders seen in the general population also occur in people with learning disabilities. Schizophrenia is three times more common among people with learning disability, and rates of depression are high. Diagnostic difficulties can present in the presence of significant language impairment, but diagnosis can be made and appropriate treatment and management provided.

Two common syndromes associated with learning disability illustrate some of the health-related issues.

- *Down's syndrome* is the commonest single chromosomal disorder in live-born infants. The learning disability can vary from mild to severe. There is an increased incidence of congenital heart disease, respiratory infections, thyroid dysfunction, visual and hearing impairment, acute leukaemia, epilepsy, and, later in adult life, a very high incidence of Alzheimer's disease and at an earlier age than usual.
- *Autism* consists of a triad of developmental impairments biologically determined, affecting reciprocal social interaction, communication and imagination, accompanied by a narrow repetitive stereotyped pattern of activities. The manifestations of this triad vary widely. Two-thirds of those with autism have a learning disability also. Others have normal to high intelligence. *Asperger syndrome* is probably a variant of the *autistic spectrum of disorder* associated with normal intelligence. People with autism can present some of the most serious and difficult-to-manage behavioural disorders. Depression is particularly common in this group.

Specialist health requirements

Specialist health services, employing the skills of psychology, psychiatry, nursing, speech and language therapy and psychotherapy, are needed to address the additional health problems found among people with learning disabilities. Good primary and secondary generic health care are required, and access to them needs to be facilitated.

Health and social care needs cannot be easily separated. The provision of good social care in the form of opportunities for employment or other day-time occupation, skills training, social integration and adequate living facilities will have considerable influence on the mental health and well-being of people with learning disability. While the biological impairment remains static, the level of disability and handicap experienced can be ameliorated by appropriate social and health care support, and this requires close working and co-ordination between all the agencies involved. Without social and health care support, the idea of 'community care' can mean care by the family alone, entailing isolation, stress and an impaired quality of life for the individual and their family.

An understanding of the wide variety of abilities and needs manifested by people with learning disabilities, together with a recognition of the importance of supporting, rather than supplanting, family and carers are essential in the process of determining appropriate services designed to improve the quality of life.

For Further Reading
Bouras, N. 1994: *Mental Health in Mental Retardation: Recent Advances and Practices.* Cambridge: Cambridge University Press.
Brown, H. and Smith, H. (eds) 1992: *Normalisation: A Reader for the 90s.* London: Routledge.
World Health Organization 1992: *The ICD-10 Classification of Mental and Behavioral Disorders: Clinical Descriptions and Diagnostic Guidelines.* Geneva: World Health Organization.

MARIE BAMBRICK

Learning Theory

Learning theory provides a set of principles to account for behavioural change in terms of interaction with the environment.

- *Respondent conditioning*, one of the three main learning principles, occurs when, following a (sometimes shocking) experience, a behavioural response becomes associated with a particular 'stimulus'. Phobias can develop this way, as when a child acquires a generalized fear of men after being assaulted by one man.

- By contrast, *operant conditioning* depends on active engagement with the environment, the consequences of the activity being the key determinant of the learning outcome. Thus, a heroin user receives an immediate 'high' after using the drug, which 'reinforces' the practice.

- A third learning principle underpins *observational learning*, where what is learnt depends on watching others. A violent home background may, for example, provide models from which children learn aggressiveness.

The key theme here is the significance of environment, which accords with social work's tendency to view problematic behaviour as a possibly reversible product of life experience. However, the social work relevance of learning theory is broadened when, drawing from cognitive psychology, detailed attention is paid to the thinking patterns which influence behaviour.

For Further Reading
Catania, A. 1998: *Learning.* New Jersey: Prentice Hall.

MALCOLM MILLAR

Least Restrictive Environment

The desire of elderly people to maintain their independence for as long as possible has led to the concept of a continuum of care, with the emphasis placed on the provision of the *least restrictive environment* that will enable them to remain in their own home. The delivery of health care, domestic services and meals makes a major contribution, together with the provision of day centre facilities, and leisure-time and other services in the community. The social work role tends to be that of an advocate or broker rather than of a service-provider. *Source*: Adapted from Suppes and Wells (1996).

Leaving Care

Leaving care refers to young people, usually aged from 16 to 19, who leave substitute care and accommodation at the end of their care careers.

The journey into adulthood

Most young people, whether they are living with their own families, or in foster care or a children's home, experience problems during their journey to adulthood. Care leavers share a lot in common with other young people, but the research evidence points to key differences:

- They have to leave care and live independently at a much earlier age than other young people leave home.
- Just over a half move regularly, and 20 per cent experience homelessness in the two years after they leave care.
- They have lower levels of educational attainment and lower post-16 further education participation rates.
- They have higher unemployment rates, more unstable career patterns and higher levels of dependency on welfare benefits.
- They enter parenthood earlier.
- They experience more mental health problems.

As regards specific groups of care leavers, the largest group of black (Afro-Caribbean, Asian, mixed heritage) young people leaving care are of mixed heritage. In comparison to white young people, black young people enter care earlier, stay longer, and, after leaving care, have similar employment and housing careers. Most black young people leaving care experience racism.

Research studies show that about 13 per cent of all young people leaving care have special needs including emotional and behavioural difficulties, learning difficulties, physical disabilities and mental health problems. Compared to other young people leaving care, those with special needs have fewer educational qualifications, are more likely to be unemployed and to experience homelessness.

The evidence from a large number of studies – see Stein (1997) for a research review – shows that young people leaving care have to cope with the challenges and responsibilities of major changes in their lives – in leaving foster and residential care and setting up home, in leaving school and entering the world of work or, more likely, being unemployed and surviving on benefits, and in being parents – at a far younger age than other young people. They have compressed and accelerated transitions to adulthood.

Recognition of the problems

The increased recognition of the problems faced by care leavers was the consequence of a number of actions – by researchers, by the small but powerful voices of young people belonging to 'in care' groups, by campaigners, and by practitioners and managers working with care leavers in the statutory and voluntary agencies. It was this awakening of leaving care in the professional and political consciousness that led to the introduction of new leaving care powers and duties through legislative change in England and Wales, Scotland and Northern Ireland during the 1990s.

Social services provision for care leavers includes specialist leaving care teams, mainstream social work support and projects for specific groups of care leavers. Specialist schemes have developed particularly since the mid-1980s to respond to what have been described as the core needs of care leavers – for accommodation, finance, careers and support networks.

The effectiveness of leaving care schemes

How effective are leaving care services? This is not an easy question to answer accurately because there are very few studies which have compared the outcomes for care leavers receiving such services with other groups of care leavers. However, the findings of a major English study are broadly consistent with a more substantial study from the USA and point to two ways of answering this question (Biehal et al., 1995).

First, leaving care schemes can make a positive contribution to specific outcomes for care leavers. They work particularly well in respect of accommodation and life skills, including budgeting, negotiating and self-care skills, and, to some extent, in furthering social networks, developing relationships and building self-esteem.

Second, researching outcomes has identified other positive influences that are independent of the specialist schemes. Successful educational outcomes are closely linked to placement stability, more often achieved in foster care placements, combined with a supportive and encouraging environment for study. Without such stability and encouragement, post-16 employment and career outcomes are likely to be very poor. Success in social networks, personal relationships and in having a positive self-image, although assisted by schemes, is also closely connected with young people having positive, supportive family relationships with family members or former carers.

Stability, continuity, and family and carer links are the foundation on which specialist leaving care schemes must build if they are to be effective. Schemes also work well by targeting the core needs of care leavers, by being committed to young people and involving them in decision making, by working with other agencies (particularly housing providers, benefit agencies, and employment and training agencies), by influencing policy at the local level and by operating within a well-developed managerial and policy framework which addresses access to schemes, equal opportunities, service delivery and scheme monitoring. However, research evidence indicates that there is great variation in the resourcing, range and quality of leaving care services within the UK (Broad, 1998).

Finally, there is a failure in much of the leaving care literature to explore theoretical perspectives. Contributions in the areas of *attachment theory*, recognizing the compensatory stability needs of young people in care, *focal theory*, identifying that the accelerated and compressed transitions of care leavers deny them the psychological opportunities of dealing with major changes over time and a *life course approach*, recognizing the interaction between the agency of young people and their wider social contexts, would further enhance our understanding.

For Further Reading

Biehal, N., Clayden, J., Stein, M. and Wade, J. 1995: *Moving On: Young People and Leaving Care Schemes*. London: HMSO.

Broad, B. 1998: *Young People Leaving Care: Life after the Children Act 1989*. London: Jessica Kingsley.

Stein, M. 1997: *What Works in Leaving Care?* Barkingside: Barnardos.

MIKE STEIN

Lesbian and Gay Issues in Social Work

Lesbians and gay men are subject to the operation of heterosexism and homophobia, but these are experienced differentially: lesbians are also women, while lesbians and gay men are distinguished by age, race, religion, disability and class.

There is no one lesbian and gay experience; the lives of lesbians and gay men are characterized by heterogeneity. General patterns or trends about lesbians' and gay men's

continued

lives are, however, discernible at the start of the twenty-first century. First, perceptions of lesbians and gay men have shifted away from a pathological model of social deviance towards a positive image of alternative lifestyle. Second, throughout the last quarter of the twentieth century, lesbians and gay men felt able to 'come out' and live openly. For social workers, this means meeting both service users and colleagues who expect to have their identities appropriately recognized and respected. For many lesbians and gay men, however, being visible has not yet become a reality. Social workers need to understand the pressures to remain hidden, and the negative consequences of living in a homophobic society.

Child care social work

In the field of child care social work, lesbian and gay parents and carers need consideration. Lesbians and gay men may apply to be assessed as foster carers or adopters, depending upon whether legislation and agencies allow this, and social workers will assess such applicants. Other lesbians or gay men may become birth parents via former relationships, co-parenting arrangements or self-insemination. Social workers will thus work with children, young people and their families where one or both parents are gay or lesbian. It is also possible that social workers will have to assess risks to children living with gay parents, but, as research demonstrates, a lesbian or gay sexuality *per se* does not pose risks.

Many lesbians and gay men first become aware of their sexuality during adolescence. Some will progress through the process of self-acceptance and the passage into young adulthood reasonably smoothly, but others will experience extreme isolation, have problems with self-acceptance and may be rejected by their peers and families, or by carers if in a *looked-after* situation. Young people also experience homophobia within the care system. Social workers can do much to support young people through an accepting and non-judgemental approach and through providing access to lesbian and gay self-help services. The parents of lesbians and gay men may respond to news of their offspring's sexuality with shock, fear, anger or guilt. Parents can also be helped through this early stage towards a gradual acceptance of their child, and can be assisted in this through involvement in self-help parents' groups.

Adult services and mental health

Within adult services, disabled people requiring support, assessment and care within the community may be lesbian or gay, but report that they are often assumed to be *asexual*. Instead, the sexuality of disabled lesbians and gay men should be taken into account in any assessment and service provision, as should the views of partners and carers. Adults accommodated in residential establishments may also be lesbian or gay, and face prejudice from other residents or staff. Denial of visiting rights to lesbian or gay partners, or the enforced separation of older lesbian and gay couples entering supported housing are two such examples. A more controversial area has been work with adults who have a learning disability. It has been assumed that such adults lack the emotional maturity to form lesbian or gay relationships, or that they have been under the influence of corrupting gay adults. Social workers therefore need to be aware that disabled adults may also be lesbians or gay men, and that the services that they require ought to acknowledge this.

In the field of mental health, homophobic oppression can create emotional and psychological difficulties and damage for some lesbians and gay men, but this is not inevitable, nor a product of the individual's sexuality. As recently as 1978, homosexuality was categorized as a mental disorder and older service users may have been subjected to inhumane treatments such as aversive shock therapy in the past in an attempt to 'cure' them of their sexuality. Social workers need to ensure that any counselling or therapeutic services do not reinforce the pathologization of lesbians or gay men.

Social work services to older people will also work with lesbians and gay men in the community. Assessments for help within the home, support services or residential accommodation will need to take older lesbians' or gay men's sexuality and partners into account. Older lesbians and gay men face problems in accessing help where they have to deal with illness or the death of partners or loved ones and bereavement counselling should acknowledge the legitimacy of such relationships.

Criminal justice social work
In the field of criminal justice, social workers work with lesbian and gay offenders within the community, in hostels, secure accommodation or prisons, and in the court. Lesbians and gay men may be particularly prone to injustices because of their sexuality: gay male sex is criminalized in legislation, lesbian mothers have lost custody of their children solely because of their sexuality, and lesbian offenders may face prejudice within the criminal justice system because of their sexuality and their gender. Social workers preparing welfare or pre-sentence reports on lesbians and gay men for the court will need to be aware of potential discrimination on the basis of sexuality. Lesbians and gay men in hostels, secure accommodation and prisons may face prejudice because of their sexuality and be at risk of physical, sexual and emotional abuses because of this.

For Further Reading
Brown, H. C. 1998: *Social Work and Sexuality: Working with Lesbians and Gay Men.* Houndmills: Macmillan.
Hicks, S. and McDermott, J. (eds) 1999: *Lesbian and Gay Fostering and Adoption: Extraordinary Yet Ordinary.* London: Jessica Kingsley.
Hunter, S., Shannon, C., Knox, J. and Martin, J. I. 1998: *Lesbian, Gay, and Bisexual Youths and Adults: Knowledge for Human Services Practice.* Thousand Oaks: Sage.

STEPHEN HICKS AND SUE WISE

The Life Course
See REMINISCENCE.

Life Expectancy
A person's *life expectancy* (sometimes called *life expectation* or *expectation of life*) is the remaining number of years he or she can expect to live. In developed countries, life expectancy at birth is typically between 70 and 80 years, and is usually a few years greater for women than men. In the UK, based on 1990–92 data, it was 73.4 years for men and 79.0 years for women (Office for National Statistics, 1997, p. 2). Life expectancy declines almost linearly with age from birth to about 50 years; thereafter the rate of decline slows (see figure 1).

Life expectancy is determined by a person's marital status (married people can expect to live longer than single, widowed or divorced persons), economic status, living conditions and environment, employment status, and lifestyle.

Demographers have also developed the idea of the expectation of a healthy life, which is the number of years a person can expect to remain free of disability or long-term illness. At birth in the UK, the expectation of a healthy life is about 59 years for men and 61 years for women.

For Further Reading
Office for National Statistics 1997: *English Life Tables Number 15* (Series DS, number 14). London: The Stationery Office.

ANDREW HINDE

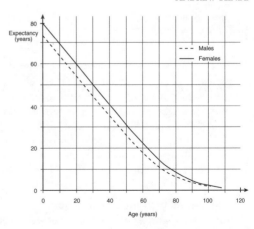

Figure 1 Life expectation (years), England and Wales, 1990–92

Life Story Work

Life story work is a structured approach to eliciting and recording the details of an individual's life with a view to identifying appropriate helping strategies. Life story work is used with older people and with people with learning disabilities, typically in institutional settings or when undergoing transitions between care and community. Talking and writing about a past life, building a record with photographs and images in a *life story book* enables adults and children to present a biography which is their own.

Used with children who have been separated from their birth parents and who may have experienced family change as well as changes in neighbourhood, schools and social workers, life story work helps them to deal with past, present and future.

Talk about the past helps a child to establish self-worth, deal with blame and develop a positive sense of identity. The life story book remains the child's possession; however, timing may depend on the child's acceptance and positive estimation of their experience of family life, and this is particularly the case when relationships with parents have involved sexual abuse.

For Further Reading

Ryan, T. and Walker, R. 1999: *Life Story Work* (revised edn). London: British Agencies for Adoption and Fostering.

JOANNA BORNAT

Lone-parent Families

The term *lone-parent family* refers to a mother or father living without a spouse or cohabitee together with never-married dependent child(ren) aged either under 16 or under 19 and undertaking full-time education.

Lone-parent families today

The 1.7 million lone-parent families in Britain make up about a quarter of all families and care for 2.9 million children – just under 1 in 4 of all children (table 9).

Table 9 Numbers of lone-parent families in Great Britain and their dependent children 1961–1997 (Thousands)

	1961	1966	1971	1976	1981	1986	1991	1996	1997[a]
Lone parent families	474	499	570	750	900	1,010	1,300	1,600	1,730
Dependent children			1,000	1,300	1,500	1,600	2,200	2,800	2,900

[a] *provisional estimate only, Labour Force Survey, 1997.*
Source: Haskey, J. 1998.

Of lone parents, 90 per cent are women, with lone fathers making up the remaining 10 per cent. Lone-parent families reflect changing family patterns throughout western societies with more couples cohabiting before both childbirth and marriage, more divorce, more re-marriage and more stepfamilies. Although the divorce rate peaked in 1993, two in five marriages ultimately end in divorce.

The number of lone-parent families has trebled since 1971. According to Marsh et al. (1977), lone parenthood is now a stage in the life-cycle lasting on average about five years, and Ford and Millar (1988) estimate that between a third and a half of all children are spending some time in a lone-parent family.

The routes into lone parenthood

Sources indicate that, in the nineteenth century, a similar proportion of families was headed by a lone parent as today, although now most lone parents are divorced or separated rather than widowed (table 10). Three in five lone parents are ex-married (either

Table 10   Routes into lone parenthood – 1998

	Percentage	Number
Lone mothers		
Divorced	31	536,300
Separated	20	346,000
Widowed	4	69,200
Single	35	605,500
Lone fathers	10	173,000
Total	100	1,730,000

Source: Office for National Statistics (2000), calcu-
lated from raw numbers supplied in a private communication to the author by staff at the General
Household Survey in the ONS.

divorced, separated or widowed). Lone fathers are mostly ex-married, usually divorced
or separated but more than twice as likely as lone mothers to be widowed. The fastest
growing group is now single or never-married lone parents although most of these are
ex-cohabitees. Less than one in seven lone parents have never married or lived with their
child's father.

The average age for a lone parent is 34; fewer than 3 per cent of all lone parents are
teenagers. Never-married lone parents are more likely to be younger than others and to
be on benefit. However, they tend to have smaller families and to take paid work and
re-partner sooner.

One contributory factor is domestic violence: 35 per cent of lone parents have
experienced violence in their last relationship with three-quarters of them sustaining
physical injuries.

Members of some ethnic minority communities are more likely to experience lone
parenthood – for example, 55 per cent of black families are headed by a lone parent
compared to 9 per cent of Indian, 17 per cent of Bangladeshi and 22 per cent of white
families.

Responsibility for children
On average, lone-parent families have fewer children (1.7) compared with couples, who
have 1.9 children. Single lone mothers have smaller families with only 1.56 children.
Nearly 40 per cent of lone mothers has a child under the age of five. This figure rises
for lone parents working under 16 hours a week and claiming Income Support, when
over 50 per cent has a child under five. Lone fathers have older children, with well over
half aged 10–15, reflecting the different routes into lone parenthood for men. By comparison, 70 per cent of lone mothers have children under 10, more than half of these
being under five.

Outcomes for children
Controversy surrounds the issue of how children are affected by relationship breakdown.
Poorer socio-economic outcomes, educational achievement, health, behavioural problems and early parenthood have all been highlighted. However, there is no simple and
direct relationship between family type and poorer outcomes as these only apply to a
minority of children in separated families, although they are twice as prevalent as in
intact families. Rodgers and Pryor's (1998) authoritative review of the evidence
has drawn attention to the complex sequence of experiences before, during and
after parental separation, concluding that poorer outcomes are by no means inevitable.

continued

Conflict, parental distress, loss of contact with a parent and repeated disruption all seem significant. Above all, the low income, poor housing and greater financial hardship experienced in lone-parent families is crucial. In the absence of poverty, it has been found that children from lone-parent families fare no worse than children in other families.

Lone-parent poverty

On separation or divorce, mothers and children usually see a substantial fall in their income averaging about £20 a week; fathers are likely to see an increase of about £10 a week. Like women in couples, those who are lone parents find that caring for young children affects their ability to take paid employment, and some prefer to be full-time mothers or work part-time. The difference is that, without a partner's income (and their help with childcare), many lone parents have to rely on state benefits to top-up their income. Currently, only one in three lone parents receives any child maintenance from the child's father and, where child maintenance is due to be collected through the Child Support Agency, only 47 per cent receive the full amount, 23 per cent receive part-payment and the remaining 30 per cent, nothing. With the exception of widows' benefits, help for one-parent families has always been through means-tested benefits paid at subsistence levels.

Typically, lone parents' incomes are less than half those of two-parent families, with average net incomes a little over £100 a week. Of lone-parent families, 50 per cent live on gross weekly incomes of less than £150 per week compared to just 4 per cent of married couples and 9 per cent of cohabiting couples.

The number of lone-parent families living in poverty has increased, overtaking pensioners as the poorest group – now 2.8 million individual lone parents and children live below the poverty line. Of lone parents, 62 per cent live in poverty (defined as having incomes below half the average income after housing costs); they are the group at greatest risk of poverty in the UK. The proportion of lone parents living in poverty has increased from 19 per cent in 1979. Now that there are more lone parents, the poverty is more visible and many would argue that the social security system has strikingly failed to deal with family change.

Why are lone parents poor?

Lone parents are disproportionately affected by poverty for a number of reasons. Chief among these are the cost of having children and the loss of earning power that results. The fact that, at present, most lone parents are women is the key to understanding the prevalence of poverty in lone-parent families: they are likely to earn significantly less than men, to be in low-paid work and to be employed in the non-standard or 'flexible' economy.

Recent government policies have emphasized paid work as the route out of poverty for lone parents. Only 44 per cent of lone mothers are in paid work, compared to 68 per cent of married women with dependent children. It is significant, however, that almost as many lone parents with children aged five and over work full-time as do married women. Worklessness in lone-parent families is closely associated with the incidence of poverty; but the inadequacy of benefits is also significant.

Housing

Bradshaw and Millar (1991) have shown that, on becoming a lone parent, 58 per cent move, usually into local authority accommodation. Many spend at least some time living with friends or relatives before finding a new place to live. 30 per cent of lone-parent families have experienced homelessness in the past ten years compared to only 3 per cent of couples with dependent children. Two-thirds of lone parents live in rented accommodation, usually social housing, compared to one-fifth of other families. Only a third are owner–occupiers compared to three-quarters of couples.

Conclusion

Lone parents have more often than not been seen as a burden on the social security budget; their reliance on benefits or 'welfare dependency' is referred to as if it were a personal choice. In fact, they are living with policies which have practically institutionalized poverty for lone parents. Their reliance on social assistance explains to a large extent the disproportionate experience of hardship in these families.

Arguably, today's lone parents are paying the price for the historic neglect of their income needs. Strikingly little progress was made in the twentieth century to right this injustice. In 1997, the Labour government committed itself to eliminating child poverty within twenty years – and it remains to be seen how far it will succeed in achieving this for children living in lone-parent families.

For Further Reading

Bradshaw, J. and Millar, J. 1991: *Lone Parent Families in the United Kingdom.* London: HMSO.

Ford, R. and Millar, J. (eds) 1998: *Private Lives and Public Responses: Lone Parenthood and Future Policy.* London: Policy Studies Institute.

Haskey, J. 1998: One-parent families and their dependent children in Great Britain. *Population Trends*, 91, London: The Stationery Office.

Marsh, A., Ford, R. and Finlayson, L. 1997: *Lone Parents, Work and Benefits.* London: The Stationery Office.

Rodgers, B. and Pryor, J. 1998: *Divorce and Separation: The Outcomes for Children.* York: Joseph Rowntree Foundation.

ALISON GARNHAM

Looked-after Children

Looked-after children is a term which was introduced following the implementation of the Children Act 1989 to denote all children placed in the care of local authorities in England and Wales. The term *looked after* is used in preference to *in the care of* because it implies a temporary provisional state. This is in line with the emphasis in the Children Act 1989 of preserving the notion of parental responsibility even when parents are not physically caring for their children.

There are two main categories of looked-after children – those described as *in care* and those referred to as *accommodated*. Prior to the Children Act, these children were described respectively as in *statutory* or *voluntary care*. There are three categories of children in care:

1 Children who are subject to court orders as a result of being abused, neglected or deemed to be beyond the control of their parents
2 Children on emergency protection orders
3 Children remanded by the courts pending further hearing

Accommodated children are those who come into care for more than 24 hours under Section 20 of the Children Act 1989 with the voluntary agreement of their parents or guardians.

The numbers involved

In 1998, there were 53,700 children being looked after in England (approximately five children per 1000) of whom 34,500 were in care (including 2,400 children on remand, on protection orders, or freed for adoption) and 19,200 were accommodated. There has

continued

199

been a gradual decline in overall numbers of looked-after children from approximately 90,000 in the early 1980s. The biggest fall has been in the numbers of older children coming into care for behavioural and offending reasons.

The statistics for numbers and types of children looked after in any calendar year give a good indication of the overall picture. In the year up to 31 March 1998, 31,700 children started to be looked after, two-thirds (21,800) under voluntary agreements, and one-third as a result of care orders (4,600), remands (1,600) and emergency protection orders (3,300). In the same year, 30,800 ceased to be looked after, two-fifths of whom had been looked after for less than eight weeks. Generally, children under voluntary agreements are looked after for relatively short periods compared with those being looked after as a result of care proceedings.

About 70 per cent of looked-after children (35,200) are placed in foster care. The remainder are living with their parents (5,700), have been placed for adoption (2,500), are in residential care (6,500) or are in lodgings and other placements (3,000). It is notable that only 12 per cent of looked-after children live in residential homes, the type of setting traditionally associated with the childcare system. The decline in numbers of looked-after children in the 1980s and 1990s was most evident in the residential sector of substitute care provision.

Deprivation as a factor

There is a wealth of debate about, and research into, issues relating to looked-after children. A key concern has been about the type of child for whom such care is provided. As has been noted already, there has been a shift away from using residential care for older children with behavioural and offending problems except in more extreme cases. Children start to be looked after for a variety of reasons, the most common being: to give relief to the parents; abuse and neglect; and the parents' health. However, government statistics miss out on what is perhaps the key issue, namely that the vast majority of children coming into local authority care are from multiply deprived backgrounds. According to a large-scale study carried out by Bebbington and Miles (1989), the odds on children aged 5–9 coming into care from financially deprived, lone-parent, mixed ethnic origin families living in overcrowded rented accommodation are as high as 1 in 10. For children where the reverse of these conditions apply, the odds are 1 in 7000.

The process of admission and placement

Much attention has been placed on the process of admissions to care. Research has pointed to the fact that these are often unplanned and are carried out in emergencies. Guidance to the Children Act 1989 places great emphasis on the need for, and the importance of, detailed planning with parents at the time of admission.

Another key issue is that of providing placements which best meet the interests of looked-after children. The Children Act 1989 requires local authorities to take into account cultural as well as religious needs in this process, and to ensure that placements for children with disabilities allow them to lead as normal a life as possible.

The Children Act 1989 placed great emphasis on the notion of parents retaining responsibility for children while in care – hence the use of the term *looked after*. This followed a period where it was felt that insufficient effort was being made to maintain links and contact with birth parents.

Measuring outcomes

Concerns about the standards of care provided for looked-after children, particularly in relation to their health and education, have led to the Department of Health introducing measures for assessing needs and measuring outcomes in relation to these and other aspects of their growth and development.

Research has shown that young people leaving care after the age of 16 are frequently poorly prepared for independence and fare badly relative to their peers who have not been in care in many spheres including further education, employment and criminal activity.

Since the early 1990s, there has been widespread concern following the discovery of a large number of cases involving the sexual and physical abuse of children in residential and, to a lesser extent, foster-care in the 1970s and 1980s. This led to much greater attention being paid to further developing complaints and monitoring systems set up by the Children Act 1989.

For Further Reading
Bebbington, A. and Miles, J. 1989: The background of children who enter local authority care. *British Journal of Social Work*, 19, 349–68.
Utting, Sir W. 1997: *People Like Us: The Report of the Review of the Safeguards for Children Living away from Home*. London: HMSO.
Ward, H. (ed.) 1995: *Looking After Children: Research into Practice*. London: HMSO.

BRIAN CORBY

Loss

Loss involves losing something or someone. The concept encompasses a range of experiences from the apparently trivial misplacement of a personal possession to the permanent loss of a loved person:

- Loss by death, or the experience of bereavement
- Loss of a parent, carer or family, not through bereavement, but through family breakdown or parental separation
- Loss of a partner, by separation or divorce
- Loss of a potential child, by miscarriage, still birth or abortion
- Loss of health, by illness, disability or accident
- Loss of a job, by unemployment, redundancy or retirement
- Loss of a role, by retirement, or, as a parent, when children become independent
- Loss of security, by being a victim of violence, rape or burglary
- Loss of a preferred milieu, by moving house, neighbourhood, geographical location or country, or by a move from home to residential or nursing care

Such losses may not be separate and distinct; loss of health, for example, may lead to the loss of a job.

Loss and attachment theory
The degree of loss experienced varies with the strength and quality of the attachment involved, and with the meaning of what has been lost to the 'loser'. Reactions to loss are analogous to the processes of mourning. Attachment theory has been described as 'a way of conceptualising the propensity of human beings to make strong affectional bonds to particular others' (Bowlby, 1979, p. 127), and the theory is pertinent to an understanding of the meaning of loss. Generally, the greater the attachment, to people, things or places, the greater the impact of the loss.

However Parkes' (1975) recognition that, in bereavement, grief is likely to be greater, the greater the feeling of ambivalence to the dead person suggests that, for adults, loss and concomitant grief may be intensified when attachment was ambivalent rather than secure.

continued

In childhood, loss has particular relevance, in that it means the loss of early attachment figures necessary for development and functioning. Loss of attachment figures in early childhood, where affectional bonds are disrupted but not replaced, may lead to significant gaps in children's physical, cognitive, and psychological development, and to maladaptive and 'stuck' patterns of behaviour.

Attachments are not confined simply to people: other attachments include pets, houses, one's homeland, and apparently minor possessions. The loss of such attachments may trigger a grief process analogous to bereavement.

Loss, change and bereavement

Marris (1974) extended the analysis of loss to an emphasis on the significance of the *meaning* of the loss to the loser, linking the concept of loss to *change*. Any change, he argued, whether voluntary or imposed, positive or negative, involves a loss for those affected. The analysis of loss prompted by change has been examined, for example, in relation to slum clearance, business innovation, becoming a university student from a non-traditional background, or moving from rural or tribal communities to cities. Such transitions involve for the participants a loss of their previously taken-for-granted view of the world, their feeling of security and their established sense of meaning and purpose.

Such a process can lead to conflict between a number of contradictory impulses:

- The need to consolidate what was valuable and important from the past
- The need to preserve the self in the face of the loss
- The need to establish a meaningful pattern of relationships in which the loss is accepted
- The need to move on and embrace the future – or *to change*

Because loss involves a tension between holding on to the past and moving on to the future, the *loser* has to detach from previous attachments, relationships and meanings of life based on them, and establish a new or changed meaning of life linked to his or her new world.

Any loss or change potentially involves similar processes to those of bereavement: alarm; searching; mitigation and denial of loss; anger; guilt; integration and acceptance of the loss; development of a new adapted identity. The bereavement model is not limited and specific to loss by bereavement, but is relevant to the full range of losses.

Loss and social work

For many users of social work services, loss is a fundamental aspect of the difficulties they may encounter, and the social worker's assessment and response should therefore include an understanding of what is involved in undergoing and adapting to loss. For example, all transitions which service users experience will involve elements of loss; in particular, the social worker should be alert to the meaning of loss when people move into, or out of, residential care, leave hospital after a long stay, or are placed in, or removed from, foster care.

The concept of loss is fundamental to social care and social work practice. Users of social work services undergo constant losses and experience many transitions and changes. Social workers, in assessment and intervention, whatever the work-setting, should be aware of the impact of loss and change on service users, the potential consequences on their lives and the grief processes they are likely to experience.

For Further Reading

Bowlby, J. 1979: *The Making and Breaking of Affectional Bonds*. London: Tavistock.
Marris, P. 1974: *Loss and Change*. London: Routledge and Kegan Paul.
Parkes, C. M. 1975: *Bereavement: Studies in Adult Grief*. Harmondsworth: Penguin.

JOYCE LISHMAN

M

Maintenance Theory

Maintenance theory is unusual in social work in that its core assertion is not drawn from psychology (as is the case with the cognitive-behavioural approach or attachment theory), sociology (as with systems theory or labelling), or political ideology (as in anti-discriminatory practice or feminist arguments), but has emerged directly from empirical research analyses of social work practice.

Maintenance theory was proposed as a way of dealing with the paradox that social work has expanded rapidly in the UK and elsewhere, despite frequent and widespread demonstrations of its therapeutic ineffectiveness. Maintenance theory proposes that the primary function of social workers is to maintain the community-based independence of adults, to protect the short- and long-term interests of children, and to contribute towards the creation of a community climate in which all citizens can maximize their potential for personal development.

The theory has been subjected to criticism from those who presumed that it *advocates* the maintenance of the *status quo*, and could therefore be deemed to be regressive in its design and its consequences. This critique, however, misconstrues the nature of theory (as understood in social psychology) and confuses it with ideology: maintenance theory is firmly based on empirical analysis, draws on a large number of research findings, and relates to what social workers do in practice – not what advocates think that social workers *should* be doing.

Good examples of maintenance theory are to be found in foster care, in the provision of respite services, family support services, parole, community care and palliative care.

For Further Reading
Davies, M. 1994: *The Essential Social Worker, Part II: The Theory and Practice of Maintenance* (3rd edn). Aldershot: Arena, 37–130.

MARTIN DAVIES

Management in Social Work

Management in social work is the process of enabling social work to achieve both its professional and organizational goals. These goals reflect the interests of different stakeholders in welfare, whose demands must be reconciled or prioritized. Their achievement requires consultation and planning, identification and deployment of resources, co-ordination of activity and support for the efforts of everyone involved. These are the key tasks of management.

Management is indivisible from the organizational context of professional practice. Much social work activity is legitimized by agency mandates derived from law. The rationale for management is the need for co-ordination of the complex organizational systems evolved to discharge these responsibilities. *Strategic management* sets the purpose and direction of the organization. *Operational management* organizes service delivery within that broad framework. The organizational agenda to which managers work may be broader than that of social work, which forms only part of the corporate function.

Models of management
At the heart of management is a fundamental tension between control and facilitation. *Control* emphasizes supervisory mechanisms for ensuring work-force compliance with task achievement. *Facilitation* emphasizes more participative processes of motivating people to maximize capabilities and commitment.

continued

This tension reflects influences from traditional management theories with differing perspectives on what makes organizations work:

- *Scientific management* proposes that organizations work best when their functions are compartmentalized and linked in rational and logical ways, each section making a predictable and standardized contribution to goal-achievement. Structure tends to be hierarchical, reflecting perceived need for strong line management to ensure co-ordination and achievement of standards.
- The *human-relations school* views organizations as human co-operative systems. Participants' search for self-fulfilment and social comfort has strong impacts on work behaviour. Co-ordination of activity is achieved through mutual adjustment. Management focuses upon making the work environment satisfying.
- *Systems perspectives* propose that organizations comprise continuously shifting, interdependent coalitions, influencing and influenced by the external environment. Management attends to the boundaries between the sub-systems and to the organization's relationship with its environment.

Influences on management in social work

Several factors influence what social work management is about. First is the nature of the welfare economy, in which markets have replaced the political structures of representative democracy as the preferred mechanism for allocating social 'goods'. Despite professional suspicion of the attempt to recast welfare users as free purchasing agents, consumerist notions of access, information, choice, representation and redress have become well-established.

Associated with marketization is public service agencies' espousal of the ethos and practices of private sector management. New public management gives managers responsibility for achieving the economy, efficiency and effectiveness deemed lacking in professionally dominated welfare bureaucracies. Its characteristics are centralized strategic control of core objectives, and delegation of the means of achieving them to operational managers, along with strict performance targets and monitoring.

Managerial and professional values may collide. The sources of legitimacy, goals and accountabilities observed by managers and social workers may radically differ. There is notable disillusionment with management among social workers who see managers, particularly senior managers, as either unfamiliar with, or hostile to, their professional task.

A further influence on managers is their organization's location in the sector. Social work is practised in a wide range of statutory and independent agencies. Managers in government agencies operating in a resource-constrained environment must balance competing demands and allocate resources by reference to some notion of collective equity. They must account for their decisions to those whose interests are served or excluded. Independent sector managers may legitimately promote specific, partisan interests, although they may struggle to retain an accountability to service users in a contract-driven environment.

Organizational structures and politics similarly influence management practice. Managers in mechanistic structures will be located precisely in a hierarchy with clear authority, span of control, vertical communication channels and accountability. Much managerial effort goes into maintaining these established patterns. Organic structures will require greater flexibility, horizontal linkages, teamwork, collaboration and networking.

Organizational politics reflect the sources and distribution of power, how interests are pursued and conflicts resolved. Managers' own power is partly derived from their formal position, but other factors, such as expertise, access to information, alliances, personal characteristics and membership of dominant or marginalized groups, also confer power. These sources of power are not confined to managers.

The third influence is who managers themselves are. Women are poorly represented in management. So, too, are black people, particularly black women. Discrimination influences career and working patterns. Women managers report experiences arising from the combined impacts of gender stereotyping, minority visibility, hostility and exclusion from male-dominated work cultures. Further, men and women managers may make different contributions, women being associated with democratic, participative and supportive styles of management, although gender may be less significant than the managerialist ethos in determining behaviour.

Managers and professional practice

The twin management aims of achieving organizational and professional goals need not be diametrically opposed. Social work managers are predominantly drawn from within the profession's ranks. Although their professional identity is no preparation for management, some individuals retain a commitment to professional values and a service user orientation while functioning in a managerial role. Effective social work management, while formulating the objectives and actions that enable the organization to achieve its overall purpose, will recognize and work with the discretion and autonomy of professional practitioners to transform or initiate policy in a process of constructive adaptation. Equally important is the need for the professional/manager dialogue not to obscure the broader participation of those outside the organization in formulating its objectives. User voices challenge both managerial and professional ownership of aims and priorities.

Managers of social work have a key role in creating space for professionals to practise. Such space involves holding social workers to account, but also entails working to place the organization's resources at the disposal of professional staff and ultimately of service users.

For Further Reading

Balloch, S., McLean, J. and Fisher, M. 1999: *Social Services: Working Under Pressure*. Bristol: Policy Press.

Coulshed, V. and Mullender, A. 2001: *Management in Social Work*. (2nd edn) London: Macmillan.

Exworthy, M. and Halford, S. 1999: *Professionals and The New Managerialism in the Public Sector*. Buckingham: Open University Press.

SUZY BRAYE

Management of Offenders in the Community

The *management of offenders in the community* refers to the structured and managed approach to the supervision of offenders. The key principles are that levels of supervision should match the risk an offender presents, that interventions should appropriately match the criminogenic factors or problematic behaviours of the offender, and that supervision resources should be allocated in a rational manner.

This approach prioritizes the reduction of reoffending and the reduction of harmful behaviours as the central objectives of supervision, rather than the reduction of client need. The approach is usually supported by formalized assessment methods and evaluation of supervision performance through the use of outcome measures such as reconviction-rates. Interventions based upon empirical studies of effectiveness are encouraged. Offenders can be managed individually or as part of structured group programmes. The range of community penalties available to sentencers reflects the emphasis upon structured, effectiveness-based interventions aimed at reducing reoffending.

Management of offenders has been associated with the rise of a managed approach to the probation service in general, increased centralized policy directives on the work of the service, and the reduction of professional discretion.

For Further Reading

McIvor, G. 1996: *Working with Offenders*. London: Jessica Kingsley.

HAZEL KEMSHALL

205

Mania and Manic Depression

See BIPOLAR AFFECTIVE DISORDER.

Market Research

Traditionally, *market research* methods are employed by commercial firms to assess sales potential or to gauge customer reaction, but similar techniques are commonly used in social work. An analysis of published social work research suggests that the market research model is more common than any other. Examples include studies which outline drug users' views about the services available, explore why foster carers cease to foster, or report on users' experience of respite services in learning disability.

Some such studies are of high quality, but many do not measure up to the disciplined market research standards demanded by indus-

try and commerce. Sampling techniques are often flawed; sample sizes tend to be small; focus groups are used superficially; and too much reliance is frequently placed on unreplicated findings. Above all, in social work, survey researchers fail time and again to take heed of the fundamental fact known to all skilled marketeers: that what respondents say – whether in interview or discussion – rarely reflects what they believe, and often conflicts with what they do in practice.

In this respect, in the field of human welfare, academic research traditions have failed to impose the same disciplinary standards that tend to be taken for granted in commercial practice.

For Further Reading

Gilovich, T. 1993: *How We Know What Isn't So*. New York: Free Press.

MARTIN DAVIES

Marriage/Relationship Counselling

Marriage counselling or *relationship counselling* is the process of addressing couple problems through a counselling relationship.

Marriage counselling is a generic term covering different approaches to helping couples with marital problems. Its defining function is to focus attention on the adult heterosexual couple relationship when responding to problems that one or both partners present for help, an orientation that is sometimes described as regarding the 'marriage as patient'. Couple or relationship counselling involves the same process, but includes couples who are unmarried and may be of the same sex. The process is constructed of three interacting variables: the setting within which counselling takes place, the clients who use the service, and the counsellors who provide it.

Agency function

Marriage/relationship counselling is available from different practice settings. The most frequently approached are specialist organizations offering counselling and/or psychotherapy services, medical settings and private practice. The UK is unusual in having specialist marriage counselling organizations delivering services through trained volunteers: Relate, Marriage Care, Jewish Marriage Council and Marriage Counselling Scotland. Some hospital departments and independent Institutes or Clinics (for example, the Tavistock Marital Studies Institute) offer marital psychotherapy. It is also becoming increasingly familiar for doctors to employ clinic-based counsellors. Many counsellors and psychotherapists working in private practice will also see couples. While these are the most commonly used settings, marriage/relationship counselling activities are not exclusive to them. Employee assistance programmes, student counselling services and counsellors in legal practices are examples of other settings in which couple help may be available.

Couple counselling may describe interventions that do not depend on the couple having identified a problem in their relationship. For example, genetic counselling may be requested by couples who are considering starting a family, and where one partner has, or may have, a genetically transmittable condition. Counselling in these terms involves obtaining specialist information and advice as part of a decision-making process. The counsellor may pay little attention to the couple's relationship. Only their joint presence in connection with a matter that concerns them both defines the encounter as relationship counselling.

A further differentiating feature occurs when the counselling process is initiated by the counsellor, or by the agency for which she or he works. This may happen as part of a broader programme of intervention being offered to and affecting the couple. Assisted conception schemes are required to offer a counselling session to couples before commencing fertility treatment. Adoption agencies may offer counselling before placing a child with a couple. An emphasis on providing information, the element of compulsion and an often accompanying hint of assessment distinguishes this form of counselling from that based on marriage/relationship models. It is a matter of debate whether such activities properly fall into what is commonly understood as a counselling activity.

User preference

Different settings will appeal to different couples according to how they see their problems. Couples may take a sexual problem to a medical setting or to an organization that they know specializes in treating sexual dysfunction. They may unconsciously 'designate' a partner to present a medical symptom at a general practice surgery, or go to a counsellor for help with relationship problems that may not, at first, be understood as such. Parents seeking help for disturbances in their children may receive help for their partnership as part of a family therapy programme. When things go well, there will be an exchange between client and selected agency that fashions a shared understanding of the nature of, and the most effective response to, the problem for which help is sought. Women are more likely than men to initiate the search for help and to involve themselves in the counselling process, although this pattern is changing.

Counsellor orientation

Counsellors take responsibility for formulating the nature of the problem which, in turn, indicates the kind of therapeutic response needed. In doing this, he or she will depend on the way couples or partners present their problems and his or her own theoretical orientation. There are well-established theoretical schools of thought offering perspectives on marital problems and informing practice. Each has its own professional training. The psychological 'maps' provided by different theories will, to some extent, reflect the personalities of the counsellors who are drawn to them. They will provide more or less suitable guides to the actual territory that they and their clients must traverse in the course of their work together. The main purpose of counselling will vary according to the relative emphasis given to support, prescription and exploration; feelings, thoughts and actions provide the raw material to be worked upon.

Therapeutic approaches to couple problems have much in common: for example, adopting a couple focus, having a non-judgemental approach and fostering the capacity for self-help. Different theoretical frameworks for understanding marital problems result in different styles of intervention. Differences are likely to be more defined across modalities than within them, whether practitioners are described as counsellors or psychotherapists. For example, psychodynamic marriage counsellors and psychoanalytical marital psychotherapists are likely to have more in common with each other than either group will have with behaviourally oriented marriage counsellors or sex therapists. Differences within the same modalities are most likely to exist in terms of training requirements, the settings within which practitioners work, their status, and the problems with which they are typically confronted.

Outcome research suggests that practitioners from different modalities may diverge less from each other than is commonly supposed; what they actually do may be more similar than what they say they do. Research also indicates that outcomes to therapy for relationship problems are positively related to what the various approaches have in

continued

common (for example, the capacity to form a therapeutic alliance), and have less to do with what differentiates between them.

For Further Reading
Butler, C. and Joyce, V. 1998: *Counselling Couples in Relationships.* Chichester: Wiley.
Hooper, D. and Dryden, W. 1991: *Couple Therapy: A Handbook.* Milton Keynes: Open University Press.
Ruszczynski, S. 1993: *Psychotherapy with Couples.* London: Karnac.

CHRISTOPHER CLULOW

Marriage
See FAMILY entries, and DIVORCE.

Masculinity
The term *masculinity* refers to the socially constructed behaviour and attitudes of men. There is a burgeoning interest within the social work field in making masculinity explicit when working with men. Within the social welfare field, there have been interesting practice developments in youth work (*boyswork*), work with a range of male offenders including perpetrators of physical and sexual violence, and work with fathers.

Apart from an increasing awareness of the connection between masculinity and mental health, there has been less work in the adult community care field that has focused on the social construction of masculinity.

An emphasis within the sociology of men on diversity and the many different ways of being a man has lead to an insistence, in some quarters, on the plural term *masculinities.* There is, however, no consensus about the appropriate theoretical basis for work with men. There is a wide range of psychological perspectives on what helps individual men to change. These are often allied to one of the competing political perspectives, which range from an assertion of men's rights to pro-feminist work which sets out to challenge men.

For Further Reading
Connell, R. W. 1995: *Masculinities.* Cambridge: Polity Press.

JONATHAN SCOURFIELD

Material Aid
Giving *material aid* is contentious and is dependent on attitudes towards:

- the 'deserving' – those without choice, older people, the sick, those with disabilities, the provision of practical support packages arranged under adult services legislation;

- the 'undeserving' – those who, according to conventional wisdom, should do better, those with choice, the able-bodied, young families, single people;
- accountability and the use of taxpayers' money, and practitioners' fear of exploitation by clients;
- dependency – the giving of material aid can conflict with social work's enduring emphasis on psychological development and use of relationship.

Poverty's known link with abusive behaviour and mental ill-health has mandated professionals to give more in kind, for example by paying day care fees; s.17 of the Children Act 1989. Family centres demonstrate the integration of therapeutic work and material aid – the provision of warmth, food, clothes, and washing facilities.

Giving money is the real test. It is clearly part of caring for children, whether in foster care or residential care, where the relationship is close and 'parental'. Children need pocket money and money with which to set themselves up for the life ahead. Working in more distanced settings or working with adults – often very dependent adults – is more problematic. Some case managers argue that giving money can be part of the casework relationship. Others who are pushed into more distanced relationships increasingly use specialists – money advisers, furniture stores. Effective professional relationships and transparent procedures are crucial whatever the setting.

For Further Reading
Vaux, G. 1991: *Don't Forget Poverty, The Children Act 1989 – Partnership with Families.* London: Family Rights Group.

CHRIS WARREN-ADAMSON

Maternal Care
See PARENTING.

Media Perspectives on Social Work

The idea that *media coverage of social work* (here defined as *print media*) was itself problematic first surfaced with the publication in 1974 of the report of the inquiry into the death of Maria Colwell. Since then, media coverage of social work has not only remained under discussion but, it has been claimed, has influenced both social work practice and legislation.

The media critique

Media, from the start, adopted a hostile tone by focusing on child abuse and blaming individual social workers for the deaths of children because of their 'bungling' and 'incompetence'. Social workers have been generally described as 'abusing trust', 'negative', 'negligent', 'failed', 'ineffective', 'misguided', 'naïve' and 'left-wing' (Franklin, 1998).

In the mid-1980s came the emergence of the so-called child abuse scandals in Cleveland, Orkney and Rochdale, when whole departments, rather than just individual staff members, were the whipping boys.

Social workers have been criticized for removing children from their families too readily, in contrast to the accusation of inertia following the child death inquiry reports. Such criticism presents social workers with a well-rehearsed dilemma, usually expressed as 'damned if we do, damned if we don't'.

It is interesting that the media criticism of social work tends to be almost wholly concerned with child care. Elderly people and adults with special needs are mostly neglected as a social services topic. Media interest in the welfare of elderly people tends to centre around matters like death from hypothermia and the level of benefits payments and pensions. Stories which feature people with learning disabilities mostly focus on their mistreatment in private homes, where the social services' role (for the media) is secondary, being concerned with matters of inspection and registration.

The exception to this obsession with child care came in the mid-1990s with media interest in homicides by people with a mental illness; but here, as much if not more attention was focused on doctors who discharged patients into the community, on policy issues like the lack of secure beds, or on the alleged failure of the policy of care in the community.

The zenith of media portrayals of social services and social workers as causing or helping to cause tragedies for children probably came with the reports of the inquiries into the deaths of Jasmine Beckford (1985), Tyra Henry (1987) and Kimberley Carlile (1987), each of which attracted sustained and highly critical media attention. Social workers were variously seen as 'easily hoodwinked' (*Daily Express*, 29 March 1985), 'too trusting with too liberal an outlook' (*The Guardian*, 19 December, 1985), and 'butterflies in a situation that demanded hawks' (*Daily Mail*, 20 December 1987). To others, they have been 'easily manipulated, brow-beaten, conned and bearded', 'authoritarian bureaucrats', 'guided by prejudice and motivated by zealotry', and 'hysterical, malignant, callow youngsters who absorb moral-free Marxoid sociological theories'.

'Political correctness'

In the late 1990s, allegations of a naïve espousal of weak left-wing or psychological theories crystallized into the shorthand of 'political correctness', which became the dominant reason for criticizing social work, particularly with regard to adoption – perhaps, by this time, the most contentious area of child care practice.

continued

Allegations of political correctness centred around social workers' alleged refusal to place black children for adoption in white families. A variant on criticism about adoption was the allegation that prospective adoptive parents had been turned down because they smoked, or were too old and or even were overweight. Fuelled by the statements of both Conservative and Labour ministers, press coverage focused on a 'crackdown on politically correct social workers'.

There is very little real evidence to support these accusations. Indeed, in one of the most celebrated cases, Jim and Roma Lawrence were allegedly turned down as adopters because, as a black woman (he was white) she said she had never experienced racism in her rural home town. The Department of Health instigated an inquiry which found that, in dealing with their application, Norfolk social services department had acted correctly. This did not stop several newspapers continuing to refer to the case as if the social services department had been in the wrong.

The effects of media criticism
Some research evidence supports the belief that adverse media coverage, in generating a damaging public perception of social work, affects how social workers do their job. Observers have posited that the media create a climate which leads to a demand for government to legislate. The shape of the Children Act 1975 and the Children Act 1989 are cited as the most prominent examples (Franklin and Parton, 1991).

For its part, social work has been unable to sustain an adequate response to media criticism, or to turn the game around by taking the initiative. Its professional associations – the British Association of Social Workers, the Social Care Association, the Association of Directors of Social Services, and the Association of Directors of Social Work – are particularly weak in this respect: none employ full-time media spokespersons. Most local authorities now have press and public relations departments, some of which have at least one staff member with a specific social services brief. Some social services departments have their own press officers.

However, press relations do not rank high on the priorities of social services departments. The evidence is that if, as social workers claim, the media fail to understand the complexities of the jobs they do, it is also true that, for their part, social workers appreciate insufficiently the motives and methods of working of journalists to allow them to make their case.

For Further Reading
Franklin, B. 1998: *Hard Pressed: National Newspaper Reporting of Social Work and Social Services.* Sutton, Surrey: Community Care/RBI.
Franklin, B. and Parton, N. (eds) 1991: *Social Work, the Media and Public Relations.* London: Routledge.
Neate, P. and Philpot, T. (eds) 1997: *The Media and the Message: A Guide to Using the Media for Everyone in Social Care.* Sutton, Surrey: Community Care/RBI.

TERRY PHILPOT

Mediation
Mediation involves bringing people with a dispute together in the presence of a neutral third party to assist them to reach an agreement. Mediation has a long history throughout the world, but has only recently developed in England and Wales, where it was first employed in resolving industrial relations disputes. It first appeared in the social work context in the mid-1970s, with the development of conciliation as a method of helping separating and divorcing parents to resolve their disagreements, often over their children, thereby limiting the harm done to children by parental conflict.

Because of a lack of public money, conciliation developed primarily within the voluntary sector, although often with the encouragement and support of family court welfare officers and the legal profession. Because of confusion with the term 'reconciliation' (helping couples stay together), *mediation* is now the preferred term and is incorporated into the name of the UK College of Mediators, founded in 1996 to co-ordinate the development and regulation of mediation practice in the context of the provisions of the Family Law Act 1996, which introduced public funding for mediation in divorce.

For Further Reading
Parkinson, L. 1997: *Family Mediation*. London: Sweet and Maxwell.

ADRIAN L. JAMES

Medical Social Work
See HOSPITAL SOCIAL WORK, PRIMARY HEALTH CARE and GENERAL PRACTICE.

Memory Loss
Memory loss can be divided into episodic/ semantic and procedural/declarative:

- *Episodic memory* relates to specific events in a person's life experience, while *semantic memory* considers facts and general information.
- *Procedural memory* considers learned motor functions and *declarative memory* the maintenance and development of language skills.

While most people forget sometimes, memory loss may be due to a variety of factors:

- Dementia
- Central nervous system infection
- Cerebral trauma
- Toxic metabolic disturbances
- Normal pressure hydrocephalus
- Neurological disorders

For Further Reading
Thompson, T. and Mathias, P. (eds) 1994: Memory. In *Lyttles Mental Health and Disorder*, London: Baillière Tindall, 207–22.

PAUL KINGSTON

Mental Handicap
See LEARNING DISABILITY.

Mental Health Inquiries

Mental health inquiries examine failings in mental health service delivery following untoward incidents. Three categories exist: internal audits of practice, independent inquiries by health authorities, and statutory inquiries set up by central government. Early inquiries focused on bad practice in long-stay psychiatric and mental handicap institutions (as they were then called). As psychiatric hospitals closed, difficulties in community-based mental health services for people with a serious mental illness emerged. Perceived failures in community care, such as the killing of a stranger by Christopher Clunis, provoked public disquiet.

This led to government guidance in 1994 making independent inquiries mandatory when someone with a history of contact with mental health services committed a homicide. The Government also established national inquiries into homicides and suicides committed by people with a known mental health history. Inquiry reports have recommended improvements in policy and practice, highlighting, among other things, the complexity of the social work role and the importance of multi-professional and multi-agency working. The inquiry into the death of Isobel Schwarz, a social worker, recommended the introduction of the Care Programme Approach; Table 11 lists this and other key inquiries in the UK.

For Further Reading
Reith, M. 1998: *Community Care Tragedies: A Practice Guide to Mental Health Inquiries*. Birmingham: Venture.

MARGARET REITH

Table 11 Mental health: Key inquiries in the UK

Year	Title	Victim	Publisher	Key findings and/or recommendations	Implications for social work
1988	Report of the Committee of Inquiry into the Care and After-Care of Miss Sharon Campbell	Isobel Schwarz (social worker)	London: HMSO	• Improve safety for social workers • Provide supervision for staff • Joint aftercare plans to include housing plans. • Need to be sensitive to issues of ethnicity	• Probably the earliest inquiry into the failings of community care • Led to the framework for the Care Programme Approach (CPA) and the development of Section 117 aftercare.
1994	The Report of the Inquiry into the Care and Treatment of Christopher Clunis	Jonathan Zito (stranger)	London: HMSO	• Importance of communication and interagency liaison • Risk assessment	• Resulted in the introduction of Supervised Discharge (Section 25, MHA 1983) and Supervision Registers
1996	The Case of Jason Mitchell: Report of the Independent Panel of Inquiry	Arthur & Shirley Wilson (strangers) & Robert Mitchell (father)	London: Duckworth	• Focus on role of Mental Health Review Tribunals.	• Importance of victim work recognized • Led to revision of guidance for social supervisors • Potential tensions in roles of social workers explored
1997	Report of the Inquiry into the Treatment and Care of Gilbert Kopernik-Steckel	Suzanne Kopernik-Steckel (mother) & himself	Croydon Health Authority	• Identifies failings in procedures, professional practice and communications within and between agencies and with family	• Implications for approved social workers and for training • Importance for social work management • Highlighted the importance of continuity of care
1998	Report of the Luke Warm Luke Mental Health Inquiry	Susan Milner (friend)	Lambeth, Southwark & Lewisham Health Authority	• Highlights importance of all agencies working together • Also emphasizes role of social supervisor being different but as important as role of psychiatric supervisor	• Identification of ingredients for effective supervision and case management • Clarification of duties of aftercare team, preparation for aftercare, detail of aftercare plans, role of housing, consultation with team – for example, when medication plans are changed

MENTAL HEALTH SOCIAL WORK

Mental Health Social Work

Mental health social work is a specialism encompassing work with people affected by mental health problems and a practice, carried out in any setting, which promotes the mental health of individuals and families. As a practice, it is rooted in awareness that problems of poverty, injustice, disadvantage, ill-health or loss of valued roles may have serious implications for mental health; and, conversely, that mental health problems such as anxiety and depression or substance abuse are pervasive, often unrecognized, and can cause or exacerbate difficulties in coping with relationships and the external environment.

Social workers aim to work in partnership with mentally distressed people and their families to improve social functioning, recognizing the complex interplay of interpersonal, intra-psychic and structural influences. While ideological debates tend to emphasize one of these factors at the expense of the others, the ability to link and relate one to another is a key characteristic of practice.

The context for mental health social work

Mental health social work is a long-established specialism, relatively small in staff numbers and expenditure but tending to have a high public profile. Various overlapping sub-specialisms can be identified: approved social work; psychiatric social work; resettlement; therapeutic and other varieties of group care, work with mentally infirm elders; forensic work; addictions; learning disabilities; child, adolescent and family mental health. No single theoretical framework is dominant, but mental health social workers tend to espouse social, rather than medical, models and aim to be responsive to user views.

During the period of genericism in the UK (1970–90), the trend was away from multidisciplinary work. Since 1990, there has been a shift in priorities towards closer relationships with the NHS, and social workers are commonly attached to multi-disciplinary or community mental health teams aligned to health service structures.

Mental health social work has always had to define itself in relation to the powerful profession of psychiatry and the larger structures of psychiatric health-care; the relationship is an ambivalent one. The historical split in the UK between the NHS and local authority services is particularly problematic in the field of mental health. While social work is recognized as a crucial component of multi-disciplinary health care, social workers are rarely employed by the health service. Their relative independence has caused much tension but can sometimes be to the benefit of service users. There is debate as to how strategic planning and decision making can be more effective in the context of continuing structural fragmentation.

Psychiatric social workers

Psychiatric social workers attached to psychiatric hospitals and child guidance clinics draw on a tradition of individualized assessment and psychotherapeutic treatment which owes much to North American models but which has gradually weakened in the UK as priorities have shifted towards the assessment and management of risk. They have a major role in the resettlement of psychiatric patients as long-stay hospital care has been replaced by short admissions and various forms of care and supervision in the community.

Approved social workers (ASWs)

ASWs are employed by UK local authorities to carry out duties under the Mental Health Act 1983, sharing with nearest relatives and doctors the responsibility for making decisions about compulsory detention in hospital. They are the only group of social workers who are required to have post-qualifying training. This high profile statutory role involves assessment of risk to the health or safety of mentally disordered people and the safety of others while ensuring that civil rights are protected. ASWs are therefore primarily concerned with people with psychotic illnesses and severe or long-term mental health problems. The Mental Health Act 1995 extended powers of supervision in the community for patients discharged or on leave from psychiatric care. Social workers have been closely involved in the debate for and against the provision of compulsory treatment in the community.

Care management and the care programme approach

Mental health social workers may act as care managers, assessing the needs of people with mental health problems and setting up care packages to meet these needs. They are also one of the main occupational groups acting as key workers within the care programme approach, a framework for delivery of services to people with mental health problems through provision of an assessment, a care plan, a key worker and regular review. Introduced in England and Wales in 1991, it has gradually been integrated with care management, usually as a tiered structure of aftercare. Intended to apply to all patients receiving psychiatric services without time limit, resource constraints restrict it mainly to people with severe mental illness. Although improved outcomes have not been demonstrated, it is a useful structure acceptable to users and professionals.

Particular concerns for mental health social work are the needs of black and ethnic communities, and of women. Some groups are over-represented in compulsory detention and forensic services while being under-represented in their use of preventative mental health services. The challenge is to eliminate discrimination in assessment and treatment, and to ensure that appropriate services are available, accessible and acceptable to people in need.

Community-based provision

Social workers have, over the years, been in the forefront of providing social care in day and residential settings. Therapeutic groups and communities, social skills training and education, group homes, employment schemes and adult fostering are some of the services staffed by social workers together with other occupational groups. The closure of long-stay hospitals has required major investment in the provision of supported accommodation tailored to individual needs, managed usually by voluntary organizations. Important developments in mental health social work include assertive community treatment teams which target reluctant users; respite and crisis services offering a user-centred alternative to hospital care; the development of advocacy schemes and user representation within service structures. Ongoing service goals include interprofessional collaboration and work in partnership with users.

For Further Reading
Heller, T., Reynolds, J., Gomm, R., Muston, R. and Pattison, S. (eds) 1996: *Mental Health Matters: A Reader*. Basingstoke: Macmillan.
Rogers, A. and Pilgrim, D. 1996: *Mental Health Policy in Britain: A Critical Introduction*. Basingstoke: Macmillan.
Ulas, M. and Connor, A. (eds) 1999: *Mental Health and Social Work, Research Highlights in Social Work 28*. London: Jessica Kingsley.

WILLIAM HORDER

Mental Illness

Mental illness is variously interpreted:

- As a physical disease state evident from specific signs and symptoms
- As a scientific construct subject to tests of its validity, such as its usefulness in making predictions
- As a social construction or label used to regulate societal definitions of normality and abnormality

The incidence of mental illness

The range of experiences that are considered as mental illnesses varies. A large-scale World Health Organization study of mental illness (Üstün and Sartorius, 1998) found that 24 per cent of people aged between 18 and 65 presenting to general health settings had a well-defined psychological problem. The most common diagnosed mental illnesses were depressive disorders, anxiety disorders, alcohol use disorders, somatoform disorders and neurasthenia. A further 10 per cent were defined as suffering from a sub-threshold condition with clinically significant symptoms and impairment. Mental illness was associated with impairments in physical and social functioning that were greater on average than disability levels among people with common chronic diseases such as hypertension, diabetes, arthritis and back pain. The study also highlighted that people with mental illnesses were neither adequately recognized nor treated by primary care physicians, the professional staff on whom the greatest burden of care falls.

Types of mental illness

Often the term *mental illness* is reserved for those experiences that would be diagnosed as psychoses (BPS Division of Clinical Psychology, 2000):

- Hearing voices speaking when there is no one there, or seeing or feeling things that other people do not – in medical terms *hallucinations*
- Holding strong beliefs which others in the person's social environment do not share, termed *delusions*.

(Hallucinations and delusions are described as the 'positive' symptoms of schizophrenia.)

- Experiencing periods of extreme depression or elation sometimes accompanied by hallucinations or delusions; associated diagnoses include *clinical depression, psychotic depression, mania, manic depression, bipolar affective disorder* and *schizoaffective disorder*
- Difficulty concentrating because of the kinds of experiences described above.

Some people may appear distracted or will talk back to the hallucinations they are experiencing. Others may talk in a way that others find difficult to follow, for example, covering many apparently unrelated topics in quick succession. The medical term for this is *thought disorder*.

- Becoming withdrawn, listless, apathetic or unmotivated often as a result of the distraction and effort of coping associated with the experiences described above

Some people may find it difficult to maintain the energy to care for themselves adequately. These are described as *negative symptoms*. Tiredness and listlessness can sometimes be a side-effect of drugs aiming to relieve the effects of the positive symptoms described above.

Such experiences are often regarded as being on a continuum with defined normality. For example, people who are recently bereaved sometimes experience hallucinations. It

continued

is only those people who find these experiences so distressing that they seek professional help, or those who come to the attention of services because others perceive their behaviour as abnormal who are likely to be diagnosed as mentally ill.

The interaction between vulnerability and stress

The very phrase *mental illness* can be interpreted as provocative of an ideological contest between those who hold mental health problems to be essentially the result of biological and genetic factors and those who emphasize social and interpersonal factors. There is a middle ground wherein mental health problems are considered to be the result of an interaction between vulnerability, usually posited as largely biological or genetic in origin, and social stressors. The social stressors include poverty, unemployment and social alienation, the effects of life events such as bereavement or divorce, and family attitudes and behaviours. For example, relapse among people diagnosed with schizophrenia is associated with family environments that are characterized by high levels of criticism or emotional over-involvement. Such stress-vulnerability models see medical and social interventions to have a complementary role in alleviating vulnerability through medication and reducing stress through psychosocial interventions or environmental interventions.

Critiques of the biological and medical emphases in mental health

However, critics of the biological basis of vulnerability to mental illness highlight the methodological problems associated with twin studies cited as evidence of the role of genetic inheritance (BPS Division of Clinical Psychology, 2000); most have failed to control for the effect of environmental influences. At best, the literature appears to support the possibility of non-specific hereditary factors such as temperamental sensitivity to unfavourable psychological environments. Research showing correlations between the experience of mental illness and chemical events in the brain or brain structure has also failed to establish the direction of causality where such correlations exist and has taken inadequate account of associated variables such as medication. The efficacy of medication is itself taken to infer a biological basis to mental illness. However, claims for the efficacy of medication are often overstated and their effects are not specific to particular diagnostic categories. Latterly, the introduction of so-called 'atypical' antipsychotic drugs appears to offer more therapeutic benefits although side-effects remain problematic.

The term *mental illness* is often associated with a *medical model* approach to diagnosis, analogous to diagnosis in general medicine, whereby a range of signs and symptoms is distilled down to a diagnosis. The diagnosis then determines the treatment that is offered. Critics of this approach have focused on the inadequacy of diagnoses as useful scientific constructs by drawing attention to the problems of reliable diagnosis, including biases arising from cultural differences between clinician and service user, and the poor validity of diagnosis concerning the prediction of behaviour or service use (Bentall, 1990). Cognitive-behavioural interventions have been developed to focus specifically on the phenomena associated with *mental illness* such as hallucinations and delusions, without necessarily seeking to distil the signs and symptoms into any given diagnosis. Diagnosis and thus the concept of *mental illness* are thereby seen as irrelevant to therapy.

For Further Reading

Bentall, R. P. 1990: The syndromes and symptoms of psychosis. In R. P. Bentall (ed.) *Reconstructing Schizophrenia*. London: Routledge.

British Psychological Society Division of Clinical Psychology (2000). Understanding Mental Illness and Psychotic Experiences. Leicester: British Psychological Society.

Üstün, T. B. and Sartorius, N. 1998: *Mental Illness in General Health Care*. London: Wiley.

STEVE ONYETT

Mentally Disordered Offenders

The term *mental disorder* occurs within mental health legislation. Although judgemental, it is defined in the law in England and Wales as referring to people who display 'abnormally aggressive or seriously irresponsible conduct'.

Social work with mentally disordered offenders involves working with people so defined by criminal courts who may be sent to secure institutions but may also be subject to supervision by social workers and/or probation officers on orders within the community. Many offenders who might be categorized as mentally disordered are never identified as such and when they commit serious offences they are likely to be sent to ordinary prisons. It has been estimated that the proportion of adult prisoners who have some form of mental illness may be as high as 37 per cent, but their conditions are not necessarily treatable and these figures include prisoners with substance addictions.

Supervision of mentally disordered offenders attracts public concern and interest, not least when grave crimes of violence are committed, albeit that these are infrequent in relation to the total numbers; a greater proportion of people suffering with a mental disorder, living in poverty and experiencing a downward spiral of health are more at risk of harming themselves than others.

The proportion of mentally disordered offenders with learning disabilities is not clearly identified although it has been suggested that, while under-represented in most violent offences, they might be over-represented as sex offenders and in offences of fire-raising. They are more frequently victimized than offending. Social work practice with mentally disordered offenders has focused on mental illness, and the problems for offenders with learning disabilities should not be assumed to be the same.

Risk/needs assessment

Social work practice is crucially involved in the assessment of risk as well as need. Risk assessment has to take account of whom the offender may harm, how seriously and in what way, and what can be done to influence these circumstances. Many of the enquiries following serious incidents of violence by mentally disordered people have highlighted the failure of agencies to communicate with each other effectively about risk and to share information across boundaries. Most of these enquiries have stressed the crucial nature of effective interagency work. Reith (1997) provides a useful overview of reports with the greatest relevance for probation practice.

Pre-court and post-conviction, social workers and probation officers are often involved, together with community psychiatric nurses, psychiatrists and police officers, in determining how the person might best be managed. Courts may request a report that offers an assessment of the person's offending behaviour, their culpability and understanding in relation to the consequences of their offending and a proposal for sentence; this may support psychiatric intervention or argue for a discharge if the offence is of a minor nature. Courts can impose a variety of community-based orders and hospital orders although there is generally an underuse of community orders for people suffering with a mental disorder. The over-representation of black people and women in secure hospitals has some worrying implications. Mentally disordered offenders serving sentences of imprisonment can be transferred to hospital if a consultant psychiatrist from the area hospital, regional secure unit or special hospital and another medical practitioner assess the prisoner as in need of, and responsive to, treatment. In practice, these arrangements are infrequently used.

The institutional setting

Social workers and probation officers are involved in working in prisons, regional secure units and special hospitals with prisoners and patients, both during their sentence, in

continued

preparation for release and post-release. The local authority has a duty to assess the need for mental health services and to invoke the care programme approach where appropriate. This includes the right to have an assessment of health and social care needs and a written care plan to meet those needs, to be involved in the drawing up of the care plan and a regular review of this plan. In the case of a mentally disordered prisoner, although the responsibility for referral for assessment should be the medical officer's, probation officers and social workers can make an important contribution to ensuring that this takes place well before release, and in facilitating communication between the prison and community psychiatric services. Social work in preparation for release also has to take account of the victim perspective, which generally involves contact by a specialist worker with the victim of the crime. In practice, this varies between areas and can be dependent on the decision of the psychiatric medical officer. Mental health service providers must maintain local supervision registers of people with severe mental illness who pose significant risk to themselves or others, although this can appear a hollow exercise if no other intervention is on offer. The establishment of the registers was largely a political move to appease criticism of community care.

Squeezed between two models

Social workers and probation officers working with mentally disordered offenders often feel squeezed between a medical model which defines the illness in esoteric terms, and a criminal model which condemns the behaviour without necessarily understanding the underlying cause. Their struggle to learn the language of psychiatry so that they can communicate with the medical profession while endeavouring also to engage with the process of gaining information and building a relationship with someone who may be seriously mentally ill is extremely challenging. Linked with this, the insufficiency of resources in the community to address or contain behaviour that breaches the commonly defined bounds of 'normality' can leave the social worker or probation officer feeling ill-equipped and fearful about responding appropriately. There is a growing awareness of the need for specialist training and interagency work to meet the needs of this particular group.

For Further Reading

Prins, H. 1995: *Offenders, Deviants or Patients?* London: Routledge.
Reith, M. 1997: Mental health inquiries: implications for probation practice. *Probation Journal*, 44 (2), 66–70.
Stone, N. 1995: *Companion Guide to Mentally Disordered Offenders*. Ilkley: Owen Wells.

CHARLOTTE KNIGHT AND BRIAN WILLIAMS

Meta-analysis

See SYSTEMATIC REVIEWS AND META-ANALYSIS and OUTCOME RESEARCH IN ADULT AND YOUTH JUSTICE.

The Mixed Economy of Care

The *mixed economy of care* exists when the state, the private sector and the voluntary sector are all involved in the provision of personal support services. In the UK, the community care reforms in the 1990s were designed to allow local authorities to shape this mixed economy through contracts placed with specific providers to produce specific services. Efficiency and user responsiveness were expected to

flow from provider competition for 'business'.

Research shows that many local authorities have been cautious in developing a mixed economy because of a lack of confidence about market making. A key tension has been over the strengths and weaknesses of 'spot' and 'block' contracts. If all purchasing of services is by care managers on a *one-off or 'spot'* basis, this is likely to be user-centred but may undermine the financial viability of providers who will lack any secure regular income. Against this, the *block purchase* of care services from established providers will limit the range of services available for the care manager to draw on.

1

For Further Reading
Forder, J., Knapp, M. and Wistow, G. 1996: Competition in the mixed economy of care. *Journal of Social Policy*, 25 (2), 201–22.

ROBIN MEANS

Mixed Race Children
Mixed race children are children whose parents are of different racial origins. In the context of British society, the term 'mixed race' is generally used to describe children with one black and one white parent. The term 'black' is used to describe people of African, Caribbean and Asian origin. Other terms used instead of *mixed race* are *mixed parentage* or *dual heritage*.

Mixed race children are over-represented in the care system. There is considerable controversy surrounding the placement of mixed race children. Many argue that mixed race children should be regarded as black children and, to help them cope with racism and facilitate the development of a positive racial identity, they should be placed with at least one black carer. Others argue that research does not tend to support the view that transracial placements necessarily damage a child's identity. The debates surrounding the identity formation of mixed race children and appropriate placements is complex, and will continue to become more so with increasing numbers of children of mixed race people requiring the services of child welfare organizations.

For Further Reading
Katz, I. 1996: *The Construction of Racial Identity in Children of Mixed Parentage*. London: Jessica Kingsley.

ANNA GUPTA

Mixed Race Placement
See TRANSRACIAL PLACEMENT IN CHILD CARE.

Mobility
Mobility in a medical and legal sense means *movement* or, in particular, *walking*. According to the World Health Organization definition, not being able to walk is construed as an *impairment*, whereas not being mobile with its inference of restrictions on 'day-to-day' normal activity is construed as a *disability*.

Society compensates individuals who have problems with mobility. Rights such as financial gains are awarded on medically assessed *incapacity*.

The medical world sees mobility in terms of physical function, which is sometimes divided into three areas: personal mobility, self-care and the performance of household tasks. Mobility can also be viewed as part of a wider concept – *independence*. Often independence is thought of as 'doing things for yourself, being self sufficient', but health professionals see their role in the achievement of independence by people with mobility problems as being to give them choice and control over their own lives. This involves the provision of an expert opinion on how best to attain a chosen goal and on whether its attainment constitutes a realistic objective; health professionals, however, have no authority over what the choice should be. If the choice involves professional intervention aimed, for example, at walking re-education, or being able to transfer from bed-to-chair-to-toilet, then this has to be the person's choice.

Giving people choice also gives them a sense of control over their own rehabilitation, and a greater sense of valuing the process.

For Further Reading
Swain, J., Finkelstein, V., French, S. and Oliver, M. (eds) 1992: *Disabling Barriers – Enabling Environments*. London: Sage.

DIANE THOMSON

Modernity

Modernity is a label denoting a particular type of society which emerged through a general social transition occurring from the seventeenth century onwards, and characterized by the emergence of distinct features and forms of organization in political, economic, social and cultural life:

- The emergence of modern nation states, which provide the institutional framework and shared legal and political norms which organize social and economic life
- The emergence of a distinct form of capitalist economy and capitalist economic relations

continued

219

- The rise of new social classes organized around capital and waged labour
- A definite separation between the 'public' and the 'private' with politics being associated with the (male) public sphere and dominated by class interests, and the 'private' being seen as the (female) area of personal relationships
- A shift from a religious to a secular world view as a foundation for social and moral values as well as the organization of political and social institutions

Social theorists identify three interlocking logics peculiar to these processes of modernization – differentiation, detraditionalization and rationalization.

Differentiation refers to the process of classifying and categorizing social life and segregating it into distinct, autonomous spheres that are separately co-ordinated and socially ordered. Thus, modernization leads to the separation of church and state, law and politics, art and science, the public and the private, economy and society, work and leisure, rationality and irrationality, fact and fiction, and so on.

Detraditionalization refers to the displacement of established customs, habits, institutions and beliefs and their substitution by seemingly impersonal and objective systems of social co-ordination. Whereas in premodern societies, communal traditions are the major vehicles through which individuals develop their self-identities, norms and moral codes, in modern societies such identities and morals are increasingly organized outside of these communal traditions by new institutions governing collective life – including the modern communications media, educational and financial institutions – and the interconnections between them. Localized traditions are supplanted by seemingly universal precepts tied to complex, bureaucratic institutions operating in the public sphere.

Rationalization is closely tied to this latter process, and involves the substitution of objective criteria and standards for subjective preferences and desires. Increasingly, social action and social institutions are organized on the basis of efficiency calculations, that is, on the basis of the extent to which they represent the most effective and instrumental means to realize a given end. Abstract rules and codes require the development of extensive systems of bureaucratic administration which, over time, come to adjudicate over, and process more and more of, individual and collective life. The development of abstract rules and codes becomes an end in itself, such that modern life is overseen by a soulless administrative machinery disconnected from individual and collective purposes, hopes and aspirations.

From this perspective, social work can be understood as one of modernity's 'expert systems'. The role of social work in classifying, managing and ordering populations, the increasing bureaucratization of practice with its emphasis on measurement, assessment, administration, quality control, audit, and so on, constitutes the application of technical and expert knowledge to the prediction and management of social problems and risks. Yet, the logic of detraditionalization, in particular, leads to a plethora of social possibilities, while expert knowledge has shown itself to be a creator of risk as much as its manager. In his work on the general themes of risk and modernity, Giddens proposes that the ever-increasing specialization of expert knowledge with a technical focus results in an impossibility to connect with other areas of knowledge and is liable to produce unintended and unforeseen consequences that 'contributes directly to the erratic, runaway character of modernity' (Giddens, 1991: p. 30). Trying to predict and manage the future is an exercise that actively creates unintended and unpredictable outcomes.

For Further Reading
Giddens, A. 1991: *Modernity and Self-Identity*. Cambridge: Polity.
O'Brien, M. and Penna, S. 1998: *Theorising Welfare – Enlightenment and Modern Society*. London: Sage, ch. 7.

SUE PENNA

Money Advice

Money advice (also known as *debt counselling*) is the process of helping with debts. It seeks to protect the debtor's rights and interests and to safeguard their standard of living when faced with demands from creditors. The approach can involve challenging the legal enforceability of debts or unreasonable or unrealistic repayment demands, and pursue the write-off of debts where repayment would either take a long time or cause harm or hardship.

For Further Reading
Ryan, M. 1996: *Social Work and Debt Problems*. Aldershot: Ashgate.

NEIL BATEMAN

Moral Panic

The term *moral panic* has entered into common English usage since its introduction by Stanley Cohen's (1972) *Folk Devils and Moral Panics* which dealt with violent mid-1960s disturbances at English holiday resorts between youth gangs known as the Mods and Rockers.

A frequent misrepresentation of the term implies that the news media are inventing or making up stories about crime and violence, or that the anxieties of the public are 'unfounded fears'. Cohen's original point was that, while clashes between rival gangs of youths were very real though spasmodic, news reports emphasized and magnified some aspects of these disturbances while diminishing others. Primarily, they were 'read' or 'constructed' as a seamless narrative of the weakening influences of youthful post-war affluence, whereas many of the participants were poorly paid manual workers. Interestingly, this preoccupation with the supposed affluence of juvenile delinquents had been well rehearsed in much earlier moments of anxiety about Victorian 'hooligans' and 'artful dodgers' (Pearson, 1983). Indeed, moral panics seem often to be associated with young people – perhaps because concerns with the rising generation are so easily interwoven with broader narratives of social change, modernity and anxieties about the future.

For Further Reading
Goode, E. and Ben-Yehuda, N. 1996: *Moral Panics: The Social Construction of Deviance*. Oxford: Blackwell Publishers.

GEOFFREY PEARSON

Motherhood

See PARENTING.

Motivational Interviewing

Motivational interviewing is a person-centred approach aiming to assist individuals in recognizing and making changes to their problematic behaviour. It is designed to support individuals in exploring their ambivalence in respect of making such changes, contrasting with more aggressive interviewing strategies which focus on confronting denial. The intention is to increase the client's own motivation to change, ideally allowing the client to make the arguments for change rather than the social worker. It is often used in conjunction with the contemplation phase of Prochaska and DiClemente's (1994) CYCLE OF CHANGE.

There are five principles of motivational interviewing:

1 Interviewers should display empathy by acceptance, reflective listening and awareness that ambivalence is normal.
2 Discrepancies between present behaviour and important goals should be developed.
3 Arguments about behaviour should be avoided as these encourage defensiveness on the part of the client.
4 Interviewers should expect some resistance and not become confrontational.
5 Interviewers should support the principle of 'self-efficacy' or 'a person's belief in his or her ability to carry out and succeed with a specific task' (Miller and Rollnick, 1991, p. 60).

For Further Reading
Miller, W. R. and Rollnick, S. 1991: *Motivational Interviewing*. London: The Guildford Press.

ELIZABETH LANCASTER

Motor Projects

Motor projects are initiatives aimed at ensuring that young people, usually offenders, use the road legally and responsibly. Techniques used on projects include banger racing, car maintenance workshops, and modules that challenge offenders' behaviour and attitudes by making them think about the consequences of their actions. By the end of 1993, 32 of the then 55 probation areas ran 60 projects. Most offenders on these projects were young males with extensive criminal records and experience of custody. Although some small-scale research has suggested that projects can be effective in reducing reoffending, a Home Office survey of 1,087 offenders who underwent projects between 1989 and 1993 came to less positive conclusions, with 79 per cent of offenders being reconvicted within two years of starting projects. Overall, actual reconviction rates were higher than predictions based on age and criminal history, with particularly poor results for racing-based schemes and for offenders who failed to complete the projects. Success was noted for offenders over 21, where actual reconviction (56 per cent) was less than the prediction (62 per cent).

For Further Reading
Sugg, D. 1998: *Motor Projects in England and Wales: An evaluation [Home Office Research Findings No. 81].* London: Home Office Research Development and Statistics Directorate.

DARREN SUGG

Multi-cultural Society, Social Work Practice in a

Social workers operate in a context of diversity, and forms of practice that do not reflect this are likely to undermine the importance of nondominant cultural patterns, beliefs and expectations. To meet the needs of culturally diverse populations, social workers must have an understanding of culturally consistent assessment, evaluation and treatment skills, as well as theoretical content. Although cultural knowledge of ethnic minority groups is important, social workers must be careful not to apply cultural information in a stereotypic way. Finally, social workers must not ignore the impact that racism and discrimination have on the lives of ethnic minority groups living in white-dominated societies. The focus here, is on three areas of social work practice in a multi-cultural society:

- Multi-cultural child development and racial identity
- Mixed-parentage children and adolescents
- Mental health issues

Multi-cultural child development and racial identity

There is now a considerable proportion of children living in the UK who belong to minority ethnic groups. However, there is a dearth of research or literature on the development of ethnic minority children in social work textbooks and journals. Most studies of child development tend to be deficiency-based and offer an Eurocentric perspective. Black psychologists (mainly in the USA) have presented alternative perspectives on minority child development.

Low self-esteem, self-hatred and a negative racial identity have been the characteristics traditionally attributed to black children and adults. A review of the literature shows that there are different perspectives on the identity development question which have produced contradictory conclusions. One body of research which dominated the psychological literature from the early 1940s to the 1950s is the black self-hatred thesis. Another body of research developed in the USA focuses on models of psychological nigrescence (the process of the psychology of becoming black). Nigrescence models are useful as they enable social workers to understand the problems of black identity confusion and to examine, at a detailed level, what happens to a person during identity change. Although most black youngsters possess the survival skills necessary for the development of a positive racial identity, there are those who experience difficulty in maintaining a positive sense of racial identity. Thus, there is a need for social workers to take an active approach in helping black children and adolescents to build positive self-image of themselves.

Mixed-parentage children and adolescents

The terms *mixed-parentage* and *mixed race* are often used to describe first-generation offspring of parents of different 'races'. It most typically describes individuals of black and white racial parentage, but it is not limited to this combination. The topic of racial/ethnic identity in mixed-parentage children has received increasing attention in recent years; this interest has been spurred by demographic trends that indicate rapid increase in the population, and by the acknowledgement that there is little well-defined research and theory in this area.

Reviews of the research suggest that few children seem to experience their situation as a painful clash of loyalties between black and white. However, there are some mixed-parentage children whose experiences give cause for concern. These are the children who are up to two-and-a-half times more likely than other children to enter local authority care. Studies have shown that some mixed-parentage adolescents in local authority care exhibit identity confusion and low self-esteem. Some authors argue that mixed-parentage youngsters should be classified as black and that they should see themselves as so; the argument is that society sees them as black and that they will be better off if that is their self-perceived identity. Although mixed-parentage children encounter the problems faced by most minorities, they also must figure out how to reconcile the heritages of both parents in a society that categorizes individuals into single groups. Thus, the development of a healthy biracial identity means not only accepting and valuing both black and white heritages and being comfortable in both the minority and majority community, but having the flexibility to accept that others may identify them as minority, majority or biracial.

Mental health issues

Here are some of the major concerns cited in the mental health literature regarding practical and research deficiencies on culturally diverse groups in the UK and the USA:

* Diagnostic errors attributed to test bias
* The lack of sufficient black psychiatrists and black psychologists
* The lack of understanding about the behaviour patterns of culturally diverse groups from their own frame of reference
* The lack of a general theory to describe normal and abnormal functioning in culturally diverse communities
* The application of majority-group-derived measures to culturally different groups

As a consequence, much of what is known about the mental health of different cultural groups must be regarded with caution. What constitutes mental health for black people needs to be understood in the context of their own culture. Eurocentric standards of mental health are often inappropriate for black people because they are based on the philosophies, values and mores of Euro-American culture, and these variables are used to develop normative standards of mental health. The reality of racism as a major force within psychiatric decision making and treatment, though often denied, is central to any understanding of black people's experience of psychiatry.

Historically and currently, social work has been strongly influenced by mainstream psychiatric thinking. Thus, social workers tend to operate within a Eurocentric model of care. It is important that social workers disentangle themselves from implicit racial and cultural stereotypes. Social workers should also be provided with frequent opportunities to examine their own feelings about ethnic minority groups. Without a conscious awareness of one's own attitudes and anxieties that may be stimulated by the presence of a black client, the effectiveness of a social worker's interventions will be seriously diminished. The process of eliminating racial bias involves an in-depth analysis of oneself and of a society that has fostered racism and oppression – it is a long-term process.

For Further Reading
Fernando, S. (ed.) 1995: *Mental Health in a Multi-ethnic Society: A Multi-disciplinary Handbook*. London: Routledge.
Robinson, L. 1995: *Psychology for Social Workers: Black Perspectives*. London: Routledge.
Root, M. (ed.) 1996: *The Multi-racial Experience*. London: Sage.

LENA ROBINSON

Multidisciplinary Practice

See INTERAGENCY WORK, INTERDISCIPLINARY PRACTICE and INTERPROFESSIONAL PRACTICE.

Multiple Disability

See DUAL DIAGNOSIS.

Munchausen Syndrome by Proxy

Munchausen syndrome by proxy is an insidious abuse incurred by victims from carers who show *factitious disorder by proxy*. Factitious disorder by proxy involves the deliberate production or feigning of physical and/or psychological symptoms in another person who is under the individual's care. Usually victims are babies or preschool children, and the perpetrators are their mothers. Children with developmental delay and elders without speech are also selected. Common abuses include inducing breathing difficulties, putting salt in food or babies' milk (causing dehydration), and forced vomiting. Perpetrators are often women with a history of abuse who are desperately attention seeking.

For Further Reading

Randall, P. E. and Parker, J. 1997: Factitious disorder by proxy: a trap for the unwary. *Journal of Social Work Practice*, 11 (1), 17–26.

PETER RANDALL AND JONATHAN PARKER

N

Narrative Metaphors

Narrative metaphors propose that people's lives are constituted by stories which they tell themselves. These stories are both cultural and personal, and they provide the frame of reference through which people interpret their lives. The effects of these stories are real, not imagined.

While a range of areas of social work including counselling, research and social theory use the narrative metaphor, Michael White and David Epston (1990) have developed particular ways of thinking and working with individuals and communities known as *narrative ways of working*. These ideas, now developed with others, particularly inform work in the field of mental health and in work with survivors and the perpetrators of abuse.

Narrative ways of working deconstruct problematic stories in people's lives often through 'externalizing' the problem from the person and mapping the history and the effects of the problem on the person and their relationships. A process of reconstruction of preferred narratives is then possible. This usually involves tracing the history of alternative personal and cultural stories that can be built on, with the assistance of others, to move towards preferred ways of being.

For Further Reading

Freedman, J. and Combs, G. 1996: *Narrative Therapy: The Social Construction of Preferred Realities*. New York: W. W. Norton.

CATHERINE HUMPHREYS

Narrative Therapy

Narrative therapy provides options for the telling and retelling of preferred stories of people's lives (their 'solutions') by deconstructing dominant cultural stories, particularly misogyny and mother-blaming stories, which marginalize and oppress service users. It challenges people's beliefs that the problem speaks of their identity – a 'totalizing' effect which conflates the person with the problem. It seeks to separate the person from the problem and to develop a sense of incongruency between the two, thus opening up new possibilities for responsibility taking and accountability.

The person's experience of the problem is explored by means of 'externalizing' conversations which provide an account of how the problem has influenced the person and what influences the person can exert on the problem. Traditional psychotherapeutic concepts are reconstructed in narrative therapy: *interpretation* is how service users can make meaning of their lives rather than be entered into stories by others; and *resistance* is the way in which they can resist the influence of the problem on their lives and relationships. The therapist relinquishes the role of expert but remains influential in the questions asked to challenge unhelpful past stories.

For Further Reading

Furman, B. and Ahola, T. 1992: *Solution Talk: Hosting Therapeutic Conversations*. New York: W. W. Norton.

JUDITH MILNER

The Nature of Social Work

The *nature of social work* emerges from a balance at any point in history between three constantly shifting views of its purpose:

1 Maintaining social order and providing services as part of a network of social agencies
2 Helping people attain personal fulfilment and power over their lives
3 Stimulating social change

continued

How social workers practise and how societies organize the social services leans towards one or other of these focuses of social work.

We cannot resolve debates about what social work is; instead, we must see the nature of social work as containing something of all three elements and as being constantly reconstructed by social change and social debate. Those social changes and debates reflect the interaction of different sources of social power. To understand the nature of social work, therefore, we have to examine first the views of social work which are in contention and then the arenas in which the changes and debates take place.

Three views of social work

Three views of social work may be identified:

1 *Individualist-reformist views* see social work as maintaining the existing social order, by providing individuals with welfare services (for example, residential care, community care), regulating individuals' social behaviour (for example, child protection) and reforming social provision to deal with social problems (for example, drug misuse).

2 *Socialist-collectivist views* see social work as transforming society by promoting co-operation, mutual support and shared learning. Such methods combat people's experience of inequality arising from social divisions, emancipate them from oppression and empower them to take control collectively of their own lives.

3 *Reflexive-therapeutic views* see social work as achieving the best well-being for individuals, groups and communities by enabling their personal growth and self-realization to the point where they feel competent as they take part in social life. As they experience being in control of their lives and decisions, they rise above suffering and disadvantage.

These views of social work are constantly in debate, and the debate represents a 'discourse' among interests in a society which seek ascendancy for their particular view. The discourse appears not only in explicit debates, but also in how people behave or in the implications of policies and practices that they pursue. So, individuals' and social institutions' preferences, leanings or policies are expressed in how they act. Each individual social work activity, the policies of social work agencies and perceptions of the social work profession all include elements of each of these views in different combinations. Thus, a social work act may lean towards achieving social maintenance, social change or personal growth. An agency may focus on social regulation, social change or personal therapy. The policy of a political party may emphasize social order, radical urban renewal or education for social inclusion.

Three debating arenas

The various arenas in which these views are in debate may be grouped into three:

1 Political and social debate within political processes, the media and general social relations in any society

2 Professional organizations and agencies: that is, organizations representing the interests of social work and those which provide social services

3 Individual clients and the communities within which they live, which have an impact because the problems they present to agencies and professionals, and how they make their demands for service, represent their interests in and views of social work

Each arena is a focus of discourse, but also influences the others, so we may see each arena as the context for discourse in the others. For example, by making demands on an agency, a group of clients with a new illness (such as AIDS in the 1980s) can make an impact on how the agency sees its job. That arena, where problems are formed by being presented to agencies, also has impact on general social and political debate.

Another example: if professionals and agencies decide that an innovation is needed, they can take part in political lobbying and use the media to stimulate debate about new needs. Alternatively, they can simply take on cases representing the new need, thus affecting how, in the community and client arena, people view the agency. Again, if politicians want social service agencies to provide a service differently, they can change law or government guidance, thus affecting the professional and agency arena. Alternatively, or additionally, they might promote the idea that clients with particular problems should go to one agency rather than another. This might cause clients and the community to define a problem as a welfare issue, rather than as, for example, a housing issue, so the client and community arena has been affected.

So, we may identify relatively limited arenas of debate and action, whose discourses affect other arenas in a broader discourse. Such discourses go on in all professional areas, so discourses about social work are affected by discourses about related professions. For example, if discourses about nursing lead it to be seen as a more valuable resource in community care than social work, the perceived boundaries between these professions may change.

Uncertainty and ambivalence

The contention that social work is a discourse of views and practices, rather than a profession with definable boundaries, knowledge base and values, accurately represents the uncertainty and ambivalence with which social work is regarded, both by practitioners and others. It represents the complex nature of any social institution such as an identifiable occupational group. It proposes that it is partial to argue that social work is one or other of the views described, and, as discourses do, such a partial view probably conceals a personal or political interest in restricting or redirecting our understanding of social work rather than acknowledging and trying to incorporate some of its complexity. Such a position proposes that occupational groups cannot be defined as 'professions' by virtue of their characteristics or traits (such as possessing an identifiable knowledge base, or a system of ethical principles). Instead, all occupational groups must be seen as in constant social negotiation about their designation and character.

For Further Reading
Ife, J. 1997: *Rethinking Social Work: Towards Critical Practice*. Melbourne: Longman.
Munro, E. 1998: *Understanding Social Work: An Empirical Approach*. London: Athlone Press.
Payne, M. 1996: *What is Professional Social Work?* Birmingham: Venture.

MALCOLM PAYNE

Need, Bradshaw's Taxonomy

Jonathan Bradshaw (1972) has argued in a seminal paper that there are four different ways of defining *social need*. Social workers should be clear about the differences – especially when engaged in the process of needs assessment.

1   *Normative need* is what the 'expert', the professional or the agency of power defines as 'need' in any given situation. It is in no sense absolute, and is likely to vary as standards of living change, as knowledge develops and as political values evolve. The idea of 'normative need' is, in a sense, paternalistic; and it runs the risk of being monocultural, but the concept is central to the principles of state welfare.

2   *Felt need* is equated with 'want'. Traditionally, it is measured by survey methods, and it is likely to reflect the extent to which each individual tends to minimize, exaggerate or reasonably assess personal expectations.

3   *Expressed need* or 'demand' is 'felt need turned into action'. In a commercial setting,

expressed need is identifiable by what people are prepared to pay for; but in the non-market context of public welfare, its identification is much less clear.

4 *Comparative need* is a measure commonly used in social policy: the level of need is found by studying the characteristics of those already in receipt of a service – either in the same geographical locality or elsewhere. 'If people with similar characteristics are not in receipt of a service then they are in need.'

The application of Bradshaw's taxonomy to a service user's potential 'need' for social care would produce the following pattern:

• *Normative need* The social services department would be expected to produce its own normative guidelines designed to influence professional assessment.
• *Felt need* Potential users can be surveyed about their attitudes towards unmet needs.
• *Expressed need* Potential users may express a level of spontaneous demand or may respond to an invitation to apply, and this can be monitored and measured.
• *Comparative need* Comparisons can be made by means of a survey between those already in receipt of social care and those not currently so served.

Bradshaw suggests that his taxonomy can 'provide a way forward in an area where precise thinking is needed for both theoretical and practical reasons' – though he acknowledges that difficult methodological problems remain.

For Further Reading
Bradshaw, J. 1972: The taxonomy of social need. In G. McLachlan (ed.), *Problems and Progress in Medical Care*, Oxford: Oxford University Press.

MARTIN DAVIES

Needs-led Policies

Needs-led policies seek to respond to identified need, either at the individual or collective level. They are frequently contrasted with service-led responses, determined by available provision rather than specific needs. In the UK, needs-led policies were given particular prominence by the NHS and Community Care Act 1990 with its emphasis on assessing the needs of the individual or community. Aggregation of unmet needs provides information for targeted development.

A number of key issues ensue: the definition of needs and of those that should be met, and whether the assessment of needs should or can be accomplished independently of resource considerations. In the attempt to distinguish *needs* from *wants*, various typologies of need have been constructed, including Maslow's hierarchy of basic needs (see NEEDS, MASLOW'S HIERARCHY), and Bradshaw's distinction of expressed, normative, comparative and felt needs. Pursuit of needs-led policies may be inhibited by resource availability; an important legal decision in 1997 (the 'Gloucestershire Judgement') confirmed that local authorities may take their resources into account when assessing the needs of a disabled person as defined under the Chronically Sick and Disabled Persons Act 1970.

For Further Reading
Doyal, L. and Gough, I. 1991: *A Theory of Human Need*. London: Macmillan.

ALISON PETCH

Needs, Maslow's Hierarchy

Much social work practice concerns an assessment of needs – brought to its apogee in the notion of a needs-led assessment. The idea of *need* is highly disputed territory within the political arena and in social policy, but Abraham Maslow has described, in psychological terms, what he perceives to be a *hierarchy of needs* with seven layers, which all human beings might ultimately seek to satisfy:

1 *Physiological needs*: the need to satisfy hunger, thirst, sex and sleep
2 *Safety needs*: the need to feel secure from physical danger
3 *The need for company*: the need to belong, to affiliate with groups, to be loved
4 *Esteem needs*: the need to be respected by others, and to enjoy self-respect
5 *Cognitive needs*: the need to have knowledge and understanding
6 *Aesthetic needs*: the need to appreciate beauty and order in art and nature
7 *Self-actualization*: the realization of one's full potential

Social work is principally concerned with the first four levels of need – exemplified respectively in the provision of material aid, child protection, referral to day care facilities, and counselling.

For Further Reading
Maslow, A. H. 1954: *Motivation and Personality*. New York: Harper and Row.

MARTIN DAVIES

Negotiation
Negotiation is the process of agreeing the best outcome which circumstances will permit for all the parties. In social work, the most frequent scenario is one in which the negotiator is acting on behalf of a client or client group. Very frequently, all parties to the process are acting on behalf of the *same* client or client group.

Negotiation is conflict resolution, not competition. It is an attempt to agree the conditions under which the parties can co-operate. In a commercial transaction, involving money for goods or services, the negotiation succeeds and all parties win if they can agree the conditions.

In most social work contexts, failure is unacceptable; the negotiation must continue until the conditions are agreed. For example, a failure between a social worker and a paediatrician to agree how to respond to an abused child cannot be allowed to happen. They must achieve agreement. If both are skilled negotiators, if they remain calm and considerate and each is clear about his or her own requirements and those of the other party, they will do so eventually.

For Further Reading
Fletcher, K. 1998: *Negotiation for Health and Social Services Professionals*. London: Jessica Kingsley.

KEITH FLETCHER

Neighbourhood
See SOCIAL SUPPORT NETWORKS.

Networking
See SOCIAL SUPPORT NETWORKS.

Neurotic Disorders
See ANXIETY DISORDERS.

New Managerialism

New managerialism reflects a set of beliefs or doctrines, relationships and management techniques aimed at enhancing the effectiveness, efficiency and productivity of the public services.

Assumptions and values
These are underpinning assumptions of new managerialism:

- Public services are inefficient and wasteful because of the lack of management, and, as a consequence, they need to be actively managed through the use of private sector management approaches.
- Increased competition, contracting-out and market-based practices are required to improve the efficiency of public services.
- A consumerist ideology suggests that, as services improve from competition between providers, the customer or consumer will have increased choice and opportunity.
- Public services need to be made more accountable by introducing management by objectives, performance indicators, greater cost-consciousness and standardization.

The values of new managerialism are: efficiency, flexibility, quality, competition, effectiveness, customer orientation and 'value for money'. Lowndes (1997) discusses three elements in new managerialism:

1 The *efficiency-based element* gives managers the right to manage, ensures the disciplined use of resources, the pursuit of objectives aimed at reducing costs and improvement of organizational performance. It also increases the use of information technology to bring about changes.
2 The *market-based element* incorporates the separation of purchaser and provider interests, contracting-out to private and non-profit organizations, compulsory
continued

competition between providers, and budget devolution with tighter budget controls or cash limits.

3   The *community-based element* emphasizes the involvement of the public in the management of services, ensures customer and user-focused services, encourages multi-agency partnerships to deliver services and ensures a greater accountability to the public and community.

Its impact on social work

During the 1980s and 1990s, new managerialism widely influenced all areas of public sector provision. Health, education, housing, social services and the probation service experienced major reforms and restructuring. New roles for social workers have emerged at all levels. The key one for managers is the purchaser–provider split which means that managers are required to purchase services from a variety of private, voluntary or other non-profit groups. The new developments have raised cost-consciousness and knowledge about purchasing services among social work staff. Social work staff are involved in managing *care packages*; many have been renamed *care* or *case managers*. Senior social workers might now be known as *team managers*. *Contracts or purchasing officers* are roles created specifically to manage devolved budgets and contracts with providers.

New managerialism encouraged a shift away from generic practice towards specialization, particularly in the areas of assessment and report writing. Other services were fragmented into special areas of practice: child protection; mental health; adult disabilities; youth justice. Areas of practice are increasingly considered in terms of *prioritization* – the need to work with or provide funding for those assessed as most needy, dangerous or risky. Accordingly, systems or routines of structured risk assessments have been introduced. Practice is more standardized with the supervision of clients programme focused: concentrating on, for example, drugs misuse, education programmes, drink/drivers courses, and anger management.

There is a language associated with new managerialism and its influence upon social work. The *client* has been renamed *offender* in probation and *customer*, *consumer* or *service user* in social work; *casework* is *care management*; an informal working relationship with another agency has become a *partnership* or *contract* or *service level agreement*. New managerialist terms familiar in social work include *national standards*, *performance* and *accountability*, *strategic planning*, *target setting*, *auditing*, *evaluation* and *monitoring*.

Relationships have also changed as a consequence of new managerialism. Large social welfare organizations have been fragmented into smaller, more varied agencies; there has been a large increase in the number of non-profit and profit-making organizations providing alternative welfare services. Social workers now arrange and organize services for their clients far more than they used to do. The relationship between senior social workers and front-line social work practitioners has changed with senior social workers less likely to meet clients face-to-face and more likely to be managers assisting and cajoling front-line staff to meet agency objectives and to keep costs down.

The relationship between social worker and clients reflects a new managerialist influence, with some clients (for example, people with disabilities) being given more independence to manage their own care, their social workers acting more like brokers or advocates; but other clients having rights and autonomy taken away – for example, offenders are more likely to end up in court for a failure to comply with national standards. Relationships with other agencies have also shifted from *ad hoc* and informal arrangements to high profile, strategic policy and practice multi-agency partnerships: for example, the introduction of youth offending teams composed of statutory and community organizations with a remit to co-ordinate and deliver youth justice services to young offenders.

A shift in power

New managerialism resulted in changes to the values, regimes and objectives of social work; it also saw a shift in power from the professionals to managers. A far-reaching restructuring of the organization, operation and delivery of social welfare has occurred. New managerialism has, however, been contested by social welfare professionals, leaving a number of paradoxes and unresolved issues:

- The increase in centralized control by government over the finances, objectives and tasks of social work agencies, yet, at the same time, the increase in decentralization of power, resources and services by social work agencies to other providers and service users
- The lack of accountability by non-elected service providers, but increased accountability of public sector social work providers to ministers and other government officials
- The gendered nature of new managerialism – most managers are male, the terminology is 'masculine' and the literature is largely written by men (management *heroes*)
- social workers feeling de-professionalized and de-skilled by the increase of task definition, standardization and technology, yet also becoming increasingly expert, specialized and adopting an evidence-based approach to promote excellence

For Further Reading
Clarke, J., Cochrane, A. and McLaughlin, E. 1994: *Managing Social Policy*. London: Sage.
Lowndes, V. 1997: Change in public service management: new institutions and new managerial regimes. *Local Government Studies*, 23 (2), 42–66.
Pollitt, C. 1993: *Managerialism and the Public Services* (2nd edn). Oxford: Blackwell.

ANITA GIBBS

Nigrescence

Nigrescence is a French word that means the process of becoming black. The psychology of nigrescence can be defined as the developmental process by which a person 'becomes black' where *black* is defined in terms of one's manner of thinking about and evaluating oneself and one's reference groups rather than skin colour *per se*.

Nigrescence models tend to have four stages; and the common point of departure is not the change process *per se* but an analysis of the identity to be changed.

1 The person is first described as functioning in an ongoing steady state with a non-black identity.
2 Following this, some event or series of events compel the person to seek and be a part of change.
3 This is followed by a period during which there is an intense struggle between the 'old' and the emerging 'new' identity.
4 Finally, the person is described as having internalized the new black identity and entering another steady state.

These models (of which that by Cross (1991) is the best known and most widely researched) are useful for social workers as they enable them to understand the potential dynamics of identity negotiation.

For Further Reading
Cross, W. E. 1991: *Shades of Black*. Philadelphia: Temple University Press.

LENA ROBINSON

Non-accidental Injury
See CHILD ABUSE.

Normalization

Normalization is a term used for a set of ideas which assert the rights of disabled people to live their lives as close to the norm as possible. Key proponents of normalization ideas include Bengt Nirje (Sweden) and Wolf Wolfensberger (USA). Originally associated with people with learning disabilities, its influence spread to practice with people with mental health problems in the 1990s.

231

This deceptively simple idea has heavily influenced policy in learning disability. It is associated with deinstitutionalization and integration in mainstream services. The normalization ideal is that people should live in an ordinary house in an ordinary street and associate with non-disabled people.

Normalization has, however, been criticized for being a top-down professionally driven movement, for assuming white male middle-class values as the norm, and because it is sometimes used to deny that people genuinely need specialist services and additional support.

For Further Reading
Brown, H. and Smith, H. (eds) 1992: *Normalisation: A Reader for the Nineties*. London: Routledge.

JAN WALMSLEY

'Nothing Works'

The phrase *'nothing works'* gained currency in social work circles – particularly among those responsible for the supervision of offenders – following the publication of a paper by Robert Martinson, an American criminologist. Martinson had been commissioned by the New York State prison service to review research on rehabilitation programmes. His paper (Martinson, 1974) drew on the results of 231 studies carried out over a 22-year period, and he concluded that, with few exceptions, none of the treatments employed had had significant impact on further offending.

Martinson's work was, understandably, viewed as controversial, and, for a time, it had a demoralizing effect on both policy makers and practitioners in the penal system. From the outset, however, there were those who argued against the legitimacy of the conclusion that 'nothing works'. In particular, a number of psychologists have pointed to the positive findings that are obtained from cognitive-behavioural programmes in work with offenders. It is emphasized, however, that such programmes must embrace four principles if they are to be successful:

1   They must target factors which have contributed to the offending behaviour.
2   They must adopt methods to which participants will respond – notably, they must have structure, encourage active involvement, and focus on concrete problem solving.
3   They must match the degree of intervention to the likely future risk of offending.
4   They must have programme integrity – avoiding drift, objective reversal, and non-compliance by staff.

For Further Reading
Vennard, J., Hedderman, C. and Sugg, D. 1997: *Changing Offenders' Attitudes and Behaviour: What Works?* London: Home Office.

MARTIN DAVIES

Nursing and its Interface with Social Work

The *interface between nursing and social work* is defined by the point at which the social and health care needs of vulnerable people are addressed jointly – either in hospital, the community and/or at discharge from hospital. This can occur with individual clients, or at team, planning or strategic level. Particular overlap occurs with children and adults at risk, disadvantaged individuals and older people where there are issues of protection, support, empowerment or transition.

The term *nurse* is used generically to include a wide range of generalist and specialist health activities. The importance of ensuring that services are targeted equitably, to agreed standards and to those most in need, is common to both nursing and social work. Both professions recognize that the assessment process is the key to the appropriate delivery of care, and both aim to reflect users' and carers' needs, though social work has more legal responsibilities and a more established focus on anti-discriminatory practice.

While there is increasing emphasis on joint and team working, differences in management structures/budgets, referral processes, accountability and places of work can constrain active partnerships.

For Further Reading
Allott, M. and Robb, M. (eds) 1998: *Understanding Health and Social Care: An Introductory Reader*. London: Sage.

SUSAN VERNON AND HILARY TOMPSETT

O

Observation in Social Work

Observation can best be understood as a complex concept which not only includes sensory processes such as seeing, but also incorporates purpose and action. An observation continuum locates informal, everyday 'tacit' processes at one end and more purposeful 'intentional' observation leading to action at the other. Social workers are involved in observation at all points in this continuum, but, in their professional roles, intentional observation can contribute to the development of good practice in a range of activities such as assessment, planning, supervision and service delivery. Observation also plays a significant part in social work education.

The Tavistock Model
Observation first became important in social work in the early 1980s when it drew on psychodynamic ideas for the development of its skill and knowledge base. This approach to observation, called the Tavistock Model, had a number of characteristics that influenced the way the observation process was carried out and the nature of the observer role. Observers were expected to watch a child, family or organization for a specific period of time, try to recall as much information as possible and to record this detailed material in narrative form after, rather than during, the observation. In the Tavistock Model, observations were repeated on a weekly basis for considerable periods of time. The material generated was discussed in small seminar groups which provided opportunities for the observer to reflect not only on the observation but also on his or her response to it.

In his or her role, the observer was expected to make use of opportunities for critical reflection by engaging with the situation while striving to be non-participant. In the world of social work, where workers frequently have to act without too much time to think, observation within the Tavistock Model provided an unaccustomed but significant space within which to reflect before acting.

Observation in training and practice
These ideas were initially applied to direct practice by means of a programme which was developed to encourage social work educators to set up child observation courses on basic training programmes. The impetus for this initiative was concern about the quality of direct work with children following a number of critical child protection reports. Observation had also been a traditional resource in family therapy both in direct work with families and in the training of therapists. However, intentional observation was not widely used in mainstream practice; it was in social work education that it played a more central role. From the late 1980s, both basic training and the post-qualifying training of practice teachers had required participants to be directly observed as part of their course. It has been suggested that this process can be characterized as a hierarchy of observation with practice assessors observing practice teachers, practice teachers observing students, and students using observation in their direct work with service users. Within this hierarchy, observation is not only used as a method of collecting evidence for assessment, but also as a means of developing knowledge and skills in the learning process.

continued

The Equality Model and other developments

Further developments in the concept of observation continue to take place against a background of change in both the theoretical ideas and the political context in which social work is located. In developing an Equality Model of observation, Le Riche and Tanner (1998) suggest that if observation is to be congruent with the values of social work then it has to incorporate a power perspective. This perspective recognizes the inequalities involved in the process of observing (between service users and workers, students and practice teachers, for example) and how these inequalities are compounded by aspects of *difference* such as race, gender and sexual orientation. However, by recognizing and working with these issues, practitioners, students and managers are mirroring their centrality to social work.

The Equality Model recognizes that an awareness of the implications of power relations has to shape all aspects of the observation process including how the observation is negotiated and the structure and content of the recorded material. Observers make use of the opportunities the observation provides to reflect critically on the dynamics of power relations and the impact of these on everyday decisions. An intentional approach to observation highlights these inevitable dilemmas of role and task, and makes them accessible to critical analysis.

Apart from the Equality Model, other developments are taking place that move observation from specific areas of social work towards the mainstream. For example, in multidisciplinary work with adults in community and social care, observation has been described as one means of counteracting rigid, bureaucratic practice. While it has traditionally contributed to assessment in social work education and in direct work with children, there are also opportunities for observation to contribute to good practice at other points of intervention. These include care planning, evaluation and service development. Similarly, managers can incorporate intentional observation into their work as one means of reducing the divisions between management and practice in social care.

This increasing flexibility suggests that observation has the potential to be used in a wider range of settings, at different points of intervention and different levels of organization. It seems probable that, while it is not a panacea, observation will continue to become an increasingly useful tool in mainstream social work and management practice.

For Further Reading

Fawcett, M. 1996: *Learning through Child Observation*. London: Jessica Kingsley.
Le Riche, P. and Tanner, K. (eds) 1998: *Observation and its Application to Social Work*: *Rather like Breathing*. London: Jessica Kingsley.
Reid, S. (ed.) 1997: *Developments in Infant Observation: The Tavistock Model*. London: Routledge.

PAT LE RICHE AND KAREN TANNER

Occupational Therapy

Occupational therapy is the treatment of people with physical or psychiatric illness or disability, through the specific use of selected occupation for the purpose of enabling individuals to reach their optimal level of function and independence in all aspects of life.

Occupation is central to the work of the therapist in three interrelated ways.

1 The occupational therapist is concerned to identify and assess the work, domestic, personal and leisure occupational needs of the individual client, with the client and their family, and plan goal directed programmes of treatment and rehabilitation.

2 Therapists have a comprehensive understanding of the physical, psychological, cultural and sociological elements of human

occupation through which appropriate programmes are devised.

3 Therapists use occupation as a treatment medium, not only as the focus of education and training, but as a means of facilitating communication, emotional expression, group interaction and self-esteem.

Occupational therapy has evolved from its original institutional role in promoting purposeful activity, to a comprehensive role in the treatment and rehabilitation of clients in hospitals, schools, prisons and the community. It provides an essential bridge between medical evaluation of physical and psychological function, and the client's perceptions of recovery and social integration.

For Further Reading
Hagedorn, R. 1997: *Foundations for Practice in Occupational Therapy* (2nd edn). Edinburgh: Churchill Livingstone.

BARBARA STEWARD

Old Age

Old age is a term that is part of the popular English vocabulary, referring to the later part of life. It has no scientific basis in that no set of biological events or changes have been identified which mark an individual's entry into a last phase in life; rather, various parts of the body deteriorate physiologically in different ways throughout life, and this process gathers pace as the individual grows older. Doctors remain uncertain as to whether old age, like illness, constitutes a 'cause' of death. In policy, practice and research literature, the term tends to be used either in its popular sense or to refer to a specific category or service defined by chronological age.

Pensionable age

Much social policy analysis relates to pensionable age (currently, in the UK, 60 years for women, 65 for men). The national census, for example, produces a volume of statistics detailing the demographic characteristics of 'people of pensionable age'. Although this is a historically specific population defined unambiguously in relation to individual age, it is often interpreted as representing 'the elderly' or 'people in their old age'. Comparisons between this and other age-specific populations tend to exaggerate contrasts between groups and to minimize those within groups.

It is widely recognized that there are many unfortunate consequences resulting from an association of pensionable age with old age. While those approaching their 60th or 65th birthday may view 'old age' with alarm, those who have continued to play an active part in society well into their pensionable years frequently protest: 'You're only as old as you feel.' The designation *OAP* (old age pensioner), explicitly linking the receipt of a pension with old age, is viewed by many with disfavour.

Statisticians and gerontologists have argued that a category of 10 million people in the UK is too large to be useful for policy analysis: it is too heterogeneous a population. Not least, it is diverse in respect to age, spanning as it does more than one generation: it is not unusual for people to reach pensionable age when their parents are still alive.

One response by those concerned to target services on 'the needy elderly' has been to associate old age with the age of 75 or 85. Some still object to this, however, in that chronological age is too arbitrary a criterion even for age-related needs: there will always be some who take advantage of such services even though not in need, whereas others, not yet old enough, are denied help they urgently need. Two implications flow from this kind of argument: there is more to age than just chronological age, and old age incorporates 'need' as well as age.

continued

Characteristics of old age

Old age is used extensively in ordinary, everyday conversation. It is popularly believed to be a self-evident aspect of ageing. Dictionaries, for example, give it a brief, unelaborated, definition (for example, 'the later part of life'), and then use it to define a wide range of other less familiar and sometimes derogatory terms (for example, *senescence*, *fogey*). Despite this, its associations in popular usage are not simple and straightforward. Like illness, old age comes to one as if from outside the self; it becomes a possession ('In my old age, ...'); and it is seen to impose undesirable changes, to cause pain and suffering and, ultimately, to be life-threatening. Nevertheless, it provides a simple explanation for changes in the body and for the emergence of related problems or constraints in everyday life. As characteristics of this 'last stage', these changes and problems are seen to be regrettable but inevitable.

A popular way of conceptualizing old age – that is rather different to thinking of it as the last of a sequence of stages – is to contrast it with youth. Over the centuries, these polar opposites have been the basis of much literature and theatre. The audience is encouraged to think positively about 'youth', and negatively about 'old age'. Many traditional images cast the old as marginal creatures (barely human), inhabiting dark, hidden, threatening spaces (as with Grandmama in Little Red Riding Hood). This view of life and the world, acquired early in life and sustained long thereafter, subsequently affects all relations between 'the young' and 'the old'.

Old age as a social construction

With a long history of popular use and without an unambiguous biological definition, old age is essentially a social construction. It is a good example of the well-known dictum: if people define situations as real, they are real in their consequences. Regardless of whether it has any biological 'reality', old age has a social reality which has consequences for the health and well-being of the person. At the societal level, chronological age is written into state policies and institutional regulations. People are barred from opportunities and services on grounds of age in a way which would not be tolerated were the criterion to be gender or ethnicity. Ageism generates a very real kind of discrimination and oppression. Some individuals cope by accepting the consequences uncomplainingly, agreeing that, as 'elderly people', they should make way for younger people, and that they should be grateful that they can enjoy a 'peaceful retirement' on a 'well-earned pension'. Others are driven into political action, believing pensions to be a policy of impoverishment and that the lifelong contribution of pensioners to society is not appropriately acknowledged.

Social work and old age

Social workers often work with older people, partly because age-related illnesses and impairments exist, and ageing does lead to certain universal and undeniable changes in the body which may cause us to seek and accept professional services and support, partly because social workers are increasingly required to assess needs and determine charges in managing these support services, and partly because older people are a substantial social resource, the bedrock of much informal care, voluntary help and community work. It is important that this is recognized and that older people are not thought of as budget-draining burdens.

Attitude is important. Older people are 'people just like ourselves' but age differences are significant: older people have lived longer, and memories, experience and historical perspectives make a difference. However, those who work with older people should be wary of interpreting this in terms of 'old age'. This is a concept that:

- legitimates age bars in the implementation of policy regulations and practice procedures;

- underpins a conceptualization of 'elderly people' which alienates *them* from *us*, often segregating them involuntarily in specially designated places (such as sheltered housing and day centres);
- sustains ageist perspectives on the life course which cause us all to fear our futures.

For Further Reading
Bernard, M. and Phillips, J. 1998: *The Social Policy of Old Age.* London: Centre for Policy on Ageing.
Bytheway, B. 1995: *Ageism.* Buckingham: Open University Press.
Phillipson, C. 1998: *Reconstructing Old Age.* London: Sage.

BILL BYTHEWAY

Old People's Homes
See RESIDENTIAL AND INSTITUTIONAL PROVISION FOR OLDER PEOPLE.

One-parent Families
See LONE-PARENT FAMILIES.

One-way Screens
One-way screens, which first came into use in the early developments in family therapy in the 1950s and 1960s, are large pieces of framed glass separating the two parts of an interviewing suite. On one side of the screen, the interviewing room, a social worker and a member or members of a family will be talking. To them, the screen looks like a mirror. On the other side of the screen sit the social worker's colleague(s) who are able to see through the screen and hear, by means of a microphone system, what is being said. There is usually a phone link between the two rooms and a facility for video recording the interviewing room discussions. In keeping with an ethical position, clients are informed of the screen and the associated technology and should be asked to give permission (signed in respect of video) for its use. Family members are often invited to meet the team behind the screen as part of a process of openness and transparency. The screen is used as part of a team approach to therapeutic work including, for example, assessment in child protection.

For Further Reading
Reimers, S. and Treacher, A. 1995: *Introducing User Friendly Family Therapy.* London: Routledge.

BARRY MASON

Open Adoption
Open adoption is the continuance of contact between a child and birth family member(s) after the legal process of adoption is complete, as opposed to the severing of all ties. Contact can be indirect, through exchange of letters or photographs, or involve direct meetings with a birth parent, grandparent or sibling. Contact allows a child to maintain links with their individual, family or ethnic history. Such openness is supported by evidence that knowledge and understanding are important for a child's overall well-being and sense of identity, and acknowledges the positive contribution that contact with the birth family can make.

CHRISTINE HARRISON

Organization

Organization refers to the structures for delivering personal social services whether in statutory agencies, not-for-profit voluntary bodies or the private sector. These range from small individual settings to large multi-purpose structures in local authority social services departments.

The primary model in the UK remains the social services – called, in Scotland, the social work – department which is an unusual example of longevity in local government. The model of a social services department responsible for a range of provision literally from the cradle to the grave (mother and baby homes to paupers' funerals) has

continued

survived since the Local Authority Social Services Act 1970. It has been under challenge throughout the period, but has survived when the structure and responsibilities of other major local authority services, notably housing and education, have been wholly transformed.

The independent sector

Social care is also delivered outside local government. The voluntary sector has a long history of welfare provision. Children's charities – the NSPCC, Barnardos, the Children's Society, National Children's Homes – have responded to the challenge of the multi-purpose social services department by positioning themselves at the forefront of innovation and research. Disability charities and those concerned with ageing have also made adjustments to their provision to maintain their position in a competitive market.

The private sector, largely fuelled by social security funding, grew threefold in the 1980s to become the dominant provider of residential and nursing home care. The private sector now provides four times more residential places than are available in local authority homes for the elderly.

The growth of the private market in the provision of social care has been strongly influenced by government policy and by a loss of confidence in directly managed services. Social services grew rapidly in the years after their establishment but faced three body-blows in the mid-1970s.

1 The economic crisis of 1976 brought an abrupt halt to the ten-year plans which had been predicated on a continuation of 10 per cent growth per annum for the full plan period.
2 The rush to embrace generic social work meant that many staff were working with vulnerable people of whom they had little prior experience.
3 The first of what has proved to be 25 years of child inquiries – that into the death of Maria Colwell – exposed social services to media scrutiny of their failings.

Specialization

The Seebohm Report (1968) has often been blamed for its advocacy of the generic social worker. In reality, the report called for a unified department and the elimination of overlapping roles, but it never advocated a multi-purpose worker, though many departments took this route. The organizational structures initially adopted were usually generic. The need for specialization has, however, increasingly been recognized. The initial division was between children's services and adult services, but this has been succeeded by sub-specialisms with separate adoption and fostering services, separate services for young offenders, services for people with disabilities, for mental health problems, and for older people. Ironically, 30 years of development has produced a *de facto* reversion to the specialist services which preceded the Seebohm reforms, albeit within a single departmental framework.

Commissioning as a dominant motif

One other trend has influenced the structure of departments. The Conservative Government's flirtation with the purchaser–provider divide was at its height when the community care changes were introduced. While the model of a rigid purchaser–provider split was adopted by some departments, the majority found it too divisive and inappropriate for the mixed economy of provision. The underlying concept – that the function of the public sector agency was to assemble a package of services to support vulnerable individuals drawing from a variety of sources – has been longer-lasting. Commissioning, whether organized for adult and children's services, or on a care group basis, or jointly with health authorities, has become the dominant motif within social services departments.

The commissioning process involves assessing the needs of the population served, mapping current services against those needs, and developing the mix of services –

public, private and voluntary – to meet those needs. While the first two aspects are a sophisticated way of describing service planning, the commissioner's budget-holding responsibility is the key differentiating factor. The government's expressed commitment to break down what has been called 'the Berlin Wall' between health and social services agencies has led to emphasis on pooled budgets and joint commissioning mechanisms to extend the range of resources available for services.

Partnership working

The emphasis on partnership working is reflected in service delivery. Community mental health teams, sometimes themselves developing sub-specialisms on assertive outreach or for homeless mentally ill people, have become the normative model for mental health services. Similar multidisciplinary teams can be found in learning disabilities and substance misuse services.

The private sector is still concentrated in residential and nursing home provision, but is becoming actively involved in domiciliary care. The 'best value' regime and the performance assessment framework with its 46 performance indicators for social services are factors likely to drive change, with an increasing share of provision being delivered through independent organizations.

Although social work constitutes just over 10 per cent of social services expenditure, its influence has been dominant in shaping the culture and values of the organization. The shift to a commissioning role threatens the direct care role of social work in local government. The threat is most acute in adult services where multidisciplinary teams and contracted-out services deliver care, while social workers tend to be employed on assessment functions. A shift to a commissioning model is also anticipated in children's services, where social work practice is under assault from politicians of all parties for 'political correctness' in adoption and fostering practice.

For Further Reading

Douglas, A. and Philpot, T. 1998: *Caring and Coping: A Guide to Social Services.* London: Routledge.

Evandrou, M. and Falkingham, J. 1998: The personal social services. In H. Glennerster and J. Hills (eds), *The State of Welfare* (2nd edn), Oxford: Oxford University Press, 189–256.

Lewis, J. and Glennerster, H. 1996: *Implementing the New Community Care.* Buckingham: Open University Press.

TERRY BAMFORD

Outcome Measures

See EVALUATION OF EFFECTIVENESS, EVIDENCE-BASED PRACTICE and OUTCOME RESEARCH IN ADULT AND YOUTH JUSTICE.

Outcome Research in Adult and Youth Justice

Outcome research seeks to establish whether intervention designed to reduce offending is achieving the desired goals relevant to its stated objectives. This area of research compares the impact of structured programmes on offenders with control or comparison groups; control groups can consist of subjects who receive no treatment, those placed on a waiting list and are seen later, or those who receive some other form of treatment. Random controlled trials remove the impact of extraneous influences, enabling conclu-

continued

sions to be drawn which specifically identify aspects of an approach which contribute to a successful outcome.

Some problems in outcome research

Random allocation can be problematic in real-life situations when allocation to programmes is normally carried out by sentencers rather than researchers. The key outcome indicators used by researchers are reconviction rates, changes in attitude, changes in behaviour, social circumstances, and programme completion. Public accountability is a further key measure which includes effective risk management, value for money and anti-discriminatory practice.

Although reconviction rates are the preferred outcome measure in most studies, they can be subject to variations in demography, police and court practices; but reconviction rates can also provide a level of objectivity, since they are usually independent of the particular method being used in the programme.

Those who work with both adult and young offenders have tended to be more interested in assessments rather than in evaluating the results of programmes and practices in any systematic way. In an outcome study of 210 structured programmes in the UK, it was found that only 11 of the projects provided evidence of rigorous evaluation practice (Ellis and Underdown, 1998).

Losel (1993) estimates that 80 per cent of studies have been conducted on young offenders despite the prevalence of persistent offending in older age groups.

Outcome research has effectively challenged the proposition that 'nothing works', a notion which was prompted by the influential North American work of Robert Martinson (1974). Canadian research first directed attention to the positive outcomes associated with programmes which combined problem-solving skills with reasoning and rehabilitation (Ross et al., 1988).

Meta-analysis

Meta-analysis is a statistical method based upon a medical approach to research which was adapted in relation to work with offenders during the 1990s. It can be used to aggregate the statistical results from programmes for offenders into large data bases and hence to measure the effectiveness of different modes of intervention designed to reduce offending. Lipsey (1995) carried out one of the most important meta-analyses in crime management: it compares the published results of 400 controlled studies of programmes designed for young offenders aged 12–21, undertaken since 1950. This represented international research involving 40,000 individual young offenders. He found a 10 per cent reduction in recidivism rates for young offenders who had been subjected to some form of structured programme which addressed their offending. In programmes which were closely monitored and paid careful attention to the selection of offenders, success rates were up to five times more successful than in programmes with less appropriate selection. The type of intervention had a considerable bearing on the outcome. Structured programmes with the aim of improving employability were found to be the most effective form of treatment. Cognitive-behavioural programmes directed at tackling offending behaviour by teaching problem-solving skills and the avoidance of problematic situations were also effective. Multi-modal programmes which combined cognitive-behavioural with other skill-based activities also produced positive outcomes. Programmes relying on various forms of individual counselling techniques did not reduce offending. It was found that some programmes such as shock incarceration could increase offending.

Losel (1993) has criticized some forms of meta-analysis, arguing that the project of synthesizing data representing a wide range of methodological techniques has led to an unacceptable subjectivity in the way in which studies have been categorized as useful or not. The majority of assessed meta-analytic studies have come from North America and are published in English. Some 57 studies in languages other than English have been produced. Meta-analytical studies examining the treatment of adult offenders in prison settings or making comparisons between prison and community interventions are rare. Notwithstanding his methodological misgivings in relation to meta-analysis, Losel confirms that cognitive-behavioural and multi-modal types of treatment appear to produce the most effective outcomes.

Three effective factors

Three factors (drawn from Raynor (1996)) are most likely to contribute to any impact on offending behaviour:

1 Programmes should be targeted at high-risk offenders, and should focus directly on the characteristics or personal circumstances which are directly related to offending behaviour. Highly structured programmes which are clearly sequenced and determined by specific learning goals enable participants to be clear about desired outcomes and what they are meant to be doing.
2 Programmes should be delivered in a consistent manner which is clearly monitored.
3 Staff should be committed and well-trained to deliver targeted and clearly structured programmes.

Although outcome research has not produced any conclusive answer as to what works best with whom and under what conditions it is still at a relatively early stage of development. It has already constituted a basis for challenging the pessimistic conclusion that nothing can be done about offending behaviour. This emphasizes the need for more methodologically sophisticated and clearly structured outcome studies that identify the mechanisms which operate in programmes that 'work'.

For Further Reading

Lipsey, M. 1995: What do we learn from 400 research studies on the effectiveness of treatment with juvenile delinquents? In J. McGuire (ed.), *What Works: Reducing Reoffending*, Chichester: Wiley.

Losel, F. 1993: The effectiveness of treatment in institutional and community settings. *Criminal Behaviour and Mental Health*, 3, 416–37.

Ross, R. R., Fabiano, E. A. and Ewles, C. D. 1988: Reasoning and rehabilitation. *International Journal of Offender Therapy and Comparative Criminology*, 32 (1), 29–35.

DAVID DENNEY

Outreach

See ASSERTIVE OUTREACH.

P

Palliative Care Social Work

Palliative care social work refers to work with people with life-threatening and non-curative conditions, and with their loved ones. It can be seen as part of a broader psychosocial approach to palliative care, which is concerned to promote people's physical, psychological and social well-being, based on a 'total care' approach and undertaken by a multi-professional team including doctors, nurses, care assistants, ministers, physio- and occupational therapists, volunteers and social workers. The goal of palliative care is the achievement of a good quality of life for patients and those close to them. Social work has always been an integral part of the multidisciplinary approach of palliative care, based on an holistic approach to care and support.

The background and context

Palliative care has its origins in the hospice movement. The concept of palliative care 'has broadened over time from "terminal care" to include the care of those who have a life-threatening disease but are not imminently dying, including people who have recently been diagnosed with advanced cancer and those who have other life-threatening diseases such as multiple sclerosis, motor neurone disease, AIDS, chronic circulatory or respiratory diseases'. (Higginson, quoted in: Oliviere et al., 1998, p. 3).

Palliative care social work is provided in a range of settings, including independent hospices, hospital support/palliative care teams, NHS hospice/palliative care units, home care teams and day hospices. In 1998, there were 228 special palliative care units in the UK, most offering social work support, and a large number of home care teams including social workers. Palliative care social workers increasingly work with people in their own homes, and there has been a growing emphasis in palliative care on enabling people to have choice in where they die, enabling more people to be supported and to die at home.

Palliative care social work has tended to be neglected in mainstream discussions of social work. It is however an important, expanding and innovatory field of practice, with its own UK organization: the Association of Hospice and Specialist Palliative Care Social Workers. It also offers insights with much wider application for social work and social care. Specialist palliative care social workers work with a very diverse population. Unlike many fields of social work, palliative care social work is potentially a universalist service because the need for palliative care cuts across social divisions including class, as well as gender, race, age, disability and sexual identity.

Because it is part of the broader palliative care movement, palliative care social work both raises key issues for interagency health/social services and statutory/non-statutory collaboration, and offers models for collaboration more generally. This context means that it draws on and seeks to negotiate both social and medical models of need. Palliative care social workers work with both adults and children, highlighting issues for both children's and adult services, impacting on both and prioritizing the need for links between the two.

The nature of palliative care practice

The political shift to the right in the 1980s, and the devaluing of the social work profession associated with it, had profound effects on the social work role, resulting in a move to more technicist, managerial and consumerist models of social work, highlighted by the role of 'care manager'. However, the role of the specialist palliative care social worker still closely reflects traditional and defining social work values, concerns and activities in its goals and process. Its practice retains a concern with both practical support (for example, over housing, income maintenance, aids and adaptations) and counselling: addressing both the 'personal' and the 'social' and offering a counter to a narrowly defined competence-based approach to practice.

Palliative care social work is unusual in that it involves work with two groups of people as direct service users: people with non-curative conditions or who are dying, and those who are bereaved. It is important to distinguish between the two groups, and for practitioners to recognize and negotiate the different, sometimes competing rights and interests of both. This demands skills and understanding relating to both loss and dying. Specialist palliative care social workers need an understanding of the physical, intellectual, spiritual, cultural, emotional and social experiences of both these conditions.

Evaluating the quality of practice

Palliative care social work generally seems to be a service valued by service users. However, as with other valued services, it appears that black people and members of minority ethnic populations are under-represented among the users of palliative care services. 'Findings highlight the need for palliative care services to provide culturally sensitive services in respect of language, religion, spiritual and dietary needs and for particular attention to be paid to providing appropriate and accessible information to these communities ... Cultural pain exists and in its widest definition colours all other pain – physical, social, spiritual, financial and psychological.' (Oliviere et al., 1998, pp. 146–7).

Specialist palliative care social work needs to be related to the different experiences of men and women, and growing recognition of the need for greater user involvement in shaping policy, services and practice. This poses particular issues in the context of palliative care because of people's ill-health and limited life expectancy. Good practice in palliative care also creates particular demands for appropriate support, supervision and consultation for staff. Suitable support systems in terms of both individual strategies and formal structures are essential.

Palliative care social work needs to be related to increasing debates and developments about euthanasia, living wills and advance directives. These, in turn, need to be set within a framework of concerns about rationing of services and support, and inadequate income maintenance denying people the quality of life that might be possible when facing debilitating and life-threatening conditions and diseases.

For Further Reading
Monroe, B. 1993: Social work and palliative care. In D. Doyle, G. Hanks and N. Macdonald (eds), *Oxford Textbook of Palliative Medicine*, Oxford: Oxford University Press.
Oliviere, D., Hargreaves, R. and Monroe, B. 1998: *Good Practices in Palliative Care: A Psychosocial Perspective*. Aldershot: Arena.
Sheldon, F. 1997: *Psychosocial Palliative Care: Good Practice in the Care of the Dying and Bereaved*. Cheltenham: Stanley Thornes.

SUZY CROFT

Panic Disorders

Panic disorders are characterized by recurrent panic attacks, which can occur with or without a precipitant, often being associated with agoraphobia. Symptoms are of intense panic with acute and severe anxiety, fear and thoughts of impending doom or death.

One year prevalence rates are 0.6 per cent for men and 1.2 per cent for women. Treatment is broadly the same as that for general anxiety disorder.

CLAIRE KENWOOD AND RAY VIEWEG

Paranoia

Paranoia is a term used to describe delusional disorders but is frequently used more widely to mean *suspicious and untrusting*, associated with the belief that others are persecuting the individual. This may take the form of a general feeling or specific beliefs, and may include beliefs of being pursued, interfered with or spoken about (delusions of reference). Such beliefs can be linked with grandiose delusions and may arise because recognition by others is not occurring. It can then be reinforced by others' negative attitudes to them that may include the unwanted involvement of mental health services and involuntary hospitalization. In delusional disorders, intricate, complex and elaborate delusional systems develop.

Paranoia can start abruptly, over a period of weeks or months, and be a symptom of schizophrenia, depression, mania or delusional disorder. Alternatively, it may form an enduring personality characteristic – a paranoid personality disorder. It is usually managed by administration of anti-psychotic medication but use of cognitive-behaviour therapy is also now being developed.

For Further Reading
Post, F. 1982: Paranoid disorders. In J. K. Wing and L. Wing (eds), *Handbook of Psychiatry 3 – Psychoses of Uncertain Aetiology*, Cambridge: Cambridge University Press.

DAVID KINGDON

Parental Contact

Parental contact with looked-after children refers to the relationship a mother or father maintains with a child cared for with parental agreement, or through court order, by a statutory agency. The form and level of indirect or direct contact may be agreed with a parent, or defined by a court. Where a parent has seriously abused a child, contact may be limited.

Maintenance of contact is regarded as critical to discharge from state care. Its significance for long-term substitute care is less well recognized, although research highlights the positive contribution contact can make to placement stability. Conversely, erosion of contact may leave young people in long-term public care without knowledge and understanding of personal history needed to develop a positive sense of identity (Ryburn, 1994).

Parents of looked-after children frequently experience discrimination and disadvantage that undermines their intention to maintain contact and makes it difficult for a parent to find a meaningful role in a child's life. To overcome these barriers requires active promotion of contact in social work practice with looked-after children, parents and carers.

For Further Reading
Ryburn, M. 1994: Research in relation to contact and permanent placement. In M. Ryburn (ed.), *Open Adoption: Research, Theory and Practice*, Aldershot: Avebury.

CHRISTINE HARRISON

Parental Rights and Responsibilities

Parental rights are the powers and entitlements adults gain by becoming parents. *Parental responsibilities* are the duties and obligations adults owe children. These reflect the history, values, social policies and child-rearing practices of cultures, from absolute patriarchal rights to arrangements balancing the rights and responsibilities of parents, children and state.

The right to parenthood is not automatic, and is easiest to establish for birth mothers or married fathers. Reproductive technologies create new questions about who is a parent. Government decisions to support families (parental leave, cash benefits) or to limit or license reproduction affect adult rights.

Societal focus on children's rights emphasizes adult responsibilities. Parents are expected to act 'reasonably'. Their power recedes with the maturing child's developing capacity for autonomy. Legislation can give parents rights in matters like residence, upbringing, education, contact and legal decision making (Children (Scotland) Act 1995 Ch. 36, PtI (s.2), Bainham, 1998, pp. 94–104). Parents failing to meet responsibilities and exercise rights reasonably may experience state intervention. Social workers can become involved if someone requests help, or alleges that a child's upbringing is inadequate or abusive. Social work's role is to support families, and assist society to balance children's and parents' rights.

For Further Reading
Bainham, A. 1998: *Children, The Modern Law*. Bristol: Jordan.

JANET SEDEN

Parenting

Parenting is the performance of all the actions necessary to promote and support the physical, emotional, social and intellectual development of a child from infancy to adult-hood. It is usually carried out by one or both birth parents, but the term refers to the activity rather than the biological relationship. It differs from child-rearing, being concerned with more than the face-to-face relationship between the child and parent, and covering a much longer time span – at least until the child achieves independence, which may not be until the mid-twenties.

The idea that bringing up children is a skilled task, which may be done better or less well and has to be learned, is comparatively recent, related to the perception that children's progress and behaviour reflect the quality of parenting they receive. Anthropological studies suggest that different parenting practices produce dramatically different personality types. Research indicates that the most successful style of parenting is authoritative without being authoritarian, setting firm but not inflexible boundaries, and having clear expectations of children within the context of a loving relationship. There is a growing consensus that physical punishment is an infringement of children's rights that should no longer be allowed, whether inside or outside the family. Hitting children is an ineffective form of discipline and conveys the message that violence is acceptable (Pugh et al., 1994).

Parenting and poverty

Parenting is influenced by culture, ethnic background, family type, and by individual beliefs and values. However, in addition, most of the people in contact with social workers are living in poverty, with an income insufficient to provide children with a healthy diet or to enable them to enjoy experiences likely to promote their educational and social development (Ferri and Smith, 1996). Activities that many parents and children take for granted may be ruled out; simply transporting children from one place to another without a car is too difficult. Providing a suitable place to do home-work may be impossible in an overcrowded flat or when heat can only be afforded in one room.

Nevertheless most parents do everything possible to minimize the impact of poverty on their children. In their anxiety not to impose inappropriate standards on poor parents or those from different ethnic backgrounds, social workers must be careful not to condone unacceptable conditions and parenting practices, which may cause serious cases of neglect or abuse to be disregarded.

Parent education and support

People need a certain level of maturity before they are ready to become parents, so that the rising number of teenage births in England and Wales, the highest in Europe, is a matter for serious concern. In discussing the options for a young girl who becomes pregnant, social workers must be realistic about the difficulties, especially for those who lack family support.

The capacity to provide good parenting is also influenced by family policy. British governments, in contrast with those of most other European countries, have usually taken a non-interventionist attitude to the task of parenting, treating it as a private matter. However, the Labour government elected in 1997 put parenting at the centre of its social policies and initiated a large expansion in education and support programmes, bringing together expertise from health, education, early years, community organization and social work. Ensuring inclusion of those who most need help can be difficult, and involves skilled and patient work over an extended time period.

continued

Family structure and parenting roles

Economic and social changes also affect parenting. The traditional gender division with the man providing income and the woman caring for children full-time has virtually disappeared. Most mothers now work outside the home and fathers take a more prominent part in the day-to-day care of children, though women continue to take on most of the organizational work of parenting. The rising divorce rate means far more children living in single-parent households or in step-families. Step-parenting has not been well researched, but there is evidence that it involves additional strains, which are reflected in child abuse statistics and conflict within families, often requiring social work intervention. One implication of these changing family structures is that social workers need to engage more effectively with men, broadening out from their traditional focus on women.

Corporate parenting

When birth parents are unable to look after their children to a 'reasonable' standard, the local authority in which they live is required by the Children Act 1989 to provide care and accommodation for them. This has come to be known as *corporate parenting*, because the tasks which for home-based children are carried out by one or two individuals are split between many different people. In the process, there is great danger that some of the most basic needs of children will be overlooked. The result is that outcomes for young people who spend long in public care are extremely poor, putting them at high risk of unemployment, homelessness, teenage parenthood, drug and alcohol misuse and involvement in crime. At least 40 per cent of young offenders have been looked after by local authorities.

During the 1990s, the Department of Health *Looking After Children* research and development team analysed the task of corporate parenting, identifying outcomes commonly desired for their children by parents in the community and finding out how they tried to achieve them. These detailed parental behaviours relating to key dimensions, such as health, education and identity, were then incorporated as questions into the *Looking After Children Assessment and Action Records* to help check that necessary tasks were being carried out and draw attention to omissions and deficiencies that needed to be remedied (Jackson and Kilroe, 1996). Social workers have the main responsibility for seeing that this happens, in collaboration with other professionals, carers, birth families and the young people themselves.

For Further Reading

Ferri, E. and Smith, K. 1996: *Parenting in the 1990s*. London: Family Policy Studies Centre.

Jackson, S. and Kilroe, S. (eds) 1996: *Looking After Children: Good Parenting, Good Outcomes*. London: HMSO.

Pugh, G., De'Ath, E. and Smith, C. 1994: *Confident Parents, Confident Children: Policy and Practice in Parent Education and Support*. London: National Childrens Bureau.

SONIA JACKSON

Parole

Parole is the discretionary release of selected prisoners on licence before the expiry of their determinate sentence. It is thus distinct from: routine remission for good behaviour; release for temporary purposes such as home leave; automatic conditional release after a standard portion of sentence; early discharge on exceptional compassionate grounds.

The contemporary parole scheme

Any parole scheme will be controversial, raising fundamental questions about the fairness of its procedures and the inevitably flawed and fallible nature of its judgements regarding liberty. The essentials of the scheme operating in England and Wales, introduced by the Criminal Justice Act 1991 and largely inspired by the Carlisle Report (1988), can be summarized thus:

- The primary consideration is the degree of risk posed to the public of a further offence being committed while the prisoner is on parole when they would otherwise be in prison. This must be balanced against the potential benefit, both to the public and to the prisoner, of early release under supervision, which might help in the prisoner's rehabilitation and so lessen the risk of reoffending.
- Any meaningful system of individual risk assessment and selection that seeks to improve on statistical estimates of prisoners' prospects of reconviction demands time and resources. Parole schemes are thus likely to focus on prisoners serving longer sentences, to allow time to assess the impact of the sentence on the prisoner. Length of sentence is not a true proxy for risk posed but those serving longer sentences, imposed for more serious offences, are likely to include the more risky offenders (56 per cent of applicants being convicted of violent or sexual crimes). The shortest eligible sentence is four years, with eligibility for parole after serving a half of the sentence and automatic early release on licence for unsuccessful applicants after two-thirds. Both parole and non-parole licences ordinarily run until the three-quarters point. The discretion zone is thus confined to one-sixth of sentence length.
- Considerations of fairness are addressed by giving applicants proper opportunity to see all reports and documents included in their dossier and to make written representations about the contents and in support of their application. They do not have any right to an oral hearing and the decision is made on the basis of the dossier alone but applicants at present have a personal interview with a member of the Parole Board to amplify their concerns and arguments. Reasons are given for all decisions, affording dissatisfied applicants some limited possibility of seeking judicial review on grounds of unreasonableness.
- Ministerial responsibility for decision making has been delegated to the Parole Board for all prisoners serving less than 15 years, so that the process is largely freed from possible political influence.
- Though the Board includes 'experts' (psychiatrists, chief probation officers and criminologists), the majority of members are 'independents' who are expected to apply informed common sense in evaluating the advice of reporting professionals within the penal system.
- Unsuccessful applicants can be reconsidered after a further twelve months if their sentence is of sufficient length (i.e. those serving 78 months or longer).

Facts and figures

Approximately four cases in ten are given parole, the average licence period (including the non-discretionary one-twelfth of sentence to which all prisoners are subject) being 15.5 months. Of prisoners under parole supervision in any year, around 11 per cent are recalled, but less than 4 per cent of parolees are recalled as a result of committing a further offence while on licence. The actual reoffending rate is somewhat higher but studies of the pre-1991 parole system indicated that the clear majority of offences committed on parole were less serious than the original offence. Overall, since parole was introduced in the UK in 1968 around 35 per cent of parolees have been reconvicted within two years of release compared with 55–60 per cent of non-parolees. This lower

continued

reoffending rate is entirely to be expected but does it arise simply as a consequence of the selection process? Though the data is by no means easy to interpret, research (reviewed by Hann et al., 1991) suggests that something about the parole process has a modest 'treatment effect', reducing reconviction. The reasons remain to be explained, whether the pay-off of investment of trust or the product of supervisory skill. Another consideration is whether denial of parole serves to worsen the post-custodial behaviour of unsuccessful applicants, but this is highly speculative.

The probation and social work role

The parole process relies heavily upon probation officers and social workers for the following:

- An analysis of the circumstances of the original offence and criminal record so that the risk assessment can be firmly grounded in a clear understanding of the offender's capacity for harmful conduct and in what circumstances
- An appraisal of the offender's willingness to consider the causes and consequences of their offending and the positive efforts made by them to reduce the risk of reoffending
- A sustained effort to build links with the prisoner through their sentence in anticipation of release and to participate actively in sentence planning in partnership with the prison – this promotes greater continuity between the custodial and the community phases of sentence
- An audit of the prisoner's positive attachments and commitments within the community that can be harnessed in promoting their successful resettlement
- A clear supervisory plan to manage and reduce risk on licence, including proposals for additional licence conditions, governing accommodation, treatment programmes and non-contact with victims
- Vigilant oversight of the licence, holding the offender to account in adhering to the objectives of supervision – this requires appropriate consultation within the supervisory agency, clear communication with other community agencies and prompt liaison with the Home Office parole unit on issues of concern that may require enforcement action through formal warning or recall
- Providing specialist support to those who have been away for longer periods in the often difficult period of readjustment to community life – ex-prisoners report that they value continuing access to supervisors who are: well informed about the realities of prison life and the demands posed in crossing the custodial divide back to freedom, able to act as their advocate in negotiating resources and to mediate constructively in their post-release encounters with the police

Parole can obviously cause greater resources to be directed for longer at those who are safer bets, with more advantages in their favour. It can also generate not insignificant uncertainty about date of release that can disrupt or inhibit planning. Overall, however, the process serves to promote forward thinking for all long-term prisoners in their anticipation of release.

For Further Reading

Carlisle, Lord (Chair) 1988: *The Parole System in England and Wales*, Cm. 532. London: HMSO.

Hann, R., Harman, W. and Pease K. 1991: Does parole reduce the risk of reconviction? *Howard Journal of Criminal Justice*, 30 (1), 66–75.

Hood R. and Shute S. 1995: *Paroling With New Criteria*, Occasional Paper Number 16. Oxford: University of Oxford Centre for Criminological Research.

NIGEL STONE

Participation
See USER PARTICIPATION.

Partnership with Service Users
The term *partnership* describes an actual or desired quality in the relationship between the service user and the social worker. Recent legislation and professional guidance in respect of social work with children and adults has emphasized its importance. It is asserted that partnership may be expressed through all aspects of social work, whether in work with individual service users or by engaging with groups of service users in planning, monitoring and evaluating services.

However, the idea of partnership between social workers and service users is inherently problematic. The notion of partnership implies equality in the balance of power: it signifies a relationship freely entered into by two or more parties of equal power or status and capable of being terminated by either party in prescribed circumstances (for example, as in a marriage or a business partnership). Relationships between social workers and service users do not necessarily have these characteristics, especially where social workers are involved in the protection of vulnerable individuals or where their role is otherwise statutorily defined.

Hence, the notion of partnership may be more of an aspirational value than a statement of the actual nature of relationships between social workers and service users.

For Further Reading
Morris, J. 1997: *Community Care: Working in Partnership with Service Users*. Birmingham: Venture Press.

STEVEN SHARDLOW

Patch
A *patch* is a geographical area which is identified for the purposes of delivering a range of public services, like housing, social services and environmental health. The term is usually associated with the decentralization of services from town halls or county halls to more local neighbourhood offices, providing greater accessibility and responsiveness to local needs. Patch social work teams usually have a strong community orientation, working closely with local groups and other agencies in the area, with the aim of improving social conditions and supporting formal and informal helping networks. A typical patch consists of approximately 5,000–10,000 residents.

GORDON JACK

Paternalism
Paternalism denotes an action or policy whereby the autonomy of persons or groups is curtailed on the grounds of their own good. The idea is analogous to the restrictions that a benevolent, responsible parent places on a child to protect him or her from dangers he or she does not fully understand. Paternalist public policies (the 'nanny state') are sometimes deemed objectionable because they prevent citizens from exercising full responsibility. In welfare practice, paternalism is often considered justified because of the vulnerability and limited understanding of children and people with various mental impairments or temporarily limited mental competence.

CHRIS CLARK

Pathological Ageing
Pathological ageing occurs when the normal changes of chronological ageing start to produce clinical symptoms or lead to complications. Ageing processes are more likely to be pathological if the person also has diseases that have similar effects to ageing changes or is taking drugs that aggravate ageing effects. As an example, bone loss with ageing is normal, but it becomes pathological when it results in curvature of the spine (kyphosis) or a broken hip or wrist following a fall. Pathological ageing is also a feature of a number of rare genetic conditions such as Werner's syndrome and progeria.

PETER CROME

Pathways
The term *pathways*, used in social work training, refers to areas of particular social work practice. Each pathway (for example, children and families, adults with specific needs) is placed within the relevant legal and organizational framework appropriate to the tasks. The primary purpose of pathways is the preparation of social workers for specialist areas of work which meet the needs of diverse and often complex groups of service users. Each pathway is deemed to be a body of knowledge, values and skills which creates competent practice in all set-

tings and sectors. Pathways are assumed to polish social workers' intellectual powers of transferring knowledge and skills from one sit-uation to another, irrespective of case, need, problem or context.

ANTONY A. VASS

Permanence

Permanence refers to a key tenet of modern child welfare theory and practice. It holds that optimum development of children relies on living in a familiar and predictable environment where they can expect to remain until independence. In preference, this should be with the birth family in security and safety, but, if this is not possible, or not in the child's best interests, a placement should be found with alternative carers who can provide stability and consistent, loving care.

The background

The prime influence on creating the *permanency movement* was the revelation that, once taken into care, large numbers of children were living in indeterminate placements with no clear plan as to whether they would remain there or be moved on. Research in the 1970s in the USA, and in the UK notably through the seminal study, *Children Who Wait* (Rowe and Lambert, 1973), confirmed that foster care could too often be a holding arrangement or, worse, lead to a chain of placement disruptions. Not surprisingly, high rates of disturbance, low self-esteem and poor academic progress were found in such children. However, high problem levels were not found in children who had acquired 'a sense of permanence'.

These findings provoked an urgent concern to secure permanent family placements for children in need of them. This meant introducing a rather different population of children with special needs to the field of adoption, formerly concerned mostly with healthy infants. That a permanence movement had to arise stands, therefore, as a salutary reminder that child welfare systems are often magnetized to the initial investigation and removal of the child, but lose forward momentum once the child is no longer in immediate danger. An important benefit of the permanence movement has been to inject a note of greater toughness of mind into the case management of looked-after children. It has led to calls for a more assertive approach, involving regular reviews, active plans, sharper decision making, time limits and contracts: all developed as an antidote to reactive and crisis-led decision making.

Permanence planning

The broad definition of permanence planning should encompass a number of placement options: remaining at home or returning home; placement with relatives or friends, foster placement or adoption; and, in some special circumstances, stable residential care. However, permanence by adoption has often been viewed as the most desirable and comprehensive solution when the child cannot live at home. It could, after all, be seen as the best attempt to re-create the features of a normal childhood: a family for life, extending beyond childhood, carrying a legal imprimatur and a socially recognized status. It is probably true that this resulted in adoption becoming the privileged route to permanence, being better resourced than options like family preservation. On the other hand, adoption involving, as it often did, severance of ties from the birth families and frequently a crossing of class, race, religion and culture boundaries has had its political opponents. Despite the heated attention adoption placement has received, a very small proportion of children, in fact, leave care for adoption.

The significance of permanence for child development

Following satisfaction of the basic needs for survival, the nature of child/caregiver relationships has emerged in psychological investigations as crucially implicated in normal development. The influence of John Bowlby and attachment theory, stressing the importance of parent/child relationships and the consequences of broken emotional ties, also contributed to a wish to preserve and not sever relationships unnecessarily. This led to an interest in the phenomenon of re-attachment. It became important to know to what extent children with a history of broken attachments and other adversities could form sufficiently strong new psychological ties and make adequate developmental recoveries.

Outcomes of permanent placements

Two key questions need to be asked about the consequences of a movement to champion permanence. First, are children living in impermanent placements to the same extent as before? Child care statistics for England show a gradual but steady fall in the total numbers of children in public care: a reduction in the numbers living in residential care and in the length of time children are looked after. Among other things, this is likely to be a reflection of the permanence philosophy and its expression in the Children Act 1989. However, behind this picture of national trends, considerable local variation is concealed, and so the struggle to prevent drift must continue.

Second, where efforts have been made to create a permanent placement, has the aim been achieved? One of the most encouraging research findings is that even late placement of ex-care children into families has proved successful for 60–90 per cent, depending largely on age at placement and the level of behavioural disturbance. Satisfactory new attachments have developed in the majority of cases although this had not been predicted previously. However, a substantial minority of placements do not succeed, many children have continuing difficulties, and the challenges to substitute parents who try to offer permanent homes to previously maltreated children can be severe.

On the other hand, studies of the consequences of returning the children home did not necessarily show that the children had achieved stability or safety. Simple comparisons of outcome are unwise, however, as differences may not be due to the placement type itself but to other factors like lack of comparability in the children placed and variations in the levels of support in different types of placement. It appears that all these options carry some level of risk of impermanence and, sometimes, subsequent abuse.

Outcome research has begun to build a more complex model of the factors determining permanence and satisfactory outcomes. The model will include factors in the placed children and their backgrounds; in the new family and new parents' handling style, with and without contact arrangements, and with different levels of support services.

Practice developments

Various new developments in permanence planning and maintenance may alter the picture. For example, one attempt to improve the chance of permanence is to adopt the model of *concurrent planning* whereby an alternative family is recruited simultaneously with attempts at rehabilitation so that, if adequate care cannot be provided by the birth family, the new carers will have undertaken to keep the child permanently and there is no sudden transfer to an unfamiliar environment. Strengthening post-placement support services and the management of contact arrangements may also increase the likelihood of permanence. The most significant tasks are to build on evidence of what determines outcome in the different types of placement, to tailor services in the light of the findings, and to provide them appropriately and equitably to the birth, kinship and unrelated families.

continued

For Further Reading

Fratter, J., Rowe, J. Sapsford, D. and Thoburn, J. 1991: *Permanent Family Placement: A Decade of Experience*. London: British Agencies for Adoption and Fostering.

Maluccio, A., Fein, E. and Olmstead, K. 1986: *Permanency Planning for Children: Concepts and Methods*. London: Tavistock Publications.

Quinton, D., Rushton, A., Dance, C. and Mayes, D. 1998: *Joining New Families: A Study of Adoption and Fostering in Middle Childhood*. Chichester: Wiley.

ALAN RUSHTON

Personal and Social Construct Theories

Constructs refer to sets of ideas and beliefs people have developed from their interpretations of their experiences of the social world. *Personal construct theory* states that an individual's social performance is determined by interpretations about events and not by the events themselves. These understandings help to predict future actions. *Social constructs* relate to shared meanings and interpretations of behaviours and events. Social constructs are dynamic and reciprocal in their influence. They change and develop in the light of shared experiences and interpretations. The importance of these theories for social work practice rests in their explanatory power that may assist practitioners in the design of effective interventions.

For Further Reading

Burr, V. 1995: *An Introduction to Social Constructionism*. London: Routledge.

PETER RANDALL AND JONATHAN PARKER

Personality Disorders

Personality disorders are defined in the International Classification of Diagnoses [ICD-10] as 'deeply ingrained and enduring behaviour patterns, manifesting themselves as inflexible responses to a broad range of personal and social situations' (World Health Organization, 1992). They are present in childhood and continue into adulthood. They represent an extreme deviation from the way an average individual thinks, feels or relates to others and are frequently, but not always, associated with various degrees of subjective distress, problems in social functioning and performance. They are not secondary to another mental disorder but may coexist with another mental disorder.

Classification

Each condition is classified according to its predominant behavioural manifestations and clusters of traits, which correspond to the most frequent or conspicuous behavioural manifestations. Personality disorders can be classified using either a dimensional or categorical approach. Dimensional classification defines the degree to which a person displays a number of personality traits and behavioural problems. The World Health Organization has adopted a categorical system of classification of personality disorders which is used clinically and assumes the existence of distinct *types* of personality disorders with distinctive features:

- *Paranoid personality disorder (F60.0)* is characterized by an excessive sensitiveness to setbacks and rebuffs. There is a proclivity to bear grudges persistently, or not to forgive insults and injuries or slights. There is usually suspiciousness and a pervasive tendency to distort and misconstrue neutral or friendly actions as hostile or contemptuous.
- *Schizoid personality disorder (F60.1)* is distinct from schizotypal disorder, which is related to schizophrenia or Asperger syndrome. It is characterized by emotional cold-

ness and detachment. There is a limited capacity to express warmth towards others or derive pleasure from any activities. This usually results in a lack of close friends or confiding relationships or indeed the desire for such relationships.

- *Dissocial personality disorder (F60.2)* was formally called antisocial, asocial, psychopathic, or sociopathic personality disorder. For diagnostic and treatment issues relating to dissocial personality disorder, see PSYCHOPATHIC PERSONALITY DISORDER. This type is often linked to aggressive behaviour producing problems which cross the child-protection, mental health and criminological interface.

- With *emotionally unstable personality disorder (F60.3)*, there is a marked tendency to act impulsively without consideration of the consequences, together with affective instability. The ability to plan ahead may be minimal, and outbursts of intense anger may often lead to violence or behavioural explosions. These are easily precipitated when impulsive acts are criticized or thwarted by others.

- Characteristic features of *histrionic personality disorder (F60.4)* are self-dramatization, theatricality and exaggerated expression of emotions. Suggestibility is present and such individuals are easily influenced by others or by circumstances. There is a continual seeking for excitement and activities in which they are the centre of attention.

- *Anankastic personality disorder (F60.5)* was formally known as obsessional personality disorder. It is characterized by feelings of excessive doubt, caution, a preoccupation with details, rules, lists, order or schedule, while perfectionism often interferes with completing the task. They are excessively conscientious, and undue preoccupation is given to productivity to the exclusion of interpersonal relationships. Included is the intrusion of insistent and unwelcome thoughts or impulses. Anankastic personality disorder is also known as obsessive–compulsive personality disorder and should be distinguished from obsessive–compulsive disorder, which is a neurotic disorder.

- With *anxious (avoidant) personality disorder (F60.6)*, the person experiences persistent and pervasive feelings of tension and apprehension. They believe that they are socially inept, personally unappealing, or inferior to others. There is an excessive preoccupation with being criticized or rejected in social situations, and an unwillingness to become involved. This restricts their lifestyle, as social or occupational activities involving significant interpersonal contact are avoided because of fear of criticism, or rejection.

- *Dependent personality disorder (F60.7)* was formally known as asthenic, inadequate, or passive personality disorder. The characteristic features include encouraging others to make their important life decisions. There is subordination of their own needs to those on whom they are dependent, undue compliance with their wishes, and an unwillingness to make even reasonable demands on people to whom they adhere. They feel uncomfortable or helpless when alone, with an exaggerated fear of their inability to care for themselves, and are preoccupied with fears of being abandoned by their 'significant other'. They are incapacitated from making everyday decisions without an excessive amount of advice and reassurance from others.

- The category of *mixed personality disorders (F61)* includes personality disorders which have features of several of the disorders in F60, but without a predominant set of symptoms that would allow a more specific diagnosis.

- The group of *enduring personality changes, not attributable to brain damage and disease (F62)* includes disorders of adult personality which develop after catastrophic experiences, or excessive or prolonged stress. The change should not be a manifestation of another mental disorder, or a residual symptom of any antecedent mental disorder. Changes due to brain damage are excluded.

continued

- The category of *habit and impulse disorders (F63)* includes behavioural disorders, not elsewhere classified, which are characterized by repeated acts that have no clear rational motivation and that generally harm the patient's own interest and those of other people. Disorders such as pathological gambling, fire setting (pyromania), stealing (kleptomania), hair pulling (trichotillomania) are included in this category.

Assessment

To diagnose a personality disorder, the person should have a pattern of behaviour which has been present since early life and persists into adulthood. This pattern should be pervasive, deviate from the patient's cultural norm and be severe enough to lead to distress in the patient or others. Early childhood history, either from old medical notes or in the form of a collateral history, is essential in distinguishing between transient and enduring patterns of behaviour.

It is necessary to rule out other psychiatric disorders, such as schizophrenia, depression or drug abuse, before a diagnosis can be made. Physical disorders such as organic brain disease will also need to be excluded.

Treatment

Intervention will clearly depend on the outcome of the assessment. The basic principles of intervention include a clear, consistent approach, with offers of help being made and delivered within realistic limits (Marlowe and Sugarman, 1997). General measures include forming a long-term therapeutic relationship with the patient; this, in itself, is usually a therapeutic goal given that this group of patients are notoriously poor at forming relationships.

Specific measures for intervention may include drug and psychological treatments. Examples of drug treatments might include selective serotonin reuptake inhibitors for borderline type emotional instability, and carbamazepine for aggressive behaviour. Psychological interventions such as cognitive-behavioural therapy, assertiveness training and anxiety management have been shown to be effective in the management of dependent and anxious patients. Anger management may be used in patients with aggressive behaviour. A comprehensive discussion of the assessment and treatability of psychopathic disorder can be found in Dolan and Coid (1993).

Personality disordered patients have a long-standing reputation of being difficult to treat. Some consider that there is an air of therapeutic nihilism when it comes to treating personality disorders, but it should always be remembered that these patients are distressed by their difficulty and a personality disorder label should not equate to untreatability. Future hopes lie in research to determine which interventions are effective in this difficult group of patients.

For Further Reading

Dolan, B. and Coid, J. 1993: *Psychopathic and Antisocial Personality Disorders: Treatment and Research Issues*. London: Gaskell.
Marlowe, M. and Sugarman, P. 1997: ABC of mental health disorders of personality. *British Medical Journal*, 315, 176–9.
World Health Organization 1992: *The ICD-10 Classification of Mental and Behavioural Disorders – Clinical Descriptions and Diagnostic Guidelines*. Geneva: WHO.

DAMIAN MOHAN

Phobias

In *phobias*, certain situations or objects, not usually seen as dangerous, provoke anxiety. The severity of anxiety and the avoidance of the trigger are seen as abnormal. Examples of phobias include claustrophobia (distress in confined spaces), social phobia (meeting people), or specific phobias (for example, a fear of animals or of flying). One-year prevalence rates are 10 per cent. Treatment is mainly behavioural and desensitization.

CLAIRE KENWOOD AND RAY VIEWEG

Physical Disability

The most widespread view of *disability* in Western society is based upon the assumption that the difficulties disabled people experience are a direct result of their individual physical and sensory impairments. This is often referred to as the *individual model* of disability. Thus the deaf person who misses the train does so because he or she failed to hear the announcement; the blind person who falls down a hole in the pavement does so because he or she failed to see it; and the person with a motor impairment is prevented from entering the building because he or she cannot walk. The effect of the physical, attitudinal and social environment on disabled people is regarded as relatively fixed and the onus is on disabled people to adapt to a disabling environment, to function as 'normally' as possible, and to accept and adjust to their situation without complaint. These expectations of how disabled people should behave have been referred to as the 'disabled role'.

The social model of disability

The conception of disability as an individual problem is something that disabled people, particularly since the growth of the Disabled People's Movement, have been increasingly challenging. The Disabled People's Movement can be regarded as one of the 'new social movements' which emerged during the second half of the twentieth century; the Women's Movement, the Black Civil Rights Movement and Gay Pride are other examples. The aim of these movements is to gain equality and social justice. Perhaps the most significant turning point for the Disabled People's Movement in Britain was the formation in 1974 of the Union of the Physically Impaired Against Segregation (UPIAS) which fought to change the definition of disability from one of individual tragedy to one of social oppression.

Within the individual model of disability, *impairment* and *disability* are terms which are used interchangeably. Within the *social model of disability*, however, *impairment* is regarded as the physical difference or malfunction of the body, such as blindness or paraplegia, and *disability* is regarded as the disadvantage disabled people experience within society because of structural, environmental and attitudinal barriers which impinge upon them, and which have the potential to impede their inclusion and progress in many areas of life, including employment, education and leisure.

- *Structural barriers* refer to the underlying norms, mores and ideologies of organizations and institutions which are based on judgements of 'normality' and 'independence' which are sustained by hierarchies of power.
- *Environmental barriers* refer both to physical obstacles within the environment – for example, steps to climb or holes in the pavement – and to the lack of resources for disabled people – for example, lack of braille or sign language interpreters. Environmental barriers may also refer to the way things are done which may exclude disabled people – for example, the way meetings are conducted, and the time allowed for various tasks in employment.
- *Attitudinal barriers* refer to the adverse attitudes and behaviour of non-disabled people towards disabled people such as pity, over-protection and hostility.

Disabled people are thus engaged in a struggle to replace the individual model of disability with a model couched in terms of civil rights. This struggle is paralleled in the Women's Movement, the Black Civil Rights Movements, Gay Pride and the survivors of the mental health system where there has also been a move away from an individual notion of deficit to a social constructionist view of oppression.

continued

Institutional discrimination

The notion of *institutional discrimination* has played an important role in the development of disability theory in recent years. It refers to the unfair or unequal treatment of individuals or groups which is built into organizations, policies and practices at personal, environmental and structural levels. Disabled people face institutional discrimination in a social and physical world that is geared by, for and towards non-disabled people. The commonalities in issues of racism, sexism, homophobia and disablism can be explored through themes such as prejudiced attitudes, power relationships, the denial of rights and discriminatory language, while also highlighting differences in the form of discrimination faced by different groups. Essential to understanding institutional discrimination is to reject individualized, or victim-blaming explanations of unjust treatment and to recognize that inequalities are woven into the very structure and fabric of society. Figure 2 depicts these barriers as the bricks in a wall of institutional discrimination.

ATTITUDINAL	Cognitive prejudice: assumptions about the (in)abilities, emotional responses and needs of disabled people		Emotional prejudice: fear	Behavioural prejudice: individual practice and praxis	CEMENTED BY
ENVIRONMENTAL	Disablist language	Institutional policies, organization, rules and regulations	Professional practices: assessment, care management	Inaccessible physical environments	IDEOLOGIES OF 'NORMALITY'
STRUCTURAL	Hierarchical power relations and structures: the disempowerment of disabled people		The denial of human, social and welfare rights	Structural inequalities: poverty	AND 'INDEPENDENCE'

Figure 2 The SEAwall of institutional discrimination
Source: Reproduced with acknowledgement from Swain et al. (1998).

In this model of institutional discrimination, attitudinal barriers are constructed on environmental barriers which are themselves constructed on structural barriers. Ideology plays a key role in the inter-reliance between each layer. The ideology of normality, for example, is manifest in all the rules, regulations, patterns of behaviour, social organization and aids to daily living that marginalize disabled people from the mainstream of society.

Disabled people throughout the world have joined forces to challenge their exclusion within society and to gain their rights as equal citizens. In 1981, Disabled People's International was formed as an international umbrella group of organizations of disabled people. It represents over 70 national assemblies of disabled people and is recognized by the UN as the representative body of disabled people internationally. The struggle of disabled people has led in some parts of the world (for example, in the USA and Australia) to comprehensive Disability Discrimination Legislation. In the UK, the first Disability Discrimination Act was passed in 1995; it is, however, weak and cannot, at present, be regarded as full civil rights legislation.

Although the individual model of disability is still prominent within society, disabled people and their allies have put forward a strong challenge in favour of the social model, and this has undoubtedly fostered major changes in their lives.

For Further Reading
Campbell, J. and Oliver, M. 1996: *Disability Politics: Understanding our Past, Changing our Future*. Routledge: London.
Oliver, M. 1996: *Understanding Disability: From Theory to Practice*. Macmillan: London.
Swain, J., Gillman, M. and French, S. 1998: *Confronting Disabling Barriers: Towards Making Organisations Accessible*. Venture Press: Birmingham.

SALLY FRENCH

Play Therapy

Play therapy is a means of creating intense relationship experiences between therapist and child or young person, in which play is the principal medium of communication. In common with other therapies, the purpose of these experiences is to bring about changes in the individual's primary relationships, which are held to have become distorted in development, so that normal developmental progress may be resumed. Play is used, in contrast to verbal approaches with adults, because it is a highly adaptive activity of childhood and has an organizing function during development, making use of largely non-verbal symbols, and is one of the main ways in which children develop understandings, explore conflicts and rehearse emotional and social skills.

Major approaches to play therapy, which developed following Anna Freud and Melanie Klein's incorporation of play into psychoanalytic sessions with children in the 1930s, include psychoanalytic play therapy, cognitive-behavioural play therapy and non-directive or child-centred play therapy. Of these, the latter, which was originally adapted by Virginia Axline from Rogerian psychotherapy, is probably the most widely practised.

For Further Reading
Wilson, K., Kendrick, P. and Ryan, V. 1992: *Play Therapy: A Non-directive Approach for Children and Adolescents*. London: Baillière Tindall.

KATE WILSON

Police Officers and the Interface with Social Work

Relationships across the *police/social work divide* are traditionally infused with tension as a result of different working practices, stereotypical ideas that each group holds about the other, and lack of trust. Where closer working relationships are facilitated, many of these barriers can be overcome. Joint training and working has become commonplace in child protection, domestic violence and sex offender work, and social workers operate alongside police officers in youth offender teams.

Although the focus of police and social work intervention is different, there are opportunities for knowledge and skills to be shared, particularly in relation to investigative interviewing. Both groups have a commitment to child protection and to ensuring that, wherever possible, young people generally and adults affected by mental ill health or learning disabilities are diverted from custody.

Some of the underlying objectives of social work and police work are broadly similar: for example, both groups regulate society by protecting vulnerable people and by investigating instances of alleged abuse. However, although police officers and social workers often work with the same individuals and families, they operate at different places on the care-control continuum.

Individually and collectively, police officers are primarily identified with law enforcement, but the relevance of their role for front-line social work should not be underestimated.

For Further Reading
Offer, J. 1999: *Social Workers, the Community and Social Interaction*. London: Jessica Kingsley, ch. 6.

ROSE BARTON

Political Correctness

Political correctness is a term commonly used to criticize social work policies supposedly based on ideology and the 'correct attitude' rather

257

than common sense or human need. These tend most frequently to concern race, adoption, professional training, and children's rights. The term is also used to criticize changes in vocabulary – *learning difficulty* or *disability* for *mental handicap*, *disabled person* for *cripple*, *mental illness* for *madness*.

Ironically, the term was first used self-mockingly by members of the Communist Party in reaction to so-called 'correct lineism'. Its more modern usage originated on the campuses of the USA in the 1960s.

It is alleged that political correctness is so prevalent in areas like social work that it encourages self-censorship; thus, alternative policies will not be put forward and unpalatable truths not expressed. Robert Hughes (1993) argues that it creates a 'linguistic Lourdes', and that change of vocabulary is seen as a substitute for action.

In opposition to this, it is said that what is called 'politically correct' is really a sensitivity to culture and gender, and a regard for the rights of others in policy formulation and service provision.

For Further Reading
Hughes, R. 1993: *The Culture of Complaint*. Oxford: Oxford University Press.
Philpot, T. (ed.) 1999: *Political Correctness and Social Work*. London: Institute of Economic Affairs.

TERRY PHILPOT

Politics and Social Work

Social work is derived from organized power and concerned with how power is used and misused in all relationships. *Politics* dominates many of our day-to-day activities and is often associated with the party politics which govern formal political decision making in most advanced Western societies.

The universality of politics

Not only is politics concerned with the governance of states; it also involves power that is mobilized in interactions within small groups like families or in decision making at work. Similarly, it is often associated with the notion of collective action and the way this is articulated, mediated and negotiated. Any definition of politics needs to encompass all these macro and micro elements. Perhaps *politics* is best understood as a process which seeks to manage or resolve conflicts of interest between people, if possible in a peaceful fashion, and to conduct relationships between organized groups within society. At the macro level, it can be seen to refer to the many and complex relationships which exist between public institutions, particularly in central and local government, and in the rest of society (Jordan and Parton, 1983). In a more general sense, however, it describes the interactions of any group of individuals and the individuals themselves in their day-to-day contexts.

In this sense, social work is heavily implicated with politics at all levels. The policy and practice of social work is influenced by, and in many respects is determined by, the changing political contexts in which it operates. In particular, political decision making – for example, by the passage of new legislation which both legitimates and proscribes the activities of the organizations that employ social workers – directly impacts on the responsibilities of social workers, and the mandate by which they operate. The introduction of new legislation or a change in the implementation of policies at central and local government levels will mobilize organized interest groups, including those of professional social workers and some service users.

The language of politics and social work

At the same time, the nature of social work practice is such that its work with individuals, families, groups and wider communities means that it is always involved in negotiating between different interests and alternative points of view. Many of the processes which social workers engage in have certain important similarities with those engaged in by others who are formally called politicians. The language of politics and the language of social work contain a number of common words such as *justice, fairness, inclusion, negotiation, participation* and *partnership*.

These should not be seen as simply technical or professional terms in either the social work or political fields; both have moral dimensions (Jordan, 1990). For example, *justice* describes both a set of principles governing processes of decision making and the outcomes that are aimed for.

Negotiation is neither an activity confined to certain formal political settings such as international summit conferences, nor is it specifically a professional social work skill: it is *the way in which* people discuss matters so as to settle apparent conflicts of interest which is important, as well as the result. Before conflicts of interest can be negotiated, some recognition has to take place that they exist, and some machinery of reconciliation be established; this applies as much to the conflicting interests of parents caught up in marital breakdown or to the different concerns of a frail and confused elderly person and their carer as it does to a meeting on arms limitation.

The same is true of the notion of *participation*: it is neither simply a description of a particular political system such as one-person-one-vote, nor of a social work method; what we mean by *participation* is that people have choices and are encouraged to exercise them in a positive way so as to further their interests and increase their welfare. It is, in this respect, that the transactions that take place between social workers and their clients or users are essentially political. While these political dimensions may not always be recognized, they are central to what it is to do social work and to understand the authority of, and the limits on the authority of, the social worker.

Social work and the state

In a wider sense, however, it is important to recognize that the growth of social work has always been closely related to its changing relationship with the state, particularly the post-war welfare state. While social workers are employed in a range of private and voluntary organizations, the majority of social workers in the UK have, since World War II, been employed in state agencies, particularly by local authorities. In this respect, they are carrying out the statutory obligations of those organizations. It is, in this sense, that social work is closely constrained by its links with formal politics itself.

Further, however, the issues, priorities and tasks developed and carried out by social workers are crucially related to the political contexts and climate in which they operate, and recent years have witnessed an increasingly hostile political climate for social work where social workers have been seen to fall down on their responsibilities, particularly their statutory responsibility in child welfare and mental health fields. The way in which social work has been represented in the media has been essentially negative, and this can be seen to have had an impact on the way it is seen by politicians, the wider public and the clients and users with whom they work. One of the consequences of this, certainly in the UK, has been that areas of professional discretion, previously associated with social work decision making, have increasingly been circumscribed by new legislation, government guidance and the introduction of specified procedures. All of these can be seen as an attempt to tighten the accountability of social workers to those in central and local government.

Another change since the late 1980s has been a growth in the role of private and voluntary organizations in the provision of social care, including that given under contract to central and local government. This has partly been an attempt to 'depoliticize' issues of care, as well as to contain costs and improve efficiency (Jordan, 1997). However, such changes simply relocate political decisions from public, democratically regulated bodies into civil society or the economy, and call forth new relations between organized interests.

continued

For Further Reading
Jordan, B. 1990: *Social Work in an Unjust Society*. Hemel Hempstead: Harvester Wheatsheaf.
Jordan, B. 1997: Social work and society. In M. Davies (ed.), *The Blackwell Companion to Social Work* (1st edn), Oxford: Blackwell.
Jordan, B. and Parton, N. (eds) 1983: *The Political Dimensions of Social Work*. Oxford: Blackwell.

BILL JORDAN AND NIGEL PARTON

Positive Regard

See UNCONDITIONAL POSITIVE REGARD.

Post-adoption Work

Adoption in the UK was first formalized in the Adoption Act 1926, although informal adoptions had served as an alternative means of building a family long before this. The purpose of the Act was to formalize the adoption process whereby parental responsibility was transferred from birth parents to adoptive parents. The adoption process at this time was seen as a 'better' option for raising children born, in most cases, out of wedlock.

During the last twenty years, however, there has been a significant shift in the way that the family and illegitimacy are viewed. Consequently, current UK legislation requires the provision of a comprehensive service that allows adopted children to have access to their birth records. It is, however, recognized that there is a conflict of interest between the different parties that makes it difficult for a single authority to provide a comprehensive *post-adoption service*.

A number of voluntary agencies have been established. The first of these was the Post-Adoption Centre in London which advocates a tripartite model that identifies post-adoption work according to the three different participant groups:

1 Birth parents can be provided with individual counselling, advocacy and support, independent of the child placement agency (normally a local authority), and intermediary work with adoptees which can facilitate a reunion. Where the adoption has been contested, a mediation service can be offered to facilitate co-operation between the parties.
2 Adoptive parents can be provided with advice, education and support relating to the parenting of adopted children, and also systemic family therapy.
3 Adoptees can be provided with counselling which will give them an opportunity to express their feelings about being adopted, access to birth records, intermediary work with their birth parents and the opportunity to attend groups before or after a reunion. For those who have been transracially adopted, specific counselling will normally provide an opportunity to explore racial identity issues.

For Further Reading
Hughes, B. 1994: *Post-placement Services for Children and Families: Defining the Need*. London: Department of Health.

MONICA DUCK

Postmodernism

Postmodernism refers to a number of strands of social theory influenced by poststructuralist epistemology and substantive concerns raised within it.

These theoretical concerns are 'post' modernism in the sense that they deal critically with the assumptions held to underlie modernist theory: that there is an underlying unity and direction to social life; that there is a common set of standards and values against which to measure progress; and that the mechanisms of social change are available to discovery by the positive sciences, so that knowledge has a key role to play in the achievement of social progress.

In postmodernist theory, the social world is seen as intrinsically fragmented, history as an uneven set of power relationships between different groups in struggle, and knowledge as a set of discourses intrinsically linked to different political projects and relations of power. There is an emphasis on the cultural construction of inequalities and the political dimension of cultural and symbolic practices.

Postmodernist theoretical concerns have led to an intense debate about whether aspirations to social progress and social justice can be achieved. Critics of postmodernism claim that the emphasis on the fragmented and conflictual nature of the social, combined with a relativist view of knowledge and ethics, leads to conservative or nihilistic political positions that abdicate responsibility for a progressive politics of welfare. These issues are addressed by Peter Leonard (1997) in a substantial examination of the modernist ideal of the welfare state as an embodiment of moral progress and humanistic concern with improving the lives of the disadvantaged. Providing a sustained analysis of the deconstructions of these ideological foundations and the role of welfare services, and discourses in constructing and maintaining relations of domination and subordination, Leonard sees emerging from debates in and with postmodernism possibilities for reconstructing an emancipatory politics of welfare, rather than a sterile stand-off between irreconcilable positions.

For Further Reading
Carter, J. (ed.) 1998: *Postmodernity and the Fragmentation of Welfare*. London: Routledge.
Leonard, P. 1997: *Postmodern Welfare: Reconstructing an Emancipatory Knowledge*. London: Sage.
O'Brien, M., Penna, S. and Hay, C. (eds) 1998: *Theorising Modernity – Reflexivity, Environment and Identity in Giddens' Social Theory*. New York: Addison Wesley Longman.

SUE PENNA

Postmodernity
The term *postmodernity* is used in a number of different senses to capture changes taking place in contemporary Western societies. These changes include: decolonization, the collapse of Soviet communism, changing patterns of consumption and employment, the decline of western economies, the declining authority of symbols of cultural and political power, changing lifestyles and political concerns, and the development of cyber time and space. Whether these and other changes represent a radical departure from the modern, a transition to a postmodern era, is vigorously disputed.

In social work, the themes of the postmodernity debate have been taken up in the work of Parton (1994) to analyse the changing nature of the organization of social work. The shift from a conception of social work as a generic activity that takes place in the context of a unified organizational structure and is characterized by an emphasis on case work, to one of fragmented, multiple service provision, purchaser–provider divisions, interagency co-ordination and case management is understood as a marker of the postmodernization of welfare institutions and practices. Here, changes in social work institutions and practices are understood as part of a more general set of transformations sweeping Western societies, transformations that suggest the emergence of a more fragmented and diverse society than the one it replaces.

Such understandings of contemporary changes are contested on three main grounds.

1 Postmodernism, a set of theoretical currents in the social sciences, proposes that diversity and fragmentation has always been a constituent feature of social life. What is new is our recognition of the differences, particularly under the impact of decolonization, multiculturalism and new social movement politics, such as feminism.
2 More mainstream theorists draw attention to a methodological problem: we can only talk about a 'post' era by drawing an over-homogenized picture of the past and ignoring continuities in the present.
3 Others argue that many of the changes that we are seeing are the outcome of modernizing logics and, thus, represent an intensification of the dynamics of modernity, rather than a transition to a postmodern era.

For Further Reading
O'Brien, M. and Penna, S. 1998: *Theorising Welfare – Enlightenment and Modern Society*, London: Sage, chs 7 and 8.
Parton, N. 1994: 'Problematics of government', (post) modernity and social work. *British Journal of Social Work*, 24, 9–32.

SUE PENNA

Poststructuralism
Poststructuralism refers to theoretical orientations inspired, in particular, by the work of Michel Foucault and Jacques Derrida. Much of

261

this work has a political focus in as much as it developed in the context of debates among left wing French intellectuals disillusioned with the direction taken by Soviet communism and with the repressive and autocratic structures of the communist party in France. The theoretical and philosophical foundations of Marxism and the 'meta-narratives' of Enlightenment theory became a focus of their work.

Foucault's concern was with the relationship of knowledge to power. In particular, he questioned any account of historical development that viewed it as a progression from barbaric to humane, or primitive to civilized. Through examinations of the organization and production of meanings – of 'madness', sexuality, crime and deviance – Foucault argued that the modern era saw an 'epistemic shift' in social thought around the eighteenth century, where new ways of thinking were conjoined to new methods of administering and regulating populations. The rise of psychology, social work, criminology and so on were, for Foucault, part of a micro-technology of power where the focus of power and control shifts from the body as the site of punishment or regulation to the psyche – an exercise in which armies of experts are drafted in to 'normalize' deviant individuals and social groups, instilling self-normalization into the population through cultural and administrative means.

Derrida's work is concerned with the many meanings contained in any text and the impossibility of any absolute or essential truth. Together with Foucault's critical appraisals of knowledge, it has generated an emphasis on the instability of meaning, the impossibility of arriving at foundational 'truths' about the world, the myth of linearity and thus the impossibility of prediction, and the role of knowledge and technologies of cultural production in oppressive exercises of power and minority subjugation.

These themes have been taken up in social work research through the deconstruction of social work documents, analysing how apparently well-intentioned expert judgements conceal prejudiced and controlling exercises in subjugating certain social groups; analysing the role of social work knowledge and practice as part of a network of micro-technologies that serve to control rather than care for or assist vulnerable groups; and examining the ways in which the normative bases of entry into welfare systems are embedded in prescrip-tive identity logics which display a cultural politics of representations and demarcations that centralize and privilege some forms of identity and social membership while marginalizing others.

For Further Reading

O'Brien, M. and Penna, S. 1998: *Theorising Welfare – Enlightenment and Modern Society*, London: Sage, ch 4.
Parton, N. 1991: *Governing the Family: Child Care, Child Protection and the State*. London: Macmillan.

SUE PENNA

Post-traumatic Stress Disorder (PTSD)

Post-traumatic stress disorder (PTSD) is a psychiatric syndrome precipitated by trauma, which is perceived by the individual to involve actual or threatened serious injury or death to themselves or others. The diagnosis is clinched in the presence of three clinical features, which persist for more than a month.

1 Repeated re-experiences of the event in the form of flashbacks, memories or nightmare
2 Avoidance of stimuli associated with the event, for example not travelling on a train if involved in a train crash
3 Hyper-arousal, including hyper-vigilance, anxiety and sleep disturbance

If the symptoms are transient and occur soon after the traumatic event then the diagnosis is of an 'acute stress reaction'. Trauma can also precipitate other conditions such as other neurotic (anxiety) disorders and depression. Not all individuals exposed to severe life-threatening situations develop PTSD. Patients with PTSD often have other psychiatric conditions such as depression or substance misuse problems.

Treatment is mainly psychological and uses graded exposure techniques. The immediate debriefing of victims after traumatic events may reduce the risk of developing PTSD. Outcome is variable and a history of psychiatric illness may confer a poorer prognosis.

For Further Reading

Gelder, M., Gath, D., Mayou, R. and Cowen, P. 1996: *Oxford Textbook of Psychiatry*. Oxford: Oxford University Press.

CLAIRE KENWOOD AND RAY VIEWEG

Poverty

Poverty is the enforced lack of those material items which a majority of people accept as essential for participation in society. People who do not already have, or because of low income are unable to purchase, the goods and services which would allow them to participate fully in society are living in poverty.

The condition is defined as relative in three senses: to an epoch; to a society; and to what counts as a reasonable standard of living. Poor people are unequal with other citizens in that they are excluded from complete participation in society. Along with a personal lack of material possessions, poor people will also be deprived of full access to services, such as leisure, transport, shopping, consumer credit, health and education. Adam Smith, the liberal economist, wrote in *The Wealth of Nations* (1776) that, besides food, the 'necessaries' of life included 'what ever the custom of the country renders it indecent for creditable people, even the lowest orders, to be without'.

Determining the threshold

The essential question is: whether there is a threshold of income above which the adequate standard of living is achieved and below which it is not. There are three objective methods of identifying and counting the poor:

1   In the *consensus* or 'Breadline Britain' approach, researchers discover what the majority of people believe are the necessities of decent life which nobody should be without. They prioritize: hot, high-protein food; weather-resistant clothing; a warm, dry dwelling. Then, they identify those people who lack a significant number of the necessities. Research can go on to determine the cost of these necessities and so seek a threshold of income which correlates with increasing deprivation of those items.
2   In the *attitudinal* approach, it is assumed that people are themselves the best judges of the minimum incomes needed to 'make ends meet'. Investigation reveals which people do not achieve such a minimum income.
3   The *budget* approach is a hybrid of empirical investigation and expert prescription. Prescription establishes a decent standard of living (a *basket of goods*) and empirical investigation reveals at what income level (the *budget*), it could be achieved. There are two ways of investigating whether the 'basket' is being purchased on the 'budget': either using households' total purchases, or just the most important items – food, housing and utilities.

These research methods do not identify a *poverty line*, but rather a high probability of low income being associated with high deprivations of the agreed goods and services. Hence, the poor have both low income and a low standard of living. Some countries – Australia and the USA, for example – use such measures to establish rates of social assistance.

Social assistance

Rates of social assistance are not necessarily any indication of a poverty line. The UK and French schemes, for example, offer no justification as to their adequacy. It is a British tradition not to claim that benefits lift recipients out of poverty, but it is certainly true that the poorest people do live on social security benefit. Whether all those claimants are in poverty is a matter for research, as there is little relationship between the rates of benefit and a minimum level of adequacy established by research.

Benefit levels are based on political decisions about how much the government is willing to pay to certain groups of people who are cast as 'dependent'. Though social

continued

assistance is by definition designed for the poor, the payments to some people may be demonstrably inadequate to provide a living standard for social participation, while other recipients may be reasonably well-off.

Who are 'the poor'?

The demographic groups most at risk of being poor are unemployed people, the oldest people, children, lone mothers, disabled people, and offenders. However, taking the *groups at risk* approach involves using data which is either a mere claimant count, or uses some other arbitrary construct such as the EU standard for 'poverty', which is half the average household income. The UK government produces an annual series, *Households Below Average Income,* which uses that standard. Around 14 million people, or a quarter of the UK population live below the standard – and, if that is poverty, a third of our children are brought up in it. The unemployed constitute a fifth of the people who live below half the average household income. They are an increasing proportion of the poor, along with lone parents, while the elderly have declined as a proportion of the poorest households. The financial circumstances of young offenders under supervision to the probation service has deteriorated to such an extent that they count among the poorest, most deprived citizens, especially when unemployment is compounded with homelessness.

Degrees of poverty

As the number of people in poverty has grown, so too has the degree of their poverty. For example, the average family with two children among the poorest tenth of households experienced a fall of £18 per week in disposable income between 1979 and 1995. The main reasons for the increase in poverty are: a growing income gap between people who are economically active and those who are not; a greater proportion of people do not have income from employment; and wage inequality has increased to the level it was in the late nineteenth century.

Developing the connection between wages and poverty, because social security payments impact with entry-level wages, recent governments have adopted the carrot and stick approach of both disciplining claimants back to work and 'making work pay' by offering in-work benefits. In 1998, 760,000 people worked for their poverty standard of living in the sense that they received means-tested in-work benefits to top-up their average £114 per week earnings to an average of £173. Politicians said that those entirely reliant on benefit income were in a 'dependency culture', to which the government's answer was – work, but at low wages with social security top-up.

Poverty is of significance in social work because it has been established that a growing majority of service users (at least two-thirds, even of those of working age) live on benefit income; the information and advice most frequently requested by them from social workers is about material help. Social workers can be effective advocates on behalf of service users, helping them obtain full benefit entitlements, discretionary payments and charity.

For Further Reading

Gordon, D. and Pantazis, C. 1995: *Breadline Britain in the 1990s.* York: Joseph Rowntree Foundation.

Nolan, B. and Whelan, C. 1996: *Resources Deprivation and Poverty.* Oxford: Oxford University Press.

Townsend, P. 1996: *A Poor Future.* London: Lemos & Crane.

JOHN STEWART

Power
See EMPOWERMENT and POLITICS AND SOCIAL WORK

Practical Help
Practical help is the identification, mobilization and provision of tangible, beneficial services, including material goods, to individuals, families or groups whose needs meet the criteria of a particular agency. Criteria may derive from legislation (for example, children in need, or carers), an agency's stated aims and objectives, and theoretical concepts concerned with human development, needs and rights. Alleviation of poverty, the promotion of social justice and the removal of external stresses may underpin this type of intervention. The level (frequency and duration) of practical help may be determined by assessment of need and the availability of resources, with local factors such as geographical remoteness playing a part.

Users of services value practical help highly because immediate material problems are addressed, and such action demonstrates care and concern. Providers need to acquire and maintain a good working knowledge of resources in their locality.

Practical help is consistent with principles of empowerment when volunteers or professionals strive to promote strengths in users' situations, as well as make up for deficits. It is valid in prevention, support and rehabilitation.

For Further Reading
Davies, M. 1994: *The Essential Social Worker* (3rd edn). Aldershot: Arena.

ELAINE ENNIS

Practice Teaching
Practice teaching is the input to a student social worker's learning, during qualification training, which takes place in a social work agency during a placement or 'practicum'. The practice teacher (sometimes called a supervisor or field instructor) has responsibility for both teaching and assessing the student, balancing the tension between helping the student to learn effectively and evaluating his/her professional competence with a pass/fail recommendation. The practice teacher seeks evidence of the student's personal skills, observes practice and invites self assessment.

The practice teacher is a social work practitioner who may supervise an individual student (a 'singleton') or several students ('dedicated'); the latter can comprise a student unit or practice learning centre. The practice teacher focuses on linking theory to practice, and developing skills, understanding and values, while supervising the student in practising social work with allocated clients, groups or projects. Arrangements can exist for a partnership between a 'long arm' practice teacher, who carries the assessment and overview, and an on-site supervisor who holds the day-to-day coaching and observation. Practice teaching itself can be assessed and accredited and requires experience and training.

For Further Reading
Shardlow, S. and Doel, M. 1996: *Practice Learning and Teaching*. Basingstoke: Macmillan.

ROBIN BURGESS

Prediction
Prediction refers to the assessment of the future behaviour of an individual, group or institution. The focus of prediction may be the nature of future behaviour, its likelihood and/or its severity. In the context of social work, prediction is most commonly associated with work with offenders, the mentally ill and child protection, and is intimately associated with the concept of *risk*.

Since the 1970s, prediction in social work and, particularly, in work with offenders, has been moving towards more formalized methods. Increasingly sophisticated statistically based instruments have been developed to increase the consistency and accuracy of prediction. These have included instruments which calculate the likelihood that an offender will receive a custodial sentence ('risk of custody' scales) as well as predictors of the likelihood of reoffending in a specific time period. Such 'actuarial' scales are typically based on a limited range of 'static' variables (for example, age and previous offending history), but more sophisticated or 'third generation' models began to emerge in the 1990s. These models incorporate 'dynamic' variables, such as employment and health status, which are amenable to change during a period of supervision.

For Further Reading
Bonta, J. 1996: Risk-needs assessment and treatment. In A. T. Harland (ed.), *Choosing Correctional Options that Work*, London: Sage, 18–32.

GWEN ROBINSON

Pre-sentence Reports

A *pre-sentence report (PSR)* is simply defined by statute as a written report 'made or submitted' by a probation officer, local authority social worker or youth offending team member, 'with a view to assisting the court in determining the most suitable method of dealing with an offender'. A court is ordinarily required by law to obtain and consider a report in determining the following sentencing issues:

- Is an offence so serious that only a custodial sentence can be justified?
- If an offence is sufficiently serious, what is the commensurate custodial term?
- In the case of a violent or sexual offence, would only a custodial term be adequate to protect the public from serious harm? If so, is a longer term required than that commensurate with the offence's seriousness?
- If an offence is serious enough to warrant a 'community sentence', is the offender suitable for certain measures?

PSRs succeeded the old form of *social inquiry reports*, which allowed huge variation from the irrelevantly biographical to the most narrowly formulaic. The form and content of reports is now closely prescribed in Home Office *National Standards* which describe their purpose thus: 'to provide a systematic assessment of the nature and causes of the defendant's offending, the risk the defendant poses to the public and the action which can be taken to reduce the likelihood of re-offending'. A report should contain four elements: an offence analysis, an offender assessment, identification of the risk of harm to the public and the likelihood of reoffending, and a conclusion.

Offence analysis

Intended to assist the court's judgement of offence seriousness, the *offence analysis* should assist the court to understand why the offender committed this offence at this time. If 'seriousness' can be conceptualized as a blend of harm caused and culpability, a report can add value to a court's assessment and the advocates' accounts by illuminating the latter element – the offender's motivation, intentions, beliefs and assumptions, their cognitive and emotional processes in approaching and pursuing the crime:

- How premeditated or spontaneous was their offending?
- What extent of harm did they anticipate?
- Was the choice of victim random or deliberate?
- Was the offence racially motivated?
- To what extent was the offender's judgement influenced or impaired by alcohol/ drugs, psychological or physical ill-health, emotional strain, unusually adverse circumstances?

The crime can thus be better located in the richness of context. Some such factors are of uncertain relevance and weight in assessing seriousness but can best be gathered by objective professional inquiry. Inquiries are normally limited to the defendant's retrospective account, using only the prosecution version of events and the reporter's experience as a foil to inevitable evasion, minimization and self-deception.

One obvious consequence of introducing another account of the crime into criminal proceedings is that the report may give a version of the facts which is substantially and materially different from that presented by the prosecution or previously accepted by the defence as the basis for a guilty plea, thus placing in doubt the factual basis for sentencing. For example, a defendant facing sentence for possession of drugs with intent to supply may tell the reporter that they were simply transporting the drugs under coercion. Or a defendant facing sentence for sexual offences against children may reveal to the reporter that their abuse was of a more serious nature than previously acknowledged. In such instances, it may be necessary for the court to hold a further inquiry, receiving evidence to determine the version of events on which to sentence.

Moving to a consideration of post-offence issues, *National Standards* expect reporters to assess the consequences of the crime, including 'the impact on any victim', a matter which the reporter has no authority to investigate. More central to the task is an evaluation of the offender's sensitivity to the victim's predicament, the extent of their remorse and their desire to make amends. Remorse beyond a guilty plea is difficult to quantify but the Court of Appeal has indicated that credit can be gained through 'hard evidence of genuine remorse and regret', and has also pointed out the relevance of a reporter's view that a defendant fails to demonstrate sufficient appreciation of their guilt. The confessional quality of the PSR encounter is thus highlighted, as well as the extent to which the reporter may lead the offender in gauging their feelings.

Offender assessment
Though an assessment of the offender's personal and social circumstances, including their family difficulties, mental disorder or substance misuse, may seem designed primarily to assist the court in deciding on the suitability of relevant sentencing options, factors addressed in respect of *the offender* also relate to seriousness, particularly in addressing the offender's motives, criminal record and response to previous intervention. The report can locate the current offence within the overall pattern of offending, perhaps by showing a propensity to offend in particular circumstances or by negating a claim of one-off opportunism or exceptional loss of self-control. A report can also identify the extent to which an offender is alert to a problem in their behaviour which they wish to tackle or, better still, have already taken steps to address. Given, too, a court's scope to take account in mitigation of any matters related to the offender as it considers relevant, a report can detail factors that may otherwise not be apparent, such as good citizenship demonstrated by the offender in other areas of their life, or opportunities now open to the offender which may be affected by sentence.

Risk of harm and likelihood of reoffending
Though the offender normally stands to be sentenced for offences committed rather than for the risk they pose of future crime, the *Standards* require reporters to give distinctive attention to the likelihood and nature of reoffending and also to identify any risks of self-harm. This can be the most speculative and tentative feature of reporting but may helpfully indicate the kind of interventive action that could serve to reduce risk and, thus, suggest the positive potential of some sentencing options.

Conclusion
Reflecting the preceding assessments, the PSR may be able to propose a suitable programme of work with the offender within the ambit of a community sentence, or to indicate their suitability for less personal measures, or otherwise to anticipate the likely consequences of custody including the adverse impact on third persons.

PSRs demand intensive assessment skills, meeting tight deadlines in anticipation of public scrutiny. They can follow the offender through the penal system as a valuable resource for further assessment. They are a tangible product by which agencies are judged on their performance.

Reporters can feel that they count for little when sentencing outcomes are inevitable on the basis of the core facts, whatever their contribution. PSRs carry greatest direct influence when concerning offenders who sit on the borderline between custodial and non-custodial sentences or in assisting courts to select the most appropriate community sentence. Perhaps their greatest understated value is to give subjects time and attention

continued

to reflect on their crimes in context within a process that can cause offenders often to feel marginalized and unheard.

For Further Reading
Cavadino, M. 1997: Pre-sentence reports: the effects of legislation and national standards. *British Journal of Criminology*, 37 (4), 529–48.
Home Office 2000: *National Standards for the Supervision of Offenders in the Community*. London: Home Office.
Stone, N. 1992: Pre-sentence reports, culpability and the 1991 Act. *Criminal Law Review*, 558–67.

NIGEL STONE

Primary Health Care, The Role of Social Workers in

The *role of social workers in primary health care* varies from simple liaison schemes to practice-based social work (PBSW) in which a social worker is based in a GP practice and provides a service for patients registered with it.

Research indicates that PBSW schemes increase the productivity of social workers and improve the quality of care received by elderly and/or disabled people. Referrals from the primary care team increase, and more clients self-refer because of the accessibility and lack of stigma of doctors' surgeries. This higher workload is manageable because of improved information exchange within the primary care team, reduced travel time (especially in rural areas), and a simpler process for allocating workload. Few PBSW schemes have involved children's services.

The success of PBSW schemes depends on shared commitment by social services and the GP practice, and the willingness of social services managers to devolve responsibility. A dispersed work-force requires social services departments to develop more explicit arrangements for supervision and quality monitoring.

For Further Reading
Cumella, S. and Le Mesurier, N. 1999: Re-designing health and social care for older people: Multi-skill case teams in primary care. *Managing Community Care*, 7 (6), 17–24.

STUART CUMELLA

Prison-based Social Work

Prison-based social work is the provision of social work services in a custodial institution. It is sometimes defined to include the use of social work skills by other people including uniformed, disciplinary staff; but, strictly speaking, social work in prisons refers to the service provided by professionally qualified staff.

There is, however, an increasing tendency to create multidisciplinary staff teams responsible for throughcare during the custodial part of prison sentences. Community-based probation officers or social workers then take over responsibility for post-release supervision and support. Throughcare often includes administrative aspects of sentence planning as well as social work input on the individual needs of the offender, and direct work aimed at rehabilitation and at challenging offending behaviour patterns.

The social work presence in prisons is not universal and it is threatened by privatization and managerialist policies in some countries, including England and Wales.

The social work role in prisons

Work may be undertaken individually or in group settings, and in liaison with other professionals such as prison officers, governors, chaplains, psychologists and teachers, and outside community groups and service providers. The social work task has to be juggled with the administrative demands of the prison, and social work values may, at times, conflict with the demands of security and risk management. For these reasons, prison-based social work is best undertaken by experienced, self-confident and committed staff who are equipped to cope with the role strain involved in balancing the various demands upon their time, and managing value conflicts in practice.

The assessment and management of risk are important aspects of prison-based social work, particularly with more serious offenders. This risk-management function includes suicide prevention work, and involvement in institutional and individual support for vulnerable inmates: risks to security and to the public have to be balanced with the risks which accompany incarceration.

Responding to prisoners' welfare needs is also important. Although there are pressures to concentrate upon delivering cognitive-behavioural programmes to as many prisoners as possible, the social work role requires staff to respond effectively and humanely to individual needs as well. The professional independence of social workers from the custodial institution is important both in validating their judgements and in facilitating appropriate relationships with prisoners and other staff. While, in many institutions, they carry keys and help to maintain security, they may only gain the trust of inmates if they maintain a degree of independence and a preparedness to challenge institutional practices when appropriate. Prisons are violent, racist, sexist institutions, many of whose inmates need social work support to help them cope with their incarceration. An important aspect of prison-based social work is the attempt to limit the damage done to individuals during their incarceration, and this is a prerequisite of more constructive engagement in many cases, when relationships are formed as a result of a relatively superficial first contact between a prisoner and a worker.

Groupwork

Groupwork programmes involve social workers to varying degrees in different institutions. Groupwork can address issues common to large groups of inmates (for example, offending behaviour, anger and anxiety management) as well as more specific concerns (such as alcohol and drug misuse, coping with life sentences, sexual offending). Tried and tested programmes are available in each of these areas of work, although it is important that they are supplemented by individual support and follow-up.

In many cases, nationally prescribed groupwork courses have been delivered in mechanistic and unhelpful ways by ill-prepared disciplinary staff without the involvement of social workers. Research-based programmes delivered by well-trained staff have been shown to increase the social competence of men who have offended sexually against children, teaching relapse-avoidance techniques while in prison. On the other hand, groups run by staff who show little respect for prisoners and simply read the content of the sessions aloud from a manual, are unlikely to have much impact. A number of prisoners have observed that anger management groups led by a prison officer known for his 'short fuse' are hard to take seriously.

Working with individual prisoners

Individual work with prisoners ranges from assistance with family problems and maintaining outside contacts, to challenging entrenched patterns of offending behaviour. It needs to be based upon a belief in the dignity and worth of all human beings, and in offenders' ability to change.

It is not always easy for prisoners to gain access to social work staff, especially in an overcrowded prison system where most people spend long periods locked in their cells. Increasingly, welfare work is entrusted to uniformed staff, often through shared work schemes which enable social workers to train and supervise them. This is progressive in so far as it broadens the discipline staff task and their view of the people they work with, but there are problems with it in practice. Some prisoners do not trust

continued

custodial staff sufficiently to confide in them; uniformed staff vary in their suitability for the work; and security tasks always come first. Some referrals are delayed by the involvement of prison officers who turn out to be too busy to deal with them, and pass them on to the social workers or probation officers who would have dealt with them in the first place.

Prison social work draws upon the same skills as social work with offenders in the community, but also on prison-based social workers' specific skills and experience of engaging with the prison system.

For Further Reading
Beech, A., Fisher, D., Beckett, A. and Scott-Fordham, A. 1998: An evaluation of the prison sex offender treatment programme. *Research Findings*, 79. London: Home Office Research, Development and Statistics Directorate.
Kemshall, H. 1997: Risk and parole: issues in risk assessment for release. In H. Kemshall and J. Pritchard (eds), *Good Practice in Risk Assessment and Risk Management 2: Protection, Rights and Responsibilities*, London: Jessica Kingsley, 233–54.
Williams, B. 1997: Work settings in social work: the prison. In M. Davies (ed.), *The Blackwell Companion to Social Work*, Oxford: Blackwell, 311–16.

BRIAN WILLIAMS

Private Residential and Day Care

Private residential and day care for vulnerable adults is part of a range of provision to enable them to continue to live in their own homes or otherwise offer them appropriate facilities. Independent 'for profit' organizations and 'not for profit' organizations, including charitable bodies, provide this care.

These services have received greater prominence in the UK with the development of the enabling role of the local authority and the implementation of community care legislation. One of the principal goals of the legislation was to stimulate the growth of private residential and day care services, thereby maximizing service user choice and reducing the significance of resources provided by local authorities.

The regulation of private residential care was initially the responsibility of inspection units in local authority social services departments. Day care facilities which are not part of a residential establishment were excluded from this process. Stronger protection for vulnerable adults through greater consistency in the application of regulation standards will be achieved through the transfer of this duty to independent bodies responsible to central government.

For Further Reading
Wistow, G., Knapp, M., Hardy, B., Kendall, J. and Manning, R. 1996: *Social Care Markets: Progress and Prospects*. Buckingham: Open University Press.

JANE HUGHES

Probation

Probation is a term used in many jurisdictions to refer to a court order, made as a consequence of a crime, which places the offender under the supervision of a probation officer for a determinate period (in England and Wales, from six months to three years).

There are variations of detail in the form probation takes in different legal systems, but there are three essential elements:

1 An order made by the court which contains requirements with which the offender must comply
2 Regular contact with a supervising officer
3 The withholding of further punishment for the offence provided that compliance with the requirements of the order is satisfactory

In Britain, the standard requirements include being of good behaviour, keeping in touch with the probation officer as instructed, receiving visits at home when required, and notifying changes of address or employment. Additional requirements are also available, such as requirements to reside in a hostel, to receive psychiatric treatment, to receive treatment for drug or alcohol problems, or to attend particular places or participate in programmes of activity as part of the probation order. Failure to comply with requirements renders an offender liable to prosecution and further punishment.

The background

Probation has its origins in local court practices in the early nineteenth century, whereby young offenders or those guilty of minor offences could be discharged or bound over if a suitable person offered to take responsibility for supervising their future conduct. In 1876, the Church of England Temperance Society, helped by five shillings from the printer Frederick Rainer of Hertford, began to maintain an active presence in some city police courts, to promote the moral reform of offenders and abstention from alcohol. Sentencers developed the practice of seeking information from the missionaries about offenders and placing some of them under informal supervision in lieu of other punishment if they seemed likely to reform. This was an opportunity to 'prove' themselves: hence the term *probation*, a proof or test.

A similar system, rooted in missionary work, charitable endeavour and the temperance movement, had developed in parts of the USA from the 1840s, and seems first to have been formalized in the legal guise of supervision by an officer of the court in Massachusetts in 1869. Developments there were eagerly studied by penal reformers campaigning for a probation law in Britain. Their efforts bore fruit in 1907 in the Probation of Offenders Act, but several more decades were to elapse before probation services everywhere in Britain were staffed by salaried public officials rather than by a mixed workforce of professionals and missionaries. By the 1950s, however, the probation service and the process of probation were coming to be regarded as an important part of the criminal justice system, as the development of the post-war welfare state reinforced a belief that, given the right forms of social treatment, the most useful approach to offenders was to try to rehabilitate them.

Community sentencing and National Standards

In England and Wales, since the Criminal Justice Act 1991, probation orders have been regarded as one of several 'community sentences' intended to provide an intermediate level of punishment for those offences too serious for a discharge or a fine, but not so serious that a custodial sentence is required. (The other community sentences are community service orders, requiring offenders to undertake socially useful unpaid work under probation service supervision; curfew orders requiring an offender to stay at home during specified parts of the day and night; and combination orders which combine a probation order with a community service order.) The supervision provided is regulated by *National Standards* issued by the Home Office which specify, for example, how frequently offenders should be seen, and when enforcement action should be taken.

In England and Wales in 1997, 50,900 probation orders were made, 47,500 community service orders and 18,900 combination orders. The probation service (which is also responsible for the supervision of many released prisoners) employed 7,149 probation officers (full-time equivalents, all grades) and 6,819 other staff. The total cost of the service was around £500 million, or one twentieth part of overall expenditure on the criminal justice system.

Towards a correctional service?

The way probation has developed since 1991 has not been uncontroversial. Traditionally, in Britain, probation has been seen as a branch of social work, and the Probation

continued

Rules have required officers to 'advise, assist and befriend' offenders (customarily, until the 1990s, referred to as 'clients'). The gradual redefinition of probation as an activity intended to 'confront offending behaviour' and to adopt a more challenging and demanding approach to supervision has presented problems of adaptation for many practitioners who regard developments like *National Standards* as an attack on professional autonomy. Against this position, it is argued that, if the use of probation rather than prison for a wider range of offenders is to receive public support, supervision needs to be accountable and rigorous and the element of punishment and restriction of liberty inherent in community sentences must be made explicit. This view tends to align probation with other 'correctional' criminal justice activities rather than with social work: the training of probation officers has accordingly been separated from that of social workers, and the possibility of a unified correctional service combining prisons and probation has been seriously considered.

After a long period since the mid-1970s, during which the received criminological wisdom was that 'nothing worked', research on the effectiveness of probation in reducing offending is beginning to show positive results from some methods and programmes, although the effectiveness of much routine work is still questionable.

The results of more recent research are being disseminated and applied in a Home Office led *Effective Practice Initiative*. The future of probation seems to lie somewhere between a bureaucratic minor punishment and an effective rehabilitation service; exactly where will depend to some extent on how well the lessons of research are applied.

For Further Reading
Brownlee, I. 1998: *Community Punishment*. Harlow: Longman.
McGuire, J. (ed.) 1995: *What Works: Reducing Reoffending*. Chichester: Wiley.
Whitfield, D. 1998: *Introduction to the Probation Service*. Winchester: Waterside Press.

PETER RAYNOR

Professional Discretion and Judicial Decision Making

Professional discretion and judicial decision making refers to the boundary between a court's power to make binding judgements under statutory provision and social workers' capacity to apply discretion in their everyday work with service users. This boundary is particularly problematic in child care cases under the Children Act 1989.

Policy and legislation presuppose that social workers will make detailed arrangements for the care of looked-after children. Courts will make decisions which have long-term consequences and which impinge on the legal status of children and their parents. There are continuing disputes, however, between the courts and local authorities where the former seek to monitor and review the implementation of social workers' care plans and to direct local authorities in the exercise of parental responsibility for children in their care.

Suspicion about local authority effectiveness in protecting children's welfare has led to judicial intervention through refusing to make requested orders, continuing to impose interim orders, attaching conditions to orders and interpreting statute law in a way which erodes the leeway for professional discretion.

For Further Reading
Smith, C. 1997: Judicial power and local authority discretion – the contested frontier. *Child and Family Law Quarterly*, 9 (3), 243–57.

CAROLE SMITH

Professional Ethics

Professional ethics comprise the more or less formalized principles, rules, conventions and customary practices that inform professionals' treatment of their clients, each other, and their relations with society at large.

Many established professions have substantial powers to regulate their own professional standards and conduct. Professional ethics may be prescribed in written codes, which the individual professional may be required to adhere to upon penalty of disciplinary action or disqualification. In social work, the status and force of professional codes is generally much weaker.

Professional ethics rest upon wider values in social work and entail specialized knowledge and expertise. The rules of social work ethics have been summarized (Clark, 2000) as follows. Practice should be:

- respectful of the individual client
- performed in a way which is honest and truthful
- carried out with proper knowledge and skill
- careful and diligent, respecting the client's trust in the professional
- based on methods which are demonstrably effective and helpful
- based on proper authority, thus legitimate and authorized
- collaborative with associates and account- able to them
- reputable in the community and of creditable status.

For Further Reading
Clark, C. L. 2000: *Social Work Ethics: Poli- tics, Principles and Practice*. Basingstoke: Macmillan.

CHRIS CLARK

Professional Fostering
Professional fostering provides family-based care for children and young people with special, often exceptional, needs. It is an alternative to main- stream or traditional fostering and is designed to deliver therapy or treatment as well as care. It is also an alternative placement service to residen- tial care. Placements tend to last longer than in mainstream fostering. Professional or *specialist* foster carers look after children and adolescents with emotional and behavioural difficulties and those with learning and physical disabilities. Many of these children will have experienced previous placement breakdowns.

Fostering agencies from both public and inde- pendent sectors manage professional fostering programmes. Professional foster carers must usually have a professional qualification – for example, in social work, teaching or applied psychology – and experience of working with challenging young people. Professional foster carers are required to observe and assess chil- dren in their care and to work alongside educa- tion, health, youth justice and social work staff. Specialist fostering schemes, therefore, provide foster carers with professional fees, status

and recognition, regular training and extensive support services such as social work consulta- tion and advice 24 hours a day. Research has shown that the provision of appropriate train- ing and support leads to the longer-term retention of foster carers and a lower risk of placement breakdown.

For Further Reading
Sellick, C. and Thoburn, J. 1996: *What Works in Family Placement?* Barkingside: Barnardos.

CLIVE SELLICK

Prostitution
Prostitution is the exchange of sexual services for money or other goods and services, such as drugs or accommodation. Causal explanations, transitions into and out of prostitution, preva- lence, the legal status of young people involved in prostitution, risk behaviour, gender, and prac- tice responses, are the main issues for social workers.

Social workers face competing views of pros- titution as a cultural and career choice in a bleak economic world, or as the oppression of young women and men. Prostitution may be viewed as including both personal choice and structur- ing by external factors. An holistic understand- ing will integrate structural dimensions of age, gender and ethnicity. Explanations of entry to prostitution depend mainly on the relative importance attached to a history of sexual abuse or problems of shelter. Sexual identities, risk behaviour, and social attitudes partly distinguish male from female prostitution.

There have been welcome trends towards decriminalizing young people involved in pros- titution, and regarding those who have sex with them as offenders. Residential care and children's services have come under frequent scrutiny for alleged failures to protect young people. Social work intervention should include participatory planning with young people, and interagency services.

For Further Reading
Barrett, D. 1997: *Child Prostitution in Britain: Dilemmas and Practical Responses*. London: Children's Society.

IAN SHAW

Psychiatric Social Work
See MENTAL HEALTH SOCIAL WORK.

Psychogeriatric Patients
See GERIATRIC MEDICINE.

Psychopathic Personality Disorder

There is little understanding of the psychopathology of *psychopathic personality disorder*. The term *psychopath* originates from Germany and means psychologically damaged. It has long been used in the UK and the USA to mean 'a type of socially damaging person' (Blackburn, 1992). Hodge (1992) has described the disorder as 'an addiction to violence'. In 1960, Scott argued that there 'was nothing to be gained by distinguishing between psychopaths and recidivists'. The diagnostic dilemma of psychopathic disorder is a complex and challenging subject.

The World Health Organization in its ICD-10 classification of mental and behavioural disorders (1992) defines personality disorders as comprising 'deeply ingrained and enduring behaviour patterns, manifesting themselves as inflexible responses to a broad range of personal and social situations'. 'Dissocial personality disorder' (which is preferred to the concept of *psychopathy*) is defined in ICD-10 as 'a gross disparity between the individual's behaviour and the prevailing social norms', and is said to be characterized by:

- callous unconcern for the feelings of others;
- gross and persistent attitudes of irresponsibility and disregard for social norms, rules and obligations;
- an incapacity to maintain enduring relationships, though having no difficulty in establishing them;
- very low tolerance to frustration and a low threshold for discharge of aggression, including violence;
- an incapacity to experience guilt or to profit from experience, particularly punishment;
- a marked proneness to blame others, or to offer plausible rationalizations, for the behaviour that has brought the patient into conflict with society.

Legal issues
Dissocial personality disorder is included in the Mental Health Act 1983 under the legal category *psychopathic disorder*. The Act defines the category of psychopathic disorder as 'a disorder or disability of mind, which results in abnormally aggressive or seriously irresponsible conduct on the part of the person concerned'.

Treatment issues
There is considerable debate about the treatment of psychopathic personality disorder and whether such treatment should take place in hospital. Those in favour argue that dissocial personality disordered patients have legitimate demands, given that they are biologically disadvantaged with higher morbidity and mortality than the general population. One argument put forward is that 'medicine is concerned about suffering and not just outcome' and that 'part of the treatment of any chronic disease, be it physical or psychosocial, is the provision of an appropriate environment' (Gunn, 1992). It is also argued that because of the higher rates of mental illness in those diagnosed as being personality disordered, this warrants a specialist service to treat the mental illness irrespective of the personality disorder (Coid, 1992).

Against the treatment of psychopathic personality disorder, it is argued that we are therapeutically impotent and that the detention of people for long periods on imprecise criteria must be wrong. Treatment of psychopathic personality disorder has been cited as 'an exercise in self-deception' (Chiswick, 1992).

Existing treatment facilities include treatment in prison, perhaps in special units such as those provided in England at Grendon Underwood. It is important, however, to remember that prisons are not primarily therapeutic institutions, but rather places of punishment. Therapeutic communities such as the Henderson Hospital provide treatment to patients who agree to voluntary admission and who pass a selection interview; a collaborative and democratic approach is adopted. Treatment is also provided in the Special Hospitals.

The Department of Health published the recommendation of a Working Group on Psychopathic Disorder in 1994 which concluded that 'a range of services in hospital and in prison was needed and these should be the focus of further research to determine which interventions are effective'. Another booklet issued by the Special Hospitals Services Authority in 1995, *Service Strategies for Secure Care*, contains a chapter on the strategy for patients with psychopathic disorder; it acknowledges that the Special Hospitals 'have a substantial role to play in the future development of services for psychopathic mentally disordered offenders' and recommends that a 'standardized assessment' be undertaken. The priorities are to identify and measure outcome, to demonstrate effectiveness of intervention and to gauge whether money is spent effectively.

For Further Reading
Blackburn, R. 1992: Criminal behaviour, personality disorder, and mental illness. *Criminal Behaviour and Mental Health, Psychopathic Disorder*, 2 (2), 66–77.
Coid, J. 1992: Diagnosis in criminal psychopaths: A way forward. *Criminal Behaviour and Mental Health, Psychopathic Disorder*, 2 (2), 78–94.
Chiswick, D. 1992: Compulsory treatment of patients with psychopathic disorder. *Criminal Behaviour and Mental Health, Psychopathic Disorder*, 2 (2), 106–23.
Dolan, B. and Coid, J. 1993: *Psychopathic and Antisocial Personality Disorders: Treatment and Research Issues*. London: Gaskell.
Gunn, J. 1992: Personality disorders and forensic psychiatry. *Criminal Behaviour and Mental Health, Psychopathic Disorder*, 2 (2), 202–11.
Hodge, J. E. 1992: Addiction to violence: A new model of psychopathy. *Criminal Behaviour and Mental Health, Psychopathic Disorder*, 2 (2), 212–13.
Scott, P. D. 1960: 'The Treatment of Psychopaths', *British Medical Journal*, 2, 1641–46.

DAMIAN MOHAN

Psychopharmacology

Psychopharmacology is the study of drugs used in clinical psychiatry. The Greek word *psychopharmakon* meaning 'a medicine for the soul' was first used in 1548. The use of drugs to alter emotion and perception is probably as old as mankind: alcohol, hallucinogens, opiates and cocaine appear to have been used from the earliest times.

Scientific psychopharmacology began with the introduction of chlorpromazine in 1952. This was the prototype antipsychotic and is still in use for the early management of schizophrenia in the UK and, to a lesser extent, elsewhere in Europe and in the USA.

There are now five main classes of psychopharmacological compounds: antipsychotics, antidepressants, mood stabilizers, anxiolytics and hypnotics, and drugs used in dementia. Psychopharmacology embraces the study of their biochemical mechanisms of action (receptor pharmacology), behavioural effects in animals, cognitive and neurophysiological effects in humans, clinical efficacy and adverse reactions (unwanted side-effects). There are seven specialist journals devoted to the subject.

For Further Reading
King, D. J. (ed.) 1995: *Seminars in Clinical Psychopharmacology*. London: Royal College of Psychiatrists.

DAVID J. KING

Psychosis

The term *psychosis* is used broadly to describe a condition characterized by lack of insight caused by mental health problems, and therefore refers to people who are experiencing delusions or are profoundly thought disordered because of severe mental health problems. Delusions are strongly held beliefs which are not in keeping with the person's cultural background, and which are not changed by simple persuasion. These beliefs may refer to hallucinations that the person perceives. However, hallucinations, in themselves, may not be psychotic; they can occur in relation to bereavement or other stressful circumstances, but insight be retained. (Sometimes they are described as pseudo-hallucinations in these circumstances.)

Thought disorder refers to where someone with severe mental health problems expresses themselves in an unintelligible way and is thus unable to communicate. *Psychotic* is sometimes used inappropriately as a term to mean *angry* or *antisocial*.

Organic psychosis occurs where the cause is of identifiable physical origin, for example, infection, dementia or drugs. Functional psychosis is a term used to describe other psychoses, such as schizophrenia, mania and delusional disorders: its prevalence is 0.4 per cent (in private households – UK).

DAVID KINGDON

Psychosocial Perspectives

Psychosocial perspectives inform those social work methodologies which aim to understand and influence the relationship between individuals and their social worlds, drawing on various syntheses of psychological, psychotherapeutic, and sociological theory and practice.

The background

Until the 1970s, psychosocial casework occupied an important position in the repertoire of recognized social work methods, but, in the UK, its psychoanalytic dimension was subjected to fierce critique by the radical social work tendency which argued that it encouraged conformity and adaptation to unequal relations of power, rather than mobilizing people as agents of social change.

In the USA, the tradition of clinically based social work practice, from which British psychosocial casework was largely derived, continued to flourish and has successfully accommodated to a political climate which emphasizes access and sensitivity to minority groups. Psychiatric social work, once the bedrock of psychoanalytically informed practice, has almost ceased to exist in the UK. Nevertheless, so central are psychosocial perspectives to any meaningful conception of social work practice that the latter cannot really be entertained without the former, and, in the 1990s, there were signs of renewed interest in social casework and psychosocial theory as well as in young child observation and attachment theory as part of basic training.

Hollis (1964) remains the classic methodological text, skilfully updated in 1981 to incorporate family systems theory. Earlier editions relied heavily on ego psychology as a basis for assessing and working with difficulties in personal, family and social relationships. The concept of the person-in-situation as the focus of intervention, and the ego as the faculty which mediates between the internal and external world, clearly differentiate this method from clinical psychotherapy with its more intense and exclusive focus on intra-psychic functioning. Yelloly's (1980) study of the history of psychoanalysis in social work remains a key source for those interested in the evolution of psychosocial perspectives in social work.

Despite a theoretical move towards a synthesis between psychoanalytic object relations and systemic theory and method, the political and material realities of the lives of social work clients always seemed remote in psychosocial literature; and even though there has been something of a revival of intellectually well-grounded psychosocial method in social work – for example, as reflected in Howe et al. (1999) – this too often fails to satisfactorily incorporate a political dimension.

The centrality of the client–worker relationship as the medium of change is a defining characteristic of psychosocial methods. However, the difficulty of researching and evidencing the link between quality of relationship and psychosocial change means that, in an instrumental political climate such as that of 'managed care' in the USA, accounts of casework in the literature are often void of qualitative depth as the pursuit of scientifically grounded data occludes the fine grain of clinical experience. Bridging the domain of subjectivity and the harder reality of service provision and outcomes is a central tension for psychosocial practice. Thus, US research in the field has been stronger on evaluation and outcome, and British research stronger on the process, meaning and inductive theorizing from small clinical studies.

Psychosocial perspectives in a managerialist climate

Important but under-theorized sites of psychosocial practice in social work can be found in group care settings and in some therapeutically oriented residential provisions. The therapeutic community 'movement' has always nurtured its own traditions of theory and practice and its principles have become widely disseminated in psychiatric day centre work and some in-patient settings. Many social workers have trained and practised in such contexts, and 'milieu' therapy constitutes a kind of microcosm in which both personal and social relations are examined as a prerequisite to change.

In the UK, with the advent of policies of care in the community for people who had previously often been consigned to institutions, the need arose for a theory and practice of psychosocial care applied to community networks and support systems. Research has examined the impact of unconscious processes in transactions between practitioners and service users, and between professional groupings; and this has provided important conceptual tools for understanding and working with the powerful emotional forces encountered in ordinary social work settings.

Overall, psychosocial perspectives have developed increasing importance for social work and other professional groups where multidisciplinary primary care has become widespread in developed welfare states and where the main challenge now stems from managerialist tendencies in welfare rather than from radical political critiques.

For Further Reading

Hollis, F. 1964: *Casework: A Psychosocial Therapy*. New York: Random House. Revised in 1981 by F. Hollis and M. Woods.

Howe, D., Brandon, M., Hinings, D. and Schofield, G. 1999: *Attachment Theory, Child Maltreatment and Family Support*. London: Macmillan.

Yelloly, M. 1980: *Social Work Theory and Psychoanalysis*. London: Van Nostrand, Reinhold.

ANDREW COOPER

Punishment

Punishment is the infliction of pain for failing to conform to rules, expectations or demands. It may take the form of *primary sanctions*, for example, reprimand, detention, withdrawal of love and personal or civil rights, banishment or death; or it may take the form of *secondary sanctions*, for example, the removal of children for protection, or keeping a register of abusive parents or perpetrators of sexual abuse which will remind the abusers of their transgression, will amplify those individuals' social culpability, disability and stigma, and will engender social exclusion.

The legitimacy of punishment is bestowed by formal means expressed in legal rights and duties involving, for example, the courts, police, social work, education or the workplace; or it is bestowed informally through moral, religious or other social codes in the family, church or mosque. Despite its assumed clarity, punishment remains a nebulous concept: the person or agency with the power to punish, is *ipso facto* in a position of power. The very idea of punishment contains at its heart the reality of an unequal social relationship. However, its nature, purpose, means, outcome and legitimacy are always a matter of definition, context and perspectives – and, in a democratic society, they are subject to political debate.

For Further Reading
Garland, D. 1990: *Punishment and Modern Society: A Study in Social Theory*. Oxford: Clarendon Press.

ANTONY A. VASS

Purchaser–provider Split

The *purchaser–provider split* refers to particular contractual and organizational relationships in the social care markets brought about by the NHS and Community Care Act 1990.

The Act required local authorities to create new roles over the provision and commissioning of care, with the aim of promoting more choice and independence for individuals and their carers. This was to be achieved by authorities becoming managing agents of care (rather than the monopolistic and inefficient suppliers they were deemed to be by the then government), obliged to buy from independent providers as well as delivering their own services. Through a purchaser–provider split, it was thought that decentralized purchasing decisions would be made by local authority care managers who would, in partnership with clients, commission from a mixed market of social services department and independent operators and, thereby, generate a more responsive and effective service.

There is no clear evidence that these reforms have been wholly successful. Guidance over contracting, purchasing skills, compliance, market management and price and quality monitoring have evolved slowly, and practices vary widely across the UK. Obtaining market stability while encouraging diversity and service innovation to meet the special needs of individuals and groups remains a challenge for many authorities. Government pronouncements on the sovereignty of the user in purchasing decisions have been equivocal and this remains an uncertain if not contested sphere of social work practice.

The emergence of the mixed market and the purchaser–provider split is well documented by Wistow et al. (1996) and its initial impact on social work practice receives critical review in Bornat et al. (1997).

For Further Reading
Bornat, J., Johnson, J., Pereira, C., Pilgrim, D. and Williams, F. (eds) 1997: *Community Care: A Reader* (2nd edn). London: Macmillan in association with the Open University.
Wistow, G., Knapp, M., Hardy, B., Forder, J., Kendall, J. and Manning, R. 1996: *Social Care Markets: Progress and Prospects*. Buckingham: Open University Press.

ANDREW PITHOUSE

Q

Quality Assurance in Social Work

Quality assurance in social work refers to processes, procedures and techniques aiming to guarantee that social work services to clients and carers meet their needs through their appropriateness, consistency and excellence.

Quality is a term indicating both the degree of excellence of goods and services, and a standard of comparison with other equivalent goods and services. Quality may mean the physical, measurable, aspects of 'fitness for purpose' of the particular product or service, and/or its ability to meet a person's needs at an affordable price.

Quality assurance may be a one-off situation-based or task-based activity, or an ongoing process akin to aspects of staff development. It may be associated with a number of different goals, such as the attempt to increase output, reduce the ratio of resources to products and services, improve effectiveness, remedy general weaknesses, or respond to specific criticisms or shortcomings.

The nature of quality assurance in social work

Quality assurance standards and processes in social work relate to a number of quality standards commonly denoted by British (BS), European (EN) and International (ISO) prefixes such as BS EN ISO 8402, and a multiplicity of approaches, among which total quality management (TQM) is one of the best known.

Standard setting is one of the main means by which quality is monitored. Quality assurance through the specification of standards of services is somewhat uneven in the personal social services, because of differences between authorities and between services. There are published standards of service in some authorities, and in some aspects of the work, yet not in others.

Published standards do not, of themselves, assure quality. In fact, failures of services rather than statements of desired outcomes have dominated debates about quality in the personal social services since the early 1970s. Inquiry reports into shortcomings in child care (especially child protection) and mental health (especially conditions in mental hospitals and special hospitals, and the community care of discharged mentally disordered offenders) have been particularly influential.

Whistle blowing makes an important contribution to quality services, but it may leave the whistle blower rather vulnerable. The findings and follow-ups of many inquiries and investigations have shown the legal and disciplinary action many individuals and groups of workers and clients risk even in questioning, let alone challenging and criticizing, existing policies and practices.

The Audit Commission and the Social Services Inspectorate, established in the early 1980s, have exercised an increasingly strong central government role in Britain in auditing and inspecting standards of services.

The legislative impact

Quality assurance mechanisms, procedures and structures were legally underpinned in British social work provision from the early 1990s, in work with families and children through the Children Act 1989, and in community care through the NHS

continued

and Community Care Act 1990. Under such legislation, overall plans for services, specifying how the needs of the local population will be assessed and met, have to be prepared, published and regularly updated; the detailed contractual arrangements for the commissioning, purchase and provision of services also require a degree of explicitness about standards which was hardly contemplated before the early 1990s. This legislation has led also to the establishment in local authorities of ongoing mechanisms such as inspection and complaints procedures to monitor the quality of services. It is debatable whether the inspectorial function can be exercised adequately from within the providing agency.

An uneven pattern of provision

Some social services departments have established quality assurance units with their own staffing, while others rely on line managers to deal with quality assurance.

Critical questions have been raised about the limitations of such quality assurance procedures:

- How far, for instance, can such measures recommend the resourcing of new and additional services where there is unmet need?
- How can they judge whether services are being delivered at prices that potential and existing clients can afford?
- How can the multiplicity of different standards for service provision in authorities throughout the UK be reconciled with the principle that all clients should have equal access to services of an equivalent quality which meet their needs?

Sometimes quality is promoted, partly through the production of quality assurance packages, as a fixed and desirable destination to be fairly straightforwardly attained by the application of specified skills to people's problems. This faith in the certainty of technical knowledge and expertise is as misplaced as it is widespread. It is more accurate to regard quality assurance, especially in social work, as unable to be de-politicized, de-problematized or made uncontroversial. In fact, debates about the quality of services take place amid a variety of value assumptions about the goodness or desirability of particular models of provision, and approaches to organizing, managing and delivering services.

The evidence of quality

Components of quality assurance systems rely on an increasingly sophisticated array of quantitative and qualitative methods of collecting data, such as check lists, schedules, systematic monitoring using statistical and other management information, recurring and one-off audits and inspection activity designed to establish whether standards are being achieved. Audits may focus on seemingly more objective measures of performance, such as financial statistics concerning budgets and resources, relating these and other data to performance criteria developed by bodies such as the Audit Commission and Social Services Inspectorate. They may also focus on qualitative aspects such as relationships between staff and management, between staff and clients and team building.

Clients' and carers' perspectives as users of services are important, but ultimate responsibility for organizing and delivering excellent, affordable services rests with staff. Even so, a balance is required between sound internal procedures and external and independent audits and checks, to maintain public and professional accountability. Auditing also should include not just the financial affairs of the organization, but all of its activities. Organizational cultures which are equality-based, open and self-critical, rooted in client and carer participation, have a greater potential for maximizing quality than techniques and procedures dominated by managers and professionals.

For Further Reading
Adams, R. 1998: *Quality Social Work*. London: Macmillan.
Evers, A., Haverinen, R., Leichsenring, K. and Wistow, G. (eds) 1997: *Developing Quality in Personal Social Services: Concepts, Cases and Comments*. Aldershot: Ashgate.
Kelly, D. and Warr, B. (eds) 1992: *Quality Counts*. London: Whiting and Birch/The Social Care Association.

ROBERT ADAMS

Quality of Life

Quality is the nature or character of a thing, its kind, standard, degree of goodness or nearness to perfection. *Life* encompasses all aspects of an individual's existence, from birth through death. The best *quality of life* estimates depict well-being in broad terms, including health and welfare.

Despite this inexact definition, the presence or lack of the 'good life' may be inferred from social, economic and behavioural indicators of external, material conditions within domains like health, employment, education, finances, living situation, leisure, social and family relations or personal safety. However, internal characteristics such as happiness, self-esteem, mental health and life-satisfaction can serve as indicators. Personal or demographic characteristics like social class, gender, age or ethnicity may be presumed to influence life quality.

These life aspects mirror the preoccupations of philanthropic, therapeutic, scientific and reformist traditions which permeate social work. Indeed, a unifying aim of social work is to promote the betterment of individuals, groups and societies by improving the material, social or political conditions in which people live or assisting people to adapt to their life circumstances, as appropriate.

For Further Reading
Oliver, J. P. J., Huxley, P., Bridges, K. and Mohamad, H. 1997: *Quality of Life and Mental Health*. London: Routledge.

JOSEPH OLIVER

R

Race and Racism in Social Work

The evolving and changing nature of the concepts of *race* and *racism* must be reflected in any attempt to define these terms. The aim is not to provide a definitive set of words of explanation, but to reflect something of the contested and shifting meanings of the terms, and to consider their relevance to policy and practice in social work. Hence, this entry is influenced by its authors' personal and professional knowledge, their values and experiences of racism and the theorizing within the social sciences. The ascribed meanings of *race* have over the last 400–500 years served the social, political and economic needs of powerful groups in Western society.

The background

Race is a word which has been used in an essentialist way as a biological, social and cultural construct to classify and distinguish one group of people from another, by using criteria such as skin colour, language and customary behaviour; it has also been used to denote status, lineage, type and sub-species. History has shown that this process of categorization has resulted in the separation, marginalization and oppression of individuals and communities.

The word is often put in inverted commas to denote the contested and developing nature of its meanings. Modern geneticists claim that there is no basis for using the term *race* as a biological category to divide people; this notion, present largely in the eighteenth and nineteenth centuries, is referred to as *scientific racism*. In coming to an understanding of the term, it is essential to take account of the historical, political, economic and geographical contexts of its usage. Ideas about *race*, in a contemporary UK context, have their roots in colonialism and empire and have a resonance in British society today. For example, the English slave trade used the idea of *race* as a biological category to assert black inferiority and thus justify the degradation and enslavement of a particular group of people. The legacy of this type of racist ideology persists in contemporary British society.

Contemporary racism

Contemporary racism, in its varying forms, can be seen to be based on changes in the meaning of the term *race*. The demise of the use of biological difference as a sound scientific basis for labelling people as different, and therefore inferior, has shifted to a focus on culture and ethnicity. Yet, these two notions are linked, and the idea of racism based on cultural difference still has, at its core, mistaken beliefs about the physical and psychological attributes and capabilities of particular groups; it includes an assumption that cultures are fixed and unchanging, and ignores the impact of globalization.

It is evident that individuals, groups and communities face discrimination and inequality based on the acceptance of the idea of 'race' as a way of categorizing and labelling people. Despite its disputed nature, academic debate regarding the experiences of racism(s) assumes the usefulness of the concept as an analytical tool. The negative connotations of a person's 'racial' identity are usually only one aspect of the experience of racism. It is important to understand how it is mediated through the other social divisions (which can also be used as markers to exclude) such as gender, class, disability, sexuality and religion.

Racism is a multidimensional and complex system of power and powerlessness. It is a process through which powerful groups, using deterministic belief systems and structures in society, are able to dominate. It operates at micro and macro levels, is developed through specific cognitions and actions, and perpetuated and sustained through policies and procedures of social systems and institutions. This can be seen in the differential outcomes for less powerful groups in accessing services in the health and welfare, education, housing and the legal and criminal justice systems.

Racism and social work

In addressing racism in social work, it is necessary to have some appreciation of its operation at individual and institutional levels. The term *institutional racism* refers to the way in which any organization, public or private, maintains and sustains, through its culture, policies, procedures and routine practices, the dominant ideologies and beliefs of the wider society. The outcome of this is the discrimination and unequal treatment of specific 'racial' groups and individuals. In a similar way, individuals working in organizations, through intentional or unintentional actions, will contribute to this system of unequal treatment. These individual actions are based on personal values and a lack of knowledge of the broader historical and political impacts of racial oppression.

Practice in social work has traditionally reflected the beliefs of the wider society, and this was seen in the design and delivery of social work. For example, social policies and legislation based on ideas of assimilation and integration as a way of managing minority ethnic communities influenced the development of social work practice in the 1960s and 1970s; this was evident in work with black children and their families. Myths about black families, originating from racist Eurocentric assumptions, influenced the assessment of need and the placement policy for children who came into the public care system. The children's racial and cultural needs were then negated in a system where assimilation and integration into the dominant and superior culture was the purpose of social work intervention.

The 1980s saw a move towards a structural analysis of racial oppression, challenging the institutional racism of social work. It required social work to shift its emphasis from individual pathology and, instead, to address the structural patterns of racial inequality and oppression. Anti-racist and black perspectives made the organization and its workers look critically at social work interventions with minority ethnic groups. This led to social work institutions having to re-evaluate the processes of policy making, recruitment and service delivery. Minority ethnic groups were given the opportunity to define their needs and shape the type of service offered.

The social work profession has had to acknowledge the impact of the inherent racism in British society and its effects on the profession as a whole. The organizations responsible for training and service delivery will have to demonstrate a continuous commitment to challenge racist attitudes, practice and procedures. This process will contribute to the provision of racially and culturally sensitive quality services.

For Further Reading

Banton, R. 1998: *Racial Theories*, (2nd edition). Cambridge: Cambridge University Press.
Barn, R. 1997: *Acting on Principle: An Examination of Race and Ethnicity in Social Services Provision for Children and Families*. London: BAAF.
Malik, K. 1996: *The Meaning of Race: Race, History and Culture in Western Society*. Basingstoke: Macmillan.

BEVERLEY BURKE AND PHILOMENA HARRISON

283

Rape

Rape is sexual assault by men or women including vaginal or anal penetration without consent of a man or woman, irrespective of marital status, or of a minor who is considered incapable of giving consent. Feminists see rape as a means by which men aim to oppress women. Although a serious crime punishable by life imprisonment, conviction rates are low, requiring proof of resistance.

Rape is an under-reported crime, particularly by marginalized and socially excluded groups. Fear of reprisal, disbelief, further trauma through medical and legal interrogation, or self-blame inhibits reporting. Investigation of the small number of cases reported by people with learning disabilities is rare. Most rape is committed by people known to complainants, taking place indoors. Many rapists are young; have previous experience of violence; choose victims of their own race and use substance abuse to confuse their victims.

Social workers can confront rapists with their behaviour. They can provide support to survivors of abuse through non-judgemental responses in collaboration with crisis centres, doctors, police and lawyers, recognizing that survivors may suffer side-effects, remember previous experiences of abuse, or report the event years later.

For Further Reading
Lees, S. 1997: *Ruling Passions: Sexual Violence, Reputation and the Law*. Buckingham: Open University Press.

JENNIFER J. PEARCE

Realist Evaluation

Realist evaluation seeks to evaluate practice within the realities of society. Practice takes place in an open system which consists of a constellation of interconnected structures, mechanisms and contexts. Realism aims to address all the significant variables involved in social work practice, through a realist effectiveness cycle which links the models of intervention with the circumstances in which practice takes place.

Realist evaluation research is about improving the construction of models and, therefore, about improving the content of the practice itself. Evidence from data gathering is used to target and adjust the content of the programme in such a way that it can have a generative impact on pre-existing mechanisms and contexts, and help to bring about the desired changes. Objectivity lies not just in the use of outcome measures, but in the extent to which the model is analogous with reality. At each cycle, a better approximation of reality is obtained, as compared with the previous cycle. In this way, realism addresses all the dimensions and questions of effectiveness of practice, including contexts, the perceptions of all involved, ethics and values, and the content of practice. The multi-method data gathering addresses the questions of what actually works, for whom and in what contexts.

For Further Reading
Kazi, M. A. F. 1998: *Single-case Evaluation by Social Workers*. Aldershot: Ashgate.

MANSOOR KAZI

Reconstituted Families

See STEPFAMILIES.

Reflective Practice

Reflective practice is an approach to learning and practice which seeks to go beyond traditional notions of applying theory to practice. Its proponents are critical of the idea of 'technical rationality' and the conventional assumptions about applying technical, professional knowledge directly to practice situations. The aim is the integration of theory (informal 'practice wisdom' gained through experience as well as the formal knowledge base) and practice (the 'messy' and often unpredictable realities of carrying out professional tasks) through the recognition of the complex interactions between the two.

Reflection takes two main forms, reflection-in-action and reflection-on-action:

- *Reflection-in-action* refers to 'thinking on one's feet', having the presence of mind to be able to reflect on situations as they are happening so that one's positive influence and impact can be maximized. This involves avoiding slipping into unthinking routines or uncritical forms of practice.
- *Reflection-on-action* refers to reflection after the event, weighing up what happened so that future plans can be developed and lessons can be learned.

Reflective practice offers a platform for continuous professional development by providing ongoing opportunities for learning and development.

For Further Reading
Thompson, N. 1995: *Theory and Practice in Health and Social Welfare*. Buckingham: Open University Press.

NEIL THOMPSON

Refugees, Social Work with

Social work with refugees involves the provision of a range of services to a group of people who, because of internal and/or external threats, have been forced to flee their homes and seek safety in another country. Such work entails the consideration and identification of some key areas of practitioner competence:

- An understanding of how the experience of being a refugee manifests itself, including an appreciation of the political, social, and cultural contexts that created the geographical dislocation
- The acquisition of enhanced skills of working with people who may be both physically and emotionally vulnerable
- The adoption of models of social work intervention sensitive to the cultural needs of refugees, including the subtle nuances of inter- and intra-cultural relations
- The use of an integrated approach to service provision that can offer swift, practical solutions to daily living problems, give appropriate help for psychological distress and promote the educational development of refugee children

Social work with refugees must recognize that the enforced movement of people will continue to have a major impact on the global community.

For Further Reading
Buckley, R. 1996: *Migrants and Refugees: Millions of People on the Move.* Berlin: Cornelsen Velag.

CATHY AYMER AND TOYIN OKITIKPI

Refuges

Refuges provide safe emergency accommodation for women and children fleeing domestic violence. The 250 refuges affiliated to Women's Aid in England alone (besides others run independently) in 1996–7 made 54,500 admissions (32,000 children) and took 145,000 calls. Associated services include helplines, outreach and aftercare. National co-ordination helps women move to safety; specialist refuges support minority ethnic women and children. Since the UK lacks a national funding strategy, demand always outstrips supply.

Refuges empower women to take control of their own and their children's lives, and do not require professional 'referral'. Workers and volunteers, often themselves survivors, advise on housing, law and benefits. Collectively agreed rules ease communal living and maintain security; most refuges do not allow men or boys above a certain age.

Specialist childworkers supplement play provision with groups, workshops and one-to-one work. 'No violence' policies encourage mothers to discipline without smacking. Because children feel safe, sexual abuse may be disclosed; refuge workers were among the first to listen to survivors and uncover the extent of abuse.

For Further Reading
Mullender, A., Debbonaire, T., Hague, G., Kelly, L. and Malos, E. 1998: Working with children in women's refuges. *Child and Family Social Work*, 3, 87–98.

AUDREY MULLENDER

Registers

In the context of social work, a *register* is a state-prescribed list of names of individuals whose identification provides a means of protecting the public from people considered dangerous, and/or of prioritizing services to people considered vulnerable.

Registers are primarily concerned with identifying people at risk either from the actions of others or where their behaviour or circumstances may cause harm to themselves or others. Sanctions are frequently employed as a means of working with people on registers.

The background
In Britain, the first use of registers was to monitor sex offenders (1933). Registers were subsequently used as a means of identifying chronically sick and disabled persons in

continued

potential or actual need of support (1971), protecting children at risk (1973), facilitating the supervision of those with mental health problems (1994), recording incidents of domestic violence (1994) and locating sex offenders (1998).

The practice is gaining momentum in the UK. The 1998 White Paper, *Modernising Social Services*, the Patients in the Community Act 1995, and the Home Office Review of Sex Offenders in 1999 have all indicated the need to maintain registers and suggest possibilities for extending the practice. This pattern of development is mirrored elsewhere in Europe and in the USA.

While there are variations in focus, operation and outcome between registers, it is possible to highlight areas of similarity:

- The listing of formal criteria for registration
- A multi-disciplinary assessment of risk and prediction of danger
- Management by a *lead* agency and the appointment of a named *keeper* to administer the register and a *key worker* to hold case responsibility
- A procedure for third-party notification of information

A climate of concern

The growth in the use of registers may be viewed as part of an increasing climate of concern with community safety and public protection. Allied to this, there is an increasing trend for vulnerable people to be treated in the community. This trend, coupled with wider media coverage of service shortfall and calls for greater public accountability, has led to efforts to regiment, regulate and control rising numbers of a potentially dangerous or vulnerable population.

One of the main aims of registers is to target scarce resources and most studies suggest that registers do provide an effective means of prioritizing services. Registers also provide a means of facilitating interagency communication.

The use of registers purports to enhance consistency of response. Problems with local variations in the quality of assessments have been well documented, but less thought has been given to the range of types of assessment employed in social care, health and criminal justice respectively. The majority of assessments rely upon clinical judgement which has been subject to criticism for its potential subjectivity, prompting an increased use of standardized assessment tools. The accuracy of such devices is subject to much debate, and the response of service users to the changing format has yet to be evaluated. Community care assessments have, however, been criticized within the profession for promoting a 'checklist mentality'.

Accountability

The use of registers is designed to provide a system of decision making that is open and accountable and can be retrospectively justified. There is considerable variation in practice: several registers operate a system of automatic registration; some have no system for appeal; and, for those that do, the procedure is often lengthy and success rates are negligible. Efforts to include service users in decision making have been made, most notably in child protection. The use of advocates has been promoted as a possible way of representing user-interests but they are not universally provided. Several studies highlight practitioner anxiety about key worker accountability.

Registers provide a means of excluding potentially dangerous practitioners from employment. The 'keepers' of registers have discretionary power to disclose details of registration to prospective employers. There are variations in the use of this discretion and some studies highlight the potential for abuse of civil liberties.

Computerization

The majority of registers are stored on computer. This raises two issues with regard to data protection and personal privacy. The first is the length of storage. According to general data protection principles, data should not be stored for longer than is useful with respect to the purposes of registration. Several registers have no system for review and it is possible for names to be retained, sometimes until after the person's death. The second issue surrounds differing security practices (physical, organizational, and system-oriented) employed within the public and private sectors. In the public sector, registration data are viewed as sensitive, but practices within the private sector are not subject to the same degree of regulation.

Some unresolved issues

Registers play an important role in targeting services to those in need and in enhancing interagency communication. However, there remain a number of practical and ethical considerations about the way in which they are managed. It remains debatable to what extent registers facilitate effective work with vulnerable people or promote public protection. Issues concerning civil liberties require serious attention. Links between different types of registers need to be made at theoretical, policy and practice levels. The involvement of users within a range of forums is equally vital. The use of registers as a means of identifying the vulnerable or the dangerous continues to grow. This form of surveillance holds potential as a tool for social work intervention, but its development must not ignore the interests of the people it purports to help or those it is intended to protect.

For Further Reading

Alaszewski, A., Harrison, L. and Manthorpe, J. (eds) 1998: *Risk, Health and Welfare*. Buckingham: Open University Press.

Campbell, J. C. (ed.) 1995: *Assessing Dangerousness: Violence by Sexual Offenders, Batterers and Child Abusers*. London: Sage.

Franklin, J. (ed.) 1998: *The Politics of Risk Society*. Cambridge: Polity Press.

PAT WILKINSON

Registration

Registration refers to the process by which social care residential provision is regulated and inspected. In the UK, the Registered Homes Act 1984 required local authorities to register and inspect independent sector homes. The NHS and Community Care Act 1990 extended the inspection function to local authority homes by the creation of *arms length* registration and inspection units. These units also have registration and inspection duties under the Children Act 1989. The structuring of these units and their incorporation into quality assurance initiatives has varied enormously.

In 1998, the government White Paper, *Modernising Social Services*, advocated change and recommended that eight independent commissions, matching existing health service regions, should be established to regulate and inspect both independent and local authority provision. Although day care services, as previously, would be excluded, fostering services, mother and baby units, maintained boarding schools, family centres and domiciliary care services, would be regulated for the first time.

The position of registration and inspection units within the mixed economy of care has been contentious. Dissension continues, with local authorities in 1999 advocating a transfer of expertise to the new commissions, while independent home representatives demanded a fresh start.

For Further Reading

Meredith, B. 1995: *The Community Care Handbook: The Reformed System Explained*. London: Age Concern.

BARBARA FAWCETT

The Regulation of Professional Social Work Practice

Professional regulation is the process by which individual social workers are held personally accountable for their standards of professional conduct and practice. Its mechanisms may include codes of conduct and practice standards, education and training requirements for entry to the profession, registers of those considered qualified and fit to practise, and remedial or disciplinary measures applied to practitioners in serious breach of the standards.

Regulation of practice can be part of a system which also includes service regulation. Here, the service agency may be subject to registration and inspection, and required to comply with specified quality standards. In professional regulation, accountability for standards of conduct and practice rests with the individual practitioner, not their employer or agency.

Social work is a regulated profession in most EU countries, as well as in North America, Israel, Japan and Australia. Typically, admission to the professional register depends on satisfactory completion of qualifying training, and may also require an initial period of supervised practice. The register may be held by a recognized professional association, or a department or agency of central or regional government. The length and level of qualifying training, and the balance between academic and practice components, differ from country to country.

The nature of regulation

Professional registration carries with it expectations that the practitioner adheres to high standards of ethical conduct and safe, knowledge-based practice. In common with other professionals, social workers are expected to place the client's or user's interest before their own, maintain and update their own professional competence, and contribute to knowledge and practice development. They should avoid bad practice and misconduct, and should not take advantage of their position or professional relationships for financial or other benefit.

Practitioners in breach of these standards may be subject to a range of remedial or disciplinary measures. These can include financial penalties, requirements for additional training, or exclusion from certain areas or levels of work. In serious cases, the practitioner's registration may be at risk of suspension or removal, normally after a formal hearing to examine evidence of misconduct and consider representations on behalf of the registrant. If registration is a condition of employment or a requirement for practice, this may put the practitioner's livelihood at stake. Where the term *social worker* is a protected title, legal sanctions can also apply to those who falsely claim to be registered, or seek to practise without registration.

The background to regulation in the UK

In the UK, progress towards regulation of social work practice has not followed a conventional path, although forms of professional self-regulation, modelled on those in medicine and nursing, developed among medical and psychiatric social workers in the first half of the twentieth century. Their professional bodies issued codes of conduct, maintained registers, inspected and approved training courses, and ensured that only registered practitioners were employed in designated social work posts. In the 1960s, responsibility for the regulation of professional training passed to the statutory Central Council for Education and Training in Social Work (CCETSW), which kept registers of those holding its qualifications, but had no powers to regulate their conduct and practice, or exclude them from its register.

In 1990, a study commissioned by the Joseph Rowntree Foundation led to the publication of Professor Roy Parker's influential report *Safeguarding Standards*. This considered the arguments for and against statutory regulation of conduct and practice standards. It concluded that there was a case for a statutory General Council to protect the public by regulating standards, not just for social workers, but for all staff working in the personal social services.

Social workers, most of them professionally qualified and employed by local authorities, comprise about 5 per cent of the UK social services work-force of 1.2 million. During the 1980s and 1990s, government policies produced an enormous increase in care staff employed by the private sector in residential, nursing home and domiciliary care services. By the mid-1990s, only a third of the social services work-force in England was employed by local authorities and subject to their personnel procedures and safeguards. Less than 20 per cent of the work-force held a formal qualification, and take-up of vocational qualifications in social care was slow to develop.

During the 1990s, support grew among employment, professional and educational interests for Parker's model of a regulatory body with a broad remit, regulating standards among social workers, child care staff and those caring for adults, including older people, in residential, day and home care services. Service users and carers, wary of professional protectionism, pressed for a regulatory body with a strong voice for users in its governance, standard setting and decision making. Public concern about standards also increased as a result of high-profile cases of poor practice, serious misconduct and abuse in social work and care services for children, elderly people, and those with sensory, learning or mental health disabilities.

The regulatory Councils

In 1997, the government announced its intention to establish regulatory Councils for England, Scotland, Wales and Northern Ireland, accountable to their respective parliaments and assemblies, and responsible for protecting the public and raising standards. They are independent statutory bodies, with a balance of users, carers, staff, employers, educationists and the public on their governing bodies. Their remit is to publish mandatory codes of conduct and practice standards for all social work and social care staff, and codes of good employment practice binding on statutory and independent sector employers. Powers of enforcement are contained in the Care Standards Act 2000.

Admission to the Councils' registers is subject to completion of approved training. Social workers, residential child care staff, and senior staff in adult care services are among the priority groups for registration, with others following as levels of training and qualification increase. The Councils' powers cover regulation of social work education and training, requirements for continuing professional development and periodic re-registration, and suspension or removal from the register in cases of serious misconduct or bad practice.

For Further Reading

Department of Health 1998: *Modernising Social Services*. London: The Stationery Office.
Harding, T. and Beresford, P. 1996: *The Standards We Expect: What Service Users and Carers Want from Social Services Workers*. London: National Institute for Social Work.
Parker, R. 1990: *Safeguarding Standards*. London: National Institute for Social Work.

DON BRAND

Reintegrative Shaming

Conceptualized first by John Braithwaite (1989), *reintegrative shaming* has attracted wide interest as an innovative approach to youth justice. In contrast to conventional responses which stigmatize the offender, it emphasizes disapproval of the deed, not the actor, and asserts that offenders should face the adverse impact of their misbehaviour and accept responsibility for making amends.

Intervention should aim to build communitarian consensus in overcoming the harm caused, harnessing family and community resources, enhancing informal social control, reducing the risk of re-offending and promoting developmental needs. Undertakings given should be monitored to ensure performance. Orders incorporating these principles are being introduced as the standard outcome for all first-time convictions in Youth Courts.

NIGEL STONE

Relationship Counselling

See MARRIAGE/RELATIONSHIP COUNSELLING.

Relationship Skills

Relationship skills are the observable behaviours to which workers resort while forming, sustaining, and terminating the *working alliance* with clients and others involved.

Exercising these skills is necessary for promoting the process of bonding among those involved in a collaborative working alliance. These skills can be learned, and include:

- listening actively
- conveying respect
- communicating empathy
- expressing oneself genuinely
- being specific, and
- sharing one's own feelings.

The combinations of skills offered will vary during the different stages of working with clients; because of this, training and supervision are needed to enhance their potential.

ODED MANOR

Religion and Social Work

Religion in social work can refer both to the impact of formal religious groups on social work values and organization and to the importance of taking account of spiritual beliefs in the delivery of services.

Early social workers were influenced by Christian values, and a number of social work organizations are based on explicitly religious principles. A growing non-Christian presence in the northern hemisphere has led to a need to take account of the social needs of religious minorities, and has raised questions such as whether to provide integrated or autonomous services. In the UK, the Children Act 1989 requires that planning for permanence for children should have regard for a child's religious background. Training organizations

increasingly recognize the reality of a multi-faith society in their publications.

A contemporary question concerns the potential conflict between social work values and some religious beliefs – for example, about the role of women in society, or about homosexuality. The major religions – Buddhism, Christianity, Hinduism, Islam and Judaism – are heterogeneous, but prejudices against some (Islamophobia, anti-Semitism) are pervasive, and this can affect the quality of social work delivery.

For Further Reading
Patel, N., Naik, D. and Humphries, B. 1998: *Visions of Reality: Religion and Ethnicity in Social Work*. London: CCETSW.

BETH HUMPHRIES

Reminiscence

Reminiscence is the conscious recollection of past experience and is undertaken by all age groups. Reminiscence among older people tended, at one time, to be associated with mental frailty and cognitive impairment. However, psychologists, following the writings of Erik Erikson, now point to the positive functions of reminiscence in old age. These include the search for meaning in late life, dealing with loss, eliciting positive memories, confronting and dealing with painful memories, coping with grief, raising self-esteem and establishing identity.

Reminiscence is regarded as an enjoyable and positive experience, but researchers and practitioners point out that, for some older people, it may not always be relevant or appropriate.

Among groups of older people, reminiscence work aims to promote social interaction and shared perceptions of previous and current lives and identities. The use of prompts such as photographs, music, games and objects helps to promote communication and recollection. Supported reminiscence plays a part in assessment processes and in the identification of appropriate care and support. It has particular relevance in work with older people with learning disability, and with people who have a dementing illness.

For Further Reading
Bornat, J. (ed.) 1994: *Reminiscence Reviewed: Perspectives, Evaluations, Achievements*. Buckingham: Open University Press.

JOANNA BORNAT

Research and Social Work

Research is a form of disciplined inquiry into a subject or problem, used to facilitate empirically based understanding and explanation, and often to inform action. What primarily distinguishes one research methodology from another is the nature of the questions addressed and the purposes of the research. Research entails commitments and decisions regarding the nature of *knowledge and evidence, methodology and methods, subject matter*, ways in which research may be *utilized*, and the relationship between *research and practice*.

Knowledge and evidence

Debate regarding the nature of knowledge and evidence has centred on three connected questions.

1 Should research represent the outworking of a particular paradigm?
2 Can we discover an objective representation of the world, or are all research accounts contingent and relative?
3 Should research be planned primarily according to the demands of scientific rigour or practice relevance?

The main paradigm positions are fallible realism, relativist constructivism, and critical research. The most common position is some form of realism, usually combined with the pragmatic belief that what matters is what appears methodologically appropriate for particular problems and settings. Realists share in common the convictions that scientific change is, on balance, progressive, and that approximate knowledge of an independent reality is made possible through research.

Methods

More recent methodological debate and development have focused on the influence of interpretive sociologies, and the continuing impact of new technologies. Qualitative methodology has become established in social work research, although relatively few fully developed social work ethnographies exist. The relationships between quantitative and qualitative methods range from equal partnership to privileged status of one or the other. Principled synthesis and creative dialectic offer the most imaginative ways of advancing multi-method research. Access to powerful data-processing capacity has enabled more sophisticated multivariate analysis, meta-analysis, and a growing application of software packages to qualitative data analysis.

Subject matter

The processes by which substantive interests develop in social work research are little understood, and the relative energy and resources devoted to different research topics do not mirror the scale or priorities of practice effort.

Utilization

Estimates of the extent to which social work research is utilized depend on views about research validity and the processes by which research is acted on or neglected. On validity judgements, the main distinction is between researchers who emphasize internal validity, plausibility, external validity and generalizability, and those who adopt interpretive or openly ideological criteria. The latter judge research in terms of its humanizing values, or catalyzing impact on the lives of the powerless.

The social work profession has been slow to respond to more realistic understandings of research use, which reflect an enlightenment model, involving a diffuse and indirect infiltration of research-informed ideas into policy and practice. However,

continued

instrumental models of research use remain important where shorter-term imme-diate applications are required, and where insider-led research is carried out. Social work researchers have sometimes claimed that the process, language and skills of practice are similar to those of research. This argument is valuable but too simplistic when stated in this way, and does not recognize the disjunctures of research and practice.

Research and practice

Arguments about the interface of research and practice have taken various forms.

- First, there is recognition of the need to apply the lessons of research to practice. Pleas for evidence-based practice take this one step further and urge a scientific ori-entation to the practice methods of social work.
- Second, social workers have been encouraged to become practitioner researchers. In the USA, this has been apparent in the empirical practice movement, the advocacy of scientific practice, and the development of single-system evaluation designs. British practitioner research has tended to draw more heavily on a methodological eclecti-cism. However, during the 1990s, arguments emerged for qualitative practitioner research.
- Third, several leading figures in US social work have illustrated ways in which the researcher may act as developer of models. For example, research on the task-centred model of practice has proceeded as a step-by-step process of development, testing and further development.

Participatory research

Participatory inquiry, reflective research, and advocacy research share a rejection of knowledge-enhancing assumptions about the relationship between research and prac-tice. They all pay attention to ways in which perspectives and methods provide a more direct exemplification of good social work practice. Each gives varying emphasis to participation by the people being studied, popular knowledge, empowerment, consciousness-raising, and political action and social transformation.

Recurring themes in participatory inquiry are subjective participation in the creation of knowledge, an emphasis on lay knowledge, an iterative testing of knowledge in live action contexts, and a prioritizing of practical knowledge. Schon's elucidation of reflection-in-action as a core practice, present in superficially different professions, has been probably the most influential and generative account of reflective practice. Redis-tributive models of welfare, feminist research and Freirian conscientization have pro-vided foundations for explicitly transformative, emancipatory visions of participatory research. Constructivism, critical theory and qualitative methodology have been com-bined in an argument that social workers should view some evaluative forms of research as direct dimensions of practice. Empirical work has shed some light on how practi-tioners seek to make evaluative sense of their day-to-day work.

The future

The contours of social work research are shaped by its infrastructure. There are a handful of research centres in the UK. Such institutions are likely to grow in number and exercise an increasing influence. However, the majority of funded research is still carried out in the older British universities. Changes in higher education have also produced shifts in British social work research. The government Research Assessment Exercise (RAE) has become the major indicator of quality and reputation. Discipline-based ranking exercises are frequent in the USA. Social work research has slowly raised its profile relative to other disciplines. The RAE has stimulated an expansion in social work refereed journals. There will continue to be moves to greater national co-ordination of research effort.

For Further Reading
Abbott, P. and Sapsford, R. 1998: *Research Methods for Nurses and the Caring Professions.* Buckingham: Open University Press.
Shaw, I. and Lishman, J. (eds) 1999: *Evaluation and Social Work Practice.* London: Sage Publications.
Sherman, E. and Reid, W. J. (eds) 1994: *Qualitative Research in Social Work.* New York: Columbia University Press.

IAN SHAW

Resettlement
See DEINSTITUTIONALIZATION and DISCHARGE PLANNING.

Residential Care

Residential care is diverse: it has varying aims, serves different client groups, keeps them for varying lengths of time, operates according to different theories or no theories at all, and achieves very varying results. Its aims may include the provision of relief for relatives, holidays for elderly people, upbringing or 'treatment' for children, normal life for people with disabilities, the provision of a homely environment for old people and 'services to the system' such as assessment or remand. Residential establishments with the same general aim can differ dramatically in their ethos and effects.

This diversity leads to problems of definition. Children's and old people's homes are commonly seen as providing residential care since they offer both care and accommodation on a group basis and on the same site; but so do prisons, hospitals, schools and hotels, none of which are seen as residential homes, while community homes with education, large foster homes, half-way houses, 'heavy-end' sheltered housing or small unstaffed establishments for adults with learning disabilities may, or may not, be seen in this way.

Critiques of residential care
Yet, despite their diversity and the lack of an agreed definition for residential care, residential establishments of all kinds are subject to remarkably uniform attacks. This critique stems, in part, from the common origins of many of them in the workhouse and, in part, from sociologists who have emphasized the oppressive commonalities of 'institutional' life. The critique, combined with the practical difficulties of staffing and paying for residential homes, raises the question of whether residential care can survive. How far is the critique justified? And what are the implications for the future of residential care?

The first plank of the critique is that residential establishments cannot provide an environment in which anyone should be expected to live. This criticism is partly based on early studies of institutions for young children, asylums, and establishments for what were then known as the 'mentally handicapped'. More recently, it has been strengthened by reports of sexual and physical abuse in children's homes and residential schools, and of exploitation and bullying in old people's homes. These accounts point to the potential dangers of any closed institution but cannot show that abuse is inevitable or is nowadays widespread. In practice, the argument has varying force

continued

depending on the client group involved and the possible alternatives. Small hostels provide a more normal and stimulating environment than long-stay wards for the psychiatrically ill. Old people's homes are generally, according to their residents, caring and comfortable places in which to live, and, whereas bullying and sexual harassment (mainly by children of each other) are widespread in UK children's homes, some are undoubtedly benign places in which to live.

The second criticism is that no one wants to go into residential care. There is some truth in this, but again it is not the whole story. Most old people want to stay in their own homes if they can – which is not to say that they do not accept the need to move in the end. By contrast, some disabled people welcome residential care as a step towards independence as do some who are psychiatrically ill. Some teenagers undoubtedly prefer it to the strains and tensions of fostering.

The third criticism is that residential care is ineffective. This criticism is largely based on studies of the attempts to prevent further delinquency among residents – as such it cannot be held to apply to other aims (for example, relieving relatives). Delinquency among young people does seem to be strongly affected by the immediate environment: it is, for example, much commoner in some residential homes than others. Thus, it is usually the home environment to which residents return rather than the preceding residential one that ultimately affects their delinquent behaviour. Nevertheless, some establishments do seem to be more effective than others in preventing future delinquency, and an integrated approach in which 'after-care' and residential treatment are linked should, theoretically, have much to commend it.

The last major criticism is that residential care is very costly. Again, this is of varying force depending on the type of residential care and the alternatives. The cost of children's homes in England is indeed extremely high: at something in excess of £500 million a year, it is in danger of distorting priorities in services for children. Yet, some residential care is cheaper than some community care for the same individuals. Moreover, the cost savings, if any, of community schemes depend on their ability to predict who would enter residential care if not provided with an expensive package. This prediction is very difficult to make. Community-based schemes will thus provide expensive packages to many who would not have entered residential care in any event. US and some British experience suggests that a determined shift to community care would be expected to lead to an increase rather than a decrease in costs.

The future of residential care
Against this background, the future of residential care is likely to display three trends.

1   There will be a continuing and welcome attempt to develop alternatives – specialist fostering, heavy packages of community care and so on.
2   There will be a recognition that, at the moment, these alternatives are expensive, hard to provide (some of those in residential care are very difficult to contain in the community) and patchily available; so residential care will continue to be provided, albeit on a shrinking scale.
3   There will be a continuing effort to ensure that provision is of as high a quality as possible. In effect, this means that the staff – above all, the head – are good at their jobs, that the establishment is (usually) small, that it has clear aims and (again, usually) a strong ethos supported by the staff, and that it is linked appropriately with surrounding services.

In this way, there will grow up a system in which the boundaries between residential care and other services are blurred, and both exist together in what is ideally an integrated and seamless network of provision.

For Further Reading
Goffman, E. 1961: *Asylums: Essays on the Social Situation of Mental Patients*. Garden City, New York: Doubleday.
Sinclair, I. A. C. (ed.) 1988: *Residential Care: the Research Reviewed*. London: HMSO.
Wagner Report, The 1988: *Residential Care: A Positive Choice; The Report of an Independent Review, Commissioned by the Secretary of State for Health and Social Services (chaired by Gillian Wagner)*. London, HMSO.

IAN SINCLAIR

Residential and Institutional Provision for Older People

Residential care involves the integration of accommodation with personal care, while nursing homes provide accommodation with nursing/health care support. The two forms of provision are often referred to as institutional care and may be provided by local authorities or the independent sector (voluntary and private agencies). Accommodation on offer is usually a bedroom with shared communal areas/facilities, although some modern schemes offer self-contained flatlets.

The background

Residential care is often seen as stigmatizing because of its development from the Poor Law workhouse of the nineteenth century. To minimize the number of destitute people seeking relief from the state, workhouses were designed to offer a harsh regime which imposed the stigma of pauperism. Elderly people became the largest group in the workhouse because they experienced high rates of unemployment and because the workhouse was often the only place available for those with long-term health and social care needs.

Workhouses were renamed public assistance institutions (PAIs) in 1929 on their transfer to local authority control. The continued harsh regimes were criticized in the early 1940s by those voluntary organizations who were establishing small 'family' homes for older people. These were often targeted at 'respectable' working-class and middle-class older people at risk of being sucked into PAIs because of disruption caused by World War II. There was also a growing acceptance that older people were ending their lives in PAIs because of the frailties of old age rather than indolence and irresponsibility in earlier life.

These concerns were responded to through the National Assistance Act 1948 which established the modern local authority residential home for those in need of 'care and attention' (those with long-term health care needs would receive free treatment both in hospital or at home through the NHS). Older residents would now be allowed to retain their pension, the majority of which they would hand over to the local authority, keeping a small amount for personal living expenses. Old regime restrictions over dress and visiting rights were to be swept away while the old large institutions were to be replaced with much smaller homes. Residential homes would be like hotels that older people could choose to go to, especially when they lacked family support.

Many of these hopes failed to materialize. Post-war shortages meant the building programme did not really start until the early 1960s. Vacancies were in short supply and so local authorities began to establish eligibility criteria as they came under pressure from the NHS to define 'care and attention' as covering ever more frail and dependent older people. Residential care work remained of low status, with little available training and with few homes run by staff with a social work qualification.

continued

The growth of the independent sector

By the 1970s, residential care was seen as consuming an excessive percentage of overall social services expenditure and hence undermining aspirations to develop a full range of domiciliary services to enable the maximum number of older people to remain in their own homes. Research evidence indicated that older people in residential care appreciated the support available but disliked the lack of privacy.

Despite this, the 1980s saw a massive expansion in the provision of private residential and nursing home care. An amendment in benefit regulations made it much easier for people in independent homes to claim their fees through the social security system. Access to this public subsidy was based solely on financial entitlement rather than on any assessment of the need for care. Such expenditure rose from £10 million in 1979 to £459 million in 1986, and to a staggering £1,812 million by 1991. This growth was driven partly by local authorities and the NHS closing down their own long-stay provision to save money and, instead, placing their clients in independent sector homes.

Central government responded to this situation through the introduction of a new funding regime in April 1993. A transfer of social security monies enabled local authorities to take over responsibility for the financial support of people in independent homes, over and above their entitlement to general benefit. Assessment was to be made on the basis of need as well as income with the monies available to be cash limited. Local authorities were encouraged to use their new money to fund care at home packages as well as residential or nursing home care.

Local authorities and the NHS continue to make extensive use of institutional care for elderly people, especially where there is an urgent need to release hospital beds. There is a concern that people still drift into such care because of the lack of adequate preventative services. The 1993 reforms confirmed that those on higher incomes and/or with capital assets such as a house would have to pay for their residential and nursing home care. Concern about this situation led to the establishment of a Commission on Long-Term Care which proposed that nursing and welfare support should be free and only the accommodation element be means tested.

For Further Reading

Means, R. and Smith, R. 1998: *From Poor Law to Community Care*. Bristol: Policy Press.
Peace, S., Kelleher, L. and Willcocks, D. 1997: *Re-Evaluating Residential Care*. Buckingham: Open University Press.
Sutherland Report 1999: *With Respect to Old Age: a Report by the Royal Commission on Long Term Care*. London: The Stationery Office.

ROBIN MEANS

Resilience

Resilience is the quality that enables some individuals to develop normally and to achieve satisfactory outcomes despite a disadvantaged background, to recover from traumatic experiences, and to continue to function competently under stress.

Longitudinal research has shown that resilience is not an innate personality trait, but the product of interaction between risk and protective factors in a person's life. For example, low birthweight is a significant risk for poor development when associated with poverty but not for children in middle-class families. A good school can compensate for a delinquent neighbourhood. No child is invulnerable; resilience is closely related to the number as well as the nature of adverse factors. Risk factors exist at individual, family, community, environmental and policy levels and may initiate risk processes, but these can be interrupted and reversed by purposeful intervention. Social workers enhance resilience by building on existing strengths (protective factors), by working to reduce risk factors, and by recognizing and using potential turning points in the lives of those they aim to help.

For Further Reading
Haggerty, R., Sharrod, L., Garmezy, N. and Rutter, M. 1994: *Stress, Risk and Resilience in Children and Adults: Processes, Mechanisms and Interventions.* Cambridge: Cambridge University Press.

SONIA JACKSON

Respite Services
Traditionally, the provision of *respite services* has been seen primarily as a way of relieving carers of the burden of looking after people with learning disabilities or with serious mental health problems, including dementia. The aim has been to give carers a break by allowing them time for themselves, for recreational activities or for medical treatment; but it can also be used to prepare the way for admission to long-term care by helping service users and carers adjust to the idea. Respite may involve short stays in a hospital or residential unit, access to community facilities, going away on holiday schemes or staying with a family. The availability of respite enables people to remain in the community longer.

There is an alternative perspective: the need for respite services to be framed around the needs and wishes of service users. It is argued that, by adopting a consumer-responsive needs-led philosophy, the perspective of the primary service user should predominate, while still providing carers with a break they are 'happy with'.

See also FAMILY-BASED RESPITE SERVICES

For Further Reading
Cotterill, L., Hayes, L., Flynn, M. and Sloper, P. 1997: Reviewing respite services: some lessons from the literature. *Disability and Society*, 12 (5), 775–88.

MARTIN DAVIES

Responsivity Principle
The *responsivity principle* states that intervention which is designed to bring about change in behaviour should take account of individual learning styles and must engage active participation.

The principle has acquired particular significance for effective probation practice, but has relevance to a range of social work interventions. By focusing on the need to secure participation, it highlights the importance attached to the quality of relationships in the intervention process, as well as the skills required for assessing the levels of risk and need so as to maximize the potential for maintaining motivation and effecting change.

Principles of anti-discriminatory practice must be adhered to both in making judgements about willingness or capacity to participate, and in enabling involvement. Attention should be paid to effective communication, incorporation of differences in learning styles and perceptions of the problems or behaviour being addressed.

The potential for both positive and negative impact of the structural context and the reasons for intervention should not be ignored, and, in particular, account should be taken of the influences of the actual or perceived power in the relationship between the individual being assessed and the practitioner seeking to intervene.

For Further Reading
Chapman, T. and Hough, M. 1998: *Evidence Based Practice.* London: Home Office.

RUTH GOATLY

Retirement Communities
Retirement communities encompass age-segregated, collective living arrangements offering residents a range of housing and care. They are specifically designed to bolster age-based identification, and are generally aimed at people over the age of 55. Key elements are a concentration on an empowering, anti-institutional, safe environment, which can offer choice and independence. The emphasis is on remaining active through social contact, togetherness and solidarity. In comparison with traditional residential and community-based populations, there are claims that retirement communities can help to combat loneliness, improve morale and increase a sense of well-being and social integration while promoting healthier lifestyles. A more pessimistic literature views retirement communities as geriatric ghettos which can also foster a denial of disability associated with age and hostility to other generations (Laws, 1997).

Schemes in the UK, for example in York, Stoke-on Trent and Chorleywood are purpose-built and consist of flats for rent or purchase. In the UK, retirement communities are provided by voluntary agencies, enlightened employers or occupational groups.

297

For Further Reading

Laws, G. 1997: Spatiality and age relations. In A. Jamieson, S. Harper and C. Victor (eds), *Critical Approaches to Ageing and Later Life*, Buckingham: Open University Press.

JUDITH PHILLIPS

Rights

See CHILDREN'S RIGHTS, COMMUNITY CARE RIGHTS and PARENTAL RIGHTS AND RESPONSIBILITIES.

Risk Assessment

Risk assessment may be defined as the process of identifying hazards which may cause an accident, disaster or harm. Linked to the process of risk assessment is risk management which seeks to improve decision making, minimizing harm and maximizing benefits. Effective assessment, communication and management should diminish the probability or likelihood of harm occurring. Some forms of risk assessment include an analysis of the positive benefits of risk taking. The objective of risk assessment is to improve decisions by making the risks explicit and by reducing unpredicted events or behaviour (Alaszewski et al., 1998).

Risk assessment and probability

The emergence of risk assessment as a professional activity in welfare services brings with it associated accountability. A narrow and technocratic interpretation of risk assessment treats risk assessment as relatively unproblematic: however, anthropological and psychological research has pointed to the ways in which different individuals and groups respond to risk and the pervasiveness of risk throughout late modern society. The forensic use of risk argues that risk is a social mechanism for allocating blame, and that it does not assist greatly in predicting normal accidents. Research on professional accountability in relation to risk assessment has identified societal pressures to allocate responsibility and blame for accidents and disasters. Influential reports on child protection (for example, Cleveland) and on mental health services (for example, the homicide of Jonathan Zito) have pointed to the dilemmas of professionals taking action following risk assessments: they are 'damned if they do and damned if they don't' take action.

Risk assessment seeks to establish or predict outcomes – and the harm and the benefits of such outcomes. It also includes reference to the probability or the likelihood of an event occurring. A series of risk assessment tools have been developed to assist professionals and to develop standardized procedures (Alberg et al., 1996).

The impact on social work practice

Within agencies, guidance has been issued concerning the screening of individuals prior to an intensive risk assessment. To develop multi-disciplinary risk assessment, much emphasis is placed on inter-professional working and communication about risk factors. Whether risk assessments are fully shared with service users appears debatable.

Risk assessment has been criticized for encouraging defensive practice. This has been attributed to the impact of media reporting of cases involving violence and abuse, and the resulting calls for policy change and increased professional control. Much of this alarm relates to risk amplification: a process distorting rational risk assessment by fuelling the imagination through an emphasis on specific high-profile incidents, for example, psychiatric homicides and 'stranger danger'. Such application can create moral panics, an exaggeration of perceived threats which play a part in scapegoating marginal groups in society, for example, New Age travellers. Risk assessment has been criticized for its limited attention to issues of values and professional discretion and expertise.

Such debates reflect broader concerns about the role of experts and public confidence in their opinions. Other critiques point to the way in which risk assessment is reduced to checklists that give a spurious appearance of certainty as seen in some health and safety practices.

Analysis of the ways in which 'risk' affects welfare points to the importance of the process of inquiry, a retrospective exploration of disasters. Within social work, a series of influential inquiries and reports have provided analyses of risk and associated decision making. These have been highly publicized and increasingly highlight issues of risk, particularly risk communication. Policy responses have encouraged the creation of risk management devices, such as registers, chronologies, monitoring and supervision systems and procedures for exchanging client information across professional and agency boundaries. From the perspectives of service users some of these devices appear to infringe civil liberties and to emphasize control measures rather than therapeutic or social supports.

Clinical or actuarial prediction?

Sophisticated risk assessments by professionals are justified by studies which show that professionals are better at prediction than decision making based on chance or lay perceptions. Such studies (Alberg et al., 1996) have been dominated by debates about violence and dangerousness, including harm to self as well as to others. Past behaviour is regarded as a high predictor of future behaviour, and much social work risk assessment is used to provide a history of behaviour and social circumstances. In some settings, formal calculations are used to inform risk assessments. Heilbrun et al.'s (1999) work on risk communication about violent behaviour points to the changing legal and ethical contexts of such interventions and, in particular, to concerns about issues of liability when clinicians fail to predict negative outcomes. They argue that, while statistical prediction has a role to play in risk assessments, the process of risk communication is an undeveloped part of the risk assessment process. Such communication may be between professionals and services, or it may include the views of service users or carers. Risk assessment as a professional activity is under pressure to deliver impossible certainties and assurances. A broader definition of the term and engagement with stakeholders can be discerned among reflective practitioners, researchers and policy makers. It is clear that risk assessment is a central part of professional activity but there is a danger that a risk-oriented approach may affect client welfare.

For Further Reading
Alaszewski, A., Harrison, L. and Manthorpe, J. (eds) 1998: *Risk, Health and Welfare*. Buckingham: Open University Press.
Alberg, C., Hatfield, B. and Huxley, P. (eds) 1996: *Learning Materials on Mental Health Risk Assessment*. Manchester: The University of Manchester and the Department of Health.
Heilbrun, K., Dvoskin, J., Hart, S. and McNeil, D. 1999: Violence risk communication: implications for research, policy and practice. *Health, Risk and Society*, 1 (1), 91–106.

JILL MANTHORPE

The Risk/Dependency Model

The *risk/dependency model* is a rationing mechanism used by some social services departments to prioritize clients for community care support. The twin concepts of risk and dependency are used to create priority bands, with those allocated to the lowest band unlikely to receive any services. The 'acceptable' cost of a care package will vary in the other bands. Thus, staff might be allowed to spend the average cost of residential care plus 20 per cent on a high-dependent person at risk of residential care, but considerably less on those from a lower band.

ROBIN MEANS

Risk Management

Risk management refers to the processes devised by organizations to minimize negative outcomes which can arise in the delivery of welfare services. Implicit in the term is the belief that risk is manageable. As such, it firmly locates responsibility for negative social outcomes within agency policy and the professional judgement of employees. In social work, the particular risks for which social care agencies and individual professionals can be held accountable will relate to their statutory duties.

These statutory duties involve fundamental considerations about risk to children and vulnerable adults. Such considerations take place within a political context, subject to differing beliefs about:

- who holds responsibility for risk in society
- how far the risk to the individual should be offset against the risk to the public at large
- the allocation of resources to manage risk.

Risk management and social work values

Risk management is not an exact science, nor is it ever likely to be. Much of the theory about risk has evolved from the context of insurance and is based on the theory of probability. Although it is central in the practice of social work, it is an area that has had little development in social work writing. The seminal text by Paul Brearley (1982) acknowledged that risk carried the possibility of gain as well as loss. There has since been a shift to only the negative meaning around loss, reflected in the way risk assessment is generally focused on danger. This change highlights that risk is a contested term and that managing risk raises issues about values.

There are different ways of conceptualizing risk. A pathological approach would be concerned with risky individuals. In work with children and families from this perspective, concerns will be focused on specific individuals and incidents in families and the potential danger of dysfunctional behaviour. The knowledge base will draw from theory about dangerous families and the cycle of abuse. However, a structural approach to risk may draw from theory about inequality and poverty and the consequences of them for health and family relationships.

From an organizational perspective, the family who are under scrutiny may see risk as arising from the stigma of being recipients of social care and enforced intervention.

Differences in perception of what constitutes risk and, subsequently, what it is that needs to be managed can be similarly explored in work with adults. Managing risk in relation to an adult with mental ill-health can focus solely on the dangers which the individual may pose to him/herself in terms of self-harm, or the possibility of physical harm to members of the public. From a structural perspective, it can also focus on the social stresses which undermine mental well-being.

In all work with adults, risk is often polarized between the risk of loss of an individual's autonomy and the agency's risk of accountability for a bad outcome.

Whose agenda determines the practice of risk management?

What is crucial is understanding whose agenda is at the forefront of the processes which are set up to manage risk, as differing stakeholders will have differing perspectives about the *how* of risk management.

At the nub of the issues which underpin the concept of risk management are:

- the degree to which there is acceptance that risk exists in any society and that a degree of risk taking is normal

- the extent to which responsibility for risk is seen to be shared collectively as a consequence of social structures
- the extent to which the society seeks to apportion individual blame for bad outcomes in relation to risk
- the location of the power to make decisions about what are bad outcomes.

By understanding and bringing into the open the differing agendas, dilemmas such as the agency's legitimate concern for accountability, the potential the agency and individual worker carry to be scapegoated for society's risks, and the perceived risks to carers can be balanced against the individual user's right to take risks.

Such a process draws out the key issue at the heart of risk management – a continuum between control, legitimate authority and empowerment.

Risk management in practice

The concept of risk can be used as a basis for the rationing of scarce resources. There are shifts and swings in most societies in beliefs about whether welfare resources should be a universal right or whether they should be rationed and targeted. Risk management is a political activity and can be linked to decisions about welfare. Identifying risk can be a way of accessing scarce resources but, where such targeting takes place, it may serve to narrow the meaning of risk management and to cut out its preventative dimension.

Because of these conflicts in risk management, it is essential that workers use those frameworks which exist to help in the assessment of risk. Braye and Preston-Shoot (1992) set out a helpful framework of questions exploring whether the law should be implemented. This identifies the differing perspectives of the key stakeholders and also makes explicit where the decision-making process may be affected by resource issues. Kemshall and Pritchard (1996) include several chapters with frameworks to assess risk for different service user groups; there is also a useful chapter in relation to the risk of violence and aggression to staff.

Because risk is a contested concept, it is imperative that agency procedures for management of risk include good staff supervision.

For Further Reading

Braye, S. and Preston-Shoot, M. 1992: *Practising Social Work Law*. London: Macmillan.
Brearley, C. P. 1982: *Risk and Ageing*. London: Routledge.
Kemshall, H. and Pritchard, J. (eds) 1996: *Good Practice in Risk Assessment and Risk Management*. London: Jessica Kingsley.
Parton, N. 1996: Social work, risk and 'the blaming system'. In N. Parton (ed.), *Social Theory, Social Change and Social Work*. London: Routledge.

ANNETTE GURNEY

Risk Management of Offenders

Risk management of offenders refers to a trend or cluster of trends according to which offenders are increasingly conceived:

- according to the *risks* rather than the *needs* they present
- according to the logic of *management* rather than *treatment*
- in *aggregate* rather than *individualized* terms.

The background

The risk management approach is generally viewed as a belated successor to the 'rehabilitative ideal'. By the late 1970s, both the legitimacy of rehabilitation as a primary penal objective and belief in the possibility of rehabilitating offenders were subject to

continued

serious doubts, but it was not until the late 1990s that the notion of *risk management* entered mainstream probation discourse.

As the term itself suggests, the origins of the risk management approach are at least twofold. First, it is evidence of the emergence of *risk* as a central cultural theme in late-modern societies. The identification of risks of all kinds is now a dominant function of 'expert' thinking across a broad spectrum of social institutions. In line with this trend, it has been observed that the policies and practices of the personal social services (including probation) are increasingly concerned with the issue of risk to the extent that the assessment, monitoring and management of risks are rapidly becoming the dominant *raison d'être* of such agencies (Kemshall et al., 1997). It is argued that, where offenders were previously conceived by criminal justice agencies in terms of the *needs* they presented, it is increasingly the case that offenders are conceived and assessed in terms of the *risks* which they present to themselves and to others.

Second, the risk management approach is related to the general growth of *managerialism* in criminal justice – a trend which, in turn, is associated with a need to deal with increasing numbers of offenders with diminishing resources. Since the 1980s, the primary concern of the criminal justice system has been the management of large numbers of offenders as efficiently as possible. For the probation service, this has meant a re-orientation from its traditional rehabilitative purpose toward a more pragmatic and less ambitious concern with relieving pressure on custodial institutions. At the level of practice, the move away from a casework toward a case management approach reflects similar concerns with *processing aggregates* rather than responding to individuals, and with *management* rather than the difficult, and expensive, task of changing people.

Risk management in practice

The risk management approach is associated with the development of increasingly sophisticated methods of risk assessment and prediction to improve the allocation of offenders to appropriate types or levels of supervision. For example, on the basis of centrally held information about the demographic characteristics and offending histories of a large sample of offenders, the Home Office has developed an instrument which provides an estimate of the statistical likelihood (i.e. the risk) of reconviction in a two-year period. This instrument can be used to aid probation officers' risk assessments at both pre- and post-sentencing stages. Garland (1997) explains that offenders have come to be 'risks to be assessed and then managed, characterised by high risk or low risk profiles, and treated accordingly'.

At the theoretical level, there is debate about whether the risk management approach represents a new paradigm in criminal justice. American criminologists, Feeley and Simon (1992), have argued that a new penology is indeed evident, the task of which 'is managerial, not transformative ... It seeks to *regulate* levels of deviance, not intervene or respond to individual deviants'. Kemshall et al. (1997) have argued that the UK probation service is part of the new penology which Feeley and Simon describe.

However, others have argued that *old* (individualized, treatment-oriented) and *new* (actuarial, managerial) approaches are not necessarily incompatible. Garland, for example, argues that while rehabilitative treatment is no longer viewed as an 'all-purpose prescription', neither has it been completely abandoned. Rather, it is targeted at those offenders who are likely to benefit most from this expensive resource. This argument is supported by the resurgence of interest in evaluating or measuring the effectiveness of probation supervision programmes, commonly known as the 'what works' movement or 'new rehabilitationism', which has challenged the idea that nothing can be done to alter patterns of offending behaviour.

RITUAL/SADISTIC SEXUAL ABUSE

Risk/needs assessment

An example of the practical integration of risk management and rehabilitation is the development of combined risk/needs assessment instruments. Such instruments, developed mainly in Canada as an alternative to actuarial approaches, provide both a prediction of the likelihood of reconviction (i.e. an actuarial assessment of risk) and information about the offender's *criminogenic needs* (i.e. those personal characteristics and areas of the offender's personal/social life which increase his or her chances of reoffending). Risk/needs assessment instruments are, thus, able to identify both *who* warrants the investment of probation resources (according to the logic of risk) and *what* needs to be changed to reduce risk (i.e. the appropriate content of rehabilitative programmes for individual offenders).

For Further Reading

Feeley, M. and Simon, J. 1992: The new penology: Notes on the emerging strategy of corrections and its implications. *Criminology*, 30, 449–74.

Garland, D. 1997: Probation and the reconfiguration of crime control. In R. Burnett (ed.), *The Probation Service: Responding to Change*, Oxford: University of Oxford Centre for Criminological Research.

Kemshall, H., Parton, N., Walsh, M. and Waterson, J. 1997: Concepts of risk in relation to organizational structure and functioning within the personal social services and probation. *Social Policy and Administration*, 31, 213–32.

GWEN ROBINSON

Risk Taking

Risk taking refers to the belief that risk and the right to take risks is a normal part of everyday living. In social work, the concept of risk taking challenges those defensive practices which give priority to an agency's concern to avoid being held accountable for any possible negative outcome, and which disregard the user's right to take risks.

The underpinning principle in such work is that of working with the service user as a citizen, who brings some expertise about him/herself rather than seeing only the worker as having expertise.

A degree of risk taking can be an empowering way of working if it is built into risk assessment and risk management. This practice requires that a risky decision is fully justified, and is based on a clear analysis from existing theory and research of why the right to take risk may be the least harmful option for the service user, having also considered social risk. Such an approach allows for an analysis of the risks inherent in social structures as well as focusing on individual behaviour.

For Further Reading

Tanner, D. 1998: The jeopardy of risk. *Practice*, 10 (1), 15–27.

ANNETTE GURNEY

Ritual/Sadistic Sexual Abuse

Definitions of *ritual abuse* have broadened from an earlier focus on the belief system – originally Satanism – to the forms of abuse and the context in which it takes place. Emphasis has shifted to the prolonged, extreme and *sadistic abuse* of children and weaker adults in group settings, conceptualized in New South Wales as 'organised sadistic abuse' (New South Wales Sexual Assault Committee, 1995).

It remains important, however, to understand the role of ritual as an expression of powerful symbolic meanings which are part of a group ideology. Where this involves reference to supernatural powers, what matters is not whether the organizers believe in it, but that those they victimize do. Thus a form of power is invoked which has the capacity to terrorize children. The use of mind-altering ritual, drugs and alcohol form a context in which many acts of deception and trickery can be practised. It is these which make accounts of ritual abuse appear 'incredible', and one of the roles of supporters is to enable survivors to recognize and unpick these deceptions, so as to diminish the 'supernatural' power they attribute to their abusers.

Scepticism about the existence of ritual abuse has become difficult to maintain in the face of documentation of sexual violence in religious cults, the conviction of perpetrators in the UK and the revelations of children being held in cages and filmed for pornography in the Belgian case involving Marc Dutroux. Debate now turns on how prevalent organised sadistic abuse is, and how much of the detail in the accounts of survivors is 'true'.

For Further Reading
Cook, K. and Kelly, L. 1997: The abduction of credibility: A reply to John Paley. *British Journal of Social Work*, 27, 71–84.

LIZ KELLY

Role Theory
Roles can only be understood in social situations. They reflect expectations and behaviours associated with a particular position or status. *Role theory* seeks to identify how people's expectations of and reactions to each other are influenced by their perceptions of their roles. The process is reciprocal and explains the responses of the person in role and of those reacting to their perceptions of that role. Roles are learned from observation and experience. They reflect our perceptions of the most appro-priate ways for persons to behave in a given situation. The theory accepts that roles exist in society, however, without challenging their underlying assumptions.

PETER RANDALL AND JONATHAN PARKER

Role-playing in Social Work Training
Role-playing in social work training is a mode of learning-by-doing, whereby, for a short while, practitioners act as if they are involved in a practice situation selected in advance. Learning is focused on exchanges related to the *roles* which are relevant to that situation more than the personalities involved. Role-playing can be used to *assess* competencies, to *enhance participants' awareness*, and to *rehearse their newly acquired skills*.

Due to being artificial, role-playing has no harmful consequences. However, participants have to be properly prepared for the enactment, and should be encouraged to fully reflect on the experience at the end.

ODED MANOR

S

Same Race Placements

Same race placements is a term which has been widely used since the 1970s to describe the placing of children with parents or carers who share the same culture, ethnicity, religion and language as the child. This practice is important for all children in promoting a positive sense of identity. It is considered particularly important for black children and is based on a belief that only black families can help children to deal with the experience of being black in a racist society and counteract the negative stereotypes of black people presented to children as a result of racism. This added dimension, over and above the quality of care which should be provided by all families, is considered by many to be essential in a permanent new family to enable black children, who will have already experienced the loss of their birth family, to develop a positive racial identity and high self-esteem.

Historically, black children were seen as 'hard to place', and most remained in residential care in the 1960s. The British Adoption Project, set up in the late 1960s, was an action research project which succeeded in placing black children in families, many of which were white, and transracial adoption became commonplace. This approach fitted with the assimilation approach to racial integration and underlined the denial of the existence of racism. The increasing political awareness of black people and the recognition of the negative impact of racism on children growing up were accompanied by a greater understanding of the strength of black families. These families' willingness to care for children separated from their parents was demonstrated by the success of targeted recruitment efforts like the *Soul Kids Campaign*. The importance of paying due attention to children's racial, religious and linguistic background was recognized in the Children Act 1989.

The policy that the placement of choice for any black child is a black family is now widely supported by statutory and voluntary child care agencies. However, there has also been a significant increase in the number of children from complex racial backgrounds, most frequently white/African Caribbean – who are believed to represent about half of the minority ethnic looked-after children. The term 'same race' is believed by many to be over simplistic. Most proponents of a same race policy, however, accept that if a black family cannot be identified within a reasonable time-scale, alternative white families should be considered, if they are able to promote and value the child's ethnicity. Lack of ethnic monitoring makes it very difficult to identify whether black children are waiting longer or indeed are less likely to experience permanent family life. Research findings on the outcome for black children who are adopted are limited and do not unequivocally support either position, although there is considerable anecdotal evidence of the difficulties and identity confusion experienced by some transracially adopted adults.

The decline in white babies relinquished for adoption and the publicity given to the poor outcomes for children growing up in public care, along with the increase in inter-country adoption, have influenced a powerful lobby from white adopters and the media who believe, erroneously, that black children and particularly infants, are languishing in residential care. Government guidance has emphasized that placement with a family of a similar ethnicity is preferable for most children.

continued

For Further Reading

Barn, R. 1999: Racial and Ethnic Identity. In R. Barn (ed.), *Working with Black Children and Adolescents in Need*, London: BAAF.

British Agencies for Adoption and Fostering 1995: *Practice Note 13: The Placement Needs of Black Children*. London: BAAF.

Department of Health 1991: *The Children Act 1989, Guidance and Regulations, Vol. 3: Family Placements*. London: HMSO.

Sumpton, A. H. 1999: Communicating with and assessing black children. In R. Barn (ed.), *Working with Black Children and Adolescents in Need*. London: BAAF.

FELICITY COLLIER

Schizophrenia

The syndrome of *schizophrenia* is a mental disorder which seriously disrupts the personality, impairing the person's ability in perceiving and interpreting their environment; it is found in all cultures.

Schizophrenia was originally described in 1911 as a group of disorders by Bleuler, after Kraepelin had proposed a distinction between dementia praecox (dementia in young adults) and affective (mood) disorders. This distinction between schizophrenia and affective disorders is not absolute and a category, *schizoaffective disorder*, is described to include patients with characteristics of both. Delusional disorders (false beliefs) also exist which consist of a single core delusional belief in the absence of other features of schizophrenia.

Symptoms

The first signs of the development of schizophrenia may be fluctuations in mood, mild eccentricity, confusion, and odd behaviour, increasing isolation, deterioration in concentration and educational performance over a period of months or years. Alternatively, there may be quite sudden development of bizarre ideas or hallucinations. The person may develop a 'delusional mood', that something strange seems to be happening about them.

Hallucinations are false perceptions, which can affect all five senses: the person hears, feels, sees, tastes or smells something that seems to be externally generated and absolutely real. This is however a misinterpretation of phenomena, either their own thoughts or sometimes, bodily sensations. Most commonly, hallucinations are heard as 'voices' speaking to the person or about them which can be derogatory, abusive, violent, sexual or neutral in content, or sometimes, positive and comforting. Sometimes, it sounds to patients that their thoughts are being echoed back to them, or that a running commentary is going on about what they are doing, or that they are being discussed by the originators of the voices.

Hallucinations can be visual as visions, or somatic as smells, or feelings of being touched, often of a sexual nature.

Delusions

Delusions have been described as irrational beliefs which are not amenable to reason and which are out of keeping with the person's cultural background. However, structured reasoning techniques can be effective. Tracing the development of the delusions with the individual often makes them understandable although the beliefs themselves are inaccurate. The themes of delusions are frequently of guilt, paranoia or grandeur.

Delusions can develop over time or sometimes quite abruptly, in response to something happening like hearing some words in a song which are taken to mean, for example, that 'I am the chosen one' (known as delusional perception). Delusions of reference are said to occur when things said by others, in the same room or street, or on the television, radio or in music, are taken to apply personally to them. Thoughts may seem to stop dead ('thought block') or patients deny they are occurring at all such that they may say that someone is taking their thoughts from them ('thought withdrawal').

Speech may be slow, repetitive, stereotyped or absent (poverty of content of speech). Sometimes, patients develop the belief that their thoughts are being broadcast to others so that they know what the person is thinking ('thought broadcasting'); this seems to occur especially where those thoughts are embarrassing to the patient, for example, sexual or violent thoughts. Similarly, they may believe that other people put thoughts into their mind ('thought insertion').

If patients describe their actions being controlled by others, for example, 'the voice made me break down my next door neighbour's door', this is described as passivity (a 'made' action). Similarly, they may describe a conviction that their thoughts or feelings are controlled by others ('made' thoughts and feelings).

Behaviour

Behavioural abnormalities can also occur. Patients can act in an eccentric way in response to the delusional ideas or hallucinations. Negative symptoms are common, characterized by poor motivation and a lack of drive to do anything. Harm to self, aggression and irritability can sometimes occur and happen significantly more often in someone with schizophrenia than in the general population. Serious offences are, however, very uncommon. Where these do occur, they are associated with acute psychosis where patients react in response to paranoid beliefs or hallucinations which command them, and are believed to have the power to make them commit an aggressive act. The use of illicit drugs and excess alcohol complicates the situation and are also major risk factors.

Causation

Schizophrenia is caused by the interaction between vulnerabilities and stressful circumstances. Genetics may contribute. Personality also seems important; people with certain personality characteristics – schizoid (cold, aloof) or paranoid traits – seem more likely to develop schizophrenia. Brain scans of groups of people with schizophrenia show some abnormalities: the areas where fluid circulates inside the brain, the ventricles, are relatively larger. Flexibility in problem solving, especially involving strategy planning and verbal fluency may be reduced. Auditory hallucinations are associated with increased blood flow in the area of the speech centre. Therapeutic and illicit drugs affect brain chemicals, for example, the neurotransmitters, dopamine and serotonin. However, specific abnormalities of the nerves or the chemicals involved have not been demonstrated conclusively. There do, however, seem to be definite signs of abnormality emerging in childhood in some people who later are diagnosed with schizophrenia – development milestones are often late and they tend to be more isolated and anxious as children.

Life events and circumstances are increased in the period before onset and relapse of illness. Some of these events are directly related to the illness itself, for example, reduction in concentration and drive can lead to losing a job, but others which seem quite independent are also increased. Other social factors are also important; for example, being brought up in an urban, as opposed to a rural, environment is a risk factor.

Incidence

One per cent of the population, both males and females, will develop schizophrenia at some time in their lives. There has been some uncertainty about whether incidence is

continued

lower in higher social classes or not, but there is certainly drift downwards before and after the illness occurs. There is an 8 per cent excess of patients who develop schizophrenia born in winter months. There is a similar incidence of schizophrenia across the world.

Treatment

Intervention in schizophrenia needs to be early. Social, especially family, interventions are very important; cognitive-behaviour therapy has been shown to be effective. Medication reduces positive symptoms and relapse in the period after an episode of schizophrenia. However, side-effects are common and include tremor, stiffness, involuntary movements and sedation. There are now a number of newer drugs, which have moderated the degree of side-effects.

Surprisingly, outcome seems to be better in developing countries compared to the developed world, with 45 per cent compared to 25 per cent clinically recovered at five years, and 75 per cent against 33 per cent with minimal or no social morbidity.

Of particular concern is suicide, which is the cause of death in 10 per cent of people with schizophrenia. Moreover, physical illness is also a significant problem with death rates two to three times higher than in the general population.

For Further Reading

Birchwood, M., Hallett, S. and Preston, M. 1988: *Schizophrenia. An Integrated Approach to Research and Treatment*. London: Longman.

Kavanagh, D. J. 1992: *Schizophrenia. An Overview and Practical Handbook*. London: Chapman and Hall.

Kingdon, D. G. and Turkington, D. 1994: *Cognitive-Behavioural Therapy of Schizophrenia*. London: Psychology Press.

DAVID KINGDON

Schools, Social Work in

See EDUCATION SOCIAL WORK.

Scientific Realism

See REALIST EVALUATION.

Sectioning

The term *sectioning* is commonly used to mean involuntary detention under a section of a Mental Health Act in designated premises, such as a hospital or nursing home. Such detention requires that the person is suffering from a mental disorder, that they are a risk to others or themselves, including to their own health, and that no available alternative to detention exists. Authorization is by one or more medical practitioners, usually including a specialist in psychiatry, and an independent authority, who may be a social worker in some countries. It may be for brief periods (for example, up to 36 hours) or for longer (for example, 1–6 months), with provision for renewal.

The courts also have specific powers for the detention of people with mental disorders, but these still require supporting medical opinion.

Independent appeal mechanisms against detention will be available and monitoring agencies exist to oversee implementation of it. Compulsory treatment may be permitted under sections providing for detention or under separate provisions. Guardianship, supervised discharge, supervision registers or commitment to outpatient treatment are included in some legislation to improve access by staff to patients' homes, enhance concordance with treatment, and ensure that support is available outside hospital, but with consequent restrictions on freedom and privacy.

For Further Reading

Hoggett, B. 1996: *Mental Health Law*. London: Sweet and Maxwell.

DAVID KINGDON

Secure Treatment in Adolescence

A small number (around 150 at any one time) of very difficult adolescents in England and Wales are placed in long-term *secure units* specifically to treat a behaviour disorder. Provision is mostly provided and managed by local authorities and is subject to Department of Health regulations and licence. Criteria for entry concern risks to self and others as specified in S. 25 of the Children Act 1989. A secure care order has to be obtained via a court. Another entry route is via a S. 53 of the Children and Young Persons Act 1933 sentence for a grave crime.

Although there are 320 secure child care places in England and Wales, only a third of these offer long-term treatment. Regimes usually follow a cognitive-behavioural approach, but a few units work on psychotherapeutic principles. Future policy changes may see shifts in the patterns and procedures for making such placements, such as greater interagency co-operation in after care and different allocations of young people to child care and prison department facilities.

For Further Reading
Bullock, R., Little, M. and Millham, S. 1998: *Secure Treatment Outcomes: The Care Careers of Very Difficult Adolescents*. Aldershot: Ashgate.

ROGER BULLOCK

Self-determination
Self-determination is the ethical principle that persons should be permitted, enabled and encouraged to make their own informed decisions about the course of their lives. It is particularly relevant in situations where the client may choose to do something that appears unwise or risky to him or herself. The concept is also applied to groups and communities (and in politics can refer to *national* self-determination, contrasted with external domination).

Self-determination rests on the concept of persons as free and rational beings who have both the mental capacity and the moral right to make moral and other choices. Protection and enhancement of the individual's autonomy is essential to the realization of a fully human life. It should not be infringed by unjustifiable compulsion or avoidable ignorance.

In social work practice, self-determination is accorded a very high priority but its power is not absolute. Individuals' rights to self-determination are restricted, on the one hand, by equivalent rights of other members of society; and on the other, in proportion to their knowledge and understanding of the choices they face.

For Further Reading
Clark, C. 1998: Self-determination and paternalism in community care: practice and prospects. *British Journal of Social Work*, 28, 387–402.

CHRIS CLARK

Self-esteem
The concept of *self-image* (or *ego identity*) refers to the way we describe ourselves, the kind of person we think we are – an account psychologists might elicit by asking the individual to answer the question 'Who am I?' many times. *Self-esteem*, unlike the self-image concept, is essentially evaluative: it has to do with the degree to which we like, accept or approve of ourselves. *Self-regard* is another term used to refer to this evaluation of self. Accounts by the person under the headings 'Myself as I am' and 'Myself as I would like to be' provide a simple indicator of the discrepancy between the idealized and actual self-image – in other words, a 'measure' of self-esteem.

Coopersmith (1967), whose book contains a questionnaire measure of self-esteem, defines self-esteem as 'a personal judgment of worthiness, that is expressed in the attitude the individual holds towards himself'. Certain characteristics or abilities have a high value in society and thus are likely to influence our self-esteem – for example, being successful, attractive, personable, as opposed to their opposites.

Low self-esteem tends to be associated with anxiety, and is a ubiquitous feature in the psychological problems of childhood, adolescence and adult life. It appears to be characteristic in, *inter alia*, drug abuse, delinquency, parenting difficulties, and many of the anxiety disorders. A central theme, therefore, in the psychological treatment of many disorders, is the self-empowerment of the client or patient, by enhancing their image of themselves and their self-confidence (or their perceived self-efficacy).

For Further Reading
Coopersmith, S. 1967: *The Antecedents of Self-esteem*. San Francisco: W. H. Freeman.

MARTIN HERBERT

Self-harm
Self-harm is a complex and controversial phenomenon where people physically self-mutilate themselves – slashing or scratching arms or legs, or head-banging – with an all-pervading sense of a profound lack of self-worth. It is associated with different psychiatric conditions – person-

ality disorders, severe anxiety disorders and people with chronic psychotic situations. It can be seen among people with severe learning disabilities where there is a lack of psychosocial stimulus and care.

Self-harm occurs more often in young women (aged 14–30), and sometimes in the victims of physical and/or sexual abuse. The person appears to disregard the pain; other people's emotional response appears to be important to the sufferer. It is a severe sign of psychosocial distress, but care is needed not to reinforce the behaviour inadvertently, and con-

siderable self-awareness by professional staff is required.

Self-harm is distinguished from 'deliberate self-harm' (or attempted suicide) by the lack of a declared intention to die, but occurs in younger patients with suicidal ideation, which further complicates these highly fraught situations.

For Further Reading
Favazza, A. and Rosenthal, R. 1993: Diagnostic issues in self-mutilation. *Hospital Community Psychiatry*, 44, 134–40.

COLIN PRITCHARD

Self-help Groups

Self-help groups are a form of collective endeavour, in which individuals sharing a common experience work together to improve their personal and common position through information-sharing, mutual support and, less universally, advocacy.

Self-help groups can be distinguished from both personal self-help and community-focused groups. Personal self-help concentrates upon the capacity of the individual to manage alone, omitting the essential principle of mutuality by which self-help groups are distinguished. Community self-help groups, such as food co-operatives and self-build schemes, focus upon the achievement of tasks and goals which lie outside the group itself, rather than upon the experiential learning which is to be derived from within its own membership and functioning.

The importance of participation
Self-help groups are self-governing and, typically, operate on a participative, non-hierarchical and democratic basis. While members might make a financial contribution to group running costs, no fees are charged. The help which members provide is free and reciprocal. The source of authority in self-help groups lies in the experiential wisdom of each member: the direct knowledge of its subject matter which all participants bring, rather than in their professional expertise.

The potential which participation provides resides in the experiential learning from one another within the group; and this, in the accounts of their adherents, is said to be the central strength of self-help groups. Participation offers individuals who have experienced problems the opportunity of giving, as well as receiving, help. As such, self-help groups can avoid the sense of stigma and powerlessness which is part of perpetual client status and can provide, instead, one of the most empowering of all experiences, that of being a helper.

As well as encompassing individuals who have personal experience of the issues which the group seeks to address, membership of self-help groups can extend also to family, friends and wider social networks of such individuals. Using that definition, but excluding groups in which professional workers play a part, research evidence suggests that at least 25 million Americans are involved in self-help groups dealing with personal and social issues.

The scope of self-help groups
The scope of self-help groups covers a wide range of issues and problems. The most numerous focus very broadly upon questions of health, including those dealing with particular physical illnesses such as diabetes, cancer or heart disease. The disability movement draws heavily on self-help groups. In the field of mental health, self-help groups

are similarly popular, while the most numerous of all are to be found in the area of substance abuse, from eating disorders, to drug and alcohol groups. A different sort of self-help group lies in the consciousness-raising tradition of women's groups, groups for men and for black people. Here, the focus is less upon a specific problem than upon a constellation of issues which impinge on the lives and prospects of participants.

The functions of self-help groups

If the values of self-help groups emphasize acceptance, mutuality and the capacity of human beings for growth and change, the functions through which such values are translated into practice may be summarized under three broad headings: the sharing and dissemination of information, mutual support and advocacy:

- The expertise of experience means that a self-help group for diabetics, for example, will hold a body of knowledge about coping strategies and self-care which becomes a *source of information* for all participants.
- The *mutual support* of self-help groups goes beyond information-sharing into the realm of emotional and therapeutic experience, enabling individuals to draw on the strength of knowing that difficulties are not to be borne alone and that a human community exists in which friendship, encouragement and a sense of personal worth can be confirmed. For many self-help groups, these essentially internally directed functions suffice.
- The third function, *advocacy*, has been deliberately avoided by some groups and has emerged more as part of a general trend towards consumerism and user-involvement in the design and delivery of services.

Despite their many advantages, self-help groups are not without difficulties. Their ideological basis is open to dispute, being capable of encompassing such diverse strands as the democratizing and participatory left and the neo-liberal right, in which self-help is regarded as a substitute for, rather than an enrichment of, the services provided by the state. Research also shows that the self-help experience is not automatically one from which individuals benefit. Many participants drop out quickly. Others may attend over an extended period but without drawing a worthwhile reward. More generally, the self-help approach is open to criticism for its focus upon the symptoms rather than the causes of difficulty, implicitly locating the need for change with the individual rather than society. Where wider advocacy strategies have been adopted, these have suffered from fragmentation, in which a plethora of small-scale groups operate in isolation, experiencing considerable difficulty in maximizing their collective effort.

Self-help groups and social work

Finally, consideration must be given to the relationship between self-help groups and professional workers. Self-help organizations are likely to hold a general suspicion of bureaucratic services and official organizations and, in some cases – such as self-help groups for survivors of tranquillizer addiction – with good reason.

Nevertheless, many self-help groups have close connections with professional workers, either through joint involvement in establishing groups, or through continuing collaboration. Fruitful relationships, however, are based upon a clear appreciation that self-help organizations are not the poor relation of their professional counterparts, in terms either of their conceptual basis or their practical achievements. Neither can self-help groups be used to fill gaps in, or substitute for, services which should be publicly funded. Rather, a relationship in which self-help groups are a grounded part of the everyday resources of professional workers, while retaining a respect for their primary loyalty to the needs and interests of their members, seems most likely to maximize the benefits for both parties.

continued

For Further Reading

Adams, R. 1996: *Social Work and Empowerment*. London: Macmillan.

Borkman, T. 1997: A selective look at self-help groups in the United States. *Health and Social Care in the Community*, 5 (6), 357–64.

Wilson, J. 1995: *How to Work with Self-help Groups: Guidelines for Professionals*. Aldershot: Arena.

MARK DRAKEFORD

Self-image, Self-regard

See SELF-ESTEEM.

Senile Dementia

See ALZHEIMER'S DISEASE.

Sentence Planning

See THROUGHCARE.

Sentencing

The Criminal Justice Act 1991 introduced in England and Wales a more coherent *sentencing framework* consisting of three bands: *custodial*, *community* and a bottom (*other*) tier without a readily distinguishable characteristic.

The primary generic principle adopted in determining sentence level is commensurability with offence seriousness (or *just deserts*, as the foundation White Paper put it, thus prompting criticism that this espouses 'expressive' retribution at the expense of 'instrumental' crime-reductive aims). Two threshold tests were set to be satisfied in determining that an offence merits the imposition of either community or custodial punishment. The Act also gave procedural prominence to pre-sentence reports (PSRs) as an essential source of information and assessment in helping sentencers make their more critical decisions.

The original relatively clear design of the Act has been rendered more fuzzy by subsequent frequent amendment and one of the more wearying features of sentencing law is the labyrinthine complexity of overlapping legislation. It nevertheless remains possible to discern the essential founding structure.

Custodial sentencing

A common approach governs the use of all custodial sentences from detention and training orders for juveniles to adult imprisonment. The core criterion justifying custody is that the offence is 'so serious' that only such a sentence can be justified for it, taking account of aggravating and mitigating factors. The Act was intended to use custodial sanctions sparingly – to increase use of alternative punishments for less serious offenders; to reduce the negative consequences of custody; to preserve expensive custodial resources for those whose offending causes the greatest harm. That parsimonious approach has not survived. For example, whereas the 1991 Act specified that a court had to adopt that test by weighing at most two offences together, the present law allows all offences for sentence to be viewed collectively.

Decisions by the Court of Appeal have not given clear leadership in gate-keeping the threshold criterion. Instead, the Court has concentrated more on increasing custodial sentences for more serious offences such as firearms or drug trafficking offences, and on policing the length rather than the principle of custody, maintaining a firm belief in the efficacy of deterrence. Custody remains centre-stage as the paramount sentencing talisman.

However, in its most recent generic guidance, the Court has sought to re-emphasize the importance of regarding crimes as more serious if they inflict personal injury or psychological trauma or if they are deliberate or premeditated. Further, the Court has reiterated that if a court determines that a custodial sentence is correct in principle, but considers that the offence need not attract more than 12 months, it should ask itself whether 'an even shorter period might be equally effective in protecting the public interest and deterring criminal behaviour'. It has also clarified that, if an offence satisfies the threshold test, it is still open to a court to impose a non-custodial measure if personal mitigation accruing to the offender justifies this course, or if the court wishes the offender to take advantage of a non-custodial opportunity that may benefit the public interest.

The proportionality principle has been clouded in other respects, including the right of courts now to take account of any previous convictions or any failure by the offender to 'respond to previous sentences', rather than concentrating attention essentially on the present offence. This amendment was pragmatically popular with sentencers who considered it artificial to view that offence in isolation, but the principled meaning of the present law lacks authoritative interpretation. Further, repeat convictions for drug trafficking or burglary now result in the automatic imposition of a minimum custodial term and a second offence of a very serious nature attracts an automatic life sentence, in both instances irrespective of commensurability.

The one explicit exception to the commensurabilty principle incorporated by the original 1991 Act is the scope to impose a longer-than-commensurate custodial term on conviction of a sexual or violent offence where this is necessary to protect the public from serious harm from the offender. Used sparingly, this power relies on careful risk assessment of dangerous offenders, particularly predatory sexual offenders against children.

Community sentencing

A community sentence incorporates one or more 'community orders' which have in common that they restrict liberty, demanding some active disciplined effort from the offender:

- Examining the causes and consequences of their offending
- Reducing risk of repetition through probation or youth offending team supervision
- Making indirect reparation through community service
- Learning useful skills at an attendance centre
- Receiving specialist counselling and monitoring under a drug treatment and testing order

These measures have in common the offender's active participation in something constructive.

The exception in the community menu is the curfew order which requires only the offender's passive presence at home, yet can be perceived as the most quasi-custodial measure in the community stable. The threshold criterion justifying restriction of liberty, that the offence is 'serious enough' to warrant such a sentence, lacks any authoritative interpretation and sentencers can side-step any rationing restraint if they consider the offender suitable for a particular measure. This serves to point up first that the one distinction that counts in judicial and popular thinking is that between the prison and freedom, and, second, that if a non-custodial measure is felt to be right for an offender, it is likely to be imposed unless a probation or social worker advising the court can persuade the sentencer otherwise.

'Other' sentencing

Whereas this bracket formerly consisted of financial penalties and discharges – measures that did not affect the liberty of the offender directly – the band has stretched to absorb liberty-restricting innovations (such as the reparation order for young offenders, com-

continued

munity service and curfew orders for adult petty persistent offenders who are considered unsuitable for a further fine), thus blurring the distinctive character of community sentences.

Special groups
Two groups of offenders command special consideration in sentencing.

1   In dealing with *a mentally disordered offender*, a court is required to seek a psychiatric assessment before passing a custodial sentence and, also, must consider the likely effect of such a sentence on the offender's mental condition and on any treatment available to them. Additionally, to preserve flexibility of approach, the normal provisions of the 1991 Act shall not operate to require a custodial sentence to be passed or to prevent the exercise of a more appropriate measure.

2   In dealing with *an offender aged under 18*, a court is required to 'have regard to their welfare', though this is no exclusive consideration. Further, courts now have to absorb that the 'principal aim of the youth justice system is to prevent offending'. It remains to be established how considerations of welfare, deserts and prevention should be juggled in the case of possible conflict but it is also intended that all young offenders on first conviction shall receive a referral order, diverting them to a community panel to agree a programme of 'restorative justice'.

For Further Reading
Ashworth, A. 1995: *Sentencing and Criminal Justice.* London: Butterworths.
Stone, N. 2000: *A Companion Guide to Sentencing.* Ilkley: Owen Wells.
Walker, N. and Padfield, N. 1996: *Sentencing: Theory, Law and Practice.* London: Butterworths.

NIGEL STONE

Separation
See DIVORCE AND FAMILY COURT WELFARE.

Service Users
See USER.

Sexism
Sexism is a form of oppression in which men exercise power over women to acquire privileges at their expense. The system of organizing social relations to control and exploit women on the personal, institutional and cultural levels is called *patriarchy*. It establishes the parameters for a dyadic relationship that endorses relations of subjugation and domination between men and women.

Sexism is closely linked to gender-based identity politics and involves the systematic devaluation of attributes associated with women and an overvaluation of those linked to men. The ensuing dyad is unstable and has to be constantly reproduced through daily exchanges that confirm women's subordinate position and men's superior one.

The affirmation of sexism cannot be taken for granted. Framed within dominant gendered discourses, men's and women's interactions within their own gender or across to the other follow one of several different paths with regard to sexism: uncritical acceptance, accommodation or rejection. Which one it is depends on the exercise of agency to achieve specific goals and upon the social and physical resources that each party brings to bear in a particular situation.

Sexism characterizes social work as 'women's work' linked to caring. It is evidenced in: a culture that condones sexual harassment and abuse; worker–client relations that reinforce sex-role stereotypes portraying women as nurturers; a work-force composed primarily of white men in managerial posts and white women on the frontline, while black workers are under-represented at all levels.

For Further Reading
Dominelli, L. 1997: *Sociology for Social Work.* Basingstoke: Macmillan.

LENA DOMINELLI

Sex Offenders

Sex offenders are persons who commit sexual offences, including rape, indecent assault, unlawful sexual intercourse, gross indecency with a child and indecent exposure. (The precise terms and definitions of sexual offences vary from one jurisdiction to another.)

Incidence

In 1993, at least 260,000 men aged 20 or over in England and Wales were convicted of a sexual offence of some kind, of whom 210,000 had convictions for a 'sexual offence with a victim' (i.e. excluding offences involving only consenting adults). Of these, 110,000 had a conviction for an offence against a child. About one in 60 in a sample of men born in 1953 had a conviction by the age of 40 for some type of sexual offence. (Home Office, 1997).

Most sex offenders are male, but studies have estimated that up to 20 per cent of abusers of boys and 5 per cent of abusers of girls are women. Most child abusers are well known to the children they abuse, with about 80 per cent of offences taking place in the home of either the offender or the victim. The literature suggests that 60 to 70 per cent of child molesters target only girls, about 20 to 33 per cent boys, and about 10 per cent children of either sex.

Most child sexual abusers were themselves abused as children (70 per cent in a Home Office study of participants in sex offender treatment programmes, but lower proportions in some other studies). However, the majority of abused children do not themselves go on to become abusers.

The effects of serious sexual offences on victims are often traumatic. Victims of such offences frequently suffer pain, fear and humiliation and their experience can lead to feelings of depression, anger, self-disgust, loneliness and helplessness. The effects of sexual abuse can include mental health problems, suicide attempts, violence and aggression, misuse of alcohol and drugs, and difficulties in making relationships. Of rape victims, 31 per cent experience post-traumatic stress disorder, 33 per cent contemplate suicide and 13 per cent attempt suicide.

Treatment programmes

A range of international studies have put reoffending rates for sexual offenders at between 15 per cent and 43 per cent, with the proportion who reoffend increasing over follow-up periods as long as twenty years. Risk assessment scales include the Rapid Risk Assessment for Sex Offence Recidivism (RRASOR) developed in Canada and the Structured Anchored Clinical Judgment (SACJ) scale developed by the Prison Service in England and Wales. In an evaluation of RRASOR, the scale identified 20 per cent of a cohort of sex offenders as high risk: in this group, recidivism was 25–50 per cent, compared with under 15 per cent in the remainder of the sample. The SACJ also successfully identified a high-risk group, of whom nearly half were reconvicted compared with under 10 per cent of the lowest risk group.

Measures which can reduce reoffending include supervision by the probation service: 93 per cent of offenders under supervision and 96 per cent of those resident in probation hostels are not reconvicted for sexual or other violent offences during the course of supervision or residence. Well-designed sex offender treatment programmes can also significantly reduce the likelihood of reconviction for a sexual offence.

Sex offenders employ distorted patterns of thinking which allow them to rationalize their behaviour. These attitudes include, for example, the view that children can consent to sex with an adult, and that victims are responsible for being sexually assaulted. Treatment programmes for sex offenders seek to tackle and change these distorted attitudes.

continued

These are the aims of such programmes:

- To counter offenders' distorted beliefs
- To increase their awareness of the effects of their crimes on victims
- To encourage offenders to accept responsibility for the results of their actions
- To assist offenders to develop ways of controlling their deviant behaviour, preventing relapse and avoiding high risk situations

Treatment programmes also seek to tackle other major factors which can contribute to sexual offending, including an inability to control anger (anger serves as the primary motivation for many sex crimes, especially for rapists), an inability to express feelings and communicate effectively, problems in managing stress, alcohol and drug abuse, and deviant sexual arousal.

Home Office research on a sample of sex offenders on probation found that the proportion of those participating in seven community-based treatment programmes who were reconvicted of such an offence within two years was around half the proportion of those under probation supervision without a treatment programme – 5 per cent as against 9 per cent. (Home Office, 1996). Research studies in the USA into treatment programmes in prisons and in the community have also identified substantial reductions in reoffending rates. In an analysis of twelve research studies into sex offender treatment programmes, 19 per cent of sex offenders who completed treatment committed further sexual offences compared with 27 per cent of sex offenders in comparison conditions (Nagama Hall, 1995).

For Further Reading
Grubin, D. 1998: *Sex Offending Against Children: Understanding the Risk*, Police Research Series Paper 99. London: Home Office.
HM Chief Inspector of Probation 1998: *Exercising Constant Vigilance: The Role of the Probation Service in Protecting the Public from Sex Offenders*. London: Home Office.
NACRO 1998: *Sex Offenders – Reducing the Risk*. London: NACRO.

PAUL CAVADINO

Sexual Abuse
See CHILD SEXUAL ABUSE, RAPE and SEX OFFENDERS.

Sexuality
Sexuality refers to the expression of erotic or sexual feelings, but also to their categorization into 'lesbian' or 'gay' (sometimes called 'homosexual' and taken to refer to same-sex relationships), 'bisexual' (having relationships with both men and women), or 'heterosexual' (relationships with members of the opposite sex). The term is sometimes understood to refer to a fixed personal identity, though others have argued that it is socially constructed.

Queer theory has argued that *sexualities* are constructed through discursive practices, being categories of knowledge rather than states of identity or being. The idea that all people fall into one or other sexual category is also debated, since some people have a range of sexual expression either simultaneously or across the lifespan.

Sexuality intersects with the dynamics of race, ethnicity, class, age, gender and disability in complex ways and has differing meanings across place and time. For social workers, the issue of sexuality is crucial to anti-discriminatory practice which should not discriminate on this basis. Anti-oppressive analyses, however, have pointed out that sexuality categories are not given equivalent worth where heterosexuality is a culturally enforced and protected norm.

For Further Reading
Hawkes, G. 1996: *A Sociology of Sex and Sexuality*. Buckingham: Open University Press.

STEPHEN HICKS

Siblings in Child Placement
At least three-quarters of the children who need to be looked after away from home will have *siblings*. For most people, sibling relationships

are significant and long-lasting. Even in very early childhood, siblings can establish important relationships with each other and be a source of continuity and emotional support.

Studies have generally found that keeping siblings together has a positive or neutral effect on placement stability. Furthermore, research has illustrated the distress of some children who are separated from familiar siblings. Given these consequences, the decision to separate established sibling groups, either temporarily or permanently, should not be taken lightly, and neither should children's needs for contact with each other be overlooked.

Many children in placement do not know their siblings because families are often fragmented and children enter care sequentially. The loss of a *potential* relationship with a sibling has been found to matter greatly to some people. Thus, it is worth considering placing children newly needing care with their siblings already in placement. It is also important to anticipate children's future identity needs by considering contact and by ensuring that good information about siblings will be available.

For Further Reading
Mullender, A. (ed.) 1999: *We are Family: Sibling Relationships in Placement and Beyond*. London: British Agencies for Adoption and Fostering.

ELSBETH NEIL

Significant Harm

Significant harm is a gauge of ill-treatment and serious developmental impairment to a child stemming from substantial deficits in parenting including maltreatment and neglect. By emphasizing the interaction between caregiving and development, future or likely harm can be anticipated. Harm can be inflicted by individuals, groups, agencies or the state.

In child abuse decision making, the language of *significant harm* represents a shift in emphasis away from a concentration on the abusive acts or neglectful behaviour of others towards the child, to the impact of such behaviour on the particular child in question.

Experiencing significant harm will influence a child's view of self and others: a child who is suffering significant harm will find it difficult to grow up to see others as reliable sources of security and comfort.

When the concept of significant harm is used in a court setting, as for example in England and Wales under the Children Act 1989, it can function as the test which has to be overcome to allow compulsory measures of care for children and state intervention in family life.

For Further Reading
Brandon, M., Thoburn, J., Lewis, A. and Way, A. 1999: *Safeguarding Children with the Children Act 1989*. London: The Stationery Office.

MARIAN BRANDON

Single-case Evaluation in Social Work

Single-case evaluation is the use of single-case designs by practitioners to track client progress systematically or to evaluate the effectiveness of their interventions or programmes.

The only fundamental requirement is the measurement of the client's target problem(s) repeatedly over time, using appropriate outcome measure(s) or indicator(s) of progress. Practitioners may use published standardized measures and/or develop their own, provided they attempt to minimize potential errors and thereby maximize reliability. In all cases where outcome measures are used repeatedly, it can be determined whether improvement was made.

In some cases, it may be possible to obtain baseline measurement before the intervention commences and/or after the intervention has ended, enabling comparisons between the baseline, intervention and/or follow-up phases. In such circumstances, it may be possible to establish a tenuous causal link between the intervention and its effects.

Single-case evaluation may be applied to one or more target problems with one client or a group of clients, and it can be used in combination with other methods, perspectives or paradigms to address wider evaluation questions.

For Further Reading
Kazi, M. A. F. 1998: *Single-Case Evaluation by Social Workers*. Aldershot: Ashgate. This text includes examples from practice settings.

MANSOOR KAZI

Single-parent Families
See LONE-PARENT FAMILIES.

Social Action
Social action is an approach to user empowerment. Social action, as an explicit practice theory and methodology, draws on several

strands of theory and practice, including the liberation education of Paulo Freire, the disability movement, black activism and the women's movement. It sits within the radical social work tradition, and can be applied to training and research as well as to direct practice with users.

Social action has two central characteristics.

1 It rejects the 'deficit blaming' and 'victim blaming' approaches which dominate social welfare, and adopts a commitment to the capacity of all people to take action to improve their life circumstances.

2 It grounds this action on a process of open participation in which people, preferably collectively, explore the underlying social issues of their circumstances as the foundation for action. Practitioners do not lead, but, through a non-èlitist highly skilled process, they facilitate members in making choices and taking action for themselves.

This formulation differs from its normal usage in North America, where social action is a generic term covering a range of forms of professional effort aimed at social change and social justice.

For Further Reading
Mullender, A. and Ward, D. 1991: *Self-Directed Groupwork: Users Take Action for Empowerment*. London: Whiting and Birch.

DAVE WARD

Social Care

Social care is a term used to describe the provision of services to adults who require assistance with aspects of daily living as a result of disability, illness or ageing. Social care workers often operate at the interface with health care where roles and responsibilities are blurred.

In the UK, it is estimated that 1.23 million social care workers are employed in statutory, voluntary and private organizations and through direct payment schemes, with many working on a part-time basis. Job titles are proliferating as services diversify: examples include support worker, project worker, residential care worker, day care assistant, home care worker and personal assistant.

Only 20 per cent of the people employed in the UK social care work-force have a qualification in social care, and a much smaller pro-

portion are qualified social workers. Although social care workers usually have more limited training opportunities, poorer working conditions and lower professional status than social workers, their input is often highly valued by service users and carers. The therapeutic potential of intervention is not a central concern of social care, although change may be an outcome of sensitive and skilled support. The aim is to maintain vulnerable people in community or residential settings by supporting them in practical ways.

Social care is also an all-embracing term for the personal social services. The transformation of the Central Council for the Education and Training of Social Workers (CCETSW) into the General Social Care Council (GSCC), and the creation of Training Organizations for the Personal Social Services (TOPSS) in England, Northern Ireland, Scotland and Wales, signals the government's intention of addressing the training needs, conditions of employment and regulation of all workers in this sector.

For Further Reading
Department of Health 1998: *Modernising Social Services*. London: The Stationery Office.

ROSE BARTON

Social Casework
See CASEWORK.

Social Class
Contemporary debates in social work theory regularly pay attention to two major systems of human categorization – gender and ethnicity – but little acknowledgement is made of the substantial significance of the idea of social class. *Social class* can be viewed either objectively (assessed, for example, by inheritance, wealth or occupation) or subjectively (gauged by where the individual places him/herself in relation to other people). In either case, 'the "class" concept has been widely used to describe the broad contours of inequality' (Crompton, 1998, p. 14).

In her extended review of the concept of *social class*, Crompton concludes that, despite problems of analysis and understanding, 'the material consequences of class inequalities continue to be highly significant … Classes may have changed but they still count … The concept of class remains essential to the understanding of our social condition' (pp. 225–9).

Despite its theoretical invisibility in social work, *class* as an idea plays an active part in most practitioners' lives – partly because the social worker's own 'professional' career route often has connotations of upward mobility, partly because the relative nature of the class relationship between worker and service user (at least in the eyes of the service user) is often relevant, and partly because the political underpinnings of social work *per se* are designed, at least in part, to counteract the negative economic and social realities in the lives of people who occupy the lowest levels of social stratification.

For Further Reading
Crompton, R. 1998: *Class and Stratification; An Introduction to Current Debates*. Cambridge: Polity Press.

MARTIN DAVIES

Social Class, its Calculation by Occupation

Traditionally in the UK, people have been allocated into one of five hierarchically structured *social classes* in the light of the information they provide for the decennial census. In 1991, social class based on occupation was defined like this:

I   Professional, etc. occupations
II   Managerial and technical occupations
III Skilled occupations: N = Non-manual;
     M = Manual
IV   Partly skilled occupations
V   Unskilled occupations

Social workers and probation officers (including managers) were placed in social class II; care assistants were allocated to social class IV.

Long-standing concern about the limitations of the method led to a major review undertaken by the Economic and Social Research Council for the Office for National Statistics (Rose and O'Reilly, 1998). In the light of this review, the 2001 census adopts a new approach known as the *National Statistics Socio-Economic Classification* (NS-SEC) It is 'based, not on skill factors, but on employment conditions and relations which are now considered to be central to describing the socio-economic structure of modern societies' (Office for National Statistics, 1999, p. 14).

The revised classification has seven major classes, together with a supplementary eighth category.

1 Higher managerial and professional occupations:

1.1 Employers and managers in large organizations
1.2 Higher professionals
2 Lower managerial and professional occupations
3 Intermediate occupations
4 Small employers and own account workers
5 Lower supervisory, craft and related occupations
6 Semi-routine occupations
7 Routine occupations
8 Never had paid work/long-term unemployed

For Further Reading
Rose, D. and O'Reilly, K. (eds) 1998: *The ESRC Review of Government Social Classifications*. London: ONS/ESRC.

MARTIN DAVIES

Social Competence
See ACTIVITIES OF DAILY LIVING.

Social Construct Theory
See PERSONAL AND SOCIAL CONSTRUCT THEORIES.

Social Construction

Social scientists use the term *social construction* in demonstrating how reality is created through social interaction. It is an approach that challenges notions of objective reality; rather reality is viewed as a negotiated outcome. The term was introduced in 1966 in *The Social Construction of Reality* by Berger and Luckman. Its use is now diverse and diffuse, not least in social work literature.

By way of example, not long ago, the term *carer* did not exist; now it is enshrined in British legislation. From the viewpoint of social construction, we can identify the processes through which 'carers' have been socially created as a category of people, and how who they are and what they do has come to acquire commonly understood meanings. This viewpoint does not deny that carers exist. Rather, it explains how situations are defined and therefore responded to. Language is a crucial part of the apparatus of social construction because it conveys meanings that have implicit consequences. If, for example, social workers define a daughter as being a carer, this will have particular consequences for her.

A social constructionist analysis is relevant to almost any social work situation and can be usefully drawn upon to develop reflective practice.

For Further Reading

Harbison, J. and Morrow, M. 1998: Re-examining the social construction of 'elder abuse and neglect': A Canadian perspective. *Ageing and Society*, 18 (6), 691–711.

JULIA JOHNSON

Social Education Centres

Social education centres are day centres, usually provided by local authorities and purpose built, which offer educational, social, leisure and work opportunities for up to 150 people with learning disabilities at any one time. They have succeeded *occupation centres*, which provided a sheltered workshop environment and skills for employment, and *adult training centres* (sometimes abbreviated to training centres) which placed an emphasis on training for work and social skills. *Community resource units* offer day services to smaller numbers each day, are usually based in buildings used for other activities within local communities, and have community integration as their stated aim.

CAROL DAWSON

Social Exclusion

Social exclusion refers to lack of participation in society and emphasizes the multi-dimensional, multi-layered and dynamic nature of the problem. Definitions of the concept emanate from diverse ideological perspectives, but most share common themes:

- *Lack of participation* Protagonists differ over which aspects of society are important and where responsibility for non-participation resides, but most are agreed that exclusion is a matter of degree, since individuals may be participating to a greater or lesser extent, and that it is relative to the society in question.
- *Multi-dimensional* Social exclusion embraces income–poverty but is broader: other kinds of disadvantage which may, or may not, be connected to low income, such as unemployment and poor self-esteem, fall within its compass.
- *Dynamic* The advent of dynamic analysis and a demand from policy makers to investigate cause, as well as effect, has generated an interest in the processes which lead to exclusion and routes back into mainstream society.
- *Multi-layered* Although it is individuals who suffer exclusion, the causes are recognized as operating at many levels: individual, household, community, and institutional.

The background

The terminology of *social exclusion* began to be used in the UK during the Thatcher years, when 'poverty' was not a recognized phenomenon in policy circles: it allowed debates about social policy to continue at a European level without offending Conservative politicians' sensitivities. By the 1990s, its use was commonplace by Labour politicians, although, in some cases, the meaning appeared to have shifted to a narrower focus on exclusion as lack of paid work.

The Social Exclusion Unit, set up in the UK shortly after the 1997 General Election, defined social exclusion as 'what can happen when individuals or areas suffer from a combination of linked problems such as unemployment, poor skills, low incomes, poor housing, high crime environments, bad health and family breakdown'. This 'official' conception fits into the tradition in British social science of investigating multiple deprivation, a tradition born out of a belief that measuring only income misses important aspects of poverty. Individuals and households have differing needs, so a given level of income may translate into different standards of living. For example, an elderly person may need to use more fuel to keep warm than a younger person: if there were no other differences between them, the elderly person would need a higher income than the younger one to achieve the same degree of comfort. In addition, there may be kinds of deprivation which have little to do with level of consumption or income, such as self-esteem or environmental factors.

Social scientists have increasingly placed emphasis on the duration and recurrence of spells in poverty. Just as the shift from income to multiple deprivation expanded the range of indicators of poverty, so the shift from static to dynamic analysis extended the range along the time dimension. Examining those in poverty at one particular time fails to differentiate between very different experiences of poverty: those who are in that state only transiently, perhaps waiting for their first pay-cheque from a new employer; those who are on the margins of benefit and work, with alternating periods of poverty and relative wealth; and the long-term poor, such as pensioners living below social assistance levels. A dynamic approach also facilitates an investigation of the processes which lead to poverty and conversely, what appears to help people to recover. For many, 'social exclusion' is a way of referring to the combination of these approaches: dynamic analysis of multiple deprivation (Room, 1995).

International perspectives

On the European continent, the term *social exclusion* has different origins. In France, 'les exclus' (the excluded) were originally those who fell through the net of social protection – in the 1970s, people with disabilities, lone parents and the uninsured unemployed – but the increasing intensity of social problems on peripheral estates in large cities led to a broadening of the definition to include disaffected youth and isolated individuals. The concept has particular resonance in countries which share with France a Republican tradition, in which social cohesion is thought to be essential to maintaining the contract on which society is founded. Where solidarity is championed, the existence of groups who feel themselves to be excluded threatens to undermine the unity of the state.

Social exclusion has yet other connotations in the USA, where it stands for the controversial idea of an underclass. The *underclass* is usually taken to consist of several generations of African–Americans, living in ghettos and in receipt of welfare, cut off from the mainstream of society, and representing a threat to it. Responsibility for the plight of the underclass tends to be put primarily on the individuals themselves – their perceived anti-social behaviour (drug taking and crime) and lack of willingness to seek employment – but also on a benefit system which encourages dependency and penalizes work. Although there are many critics of the emphasis on behavioural factors and personality traits, research on the underclass has drawn attention to the possibility that geographical concentration may play a part in social exclusion, and that inter-generational effects cannot be ignored.

In the international arena, the UN Development Programme has been at the forefront of attempts to conceptualize social exclusion across the developed and developing world (Gore and Figueiredo, 1997). A series of country studies led to the formulation of a rights-focused approach, which regards social exclusion as lack of access to the institutions of civil society – the legal and political systems – and to the basic levels of education, health and financial well-being necessary to make access to those institutions a reality.

For Further Reading

Atkinson, A. B. and Hills, J. (eds) 1998: *Exclusion, Employment and Opportunity*, CASE Paper 4. London: Centre for Analysis of Social Exclusion, London School of Economics.
Gore, G. and Figueiredo, J. 1997: *Social Exclusion and Anti-Poverty Policy: A Debate*. Geneva: International Institute for Labour Studies, UN Development Programme.
Room, G. (ed.) 1995: *Beyond the Threshold: The Measurement and Analysis of Social Exclusion*. Bristol: The Policy Press.

TANIA BURCHARDT

The Social Model of Disability

The *social model of disability* is the model created and adopted by the disabled people's movement in the UK. It states that people are disabled, not by their impairments but by barriers erected within society. The social model removes the disability from the person with the impairment, and represents people as disabled by society. It becomes society's responsibility to remove these barriers, not disabled people's responsibility to transcend them.

The barriers erected within society include the built environment and public transport, when people with physical impairments are prevented from undertaking activities open to everyone else. Segregation in education and employment through policy and discrimination are obstacles to equality, and poverty arising from these further contributes to social exclusion. Discrim-inatory media representation and attitudes are other social barriers.

The social model of disability replaces the *medical model* which defines people as faulty, the *charity model* which depicts them as in need of paternalist help, the *religious model* which can hold people responsible for their impairments, and the *tragic model* used by large charities and the media to raise funds that should be provided by right. The social model of disability is, above all, a rights-based model.

For Further Reading
Oliver, M. 1996: *Understanding Disability: From Theory to Practice*. Basingstoke: Macmillan.

VIVIEN LINDOW

Social Networks
See SOCIAL SUPPORT NETWORKS.

Social Policy

An identifiable field of government activity called *social policy* developed slowly from economic policy, home affairs and local authority administration as central government became more involved in creating and delivering welfare services and benefits in the early decades of the twentieth century.

The background
As an academic subject, *social policy* emerged from the *social administration* which was taught from 1912 at the London School of Economics (LSE) as part of training courses for people who intended to work in the statutory and voluntary social services. Social administration was mainly descriptive of public and charitable services intended to improve people's well-being and was prescriptively supportive of collective action directed to that end.

The social policy which emerged from social administration initially focused on the institutional areas of housing, health, social security, education and the personal social services (or social work). The early social policists in government, and at the LSE, were mostly Fabians and hence strongly attached to state services, collective provision and intervention in those institutional areas by professional expert elites.

After World War II, Richard Titmuss argued that the social problems, which Beveridge had characterized in 1942 as the 'giant evils on the road to social reconstruction' of poverty, ignorance, squalor, disease and idleness, each believed to be largely byproducts of free market economics, could best be dealt with through collective action. For example, addressing poverty required a redistribution of income according to need in a mode which would also have a socially integrative function, rather than seeking to divide, stigmatize and demean the poorest people, as the Poor Laws had done. The welfare state should be a system which would promote altruism through mutually beneficial services; it should be integrative, reducing the diswelfares of capitalist production such as unemployment and pollution, but also be an investment through public expenditure in providing business with a healthy and educated work-force.

The radical reappraisal

A radical reappraisal of the academic subject emerged in the late 1970s as the whole welfare state project staggered beneath the oil and associated economic crises. A political consensus regarding the development of welfare had been predicated on economic expansion to fund its increasing cost. In academic debates, the consensus about welfare aims and objectives evaporated as investigators revealed how the welfare state had failed to deliver greater equality. The welfare state itself was building the new slums in high-rise dwellings and on outer estates and undermining old communities in the process. Homelessness was growing rapidly. Poverty had not been abolished, nor had the NHS brought equality in health care. Until the late 1970s, it was still widely assumed by social policy traditionalists that more of the same type of welfare medicine would effect a cure.

Three critiques assailed such complacency. First, Marxists pointed out the failure to see welfare as a device which supported capitalism by incorporating the proletariat into a compliant work-force. Hence, modern social security was in direct line of descent from the overt labour discipline which had been maintained by the Poor Laws since 1834. Capitalism needed welfare to reproduce a trained, healthy and socialized work-force, but the relationship produced a contradiction of interests because welfare also allowed the development of non-capitalist interests which had direct costs on capital accumulation.

Second, feminist theorists argued that the welfare state was an institutional embodiment of patriarchal power, based on assumptions about the particular contribution which women were meant to make to the economy and the family. The assumption was that women are at home looking after male breadwinners and other dependents. As Beveridge put it (wrapping up patriarchy with racism): 'In the next thirty years housewives as mothers have vital work to do in ensuring the adequate continuance of the British race and of British ideals in the world.'

Third, though, the seriously damaging critique of the 1970s which actually changed welfare for the Millennium came philosophically from the neo-classical liberal economic disciples of Hayek linked to the 'new public management theory'. Their policy critique was that consensual welfare had undermined the ability of western capitalist democracies to advance economic production and profitability. Welfare was unproductive, denied freedom of choice and was ineffectively managed – mainly in the interests of its employees. The policy answer was to reduce spending on social services and to reduce the power of welfare bureaucracies by opening them up to market forces. The ideology found eager political advocates in the UK (Thatcher) and in the USA (Reagan and Bush) through the 1980s to the mid-1990s; they busily cut welfare budgets, abolished or privatized services, created 'quasi-markets' in health and education, while moralizing about an 'underclass' of people living in a culture of welfare dependency. Following that onslaught, what Giddens called a 'third way' between state interventionist socialism and free-market liberalism was navigated by social democrats in the late 1990s. Borrowing its morality from neo-classical liberalism, its economics from 'regulation approach' and its social justice from Christian socialism and communitarianism, the central nostrum of the *third way* seems to be that everybody should work in the formal economy. The 'New Deal of Welfare to Work' was the major welfare policy of the Labour administration under Blair.

The impact of globalization

It has been argued that policy makers now respond to globalization – the emerging ability of capital to maximize its international mobility, while the movement of labour is still restricted by migration regulations. An interventionist, redistributively orientated

continued

welfare nation state is undermined by the globalization of capital. The right climate for mobile capital is a flexible labour market with low social costs, characterized by politicians as being 'internationally competitive'. Hence, the thrust in social policy will be to scale down tax-costly public pensions, while concentrating on transferable training, rather than education. The interaction between market forces and common human needs is complex. The manner in which regulatory social policies influence this relationship can be geared as much to economic interests as to social needs.

For Further Reading
Franklin, J. (ed.) 1998: *Social Policy and Social Justice*. Cambridge: Polity Press.
O'Brien, M. and Penna, S. 1998: *Theorising Welfare: Enlightenment and Modern Society*. London: Sage.
Pierson, C. 1998: *Beyond the Welfare State?* (2nd edn). Cambridge: Polity Press.

JOHN STEWART

Social Psychology

Social psychology is the scientific study of the reciprocal influence of the individual and his or her social context. Through the behavioural expression of his or her thoughts and feelings, the individual can have an impact on the social environment. The social environment, in turn, contains many factors that serve to encourage or constrain the individual's behaviour.

Within this general concern with the interface between the individual and his or her social context, the topics studied by social psychologists include:

* *interpersonal processes*, for example, how we perceive, feel and think about other people
* *interpersonal relations*, for example, aggression, attraction, helping behaviour, interdependence, friendship and other relationships
* *intergroup behaviour*, for example, stereotyping, prejudice and intergroup conflict
* *societal analyses*, for example, the beliefs shared by large numbers of people within a society, or social representations.

Origins of social psychology
The modern discipline developed mainly in the social and scientific climate of the USA, after World War I and, particularly, World War II. It was after World War I that social psychology became a 'science of the individual', the individualist conception coinciding with an experimental-behavioural methodological orientation. This combination of individualism, behaviourism, and experimentalism was intended to make social psychology a scientifically respectable discipline; thus it relied heavily on studying the effect of a manipulable social environment upon individual behaviour under laboratory conditions.

Research methodology
Social psychologists employ a wide range of methodological techniques depending on the topic studied. Methods include attitude measurement, surveys, interviews, systematic observational methods, field studies, field experiments and, most prominently, laboratory experiments.

The laboratory experiment has become 'the core research method in social psychology' (Aronson et al., 1985) because it is the method best suited to testing theory rather than merely describing the world as it is. It permits experimenters a great degree of control over possible random variation and, even more advantageous, allows them to assign research participants at random to experimental conditions. To its proponents, laboratory experimentation, allied to probabilistic statistics, has led to the discovery of reliable, counter-intuitive effects, often specified in the form of an interaction between manipulated variables. However, the use, abuse and overuse of laboratory experiments has also fuelled a long-running controversy in the discipline.

Laboratory experimentation and its discontents

According to its critics, social psychology in the 1960s and 1970s stumbled into a 'crisis' about its goals, methods and accomplishments. Many of the critiques originated from outside social psychology and centred on three areas: the ethics involved in, the artefacts undermining, and the doubtful relevance of laboratory experimentation. In fact, none of these critiques is peculiar to laboratory experimentation, but, more than any other method, it came to be the focus of discontent.

Ethical concerns arise in experimentation whenever deception is used and, more generally, whenever anxiety, pain, embarrassment, guilt, or other intense feelings are aroused in research participants. Aronson et al. (1985) suggest that these issues arise in any procedure that enables participants to confront some aspect of themselves that may not be pleasant or positive. The purpose served by deception is to eliminate or weaken contaminating artefactual variables, often by means of a 'cover story' which provides the participant with a sensible rationale for the research. Alternatives to deception have been suggested, but the ethical issues involved are more general. Partly as a result of the furore surrounding Milgram's (1974) studies of obedience, which both deceived and distressed participants, weaker forms of deception now tend to be used. There has also been a public debate on the pros and cons of deception in social psychological research and a rapid growth of professional and governmental regulations on the protection of human research participants.

By its very nature, the placement of a 'participant' under the control of an 'experimenter' in an experimental setting can result in behaviour that may not occur in other settings. The term 'demand characteristics' refers to cues in the experimental setting that convey to the participant the nature of the experimenter's hypothesis and thus vitiate the results of social-psychological research. It is also possible that the experimenter's own behaviour may provide cues that influence the responses of participants. This inadvertent influence of the experimenter, via verbal and nonverbal cues, can suggest covertly to the participant the experimenter's own expectations concerning the outcomes of an experiment.

The relevance of social psychology

The tendency of social psychologists slavishly to emulate natural science techniques has led to the charge of irrelevance, based on three claims: the supposed artificiality of the laboratory experiment; the asocial nature of much social psychology; and limitations of social psychology as a trans-historical enterprise. The claim that laboratory experiments are 'artificial' tends to confuse two ways in which an experiment can be said to be realistic: an experiment has 'experimental realism' if the situation is involving to participants and has 'impact'; it has 'mundane realism' if the events occurring in the research setting are likely to occur in the normal course of a participant's life (Aronson et al., 1985). The successful laboratory experiment depends only on the establishment of experimental realism, thus side-stepping some of its critics who tend to ignore the fact that the artificiality of laboratory experiments is a common characteristic of any science.

Experiments may also be seen as artificial in terms of their unrepresentative samples of participants, who are often volunteers and/or undergraduate students. Certainly, these samples are not representative of the general population, but critics sometimes fail to

continued

recognize that social psychologists typically do not attempt to generalize findings from their laboratory experiments with student participants to the general population in other settings.

The view that much social psychology is rather asocial was neatly captured by Tajfel's (1981) observation that too many experiments were conducted 'in a social vacuum'. Instead of advocating the abandonment of experimental methods, Tajfel argued that social psychologists should be more inventive in bringing society into the laboratory. This inventiveness, he argued, should include more attention to the 'intergroup' aspects of social life, and not merely the 'interpersonal' ones.

The third strand to the argument about the discipline's relevance equates social psychology with history. Gergen (1973) proposed that human behaviour is culturally and historically relative, at best characterizing a particular sample, in a particular setting, at a particular time. He argued, moreover, that social psychological findings enlighten the public, thus making the observed behaviour less likely in the future. The historical nature of social psychology means, according to Gergen, that no general laws can be, or have been, established by the discipline. However, this view tends to ignore the heterogeneity of research approaches and objectives within the field which increase the generalizability of social-psychological research.

The generalizabilty of social-psychological research

All these criticisms of experimentation converge on the questions of whether social-psychological research has provided generalizable results, and how to achieve, or improve progress toward, that goal. As Aronson et al. (1985) argued, all experiments should be conducted in a variety of settings, and hypotheses should be tested in both the laboratory and the field. These authors refer to the interplay between laboratory and field experimentation as 'programmatic research', a research programme that capitalizes on the advantages of each approach. This solution is best understood in terms of the distinction between internal and external validity: internal validity refers to the confidence with which one can draw cause and effect conclusions from research results; external validity refers to the extent to which a causal relationship, once identified in a particular setting with particular participants, can be generalized to other times, places, and people. Aronson et al. proposed that many different experimental procedures should be used to explore the same conceptual relationship, thus replacing the profusion of single, isolated studies with systematic, conceptual replications.

It should be clear that neither laboratory nor field studies should be preferred: both are necessary. Hypothesis tests carried out under artificial, laboratory conditions are best at telling us whether or not x can cause y under favourable circumstances; they can thereby promote theoretical progress. Once this relation is established, the criterion of successful research should shift to the validity of the proposition in everyday life. It should, furthermore, be realized that it is theories, not empirical findings, that should be generalized to realistic settings. An adequate social psychology should, then, continually move back and forth between the laboratory and the field.

Conclusions

Although laboratory experiments, with undergraduate students as research participants, remain the most popular research method, the commitment to a scientific social psychology has not overlooked applications. Social psychology, as an empirical, primarily experimental, discipline, is eminently applicable to the major social issues of the day, be they ethnic relations, health issues or the evaluation of new government programmes. What social psychology must not lose is its unique perspective on, and contribution to, the behavioural sciences: the subjective view of the individual in a social context.

For Further Reading
Aronson, E., Brewer, M. B. and Carlsmith, J. M. 1985: Experimentation in social psychology. In G. Lindzey and E. Aronson (eds), *Handbook of Social Psychology*, vol. 1 (3rd edn), 441–86, New York: Random House.
Gergen, K. J. 1973: Social psychology as history. *Journal of Personality and Social Psychology*, 26, 309–20.
Tajfel, H. 1981: *Human Groups and Social Categories: Studies in Social Psychology*. Cambridge: Cambridge University Press.

MILES HEWSTONE

Social Role Valorization

Social role valorization (SRV) was defined in a 1998 monograph by its originator, Wolf Wolfensberger, as 'the application of what science has to tell us about the defense or upgrading of the socially perceived value of people's roles'. The definition reveals the continuing evolution of SRV from its predecessor term, *normalization*: the first part places SRV in the realms of social science; the second reveals SRV's analysis of the power of perceived social roles in the devaluation of individuals and groups.

Both NORMALIZATION and SRV are responses to the multiplicity of devaluing experiences of individuals and groups perceived as different, including rejection, segregation, and being cast into negatively valued roles such as 'object of pity or ridicule' or 'non-human'.

SRV suggests strategies to think about addressing the physical and social conditions of vulnerable people so as to increase the likelihood of their social image being perceived positively by others, and to maximize opportunities for their development of real and perceived competencies. Such strategies lead to, and are reinforced by, more valued social roles and less, or less powerful, devalued ones, counteracting the negative perceptions that feed devaluation.

For Further Reading
Race, D. G. 1999: *Social Role Valorization and the English Experience*. London: Whiting and Birch.

DAVID G. RACE

Social Security

By *social security* is meant the state benefit system. In the UK, this involves a complex set of relations between benefits which are contributory (such as the old age pension); means-tested (for those deemed to need financial help as a result of unemployment, low pay, age, disability or caring responsibilities); or which, mainly in the context of disability, are awarded without contribution or means tests.

The benefit system interacts with social care in many ways. In the UK, some of this is highly structured. Within the residential care and nursing home sector, there is a complicated legally defined relationship between benefit and charging rules. Charges for other types of supported accommodation and for home and day care, although more diverse, entail an analogous interaction. The post-April 1993 community care system was, in large part, financed by a transfer from the social security to the personal social services budget.

Co-operation between benefit and social work staff over service-users' and carers' needs is increasingly encouraged. Benefits, because they reduce poverty, play an important part in helping service users to remain in the community.

For Further Reading
Fimister, G. 1995: *Social Security and Community Care in the 1990s*. Sunderland: Business Education Publishers.

GEOFF FIMISTER

Social Skill Development

Social skill development is a lifelong growth of the ability to interact effectively with other people. This depends on awareness of one's own feelings and rights, and a respect for others' rights.

Many practitioners consider social skill deficits to be an integral part of learning difficulty, and follow Argyle, who analysed social skills into component non-verbal and verbal behaviours. There is a range of social skills training (SST) tools which can be helpful, provided the individual is in control of his/her own goals and learning. (See Hargie et al. (1994) re social skills *per se*.)

A model based on social interaction, rather than on individual deficits, reveals how communication is related to the social situations encountered. This applies equally to people with or without verbal ability. Appropriate and differentiated social skill depends on a widening of roles and challenges: moving to the community, having friendships, having a job and taking part in self-advocacy are more important than SST alone. (See Firth and Rapley (1990) re learning disability.)

A cognitive approach emphasizes self-confidence and understanding. Social skills are reciprocal, and are developed on the basis of equality. People have a right to be 'different but equal', and no authors have described a fixed social standard to which everyone must aspire. A positive self-identity, built on respect and value from others, is the basis for development.

For Further Reading
Firth, H. and Rapley, M. 1990: *From Acquaintance to Friendship*. Kidderminster: BIMH Publications.
Hargie, D., Saunders, C. and Dickson, D. 1994: *Social Skills in Interpersonal Communication*. London: Routledge.

VAL WILLIAMS

Social Support Networks

A *social support network* is a set of interconnected relationships among a group of people which provides help in coping with the demands of daily living. The members of a social support network may include relatives, friends, neighbours, work colleagues, volunteers and professionals.

Distinguishing between *networks* and *support*
It is helpful from the outset to distinguish between two concepts contained within the term *social support networks*, namely 'social networks' and 'social support'.

Social networks are the webs of relationships which exist between groups of people, whether they are supportive or not. They vary according to a range of different characteristics, including the total number of people in a particular network, the degree of interconnectedness between them, the nature of the relationships, the frequency of contacts within the network, the quality and duration of the relationships and the degree to which they are supportive or undermining of personal functioning.

Networks also vary, in fairly consistent ways, according to a range of structural factors, including socio-economic circumstances, educational background, family composition, age, gender, disability, ethnic origin and employment status. Gender, for example, influences the quality of relationships, with men's relationships with men tending to be less intimate and emotionally supportive than women's same sex relationships.

Family composition also plays a significant role. Women with pre-school children at home tend to have smaller, less reliable and more localized networks, involving fewer social activities than similar women without young children at home. Furthermore, single mothers with pre-school children at home generally have less supportive social networks than similar married women.

Socio-economic conditions also exert a powerful influence over social networks, with poorer communities tending to display a general paucity of interactions between neighbours and fewer neighbourhood organizations in which residents can participate. Poor families are generally more reliant on local family members than their more affluent counterparts, who enjoy a wider range of contacts with friends over a wider geographical area. Finally, people with experience of higher education and those in employment generally have richer social networks.

Network relationships are not, however, necessarily supportive. They can be stressful and contribute in various ways to undermining personal functioning as well. Certain social networks may also serve to insulate individuals from the norms and expectations of the wider community. For example, the use of illegal drugs and other forms of criminal activity are commonly sustained by such networks and some forms of child abuse are supported, rather than challenged, by the social networks within which they occur. This is why it is necessary to make the distinction between *social networks* and *social support*.

Dimensions of social support

Several different dimensions of social support are identified in the literature, the most significant of which are *emotional support, practical support* and *social integration*. These different aspects of social support are associated with a wide range of potential psychological and physical benefits to individuals, including recovery from physical illness, protection from depression and the enhancement of the ability to cope with stressful life events. They operate either through *direct effects*, which enhance well-being irrespective of other factors or *buffering effects*, which protect health in the face of stressful life events.

The potentially harmful effects of lack of social integration are illustrated by the consistently higher rates of some types of child abuse and neglect found to be associated with parents who are socially isolated. Conversely, practical and emotional support have been shown to have beneficial effects for all parents in bringing up their children. Even the perception that support is available if needed, especially from a partner or close friend, has a protective effect at times of stress, especially for parents living in impoverished circumstances.

The impact of social support networks

Bringing these two concepts together, we can look at the influences exerted by social support networks over people's daily lives. Again, using the effects on parenting as an illustration of these influences, a number of studies have shown that lower rates of reported child abuse are found in neighbourhoods which have stronger formal and informal networks providing social support, and higher rates of abuse are found in areas where the social environment is impoverished.

Socio-economic factors play a significant role here, but some differences persist even when socio-economically matched areas are compared. Garbarino's work in the USA, for example, has shown that areas with higher than predicted rates of child maltreatment, according to their socio-economic profile, lack supportive networks, and are perceived by their residents to be characterized by insular and unstable relationships, with lower levels of community participation and neighbour interactions. By contrast, the lower-risk neighbourhoods are perceived to be 'poor but decent' places to live, where neighbours are willing to provide mutual help with child care, looking after one another's children in emergencies and keeping an eye on children in the community, intervening to protect their safety if necessary.

The implications for social workers of the known benefits of social support networks are fairly self-evident. In the socially impoverished environments in which social workers are usually to be found, residents are likely to benefit from the creation and maintenance of a wide range of socially supportive network relationships in the locality. A community orientation, rather than a purely individualistic approach, is indicated, which helps local people to participate in such activities as play groups, youth clubs, women's groups, food co-operatives, luncheon clubs and adult education classes. The relationships formed can help individuals to develop competence, build self-esteem, participate in reciprocal exchanges and provide a sense of belonging, all of which are likely to improve their health and well-being in significant ways.

continued

For Further Reading

Garbarino, J. and Kostelny, K. 1992: Child maltreatment as a community problem. *Child Abuse and Neglect*, 16, 455–64.

Jack, G. 1998: The social ecology of parents and children: implications for the development of child welfare services in the UK. *International Journal of Child and Family Welfare*, 98 (1), 74–88.

Wilkinson, R. 1996: *Unhealthy Societies: The Afflictions of Inequality*. London: Routledge.

GORDON JACK

Social Theory and Social Work

A *social theory* is best understood as a general framework which attempts to describe, analyse and interpret both society itself and society's relationship to the activities of people within it.

The attempt to map and explain the *social* can be traced to the eighteenth century in Western Europe, when there was a general drive towards rationality and reason through the critical appraisal of existing ideas, which has become known as the Enlightenment. Thus, social theory is closely related to political theory and to philosophy. Today, there are many competing social theories, but, in spite of this diversity, the questions with which theorists have sought to grapple are often very similar. It is the answers provided by each theory that differ.

Three questions relevant to social work

There are some recurrent questions (or clusters of analytic problems) that continue to preoccupy social theorists which have particular relevance to social work. These questions are not mutually exclusive; each relates to the others and the answers work together to provide frameworks or lenses for understanding society. There are three main questions:

1   What is the relationship between society and the individuals within it? Do individuals create society through their actions or is it an entity which imposes certain forms of behaviour, life chances or choices upon them? This is often known as the structure (society and its institutions) versus agency (people and their activities and interactions) debate.

2   How do everyday events taking place between individuals within homes, organizations, schools, shops, hospitals and so forth relate to the 'big' institutions of society such as the state, government, the law, the economy, and increasingly the international institutions and corporations? Can we have a theory which is adequate to explain both realms? This is known as the micro/macro divide.

3   How is control exercised over the individuals in society? That is, what is power? Where does it come from? How is it legitimately or illegitimately exercised? How are we to make judgements about the rightness or wrongness of attempts at social control? Are there winners and losers (oppressors and oppressed)?

These questions have been answered in various ways and the different frameworks which result have, in turn, been applied to the study of the professions, including social work. Moreover, social work has itself expropriated certain ideas from social theory and incorporated them into its own ways of thinking about, and understanding, its own role and the experiences of service users.

The Marxist influence

To illustrate the relevance of these debates for social work, it will be helpful to look at the ways in which the questions have been answered by a particular theory. During the late nineteenth century, Karl Marx analysed capitalist society and argued that it was the structures derived from the economy and the technologies associated with the industrial revolution which could best explain how society hangs together and why some people are powerful, and others are not. Marx's theory is very complex and he deals with the role of institutions and language in the transmission of these structures, but individuals are generally seen as constrained by the demands of capitalism and its grip on institutions. He resolves the structure/agency problem in favour of structure. Some varieties of feminism can also be seen as structuralist in that they argue that the institutions associated with centuries of male domination (patriarchy) sustain women's oppression. Marxist ideas have been very influential in the analysis of the professions. Understood from this perspective, social workers are often portrayed as the unwitting servants of the capitalist state, policing, controlling and diffusing the discontents of the oppressed. Here, the emphasis is on the ways in which 'macro' social structures directly and indirectly control 'micro' encounters between social workers and service users. Power derived from the capitalist system is seen as essentially oppressive. Thus, Marxist structuralism has been very influential, not only in analyses of social work, but in social work's own analysis of power and oppression. It spawned the radical social work movement of the 1970s. Moreover, the drive to promote anti-oppressive practice in the 1990s derives its understanding of power almost exclusively from such social theory.

The Weberian view of power

However, there are other ways of understanding social work and its activities. For example, Max Weber answered the structure/agency problem very differently. He placed a much greater emphasis on human beings as 'agents' who have effects upon society in various ways. Weberian analyses of the professions, for example, focus on the actions taken by members of the occupation which result in 'professionalization'. Professions become dominant, not simply because they serve the purposes of capitalism, but because their members themselves control access to training, become self-regulating (like the British Medical Association, for example) and carve out areas of monopoly expertise. Viewed in this way, social work may be seen as unsuccessful in achieving full professional status and as subordinate to other professions such as medicine and the law. From a Weberian perspective, power is much more of a negotiated phenomenon, dependent for its existence on the action of individuals.

Another major classical social theorist is Emile Durkheim. Durkheim, like Marx, can be classified as a structuralist, but instead of conflict, he stressed social solidarity. Society was more than just a sum of individuals and was held together by a 'collective conscience', a system of rituals and rules which work together to give cohesion and stability. Durkheim's ideas were developed by Talcott Parsons who produced a structural 'functionalist' analysis of the professions. Here, professions like social work are seen as functional for society – they are part of the cement which holds it together.

Developments in the late twentieth century

All of the classical social theories have been subject to critique, debate and development and the late twentieth century produced some interesting developments. Some theorists (for example, Anthony Giddens, Pierre Bourdieu) have drawn on some of these classical works to produce theories which give a more central role to language as a medium of transmission and reproduction of ideas in society, and which attempt to bridge the structure/agency and macro/micro divide in various ways. These works can be used to

continued

understand both social work's location among, and interdependence with, other parts of society such as the law, and also the active role its agents play in shaping their own practices.

Alongside these developments, others have argued that society has now become so complex that any attempt to provide a theory of everything in it is hopelessly naïve and outdated. This view is sometimes called POSTMODERNISM. Moreover, it has been argued that social theory is, itself, merely an artefact of white, male, Eurocentric preoccupation with the nation state. However, these developments have themselves bequeathed a renewed focus on language which can be useful in understanding the way in which social workers exercise their power but are, at the same time, themselves controlled.

By using theories as lenses on the world, social workers can expand their understanding of their roles and tasks, and learn to think about the processes of continuity and change within their profession in new ways.

For Further Reading
Craib, I. 1997: *Classical Social Theory: An Introduction to the Thought of Marx, Weber, Durkheim and Simmel*. Oxford: Oxford University Press.
Layder, D. 1994: *Understanding Social Theory*. London: Sage.

SUE WHITE

Social Welfare Law
See LAW AND SOCIAL WORK.

Social Work Theory

Social work theory is a body of thought which provides an organized description and explanation of the purposes and content of social work as both a social phenomenon and as an activity. Some writers reserve the term *theory* to thinking which offers explanation, but most would also accept the inclusion of organizing concepts and description.

Theory's three categories
Social work theory may be divided into three categories: theories of the *nature* of social work; theories of *practice*; and theories of the *client world*. Each affects the others. For example, as ideas on the nature of social work change, they press practice theories to develop to meet new purposes, drawing on different theories of the client world. These mutual influences may be seen in the following summary of important theoretical debates within twentieth-century social work.

Theories of the *nature of social work* are perspectives, drawn from general social and political philosophies, on the social functions, aims and values of social work. These counterpose three purposes:

1 Service provision and social regulation of individuals on behalf of organized society, mainly represented by the state
2 Individual growth in personal satisfaction and social stability
3 Social change and improvement

Practice theories are relatively discrete sets of ideas prescribing appropriate social work actions in particular situations. Psychological or social explanations of human behaviour are applied to social work situations, and actions are prescribed, based on the worker's assessment of the situation. Practice theories are usually formulated as separate, relatively complete and coherent sets of ideas. However, aspects of them are often used eclectically, in combination.

Theories of the *client world* are ideas about human behaviour and social life, drawn mainly from theory and research in management, philosophy, psychology, social policy and sociology. These theories describe and explain why people act as they do in particular circumstances, and how social phenomena arise. These inform the prescriptions of practice theories.

The background to social work theory

Theories of social work's nature in the nineteenth century saw it as organizing and focusing charitable assistance. Its aim was the moral improvement and effective regulation of disorganized and stigmatized working-class people. Practice theories emphasized investigation providing evidence of need and worthiness for help and 'social diagnosis'.

Socialist thought sought social change through political means, by introducing social security, and improved education, health care and housing. This position criticized the moralistic goals and limited effectiveness of more individualistic social work. In less radical form, as 'social improvement', thinking about the nature of social work incorporated social change as an objective, without its being adequately connected to practice theory prescriptions.

Between the 1920s in the USA (the 1940s in the UK) and the 1960s, psychodynamic theory, based on the work of Freud and his followers, dominated social work thinking. Social problems were ascribed to behavioural difficulties arising from irrational drives. Social work's purpose was to adjust social work clients' behaviour to fit with social expectations. This theoretical position on the nature of social work, while concerned with individual help and social regulation, also incorporated elements seeking personal growth towards social and psychological health. Psychosocial theory, the most recent implementation of psychodynamic theory, proposes that social work focuses on the 'person-in-situation', that is, how clients deal with the social environment in which they live. These ideas were criticized, particularly in the recession of the 1930s, for failing to respond to the social distress of extreme poverty arising from economic movements.

In the mid-twentieth century, there was a period of economic expansion and political consensus about the value of improving social provision. Social work was incorporated into these aims, becoming an accepted instrument of social improvement, integrating this purpose somewhat with formerly unconnected individualistic practice. This higher profile raised questions about the adequacy of social work's practice methods and whether seeking social change was consistent with a focus on personal change.

Psychodynamic theory was, therefore, challenged in the 1960s and 1970s by two trends. First, the 'empirical practice movement', derived from behavioural psychology, sought to target interventions more precisely on specific behaviours in a practice theory more strongly based on empirical research. However, this was criticized as being too mechanistic, although derivatives like task-centred practice theory mitigated this tendency. Behavioural social work was modified in the 1970s by social learning theory and, in the 1980s, by cognitive theory. These introduced learning from observation, modelling behaviour on others and applying rational thought to change behaviour.

The other challenge to psychosocial theory in the 1970s criticized its failure to incorporate social factors in its explanations of human behaviour and social change into its purposes. Practice theories based on systems theory responded to this critique. Ecological systems theory, influential in North America, focused on the 'person-in-environment', extending social work concerns beyond the immediate social surroundings of clients, typical of psychosocial work. However, the focus was still primarily personal.

continued

Theories of the client world were also strongly influenced in the 1970s by Marxist theory, particularly in Europe and Latin America. This perspective focused on the social change objective within the nature of social work. Radical practice theories with these objectives and drawing on these theories of the client world proposed that social distress arises from the oppression of working class people by capitalist elites. Social work should promote experience of co-operation and mutual support among working class people, particularly in class-based community and trade union organizations. Subsequent developments have incorporated social divisions arising from other factors, such as discrimination arising from gender, 'race', sexual orientation and disability. Consequently, anti-discriminatory or anti-oppressive practice theories seek to help clients to gain an insight into how oppression adversely affects their lives, and promote various strategies for challenging discrimination and gaining mutual support. Practice also seeks to prevent agencies from being discriminatory.

Social work theory today

Several emphases are thus now available to social work within psychosocial, empirical cognitive-behavioural systems, and radical, anti-discriminatory practice theories. These represent the current outcome of the discourse on the nature of social work and the influence of a range of theories of the client world.

For Further Reading

Parton, N. (ed.) 1996: *Social Theory, Social Change and Social Work*. London: Routledge.
Payne, M. 1997: *Modern Social Work Theory* (2nd edn). London: Macmillan.
Soydan, H. 1999: *The History of Ideas in Social Work* (British edn). Birmingham: Venture.

MALCOLM PAYNE

Sociology

Sociology is the study of patterns of social relationships and of the institutionalized organization generated and sustained by those relationships.

The background

The impetus for the development of sociology as a discipline came with the rise of industrial capitalism and democratic politics in northern Europe in the nineteenth century, and in the USA in the early twentieth century. As well as new social and political concerns, the radical transformations of life brought about by industrialization and urbanization led to new intellectual questions being posed which required fresh modes of interpretation and understanding. The achievements of the classic sociological innovators of these eras – Marx, Weber, Durkheim, Simmel, the Chicago School, among others – were that they developed rigorous analytical frameworks that allowed the changes occurring in social and economic life to be better comprehended. Through their work, the organization of social life became a legitimate focus of enquiry and the discipline of sociology as it is now recognized emerged. Since then sociology has, like society itself, become more complex and more global. Its concern is still with understanding the transformations affecting social and economic life in different societies, though its subject matter is now generally quite highly differentiated. Indeed, the maturity of contemporary sociology is reflected in the wide range of substantive specialisms which now characterize the discipline, as well as in its theoretical and methodological diversity. In this respect, sociology is all-embracing: all manner of social activity – from aesthetics to family conflict, from ideological commitment to labour processes – is now open to critical sociological scrutiny.

Yet, as efforts to understand the structural transformations occurring at the beginning of the twenty-first century indicate, sociology also remains committed to a more global view in which changes in one sphere are seen as integrally related to changes in others. Be the contemporary period labelled 'post', 'late' or 'high' modernity, the impact of such factors as rapidly shifting technologies, globalization, and radical economic restructuring has led to old certainties being contested just as fully as previously dominant ideas were challenged by the rise of urban, industrial capitalism in the nineteenth and early twentieth centuries.

Structures and personal choice

It is sometimes wryly suggested that, if economics is about the choices people make, sociology is about why they have no choices open to them. There is an element of truth in this. Fundamentally, sociology is concerned with examining how people order their lives within the structural constraints of their setting. Of course, people have the power to make choices – in more technical language, they have *agency* – but, equally, that agency is enacted in a world in which economic and social structures constrain how they behave in ways over which they as individuals have little control or influence. Thus the institutionalized arrangements occurring in any society appear to operate independently of the individuals involved, though ultimately they are constructed through people's collective activities. Similarly, these arrangements alter over time, but not necessarily in ways that are planned or foreseen.

Language is a good example. For each of us it is 'given', out there independently of our use of it, but, at the same time, it exists only because people like us do use it and, moreover, gradually modify it through our creative constructions. So, too, all other social patterns appear 'external', yet, in reality, are constructed through human agency. It is the interplay of agency and structure that lies at the heart of sociology.

The inequality of influence

However, it is also important to recognize that individuals are not all able to influence social order to the same degree. Some people hold more power than others, and have greater access to significant resources. A focus on social and economic inequalities has certainly been central to the development of British sociology. Whether rooted in Fabianism or in more theoretical Marxist or Weberian perspectives, much attention was – and continues to be – paid to the systematic structuring of poverty and class inequality, though more recently, in line with broader social movements, gender, ethnic and other social divisions like disability have also been the focus of extended sociological analysis.

Arguably, it is in these concerns with inequality that sociology has most obviously influenced social work theorizing and practice. Rather than being premised on individual pathology, many of the difficulties social work clients face are consequent upon the systematic material inequalities of class, gender and ethnicity inherent in the social and economic ordering of contemporary society. Understanding the nature of these inequalities, and the impact they have on the actions and behaviour of individuals, has thus become an integral element of social work practice and training.

As the transformations currently associated with 'late' or 'high' modernity illustrate, social and economic structures are emergent rather than static. Change is normal. So too, the practice of social work evolves as new ideologies, and accompanying legislation, emerge to reframe its substance. In turn, the training which social workers receive is modified to reflect the new demands made of practitioners. Currently, there is much emphasis on technical competence and expertise reflecting the need for knowledge of complex legislation and recommended codes of practice, together with financial and other new managerial skills.

continued

Within this climate, the desirability of social workers understanding sociological frameworks and perspectives may seem less critical. Yet, many would argue this is far from the case. Social work cannot fulfil its mission if it is interpreted as simply the application of guidelines and rules. For social work intervention to be effective, the varied constellations of factors influencing an individual's actions need to be understood. This entails a recognition that individual agency is framed by structural constraint. Be the concern with social exclusion, elder care, new patterns of family solidarity, or whatever, individual actions occur within a social and economic context. If social workers are to offer appropriate support, it remains imperative that they appreciate the structure and dynamics of that context.

For Further Reading

Abbott, P. and Wallace, C. 1996: *An Introduction to Sociology: Feminist Perspectives*. London: Routledge.
Bauman, Z. 1990: *Thinking Sociologically*. Oxford: Blackwell Publishers.
Crompton, R. 1998: *Class and Stratification*. Cambridge: Polity Press.

GRAHAM ALLAN

Solution Focused Therapy

Solution focused therapy constructs solutions rather than deconstructs problems. It is based on the idea that all problems have exceptions – times when the problem could have happened but somehow did not. Discovering these exceptions enables the identification of the seeds of a solution in a service-user's current repertoire, constructing a picture of a possible future without the problem. The therapy develops and utilizes people's strengths in the present, assuming that it is not necessary to understand a problem to arrive at a solution.

Although based on a simple idea, solution focused therapy is not simplistic. As there is no concept of resistance or denial, the therapist has to abandon subjective interpretation and hypothesis based on existing theories of knowledge about the nature of people, developing instead a respectful curiosity about the individual meanings of behaviour and emotion, and discovering service-users' unique ways of co-operating.

In building on strengths rather than attempting to repair deficits, the therapist is relinquishing traditional models of expertise but developing communication skills and empowering service users by offering them choice and control over their own preferred solutions.

For Further Reading

George, E., Iveson, C. and Ratner, H. 1999: *Problems to Solutions*, (revised edn). London: Brief Therapy Press.

JUDITH MILNER

Special Needs Children

Special needs children is a collective term used to describe children with physical or intellectual impairments who need specialist help and equipment to facilitate their education. The local education authority issues a *statement* (Friel, 1997) identifying the nature of these special needs, and this often results either in selective education in a dedicated special school or in the provision of additional help within mainstream schools. Parental comment is invited on the statement before it is agreed: it is reviewed annually.

Special needs children attending mainstream schools are the responsibility of a Special Educational Needs Co-ordinator (SENCO), appointed by the school. A support worker for the child is available in the classroom, plus aids and equipment designed to ensure that reasonable educational progress is possible. The aim is to reduce, as far as possible, any element of disadvantage that children with special needs might experience compared with their non-disabled peers.

The term *special needs* also concerns work with the children's families, where professional guidance through the health, welfare and educational services is necessary.

For Further Reading

Friel, J. 1997: *Children With Special Needs: Assessment, Law and Practice – Caught in the Acts*, (4th edn). London: Jessica Kingsley.

PETER BURKE

Specialist Foster Care

See PROFESSIONAL FOSTERING.

Statutory Context of Social Work

See LAW AND SOCIAL WORK.

Stepfamilies

A *stepfamily* is formed when two adults form a couple in which either or both have a child or children from a previous relationship or relationships.

The 'step' stem of this word is associated with the death of a parent, and originated when most step-relationships came about by this means. Most modern stepfamilies are created following the divorce or separation of a couple. Considerable stigma may attach to stepfamilies due to the loss of idealized relationships between children and their birth parents. The term is usually associated with heterosexuality, but may also apply to the families of same-sex couples. The stigma attached to step-relationships often means that people living in stepfamilies do not use the term.

There are important cultural and religious differences when considering the meanings attached to birth and non-birth parental roles. In stepfamilies, attachments often form across households as children move between birth parents and their new partners. Calculations by the National Stepfamily Association suggest that 2.5–3 million children and young adults in the UK are now stepchildren.

For Further Reading
Gorell Barnes, G., Thompson, P., Daniel, G. and Burchardt, N. 1998: *Growing Up in Stepfamilies*. Oxford: Clarendon Press.

BRIAN DIMMOCK

Stigma

Stigma is the moral disapprobation, social devaluation or exclusion associated with certain attributes, traits, conditions, behaviours, or group membership. It has been applied variously to 'a property, a process, a form of social categorization, and an affective state' (Coleman, 1997, p. 216).

Stigma involves the systematic production of spoiled identities arising out of specific societal responses to the violation of cultural norms. It implies inferiority, and marks the boundaries of the acceptable and the unacceptable. Stigma cannot be understood outside of its social context; it resides less in the individual or behav-

iour than in the relationship between the parties to the interaction.

It is arguable that all involvement with social work is potentially stigmatizing given its associations with dependency and low status. This prompts four responses:

1 To modify the stigma-inducing attributes of individuals or groups
2 To challenge prevailing social norms through a programme of public education
3 To address those aspects of service provision and practice that create or reinforce stigma
4 To keep individuals out of the system wherever possible

For Further Reading
Coleman, L. 1997: Stigma: An enigma demystified. In L. Davis (ed.), *The Disability Studies Reader*, London: Routledge.

DAVID MAY AND MURRAY SIMPSON

Substance Abuse

Within the phrase *substance abuse*, *substance* can mean anything taken into the body that affects mood, irrespective of whether the substance is legal. Thus alcohol, tobacco, caffeine, glue sniffing and other solvents, prescribed sleeping pills, anabolic steroids, and the whole range of illegal drugs are included.

The notion of *abuse*, however, is entirely subjective; there is no precise clinical or legal definition as to what constitutes substance or drug abuse. There are many differences of opinion over the use of terms such as *abuse*, *misuse* and *use*. For example, smoking one cannabis cigarette might be defined by somebody as *abuse* simply because cannabis is an illegal drug. Others would argue that drinking ten cups of coffee a day or smoking 40 cigarettes is much closer to a common-sense definition of abuse. Such a view would establish substance abuse as that which causes demonstrative harm to the body either over the short term (such as taking 20 ecstasy tablets over a weekend) or in the longer term as in heavy drinking which results in alcohol dependency and physical harms such as cirrhosis of the liver.

For Further Reading
Institute for the Study of Drug Dependence 1999: *Drug Abuse Briefing*, (7th edn). London: ISDD.

HARRY SHAPIRO

Suicide

Suicide is the deliberate act of killing oneself. In law and practice, this definition can be problematic as the intention and the action may not match: that is to say, behaviour intended to be fatal might be incomplete, while lethal outcomes might not have been intended.

Incidence

The stigma surrounding suicide sometimes influences coroners to bring in an open verdict to protect family sensitivities; hence, the number of suicides recorded is probably an under-estimate.

It is estimated that the lifetime risk for suicide among people suffering from an affective disorder is more than 80 times, among alcohol abusers 90 times and among schizophrenics 50 times that in the general population. Suicide is the ninth highest cause of death; 4,315 people killed themselves in the UK in 1995. Suicide by age and gender is shown in table 12.

Table 12   Suicide in the UK, 1995 (rates per million population)

Age	5–14	15–24	25–34	35–44	45–54	55–64	65–74	75+	All ages
Male	2	110	179	180	143	119	113	157	117
Female	1	22	31	47	42	40	43	57	32
M:F ratio	2.00	5.00	5.77	3.83	3.40	2.98	2.63	2.75	3.66

Source: World Health Organization (1998).

Suicide is extremely rare below the age of 15. Ageist attitudes about elderly suicides are pervasive, as healthy people project their belief about the value of life after a certain age; yet, even in respect of terminal illness, only 18 per cent of elderly people and 25 per cent of families supported 'physician assisted suicide'. In one study of people aged 70–105, 22 per cent said they wanted to die; but almost all of these were suffering from psychiatric and/or psycho-socio-physical disturbance (Linden and Barnow, 1997).

Men kill themselves more frequently than do women at all ages, but especially so among young adults, when the ratio is greater than 5:1.

Patterns of suicide

The factors related to suicide are schematically divided into those which are *psychiatric*, and those which are *social*.

Psychiatric-related factors in suicide

There are four contributory elements:

1 Affective disorders
2 Deliberate self-harm (DSH)
3 Substance abuse
4 Personality disorder

Research confirms the close link of suicide with psychiatric disorder, especially the *affective disorders*. The dominant emotion surrounding suicide is depression, followed by hopelessness, with a catastrophic collapse of self-esteem which often means the person feels unworthy of help and avoids assistance. Almost one-third of suicides saw a medical practitioner within the three months prior to death, highlighting the importance of active psychosocial outreach.

About 30 per cent of all suicides have been involved in an incident of *deliberate self-harm* (DSH), behaviour which is no longer described as 'attempted suicide' because, while it is self-damaging, the intention behind the act is often uncertain. Yet 15–20 per cent of all DSH patients repeat within a year, of whom 2 per cent die. Deliberate self-harm is substantially more common than suicide: 80 times more frequent among under-20s and 40 times more common among under-30s. The gender ratio is reversed: there are three female DSHs to every male. Deliberate self-harm is the second highest reason for young female (aged 15–24) hospital admissions (pregnancy is the commonest reason for admission); 15 per cent of all probation and social services clients have been involved in acts of DSH. Consequently, a DSH always requires an in-depth individualized analysis and the significance of the 'cry-for-help' should never be minimized.

The presence of either illegal drugs or alcohol invariably makes a difficult situation worse, and, where *substance abuse* appears to be a means of alleviating psychosocial distress, the risk of suicide or deliberate self-harm should always be taken into consideration.

Personality disorder is associated with suicidal behaviour. It reflects an inability in the patient to make or sustain relationships, out of which aggressive behaviour emerges. At the extreme can be cases of *homicide-followed-by-suicide*; indeed, suicide follows about one in every ten unlawful killings.

In practice, these four features are often interrelated and, in the crises of people's lives, different aspects predominate. Crucially the cumulative presence of any of the features increases the risk of death considerably.

Socially related factors in suicide

Here, eight factors can be identified:

1 While being jobless does not cause suicide, after gender and age, it is the strongest associated social correlate. Within the western world, as *unemployment* fluctuates, the suicide rate follows the same direction.
2 *Marital status* Being married is a barrier to suicide for men, but not for women. Divorce and/or a turbulent separation are statistically linked with suicidal behaviour.
3 *Social isolation and homelessness* is indicative of psychosocial disruption, as people living alone invariably have fewer significant others, and this exposes them to particular vulnerability.
4 *Psychology* Low self-esteem, hopelessness and *learned helplessness* are found in clinical affective disorders and in so-called 'reactive depression'. They contribute to the depressed mood which invariably under-pins the suicidal ideation.
5 *Physical illness* is statistically linked to suicidal behaviour, especially chronic conditions or those terminal situations where there is inadequate pain relief.
6 With *child neglect and abuse*, there is a complex link with suicidal behaviour for both victim and assailant, reflecting an important interface between child protection and psychiatry.
7 *Religion* Durkheim's views on the influence of religion no longer hold: it is community involvement which provides the protective mechanism, rather than religious allegiance *per se*. However, the Roman Catholic and Orthodox faiths, along with Islam, still have overt theological sanctions against suicide with the concomitant social stigma.
8 *Ethnicity* Most research on suicide is western based, but there are important ethno-cultural variations. Suicide is substantially lower in Islamic countries. Asians in western countries reverse the gender profile, as more Asian women kill themselves than men. The pervading influence of ethno-cultural features is seen in countries where there has been heavy migration, such as the USA and Australia; there, various ethnic group's suicide rates, even after two generations, are closer to the rates prevalent in the families' original country than the current national average.

continued

Conclusion

Suicide is the 'ultimate rejection'. The deceased reject their family and society, while society often rejects the vulnerable 'alternative-life-style' citizen. This is seen in the increased suicide rates of the mentally disordered, the psycho-socio-physically distressed elderly, the physically disabled, people with AIDS, the homeless, offenders and the unemployed; yet most of these conditions are amenable to amelioration.

For Further Reading

Bagley, C. and Ramsay, R. 1997: *Suicidal Behaviour in Adolescents and Adults.* Aldershot: Ashgate.

Linden, M. and Barnow, S. 1997: The wish to die in very old persons: A psychiatric problem? Results from the Berlin Ageing Study. *International Psychogeriatrics*, 9, 291–307.

Pritchard, C. 1996: *Suicide: The Ultimate Rejection: A Psychosocial Study.* Buckingham: Open University Press.

COLIN PRITCHARD

Supervision as a Social Work Role

Supervision is the monitoring of individuals or families where there is concern about their ability to care for either themselves or others. It is seen as being at the control end of the social work spectrum, and there will often be a legal mandate that dictates the intervention.

When working with children subject to care proceedings, a supervision order may be granted by the courts. This places duties on a local authority that include advising, assisting and befriending the supervised child. In youth offending teams, a supervision order can be made against young people who have committed offences. It can be used as an alternative to custody by placing restrictions on young offenders which act as a punishment designed to correct their conduct. The social worker's role is to ensure that the young person adheres to the conditions imposed by the order and to breach any non-compliance.

In mental health, a patient may receive aftercare under supervision which aims to keep a former detained patient out of hospital after discharge. The role of the supervisor is to ensure that the individual complies with a community care programme by imposing conditions, for example around treatment, to prevent a deterioration in their mental health.

For Further Reading

Brayne, H. and Martin, G. 1997: *Law for Social Workers,* (5th edn), London: Blackstone Press.

ASHOK CHAND

The Supervision of Social Workers

Social work supervision is a relationship-based activity which enables practitioners to reflect upon the connection between task and process within their work. It provides a supportive administrative and developmental context within which responsiveness to clients and accountable decision making can be sustained.

Supervision typically takes the form of a dialogue in which emotional, cognitive and ethical issues arising from the triadic relationship of client, practitioner and agency can be addressed. In principle, its relationship to management is one of complementarity. Both are ultimately concerned with professional effectiveness but, whereas management departs from the instrumental goal-orientation of the agency, supervision is concerned with meaning and understanding, and is thus central to the maintenance of a communicative culture within the organization. It draws theoretically on traditions that inform social work practice such as psychodynamic theory and systems theory.

In many agencies, supervision is the responsibility of the line-manager. This may obscure its distinctiveness, but is thought to facilitate negotiation of the tension between needs and resources. Alternatively, it can be carried out with specialist practice supervisors who are normally agency-based, or within the context of teams or professional peer groups.

For Further Reading

Hughes, L. and Pengelly, P. 1997: *Staff Supervision in a Turbulent Environment.* London: Jessica Kingsley.

LYNN FROGGETT

Supervision Registers

See REGISTERS and THE CARE PROGRAMME APPROACH (CPA).

Support Systems

See SOCIAL SUPPORT NETWORKS.

Survey Research

Survey research involves the systematic collection and analysis of information on more than one case. The variables must be collected in a consistent manner so that the cases can be compared, whether they are individuals, referral files, organizations or countries. Survey research is the most widely used method of investigation in the social sciences, and it provides the primary mechanism for establishing causality in social work research. Survey research seeks to understand the causes of a social phenomenon (such as child abuse) by comparing cases and identifying other characteristics that are systematically associated with it (such as parental alcoholism).

Survey research usually involves the use of questionnaires to collect social facts although other methods of data collection may be used, such as interviews, content analysis and observation. Designing a valid questionnaire (one that can accurately measure the phenomena of interest) and obtaining a reliable sample (one that is representative of the phenomena of interest) are usually the primary problems that a survey researcher must solve. The 1990s has witnessed increased use of cognitive methods to improve questionnaire design and aid the interpretation of survey results.

For Further Reading

Moser, C. A. and Kalton, G. 1972: *Survey Methods in Social Investigation*, (2nd edn). New York: Basic Books.
Tanur, J. M. (ed.) 1994: *Questions About Questions*. New York: Russell Sage Foundation.
Waksberg, J., Ferber, R., Sheatsley, P. and Turner, A. 1995: *What Is a Survey?*, (Three volumes). Alexandria: American Statistical Association. (Available free of charge at http://www.stat.ncsu.edu/info/srms/srms.html)

DAVID GORDON

Survivors

Those who have suffered sexual abuse use the term *survivors* to describe themselves, challenging perceptions of them as victims. Survivors present themselves to mental health, child care, criminal justice, police and medical services, with incidence figures of 6–60 per cent, depending on definitions of abuse. Most data suggest that females are three times as likely to be victimized as males. Of perpetrators, 90 per cent are male and are usually known to victims.

Impact is linked to the meaning the abusive relationship had for the victim and the degree to which the perpetrator sought to undermine self-esteem. Survivors are particularly susceptible to depression, substance addiction and self-destructiveness. Disclosure is rarely volunteered and can require specific inquiry; a history can be triggered by life events or remain hidden for decades; immediate post-disclosure symptoms can include vivid flashbacks, panic and denial.

Recovery is closely linked to a professional's capacity to hear stories and give genuine permission for their telling. It is work for skilled practitioners, who themselves require supportive management. The concept of *false memory syndrome* has attracted attention although prominent clinicians are adamant that false disclosures are rare.

For Further Reading

Draucher, C. B. 1992: *Counselling Survivors of Childhood Sexual Abuse*. London: Sage.

JIM ENNIS

Systematic Reviews and Meta-analysis

Research summaries play an important role in helping practitioners to keep abreast of research trends, and in promoting an evidence-based approach to policy and practice. However, like single studies, literature reviews can be susceptible to bias and error; what, at first sight, might appear to be a useful summary can, in fact, be a highly flawed and misleading representation of the 'state of play'.

Bias can invalidate attempts to summarize research studies in a number of ways; for example, it can influence the identification of studies when authors limit searches to English language sources or rely on a single method such as electronic searching (Dickersin et al., 1995). Bias can also influence decisions regarding which studies to include and which to exclude, given a natural human tendency to be more methodologically forgiving of studies which support a preferred or favoured view than of those which do not. Relying on experts in a particular area is not necessarily the answer to such problems as experts may be less objective than non-experts in evaluating work in their own field.

To overcome such problems and to minimize error, methods have been developed which enable reviewers to apply scientific principles to the synthesis of research. Such products are generically referred to as *systematic reviews*. When augmented with statistical analyses, they are known as *meta-analyses*.

Transparency and replicability are the hallmarks of systematic reviews, which require reviewers to state clearly their decision-making rules for each stage of the review process at the outset. The end result, a *review protocol*, provides readers with information about such things as:

- the search strategy
- inclusion and exclusion criteria
- the criteria used to judge methodological quality (study validity)
- the ways in which data were extracted
- how these were combined and analysed.

Readers can then make an informed judgement about the faith they can place in the conclusions of the review, assess its relevance to their clients and work setting, and can take issue with the reviewers if this seems appropriate. Should they wish, they can re-run the review and check its reliability. In electronic form, reviews can be updated in line with new evidence, thus ensuring that policy makers and practitioners are not making sub-optimal or erroneous decisions based on out-of-date evidence.

For Further Reading
Chalmers, I. and Altman, D. G. (eds), 1995: *Systematic Reviews*. Plymouth: BMJ Publishing Group.
Dickersin, K., Scherer, R. and Lefebvre, C. 1995: Identifying relevant studies for systematic review. In Chalmers and Altman (1995, pp. 17–36).
The Cochrane Handbook: http://www.cochrane.org/cochrane/hbook.htm

GERALDINE MACDONALD

Systems Theory

Systems theory describes how a designated set of parts have no meaning unless they are connected together to become one functional dynamic unit. In social work, four basic systems have been identified: the change agent system, the client system, target systems and the action system. The common objective of all these systems is to enable the social worker to promote change through means which are dynamic and which respect cultural diversities.

Systems theory has a clearly defined framework to help social workers, users and other professionals understand the relationship between different parts of a system and between different systems, so that the impact of action 'here' can be understood in relation to its impact 'there'. The strength of systems theory lies in its ability to explore the complex interconnectedness of different sub-systems. It is analytical, creative and innovative in seeking desired outcomes.

Systems theory has been criticized for being functional, i.e. for only describing what is rather than what might be, and for placing insufficient emphasis on differences in power within the various systems.

For Further Reading
Payne, M. 1997: *Modern Social Work Theory*, (2nd edn). London: Macmillan.

VAL SYLVESTER

T

Tagging

Tagging or electronic monitoring is used to check on an individual's movements. It is usually applied to offenders, although there have been experiments in its use for older people in residential care.

Courts in England and Wales were empowered to make curfew orders with tagging, alone or alongside a probation order, in the late 1990s, and it was later made a condition for the early release of some short-term prisoners.

Tagging works as follows: monitoring equipment is installed in the offender's home, and the offender is required to wear a 'tag' on the wrist or ankle, which sends a signal to the monitoring unit. If the offender moves out of range of the signal, an electronic message is sent to the monitoring centre, and action may be taken for breach of the order. The most common form of restriction is to require an offender to remain at home for a specified period of the day or night. Criticisms of tagging have concentrated on the Orwellian implications of electronic surveillance, and on the increased scope it provides for private sector involvement in criminal justice, but offenders and their families have generally welcomed it when they see it as an alternative to imprisonment.

For Further Reading
Whitfield, D. 1997: *Tackling the Tag*. Winchester: Waterside Press.

DAVID SMITH

Task-centred Social Work

Task-centred social work is a practice method which provides a clear framework to guide professional intervention. It is a here-and-now, problem-solving method which builds on people's strengths. It is centred around a carefully negotiated *agreement* which covers the nature of the problems experienced, the agreed goals and a time limit for the work. Task-centred practice aims to develop a partnership between all those who are involved in the agreement. Its practical guidance in terms of process is balanced by a strong commitment to evaluating outcomes.

Tasks and time limits
Two central components of this practice method are *tasks* and *time limits*.

- *Tasks* are the sequence of actions which help all those involved to reach the agreed goals; taken together, over time, they constitute 'a ladder' from the present problem to the future goal. It is their incremental nature which differentiates them from the kinds of everyday task which are a regular part of all professional practice (and which sometimes leads to an intervention being called 'task-centred' when it is not).
- The setting of a *time limit* is an important boundary to the intervention. Indeed, the method's origins as 'brief casework' arose from a research study which was premised on the belief that extended social work would be *more* effective than brief work, whereas the two were found to be equally effective (Reid and Shyne, 1969). Only later was a practice methodology devised around the virtue of a deadline with even more promising results (Reid and Epstein, 1972). The model is uniquely 'home-grown', as a direct result of research into time-limited social work practice.

During the 1970s, the task-centred model and method continued to expand in the USA, inspired by the combined influence of systems theory and learning theory. A British

continued

variant was developed, sustained by a training model devised at the National Institute for Social Work, and further research into its effectiveness in different settings. Task-centred *casework* developed into a broader task-centred *practice* which incorporated groupwork and family work, with a growing emphasis on the significance of context and techniques specific to the method, such as *The Task Implementation Sequence* and *Headlining* (Doel and Marsh, 1992).

Essential elements in the model

In addition to tasks and time limits, what are the essential elements which make a piece of practice *task-centred* and which connect one piece of task-centred work to another in ways which make them comparable? The factors common to any practice method provide a useful way of exploring these components.

An identifiable sequence

A sequence of task-centred practice features a number of distinct stages. It involves the careful exploration of problems with the people concerned, both from their perspective and from others. This stage in the work is an essential foundation for the next, which focuses not on what is wrong, but on what is wanted; realistic goals for the work are negotiated, including an understanding by all involved of how successful achievement of the goals will be recognized. The rest of the work is what gives the method the 'task-centred' monicker, as participants develop, carry out and review tasks which help take them, step-by-step, to the achievement of the goals. Finally, the work is evaluated by all concerned in a way which helps practitioners to learn more about their own practice, agencies to monitor the quality of their services and, even more important, service users to deploy the method as a problem-solving process for themselves.

An explicit value base

Most methods of social work practice would aspire to partnership, empowerment and anti-oppression, as does the task-centred. However, the task-centred method is relatively unusual in that its effectiveness depends in large part on the way in which the very processes of the work are understood by the service users themselves. In effect, they are participants in a short training course in problem solving. This gives reality to the aspirations of empowerment, partnership and anti-oppression.

The method also helps practitioners to consider what grounds they have for intervention with the service users (the 'mandate' for practice). When the method is unhooked from this value base of openness and partnership, it becomes capable of being misused.

A knowledge base founded on researched practice

The task-centred bibliography is impressive in its scope, demonstrating its usefulness with a great variety of user groups in many different settings and circumstances with 'hard-to-reach' populations. Task-centred practice is a member of the family of problem-solving methods and its knowledge base derives largely from a combination of systems and learning theory. Task-centred practice is primarily about *learning*. Indeed, the task-centred encounter between social workers and service users can be likened more to a teaching session than, say, a medical consultation, an administrative interview, a salesperson's pitch or a therapy session. The task-centred encounter has the feel of a highly participative workshop.

A specific 'technology' which gives clear guidance to practitioners

A practice method should provide guidance as to how to do it. This is not to say that the method can or should be pursued in a 'painting by numbers' fashion, but that it is possible and desirable to accelerate a working knowledge of the method by learning key techniques. Task-centred practice has developed its own and has borrowed from elsewhere, all of which can be used with the individual artistry of each practitioner.

Summary

The task-centred practice method has adapted to meet different contexts of social work practice and has proved effective in helping people with 'problems of living', at the local rather than the policy level. It is rightly considered to be a *practical* method, and is one of the few practice methods which almost every practitioner and student of social work can name, so it appears to be popular. Its ability to fulfil many different agendas has attracted approval for its potential for partnership and anti-oppressive practice as well as some opprobrium for being 'managerialist'. However, as the boundaries between social work, social care and other related professions continue to blur, the task-centred methodology is well placed to provide a unifying and effective model for professional practice.

For Further Reading

Doel, M. and Marsh, P. 1992: *Task-Centred Social Work*. Aldershot: Ashgate.
Reid, W. J. and Epstein, L. 1972: *Task-Centred Casework*. New York: Columbia University Press.
Reid, W. J. and Shyne, A. W. 1969: *Brief and Extended Casework*. New York: Columbia University Press.

MARK DOEL

Team Leadership/Team Management

Team leadership or *team management* is providing a group of workers with individual professional supervision and consultation, together with developing participatory group relations among them, enhancing mutual support and enabling individual group members to make complementary contributions to achieving shared aims more successfully than individuals could do alone. The team may comprise only social workers, or social workers and para-professional or non-professional personnel, or people from several professions working together in a multi-professional team.

Leadership or management?

Are team leadership and team management the same? Cockburn (1990, p. 105) proposes that management is concerned with achieving pre-defined corporate goals, while leadership is about interpreting complex and conflicting social requirements involving different groups and interests within an organization. Thus, he separates achieving organizational goals (management) from participation and commitment (leadership). However, this is an artificial distinction: team management always involves both. Corporate goals are defined by social processes involving those within an organization. This clearly requires leadership and participation, and is part of the leadership function, rather than being separate from it and pre-defined. Also, leadership implies being responsible for, or wanting to achieve, outcomes, and so therefore must involve management in Cockburn's sense.

Concern for team leadership derives from human relations management thinking, as opposed to the scientific or 'Taylorist' school of management thought. Scientific management proposes that rational planning of an organization and its systems are the main factors in management success. Human relations management thinking argues that concern for workers' motivation and social relations at work is essential to achieving organizational goals. An important source for human relations ideas is the Hawthorne experiments in a US factory in the 1930s. Here, it was found that grouping workers with a manager who took an interest in their work and interpersonal relations improved

continued

345

productivity. Development of these ideas took place in the 1950s and 1960s, as management science grew up in the universities.

Much social work until the 1960s was individualistic. Social workers worked with individual clients, often isolated in larger organizations dominated by other professions. However, the growth of local government social work services in the 1950s, and their merger into social services departments in the 1970s, proved the foundation for dividing workers into groups covering particular geographical areas or client specialisms. Each group would have a leader or manager, responsible for 6–8 workers.

The hierarchical model

One model of teamwork practice came from the medical profession, where social workers were part of multi-professional teams. Medical teams had a hierarchical model, stemming from the development of hospitals through nineteenth-century military medicine, and later introduced into the NHS when it was formed. The surgeon took professional responsibility for the operation, assisted by ancillary workers. In the 'ward round', doctors instruct and direct other workers involved in the case. Among family practitioners, teams of ancillary health workers, sometimes including a social worker, grew up, with the doctor again at the centre. The personal clinical responsibility of the doctor maintains this hierarchical model, sustained by hierarchical gender assumptions: most senior doctors are men, and most professions allied to medicine are mainly female. Doctors saw teamwork as a way of implementing their treatment effectively, while other professions saw it as a process which enabled them to influence medical decisions. This conflict of perception again encapsulates the central tension in team management between achieving the organization's objectives and facilitating participation.

The emergence of teamwork

In the social services, interest in teamwork and team leadership grew in the 1970s as area teams of social workers were formed. These were generic, with social workers having relatively non-specialist roles, often learning from each other and involved in great professional and organizational change. As a result, the mutual support aspect of team membership became important. Workload management, priority-setting and allocation systems developed, to control increasingly stressful workloads. There was also interest in 'differential manpower use', employing a range of non-social work staff, or volunteers, to undertake tasks which did not require highly trained professionals. Specialized types of team grew up, such as intake teams to manage the heavy bombardment of work in social services departments. Residential care work stimulated interest in teamwork where members co-operated together daily. All this reduced the individualistic focus of social work management.

Management thinking during the 1980s followed political trends and emphasized individuality and competition, contesting work-force participation. To reduce organizations in size in economic recessions, a more assertive form of management was required. In the public services, financial constraints and greater demands for explicit achievement of outcomes invoked similar trends. Top–down communication methods were in vogue. 'Team briefings', for example, 'cascaded' information down an organization from the top (and theoretically, but less commonly, facilitated responses from below upwards) by a series of planned group meetings. These emphasized the role of team manager implementing the organization's requirements, rather than participating in group relations. Group participation, drawing on Japanese practice, focused on 'quality circles' where the emphasis was on work planning, rather than interpersonal relations and support.

In the 1990s, 'self-directed' teamwork developed. This idea proposes allocating responsibility for an activity to a group of workers. At the same time, in the public services, 'citizens charters' for various services led to an emphasis on individual and group responsibility for 'customer care'. The focus of team management shifted through these movements towards ensuring accountability for effective service provision in compliance with clear achievement targets and defined objectives. An emphasis on group responsibility for team members achieving explicit outcomes builds on all these trends.

The focus of team leadership and management has shifted with trends in management thinking and as social conditions have changed, but always reflects a balance between maintaining group participation and interpersonal support and achieving the task of the organization. While team members emphasize the value of support, agencies see team management and leadership as a means of implementing their objectives effectively.

For Further Reading
Cockburn, J. 1990: *Team Leaders and Team Managers in Social Services*. Norwich: Social Work Monographs.
Øvretveit, J. 1993: *Coordinating Community Care: Multidisciplinary Teams and Care Management*. Buckingham: Open University Press.
Payne, M. 2000: *Teamwork in Multiprofessional Care*. London: Macmillan.

MALCOLM PAYNE

Teamwork

Teamwork concerts the different capacities of individuals in a group of workers through complementary contributions which achieve shared aims more successfully than individuals could alone. It may involve close group relationships or a more diffuse network of connections between workers.

The team's mission and important decisions should be agreed participatively. Conflicts and difficulties should be overcome openly. Improving communication and sharing knowledge and information enhances teamwork. Early in a team's development, professional or specialist roles may be blurred, but teamwork is more effective if clear role divisions are negotiated and maintained. Team members often provide emotional support for each other. Teamwork allows agency tasks to be divided efficiently, and limits the number of workers a manager supervises. Teams are managed collectively as well as by individual supervision.

Where clients with complex needs are helped by several workers, perhaps from different agencies, teamwork across agency, professional and discipline boundaries may increase cooperation, although clients may also become confused about who carries particular responsibilities. Some people fear that teamwork will inhibit individual initiative and freedom, and make accountability for actions more difficult to identify.

For Further Reading
Payne, M. 2000: *Teamwork in Multiprofessional Care*. London: Macmillan.

MALCOLM PAYNE

Teenagers in Care

Teenagers in care, other than those in residential schools, tend to underachieve educationally. The stigma of being in care, coupled with frequent changes of placement, erodes self-esteem and partly explains this outcome.

Many teenagers in care have always experienced difficulties at school. In November 1998, the UK government estimated that one in four looked-after children either do not attend school regularly or have been excluded; 30 per cent have statements of special educational need; 25 per cent leave care with no educational qualifications; and 67 per cent have an identifiable mental health problem.

Some young people in care have difficult histories around sexuality, and all experience puberty and the progression to sexual maturity in a context dissimilar to most others. On average, 19.5 per cent of young women leaving care are pregnant or have a child, compared to 3 per cent of 20-year-old women in the general population who are mothers. It is possible that the sexual behaviour of young men in care also contrasts with that of the general population.

The experience of coming into and growing up in care is complex and traumatic. Young people's needs around identity and culture may be overlooked if other, seemingly more urgent, relationship difficulties or behavioural problems take precedence.

For Further Reading
Department of Health 1998: *Modernising Social Services: Promoting Independence, Improving*

Protection, Raising Standards, Cm 4169. London: The Stationery Office.

MARK PEEL

Territorial Justice

Territorial justice exists when levels of publicly financed provision, expenditure or outcomes across geographical areas are proportional to the sum of the needs of the areas' population, because the expected publicly provided provision/expenditure for persons with the same 'needs' are the same in all areas.

Invented in British social administration when the concept of *social justice* was often used in policy and politics, prime minister Harold Wilson made improving territorial justice a policy commitment. Barbara Castle used the concept when initiating the attempt to reallocate NHS spending. Territorial need indicators were developed for various policy areas, including the provision of social services for children and elderly people, and they influenced the development of other tools used by government.

First generation indicators, focused on provision or expenditure (uncorrected for price differences), have been used to describe, evaluate and explain patterns of variation in several countries by geographers, political scientists and researchers in social policy and social work; an example is provided by Powell (1992). Second generation indicators have allowed for price differences and more clearly distinguish technical relationships from priorities. They have been incorporated into the methodology for allocating central grant to authorities.

For Further Reading

Powell, M. 1992: Hospital provision before the NHS: territorial justice or inverse care law? *Journal of Social Policy*, 21, 145–63.

BLEDDYN DAVIES

Theory

See SOCIAL THEORY AND SOCIAL WORK and SOCIAL WORK THEORY.

Therapeutic Intervention

Therapeutic intervention is the help given at an emotional, cognitive and/or behavioural level through means of a professional relationship to individuals, whether on their own, in families or in groups, to enable them better to recognize, manage and resolve their current difficulties. These may arise from distortions in primary relationships which have occurred during development, other relationship problems or problems arising from their environment.

Although a brief intervention for a different purpose, such as assessment, may be found helpful and therefore therapeutic, normally therapeutic intervention is provided in the context of a sustained relationship. The terms *therapeutic intervention, therapy* and *counselling* are often used interchangeably: where they are differentiated, therapy is seen to be conducted by clinicians with more extensive training. Within social work, a further distinction may be made between *therapeutic intervention* and the traditional term *casework*, the former being geared to specific psychological, relationship or behavioural problems, and the latter including in addition the delivery of agency services.

The background

In the UK, social workers have traditionally provided therapeutic help as part of their role, recognized in statute. This is in contrast to other European countries where professional activities are more strictly demarcated, and where social workers are not considered qualified to undertake therapeutic work. It also contrasts with US social work, where the provision of statutorily defined social services has been separated from much social work practice.

The therapeutic role for the social worker in the UK developed between the two World Wars from the more practical, Poor Law based activities of Victorian social work, and was heavily influenced by psychological, especially Freudian, theory. This seemed to offer the possibility of penetrating beyond superficial social characteristics by focusing on universal patterns in human relationships, and dealing with problems at any social level or with any social group. The use of psychological theory as a basis for casework strengthened the movement towards professionalism in social work, itself given impetus chiefly by middle-class women seeking philanthropic and occupational opportunities. It was further influenced by casework theorists from the dominant *diagnostic* or mainstream Freudian school of social work from the USA, where professional social work was already established.

In contrast to Britain, social services in the USA were not generally available through statutory machinery, thus encouraging greater emphasis on the provision by social workers of psychological rather than practical help. During this period, until the early 1960s, social work educators on both sides of the Atlantic concentrated exclusively on casework theory: theories of intervention based on psychological, usually psychoanalytical principles, regarded as applicable to a wide range of settings and problems. The extent to which maingrade British social workers (whether in child care, probation, psychiatric, health or welfare settings) did, in practice, offer therapeutic help is perhaps doubtful, (in one study of rank and file practice in the early 1960s, only 5 out of 72 social work employees were professionally trained), but contemporary professional discourse nonetheless considered it to be central.

By the early 1970s, a number of evaluative research studies began to question the efficacy of therapeutic work undertaken by social workers, and any 'therapeutic' work began to be regarded with scepticism. Nonetheless, many of the major therapeutic innovations introduced during the ensuing decades (for example time-limited intervention, task-centred casework, crisis intervention, cognitive-behavioural approaches, family therapy, 'direct work' with children) derived from or were developed in social work practice and were employed as techniques to a greater or lesser extent by social workers, who received training, albeit at a rather rudimentary level, in many of these approaches on their qualifying programmes. In addition, the *core conditions*, derived from Rogerian person-centred counselling of *genuineness*, *authenticity*, *accurate empathy* and *nonpossessive warmth*, have been widely accepted as the bedrock of much social work practice.

Losing the therapeutic focus?

Major changes in organizing the provision of services, embodied principally in the NHS and Community Care Act 1990 and the Children Act 1989, and dividing service provision into purchasers and providers, have meant that social work as a state controlled activity has become increasingly managerial (Parton, 1996). As a result, social work has appeared somewhat rapidly to cede to modern counselling 'the practice ground which made clear a significant part of its expertise and offered it potential credibility' (England, 1986). Social workers as employees of the state seem increasingly to be becoming case managers, developing and purchasing individually tailored packages of services to promote, for example, the care of children and to prevent the breakdown of family relations, rather than themselves offering therapeutic help, at least in terms of a sustained intervention.

Nonetheless, therapy is still provided by social workers employed in specialist settings such as family centres or other centres in the voluntary or private sector. There is also a developing knowledge about the effectiveness and appropriateness of different forms of help, and the framework needed to support these. Skilled social workers, even in settings where they are confined to a largely managerial, purchasing or assessment role, need to be familiar with the different forms of therapy available and clear about the different tasks which need to be undertaken by case manager and therapist; they may also, periodically, find it appropriate themselves to offer therapeutic help.

continued

Therapeutic intervention, in the sense of providing sensitive, helping professional relationships, remains at the heart of good social work practice. Social workers, by nature of their training, experience and usually their personal interests and strengths, are well-suited to taking an active role in such intervention. Were social workers to lose their therapeutic role, it would be difficult to reclaim it at a later stage, and social work would be the poorer.

For Further Reading
Cigno, K. and Wilson, K. 1994: Effective strategies for working with children and families: Issues in the provision of therapeutic help. *Practice*, 6 (4), 285–97.
England, H. 1986: *Social Work as Art*. London: Allen and Unwin.
Parton, N. (ed.) 1996: *Social Theory, Social Change and Social Work*. London: Routledge.

KATE WILSON

The 3Es
See AUDIT IN THE PUBLIC SECTOR.

Throughcare
Throughcare refers to continuity of work between time spent in an institution and the period after discharge.

In principle, the concept could apply to any kind of residential institution, but throughcare is generally applied to preparing prisoners for release and supporting them afterwards, and is sometimes contrasted with after-care. The idea became prominent in the 1960s, when probation officers began to be seconded to work in prisons, and it was important in the development and implementation of parole, introduced in 1968.

Continued problems of communication between prison-based staff and probation staff outside meant that interest in throughcare faded in the 1980s, but it revived with the introduction in the early 1990s of a new system of early conditional release and efforts to develop a more constructive, welfare-oriented role for prison officers. The new term for throughcare was 'sentence planning', which is meant to entail consistency in intervention from the start of the sentence until the end of post-release supervision. Throughcare is a more optimistic concept than after-care, since it implies that something positive can be achieved during a prison sentence, while 'after-care' suggests that remedial work will be needed to undo the damage caused by a period in custody.

For Further Reading
Maguire, M., Peroud, B. and Raynor, P. 1996: *Automatic Conditional Release: The First Two Years*. London: Home Office.

DAVID SMITH

Time Studies in Social Work
Time studies have consistently revealed similar patterns in the average shape of the social worker's week: about one-third of the time is spent on face-to-face service-user contact; 20 per cent – or one day a week – is devoted to record-keeping, with a further 10 per cent given to administration; 20 per cent involves time spent in meetings or in consultation with professional colleagues (including those in other agencies); 10 per cent goes on travelling time and the residue is usually listed as being linked to a range of miscellaneous activities. The work patterns of individual social workers can vary greatly within this common framework.

MARTIN DAVIES

Training for Social Work
See EDUCATION AND TRAINING FOR SOCIAL WORK and PRACTICE TEACHING.

Transactional Analysis (TA)
Transactional analysis (TA) is a systematic theory of personality and human interaction which integrates psychodynamic theory and social psychology within a humanistic-existential framework. This theory gives rise to a specific method of counselling and psychotherapy as well as models and practice used widely in the helping professions, educational and organizational fields.

Dr Eric Berne (founder of TA) believed that people naturally seek growth and self-expression, that we can live autonomously and co-operatively, and that change is possible. He stressed the importance of the treatment contract – a mutual agreement about therapeutic goals and methods – as a primary tool in the therapeutic relationship. This helps to ensure that all practice is grounded in the respectful relationship. Particular emphasis is placed on empowerment of both parties by using accessible language and concepts.

Through careful clarification of the contracts, TA offers ways of understanding and intervening in complications which occur in three-cornered relationships such as exist between social worker, agency and client. Berne also invented the idea of psychological games as played out between people in predictable and recurrent patterns. Together with the ability to analyse and avoid becoming a participant in the games clients play, TA teaches how to intervene in these games and how to avoid introducing our own into the field. This has been well documented – for instance, with respect to alcohol abuse.

For Further Reading
Stewart, I. and Joines, V. 1987: *TA Today.* Nottingham: Lifespace.
GRAHAM PERLMAN AND CHARLOTTE SILLS

Transition

Transition is a term which describes a process of change and passage that implies movement from one level or state to another, whether it be from a physical, emotional, behavioural, psychological, spiritual or social perspective – for example, entry into or departure from residential care.

Notable transitions for people with learning disabilities include *chronological transitions* from childhood through adulthood to old age. These may be difficult due to negative or paternalistic attitudes, the lack of appropriate adult-orientated opportunities, or the absence of associated symbolic rites of passage – for example, in employment or marriage. People with learning disabilities need to be actively involved in the transitional process where advantages, disadvantages, implications and emotions can be identified, acknowledged and explored in an open and supportive manner.

Another process of transition is that from care-giver to care-receiver: this occurs when someone who has previously cared for ageing parents, after their death then moves on to become the receiver of care. Bereavement may be a major factor in this transitional process. All such transitions present challenges to both services and service providers.

For Further Reading
Booth, T., Simons, K. and Booth, W. 1990: *Outward Bound: Relocation and Community Care for People with Learning Disabilities.* Buckingham: Open University Press.
SUE READ

Transracial Placement in Child Care

Transracial placement refers to the placement of children across racially defined groups such that a child from particular racial origins is placed with carers of a different race. In contradistinction, *same race placements* require children to be racially matched with their carers.

Social work practice has simplified and refined the definition of transracial placements to characterize those situations where black children are cared for, most frequently, by white adoptive parents and foster carers. The term *black* is employed both politically and inclusively to refer to people of non-white racial origins, most notably Asian, African and Afro-Caribbean, who experience discrimination on the grounds of race.

Although the terms have different meanings, social workers commonly bracket race and ethnicity when matching black children with substitute carers. Race indicates the categorization of people on the basis of physical and mental characteristics which are supposedly shared and genetically transmitted. Ethnicity, however, incorporates beliefs, ideas, values and a sense of identity which relate to an individual's cultural affiliation and which are essentially learned rather than genetically determined. The short-handed usage of transracial placement, where this denotes the practice of placing black children with white carers, conflates complex and contestable concepts, and subsumes different racial and ethnic backgrounds under inclusive categories of black

continued

351

and white; see Macey (1996) for a discussion of the analytical confusion associated with transracial placement.

The background

The practice of transracial placement, particularly involving the adoption of black children by white families, developed gradually in the UK and the USA during the 1960s. Contextually, the acceptability of transracial placements reflected a philosophical and political drive towards racial integration, an increasing mismatch between families motivated to adopt and healthy white babies available for adoption, and a growing conviction that, where children could not grow up with their birth families, their needs could only satisfactorily be met by permanent placement in substitute families.

By the early 1970s in the USA, and the early 1980s in the UK, increasingly separatist attitudes toward race and ethnicity and concern about the future well-being of transracially adopted children led to a practice emphasis on recruiting racially matched families for black children. National legislation in several countries effectively prohibits the transracial adoption of native black children and many placement agencies in Britain and abroad pursue local policies which require same race placements; see chapters in Gaber and Aldridge (1994) for a history of transracial placement in the UK and the USA.

Four propositions

The widespread rejection of transracial placements derives from four propositions:

1 Black children placed in white families will fail to develop an adequate sense of their black identity and will, as a consequence, suffer identity confusion.
2 Given their affiliation to a white culture, black children will be unable to relate to black people but will, at the same time, be subject to discrimination from their white counterparts.
3 White families lack the experience and skills to equip black children with techniques for coping with institutionalized racism.
4 Transracial placements deprive black children of their cultural heritage and deprive black communities of their most valuable human asset.

The contrary argument

It is argued by some commentators, however, that policy and practice which prohibits transracial placements must be challenged on the basis of extensive research findings, particularly relating to adoption, and evidence that black children experience placement delays while waiting for black families to become available. Outcome research on transracially adopted children and young adults does suggest that, while acknowledging their racial origins, they do not uniformly identify themselves as black or prioritize blackness as a valued characteristic. Studies of young black children growing up in their birth families also indicate a tendency for children to misidentify themselves and to prefer the attributes of white people. Some researchers, therefore, suggest that these findings are associated with relative socio-economic status and the experience of growing up in a white majority culture, rather than with fundamental identity confusion or transracial placement arrangements. Overall, research indicates that transracially adopted children grow up with high levels of self-esteem, a positive attitude towards their racial origins, an attachment to their adoptive families and educational and emotional functioning which is comparable to that of their peers. Studies of transracial and same race adoptions (both in black and white families) show comparable findings on all outcome measures and indicate an absence of significant developmental difficulties in around 75 per cent of families.

Policy

Policy as determined in the UK by the Children Act 1989 and government guidance, and influenced internationally by the UN Convention on the Rights of the Child, points to the importance of children's racial, ethnic, religious and linguistic backgrounds when matching them with adoptive or foster families or placing them in residential care. It is considered that children's best interests can most effectively be protected by attention to race and ethnicity, among other significant matching factors, when making placements. Same race placements are preferred, where this practice is not reduced to inclusive reference to black children and white carers but where other factors such as the child's wishes and feelings, the availability of families, and the child's socio-emotional needs, may indicate the acceptability of transracial arrangements.

For Further Reading
Gaber, I. and Aldridge, J. (eds) 1994: *In the Best Interests of the Child*. London: Free Association Books.
Macey, M. 1996: In the best interests of the child? Race and ethnic matching in adoption and fostering. *Representing Children*, 9 (2), 83–98.
Triseliotis, J., Shireman, J. and Hundleby, M. 1997: *Adoption: Theory, Policy and Practice*. London: Cassell.

CAROLE SMITH

Triple Jeopardy

Triple jeopardy is a broad term used to analyse the risk of disadvantages faced by groups or individuals and their multiple effects. Particularly applied to ethnic minority elders, it identifies disadvantages in areas of their advanced age, poor environments and problems over accessible services. An influential report, *Triple Jeopardy*, by Alison Norman in 1985 highlighted the issue, building on earlier work on double jeopardy in the USA. Triple jeopardy conceives of disadvantages as possibly multiple and dynamic but, as yet, lacks significant empirical evidence. Its problem focus fails to engage with strengths within ethnic communities and often side-steps issues of racism.

For Further Reading
Blakemore, K. and Boneham, M. 1994: *Age, Race and Ethnicity*. Buckingham: Open University Press.

JILL MANTHORPE

Truancy

Truancy refers to illicit non-attendance at school. It tends to involve older and poorer pupils, and may affect in a serious way up to 2 per cent of students by Year 11 in UK schools.

Chronic truancy may be associated with educational failure in terms of poor attainment or early leaving, with consequent effects on self-esteem, social inclusion and job prospects. It may also deprive the young person of important opportunities and supports which schools may offer in nurturing social skills, talents, interests, hobbies and social responsibility.

It is increasingly accepted that a systemic or ecological view should be taken of the causation of truancy. Problems and solutions are more likely to lie in the child–family–school–community ecology. Key variables in pathways in and out of truancy include the young person's motivation and attachment to the school as a community, parental perceptions of school and education, the climate of home–school–community relations, cultural distance between teachers and students, the child's behaviour, the school's construction of, tolerance of and strategies in relation to challenging behaviour, general supports to the teachers, and pupil exclusion policies. Social workers have an important part to play in vital interprofessional and interagency strategies to promote mutual commitment in the school–child relationship.

For Further Reading
Gilligan, R. 1998: The importance of schools and teachers in child welfare. *Child and Family Social Work*, 3 (1), 13–25.
Social Exclusion Unit 1998: *Truancy and School Exclusion*. London: Stationery Office.

ROBBIE GILLIGAN

U

Unconditional Positive Regard

Carl Rogers identified the concept of *unconditional positive regard* in relation to two different but interlinked spheres of behaviour. He first defined it as the full, free and total affirmation of the child which should characterize all parental relationships, and the lack of which seemed to be the root cause of the problems which brought people into therapy. He then came to see it as an essential characteristic of the therapeutic relationship without which the therapeutic endeavour could not prosper.

Criticized as idealistic in respect of clients presenting abusive or challenging behaviour, the response is to advocate regard for the person, not their behaviour.

CAROL KEDWARD

The UN Convention on the Rights of the Child

The UN Convention on the Rights of the Child, drafted over ten years, and adopted by the UN General Assembly in November 1989, has been ratified, with unprecedented support for a human rights treaty, by 191 countries (excluding only the USA and Somalia).

It is comprehensive, embodying social, economic, cultural and civil and political rights, which are both universal and indivisible. On ratification, nation-states undertake:

- to implement fully the principles and standards it contains
- to ensure that adults and children are aware of its provisions and implications
- to report two years after ratification, and then every five years, to the Committee on the Rights of the Child, which monitors governments' progress on implementation.

The Convention has succeeded in raising awareness of children as subjects of rights both nationally and internationally. The UK Government ratified the Convention in December 1991, and made its first report to the Committee on the Rights of the Child in January 1995. In its response, the Committee identified areas of concern, including the growth in child poverty and inequality, the extent of violence towards children, the increasing use of custody for young offenders, the low age of criminal responsibility and the absence of opportunities for children and young people to express their views and have them taken seriously in schools, home and community.

For Further Reading

Children's Rights Office 1995: *Making the Convention Work for Children: Explaining the History and Structure of the UN Convention on the Rights of the Child and its Application in the UK*. London: Children's Rights Office.

JANE TUNSTILL

User-friendly Practice

User-friendly practice is a style of conducting social work that is transparent to service users and empowers them to be involved in the definition of the service they receive. The emphasis in user-friendly practice is on making the service user the centre of an informed decision-making process. Thus, in an assessment for services, or in the construction of a particular package of provision, the more involved the service user, the more user-friendly is the practice.

Some factors which can aid transparency in social work and thereby make the practice more user-friendly include:

- clear verbal interaction
- minimal written contact
- the use of interpreters
- negotiated intervention

Agencies that deliver social work can also involve service users in the evaluation and, hence, the definition of their provision. User-friendly practice requires that service users involved in such activities should be treated with respect and should benefit from a continuous commitment to their involvement built on mutual trust. The importance of user-friendly practice stems from its relationship to concepts of ethics, citizenship and anti-oppressive practice.

For Further Reading
Beresford, P. and Turner, M. 1997: *It's our Welfare: Report of the Citizens' Commission on the Future of the Welfare State*. London: National Institute for Social Work.

AIDAN WORSLEY

User-led Policy

User-led policy is policy that is directly informed by the participation of service users in the planning, delivery and evaluation of those services. Approaches to user-led models range from the consumerist models broadly associated with the reforms in health and social welfare of the 1980s and 1990s, to collectivist models in health and social services more generally associated with community work and self-help groups. The common theme in all approaches is the empowerment of users.

User-led policy represents a radical departure from the traditional paternalistic model of policy in which recipients of services are regarded as passive clients or patients, whose choice is limited and mediated by the decisions of service providers. Ideally, in a user-led model, it is users' self-definitions of need that shape the delivery of services.

User-led policy has some contentious areas. One is the problem of defining which people should be considered representative of users. Another arises from the fact that some recipients of services are not willing or voluntary users. Finally, decisions about competence to express a view may be necessary.

For Further Reading
Lindow, V. and Morris, J. 1995: *Service-user Involvement: A Synthesis of Findings in the Field of Community Care*. York: Joseph Rowntree Foundation.

BRIGID DANIEL AND MURRAY SIMPSON

User Participation

User participation implies active involvement in the social sphere and refers to a range of involvements which individuals and groups may have in organizations, institutions and decisions affecting them and others. These extend from having control to being a source of information or legitimation. Participation is crucially judged by the extent to which people can exert influence and bring about change.

The background
In the fields of social work and social care, participation, generally framed in terms of 'user involvement', emerged in the late twentieth century as a key idea, policy, practice and goal, required by legislation and government guidance. While participation in social care is generally associated with service users, it also relates to the involvement of workers and other citizens, and the negotiation of their different rights and interests.

The concept of public participation developed in the context of land-use planning in the 1960s, became a key concern of community development, and is central in a growing number of discussions and developments, including the emergence of new social movements, postmodernism, the rekindling of interest in citizenship, human need, social exclusion, and the search for a new more participatory politics.

Because it is an inherently political concept, participation is contentious, without clear or agreed definition. There is no consensus about terminology, with different words used, including *citizen participation, self-advocacy* and *consumer involvement*, sometimes synonymously, sometimes to impart different meanings. The term *participation* itself is used both as an umbrella term and to denote a *degree* of involvement.

Consumerist and democratic approaches
The emergence of the idea of user involvement relates to two frequently opposed and broader developments:

continued

1   The shift to the political right in the UK and internationally, associated with a retreat from state welfare and increasing emphasis on the market and individual responsibility; this is linked with the philosophy and rhetoric of consumerism, including purchase of service, consumer choice and involvement.

2   The development of increasingly powerful and influential movements of disabled people, psychiatric system survivors, older people and other recipients and users of social work and social care, with their own democratically constituted local, national and international organizations and groupings.

This has resulted in two competing approaches to user involvement in social care: the first, from the state and service system, reflecting the consumerist concerns of improving the efficiency, effectiveness and economy of services, and the second, from the disabled people's and service-users' movements committed to people speaking for themselves and securing and safeguarding the human and civil rights, choices and quality of life of the subjects of policy and practice. The first approach starts with the *service system*; the second with people's *lives*. These two approaches to participation, the *consumerist* and *democratic* approaches, do not sit comfortably. One is managerial and instrumental in purpose, without any commitment to the redistribution of power or control; the other liberational, with a commitment to empowerment.

Differences of strategy

They are also associated with different strategies for participation. The consumerist preoccupation with service-user feedback is reflected in an emphasis on consultation and data collection exercises focusing on the planning, management and market testing of specialist services. The experience of service users and their organizations is that such exercises have very limited effects in improving their lives and services, while making significant demands upon them. Their concern is with bringing about direct change in people's lives through collective as well as individual action. The disabled people's movement bases its approach to participation on the social model of disability, using both parliamentary and direct action. It has prioritized civil rights and freedom of information legislation and the provision of adequate support for organizations controlled by disabled people themselves, establishing the independent living movement to ensure that disabled people maintain control over their personal support through direct payment schemes.

Key routes to more user-led social care policy and practice identified by service users and their organizations include:

• the resourcing of their organizations
• the systematic and central involvement of service users in professional education and training
• service-users' equal access and opportunities as social care practitioners
• a participatory approach to care management, including self-definition of needs and design of support systems
• user-led standard setting and definition of outcomes in policy and practice
• user-led monitoring and evaluation of provision.

While participation is generally associated with the public sphere, it is also affected by people's circumstances and responsibilities in the *personal* sphere. This can limit the participation of many groups, notably women. Two components are essential if people are to have a realistic chance of participating and all groups are to have equal access to involvement. These are *access* and *support*. Experience indicates that without support only the most confident, well-resourced and advantaged people and groups are likely to become involved, while without access, efforts to become involved are likely to be arduous and ineffective. Access includes equal access to the political structure at both central and local state levels and to other organizations and institutions which affect people's lives. Support includes increasing people's expectations and confidence; extending their skills; offering practical support like child care, information, advocacy and transport; enabling people to meet together in groups; and ensuring that minority ethnic groups and others facing discrimination can be involved on equal terms.

While participation is generally presented in positive terms it also has a regressive potential. Participatory initiatives frequently serve to obstruct rather than increase people's involvement, being used to tokenize and co-opt people, delay decisions and action, and to legitimate predetermined agendas and decisions. This relates to a more general tension which exists when arrangements for participatory or direct democracy exist in a political structure based primarily on a system of representative democracy.

For Further Reading

Beresford, P. and Croft, S. 1993: *Citizen Involvement: A Practical Guide for Change.* Basingstoke: Macmillan.
Beresford, P., Croft, S., Evans, C. and Harding, T. 1997: Quality in personal social services: The developing role of user involvement in the UK. In R. Haverinen and K. Leichsenring (eds), *Quality Development in Personal Social Services*, Austria: European Centre.
Taylor, D. (ed.) 1996: *Critical Social Policy: A Reader*. London: Sage.

PETER BERESFORD AND SUZY CROFT

User Perspectives on Social Work

Users of personal social services are a diverse group who do not speak with one voice. Attempts to elicit service-user views often do not take this diversity into account. However, movements of disabled people, people with learning disabilities, mental health system survivors and other groups have developed new analyses and models which have begun to inform the thinking and practice of social workers and the managers of personal social services.

The most powerful of these analyses is the social model of disability. Mental health service users are also developing a human rights based model to counterbalance the heavy medical dominance of services intended to meet their needs. One consequence of full acceptance of these models would be the reorganization of social work so that different impairment groups are not treated separately. Disabled people of all ages, mental health service users, parents and children in need of support would all be served from the perspective of people entitled to resources to help them to embrace life from a position of equality with everyone else.

The concept of need has been brought into question, on the basis that social needs tend to be defined by others. Focusing on needs tends to individualize issues that might more fruitfully involve changes in wider society to remove barriers to full social participation by everyone. These changes would include: changes to attitudes giving equal status and access to members of minority ethnic communities; access to the built environment and to information; access to employment, housing and education, and to an income that would give disabled people the right to purchase the support they need to take their place in society.

The controlling social worker

Many service users experience personal social services as controlling rather than supportive. Some obvious reasons for this are statutory duties in child protection, where

continued

children can be separated from parents and put up for adoption, and in mental health, where citizens can be locked away when they have done nothing wrong. The role of social workers in rationing scarce resources is another obvious situation where they are experienced as controlling.

Other instances of control are occasions when social workers feel that their duty of care requires them to override the decisions of service users about their own lives. Acting against people's wishes or consent in their 'best interests' arises when a paternal or medical model is in operation, and seems extraordinary to those who know from experience what would help them. Once the social model of disability is invoked, people are free to make their own decisions (and sometimes mistakes) and the duty of society is to remove barriers to independent action. Clearly, this model would also prevent social workers from being blamed for the actions of their fellow citizens.

Traditional social work attitudes have led to what has been described as 'clientism'. By virtue simply of being a client of social services, people's judgements about themselves and their needs are seen as inferior to those of social workers. Another aspect of this attitude is a tendency to pessimism about a person's potential, compared with the optimism about each other that can be found in organizations of disabled people, people with learning disabilities and mental health system users/survivors.

This pessimism may partly arise from the compartmentalized thinking that characterizes service delivery. This is often imposed by legislation (based on preventing something rather than enabling independence) or by management systems (care management and assessment methods that do not incorporate user views in their processes and outcomes). Treating people in separate groups according to age or impairment can powerfully enhance social stereotypes, decreasing individual rights for support, to live independently or to become or continue as parents.

Where the attitudes and practice of social workers change in line with the social and human rights models, attitudes to social workers have become more positive. The most obvious examples of such change are direct payments, when accompanied by support to become an employer. Direct payments recognize that people are experts in their own lives and enable them to acquire the support that they judge they need, at the times they need it.

The need for respect and support

Respectful, supportive relationships are another aspect of social work that elicit service-user praise. Receiving services from the same individual rather than a series of social workers is highly valued, as long as that individual is acceptable to the service user. An understanding of power differentials is a feature that underpins such good relationships. Social workers who do not recognize that control of resources as well as a steady job with a salary confer power on them are unlikely to make respectful relationships with service users.

The rhetoric of user involvement has resulted in some fruitful partnerships between independent, democratic organizations of service users and social work professionals. More often, though, organizations have not been resourced to develop their own agendas and to reach out to the most marginalized groups of service users. This means that agendas are developed from the top down, user 'representatives' are not given the resources to be accountable to their constituencies, and those constituencies exclude the more marginalized groups of service recipients.

For user perspectives on social work to inform practice fully, both large and small changes are necessary. Some of the small changes can be implemented relatively easily: adopting a more holistic approach, giving sufficient information in accessible formats to enable informed decisions, being honest about limitations and consequences. The larger changes await government policies that are less driven by the tabloid press and more driven by the expertise of those who know best: service users. Alliances between service users and social workers can promote faster change.

For Further Reading
Campbell, J. and Oliver, M. 1996: *Disability Politics*. Routledge: London.
Read, J. and Reynolds, J. 1996: *Speaking Our Minds: An Anthology of Personal Experiences of Mental Distress and its Consequences*. Basingstoke: Macmillan.
Turner, M. (ed.) 1998: *It's Our Day: Report of a National User Conference*. London: National Institute for Social Work.

VIVIEN LINDOW

V

Value for Money
See AUDIT IN THE PUBLIC SECTOR.

Values in Social Work

In social work, the term *values* commonly denotes the summit aspirations of the professional commitment; values are held aloft as the ultimate and, perhaps, never wholly attainable ends of policy and practice. The ideal principles of practical service provision are also represented as values.

Values are entailed in the attitudes, methods and practices of practitioners and their agencies. Values can equally be thought of as attributes of persons, groups or social institutions, but care should be taken not to treat values as detachable entities: values are always the ongoing accomplishments of knowledgeable and reflective human intelligences immersed in a social world. Although it is widely agreed that no practice can be value free, the usage of 'values' is not neutral: references to values signal a normative concept of the morally good, while bad values remain largely implicit.

No consensus, no resolution

There is no dependable consensus about what type of concept, principle or precept merits the implied high status of a social work 'value', and there are different views about the specific character of social work values. These are sufficient reasons to explain why there is no universally accepted, definitive set of social work values. Overlaid on the conceptual ambiguity lies the diverse range of substantive beliefs and theories, religious outlooks, moral values, political principles and general world-views to be found among social workers just as among any comparable section of society. There is no evidence for a stronger consensus on moral, social and political questions among social workers than among any other comparable group in modern pluralist and multicultural societies. Moreover, most versions of social work values strongly recommend the acceptance and positive valuation of diverse ways of life, making the identification of essential values even more elusive. For example, social workers usually claim to value both ethnic and cultural diversity, and equal rights for women. Where cultural standards deny gender equality, the issue cannot be resolved by appealing to social work values.

The conceptual framework for apprehending values is ambiguous and contested; the evidence for the existence of a distinctive and coherent set of normative professional social work values is extremely tenuous; and the actual range and content of social workers' personal and professional values can be conjectured from the professional literature but is not evidenced by any significant body of empirical social research. The identification of social work values can therefore be no more than approximate, provisional and inherently controversial. In broad terms, the values of social work are clearly rooted in Christian ethics blended with modern western secular liberal individualism. They share their origins with the dominant western tradition of morality. This broad tradition does, of course, accommodate numerous divergences of outlook, controversies and even unresolvable contradictions.

Because of the all-encompassing scope of values and the unresolved questions about their nature, useful conceptions of social work values are best restricted to a handful of truly essential and illuminating principles. The tendency to label any or every aspect of theory and practice as a value merely debases the currency.

There are four essential principles that, between them, accommodate the important insights contained in typical statements of social work values:

1   The worth and uniqueness of every person
2   The entitlement to justice
3   The claim to freedom
4   The essentiality of community

As already indicated, these are not specific to social work, but reflect the religion, theory and culture of the wider societies that support social work. It must be grasped that all of these principles are highly contested. They can be thought of as generic values: accepting them does not settle the question of social work values but does serve to focus the controversies in relevant fields. Thus for example, some concrete differences in claimed values are rooted in competing concepts of the person or contradictory notions of the good community.

The worth and uniqueness of every person
Every human person is, in certain respects, unique and individually precious. All should be treated with utmost care and respect. All persons have equal value irrespective of such contingencies as age, gender, ethnicity, physical or intellectual ability, wealth, contribution to society, etc. Respect is active, not passive: our treatment of persons should positively demonstrate respect founded on understanding the worth of the individual.

The entitlement to justice
Every person and social group is entitled to treatment on agreed principles of justice. Justice is complex and multifaceted, but requires at least the protection of essential liberties; a theory of human need; a theory of fair distribution; a theory of desert; and fair and effective procedures for its implementation. Justice is interventionist; it does not countenance the neglect of manifest injustice.

The claim to freedom
Every person and social group is entitled to their own beliefs, pursuits and projects without interference, except as necessary for the like freedom of others. This includes freedom of speech, assembly, religion, etc. To achieve greater ultimate freedom, it is sometimes necessary to impose restrictions, for example by requiring children to attend school. The understanding of freedom depends on a theory of human nature.

The essentiality of community
The human life can only be realized interdependently in communities, from the micro level of the family or its equivalent to the larger community of the nation. Much of social work is dedicated to the restoration or improvement of specific communities. Human communities embrace a very wide and not infrequently contradictory range of beliefs, practices and ways of life; to enable fulfilled lives, these must be respected; but the principles of respect, justice and freedom may sometimes conflict with community values.

The substance of values varies with developing scientific knowledge and changing social standards and priorities. The banner of values signals the orientation of social work. Implementing values in practice is facilitated by systems of PROFESSIONAL ETHICS.

continued

For Further Reading
Banks, S. 1995: *Ethics and Values in Social Work*. Basingstoke: Macmillan.
Clark, C. L. 2000: *Social Work Ethics: Politics, Principles and Practice*. Basingstoke: Macmillan.
Hugman, R. 1998: *Social Welfare and Social Value*. Basingstoke: Macmillan.

CHRIS CLARK

Victims

While it is widely agreed that *victims* have been unduly marginalized in criminal justice, the challenge has been to accord them greater recognition without imposing an unfair burden of responsibility in offender-centred decisions or intervention. Initiatives to aid victims in coping with the immediate aftermath and longer-term distress of crime, to inform them of police/prosecution progress and to offer support at court if they are required to give evidence are self-evidently sound, provided that recipients do not feel stereotyped. It is more controversial whether information from victims should influence sentencing decisions. For example, should an offender be advantaged or disadvantaged by the chance factor that their victim is particularly resilient, especially vulnerable or generous-mindedly forgiving?

Probation and social workers need to be victim-minded:

- By helping offenders to appreciate better the impact of their actions on victims and by reflecting offenders' extent of empathy and regret in advice to sentencers and in risk assessments
- By being alert to the potential for victim–offender mediation, in a spirit of 'restorative justice', provided that victims are not pressured to participate for the offender's 'good'
- By fulfilling Victims' Charter responsibilities to keep concerned victims informed about offenders in custody, particularly release/home leave decisions, to avoid the shock of unanticipated encounters
- By recommending and enforcing licence conditions that seek to protect victims from unwanted attention

For Further Reading
Nettleton, H., Walklate, S. and Williams, B. 1997: *Probation Training with the Victim in Mind*. Keele: Keele University Press.

NIGEL STONE

Video Evidence in Child Care Cases

In child care cases, *video evidence* usually means the videotape of an interview that someone has earlier conducted with the child, but the phrase may also mean a child's live evidence given from outside the courtroom by a video link (alias *a live television link*). Originally, videotapes of previous interviews with children were inadmissible in evidence because of the hearsay rule. In civil proceedings, in both England and Scotland, the hearsay rule has been progressively abolished, with the incidental consequence of making video evidence freely admissible.

In criminal proceedings, the hearsay rule in principle survives. However, for England, the Criminal Justice Act 1991 provides that, in certain types of case, a criminal court can receive as evidence a videotape of a previous interview with a child witness, provided he or she comes to court for a live cross-examination. This reform enacted (in diluted form) a proposal of the Advisory Group on Video Evidence (The Pigot Committee, Home Office, 1989). In criminal cases, videotapes are usually those of interviews made under the Home Office *Memorandum of Good Practice on Video Recorded Interviews with Child Witnesses for Criminal Proceedings*.

For Further Reading
Spencer, J. R. and Flin, R. 1993: *The Evidence of Children, the Law and the Psychology* (2nd edn). London: Blackstone, ch. 7.

JOHN R. SPENCER

Violence against Social Workers

Violence at work may take the form of physical assaults, threats of assault, or verbal abuse. The 1992 British Crime Survey (Mayhew et al., 1993) showed that 'welfare workers' are three times more likely than the average employee to be physically attacked or threatened.

Evidence about the nature and extent of violence within the social services has come from research carried out at the National Institute for Social Work (Balloch et al., 1999). This suggested that three-quarters of the social services work-force have been shouted at or insulted at work, a third have been threatened with violence, and a third have been physically attacked. Those who work in residential homes are most at risk, while home care workers are least likely to be attacked. Social workers are slightly less likely to experience violence at work than the average member of the social services work-force, with about a quarter having been physically attacked in their present jobs. Men are more at risk than women, and younger people than older members of staff. Constructive responses on the part of employers include setting up systems to record and analyse incidents of violence, training staff in methods of prevention and self-protection, and providing support and counselling for those who have experienced violence.

For Further Reading
Balloch, S., McLean, J. and Fisher, M. 1999: *Social Services: Working Under Pressure.* Bristol: Policy Press.

JAN PAHL

Violent Men

Men's violence against women partners refers to the physical and/or sexual abuse of a woman partner and may include psychological abuse and other forms of controlling, aggressive and intimidating behaviours.

The background
The problem was brought to public attention by the women's movement during the 1970s and was recognized as an issue of human rights at the 1995 UN Conference in Beijing. Throughout the world, the most widespread response is the provision of refuges for abused women and their children. Responses to abusers are less developed and range from relative indifference to protection orders and/or arrest. Since the 1980s, some police departments have introduced special units to deal more sensitively with abused women and various programmes for abusers have been introduced.

Abuser programmes began in North America where hundreds now exist. Many are attached to the justice system through probation orders, while some are voluntary. The Duluth Domestic Abuse Intervention Project (DAIP), founded in Minnesota in 1980, is one of the most influential, and its philosophy and content informed the development of the first two criminal justice based abuser programmes in the UK (CHANGE, established in 1989, and the Lothian Domestic Violence Probation Project, established in 1990). This model combines feminist knowledge and perspectives with cognitive-behavioural methods, and uses an educational rather than a psychodynamic approach.

Men using their power
The terms *pro-feminist* and *cognitive-behavioural* are often used to describe the same programmes and reflect the view that this violence is generated within a context of gender relations and social learning. As learned behaviour, it requires re-education or the learning of new orientations and behaviours relating to the use of violence and aggression and new orientations to intimate relationships. Abusers are seen as acting within the context of relationships between husbands and wives, where men have greater power and control, and violence is used to punish women and maintain authority. Violence is intentional and usually occurs along with intimidation, coercion and other forms of aggressive and controlling behaviours. Violence is learned and is chosen as a resource when settling disputes or maintaining authority. The issues in dispute typically involve:

continued

- possessiveness and jealousy
- the man's sense of ownership
- domestic work and child care
- the distribution and use of household resources including money, mobility and time
- contests over power, control and authority.

Abusers are usually extremely self-oriented, lack empathy, frequently deny responsibility for the violence, minimize the harm done and deflect blame onto others, particularly the woman.

Programme responses

Abuser programmes focus on the violence, the man's responsibility for his violent behaviour and his need to change. Violent events are examined in detail to gain insight into the development of an event from initial conflict to violent attack and to consider decisions and choices made at each stage. Groupwork is used and men are challenged to accept responsibility for their own behaviour and to acknowledge the consequences of their violence. These are deemed to be essential starting points without which men are unlikely to see a need for change. Abuser programmes are highly structured, educational in approach and include skills training. Men learn to monitor their own behaviour and orientations using various techniques including daily homework reported back to the group.

Some other programmes also adopt a cognitive-behavioural approach to the learning of new behaviours and cognitions, but do so without using the feminist analysis of the phenomenon of violence with its focus on power and gender relations. For example, some anger management programmes emphasize control of emotions and teach techniques for dealing with anger once aroused but do so without considering the issues that give rise to the anger itself. The anger is thereby decontextualized and one of its principle sources, gender relations, is neither addressed nor modified.

Sentencers using such programmes want them to be clearly structured, to have an effect on the offending behaviour and to provide relevant information for the courts and probation. While only a few valid evaluations of abuser programmes now exist, the results suggest that an intervention combining a criminal justice sanction with a cognitive-behavioural programme focused on the offence and the offending behaviour is more successful than other sanctions at eliminating subsequent violence, and that such changes are more likely to be sustained over a longer period of time.

For Further Reading

Dobash, R. E. and Dobash, R. P. 1998: Violent men and violent contexts. In R. E. Dobash and R. P. Dobash (eds), *Rethinking Violence against Women*, London: Sage.

Dobash, R. P., Dobash, R. E., Cavanagh, K. and Lewis, R. 2000: *Changing Violent Men*. London: Sage.

Morran, D. and Wilson, M. 1997: *Men who are Violent to Women: A Groupwork Practice Manual*. Lyme Regis: Russell House Publishing.

RUSSELL P. DOBASH AND R. EMERSON DOBASH

Vision-impairment

Although severe *vision-impairment* affects over two million people of all ages, over 80 per cent of vision-impaired people referred to social work agencies are over 65-years-old. Sight loss is usually assessed by clinical ophthalmologists who certificate individuals as *blind* or *partially sighted*. Certificated individuals are then referred to their local authority, who should seek their permission to be placed on a register of blind and partially sighted people.

A needs assessment, incorporating an assessment of useful vision, should be undertaken by a trained worker in vision-impairment. The usefulness of remaining vision is not the only determinant of need. Many factors will affect an individual's ability to manage their sight loss, including aetiology, speed of sight loss, age, physical and emotional well-being, life-experience, attitude, motivation, support systems, lighting, daylight, and other environmental circumstances.

Blind and partially sighted adults often require specialist support to enable them to adapt existing skills and experience regarding mobility, independent living, communication and personal management. Children generally require more complex support to help them to develop basic life-skills and concepts. Severe sight loss frequently affects sleeping patterns, posture, physical and emotional well-being, and can be extremely distressing for those concerned.

For Further Reading
French, S., Gillman, M., and Swain, J. 1997: *Working With Visually-disabled People: Bridging Theory And Practice*. Birmingham: Venture Press.

JOHN IRVINE

Voluntary Organizations and Societies

The Report of the Commission on the Future of the Voluntary Sector (National Council for Voluntary Organizations, 1996) defined *voluntary organizations* as 'the voluntary coming together of individuals to engage in mutual undertakings for the common good' (p. 15). Voluntary organizations, which represent one of the oldest and most basic forms of human activity, constitute the infrastructure of civil society. In the USA, voluntary organizations are known as *the third sector,* whereas in the UK the terms *voluntary sector* or *community sector* tend to be employed. On the other hand, Europeans use the terms *associations* or *social economy organizations*. International voluntary organizations call themselves non-governmental organizations (NGOs).

Voluntarism, citizenship and empowerment
The scope of voluntary activity ranges from local and national concerns with social provision for marginalized groups, community development and social action to more global issues such as environmental protection and Third World poverty. At the heart of volunteering is empathy, compassion, trust and participation – or, in other words, an active belief in social solidarity.

The renewal of interest in civil society has been associated with demands for a larger role for voluntary welfare provision in both western society and the former soviet block. The voluntary sector is perceived as an alternative to state bureaucracy and professional elitism, as well as constituting a public space between government and market. Voluntarism in its modern form is presented by its advocates as a democratic movement, based upon the concept of active citizenship, as opposed to the dependent status imposed by the entitled citizenship of the welfare state. The emphasis in active citizenship is on participation in the decision-making process leading to empowerment of the citizen.

Critics of voluntarism point out that the real emphasis is on the dutiful citizen engaged in self-help. In the context of the atomized individualism and fragmented social order in which we live, there is an element of unreality about the larger claims made for the concept of voluntarism as an alternative to state welfare. Clearly, voluntary organizations cannot provide an alternative to the social protection offered by the welfare state. In reality, voluntary organizations in the social services sector have a symbiotic relationship with the state, largely depending on it for funding.

continued

A global voluntary sector

Nonetheless, Salaman (1994, p. 5) suggests that a 'virtual associational revolution' is taking place throughout the world, creating a global voluntary sector. It is defined by several core characteristics: structured organizations; located outside the formal apparatus of the state; not intended to distribute profits from activities to a set of shareholders or directors; self governing; involving significant private, voluntary effort. Those characteristics make the voluntary sector a much more flexible form of social provision capable of innovation.

There are four basic types of voluntary organizations.

1 Mutual organizations that consist of a membership where the participants are both the essential producers and consumers of the group's activities (for example, self-help welfare groups)
2 Voluntary organizations in which the members are essentially the beneficiaries of services and activities provided by other people on a voluntary basis (for example, the Samaritans)
3 Campaigning/representational organizations that represent interest groups outside the established party political structures (for example, Shelter and the Child Poverty Action Group)
4 'Intermediaries' that provide services for other organizations in the voluntary sector, for example, the National Council for Voluntary Organizations (NCVO) in the UK

Comparative European research would seem to indicate that similar patterns are evident across several countries. After reviewing the research findings on the extent of volunteering in Belgium, Bulgaria, Denmark, France, Germany, Great Britain, Ireland, Netherlands, Slovakia and Sweden, Gaskin and Smith (1995, p. 63) concluded that volunteering includes diverse social groups with a wide variety of personal characteristics. However, in both Britain and Ireland, volunteering tends to be somewhat skewed towards the middle classes with all the negative connotations of Lady Bountiful. In reality, such a caricature belies the diverse and complex nature of voluntary associations in contemporary society that are often at the cutting edge of social progress.

A partnership in civic renewal?

In the UK during the second half of the twentieth century, voluntary activity has expanded. While many traditional voluntary organizations have declined, they have been replaced by new forms of voluntary association, notably self-help and environmental groups. Women have become much more actively involved in voluntary associations. In 1991, there were in excess of 160,000 charitable groups registered in Britain, with 20 per cent of the population engaging in some form of voluntary activity during the year – 10 per cent on a weekly basis. Young people continue to be as actively involved as in previous generations (Giddens, 1998, pp. 81–2).

The roots of social work are in the voluntary sector, notably the Charity Organization Society, founded in London in 1870. In the post-war era, social work has been largely incorporated into the apparatus of the welfare state. However, the practice of social work continues to be intimately associated with civil society through its involvement with voluntary organizations and community groups. Moreover, social work shares the core values of the voluntary sector. This has tended to make its relationship with the state at times conflictual, since social work embodies the spirit of the civic as opposed to the political realm of society – humanism as opposed to the Leviathan.

The future of voluntary organizations is likely to reflect the changing nature of society. As we move away from *dirigiste* models of social democracy, the concepts of civil society and active citizenship are likely to be thrust into the foreground of societal concerns, notably in *third way* politics (Giddens, 1998, pp. 69–98). In this context, voluntary organizations are certain to have an important role to play, not as an alternative to the welfare state, but in a partnership of civic renewal.

For Further Reading
Gaskin, K. and Smith, J. 1995: *A New Civic Europe? A Study of the Extent and Role of Volunteering*. London: Volunteer Centre.
Giddens, A. 1998: *The Third Way*. Cambridge: Polity.
Salaman, L. 1994: *The Global Association Revolution*. London: Demos.

FRED POWELL

Volunteers and Volunteering

Volunteering involves making an offer of a service or providing assistance. Within social work, a volunteer is an individual who is unpaid and who provides, by choice, direct services for another person's benefit, through an organizational context – whether statutory or voluntary.

In the 1980s, research suggested that volunteers were typically white, middle class, middle-aged, educated and female. However, now women are turning to paid rather than voluntary work, young people and adults volunteer as a stepping stone to paid work, and more volunteers are older and are motivated by reasons such as the need to combat loneliness or depression in themselves.

Recent policy in the UK, regardless of party, has promoted volunteering. As a result of community care legislation, volunteers work with frailer and more dependent clients, undertaking tasks previously done by paid staff.

More formal methods of deploying and managing volunteers, including selection, training and written agreements have been introduced. This can blur the boundaries between the role of paid staff and volunteers, and may alienate potential volunteers motivated by social and informal reasons.

For Further Reading
Wardell, F., Lishman, J. and Whalley, L. J. 1997: Volunteers: Making a difference. *Practice*, 9 (2), 21–34.

JOYCE LISHMAN

Vulnerable Adults

Vulnerable adults has come to be used as an umbrella term for adults who are eligible to use social services, particularly in relation to issues of abuse and protection. The term embraces all adult client groups, including people with learning disabilities or mental health problems, older people and disabled people. Service users may be deemed 'vulnerable' particularly when their situation is complicated by additional factors, such as physical frailty or chronic illness, sensory impairment, challenging behaviour, social or emotional problems, poverty or homelessness.

The Law Commission's consultative document
The notion of 'vulnerability' was first proposed and defined in a consultative document issued by the Law Commission in 1995 on decision making for 'mentally incapacitated' adults. The term has crept in from this point and has come to be used as shorthand in areas of social work where generic policies apply across adult client groups.

The Law Commission defined a vulnerable adult as a person over 18 years of age who 'is or may be in need of community care services by reason of mental or other disability, age or illness and who is or may be unable to take care of himself or herself, or unable to protect himself or herself against significant harm or serious exploitation' Law Commission (1995, p. 207).

continued

This new collective term identified a broader group of people who should be the focus of protection and substitute decision making than those who traditionally lacked 'capacity'. However, while this widened the scope for intervention, the Commission advocated more sensitive and functional assessment of capacity in relation to specific decisions. 'Mental incapacity' was otherwise a blunt legal concept that led to individuals losing control over *all* their affairs, rather than only those decisions that were too complex for them.

Until new legislation is enacted, issues of consent to treatment and personal decision making continue to be decided in a legal vacuum, and this is often critical in cases of potential abuse. For example, where someone becomes involved in a sexual or financial transaction or a relationship which they do not or cannot understand, this would be viewed as exploitative. At present, social services have no specific duties or powers to intervene when a vulnerable adult is being abused, but they are required to work together with other agencies and to develop policies and procedures. The Commission had urged the government to provide extra powers for assessment and removal of a vulnerable adult to a place of safety where there were significant concerns.

Some issues prompted by the document

A problem in the Law Commission's definition is that it links the assumption of vulnerability to an individual's eligibility to receive services. Resource constraints have seen eligibility criteria revised with a view to targeting resources on the most disadvantaged, and this has led to some very vulnerable people living without support on the margins of their communities. These people might not be deemed 'vulnerable' or entitled to intervention or protection.

The term raises other issues. It flies in the face of other current terminology, which seeks to reflect a less stigmatized, more equal and assertive role for service users. It is likely that the term will be challenged by user groups for this reason. On the other hand, inclusive language tends to downplay the extent to which individuals are vulnerable to abuse, exploitation or neglect in their homes, services and neighbourhoods. Far from helping them in these circumstances, denial of impairment or disadvantage works against the interests of service users and can leave them without ordinary safeguards which would be taken for granted by other people.

Moreover, the term is problematical in locating vulnerability with the individual client rather than conceptualizing it as a function of wider systems and structural inequalities. Theoretical models that explore causes of abuse address power and inequality within society, the family and service provision. Institutional models of care create contexts in which abuse may be endemic. These theorists would argue that individuals are not intrinsically vulnerable but are *made so* by poverty, inadequate housing, poor service provision and weak regulation. Similarly, within the wider community, women, black people, gay men and lesbians are made vulnerable as a result of racism, sexism and homophobia. Moreover, people with complex needs, severe impairments or challenging behaviour are made vulnerable by lack of understanding and expertise on the part of practitioners. So, the term may inadvertently personalize rather than problematize or politicize vulnerability.

Data gathered about usage of policies on abuse of vulnerable adults in Kent and East Sussex (Brown and Stein, 1998) suggest that it is primarily older people and people with learning disabilities who are the focus of concerns which are channelled through social services policies. Concerns relating to people with mental health problems are more likely to be addressed through the care programme approach within the health service although often these assessments focus on dangerousness rather than vulnerability. Disabled people may or may not feel that they need additional help in accessing protection and might be better served by advocacy geared towards their inclusion in mainstream services for people who have been the victims of personal, domestic and/or community violence.

Nevertheless, it might be argued that acknowledging the additional vulnerabilities of people who use services and the barriers which exist when they seek to access support, redress or protection, is a step forward. Time will tell if this formulation proves to be durable and/or acceptable to users, practitioners and their managers.

For Further Reading

Brown, H. and Stein, J. 1998: Implementing adult protection policies in Kent and East Sussex. *Journal of Social Policy,* 27 (3), 371–96.

Department of Health 2000: *No Secrets: Guidance on Developing and Implementing Multi-agency Policies and Procedures to Protect Vulnerable Adults from Abuse.* London: The Stationery Office.

Law Commission 1995: *Who Decides? Making Decisions on Behalf of Mentally Incapacitated Adults.* Report 231. London: Lord Chancellor's Department.

Macreadie, C. 1997: *Update on Research in Elder Abuse.* London: Age Concern/Institute of Gerontology, Kings College.

HILARY BROWN

W

Welfare Rights

Welfare rights work aims to maximize service users' social security income by giving them information and advice and advocating on their behalf; advocacy is particularly employed when a benefit has been denied. When undertaking welfare rights work, the social worker is consciously acting on behalf of service users as their advocate.

Welfare rights work may also be practised in non social work settings – for example, in housing organizations; specialist welfare rights advisers may not have a social work background, though they are likely to be knowledgeable about debt and money advice, housing rights and perhaps about community care, employment law or immigration.

Welfare rights work consists of:

- the provision of individual advice, advocacy and representation at social security tribunals
- organizing publicity to improve benefit take-up, usually targeted at groups of potential benefit claimants who may be missing out; this may include individual advice work
- providing training and consultancy to develop other peoples' welfare rights skills
- policy development to improve social security administration and entitlement, using evidence from individual cases.

Welfare rights work is often a key part of local authority anti-poverty strategies because it is a practical response to poverty and it involves recognizing the priorities for people on low incomes. The rationale for this is described by Alcock and Craig (1996):'A majority of those now on benefits now experience competing demands on their weekly budgets for food, children's clothing and bills. Poor families are thus forced to adopt desperate strategies to survive, frequently involving multiple debts which cannot be repaid regularly and adaptations and cutbacks in diet which could have longer term implications for health and well-being. Given the growing proportion of poor households which include children, these changes have put particular pressures on parents' ability to cope with the need to provide an upbringing for their children which does not mark them out from their peers at an early age … This paints a rather depressing picture of widening divisions, increasing deprivation and deepening desperation for a significant proportion of the British population.'

Skills required for welfare rights work

To undertake welfare rights work, the social worker needs good advocacy skills, a good understanding of the legal and technical aspects of social security law, as well as an understanding of the social policy context of social work practice and the effect of poverty and social exclusion on service users.

Advocacy skills have been identified as including:

- an understanding of the ethical basis of advocacy – acting in the service user's best interest, giving frank, impartial advice, carrying out the service user's instructions with diligence and competence

- effective interviewing skills that look behind the immediate financial problem to understand the whole financial scenario
- legal research skills
- the ability to organize and manage oneself
- good, assertive negotiation skills
- the ability or willingness to litigate matters and/or refer on to specialists.

The background

Some form of welfare rights work has existed since formal rules of social security were established, and its existence goes back beyond the origins of social work. In Britain, there were legal challenges to the excesses of the Poor Law as a result of liberal minded lawyers working in partnership with clergy, trade unionists and people involved in the Settlement Movement. In the nineteenth century, Settlements were also campaigning for state pensions.

In the 1920s and 1930s, the National Unemployed Workers Movement undertook benefit take-up campaigns as well as representation at the equivalent of Tribunals to challenge the worst effects of the means test. In the 1940s and 1950s, the growth of full employment and the welfare state reduced the need for welfare rights activity, though it remained a feature of social work practice to some extent or another and was often undertaken by Citizens Advice Bureaux. In the late 1960s and 1970s, influenced by the growth of welfare rights activity in the civil rights movement in the USA, it featured in community-based social work, particularly among adherents of radical practice, as well as in grass roots organizations like claimants unions.

1969 saw the appointment of the first paid welfare rights worker in a social services department following the founding of the Child Poverty Action Group in 1965 to campaign on poverty issues and be a source of expertise for those representing individuals against the social security system.

There has always been a debate among practitioners as to whether welfare rights work is a legitimate part of the social work task. However, the impact of increased poverty on service users, the inadequacy of benefit levels and variable standards of benefits administration mean that resolving social security problems and using welfare rights skills to try to push back the boundaries of benefit restrictions is an inevitable and continuing activity for social workers. It is also a way to develop empathy with service users and so engage them in the social work task.

Welfare rights work has become a feature of many social work organizations with over 300 welfare rights specialists employed by local authorities in the UK.

Internationally, Canada, the USA and Australia have long-established welfare rights organizations, and welfare rights advocacy takes place in many other countries including Ireland, Scandinavia, the Netherlands, Spain, Belgium, Germany, France and the Czech Republic, with varying degrees of involvement by social work practitioners. Wherever there are rules determining welfare, there will be a need for advocacy to support rights to welfare.

For Further Reading

Alcock, P. and Craig, G. 1996: *Combating Local Poverty*. London: Local Government Management Board.
Bateman, N. 2000: *Advocacy Skills for Health and Social Care Professionals*. London: Jessica Kingsley.
Disability Rights Handbook. London: Disability Alliance.
Welfare Benefits Handbook, released annually. London: Child Poverty Action Group.

NEIL BATEMAN

Whistle-blowing

Whistle-blowing refers most frequently to an insider, often a social worker or nurse, 'blowing the whistle' on perceived abuses and misuses of power, sometimes by colleagues, usually in the setting which employs them. For example, they might complain formally to their local authority service managers about allegations of physical and sexual abuse by group home staff on residents with learning disabilities. Whistle-blowing is advocacy aimed at remedying specific structural and ethical failures, and involves the disclosure of information available through a professional role.

Whistle-blowing complainants are frequently scapegoated, and can pay a high price for their diligence and ethical concerns through personal vilification. There is a long history of whistle-blowers being punished, even dismissed, rather than securing the effective investigation of complaints made. Services close ranks against complainants seen as 'disloyal' and violating internal codes of secrecy.

Very considerable attention has been paid over recent years to turning a so-called vice into a virtue. Most authorities now formally welcome whistle-blowing in their formal guidance to staff, but, in practice, it is still seen as violating profound aspects of most service cultures and complainants receive punishment rather than praise.

For Further Reading

Hunt, G. (ed.), 1998: *Whistleblowing in the Social Services*. London: Edward Arnold.

DAVID BRANDON

Withdrawal

Withdrawal is the body's reaction to the sudden absence of a drug on which the user has become physically dependent. The nature and severity of withdrawal symptoms vary with the drug. With heroin, the effects last several days and are equivalent to a very bad dose of flu with stomach cramps and sweating, but it is not life-threatening. However, withdrawal from drugs such as alcohol or barbiturate sleeping pills can include fitting and convulsions which have proved fatal. Those withdrawing from stimulants (cocaine, amphetamine) will not exhibit such marked physical symptoms, but may become chronically depressed or even suicidal.

HARRY SHAPIRO

Women and Social Work

Until the early 1980s, the commonly employed social work term 'client' had the effect of making *women* invisible in all except the stereotypical roles of mother, wife, daughter and in respect of adolescent sexual behaviour. Feminist research at that time similarly highlighted the fact that, hidden in the linguistic device of *carer* and *parent*, are women: wives, daughters, sisters, mothers.

Women as service users and social workers

Women were expected to take, and usually assumed that they should take, the main responsibility for the provision of care and support for children and adults. These expectations continued through the 1990s and still underpin community and childcare policies today. Although women *per se* do not form a service-user category, nor are there any specific statutory social work responsibilities towards them, there is a coherence between the expectations of women as carers and the responsibilities of social care organizations. It is no surprise that women make up the majority of people using social care services.

Women also predominate in the social services work-force. They make up 86 per cent of the staff employed, with very few men working in home care services. As in other occupations, men are in the majority in senior management. Thus, men are making policies predominantly for women using the services, while women are responsible for carrying them out.

Although there are consistent patterns historically, there have also been major changes in the last quarter century. During the 1980s, it was not easy to integrate the idea of employment into any analysis of the relationship between women and social work: the assumed framework for practice was that women were available on demand to provide care for children and support for adults whenever it was required; employment took the woman away from these responsibilities and this was perceived to present as big a problem for women as the fact of unemployment did for men. This assumption operated even though the work-force in social care was itself primarily female. By the late 1990s, however, the position had dramatically changed and successful womanhood came to be seen as being achieved through the ability to combine employment with caring even if this came about through the purchase of care.

Commonalities and diversities

Training for social work and social care often emphasizes the differences between the women who use services and those who work in them. Hanmer and Statham (1999) argue, however, that gender brings with it commonalities as well as the diversities between women workers and women service users: most women share the experience of caring for children, supporting adults and living with men. The woman worker may go home to face similar, even if sometimes less severe, problems to those faced by the women she has worked with during the day: the breakdown of relationships with men and children, domestic violence, or problems about the allocation of money within the household.

Gender, like race and visible impairments, is obvious from first contact and cannot be shared at the worker's or the service user's pace. Diversities between women are based on the differential access each has to economic and social resources, on race, disability, social class and age. Awareness of commonalities and diversities between the woman worker and the service user is an essential resource for practice.

Woman-centred practice

Woman-centred practice is an approach rather than a technique. The full range of social work methods should be available to women: individual counselling, therapy (including family therapy), methods based on learning theory, groupwork and community work. In the 1980s, woman-centred practice was radical in that it challenged the expert approach through attempting to recognize the impact of power differentials on relationships and aimed to be non-hierarchical. Some of these elements have now been incorporated into mainstream practice. There is an increased emphasis on the provision of services which focus on the outcomes for the person using the services rather than on service-led or expert-determined processes. Many of the principles underpinning this practice are well established in work that has been based on the women's, the black and the disabled people's movements:

- An emphasis on what would make a difference in the user's or carer's life
- The use of users' and carers' experience and expertise
- Open and accountable practice
- The need to keep up-to-date with changes in practice and with the knowledge and skills that underpin it

The 1990s saw an outpouring of literature on 'girl power', and an emphasis on the advances that some women had made in educational attainment, in access to the professions and into employment. The view gained ground that women had secured power and that attention needed to be given to the position of men. This is not the experience

continued

of most of the women who use social work services or who are required to use them. Many are unemployed and are without formal educational qualifications. Olive Stevenson in her work on child neglect saw the need to improve the mother's self-esteem as an important focus in improving mothering.

Key areas for practice remain:

- Working to raise women's self-esteem
- Increasing resources to reduce the impact of family and environmental poverty
- Supplementing care for children and adults

Groupwork provides women with the opportunity to share their experience and their expertise with each other, and to reduce their sense of isolation. Woman-centred practice cannot always be achieved through the statutory agencies whose focus is to a large extent on monitoring how women carry out their caring responsibilities. The concept of the 'fit mother' is not matched by that of 'fit fatherhood' even though the state now expects fathers to fulfil their financial responsibilities to their children. An illustration of how the concept of *fit motherhood* operates in practice is seen in the way that mothers are expected to take responsibility for protecting their children from the men who abuse them. Voluntary organizations such as Women's Aid, Rape Crisis, women's help lines and therapy and health centres all work with and for women; groups for black and minority ethnic women and for disabled women are key resources for practice. Unlike workers in the statutory sector, they can unequivocally take a woman-centred approach.

For Further Reading
Hanmer, J. and Statham, D. 1999: *Women and Social Work: Towards Woman-centred Practice*. Basingstoke: Macmillan.
Stevenson, O. 1998: *Child Neglect: Issues and Dilemmas*. Oxford: Blackwell.
Van den Berg, N. (ed.) 1995: *Feminist Practice in the 21st Century*. Washington: National Association of Social Workers.

DAPHNE STATHAM

Workfare

Workfare is an umbrella term for a range of employment, training and job-search programmes that are compulsory for welfare recipients. Coined in the USA in the late 1960s, workfare originally referred in a narrow fashion to 'work-for-the-dole' programmes in which welfare recipients were required to perform menial labour in exchange for their benefits. Since this time, workfare has assumed an increasingly generic and elastic meaning, as a summary term for work-based welfare reform, welfare-to-work programming and even, at a systemic level, as a successor to the welfare state ('workfare state').

Outside the USA, workfare often has pejorative and/or punitive connotations, and, as such, is often used by critics of work compulsion and benefit conditionality. So, while the Blair Government's New Deal programme was consistent with the broad principles of workfare, ministers would resist such a characterization. Within the USA, the term is less controversial, particularly since the bipartisan 'workfare consensus' established in the Family Support Act 1988 and the Personal Responsibility and Work Opportunities Reconciliation Act 1996. Here, in fact, it has become more common for 'welfare' to be used as a political attack term.

For Further Reading
Mead, L. M. 1997: *The New Paternalism*. Washington, DC: Brookings Institution Press.

JAMIE PECK

The Working Alliance

The *working alliance* is the collaborative aspect of the relationship between worker and client, as well as other people involved with both, in pursuing agreed goals.

Collaborating (sometimes referred to as *partnership*) means that, to some extent at least, clients and others involved with them, actively influence the nature of social work intervention. Other aspects may well be included in this endeavour, but some degree of collaboration is vital for reaching desired outcomes. The collaborative underpinning of social work interventions may not always be visible; for example, sometimes workers have to enter into conflict with clients and other people involved with the clients. However, workers should handle such conflicts with the long-term interests of clients in their minds.

The understanding of the working alliance has undergone considerable changes over time. Broadly speaking, it is possible to identify three perspectives: individual, interpersonal, and contextual. The contextual view of the working alliance includes the earlier concern with the personality of each worker and each client. This view also embraces the interpersonal emphasis on training social workers in relationship skills that help to engage clients. The added contextual slant expands the individual and interpersonal perspectives, and encourages the worker to liaise with all those who may influence the efforts to reach the identified goals.

The systems approach

Grounded in the systems approach (Pinsof, 1994), the contextual view helps workers take into account the mutual influences among sub-systems: a change in one is likely to effect changes in all the others. For example, the social worker's relationships with teachers of a certain school (as one sub-system), may effect changes in the ways another sub-system – perhaps, for example, family members – handle their child's attendance at that school.

Furthermore, the systems approach directs workers to take care of each sub-system separately while also minding the quality of the arrangement as a whole. In practice, workers are encouraged to properly engage each of the parties involved while striving to ensure that these parties also collaborate among themselves. Of course, all these relationships have to be geared to enhancing progress towards the identified goals. Therefore, each worker has to have an overall map of the systems as a whole, while creating, sustaining, and terminating the working alliance.

Such an overall map comprises at least three levels: personal, interpersonal, and social.

1 At the personal level, the worker has to properly engage each client as an individual with his or her own strengths and his or her own vulnerabilities.
2 At the interpersonal level, the worker has to engage the people with whom the client is most closely involved, be they intimate partners, close friends, children, or relatives.
3 At the social level, the worker has to liaise with various sub-systems that influence the client, for example, school, hospital, police, church, or a voluntary club.

Goals, methods and bonding

At each of these levels, at least three clusters of concerns may have to be addressed: goals, methods, and bonding.

The *goals* refer to the purpose of the worker's involvement and the outcomes that can be realistically expected of this piece of work. Such goals may be quite small (for example, the client making a few more friends) or they may be quite central (for example, the client's child returning to live with the family). No matter how small or large, these goals have to be worked out from the outset. Clarifying goals is important because

continued

clients, and others, are likely to increase collaboration when they know, in quite concrete terms, what they may expect to be different at the end of their involvement with the worker.

The *methods* spell out how the identified goals may be pursued – what each party may actually do to help to achieve these goals. These ways and means of working together can be described in simple and jargon-free terms from the beginning. Workers can usually describe what they may do: for example, they may try to understand, to provide information, or to suggest alternative steps. As part of these explanations, workers should be quite open about their legal obligations, in regard to confidentiality as well as those factors involving the courts. Workers can also say what clients may do: for example, they might be expected to turn up to sessions at the agreed times, to directly express their feelings and thoughts, or to carry out homework assignments.

For a collaborative relationship to emerge, each person has to feel validated; that is, they have to feel understood, respected, and encouraged, as individuals and as members of a group. The experience of being validated can be facilitated by recognizing people's strengths before fully exploring their distress. In addition, resorting to well-identified relationship skills is of considerable value in fostering such *bonding*. These skills include active listening, conveying respect, communicating empathy, expressing oneself genuinely, being specific, and sharing one's own feelings (Egan, 1998). Each of these skills has to be offered selectively during the various stages of the work: at the beginning, in the middle, and towards the end.

Some aspects of the worker's personality may influence the process of bonding too. While these aspects may interfere with the process of bonding, the worker may not always be conscious of them. Over-involvement with clients as much as unintended detachment, impatience as well as aimless meandering – any of these may be the result. This is why it is often helpful to resort to supervision where unconscious processes that disrupt bonding can be clarified (Preston-Shoot and Agass, 1990).

It is vital to remember that each worker has to apply these aspects of the working alliance differently; bearing in mind structural inequalities involved in relation to gender, ethnic origin, sexual orientation, religious beliefs, and various special needs.

For Further Reading

Egan, G. 1998: *The Skilled Helper: A Systematic Approach to Effective Helping* (5th edn). Pacific Groves, CA: Brooks/Cole.
Pinsof, W. M. 1994: An integrative systems perspective on the therapeutic alliance. In A. O. Adams and L. S. Greenberg (eds), *The Working Alliance: Theory, Research and Practice*, New York: John Wiley, 173–95.
Preston-Shoot, M. and Agass, D. 1990: *Making Sense of Social Work: Psychodynamics, Systems and Practice*. London: Macmillan.

ODED MANOR

Working Carers

Working carers informally care for dependent children, persons with disability and/or frail elderly people, as well as engage in paid employment.

In 1998, 47 per cent of carers were in paid employment in the UK. Although the majority of working carers are women, men are increasingly balancing work and caregiving. The ageing of the population as a whole and the work-force in particular, combined with increasing numbers of women returning to work after childbirth, will lead to an increase in the number of working carers.

Evidence shows that the balance of work and care can have positive effects for carers, care recipients and employers. The negative effects centre on psychological aspects of caregiving, such as stress, which affect the carer and employer as employees take time off work or forego promotion or mobility opportunities.

Programmes and policies, such as day care and flexileave have been developed in the workplace to assist carers, although in the UK such schemes are limited to large employers. The changing contexts of work and caring have implications for social work assessment and service delivery.

For Further Reading
Phillips, J. (ed.) 1995: *Working Carers*. Aldershot: Avebury.

JUDITH PHILLIPS

Workload Management

Workload management is a means of measuring, allocating, monitoring, prioritizing and rationing the tasks undertaken by social workers. It occurs at a number of levels: the individual, the team and the organizational. At its simplest, it involves counting the cases (i.e. the caseload) allocated to a worker; this is a system of workload *measurement*. More sophisticated systems use nationally tested and agreed scales which capture all tasks required of a worker and estimate the time needed to perform them.

The aim of workload management is to use measurement scales to ensure the equitable distribution of tasks, to protect workers from stress and to enable them to perform to the best of their ability, thereby ensuring the quality of services to users/clients. This is achieved by systematic monitoring, operating workload ceilings and having an organizational response to workload crises: for example, prioritizing work, rationing services, closing cases, introducing waiting lists. Effective workload management incorporates risk assessment and shared decision making between worker and line manager.

Properly operated schemes are incorporated into resource allocation systems, justifying requests for more staff. They can also be invoked when calculating the cost of services purchased from provider agencies in the community.

For Further Reading
Orme, J. 1995: *Workloads: Measurement and Management*. Aldershot: Avebury.

JOAN ORME

Work Satisfaction in Social Work

Work satisfaction is the sense of gratification, fulfilment, pleasure and achievement an individual experiences from carrying out work-related tasks. Work satisfaction varies according to occupational level and job type. Different elements are important to different people: individuals vary in the satisfaction they obtain from work tasks as much as from different sources in other areas of life.

High satisfaction is associated with higher commitment, higher job control and lower stress. Jobs which allow autonomy and rewards in proportion to effort provide the greatest satisfaction. Low satisfaction is associated with aspects of work outside an individual's control, particularly aspects pertaining to the employer or organization. Jobs which combine high levels of responsibility with conflicting demands are generally the least satisfying.

Social services staff experience very high levels of satisfaction from their work, particularly from feeling they have helped people or made a difference to people's lives. Direct care staff, especially home care workers are the most satisfied; middle managers and social work staff generally tend to be less satisfied (Balloch et al. 1999).

For Further Reading
Balloch, S., McLean, J. and Fisher, M. 1999: *Social Services: Working Under Pressure*. Bristol: Policy Press.

JOHN MCLEAN

Writing Skills

The *written word* is a major form of communication in social work, both within and without the profession. It is also the one most likely to remain as a permanent record. *Writing skills* are therefore fundamental to good practice. In developing their skills, practitioners must have in mind the intended audience and the purpose of the communication. Clear structure aids the presentation of information, arguments, assessments and plans. Unnecessary jargon should be avoided. More than one draft is recommended. Reading good authors and observing their style, coupled with much practice, improves writing.

DAVID HOWE

Y

Young Carers

Young carers are children and young persons under 18 who provide, or intend to provide, care, assistance or support to another family member. They carry out, often on a regular basis, significant or substantial caring tasks and assume a level of responsibility which would usually be associated with an adult.

The person receiving care is often a parent but can be a sibling, grandparent or other relative who is disabled, has some chronic illness, mental health problem or other condition connected with a need for care, support or supervision.

Factors which influence the extent and nature of young carers' tasks and responsibilities include the illness/disability, family structure, gender, culture, religion, income, and the availability and quality of professional support and services.

Where children and families lack appropriate professional support and adequate income, then some young carers experience impaired psychosocial development, including poor educational attendance and performance, and restricted peer networks, friendships and opportunities. These will have implications for their own adulthood. Young carers have rights to an assessment and support under legislation. Specialist projects are one way of meeting their needs.

For Further Reading
Becker, S., Aldridge, J. and Dearden, C. 1998: *Young Carers and their Families*. Oxford: Blackwell Science.

SAUL BECKER

Youth Justice

Youth justice is an umbrella term which encompasses the differential treatment of young offenders as compared with adults within criminal justice systems. The simplicity of that definition belies the complex, contradictory and unpredictable nature of youth or juvenile justice systems – the terms are interchangeable – in which police, specialist courts, and welfare agencies seek to control and reform children who commit criminal offences. The complexity is compounded in that the youth justice system co-exists and may conflict with parallel processes such as education, health, and child care. Additionally, within the UK, young offenders in England and Wales are, for reasons related more to historical accident than to ideological disparity, treated very differently from children committing criminal offences in Scotland (*see* CHILDREN'S HEARINGS SYSTEM). Such is the multi-faceted nature of the topic that the state of youth justice in England and Wales at the beginning of the twenty-first century invites comment from both a legal and a social work practice perspective.

Historical context
The separate treatment of young offenders developed disparately throughout western jurisdictions during the late nineteenth and early twentieth centuries. Before that, apart from a general recognition that there was an age below which children could not be regarded as criminally responsible, young offenders were tried in the same courts and suffered the same punishments as adults. With major reforms initially introducing a separate juvenile court, and subsequently shifting from due process to a more welfare-based approach to youth offending and back again, developments in youth justice in common law jurisdictions throughout the twentieth century, for the most part, reflected parallel ideological approaches to criminal justice in general.

In England and Wales, the early 1990s exemplified one of those cyclical periods of heightened public concern and media interest in young offenders, tellingly catalogued by Pearson (1983) in his *Hooligan: A History of Respectable Fears*. The decade was also one in which, for the first time, the pressures for legislative change, resulting in six youth justice related statutes in nine years, appeared to be overtly political, rather than ideological. Policy statements and reforming provisions of this time were not only populist, but bifurcated. They responded punitively to youth offending as a rational activity – whereas the overwhelming bulk of research evidence suggests that youth crime is essentially opportunistic, and that there is a high correlation between social disadvantage and crime (Newburn, 1997). They also, with the creation of a policy-making national Youth Justice Board, and a declared commitment to the principles of restorative justice, represented an attempt to provide a credible response to a damning critique of the youth justice system by the Audit Commission (1996).

The international and domestic regulation of youth justice
Growing international interest in the recognition and protection of the human rights of children led to the UN Convention on the Rights of the Child. This treaty, to which almost all states are signatories, includes principles of child welfare-oriented provision for the separate and humane treatment of young offenders. The Convention sets standards which many youth justice systems fail to satisfy. The system in England and Wales, for instance, has been roundly criticized for its low age of criminal responsibility and high use of custody.

Other legislative changes have removed safeguards formerly provided for very young children. The historical protection provided to children aged 10–13 under the presumption of *doli incapax*, which required courts trying children to be satisfied that they knew that what they were doing was 'seriously wrong' before the case could go ahead, was removed in 1998. Earlier the Crown Court's jurisdiction to try to sentence young people for grave crimes was extended to include 10–13-year-olds, and a new custodial sentence for 12–15-year-olds was introduced. In 1999, the wide police discretion to administer cautions was replaced by a statutory system of a single reprimand followed by a final warning. All these amendments have further compounded the complexity of statutory provision, so that the legal framework of youth justice is as badly in need of clarification and consolidation as was child care law prior to the Children Act 1989.

The social work role in youth justice
These developments provide local authority social workers with a dilemma, but there is no doubt that they are still expected to play a leading role in the youth justice system:

- They may be required to act as *appropriate adults* when children are being questioned by the police.
- Young offenders given a final warning by the police – S.65 of the Crime and Disorder Act 1998 – may be subject to diversionary intervention organized by local youth offending teams, which include local authority social workers.
- Social workers may be members of panels to which youth courts have to refer most first time offenders for a contracted programme of behaviour designed to achieve an element of reparation to individual victims or the community, and prevent further offending.
- Social workers prepare pre-sentence reports when requested to do so by youth courts, and supervise young offenders made the subject of community orders.

These roles may in part be the traditional welfare ones of protecting young offenders from the full effects of involvement in the criminal justice system; in essence, however, they appear to be more about control than welfare.

continued

For Further Reading
Audit Commission 1996: *Misspent Youth: Young People and Crime*. London: Audit Commission.
Ball, C., McCormac, K. and Stone, N. 2000: *Young Offenders: Law, Policy and Practice*, (2nd edn). London: Sweet and Maxwell.
Newburn, T. 1997: 'Youth, crime and justice'. In M. Maguire, R. Morgan and R. Reiner (eds), *The Oxford Handbook of Criminology*, (2nd edn). Oxford: Oxford University Press.

CAROLINE BALL

Youth Social Work

Youth social work is social welfare practice with young people in their teenage and adolescent years. It refers to the range of services in contact with young people and, albeit less universally, to the particular character of that contact. This form of intervention is based on a version of systems theory and it suggests, essentially, that effort to change outcomes in social welfare is better directed towards the systems in which young people are caught up than at young people themselves. The techniques of maximum diversion, minimum intervention and systems management were most thoroughly applied in the field of juvenile and youth justice in the 1980s, but were influential elsewhere.

During the 1990s, the social rights of young people were progressively eroded and the climate of opinion towards those in trouble worsened sharply. 'Avoidance of harm', previously the primary ambition of youth social workers, was now joined by a revived interest in 'doing good' in the lives of young people. Early intervention and preventative work re-entered official vocabulary, although with little apparent understanding of the achievements of the 1980s, or the dangers of drawing young people prematurely into the welfare net.

For Further Reading
Furlong, A. and Cartmel, F. 1997: *Young People and Social Change*. Buckingham: Open University Press.

MARK DRAKEFORD

Contributors

Malcolm Adams
University of East Anglia, Norwich

Professor Robert Adams
University of Lincolnshire and Humberside, Hull

Dr Graham Allan
University of Southampton

Dorothy Atkinson
The Open University, Milton Keynes

Cathy Aymer
Brunel University, Twickenham

Professor Chris Bagley
University of Southampton

Dr David S. Baldwin
University of Southampton

Dr Mark Baldwin
University of Bath

Professor Norma Baldwin
University of Dundee

Dr Caroline Ball
University of East Anglia, Norwich

Dr Marie Bambrick
Lifespan Heathcare NHS Trust, Cambridge

Terry Bamford
Consultant; formerly Executive Director, Kensington and Chelsea Housing and Social Services

Professor Hugh Barr
University of Westminster

Rose Barton
The Open University, Milton Keynes

Neil Bateman
Suffolk County Council Social Services Department and Suffolk Health Authority

Dr Saul Becker
Loughborough University

Clare Beckett
Leeds City Council

Professor Peter Beresford
Brunel University and Open Services Project, London

Denise Bevan
St Rocco's Hospice, Warrington

Dr Jackie Blissett
University of Birmingham

Professor Eric Blyth
University of Huddersfield

Dr Joanna Bornat
The Open University, Milton Keynes

Greta Bradley
University of Hull

Don Brand
National Institute for Social Work, London

Professor David Brandon
TAO, Cambridge

Marian Brandon
University of East Anglia, Norwich

Suzy Braye
Staffordshire University, Stoke-on-Trent

Professor Roger Briggs
University of Southampton

Professor Hilary Brown
Salomons, Canterbury
Christ Church University College, Tunbridge Wells

Philippa Brown
University of Hertfordshire

Dr Helen Buckley
Trinity College, Dublin

Roger Bullock
Dartington Social Research Unit

Tania Burchardt
London School of Economics

Robin Burgess
University of Stirling

Beverley Burke
Liverpool John Moores University

Peter Burke
University of Hull

Professor Ian Butler
University of Keele

Dr Bill Bytheway
The Open University, Milton Keynes

Paul Cavadino
NACRO, London

Professor David Challis
University of Manchester

Ashok Chand
University of Central England, Birmingham

Chia Swee Hong
University of East Anglia, Norwich

Isabel Clare
University of Cambridge

Dr Chris Clark
University of Edinburgh

Dr Christopher Clulow
Tavistock Marital Studies Institute, London

Felicity Collier
*British Agencies for Adoption and Fostering,
London*

Dr Stewart Collins
University of Wales, Bangor

Margaret Coombs
*Oxfordshire Community Care Advice and
Action Group, Oxford*

Professor Andrew Cooper
Tavistock Clinic, London

Brian Corby
University of Liverpool

Suzy Croft
*St John's Hospice and Open Services Project,
London*

Peter Crome
University of Keele

Adrian Crook
Wigan Metropolitan Borough Council

Dr Stuart Cumella
University of Birmingham Medical School

Jane Dalrymple
University of the West of England, Bristol

Dr Brigid Daniel
University of Dundee

Professor Bleddyn Davies
University of Kent, Canterbury

Professor Martin Davies
University of East Anglia, Norwich

Dr Carol Dawson
Independent lecturer and trainer, Norwich

Dr David Denney
*Royal Holloway and Bedford New College,
University of London*

Dr Karola Dillenburger
The Queen's University of Belfast

Brian Dimmock
The Open University, Milton Keynes

Professor Rebecca Emerson Dobash
University of Manchester

Professor Russell P. Dobash
University of Manchester

Professor Mark Doel
University of Central England, Birmingham

Professor Lena Dominelli
University of Southampton

Dr Mark Drakeford
University of Wales, Cardiff

Mark Drinkwater
Single Homeless Project, London

DrugScope, *London*

Monica Duck
Post-Adoption Centre, London

Elaine Ennis
University of Dundee

Jim Ennis
University of Dundee

Dr Barbara Fawcett
University of Bradford

Brid Featherstone
University of Huddersfield

Geoff Fimister
Child Poverty Action Group, London

Keith Fletcher
Social Services Strategic Planning, Caerphilly

Dr Sally French
The Open University, Milton Keynes

Lynn Froggett
University of Central Lancashire, Preston

Alison Garnham
National Council for One Parent Families, London

Jane Gibbons
Centre for Social Policy, Dartington

Dr Anita Gibbs
University of Otago, New Zealand

Robbie Gilligan
Trinity College, Dublin

Ruth Goatly
University of Hertfordshire

Dr David Gordon
University of Bristol

Dr Helen Gorman
University of Central England, Birmingham

Leonne Griggs
University of Lincolnshire & Humberside, Hull

Anna Gupta
Royal Holloway and Bedford New College, University of London

Annette Gurney
University of Central England, Birmingham

Elizabeth Harlow
University of Bradford

Christine Harrison
University of Warwick

Philomena Harrison
Liverpool John Moores University

Dr John Haskey
Office for National Statistics, London

Paul Henderson
Community Development Foundation, Leeds

Professor Martin Herbert
University of Exeter

Joanna Heslop
University of Hull

Professor Miles Hewstone
Cardiff University

Dr Stephen Hicks
University of Central Lancashire

Professor Malcolm Hill
University of Glasgow

Dr Andrew Hinde
University of Southampton

Christopher Holden
Brunel University, Twickenham

Dr Clive Holmes
University of Southampton

Paul Holt
West Midlands Probation Service

383

William Horder
Goldsmiths College, University of London

Jan Horwath
University of Sheffield

Professor David Howe
University of East Anglia, Norwich

Barbara L. Hudson
University of Oxford

Jane Hughes
University of Manchester

Dr Catherine Humphreys
University of Warwick

Dr Beth Humphries
Manchester Metropolitan University

John Irvine
University of Central England, Birmingham

Professor Dorota Iwaniec
Queen's University, Belfast

Gordon Jack
University of Exeter

Professor Sonia Jackson
University of Wales, Swansea

Professor Adrian L. James
University of Bradford

Julia Johnson
The Open University, Milton Keynes

Sue Jones
Manchester Metropolitan University

Professor Bill Jordan
Universities of Exeter and Huddersfield

Mansoor Kazi
University of Huddersfield

Carol Kedward
University of Sussex, Brighton

Dr Liz Kelly
University of North London

Professor Hazel Kemshall
De Montfort University, Leicester

Gena Kennedy
Audit Commission, Bristol

Dr Claire Kenwood
University of Southampton

Dr Kenneth Kim
University of East Anglia, Norwich

Professor David J. King
The Queen's University of Belfast

Professor David Kingdon
University of Southampton

Dr Paul Kingston
University of Keele

Charlotte Knight
De Montfort University, Leicester

Juliet Koprowska
University of York

Rod Lambert
University of East Anglia, Norwich

Dr Elizabeth Lancaster
University of Bradford

Hilary Lawson
University of Sussex, Brighton

Dr Pat Le Riche
Goldsmiths College, University of London

Vivien Lindow
University of Bristol

Professor Joyce Lishman
The Robert Gordon University, Aberdeen

Dr Michael Little
*Dartington Social Research Unit and
University of Chicago*

Professor Walter Lorenz
University College, Cork

Barry Luckock
University of Sussex, Brighton

Dr Carol Lupton
University of Portsmouth

Mark Lymbery
University of Nottingham

Dr Andrew McCulloch
The Sainsbury Centre for Mental Health, London

Professor Geraldine Macdonald
University of Bristol

Peter McGill
University of Kent, Canterbury

Professor Gill McIvor
University of Stirling

John McLean
National Institute for Social Work, London

Eileen McLeod
University of Warwick

Dr Oded Manor
Middlesex University

Jill Manthorpe
University of Hull

Deborah Marks
University of Sheffield

Professor Peter Marsh
University of Sheffield

Barry Mason
Institute of Family Therapy, London

David May
University of Dundee

Professor Robin Means
University of the West of England, Bristol

Professor Laura Middleton
Independent Consultant, Lancashire

Dr Malcolm Millar
University of Liverpool

Judith Milner
Northorpe Hall Trust, Mirfield, Yorkshire

Dr Damian Mohan
University of Southampton and Broadmoor Hospital

Ann Mooney
Institute of Education, London University

Dr Emanuel Moran
The National Council on Gambling, London

Professor Audrey Mullender
University of Warwick

Teresa Munby
Ruskin College, Oxford

Elsbeth Neil
University of East Anglia, Norwich

Toyin Okitikpi
Brunel University, Twickenham

Dr Joseph Oliver
University of Manchester

Steve Onyett
NHS Executive, Department of Health, Bristol

Professor Joan Orme
University of Glasgow

Terence O'Sullivan
University of Lincolnshire and Humberside

Professor Jan Pahl
University of Kent at Canterbury

Jonathan Parker
University of Hull

Emeritus Professor Phyllida Parsloe
University of Bristol

Professor Nigel Parton
University of Huddersfield

Professor Malcolm Payne
Manchester Metropolitan University

Jennifer J. Pearce
Middlesex University

Professor Geoffrey Pearson
Goldsmiths College, London University

Professor Jamie Peck
University of Wisconsin-Madison, USA

Mark Peel
University of Loughborough

Bridget Penhale
University of Hull

Dr Sue Penna
University of Lancaster

Graham Perlman
Metanoia Institute, London

Professor Alison Petch
University of Glasgow

Dr Judith Phillips
University of Keele

Professor Chris Phillipson
University of Keele

Terry Philpot
Editor in chief, Community Care

Dr Andrew Pithouse
University of Wales, Cardiff

Professor Fred Powell
National University of Ireland, Cork

Professor Michael Preston-Shoot
Liverpool John Moores University

Dr Katie Prince
Lincolnshire Social Services Department

Professor Colin Pritchard
University of Southampton

Dr David G. Race
Salford University

Jackie Rafferty
University of Southampton

Dr Peter Randall
University of Hull

Professor Peter Raynor
University of Wales, Swansea

Sue Read
University of Keele

Margaret Reith
South Wales Forensic Mental Health Service, Bridgend

Gwyneth Roberts
University of Wales, Bangor

Gwen Robinson
University of Wales, Swansea

Dr Lena Robinson
University of Birmingham

Professor Vincenzo Ruggiero
Middlesex University

Dr Alan Rushton
The Maudsley Hospital/Institute of Psychiatry, King's College, London

Catherine Sawdon
Independent Training Consultant, and Wakefield Housing and Social Care Department

Gillian Schofield
University of East Anglia, Norwich

Jonathan Scourfield
University of Wales, Cardiff

Janet Seden
The Open University, Milton Keynes

Clive Sellick
University of East Anglia, Norwich

Harry Shapiro
DrugScope, London

Steven Shardlow
University of Sheffield

Dr Ian Shaw
Cardiff University

Professor Brian Sheldon
University of Exeter

Charlotte Sills
Metanoia Institute, London

Murray Simpson
University of Dundee

Professor Ian Sinclair
University of York

Bijal Sisodia
*Leicestershire and Rutland Probation Service
and De Montfort University, Leicester*

Carole Smith
University of Manchester

Professor David Smith
University of Lancaster

Professor Nigel South
University of Essex

Professor John R. Spencer
Selwyn College, Cambridge University

Dr Kirsten Stalker
Scottish Human Services Trust, Edinburgh

Nicky Stanley
University of Hull

Professor Daphne Statham
National Institute for Social Work, London

Professor Mike Stein
University of York

Professor Olive Stevenson
University of Nottingham

Barbara Steward
University of East Anglia, Norwich

John Stewart
University of Lancaster

Nigel Stone
University of East Anglia, Norwich

Darren Sugg
*Home Office Research and Statistics
Directorate, London*

Val Sylvester
University of Central England, Birmingham

Karen Tanner
Goldsmiths College, University of London

Professor June Thoburn
University of East Anglia, Norwich

Dr Neil Thompson
Ashley Maynard Associates, Wrexham

Paul Thompson
University of East London

Diane Thomson
Kings College, London University

Professor Anthea Tinker
Kings College, London University

Hilary Tompsett
Kingston University

Professor John Triseliotis
University of Strathclyde

Professor Jane Tunstill
Royal Holloway, University of London

Professor Antony A. Vass
Middlesex University

Susan Vernon
*St George's Hospital Medical School and
Kingston University*

Dr Ray Vieweg
Portsmouth Healthcare NHS Trust

Dr Jan Walmsley
The Open University, Milton Keynes

Professor Dave Ward
De Montfort University, Leicester

Martin F. Ward
RCN Institute, Oxford

Chris Warren-Adamson
University of Brunel, Uxbridge

Professor Lorraine Waterhouse
University of Edinburgh

Dr Sue White
University of Manchester

Dr Colin Whittington
Whittington Research & Development, London

Pat J. Wilkinson
University of Bradford

CONTRIBUTORS

Dr Brian Williams
De Montfort University, Leicester

Professor Bryan Williams
University of Dundee

Val Williams
University of Bristol

Kate Wilson
University of York

Dr Sue Wise
University of Lancaster

Aidan Worsley
Liverpool John Moores University

References

This list includes those titles specifically mentioned by contributors in their encyclopaedia entries; it does not include titles only listed as being 'for further reading'.

Alaszewski, A., Harrison, L. and Manthorpe, J. (eds) 1998: *Risk, Health and Welfare*. Buckingham, Open University Press.

Alberg, C., Hatfield, B. and Huxley, P. (eds) 1996: *Learning Materials on Mental Health Risk Assessment*. Manchester: The University of Manchester and the Department of Health.

Alcock, P. and Craig, G. 1996: *Combating Local Poverty*. London: Local Government Management Board.

Andrews, D. A. 1995: The psychology of criminal conduct and effective treatment. In J. McGuire (ed.), *What Works: Reducing Reoffending. Guidelines from Research and Practice*, Chichester: John Wiley.

Aronson, E., Brewer, M. B. and Carlsmith, J. M. 1985: Experimentation in social psychology. In G. Lindzey, and E. Aronson (eds), *Handbook of Social Psychology* (3rd edn), New York: Random House, l, 441–86.

Audit Commission 1996: *Misspent Youth: Young People and Crime*. London: Audit Commission.

Bainham, A. 1998: *Children, The Modern Law*. Bristol: Jordan.

Balloch, S., McLean, J. and Fisher, M. 1999: *Social Services: Working Under Pressure*. Bristol: Policy Press.

Baraclough, I. 1995: A cause for celebration. *A Hundred Years of Health Related Social Work. Professional Social Work (Special Supplement)*, January, 9–12.

Baumhover, L. A. and Beall, S. C. (eds) 1997: *Abuse, Neglect and Exploitation of Older Persons: Strategies for Assessment and Intervention*. Baltimore: Health Professions Press.

Bebbington, A. and Miles, J. 1989: The background of children who enter local authority care. *British Journal of Social Work*, 19, 349–68.

Bennett, G. and Ebrahim, S. 1995: *Health Care in Old Age*. London: Edward Arnold.

Bennett, G., Kingston, P. and Penhale, B. (eds) 1997: *The Dimensions of Elder Abuse: Perspectives for Practitioners*. Basingstoke: Macmillan.

Bentall, R. P. 1990: The syndromes and symptoms of psychosis. In R. P. Bentall (ed.), *Reconstructing Schizophrenia*, London: Routledge.

Berger, P. and Luckman, T. 1966: *The Social Construction of Reality*. New York: Doubleday.

Berkowitz, N. (ed.) 1996: *Humanistic Approaches to Health Care: Focus on Social Work*. Birmingham: Venture Press.

Berridge, V. 1998: *Opium and the People*. London: Free Association Books.

Biehal, N., Clayden, J., Stein, M. and Wade, J. 1995: *Moving On: Young People and Leaving Care Schemes*. London: HMSO.

Blackburn, R. 1992: Criminal behaviour, personality disorder, and mental illness. *Criminal Behaviour and Mental Health, Psychopathic Disorder*, 2 (2), 66–77.

Blyth, E. and Milner, J. 1997: *Social Work with Children: The Educational Perspective*. Harlow: Longman.

Bornat, J., Johnson, J., Pereira, C., Pilgrim, D. and Williams, F. (eds) 1997: *Community Care: A Reader*, (2nd edn). London: Macmillan in association with the Open University.

Bowlby, J. 1979: *The Making and Breaking of Affectional Bonds*. London: Tavistock.

Braithwaite, J. 1989: *Crime, Shame and Reintegration*. Cambridge: Cambridge University Press.

Braye, S. and Preston-Shoot, M. 1992: *Practising Social Work Law*. London: Macmillan.

Brearley, C. P. 1982: *Risk and Ageing*. London: Routledge.

Broad, B. 1998: *Young People Leaving Care: Life after the Children Act 1989*. London: Jessica Kingsley.

Brown, H. and Stein, J. 1998: Implementing adult protection policies in Kent and East Sussex. *Journal of Social Policy*, 27 (3), 371–96.

Bytheway, B. and Johnson, J. 1998: The social construction of informal carers. In

A. Symonds and A. Kelly (eds), *The Social Construction of Community Care*, Basingstoke: Macmillan.

Cannan, C. and Warren, C. (eds) 1997: *Social Action with Children and Families: A Community Development Approach to Child and Family Welfare*. London: Routledge.

Carlisle, Lord (Chair) 1988: *The Parole System in England and Wales*. Cm. 532, London: HMSO.

Challis, D. 1993: The effectiveness of community care. *Clinical Gerontology*, 3, 97–104.

Challis, D. and Davies, B. 1986: *Case Management in Community Care*. Aldershot: Gower.

Challis, D., Darton, R. and Stewart, K. (eds) 1998: *Community Care, Secondary Health Care and Care Management*. Aldershot: Ashgate.

Challis, D., Darton, R., Johnson, L., Stone, M. and Traske, K. 1995: *Care Management and Health Care of Older People*. Aldershot: Ashgate.

Chiswick, D. 1992: Compulsory treatment of patients with psychopathic disorder. *Criminal Behaviour and Mental Health, Psychopathic Disorder*, 2 (2), 106–23.

Clark, C. L. 2000: *Social Work Ethics: Politics, Principles and Practice*. Basingstoke: Macmillan.

Cockburn, J. 1990: *Team Leaders and Team Managers in Social Services*. Norwich: Social Work Monographs.

Cohen, S. 1972: *Folk Devils and Moral Panics*. London: McGibbon and Kee.

Coid, J. 1992: Diagnosis in criminal psychopaths: A way forward. *Criminal Behaviour and Mental Health, Psychopathic Disorder*, 2 (2), 78–94.

Coleman, D. and Salt, J. 1992: *The British Population: Patterns, Trends and Processes*. Oxford: Oxford University Press.

Coleman, L. 1997: Stigma: An enigma demystified. In L. Davis (ed.), *The Disability Studies Reader*, London: Routledge.

Corr, C. A., McNabe, C. M. and Corr, D. M. 1996: *Death and Dying, Life and Living*. Pacific Grove: Brooks/Cole.

Crompton, R. 1998: *Class and Stratification: An Introduction to Current Debates*. Cambridge: Polity Press.

Daugherty, H. G. and Kammeyer, K. C. W. 1995: *An Introduction to Population*. New York: The Guildford Press.

Davies, M. and Connolly, J. 1995: The social worker's role in the hospital. *Health and Social Care in the Community*, 3 (5), 301–9.

Department of Health 1989: *Discharge of Patients from Hospital*. HC (89) 5 and LAC (89) 7. London: HMSO.

Department of Health 1995a: *Child Protection: Messages from Research*. London: HMSO.

Department of Health 1995b: *Hospital Discharge Workbook*. London: HMSO.

Department of Health 1998: Modernising Social Services. London: The Stationery Office.

Department of Health 1999: *Working Together to Safeguard Children*. London: The Stationery Office.

Dickersin, K., Scherer, R. and Lefebvre, C. 1995: Identifying relevant studies for systematic review. In I. Chalmers and D. G. Altman (eds), *Systematic Reviews*, Plymouth: BMJ Publishing Group.

Doel, M. and Marsh, P. 1992: *Task-Centred Social Work*. Aldershot: Ashgate.

Dolan, B. and Coid, J. 1993: *Psychopathic and Antisocial Personality Disorders: Treatment and Research Issues*. London: Gaskell.

Edwards, G. and Grant, M. (eds) 1977: *Alcoholism*. Oxford: Oxford University Press.

Egan, G. 1998: *The Skilled Helper: A Systematic Approach to Effective Helping*, (6th edn). Pacific Groves, CA: Brooks/Cole.

Ellis, T. and Underdown, A. 1998: *Strategies for Effective Offender Supervision*. London: Home Office.

Emerson, E. 1995: *Challenging Behaviour: Analysis and Intervention in People with Learning Disabilities*. Cambridge: Cambridge University Press.

England, H. 1986: *Social Work as Art*. London: Allen and Unwin.

Featherstone, B. and Trinder, L. 1997: Familiar subjects? Domestic violence and child welfare. *Child and Family Social Work*, 2 (3), 147–59.

Feeley, M. and Simon, J. 1992: The new penology: Notes on the emerging strategy of corrections and its implications. *Criminology*, 30, 449–74.

Fein, E. and Staff, I. 1993: Last best chance: Findings from a reunification services program. *Child Welfare*, 62 (1) 25–40.

Ferri, E. and Smith, K. 1996: *Parenting in the 1990s*. London: Family Policy Studies Centre.

Franklin, B. 1998: *Hard Pressed: National Newspaper Reporting of Social Work and Social Services*. Sutton, Surrey: Community Care / RBI.

Franklin, B. and Parton, N. (eds) 1991: *Social Work, the Media and Public Relations.* London: Routledge.

Freire, P. 1972: *The Pedagogy of the Oppressed.* Harmondsworth: Penguin.

Friel, J. 1995: *Children with Special Needs: Assessment, Law and Practice – Caught in the Acts*, (3rd edn). London: Jessica Kingsley.

Frith, U. 1991: *Autism and Asperger Syndrome.* Cambridge: Cambridge University Press.

Gaber, I. and Aldridge, J. (eds) 1994: *In the Best Interests of the Child.* London: Free Association Books.

Gant, L. M. 1998: Essential facts every social worker needs to know. In D. M. Aronstein and B. J. Thomson (eds), *HIV and Social Work: A Practitioner's Guide*, Birmingham, New York: The Harrington Park Press.

Garland, D. 1997: Probation and the reconfiguration of crime control. In R. Burnett. (ed.) *The Probation Service: Responding to Change*, Oxford: University of Oxford Centre for Criminological Research.

Gaskin, K. and Smith, J. 1995: *A New Civic Europe? A Study of the Extent and Role of Volunteering.* London: Volunteer Centre.

Gaudin, J. 1993: *Child Neglect: A Guide for Intervention.* Washington: National Center on Child Abuse and Neglect, US Department of Health and Human Services.

Gergen, K. J. 1973: Social psychology as history. *Journal of Personality and Social Psychology*, 26, 309–20.

Gibbons, J. with Thorpe, S. and Wilkinson, P. 1990: *Family Support and Prevention: Studies in Local Areas.* London: HMSO.

Giddens, A. 1991: *Modernity and Self-identity.* Cambridge: Polity.

Giddens, A. 1998: *The Third Way.* Cambridge: Polity.

Gilligan, R. 1998: The importance of schools and teachers in child welfare. *Child and Family Social Work*, 3, 13–26.

Goffman, E. 1961: *Asylums: Essays on the Social Situation of Mental Patients.* Garden City, New York: Doubleday.

Gore, G. and Figueiredo, J. 1997: *Social Exclusion and Anti-Poverty Policy: A Debate.* Geneva: International Institute for Labour Studies, UN Development Programme.

Griffiths, Sir R. 1988: *Community Care: An Agenda for Action.* London: HMSO.

Gunn, J. 1992: Personality disorders and forensic psychiatry. *Criminal Behaviour and Mental Health, Psychopathic Disorder*, 2 (2), 202–11.

Hanmer, J. and Statham, D. 1999: *Women and Social Work: Towards Woman-centred Practice.* Basingstoke: Macmillan.

Hann, R., Harman, W. and Pease K. 1991: Does parole reduce the risk of reconviction? *Howard Journal of Criminal Justice*, 30 (1), 66–75.

Haskey, J. 1998: One-parent families and their dependent children in Great Britain. *Population Trends*, 91. London: The Stationery Office.

Heilbrun, K., Dvoskin, J., Hart, S. and McNeil, D. 1999: Violence risk communication: Implications for research, policy and practice. *Health, Risk and Society*, 1 (1), 91–106.

Hodge, J. E. 1992: Addiction to violence: A new model of psychopathy. *Criminal Behaviour and Mental Health, Psychopathic Disorder*, 2 (2), 212–3.

Hollis, F. 1964: *Casework: A Psychosocial Therapy.* New York: Random House. Revised in 1981 by F. Hollis and M. Woods.

Holman, R. 1992: Family Centres. *Highlight*, 111. London: National Children's Bureau.

Home Office 1995: *National Standards for the Supervision of Offenders in the Community.* London: Home Office.

Home Office, 1996: *Does Treating Sex Offenders Reduce Reoffending?*, Research Findings 45. London: Home Office.

Home Office 1997: *The Prevalence of Convictions for Sexual Offending*, Research Findings, 55. London: Home Office.

Hornby, S. 1993: *Collaborative Care: Interprofessional, Interagency and Interpersonal.* Oxford: Blackwell Science.

Howe, D., Brandon, M., Hinings, D. and Schofield, G. 1999: *Attachment Theory, Child Maltreatment and Family Support.* London: Macmillan.

Hughes, R. 1993: *The Culture of Complaint.* Oxford: Oxford University Press.

Institute for the Study of Drug Dependence (ISDD) 1999: *Drug Abuse Briefing*, (7th edn). London: ISDD.

Iwaniec, D. 1995: *The Emotionally Abused and Neglected Child: Identification, Assessment and Intervention.* Chichester: John Wiley.

Jackson, S. and Kilroe, S. (eds) 1996: *Looking After Children: Good Parenting, Good Outcomes.* London: HMSO.

Jordan, B. 1990: *Social Work in an Unjust Society*. Hemel Hempstead: Harvester Wheatsheaf.

Jordan, B. 1997: Social work and society. In M. Davies (ed.), *The Blackwell Companion to Social Work*, (1st edn). Oxford: Blackwell, 8–23.

Jordan, B. and Parton, N. (eds) 1983: *The Political Dimensions of Social Work*. Oxford: Blackwell.

Kemshall, H. 1996: *Reviewing Risk: A Review of Research on the Assessment and Management of Risk and Dangerousness – Implications for Policy and Practice in the Probation Service*. London: Home Office Research and Statistics Directorate.

Kemshall, H. and Pritchard, J. (eds) 1996: *Good Practice in Risk Assessment and Risk Management*. London: Jessica Kingsley.

Kemshall, H., Parton, N., Walsh, M. and Waterson, J. 1997: Concepts of risk in relation to organizational structure and functioning within the personal social services and probation. *Social Policy and Administration*, 31, 213–32.

Kohlberg, L. 1963: The development of children's orientations towards a moral order. I: Sequence in the development of moral thought. *Vita Humana*, 6, 11–33.

Langan, M. and Day, L. (eds) 1992: *Women, Oppression and Social Work*. London: Routledge.

LaVigna, G. W., Willis, T. J. and Donellan, A. M. 1989: The role of positive programming in behavioral treatment. In E. Cipani (ed.), *The Treatment of Severe Behavior Disorders*, Washington DC: AAMR Monographs, 12.

Law Commission 1995: *Who Decides? Making Decisions on Behalf of Mentally Incapacitated Adults*, Report 231. London: The Lord Chancellor's Department.

Laws, G. 1997: Spatiality and age relations. In A. Jamieson, S. Harper and C. Victor (eds), *Critical Approaches to Ageing and Later Life*, Buckingham: Open University Press.

Leonard, P. 1997: *Postmodern Welfare: Reconstructing an Emancipatory Knowledge*. London: Sage.

Le Riche, P. and Tanner, K. (eds) 1998: *Observation and its Application to Social Work: Rather like Breathing*. London: Jessica Kingsley.

Linden, M. and Barnow, S. 1997: The wish to die in very old persons: A psychiatric problem? Results from the Berlin ageing study. *International Psychogeriatrics*, 9, 291–307.

Lipsey, M. 1995: What do we learn from 400 research studies on the effectiveness of treatment with juvenile delinquents?. In J. McGuire (ed.), *What Works: Reducing Reoffending*, Chichester: Wiley.

Little, M. and Mount, K. 1999: *Prevention and Early Intervention for Children in Need*. Aldershot: Ashgate.

Losel, F. 1993: The effectiveness of treatment in institutional and community settings. *Criminal Behaviour and Mental Health*, 3, 416–37.

Lowndes, V. 1997: Change in public service management: New institutions and new managerial regimes. *Local Government Studies*, 23 (2), 42–66.

Macdonald, G. M. 1998: Promoting evidence-based practice in child protection. *Clinical Child Psychology and Psychiatry*, 3 (1), 71–85.

Macey, M. 1996: In the best interests of the child? Race and ethnic matching in adoption and fostering. *Representing Children*, 9 (2), 83–98.

Marlowe, M. and Sugarman, P. 1997: ABC of mental health disorders of personality. *British Medical Journal*, 315, 176–9.

Marris, P. 1974: *Loss and Change*. London: Routledge and Kegan Paul.

Martinson, R. 1974: What works? Questions and answers about prison reform. *Public Interest*, 10, 22–54.

Mayhew, P., Maung, N. and Mirrless-Black, C. 1993: *The 1992 British Crime Survey*. London: HMSO.

Milgram, S. 1974: *Obedience to Authority: An Experimental View*. New York: Harper and Row.

Miller, W. R. and Rollnick, S. 1991: *Motivational Interviewing*. London: The Guildford Press.

Milner, K. 1998: The etiology and epidemiology of HIV disease. In M. D. Knox and C. H. Sparks (eds), *HIV and Community Mental Health Care*, London: John Hopkins University Press.

Nagama Hall, G. C. 1995: Sex offender recidivism revisited: A meta-analysis of recent treatment studies. *Journal of Consulting and Clinical Psychology*, 63: 802–9.

National Council for Voluntary Organizations (NCVO) 1996: *Report of the Commission on the Future of the Voluntary Sector*. London: NCVO.

Newburn, T. 1997: Youth, crime and justice. In M. Maguire, R. Morgan and R. Reiner (eds), *The Oxford Handbook of Criminology*, (2nd edn), Oxford: Oxford University Press.

New South Wales Sexual Assault Committee 1995: *Organised Sadistic Abuse: Current Knowledge, Controversies and Treatment Issues*. Sydney: Ministry for the Status and Advancement of Women.

Norman, A. 1985: *Triple Jeopardy: Growing Old in a Second Homeland*. London: Centre for Policy on Ageing.

Oakley, A. 2000: *Experiments in Knowing: Gender and Method in the Social Sciences*. Cambridge: Polity Press.

O'Brien, J. 1986: A guide to personal futures planning. In G. T. Bellamy and B. Wilcox (eds), *A Comprehensive Guide to the Activities Catalog: An Alternative Curriculum for Youth and Adults with Severe Learning Disabilities*, Baltimore, Maryland: Paul J. H. Brooks.

Office for National Statistics 1997: *English Life Tables Number 15*, DS 14. London: The Stationery Office.

Office for National Statistics 1998: *Population Trends*, 91. London: The Stationery Office.

Office for National Statistics 1999: *Census News*, 41, March, 14. London: The Stationery Office.

Oliviere, D., Hargreaves, R. and Monroe, B. 1998: *Good Practices in Palliative Care: A Psychosocial Perspective*. Aldershot: Arena.

Øvretveit, J. 1993: *Coordinating Community Care: Multidisciplinary Teams and Care Management in Health and Social Services*. Buckingham: Open University Press.

Parker, R., Ward, H., Jackson, S., Aldgate, J. and Wedge, P. 1991: *Looking After Children: Assessing Outcomes in Child Care*. London: HMSO.

Parkes, C. M. 1975: *Bereavement: Studies in Adult Grief*. Harmondsworth: Penguin.

Parton, N. 1994: Problematics of government, (post) modernity and social work. *British Journal of Social Work*, 24, 9–32.

Parton, N. (ed.) 1996: *Social Theory, Social Change and Social Work*. London: Routledge.

Pearson, G. 1983: *Hooligan: A History of Respectable Fears*. London: Macmillan.

Piaget, J. 1950: *The Psychology of Intelligence*. London: Routledge.

Pigot Committee 1989: *The Report of the Advisory Group on Video Evidence*. London: The Home Office.

Pinsof, W. M. 1994: An integrative systems perspective on the therapeutic alliance. In A. O. Adams and L. S. Greenberg (eds), *The Working Alliance: Theory, Research and Practice*, New York: John Wiley, 173–95.

Pithouse, A., Lindsell, S. and Cheung, M. 1998: *Family Support and Family Centre Services: Issues, Research and Evaluation in the UK, USA and Hong Kong*. Aldershot: Ashgate.

Prochaska, J. O. and DiClemente, C. C. 1994: *The Transtheoretical Approach: Crossing Traditional Boundaries of Therapy*. Malabar, Fla.: Krieger.

Pugh, G., De'Ath, E. and Smith, C. 1994: *Confident Parents, Confident Children: Policy and Practice in Parent Education and Support*. London: National Children's Bureau.

Raynor, P. 1996: Evaluating probation. In T. May and A. A. Vass (eds), *Working with Offenders*, London: Sage.

Reid, W. J. and Epstein, L. 1972: *Task-centred Casework*. New York: Columbia University Press.

Reid, W. J. and Shyne, A. W. 1969: *Brief and Extended Casework*. New York: Columbia University Press.

Reith, M. 1997: Mental health inquiries: implications for probation practice. *Probation Journal*, 44 (2), 66–70.

Richmond, M. 1917: *Social Diagnosis*. New York: Russell Sage Foundation.

Room, G. (ed.) 1995: *Beyond the Threshold: The Measurement and Analysis of Social Exclusion*. Bristol: The Policy Press.

Rose, D. and O'Reilly, K. (eds) 1998: *The ESRC Review of Government Social Classifications*. London: ONS/ESRC.

Ross, R. R., Fabiano, E. A. and Ewles, C. D. 1988: Reasoning and rehabilitation. *International Journal of Offender Therapy and Comparative Criminology*, 32 (1), 29–35.

Rowe, J. and Lambert, L. 1973: *Children Who Wait*. London: British Agencies for Adoption and Fostering.

Rowlands, O. 1998: *Informal Carers*. London: The Stationery Office.

Ryburn, M. 1994: Research in relation to contact and permanent placement. In M. Ryburn (ed.), *Open Adoption: Research, Theory and Practice*, Aldershot: Avebury.

Salaman, L. 1994: *The Global Association Revolution*. London: Demos.

Scott, P. D. 1960: The treatment of psychopaths. *British Medical Journal*, 2, 1641–6.

Seebohm Report 1968: *The Report of the Committee on Local Authority and Allied Personal Social Services*. London: HMSO.

Shaw, C. 1998: 1996-based national population projections for the United Kingdom and constituent countries. *Population Trends*, 91, 43–9.

Social Services Inspectorate / Social Work Services Group (SSI/SWSG) 1991: *Care Management and Assessment: Managers Guide*. HMSO: London.

Social Services Inspectorate 1993: *Social Services for Hospital Patients*. London: Department of Health.

South, N. (ed) 1999: *Drugs: Cultures, Controls and Everyday Life*. London: Sage.

Stein, M. 1997: *What Works in Leaving Care?* Barkingside: Barnardos.

Stevenson, O. 1998: *Neglected Children: Issues and Dilemmas*. Oxford: Blackwell Science.

Suppes, M. A. and Wells, C. C. 1996: *The Social Work Experience*. New York: McGraw-Hill.

Swain, J., Gillman, M. and French, S. 1998: *Confronting Disabling Barriers: Towards Making Organisations Accessible*. Birmingham: Venture Press.

Tajfel, H. 1981: *Human Groups and Social Categories: Studies in Social Psychology*. Cambridge: Cambridge University Press.

Thompson, N. 1997: *Anti-Discriminatory Practice*, (2nd edn). London: Macmillan.

Thompson, N. 1998: *Promoting Equality: Challenging Discrimination and Oppression in the Human Services*. London: Macmillan.

Trevillion, S. 1993: *Caring in the Community: A Networking Approach to Community Partnership*. London: Longman.

Üstün, T. B. and Sartorius, N. 1998: *Mental Illness in General Health Care*. London: Wiley.

Ward, A. 1993: *Working in Group Care: Social Work in Residential and Day Care Settings*. Birmingham: Venture Press.

White, M. and Epston, D. 1990: *Narrative Means, Therapeutic Ends*. New York: W. W. Norton.

Wilson, E. O. 1975: *Sociobiology*. London: Harvard University Press.

Wise, S. 1995: Feminist ethics. In R. Hugman and D. Smith (eds), *Ethical Issues in Social Work*, London: Routledge.

Wistow, G., Knapp, M., Hardy, B., Forder, J., Kendall, J. and Manning, R. 1996: *Social Care Markets: Progress and Prospects*. Buckingham: Open University Press.

World Health Organisation 1992: *The ICD-10 Classification of Mental and Behavioural Disorders – Clinical Descriptions and Diagnostic Guidelines*. Geneva: WHO.

World Health Organisation 1998: *World Health Annual Statistics*. Geneva: World Health Organisation.

World Health Organisation, http://www.who.ch/emc/diseases/hiv Accessed 8/9/99

Yelloly, M., 1980: *Social Work Theory and Psychoanalysis*. London: Van Nostrand, Reinhold.

Index of Names

Indexed reference pages **in bold typeface** indicate Encyclopaedia entries

Index of Subjects

The index of subjects should be used in association with the Lexicon where a listing of major topics can be found, together with a note of the relevant entries (pages ix–xvi). In the index of subjects, topics covered alphabetically in the Encyclopaedia, together with the relevant page reference, are indicated in **bold**.